Palgrave Studies in the History of Social Movements

Series Editors

Stefan Berger
Ruhr University Bochum
Bochum, Germany

Holger Nehring
University of Stirling
Stirling, United Kingdom

INSTITUT FÜR
SOZIALE
BEWEGUNGEN

Around the world, social movements have become legitimate, yet contested, actors in local, national and global politics and civil society, yet we still know relatively little about their longer histories and the trajectories of their development. This series seeks to promote innovative historical research on the history of social movements in the modern period since around 1750. We bring together conceptually-informed studies that analyse labour movements, new social movements and other forms of protest from early modernity to the present. We conceive of 'social movements' in the broadest possible sense, encompassing social formations that lie between formal organisations and mere protest events. We also offer a home for studies that systematically explore the political, social, economic and cultural conditions in which social movements can emerge. We are especially interested in transnational and global perspectives on the history of social movements, and in studies that engage critically and creatively with political, social and sociological theories in order to make historically grounded arguments about social movements. This new series seeks to offer innovative historical work on social movements, while also helping to historicise the concept of 'social movement'. It hopes to revitalise the conversation between historians and historical sociologists in analysing what Charles Tilly has called the 'dynamics of contention'.

More information about this series at
http://www.springer.com/series/14580

Stefan Berger • Holger Nehring
Editors

The History of Social Movements in Global Perspective

A Survey

palgrave
macmillan

Editors
Stefan Berger
Ruhr University Bochum
Bochum, Germany

Holger Nehring
University of Stirling
Stirling, United Kingdom

Palgrave Studies in the History of Social Movements
ISBN 978-1-137-30425-4 (hardback)   ISBN 978-1-137-30426-1   (paperback)
ISBN 978-1-137-30427-8   (eBook)
DOI 10.1057/978-1-137-30427-8

Library of Congress Control Number: 2016960746

Cover icons created by Tl| William Jean; Cesar Reynoso; Rflor; Mike Jewett from the Noun Project

Printed on acid-free paper

This Palgrave Macmillan imprint is published by Springer Nature
The registered company is Macmillan Publishers Ltd.
The registered company address is: The Campus, 4 Crinan Street, London, N1 9XW, United Kingdom

CONTENTS

1   Introduction: Towards a Global History of Social
    Movements   1
    Stefan Berger and Holger Nehring

Part I   Conceptual, Methodological and Theoretical
         Considerations   37

   2   Studying Social Movements: Some Conceptual Challenges   39
       Dieter Rucht

   3   Subaltern Studies as a History of Social Movements
       in India   63
       Rochona Majumdar

   4   Transpacific Feminism: Writing Women's Movement
       from a Transnational Perspective   93
       Seonjoo Park

v

Part II   Continental Perspectives on the History of Social
Movements   113

 5   Social Movements in Latin America: From the Nineteenth
     to the Twenty-First Century   115
     Claudia Wasserman

 6   Dissident Political History: Social Movements in North
     America   145
     Felicia Kornbluh

 7   European Social Protest, 1000–2000   175
     Marcel van der Linden

 8   Social Movements in Africa   211
     Andreas Eckert

 9   Popular Movements in the Middle East and North Africa   225
     John Chalcraft

10   Social Movements in India, 1800 to the Present   265
     Arvind Elangovan

11   Subjectivation and Social Movements in Post-Colonial
     Korea   297
     Jung Han Kim and Jeong-Mi Park

12   The History of Social Movements in Australia   325
     Sean Scalmer

Part III   Social Movements in Transnational Historical
           Perspective   353

13   From Cultural Wars to the Crisis of Humanity: Moral
     Movements in the Modern Age   355
     Alexandra Przyrembel

14   Labour Movements in Global Historical Perspective:
     Conceptual Eurocentrism and Its Problems   385
     Stefan Berger

15   Myths, Big Myths and Global Environmentalism   419
     Frank Uekötter

16   Equality, Difference and Participation: The Women's
     Movements in Global Perspective   449
     Ilse Lenz

17   Peace Movements   485
     Holger Nehring

18   1968: A Social Movement *Sui Generis*   515
     Gerd-Rainer Horn

19   Terrorism between Social Movements, the State
     and Media Societies   543
     Klaus Weinhauer

20   Fascism as a Social Movement in a Transnational Context   579
     Kevin Passmore

21   Post-Fascist Right-Wing Social Movements   619
     Fabian Virchow

22 The Global Justice Movement: Resistance to Dominant
Economic Models of Globalization 647
Britta Baumgarten

23 The 'Arab Spring' in Global Perspective: Social
Movements, Changing Contexts and Political
Transitions in the Arab World (2010–2014) 677
Nora Lafi

Index 703

NOTES ON CONTRIBUTORS

Britta Baumgarten is a contracted post-doctoral researcher at CIES-IUL, Lisbon and a lecturer on protest politics and collective action at ISCTE, Lisbon. She works on civil society and social movements in Portugal and in Brazil in a transnational perspective. Her recent publications include 'Geração à Rasca and Beyond. Mobilizations in Portugal after 12 March 2011', *Current Sociology* 4 (2013); *Conceptualizing Culture in Social Movement Research* (Palgrave Studies in European Political Sociology Series, ed. with Priska Daphi and Peter Ullrich, 2014); The Portuguese translation of her contribution in this volume was published as *Resistência ao modelo neoliberal—do Movimento alterglobalização aos protestos atuais contra a Troika*, in PerCursos, FAED/UDESC, Brazil, 2014 (online: www.periodicos.udesc.br/index.php/percursos/issue/view/305).

Stefan Berger is Professor of Social History and Director of the Institute for Social Movements, Ruhr-Universität Bochum as well as Executive Chair of the Foundation History of the Ruhr. His main research interests are comparative labour history, history of historiography, history of nationalism and industrial heritage. He recently published *The Past as History: National Identity and Historical Consciousness in Modern Europe* (2015, with Christoph Conrad) and he co-edited, with Alexei Miller, *Nationalizing Empires* (2015).

John Chalcraft is Associate Professor in the History and Politics of Empire/Imperialism at the London School of Economics and Political Science (LSE). Previous posts include a Lectureship at the University of Edinburgh and a Research Fellowship at Gonville and Caius College, Cambridge. His research focuses on labour, migration and contentious mobilization in the Middle East. He is the author of *The Striking Cabbies of Cairo and Other Stories: Crafts and Guilds in Egypt, 1863–1914* (2004) and *The Invisible Cage: Syrian Migrant Workers in*

Lebanon (2009). His new book *Popular Politics in the Making of the Modern Middle East* was published in 2016.

Andreas Eckert is Professor of African History at the Institute of Asian and African Studies at the Humboldt University Berlin. Moreover, Eckert is Director of IGK Work and Human Life Cycle in Global History, Berlin. His main research interests are contemporary African history, history of colonialism and history of work. Most recently he co-edited with Babacar Fall and Ineke Phaf-Rheinger *Travail et culture dans un monde globalisé. De l'Afrique à l'Amérique latine [Work and Culture in a Globalized World: from Africa to Latin America]* (2015) and currently he is working on two book manuscripts: a history of Africa since 1850 (German) and *A Short History of Colonialism* (English).

Arvind Elangovan is Assistant Professor in the History Department at Wright State University in Dayton, Ohio, USA. He completed his Ph.D. at the University of Chicago in 2012 and is interested in political, constitutional, and institutional histories of the late British Empire in South Asia and post-colonial India. He has previously published 'The Making of the Indian Constitution: A Case for a Non-Nationalist Approach', *History Compass* (12/1 January 2014). He is currently working on a book manuscript tentatively titled *Norms and Politics: Sir Benegal Narsing Rau and the Making of the Indian Constitution, 1935–1950* and an edited collection, tentatively titled *An Empire of Possibilities: Social Movements in India, 19th and 20th Centuries.*

Gerd-Rainer Horn is Professor of Twentieth Century History at the Institut d'Études Politiques de Paris (Sciences Po). He specializes in the study of twenti-eth-century continental western European social movements from a transnational perspective. His most recent monographs are *The Spirit of '68: Rebellion in Western Europe and North America, 1956–1976* (2007); *Western European Liberation Theology: The First Wave (1924–1959)* (2008); *The Spirit of Vatican II: Western European Progressive Catholicism in the Long Sixties* (2015).

Jung Han Kim is Research Professor of Research Institute of Korean Studies at Korea University. His publications include *The Masses and Violence* (1998) and *Insurrection of the Masses and its Democracy in 1980* (2013).

Felicia Kornbluh is an Associate Professor of History and of Gender, Sexuality, and Women's Studies at the University of Vermont, Burlington, VT. Her recent publications include 'Food as a Civil Right: Hunger, Work, and Welfare in the South after the Civil Rights Act', *Labor: Working-Class History of the Americas* (2015) and 'Siting the Legal History of Poverty' (with Karen Tani), in the *Blackwell Companion to American Legal History* (2013). She is the co-author of the forthcoming books, *Rethinking the Disability Rights Movement* (with Audra Jennings) and *Ensuring Poverty: Welfare Reform after Twenty Years*, with political scientist Gwendolyn Mink. She is the president of United Academics, the union that represents 800 faculty at the University of Vermont and is a local of the American Federation of Teachers and American Association of University Professors.

Nora Lafi is Researcher at the Zentrum Moderner Orient (ZMO) Berlin. Currently, she is researching about Ottoman and post-Ottoman cities. She co-edited several books, most recently *Urban Violence in the Middle East. Changing Cityscapes in the Transition from Empire to Nation State* (with U. Freitag, Nelida Fuccaro and Claudia Ghrawi, 2015).

Ilse Lenz is Professor emirita of Sociology at the University of Bochum. She published on Feminist movement and gender based inequalities in Japan and Germany. Most recently, she published *Die Frauenbewegung in Japan* [*The Women's Movement in Japan*] (ed. with Michiko Mae, 2010). Upcoming is a book on German society and the influence of immigration on it.

Rochona Majumdar is Associate Professor at the University of Chicago. Her research focusses, among other things, on gender and marriage in colonial India, on the history of Indian cinema, and contemporary Indian intellectual thought. Her most recent book is *Writing Postcolonial History* (2010) and currently she is working on two book projects: a history of the film society movement in India and an intellectual history of Hindu/Muslim Bengali in nineteenth- and twentieth-century India.

Holger Nehring is Professor of Contemporary European History at the University of Stirling. He is mainly interested in the history of social movements in Great Britain and West Germany, the history of the Cold War and in environmental history. He co-edited with Patrick Bernhard *Den Kalten Krieg denken: Beiträge zur sozialen Ideengeschichte seit 1945* [*Thinking the Cold War. Contributions to the Social History of Ideas since 1945*] (2014) and published in 2013 *Politics of Security. The British and West German Protests against Nuclear Weapons and the Early Cold War, 1945–1970* (2013).

Jeong-Mi Park is Ph.D. in Sociology and a lecturer at Chungbuk National University. She served as a Kluge Fellow at the Library of Congress and a Research Assistant Professor at Hanyang University. Her recent publications include 'A Historical Sociology of the Korean Government's Policies on Military Prostitution in US Camptowns, 1953–1995' (*Korean Journal of Sociology*, 2015) and 'Paradoxes of gendering strategy in prostitution policies' (*Women's Studies International Forum*, 2013).

Seonjoo Park is Associate Professor at Inha University, South Korea. Her research interests are transnational fiction, comparative literature, cultural studies and gender theory. Her recent publications are '(In)appropriate Crossings: Gender-ing

Translation, Gender in Translation' (in Korean, 2012); 'Comfort Women and Emma Bovary: The Historical Construction of the "Unspeakable" in Transnational Subalternity' (in Korean, 2014); 'Abandoning Imagination: The Genealogical Aberration in Magical Realism and Karen T. Yamashita's *Tropic of Orange*' (in Korean, 2016).

Kevin Passmore is Professor of History at Cardiff University. His research interests are French history since 1870, fascism and historiography. Recently he co-edited with Chris Millington *Political Violence and Democracy in Western Europe 1918–1940* (2015) and published the second edition of *Fascism: a Very Short Introduction* (2014). Currently, he is working on the history and memory of the Maginot Line and the reception of fascism in France.

Alexandra Przyrembel is Professor of Modern European History at the University of Hagen. She is especially interested in global history of capitalism, history of knowledge and the history of humanitarian movements. She co-edited with Rebekka Habermas *Von Käfern, Märkten und Menschen. Wissen und Kolonialismus in der Moderne* [*Of Beetles, Markets and People. Colonialism and Knowledge in the Modern Age*] (2013) and published *Verbote und Geheimnisse. Das Tabu und die Genese der europäischen Moderne* (1784–1913) [*The Secret and the Prohibited: Taboo in the Age of Modernity*] (2011).

Dieter Rucht retired in July 2011. He was co-director of the research group 'Civil Society, Citizenship and Political Mobilization in Europe' at the Social Science Research Centre, Berlin, and Professor of Sociology at the Free University of Berlin. His research interests include political participation, social movements, political protest and public discourse. He recently published *Meeting Democracy: Power and Deliberation in Global Justice Movements* (ed. with Donatella della Porta, 2013).

Sean Scalmer is Associate Professor in the School of Historical and Philosophical Studies, University of Melbourne, Australia. His books on social movements include *Dissent Events: Protest, the Media and the Political Gimmick in Australia* (2002); *Activist Wisdom: Practical Knowledge and Creative Tension in Social Movements* (with Sarah Maddison, 2006); *The Little History of Australian Unionism* (2006) and *Gandhi in the West: The Mahatma and the Rise of Radical Protest* (2011).

Frank Uekötter is Reader in Environmental Humanities at the University of Birmingham. His research focusses on environmental history. He has published several books, most recently *Comparing Apples, Oranges, and Cotton: Environmental Histories of the Plantation* (ed.) (2014) and *Deutschland in Grün: eine zwiespältige Erfolgsgeschichte* [*Germany in Green: An Ambivalent Success Story*] (2015).

Marcel van der Linden is a fellow and former Research Director of the International Institute of Social History, and Professor of Social Movement History at the University of Amsterdam. He published widely on the history of ideas and on labour and social history. Recent publications include *Transnational Labour History* (2003); *Western Marxism and the Soviet Union* (2007); *Workers of the World* (2008) and *Capitalism: The Resurgence of a Historical Concept* (2016; ed. with Jürgen Kocka).

Fabian Virchow is Professor of Social Theory and Theories of Political Action at the University of Applied Sciences, Dusseldorf, as well as the Director of its Research Unit on Right-Wing Extremism. His research is on protest and social movements, the extreme right, and on cultural representations of the military. His most recent publications include *Rechter Terrorismus in Deutschland* [*Right Wing Terrorism in Germany*] (2015); *Cultural Dimensions of Far Right Politics and Lifeworld* (edited with Cynthia Miller-Idriss, 2015) and *Transnational Extreme Right Networks* (edited with Graham Macklin, upcoming).

Claudia Wasserman is Professor of Social History at the Federal University of Rio Grande do Sul (UFRGS), Ph.D. in Social History at Federal University of Rio de Janeiro (UFRJ), Fellow Researcher of the National Counsel of Scientific and Technological Development of Brazil (CNPq). She has experience in Latin American and Brazilian contemporary history. Her most recent publications include 'Transição ao socialismo e transição democrática: os exilados brasileiros no Chile' [Transition to Socialism and Democratic Transition: Brazilian Exiles in Chile], *Revista de História Unisinos* (2012), 'Intelectuales y transición: años 1980' [Intellectuals and Transition: 1980s', in *Cuadernos del CILHA* (2013) and 'Transformações no ensino superior e interdição ao marxismo (anos 1980)' [Transformations in Higher Education and Interdiction to Marxism], *Pacarina del Sur* 21 (2014).

Klaus Weinhauer is Professor of Modern History at Bielefeld University. He was Fellow at the Netherlands Institute for Advanced Study (NIAS), at the Modern European History Research Centre (MEHRC), Oxford, and at the Centre for Interdisciplinary Research (ZIF), Bielefeld. His most recent publications include *Terrorism, Gender, and History since the Nineteenth Century* (special issue of *Historical Social Research* 3 (2014), (edited with Sylvia Schraut); *Germany 1916–1923. A Revolution in Context* (ed. with Anthony McElligott and Kirsten Heinsohn, Bielefeld, 2015; 'Imaginaries of Urban Threat: Perceptions of Collective Protest and Violence in the USA and in Argentina during the Twentieth Century', *Forum for Inter-American Research* (FIAR) (2) 2016 (Online Journal).

LIST OF FIGURES

Fig. 2.1   Typology of movement-related organizations   53

List of Tables

Table 2.1   Reference points for social movement theories   51
Table 22.1   GJM events   654

CHAPTER 1

Introduction: Towards a Global History of Social Movements

Stefan Berger and Holger Nehring

Protests and social movements are back: Occupy, the 'Arab Spring', and a rise in protest movements and demonstrations around the world seem to suggest that we have entered a new democratic age that is no longer characterized by the dominance of political parties and interest groups and no longer confined to the territory of the nation-state, but that has a truly global shape.[1] Just as social scientists diagnosed the arrival of 'new' social movements in the 1970s and 1980s that replaced the labour movements as the key representatives of social conflict within a post-materialist and potentially post-industrial society, today they discover the arrival of global social movements that accompany our age of globalization.[2]

---

[1] See, for example, Manuel Castells, *The Rise of the Network Society* (Oxford: Wiley-Blackwell, 2nd edn, 2010); Benjamin Tejerina et al., 'From Indignation to Occupation: A New Wave of Global Mobilization', *Current Sociology* 4 (2013), pp. 377–392.

[2] The emphasis on novelty is strongest with Alain Touraine, *The Post-Industrial Society. Tomorrow's Social History: Classes, Conflicts and Culture in the Programmed Society* (New York: Random House, 1971), although weaker in his more recent *After the Crisis* (Cambridge: Polity, 2014); and Alberto Melucci, *Nomads of the Present. Social Movements and Individual*

S. Berger (✉)
Department of History, Ruhr University Bochum, Bochum, Germany

H. Nehring (✉)
Divion of History and Politics, University of Stirling, Stirling, UK

© The Author(s) 2017
S. Berger, H. Nehring (eds.), *The History of Social Movements in Global Perspective*, DOI 10.1057/978-1-137-30427-8_1

1

This interpretation seems to have become part of our common knowledge. *The Economist*, for example, in 2013 sketched out a direct genealogy from the French Revolution, across the revolutions of 1848, via the movements around 1968, the peace and human rights movements of around 1989 and the protests in many cities in 2013. The cover picture showed the embodiments of these protests: The French Marianne with the *Tricolore*, a hippy with a Molotov cocktail, a Lech Wałęsa lookalike with a candle, and a woman in tight jeans waving an iPhone. The leader writer interpreted this as the global march of democracy towards areas of the world where authoritarianism still reigned.[3] A bit more than half a year later, however, the same magazine sounded a more pessimistic note and wondered what had 'gone wrong with democracy', amidst the rise of populism in Europe and around the world and the seeming descent of stable countries into chaos in North Africa and the Middle East.[4]

These recent interventions rehearse some key liberal themes in the history of social activism: the story of social movement as one of modernization and specifically as one where social movements embody that modernization—in effect they often become paradigmatic of modernity. As such, their existence is, by definition if not in social reality, global: their claims and utopias that become connected with them purport to have universal applicability. They are also connected to the growth of a public sphere, and their existence is itself seen as proof for the importance of deliberative democracy and its cosmopolitan potential.[5] At the same time, however, social movements have also been seen as signs of decline and decay, often precisely because they seem to lack a territorial place and precisely because they cannot be fixed in time or in space: movement here

Needs in Contemporary Culture (London: Radius, 1989) as well as Castells, *Rise*. This novelty refers to 'the dominant patterns of social conflictuality' rather than the fact that movements that have emerged in the 1970s have no antecedents, as pointed out by George Steinmetz, 'Regulation Theory, Post-Marxism, and the New Social Movements', *Comparative Studies in Society and History* 1 (1994), pp. 176–212, here pp. 179–180.

[3] 'The March of Protest', *The Economist*, June 29, 2013. For empirical evidence on the spread of social movement activism see Jackie Smith, 'Characteristics of the Modern Transnational Social Movement Sector', in eadem, Charles Chatfield and Ron Pagnucco, (eds), *Transnational Social Movements and Global Politics* (Syracuse, NY: Syracuse University Press, 1997), pp. 42–58.

[4] 'What's Gone Wrong with Democracy', *The Economist*, March 1, 2014, pp. 47–52.

[5] Werner Hofmann (with assistance from Wolfgang Abendroth), *Ideengeschichte der sozialen Bewegung* (Berlin: de Gruyter, 1971).

becomes synonymous with menace.[6] Current discussions also make it clear that 'social movement' is not merely an abstract concept from the social sciences. It is a concept that performs work in everyday politics as well, and is connected with associations of utopias of community and belonging and social transformation. This double status of social movement is not new. It has accompanied the movements from when the term was first coined in the context of the French Revolution.[7] We lack, however, specific knowledge about '*this* existing world and how it has come about'.[8]

Despite the recent boom in global history, historical research that seeks to connect these conceptual and everyday histories of activism to specific historical experiences is still in its infancy. This is especially so because the subject matter of social movements has become somewhat unfashionable: conceptually speaking, references to holistic notions of 'society' or 'the social' are seen as out of date, so that social history is only seen to be happening in everyday experiences rather than in reference to political utopias.[9] This also means that the historical sociology that enabled so much innovative research on social activism and movements has been replaced by references to the profoundly ahistorical and self-referential theories of Niklas Luhmann and others, who have argued that protest and social movements were fundamentally about their opposition against social differentiation as the key hallmark to modernity.[10] Social movements, then, tend to become part of what Ingolfur Blühdorn has described as 'simulative democracy':

[6] Cf. Stefan Jonsson, *Crowds and Democracy. The Idea and Images of the Masses from Revolution to Fascism* (New York, NY: Columbia University Press, 2013) and Christian Borch, *The Politics of Crowds. An Alternative History of Sociology* (Cambridge: Cambridge University Press, 2012). A masterful survey of radical movements as key drivers of democracy in Europe is provided by Geoff Eley, *Forging Democracy. The History of the Left in Europe 1850–2000* (New York: Oxford University Press, 2002).

[7] Otthein Ramstedt, *Soziale Bewegung*, Frankfurt/Main: Suhrkamp, 1978, p. 7 and pp. 27–28 on these two dimensions.

[8] Michael Geyer and Charles Bright, 'World History in a Global Age', *The American Historical Review* 4 (1995), pp. 1034–1060, here p. 1059.

[9] See, for example, the contributions in Thomas Mergel and Thomas Welskopp (eds), *Geschichte zwischen Kultur und Gesellschaft. Beiträge zur Theoriedebatte* (Munich: Beck, 1997). Cf. the scathing critique of this by Geoff Eley and Keith Nield, *The Future of Class in History. What's Left of the Social?* (Ann Arbor, MI: University of Michigan Press, 2007) and the plea by George Steinmetz, 'The Relations between Sociology and History in the United States: The Current State of Affairs', *Journal of Historical Sociology* 1/2 (2007), pp. 1–12.

[10] Niklas Luhmann, *Ecological Communication* (Cambridge: Polity Press, 1989); idem, 'Umweltrisiko und Politik', in Kai-Uwe Hellmann (ed.), *Protest. Systemtheorie und soziale Bewegungen* (Frankfurt/Main: Suhrkamp, 1996).

an ultimately meaningless activity in a post-democratic age.[11] But such system-theoretical and functionalist analyses are historically unspecific, and they are especially problematic in that they ignore the historical and ideological boundedness of their own observations. Equally problematic are presentist accounts which create and reify heroic movements by providing us with thick and often nostalgic descriptions of their activism, but do not make specific the boundaries power structures in which they are embedded.[12]

Research on global social movements can, we believe, make visible, and thereby open for discussion, the ways in which we might conceptualize this relationship between agency, structure, and political, social, cultural and material contexts more precisely, a relationship that has also provided the ground for the debates on the many 'turns' that has accompanied debates in the historical social sciences over the last decades.[13] In particular, they throw the question of what happens to the social if it is conceptualized from the perspective of a global horizon into particularly sharp relief.[14]

Against this backdrop, this volume takes on the challenge which Michael Geyer and Charles Bright developed in a brilliant keynote article more than a decade ago: the purpose of this volume is, with respect to the global history of social movements, 'to shatter the silence surrounding global practices, by tracking them, describing them and presenting them historically, [...] recognizing with Georg Simmel that, in an integrated world, we only encounter more strangers'. Accordingly, our global approach to the history of social movements does not seek to provide a coherent interpretation or even line of enquiry. Instead, we wish to highlight the

[11] Ingolfur Blühdorn, *Simulative Demokratie. Neue Politik nach der postdemokratischen Wende* (Berlin: Suhrkamp, 2013) p. 44; idem, 'Self-description, Self deception, Simulation: A Systems-Theoretical Perspective on Contemporary Discourses of Radical Change', *Social Movement Studies* 1 (2007), pp. 1–20; Cf. also Slavoj Žižek, *Living in the End Times* (London: Verso, updated edn, 2011); Jacques Rancière, *La haine de la démocratie* (Paris: La Fabrique, 2011).

[12] See, for example, David Graeber, *The Democracy Project: A History, a Crisis, a Movement* (Harmondsworth: Penguin, 2014).

[13] See, for example, Gary Wilder, 'From Optic to Topic: The Foreclosure Effect of Historiographic Turns', *American Historical Review* 3 (2012), pp. 723–745, and Victorian Bonnell and Lynn Hunt (eds), *Beyond the Cultural Turn. New Directions in the Study of Society and Culture* (Berkeley, CA: University of California Press, 1999).

[14] See the conceptual remarks in Emily S. Rosenberg, 'Transnationale Strömungen in einer Welt, die zusammenrückt', in eadem (ed.), *Geschichte der Welt, 1870–1945. Weltmärkte und Weltkriege* (Munich: C.H. Beck, 2012), pp. 815–998, here pp. 819–824.

'multiplicity of the world's pasts', the 'colliding, interacting, intermixing' that moves against 'the history of a homogenous civilization',[15] so that 'the whole and the fragment are not opposed but understood in dynamic and historical relation'.[16] This means that the contributions in this volume do not subscribe to a view that regards social movements as agents of modernization across the board. The global perspective adopted here cautions in particular against a perspective that emphasizes the 'liberating potential of social movements' and portrays protesters 'marching lock-step toward human emancipation'.[17] Such a perspective would reify specific notions of freedom, liberation and movement, and would also reify the protesters' agency.[18]

This volume, then, seeks to contribute to the field in three ways: a dialogue between history and social sciences, the conceptualizations of social movements from a global perspective, and, empirically, to global history. First, this book, like the book series in which it appears, seeks to revive the dialogue between history and the social sciences in their attempts to conceptualize and analyse social phenomena that was so impressively begun by Craig Calhoun, Charles Tilly and others in the 1960s and 1970s.[19] Like global history more generally, a global perspective on the history of social movements problematizes and historicizes reified notions of society and their links to (nation-) statehood that have undergirded some of the

---

[15] Geyer and Bright, 'World History', p. 1059 and p. 1043. Cf. also Geoff Eley, 'Historicizing the Global, Politicizing Capital: Giving the Present a Name', *History Workshop Journal*, 63 (2007), pp. 154–188.

[16] Nico Slate, *Colored Cosmopolitanism. The Shared Struggle for Freedom in the United States and India* (Cambridge, MA: Harvard University Press, 2012), p. 251.

[17] Richard G. Fox and Orin Starn, 'Introduction', in idem, *Between Resistance and Revolution. Cultural Politics and Social Protest* (New Brunswick, NJ: Rutgers University Press, 1997), pp. 1–16, here p. 11.

[18] As an example for such an approach see the contributions Robin Cohen and Shirin M. Rai, *Global Social Movements* (London: Continuum, 2000). For a brilliant example that historicizes such images of totemic agency see Quinn Slobodian, *Foreign Front: Third World Politics in Sixties West Germany* (Durham, NC: Duke University Press, 2012).

[19] Charles Tilly, *The Vendée: A Sociological Analysis of the Counter- Revolution of 1793* (Cambridge, MA: Harvard University Press, 1964); idem, *Popular Contention in Great Britain, 1758–1834* (Cambridge, MA: Harvard University Press, 1995); Craig Calhoun, *The Question of Class Struggle: The Social Foundations of Popular Radicalism during the Industrial Revolution* (Chicago: University of Chicago Press, 1982) and his more recent *The Roots of Radicalism. Tradition, the Public Sphere and Early Nineteenth-Century Social Movements* (Chicago: University of Chicago Press, 2012).

classical social history and social theory.[20] At the same time, a social movement perspective, because of its emphasis on protests, is especially good at highlighting how 'the condition of globality has always been organized locally, in one place after the other, according to particular circumstances and conditions that happen to obtain'.[21]

Second, we wish to encourage developing the conceptual tools of social movement history further. Historical research is 'in need of theory'.[22] But sociological research can also benefit from the rich insights of historical research in order to test its theoretical assumptions. A significant weakness of Tilly's approach to social movement studies is that he conceptualizes movements from the perspective of 'dynamics of contention' in which 'repertoires of action' are mobilized through certain 'mechanisms'.[23] Historically (and perhaps also sociologically) this is not satisfactory. Tilly's is an analysis of movements with the movement left out: it is action without agency.[24]

Although such analyses are grounded in time, they ignore the temporality of the movements' claims-making. A global perspective on social movements enable us to highlight the ways in which social movements expressed 'imaginary futures' that cannot easily be slotted into the rise of either the nation-state of a historical form or a homogenous form of globality and other stories of modernization. They were utopias, non-places, in the original sense of the word, but they nonetheless were promoted by specific actors in specific locales and in specific contexts.[25] In the practices of protest, however, such utopias turned into what Manuel Castells has called 'timeless time' that 'combined two different types of experience': the 'day by day' experiences in the occupation or protest camps and on

---

[20] For another field see George Steinmetz (ed.), *Sociology and Empire. The Imperial Entanglements of a Discipline* (Durham, NC: Duke University Press, 2013).

[21] Geyer and Bright, 'World History', p. 1057.

[22] Reinhart Koselleck, 'Über die Theoriebedürftigkeit der Geschichtswissenschaft', in Werner Conze (ed.), *Theorie der Geschichtswissenschaft und Praxis des Geschichtsunterrichts* (Stuttgart: Klett Cotta, 1972), pp. 10–28.

[23] Doug McAdam, Sidney Tarrow and Charles Tilly, *Dynamics of Contention* (Cambridge: Cambridge University Press, 2001).

[24] See the critique by James M. Jasper, 'Social Movement Theory Today: Toward a Theory of Action?' *Sociology Compass* 11 (2010), pp. 965–976, especially p. 974.

[25] Manu Goswami, 'Imaginary Futures and Colonial Internationalism', *American Historical Review* 5 (2012), pp. 1461–1485.

demonstrations, and the 'unlimited horizon of possibilities of new forms of life and community emerging from the practice of movement'.[26] The global history of social movements is therefore not simply limitless, it still takes place, quite literally. It allows us to 'read time into space' and to identify the spaces at which history unfolds.[27] Our contributions are therefore sceptical of approaches that posit a 'world culture' as the basis for global social activism. Although John Boli, George Thomas and others make it clear that they do not wish to suggest the homogeneity of assumptions of culture, the approach nonetheless risks positing a globally valid framework of understanding as a priori, rather than opening it up for historicization and interpretations. In our view, their approach also does not take sufficient account of the way in which global imaginaries were just as much interpretations of specific cultural assumptions rather than universals, and gave rise to specific utopian longings of the future, rather than generic ones.[28]

These futures were often expressed locally, through the occupation of very particular spaces and by creating very specific places. Such spaces have created communities of belonging that make visible symbolically the

[26] Manuel Castells, *Networks of Outrage and Hope. Social Movements in the Internet Age* (Cambridge: Polity, 2012), p. 223.

[27] See the imaginative account by Karl Schlögel, *Im Raume lesen wir die Zeit. Über Zivilisationsgeschichte und Geopolitik* (Munich: Hanser, 2003), whose title is inspired by the geographer Karl Ratzel. An excellent summary of the sociology of spaces and places is provided by Markus Schroer, *Räume, Orte, Grenzen. Auf dem Weg zu einer Soziologie des Raums* (Frankfurt/Main: Suhrkamp, 2006). As case studies see James Epstein, 'Spatial Practices/ democratic vistas', *Social History* 3 (1999), pp. 294–310, especially pp. 309–310 and Sebastian D. Schickl, *Universalismus und Partikularismus. Erfahrungsraum, Erwartungshorizont und Territorialdebatten in der diskursiven Praxis der II. Internationale 1889–1917* (St. Ingbert: Röhrig, 2012); Davina Cooper, *Everyday Utopias. The Conceptual Life of Promising Spaces* (Durham, NC: Duke University Press, 2014); Francesca Polletta, '"Free spaces" in Collective Action', *Theory and Society* 1 (1999), pp. 1–38.

[28] John Boli and George M. Thomas, *Constructing World Culture. International Nongovernmental Organizations since 1875* (Palo Alto, CA: Stanford University Press, 1999). For a theoretical critique see Rudolf Stichweh, *Die Weltgesellschaft. Soziologische Analysen*, Frankfurt/Main: Suhrkamp, 2000), pp. 19–23; Bettina Heintz, Richard Münch, Hartmann Tyrell (eds), *Weltgesellschaft. Theoretische Zugänge und empirische Problemlagen* (Stuttgart: Lucius & Lucius, 2005); and Janet Wolff, 'The Global and the Specific: Reconciling Conflicting Theories of Culture', in Anthony D. King (ed.), *Culture, Globalization and the World System* (Binghamton, NY: State University of New York Press, 1991), pp. 161–173, and empirically Oscar Handlin, *One World: The Origins of an American Concept* (Oxford: Oxford University Press, 1974); cf. Geyer and Bright, 'World History', p. 1047 and p. 1055.

movements' claims to power and are also public.[29] It is a well-known fact that social movements depend on the (mass) media to reproduce themselves, to frame their messages and to broadcast their aims.[30] The question that arises from this is whether the development of information technology and the possibilities of instant communications have fundamentally changed this relationship by making global connections more efficient and effective.[31] The contributions by John Chalcraft and Nora Lafi on the social movements in the modern Middle East express deep scepticism about such interpretations and highlight the importance of real over virtual networks; and a mere cursory glance at historical revolutionary conjunctures suggests that the mechanisms whereby global futures become embedded in specific local contexts that we can observe today also have their histories.[32] The question remains, though, whether the new technologies have, by reshaping the nature of power and statehood, also had an impact on the nature of protest, enabling new interactions between virtual and real connections.[33] The network metaphor has itself a fascinating history that was deeply embedded in the history of global movement activism and that deserves further exploration in this context.[34]

History, and global history in particular, allow us to bring agency and time back into sociological research on social movements and might provide crucial evidence to develop further action-theoretical accounts of social movements that take full account of the role of emotions and culture in social movement activism.[35] A conversation between historians

[29] See Castells, *Networks*, pp. 10–11.

[30] William Gamson and Gadi Wolfsfeld, 'Movements and Media as Interacting Systems', *Annals of the American Academy of Political and Social Science* 528 (1993), pp. 114–125.

[31] See, for example, the differentiated take by Jeffrey S. Juris, *Networking Futures. The Movements against Corporate Globalization* (Durham, NC: Duke University Press, 2008).

[32] See, for example, the remarks on a 'globalization from below' in the context of the Paris Commune by Kristin Ross, *Communal Luxury: The Political Imaginary of the Paris Commune* (London: Verso, 2015) and, with a specific emphasis on the temporality of these imaginaries Lucian Hölscher, *Weltgericht oder Revolution. Protestantische und sozialistische Zukunftsvorstellungen im deutschen Kaiserreich* (Stuttgart: Klett Cotta, 1989).

[33] Castells, *Networks*, p. 15.

[34] Sebastian Gießmann, *Die Verbundenheit der Dinge. Eine Kulturgeschichte der Netze und Netzwerke* (Berlin: Kadmos, 2014) and the critique of the concept by Marilyn Strathern, 'Cutting the Network', *The Journal of the Royal Anthropological Institute* 3 (1996), pp. 517–535.

[35] Cf. Britta Baumgarten, Priska Daphi and Peter Ullrich (eds), *Conceptualizing Culture in Social Movement Research* (Basingstoke: Palgrave Macmillan 2014), especially the chapter by James M. Jasper, 'Feeling–Thinking: Emotions as Central to Culture', pp. 23–44.

and social scientists will enable us to avoid 'the danger of substituting the dogmatic structuralism of older forms of social history with a more accidental, but nevertheless exaggerated actor-centeredness'.[36] They will help to highlight in particular the multiple interactions between actors, their values, the political and social structures, as well as the processes within which they operated.[37] Within this general framework, the 'globality' of social movements might pertain to one of these aspects, but not to the others, so that the global nature and reach of the movements may often be smaller than the term suggests.[38]

Our volume, therefore, brings together historical studies that stem from a variety of theoretical traditions, although none of our chapters adopts only one particular theoretical model by, say, prioritizing political opportunity structures or the mobilization of resources over social and economic conditions. Historical research, in particular, highlights the importance of framing as well as cognitive aspects to social movement studies, while not reducing these activities to strategic choices made by rational actors.[39] For most of the sociological approaches, 'globalizing' social movement theory means investigating whether and to what extent global connections have had an impact of the nature and efficacy of social movement activism. The domestic theoretical toolkit is essentially transferred to the global arena.[40] Social movements often appear primarily as international non-governmental organizations or as domestic non-governmental organizations that act

---

[36] Wolfram Kaiser, 'Transnational Mobilization and Cultural Representation: Political Transfer in an Age of Proto-Globalization, Democratization and Nationalism 1848–1914', *European Review of History* 2 (2005), pp. 403–424, here p. 416.

[37] On these analytical distinctions see Carlos R. S. Milani and Ruthy Nadia Laniado, 'Transnational Social Movements and the Globalization Agenda: A Methodological Approach Based on the Analysis of the World Social Forum', *Brazilian Political Science Review* 1 (2007), pp. 10–39, here pp. 14–17, available at: http://socialsciences.scielo.org/pdf/s_bpsr/v2nse/a01v2nse.pdf.

[38] A point made forcefully by Frederick Cooper, 'What is Globalization Good for? An African Historian's Perspective', *African Affairs* 100 (2001), pp. 189–213.

[39] Cf. Doug McAdam, John D. McCarthy and Mayer Zald (eds), *Comparative Perspectives on Social Movements. Political Opportunities, Mobilizing Structures, and Cultural Framings* (Cambridge: Cambridge University Press, 1996); Ron Eyerman and Andrew Jamison, *Social Movements. A Cognitive Approach* (Cambridge: Polity, 1991).

[40] Cf., for example, John D. McCarthy (ed.), 'The Globalization of Social Movement Theory', in Jackie Smith, Charles Chatfield and Ron Pagnucco (eds), *Transnational Social Movements and Global Politics* (Syracuse, NY: Syracuse University Press, 1997), pp. 243–259 and Jackie Smith, 'Social Movements and World Politics. A Theoretical Framework', pp. 59–77 in the same volume.

internationally, so that their main activity appears as one of pressure groups that campaign for specific policy outcomes rather than as movements that try to promote broader programmes of social and cultural change.[41] Tilly's analysis of social movements has also, broadly, been embedded within a modernization-theoretical account of social movement activism. Given the emergence of 'world history in a global age' that has highlighted the complexity of multiple modernities that coexisted side by side, such an account no longer seems reasonable.[42] This is why, third, we contend that the renewal of the history of social movement can only happen from the perspective of global history that takes account of the rich literature in transnational and global history that has developed over the recent decade or so.[43] A global perspective is especially adept at bringing to light both the structures of power and the power of contestation stemming from social movements that operate across national boundaries: domestic social movements challenge the boundaries of the political vested in a regime of territorial sovereignty,[44] social movements that operate in the global domain do this even more. In this context, it is important to be aware that the metaphor of 'flow' that is often used to described the global connections and reach of these movements was itself embedded in these networks of power and contestations and has the tendency to efface that power and the agencies that are associated with it. The metaphor opens up a 'rhetorical dichotomy that locates agency and dynamism in global systems all

[41] See the pathbreaking book by Margaret E. Keck and Kathryn Sikkink, *Activists Beyond Borders. Advocacy Networks in International Politics* (Ithaca, NY: Cornell University Press, 1998).

[42] Geyer and Bright, 'World History', as well as the magisterial study by Jürgen Osterhammel, *The Transformation of the World. A Global History of the Nineteenth Century* (Princeton, NJ: Princeton University Press, 2014) as well as and volumes by Emily S. Rosenberg (ed.), *A World Connecting* (Cambridge, MA: Harvard University Press, 2012); Akira Irye (ed.), *Global Interdependence. The World after 1945* (Cambridge, MA: Harvard University Press, 2014) and the textbook by John Coatsworth et al., *Global Connections. Politics, Exchange and Social Life in World History* (Cambridge: Cambridge University Press, 2015), vol. 2: Since 1500.

[43] See only Akira Iriye and Pierre-Yves Saunier (eds), *The Palgrave Dictionary of Transnational History. From the Mid-19th Century to the Present Day* (Basingstoke: Palgrave Macmillan, 2009).

[44] Charles S. Maier (ed.), *Changing Boundaries of the Political* (Cambridge: Cambridge University Press, 1987), especially the chapter by Claus Offe.

at the larger scales while treating small scales, such as the level of human experience, as essentially passive and reactive'.[45] Global social movements therefore bring to light the 'alternative world destroyed and suppressed' within a global system of states.[46] We wish to stress in particular that it is not only progressive but also reactionary movements that make use of this global sphere of operations.[47] It is also this crossing of borders, real or imagined, that makes the legitimacy of global social movements so contested: they often operate outside the coordinates of domestic politics, while at the same time appearing as alien influences in domestic politics. They are, to use Sidney Tarrow's phrase, doubly 'strangers at the gate'.[48] This is why a global history of social movements cannot do without taking the history of power and its legitimacy into account. It can only be written as a socio-cultural history of politics.

But this alienation effect that a global perspective might have also applies to historical research itself: Park Chung Hee's conceptual chapter on Korean feminism demonstrates the vast creative conceptual potential of a global optic. As Andreas Eckert's contribution mentions, there has been an intensive and highly productive debate about whether a Western notion of 'social movement' can be applied to African countries, given the nature of statehood and the legacy of colonialism there. This debate essentially revolved around the nature of post-colonial agency and was a sub-set of the wider debate surrounding the theme of 'national liberation [as] a western derived project'.[49] Furthermore, it enquired whether there could be 'African' movements *sui generis*. This debate has resulted in a number of productive interventions on a 'politics from below' that crossed

---

[45] Stuart Alexander Rockefeller, 'Flow', *Current Anthropology* 4 (2011), pp. 557–568, here p. 564.

[46] Michael J. Schapiro, 'Moral Geographies and the Ethics of Post-Sovereignty', *Public Culture*, 6 (1994), pp. 479–502, here p. 481.

[47] See, for example, the ERC project by Robert Gerwarth on paramilitary violence in the context of the First World War and its aftermath: http://www.ucd.ie/warstudies/research-projects/demobilization/ as well as the contributions by Kevin Passmore, Klaus Weinhauer and Fabian Virchow in this volume.

[48] Sidney Tarrow, *Strangers at the Gate. Movements and States in Contentious Politics* (Cambridge: Cambridge University Press, 2012). Cf. also Olaf Kaltmeier, *Politische Räume jenseits von Staat und Nation* (Göttingen: Wallstein, 2012), p. 70.

[49] See John D. Kelly and Martha Kaplan, 'Nation and decolonization. Toward a New Anthropology of Nationalism', *Anthropological Theory* 4 (2001), pp. 419–437, here p. 419.

national boundaries.[50] But this debate has also brought to light questions of power and influence and their legitimatizing discourses that frequently remain hidden in social movement scholarship and that can provide important clues for conceptual scholarship elsewhere. Marie-Emmanuelle Pommerolle, following Jean-François Bayart, has suggested an analysis that places 'dependency as a mode of action' centre stage and that regards the global and international orientation of social movements in Cameroon as the 'extraversion of African political spaces'. Here, 'the international sphere should not be viewed as external to national political space—it is, in fact, a constituent part of it'. In short: the global is already part of the national. This constellation has had highly contradictory effects: access to the global sphere is the result of contestations, and success or failure have had consequences on the distribution of domestic power.[51]

A global perspective on social movements therefore opens up the fixed Western meanings of some of the movements that are included in this volume for deeper historicization by asking how some of the universal languages and claims came 'with their own set of inclusions and exclusions' and how such more restrictive languages could nonetheless transform social relations in places like Africa. Our perspective therefore draws attention to the different meanings of 'equality', 'freedom', 'peace' and so on, while nonetheless bringing them together within a common frame of reference that help to create connections across the globe.[52] It

[50] Jean-François Bayart, Achille Mbembe and Comi Toulabor, *Le politique par le bas en Afrique noire* (Clamecy: Karthala, new edition, 2008).

[51] Marie-Emmanuelle Pommerolle, 'The Extraversion of Protest: Conditions, History and Use of the 'International' in Africa', *Review of African Political Economy* 125 (2010), pp. 263–279, here p. 264 citing Jean-François Bayart, 'L'Afrique dans le monde: une histoire d'extraversion', *Critique Internationale* 5 (1999), pp. 97–120. For a global history of social movements that places power at the centre see Susan Zimmermann, *GrenzÜberschreitungen. Internationale Netzwerke, Organisationen, Bewegungen und die Politik der globalen Ungleichheit vom 17. bis zum 21. Jahrhundert* (Vienna: Mandelbaum, 2010).

[52] Frederick Cooper, 'Networks, Moral Discourse, and History', in Thomas Callaghy, Ronald Kassimir and Robert Latham (eds), *Intervention and Transnationalism in Africa. Global–Local Networks of Power* (Cambridge: Cambridge University Press, 2001), pp. 23–46, especially p. 24 and p. 35. As case studies see, for example, Janet Polasky, *Revolutions without Borders. The Call to Liberty in the Atlantic World* (New Haven, CT: Yale University Press, 2015); Laurent Dubois; *A Colony of Citizens. Revolution and Slave Emancipation in the French Caribbean, 1787–1804* (Chapel Hill, NC: University of North Carolina Press, 2004) and on the specific regime of temporality Malick W. Ghachem, *The Old Regime and the Haitian Revolution* (Cambridge: Cambridge University Press, 2012).

highlights how 'projections of Western power were [...] locally articulated as self-mobilizations and absorbed into the very fabric of local affairs'.[53] Analysing social movement activism within a global framework therefore also enables us to unpack the meaning of some of the metaphors within the context of the (co-) production of social relations: rather than starting with preconceived notions of what 'the social' in the social movements is, a global perspective encourages us to follow and trace, unpack and unpick, the protests, networks, flows and stories as they occur, thus 'reassembling the social'.[54] We also believe that global approaches to the history of social movement are especially adept at showing how notions of class and gender were directly connected with notions of race and political domination.[55] In particular, a global perspective enables us to glimpse how the forms that social movements took were themselves embedded in and related to specific global formations, such as imperialism and colonialism.[56]

The conceptual history of (global) social movements developed in synch with the actual history of social movements, but has always been in a complex relationship with it. In particular, the concept 'social move-ment' emerged in the context of the conceptual changes in the wake of the French Revolution, so that the concept comes with intimate connections to the history of the European Enlightenment.[57] 'Social movement' always refers to both an abstract conceptualization and the actual occurrence of protests. Early conceptualizations of 'social movement' emerged in France around the French Revolution. For Saint-Simon and others writing in France in the 1820s, 'social movement' became a shorthand for progres-sive social change as such. After the July Revolution of 1830, the concept travelled to Germany, and French theorists instead discussed society from

---

[53] Geyer and Bright, 'World History', p. 1049.

[54] Bruno Latour, *Reassembling the Social. An Introduction to Actor–Network-Theory* (Oxford: OUniversity Press, 2005).

[55] See the important conceptual interventions on the mutual imbrication of gender and class by Kathleen Canning, Gender History in Practice: Historical Perspectives on Bodies, Class, and Citizenship (Ithaca, NY: Cornell University Press, 2006).

[56] Cf., for example, the case study by Matthew Hilton, 'Ken Loach and the Save the Children Film: Humanitarianism, Imperialism and the Changing Role of Charity in Britain', *Journal of Modern History* 2 (2015), pp. 357–394 and Gary B. Magee and Andrew S. Thompson, *Empire and Globalisation. Networks of People, Goods and Capital in the British World, c. 1850–1914* (Cambridge: Cambridge University Press, 2010).

[57] On the French Revolution as a moment of conceptual change see Reinhart Koselleck, *The Practice of Conceptual History: Timing History, Spacing Concepts* (Palo Alto, CA: Stanford University Press, 2002).

the perspective of 'the masses' posing a threat to the stability of social order. In Germany, however, the concept 'social movement' found resonance among Hegel and his followers, where it became shorthand not for any specific social processes, but the dialectical movement of history as such. It is only in the context of the left-wing Hegelians that 'social movement' regained its critical potential, when Bruno Bauer began to conceptualize 'movement' as the 'negation' of existing social conditions. It was in the critical engagement of Karl Marx and Friedrich Engels with Bauer's writing that 'social movements' became connected to a specific social formation, the working class. In the conceptualization in the *Communist Manifesto* (1848), Marx and Engels connected the concept of 'social movement' with a positive rendering of 'masses', so that the emerging proletariat became the archetype of a social movement. By the end of the nineteenth century, 'social movement' was no longer in fashion, as the specifics of the labour movement came into view: Lorenz von Stein, for whom the concept had carried notions of holistic social change in the 1840s, refocused his inter-pretation of 'social movement' primarily on its empirical existence rather than any world-historical conclusions. In the wake of the First World War, 'social movement' then became a concept that was used both conceptually and in empirical practice as a counter-concept to 'revolution'. It was mainly connected to the rise of fascist movements that now occurred in specific protest events, a meaning that lingers on in the early socio-psychological work on collective behaviour in the 1950s as well as in the various incar-nations of theories of totalitarianism.[58] As such, global movements and their (social-scientific) conceptualization have influenced the images of the social and of society that have circulated at any given time.[59]

Any serious attempt at writing the global history of social movements requires an awareness of the 'historical sociology of concept formation' and the 'epistemological unconscious' that is constantly brought into con-versation with the empirical evidence.[60] In that sense, rather than regarding

[58] Wolfgang Schieder, ed., *Faschismus als soziale Bewegung* (Göttingen: Vandenhoeck & Ruprecht, 1982) and the chapter by Kevin Passmore in this volume.

[59] For the preceding paragraph see Otthein Ramstedt, Soziale Bewegung (Frankfurt/Main Suhrkamp, 1978), p. 7, 27, 30, 43, 47–55, 59–61, 75–77, 105, 107–108, 110–112; Borch, *Politics of Crowds*; and Gabriele Klein (ed.), *Bewegung. Sozial- und kulturwissenschaftliche Konzepte* (Bielefeld: transcript, 2004).

[60] See Margaret R. Somers, *Genealogies of Citizenship. Markets, Statelessness, and the Right to Have Rights* (Cambridge: Cambridge University Press, 2008), p. 173; George Steinmetz, 'Introduction: Positivism and its Others in the Social Sciences, in idem (ed.), *The Politics of*

the concept of 'social movement' as evidence of what Lutz Raphael has called the 'scientization of the social', it may be more apposite to regard 'global social movement' as a concept or category that performs specific knowledge work, both conceptually and empirically.[61] While not all chapters in this volume seek to engage in such an effort explicitly, they jointly, together with the conceptual contributions, seek to encourage a debate in this direction.

Social movements have played a vital role in determining the course of world history at many important junctures. They comprised many organizationally and ideologically different movements, including socialist and communist movements but also fascist ones. They go back deep into history, as the chapter by Marcel van der Linden in this volume particularly exemplifies, and yet they are often treated as extremely recent phenomena. The latter has much to do with the dominance of social movement studies, a field in which social scientists look mainly at contemporary social movements.[62] When representatives of social movement studies talk about taking a historical approach, they often go back to the new social movements of the 1970s, which are widely perceived as the origins of today's social movements. In particular, the big three social movements—women's movements, peace movements and environmental movements—have been studied extensively over recent years. The main academic journals in the field in English are oriented towards social science, in particular *Social*

Method in the Human Sciences. Positivism and its Epistemological Others (Durham, NC: Duke University Press, 2005), pp. 44–45. For a conceptual history of 'globalization' see Olaf Bach, *Die Erfindung der Globalisierung. Entstehung und Wandel eines zeitgeschichtlichen Grundbegriffs* (Frankfurt/Main: Campus, 2013).

[61] Cf. Jakob Vogel, 'Von der Wissenschafts- zur Wissensgeschichte. Für eine Historisierung der "Wissensgesellschaft"', *Geschichte und Gesellschaft* 4 (2004), pp. 639–660 vs. Lutz Raphael, 'Die Verwissenschaftlichung des Sozialen als methodische und konzeptionelle Herausforderung für eine Sozialgeschichte des 20. Jahrhunderts', *Geschichte und Gesellschaft* 2 (1996), pp. 165–193. Cf., as an example for such a coproduction of knowledge: Tova Benski et al., 'From the Streets and Squares to Social Movement Studies: What Have We Learned?' *Current Sociology* 4 (2013), pp. 541–561.

[62] Good introductions to social movement studies in English include Donatella della Porta and Mario Diani, *Social Movements. An Introduction*, 2nd edn (Oxford: Blackwell, 2006); Hank Johnston, *What is a Social Movement?* (Cambridge: Polity, 2014); David A. Snow, Sarah A. Soule and Hanspeter Kriesi, *The Blackwell Companion to Social Movements* (Oxford: Blackwell, 2004); Sidney Tarrow, *Power in Movement: Social Movements and Contentious Politics* (Cambridge, Cambridge University Press, 2011); Charles Tilly and Lesley J. Wood, *Social Movements, 1768–2008*, 2nd edn (New York: Paradigm, 2009). Only Tilly and Wood, as historical sociologists, take a deep historical perspective.

Movement Studies, Mobilization and *Interface: A Journal for and about Social Movements*. By contrast, there is only one historical journal dedicated to exploring the deep history of social movements in their social history context—*Moving the Social. Journal of Social History and the History of Social Movements*.[63]
Whilst social scientists have been doing and continue to do a sterling job exploring contemporary social movements and their origins in contemporary history, it seems timely to explore in greater depth the deep history of social movements and to do so in global perspective. We take particular inspiration from Craig Calhoun's masterly attempt to trace the roots of radical social movements back to the early nineteenth century.[64] The Institute for Social Movements at Bochum University is dedicated to the task of historicizing social movements, although it also hosts social scientists and therefore develops deep historical analysis in close alliance with the perspectives from social-science oriented social movement studies.[65] Its current director, Stefan Berger, has joined forces with one of the foremost historians of social movements in Britain, Holger Nehring, to set up a new book series with Palgrave Macmillan, entitled *Palgrave Studies in the History of Social Movements*, which has already published several volumes on social movements on different parts and at different times in world history.[66] The current volume, coedited by Berger and Nehring,

[63] For *Social Movement Studies*, see: http://www.tandfonline.com/toc/csms20/current#. VSqM4JO1eVM; for *Mobilization*, see: http://www.mobilization.sdsu.edu/; for Interface, see: http://www.interfacejournal.net/; for *Moving the Social*, see: http://moving-the-social.ub.rub.de/; of course, we also have a range of journals dealing with social movements in other languages: in German, see, for example *Forschungsjournal Soziale Bewegungen*: http://forschungsjournal.de/, and in French, the journal *Le Mouvement Social*: http://www.cairn.info/revue-le-mouvement-social.htm. [all accessed 12 April 2015]

[64] Craig Calhoun, *The Roots of Radicalism: Tradition, the Public Sphere and Early Nineteenth-Century Social Movements* (Chicago: University of Chicago Press, 2012).

[65] http://www.isb.rub.de/isb/ [accessed 12 April 2015]. One of the most recent publications in the Institute's German-language book series also calls for the more thorough historicization of social movement studies, whilst at the same time urging historians to make use of the theoretical and conceptual arsenal provided by social movement studies. See Jürgen Mittag and Helke Stadtland, 'Soziale Bewegungsforschung im Spannungsfeld von Theorie und Empirie: einleitende Bemerkungen zu Potenzialen disziplinärer Brückenschläge zwischen Geschichts- und Sozialwissenschaft', in Jürgen Mittag and Helke Stadtland (eds), *Theoretische Ansätze und Konzepte der Forschung über soziale Bewegungen in der Geschichtswissenschaft* (Essen: Klartext, 2014), pp. 13–60.

[66] For the range of titles published in the Palgrave Studies in the History of Social Movements, see: http://www.palgraveconnect.com/pc/browse/listsubseries?subseries=

is meant to provide a state-of-the-art overview on social movements in a deep historical perspective, first of all, because any such overview is missing and secondly, because the editors hope to inspire more work in the history of social movements by showing what a fascinating and exciting field of research this currently is.

Any deep historical turn in social movement studies raises the question: How deep is this turn supposed to be? This leads us straight to the question of whether and to what extent social movements are modern phenomena and how we intend to define modernity. Our position is that social movements go back to the beginnings of society—social protest is as old as the first communities of human beings setting up their settlements and constituting a field of the social. However, we have no wish to deny that something of fundamental importance happened in the century between roughly 1750 and 1850, and it happened in the West, i.e. mainly in Europe and North America. What happened can be described in terms of two processes: industrialization and democratization. Much ink has been spilt over the question why the Industrial Revolution happened in Europe and not in China, and whilst the debate on the 'Great Divergence' is far from over and decided in all of its details, industrialization in the West provided the basis for the West's global dominance.[67] But the fundamental change in the eighteenth and nineteenth centuries was not just technological and industrial; it involved massive social change as well. A society, ordered into estates, into which people were born and out of which they could not move, in other words, a relatively static society, gave way to a society of equals, which was theoretically meritocratic and where the abilities and potentials of the individual determined its position in society. Of course, there were many other factors, such as wealth, education and networks which determined positions in society, but the social sphere became more fluid. The dual political revolutions in North America and France in the late eighteenth century emancipated 'the third estate' and formulated for the first time the equality of citizens who were all, without distinction, equal members of a posited national community. As people were emerging from estates-based societies, they attempted to organize their own lives, societies and social conditions through forms of

Palgrave%20Studies%20in%20the%20History%20of%20Social%20Movements&order_by=publish-date [accessed 12 April 2015].

[67] Roman Studer, *The Great Divergence Reconsidered: Europe, India and the Rise to Global Economic Power* (Cambridge: Cambridge University Press, 2015), pp. 13–17.

organization, thereby paving the way to modern forms of mass societies. These emerging forms of bourgeois associationalism also can be understood as an important boost for social movements in Europe and the Western world.[68] The birth of modern nationalism went hand in hand with the birth of some of the most cherished principles of modern democracy.[69] The political and industrial revolutions in Europe and North America marked a watershed in world history and reconstituted the world, as it was known by contemporaries. Hence, under the new conditions of citizenship and industrialization, the character of social movements also changed significantly as they had to take into account the fundamental change in the self-understanding and constitution of societies transitioning from an 'old' world into a 'new' one. This is also why we asked authors in this volume to concentrate on the modern history of social movements, i.e. the last 250 years. Whilst, some, notably Marcel van der Linden, challenged that idea and self-consciously presented an even deeper history of social movements, most adhered to our framework. It still presents, we would argue, a significant enrichment of our understanding of social movements, as we intend to contribute to add to the existing and flourishing study of social movements the field of social movement history.

One intriguing question is whether it is possible to identify waves of mobilization of social protest through social movements on a global level.[70] On the basis of the articles assembled in this volume we would like to suggest that it is difficult to talk about such waves in strict synchronic ways. Sometimes we can identify global moments of protest, e.g. the revo-

---

[68] In Germany, the rise of bourgeois society has been analysed in great detail in massive research projects based independently at the universities of Bielefeld (under Hans-Ulrich Wehler and Jürgen Kocka) and Frankfurt/Main (under Lothar Gall). See, for example, Jürgen Kocka, *Industrial Culture and Bourgeois Society: Business, Labor and Bureaucracy in Modern Germany* (Oxford: Berghahn Books, 1999); Lothar Gall, *Bürgertum in Deutschland* (Berlin: Goldmann, 1996); Peter Lundgreen (ed.), *Sozial- und Kulturgeschichte des Bürgertums: eine Bilanz des Bielefelder Sonderforschungsbereichs* (Göttingen: Vandenhoeck & Ruprecht, 2000).

[69] John Breuilly (ed.), *The Oxford Handbook of the History of Nationalism* (Oxford: Oxford University Press, 2013), Chaps. 5 and 6.

[70] Dieter Rucht, for example, has tried to trace protest waves in West Germany after 1949. See his 'Zur Wandel politischen Protests in der Bundesrepublik', *vorgänge* 4 (2003), pp. 4–11; Stefan Berger has tried something similar for Western Europe in his 'Social Movements in Europe since the End of the Second World War', in Jan-Ottmar Hesse, Christian Kleinschmidt, Alfred Reckendrees and Ray Stokes (eds), *Perspectives on European Economic and Social History* (Wiesbaden: Nomos, 2014), pp. 15–46.

lutionary period between 1905 and the early 1920s, the 1968 protests, or the anti-globalization protests of the 1990s and 2000s. But beyond such moments there are also many longue-durée and diachronic waves, forming around particular issues or themes. Here, for example, we can identify, first, waves of mobilization around the constitution of bourgeois society and its delineation from older aristocratic societies, lasting from the middle of the eighteenth to the middle of the nineteenth century and largely restricted to the Western world. Secondly, we can identify waves of mobilization against the expansion of the Western world to 'the rest', i.e. against colonialism and imperialism, which stretch from the early modern period right to the present, but had a particular strength from the late nineteenth century to the post-Second World War period. Third, we can identify waves of mobilization around labour protests against diverse regimes of labour associated with the expansion of industrial capitalism: starting in Europe and the West in the nineteenth century they reached other parts of the globe later in time and today still form a major backbone of social movement contention in places like Latin American and Asia. Fourth, social protests against war are perhaps as old as war itself, but in the Cold War conflict during the second half of the twentieth century, the real possibility of mutual annihilation of mankind and global destruction led to a massive wave of social movement protest. Not only 'the bomb' threatened the very survival of mankind from the second half of the twentieth century onward, environmental destruction at the same time plumbed new depths and threatened the ecological collapse of the planet, spawninga many-faceted environmental protection movement that is still riding the crest of a massive and truly global protest culture.[71] Sixth, the search for equal rights for women saw a first wave of protest in the late nineteenth and early twentieth century, and a second wave during the 1960s and 1970s.

Sometimes, waves of social movement mobilization have been connected to political generations, although this connection has never been a straightforward reflection of age differentials within society.[72] Thus, we

---

[71] See Joachim Radkau's magisterial account *The Age of Ecology. A Global History.* (Cambridge: Polity, 2014).

[72] Holger Nehring, '"Generation" as Political Argument in West European Protest Movements in the 1960s', in S. Lovell (ed.), *Generations in Twentieth-Century Europe* (Basingstoke: Palgrave Macmillan, 2007), pp. 57–78. See also, more generally, Mark Roseman (ed.), *Generations in Conflict: Youth Revolt and Generation Formation in Germany 1770–1968* (Cambridge: Cambridge University Press, 2004).

may speak of a revolutionary generation, influenced by the double revolution of US independence of 1776 and the French revolution of 1789, an 1832 and an 1848 generation, influenced by revolutionary events that spanned many parts of Europe in those years. Nationalist social movements are often connected to key events in the formation of modern nation-states, e.g. 1871 in Germany, 1867 in Hungary, 1905 in Norway etc. In a transnational Western vein, it makes sense to talk of a First World War and a Second World War generation, perhaps also a Great Depression generation. In the second half of the twentieth century, other generational caesuras spring to mind: the 1945 generation, the 1968 generation, and the 1989 generation.[73] Whilst 'generation' is rarely an exclusive explanatory factor in the formation and success of social movements, in many different ways generation can be usefully employed as a heuristic and analytical tool for a better understanding of social movement development.

No one volume can offer a complete history of everything, especially in sub-field where research is still in its infancy. Perhaps the most obvious omission in this volume is the absence of a chapter on anarchism, part of the movements for social reform that emerged around the world from the 1880s to the 1920s. Anarchism was especially adept at crossing boundaries and establishing global connections.[74] In a number of regions, the translation of anarchism into local movements and societies 'forged a culture of contestation [...] which [...] challenged existing and emerging class boundaries, redefined notions of foreignness and belonging, and promoted alternative visions of social and world order' that lay outside the traditional remit of the organized labour movement and depended on the appropriation and translation of culture as much as on direct political exchanges. It was frequently connected to 'nodal cities' that became connected through improved means of communication and cross-migration.[75] Likewise, we

---

[73] A. Dirk Moses, *German Intellectuals and the Nazi Past* (Cambridge: Cambridge University Press, 2009), pp. 55–73 on the 'forty fivers'; Dorothee Wierling, *Geboren im Jahr eins. Der Jahrgang 1949 in der DDR. Versuch einer Kollektivbiographie* (Berlin: C. H. Links, 2002); Jürgen Reulecke (ed.), *Generationalität und Lebensgeschichte im 20. Jahrhundert* (Munich: Oldenbourg, 2003); Mary Fulbrook, *Dissonant Lives: Generations and Violence through the German Dictatorships* (Oxford: Oxford University Press, 2011).

[74] Benedict Anderson, *Under Three Flags. Anarchism and the Anti-Colonial Imagination* (London: Verso, 2005).

[75] Ilham Khuri-Makdisi, *The Eastern Mediterranean and the Making of Global Radicalism, 1860–1914* (Berkeley, CA: University of California Press, 2010), p. 1 and p. 26. Cf. also Constance Bantman, *The French Anarchists in London 1880–1914. Exile and Transnationalism in the First Globalisation* (Liverpool: Liverpool University Press, 2013); Nicola Pizzolato,

might have also included a chapter on the global trajectories of revolutions and revolutionaries.[76] The volume also does not include a chapter on global religious movements. While it becomes clear in some of the chapters that religion was a crucial force,[77] our volume does not engage with the global movements for religious awakenings, nor with the global nature of connections that religious movements were able to provide.[78] Religious movements, in particular, were deeply imbricated in colonial rule. But the social contexts in terms of race, class and gender in which the missionaries operated were never fixed; they changed as the missionaries travelled. The Catholic Church, in particular, has not only provided an organizational framework for these groups:[79] it has, through this organizational context, provided

---

Challenging Global Capitalism. Labor Migration, Radical Struggle, and Urban Change in Detroit and Turin (New York, Palgrave Macmillan, 2013). On the specific task of 'translation' see Sean Scalmer, 'Translating Contention: Culture, History, and the Circulation of Collective Action', *Alternatives: Global, Local, Political* 4 (2000), pp. 491–514.

[76] See, for example, Polasky, *Revolutions;* Peter Linebaugh and Marcus Rediker, The Many-Headed Hydra: *Sailors, Slaves, Commoners, and the Hidden History of the Revolutionary Atlantic* (Boston, MA: Beacon Press, 2000); Matthew D. Rothwell, *Transpacific Revolutionaries: The Chinese Revolution in Latin America* (New York: Routledge, 2013), Padraic Kenney, *1989. Democratic Revolutions at the Cold War's End: A Brief History with Documents* (New York: Bedford/St Martin's, 2009).

[77] For example Holger Nehring's on peace movements and Alexandra Przyrembel's on moral reform movements.

[78] For summaries see Rosenberg, 'Strömungen', pp. 870–879 (published separately in English as *Transnational Currents in a Shrinking World: 1870–1945* (Cambridge, MA: Belknap, 2014) and Osterhammel, *Transformation*, Chapter 19. For case studies see Abigail Green and Vincent Viaene (eds), *Religious Internationals in the Modern Age: Globalization and Faith Communities since 1750* (Basingstoke: Palgrave Macmillan, 2012); David Bebbington, *Victorian Religious Revivals: Culture and Piety in Local and Global Contexts* (Oxford: Oxford University Press, 2012); Rebekka Habermas, 'Mission im 19. Jahrhundert. Globale Netze des Religiösen', *Historische Zeitschrift* 56 (2008), pp. 629–679; Harald Fischer-Tiné, 'Global Civil Society and the Forces of Empire: The Salvation Army, British Imperialism, and the "Prehistory" of NGOs (c 1880–1920)', in Sebastian Conrad and Dominic Sachsenmaier (eds), *Competing Visions of World Order: Global Moments and Movements* (New York: Palgrave Macmillan, 2007), pp. 29–68: Alexandra Przyrembel, 'The Emotional Bond of Brotherliness: Protestant Masculinity and the Local and Global Networks among Religious in the Nineteenth Century', *German History* 2 (2013), pp. 157–180.

[79] Markus Friedrich, *Der lange Arm Roms?: Globale Verwaltung und Kommunikation im Jesuitenorden 1540–1773* (Frankfurt/Main: Campus, 2011); Vincent Viaene, *The Papacy and the New World Order: Vatican Diplomacy, Catholic Opinion and International Politics at the Time of Leo XIII (1878–1903)* (Leuven: Leuven University Press, 2006).

a powerful backdrop to social movement activity.[80] Likewise, one might have also included chapters on the global history of nationalism in this volume, especially in the context of pan-Arabism and pan-Asianism. These movements highlight especially well the fracturedness of the global history of social movements, where global connections do not lead to the emergence of global utopias, but, rather, reinforce particularist visions. We hope, however, that this theme is made sufficiently clear in the other chapters to this volume.[81]

It seems appropriate to start the volume with one of the foremost theoreticians and practitioners of social movement studies, Dieter Rucht, who has been active in this field for many decades and who provides us with some conceptual and theoretical guidance. Thus, he discusses various attempts to define social movements and provides us with his own lucid and convincing definition. Rucht goes on to differentiate between descriptive questions and causal explanations in social movement questions, introducing the 'triple C'—characteristics, conditions and consequences. He also problematizes the normativity of much social movement studies research. Furthermore, he reinforces the need to theorize social movement studies and gives examples of the usefulness of a diverse body of theories helping to answer specific questions. After discussing some of the most common methods of and sources for research on social movements, he concludes his chapter by discussing ways of interpreting and contextualizing social movement research.

Rucht's conceptual chapter is accompanied by two chapters which apply a particular body of theory to social movement research in specific regions of the world. Rochona Majumdar underlines the fruitfulness of applying a subaltern studies perspective to the history of social movements. Subaltern studies scholars started out with a strong interest in popular movements,

---

[80] Cf., for example, Christian Smith, *The Emergence of Liberation Theology: Radical Religion and the Social Movement Theory* (Chicago: University of Chicago Press, 1991).

[81] See, for example, Amira K. Bennison, 'Muslim Universalism and Western Globalization', in A.G. Hopkins (ed.), *Globalization and World History* (London: Pimlico, 2002), pp. 74–97; Cemil Aydin, *Politics of Anti-Westernism in Asia. Visions of World Order in Pan-Islamic and Pan-Asian Thought, 1882–1945* (New York, NY: Columbia University Press, 2007; Hasan Kayali, *Arabs and Young Turks: Ottomanism, Arabism, and Islamism in the Ottoman Empire, 1908–1918* (Berkeley, CA: University of California Press, 1997); Ali Raza, Franziska Roy and Benjamin Zachariah (eds), *The Internationalist Moment: South Asia, Worlds, and World Views 1917–39* (New Delhi: Sage, 2014); Vijay Prashad, *Darker Nations. A People's History of the Third World* (New York: New Press, 2007).

on the Indian sub-continent in particular an interest in peasant movements. Their desire to give 'the subaltern' their rightful place in history has been a strong motivation for studying social movements. Furthermore, peasant identities were often seen as bedrock of a range of other identities informing social movements by industrial workers, craftsmen and religious communities. Hence, from the interest in the subaltern peasant spread the interest in other post-colonial social movements. Finally, the emphasis by subaltern studies scholars on the agency of the subaltern had important theoretical repercussions for the understanding of social movements and their agency both in the metropole and the colonial peripheries. It challenged both the statism and the methodological nationalism of more traditional social movement studies in India and elsewhere in the world.

Senjoo Park problematized the way in which Western feminism has successfully styled women's rights as human rights, thereby achieving a de facto unparalleled globalization of women's issues but at the same time providing both the women's movements and their historians with a totally Western-centric view on the history of women. Her chapter is critical of such universalizing feminist theory. Instead it seeks to explore the rich diversity of women's protest forms and resistances in the realm of 'transpacific feminism' without wanting to fall back on national trajectories of such resistances and protests. The challenge, according to Park, is to avoid both nationalist tunnel-vision and Western-centric universalism.

The second part of this volume assembles a set of chapters providing surveys on the development of social movements in distinct continents. Some readers may find the 'continental' approach to the geography of social movements that undergirds one of the sections irritating: we agree that the designation of continents is itself part of the history we wish to unpack.[82] But we feel that our contributions, although written from within the geographical framework of the world's continents, still highlight the flows in and out of these countries and problematize the ways in which these continental histories are constructed, through contestations and the ways in which 'racial inscriptions' might be contained in such practices.[83]

---

[82] Martin W. Lewis and Kären Wigen, *The Myth of Continents: A Critique of Metageography* (Berkeley, CA: University of California Press, 1997) and Johannes Fabian, *Time and the Other. How Anthropology Makes its Object* (New York: Columbia University Press, 1983).

[83] Geyer and Bright, 'World History', p. 1035, fn 5. Cf. Thomas McCarthy, *Race, Empire and the Idea of Human Development* (Cambridge: Cambridge University Press, 2009).

Starting in the Americas, Chapter 5 explores a wide range of social movements in Central and Southern America. Claudia Wassermann introduces a periodization of their development which distinguishes between, first, post-independence movements from 1810 to 1870. They were led by indigenous peasants in times of great political instability. The peasants sought to defend themselves against the expansion of large European-owned landed estates and fought the compulsory labour regimes introduced for indigenous peasant populations. Secondly, anti-oligarchical social movements surfaced between the last third of the nineteenth and the first third of the twentieth century. They comprised traditional peasant groups but also traditional labour movement organizations and even urban middle-class protest groups: what united them was their enmity towards authoritarian oligarchies wielding power in post-independent Latin American states. Thirdly, nationalist social movements were prominent from the 1920s onwards. They were either inspired by European fascisms or by diverse forms of anti-imperialism. Fourthly, revolutionary social movements resisting right-wing dictatorships could be found in many Latin American countries during the second half of the twentieth century. Fifthly, new social movements, such as the women's and environmental movements as well as contemporary anti-capitalist anti-globalization movements emerged from the 1970s onwards.

A North American perspective is provided by Felicia Kornbluh's chapter. She acknowledges in her introduction the strength of methodological nationalism in studies on social movements in North America. It is a timely reminder of the strength of national research traditions in different parts of the world, albeit one that is hardly unique to the United States. While she is therefore almost forced to focus on developments in the United States she tries to look occasionally towards Canada and Mexico to put developments in North America into a more transnational perspective. Another bias of her chapter are the new social movements of the second half of the twentieth century. She explores to what extent the distinction between new and old social movements is a helpful one and finds it less helpful in the case of the US than in the cases of Canada and Mexico. After giving a survey of major social movements in the three countries under discussion, albeit with a clear focus on the US, she concludes that much of twentieth-century social change in North America cannot be properly understood without taking account of the multitude of social movements campaigning for such social change.

This is a conclusion that Marcel van der Linden's survey on social movements in Europe from 1000 to 2000 would concur with. Referring to the theoretical framework provided by resource mobilization, opportunity structure and framing, he emphasizes three long-term processes and their impact on the formation of social movements in Europe: state formation, capitalism and urban development. Whilst providing us with a longue-durée picture of social protest in Europe, van der Linden does distinguish pre-Modern from Modern protests. The Middle Ages and the Early Modern era, he argues, were divided from the Modern period by the transition from a predominantly agrarian to a predominantly industrial society. His survey focusses on forms of open and public protests: peasant protests, spanning all periods from the medieval to the twentieth century; guild battles that tended to peter out with the decline of the guilds in the Early Modern period; food riots, which again is a continuum throughout all periods of time; workers' and journeymen's struggles that van der Linden can also trace to the high Middle Ages; millenarian movements, spanning once again the pre-Modern and the Modern; social revolutions that he also traces to the high Middle Ages. Social protests under conditions of modern capitalism are then discussed with reference to the anti-slavery movement, the modern labour movement, and the women's movement. Van der Linden also gives us an intriguing glimpse into social protests under the twentieth-century communist regimes in Europe. He concludes by asserting three common threads that united social protest movements in Europe: the search for social security, social justice and respect.

Andreas Eckert's chapter on sub-Saharan Africa is a stark contrast to the chapters on the Americas and Europe. Whereas Wassermann, Kornbluh and van der Linden clearly struggled to provide a brief survey of immensely rich movements and their historiographies, Eckert states that there is an extreme dearth of studies on sub-Saharan African social movements—with the exception of the struggle against apartheid in South Africa. In his attempt to provide chronological caesuras, Eckert distinguishes a post-independence period from the 1960s to the 1980s, in which national liberation movements often turned dictatorial, from a period of democratization in the 1990s and a third period, in which civil society groups and international agencies joined forces to form a network of institutions furthering the overall aim of development. For a long time the sparse research on social movements was framed within the wider research focus on African civil society, or rather the absence of such a civil society and the need to develop one. The Western concept of civil society points to a more fundamental problem of social movement research in Africa—the concepts of civil society and social movement are adopted from the West, meaning that certain movements, especially Muslim movements, that could easily be classed as authentic African movements, did not come into the focus of social movement researchers. In line with developments in the West, social movements in Africa have more recently shifted their emphasis from the productive sphere to the sphere of consumption and from more material issues to issues of identity. Eckert goes on to argue that there is much scope in discussing African labour and nationalist movements under the rubric of social movements—something that so far has rarely happened. But the history of both movements would focus attention on the colonial state and on the labour question, two areas of central significance for any understanding of modern sub-Saharan African history. Thus, Eckert concludes, the potential for histories of social movements in sub-Saharan Africa is huge and as yet largely untapped.

Popular protest movements in North Africa and the Middle East, as discussed by John Chalcraft, have been much better served by a rich stream of historiography that was again boosted by the impact of the recent Arab Spring. Chalcraft's periodization distinguishes between a nineteenth century, ending in 1911 and characterized by imperialist interventions and reactions against it, a second period from 1911 to 1939, characterized by nationalism, wars and invasions, a third period from 1939 to 1979, in which Third Worldism, national liberation, socialism and neo-colonialism marked important themes and a fourth period from 1979 onwards, in which he sees Islamism, people's power and neo-liberalism as forces dominating the landscape of social movement activity. Chalcraft lays out a rich tapestry of traditions of social protest, which were almost always translocal in character and evolved in a transnational imperialist dynamic that very much determined the development of the region. Colonialism and its legacy, processes of state formation, geopolitics and the cultural dynamics inherent in specific historical contexts are here highlighted as the most important determinants for the development of social movements in North Africa and the Middle East. Like many of the other chapters in this volume, Chalcraft's study concludes that it is impossible to understand the history of the region without understanding the history of its social movements.

Whilst we have sub-divided the African continent into two units each comprising many nation-states, it was impossible to find authors to provide us with a survey or surveys on Asian social movements. Hence the editors settled for two Asian case studies which focus on nation-states. Arvind Elangovan can also draw on a rich historiography on social movements in India, and, like Chalcraft, he emphasizes the importance of imperialism and colonialism for the shape of social movement development in the modern period. He distinguishes three periods, first, the imperial dependency of India, secondly, the nationalist self-determination of India and thirdly, post-colonial India. For each of the periods he focusses on one case study of a social movement: for the nineteenth century he chooses the socio-religious reform movement of Raja Ram Mohan Roy; for the nationalist period he focusses on the socio-political reform movements of Mahatma Gandhi and Bhim Rao Ambedkar, and for the post-colonial period he analyses the environmental movement, Chipko. He thereby traces a development from socio-religious to socio-political social movements over the course of two centuries. The relationship of state and society was crucial in determining the shape and outlook of social movements throughout, but only in the post-colonial period, he argues, did the fate of social movements become inextricably intertwined with political parties.

In Chapter 11 on post-colonial Korea, Jung Han Kim seeks to underline that in dictatorial post-colonial contexts spontaneous mass protests lead to the creation of a political subject that subsequently finds expression in organized social movements. The chapter clearly shows how the forces of nationalism and modernization shaped Korean social movements under conditions of civil war, Cold War and the dictatorial regime of Park Chung Hee. Labour protests and the alliances between student and workers' protests from the 1970s onwards were powerful social movements contributing to the end of the dictatorship in South Korea and paving the way for the transition to democracy. The influential democracy movement in Korea is analysed in some detail before the chapter turns to the development of social movements in a post-democratic South Korean society. Here the impact of the New Left on South Korean social movements is assessed and the case study of the Korean's women's movement as an important new social movement is introduced. Kim concludes that South Korea might well serve as an example of the importance of social movements to post-colonial laboratories of democracy in a post-independence period.

The final chapter of Part II of this volume deals with both an entire continent and a nation-state, Australia. Here, as Sean Scalmer underlines, the colonial setting was vital in shaping social movements, in particular the important role of the colonial state and the manifold transnational connections that the British empire provided. Violent resistance of the indigenous population to colonial rule, and violent insurrections by convicts in the penal colony, characterized the early history of European settlement in Australia. Soon, less violent forms of protest, including petitions and the formation of movements by settlers or by miners demanding land rights and self-government could be found. They were inspired by the nineteenth-century European trend to form social movements in order to obtain certain rights and get what they regarded as their just demands fulfilled. The emergence of representative democracy in Australia and a relatively open society with many possibilities for social mobility turned out to be a positive environment for the formation of social movements. This is evident in the thriving of both the labour and women's movements and the emergence of an early welfare state. However, the more radical socialist and communist strands of the labour movement faced the full force of the state in an attempt to channel the labour movement in a parliamentary and reformist direction. Scalmer also introduces the repercussions of 1968 in Australia and talks at greater length on the campaign for aboriginal rights starting to gain momentum from the 1980s onwards. Together with the chapters on the Americas, the chapter on Australia confirms the basic distinction between colonial settler societies, in which white Europeans settled and dominated the post-colonial state and society, and colonies in which only a small colonial elite settled, where the Europeans withdrew after independence, leaving an indigenous, albeit often European-trained, elite in charge of the post-colonial state and society.

Following the survey chapters on diverse geographical regions of the world, Part III explores the history of social movements thematically. It starts off with Alexandra Przyrembel's chapter on 'moral movements', a diverse and wide-ranging array of largely middle-class and often aristocratic philanthropic societies that were motivated by a sense of bringing about moral improvement, be it in the field of the abolition of slavery, temperance reform, or the prevention of cruelty to animals. Such moral sentiments, Przyrembel shows, were intertwined with the formation of social movements from the Middle Ages to the twenty-first century. In her article she focusses on the nineteenth and early twentieth centuries, examining fields in which such transnational, albeit Western-centric, moral movements were active. They include the movement for the abolition of slavery, the Red Cross movement, and diverse movements aimed at morally uplifting the working classes. In the second part of the article, she deals with the global rise of human rights discourse and its impact on diverse moral movements. She uses two examples—aid efforts in connection with the Armenian genocide in the context of the First World War, and the formation and rise of Amnesty International—to underline the diverse ways in which the language of human rights influenced the formation of social movements. Overall, her article is a powerful reminder of the impact of moral and often religious sentiments on movements intent on helping strangers who are perceived to be in need. These movements developed a range of powerful activities in pursuit of her objectives and sought manifold alliances. With hindsight they formed some of the most successful and wide-ranging social movement campaigns in the modern age.

Although Karl Marx and Friedrich Engels mocked the moral sentiments of middle-class social movements, the labour movement can indeed be understood as a moral movement, although most of the activists here came from the working classes. Stefan Berger's chapter starts off with a criticism of the Western-centric nature of labour history and its concern with industrial wage labour. Its tunnel vision did not take into account the full diversity of labour regimes and protest forms associated with those labour regimes in different parts of the world. His survey of the emergence and development of labour movements across five continents seeks to take into account those local differences, but his survey also highlights transnational moments in the development of labour movements in different parts of the world. In fact, his attempt to highlight global moments in the development of labour movements, somewhat counter to recent trends in global history, argues that as labour movements emerged as Western phenomena, Western movements had an overwhelming influence on the development of labour movements elsewhere in the world, although non-Western labour movements always adapted those moments in the context of their local specificities. Berger concludes with a section discussing contemporary problems of labour movements in a world in which industrial wage labour is declining in Europe and North America and increasingly shifting to Latin America and Asia.

Labour movements have, of course, for a long time not even been understood as social movements, as they consisted of formal organizations, such as political parties, trade unions and cooperatives, which, in themselves were organizationally different from the much looser networks usually associated with 'new social movements'. This is also why labour movements are sometimes described as 'old' social movements, especially as they were allegedly less concerned with identity issues and more attuned to productivist and materialist concerns of their supporters. Such a view is criticized in Sean Scalmer's chapter, and Berger also underlines the firmly based status of labour movements as members of the family of social movements. In fact, a stream of articles on movements, usually referred to as 'new social movements', demonstrate that, in historical perspective they were not so new. In fact, the women's, the environmental and the peace movement, to name just the big three social movements, all had origins and roots that go back to the nineteenth century.

Frank Uekötter sets out to deconstruct the notion of a global environmental movement. From the beginning, the label 'environmentalism' covered a wide variety of fundamentally different and diverging movements. It was viewed differently in the global North and the global South, and the success of the movement and its consequences also varied enormously over space and time. Uekötter begins his survey with critical historiographical remarks stating how much of the existing literature is of relatively recent origin and how it tends to follow teleological narratives of progress. In the history of the environmental movement, as with movements discussed in other chapters, the state features large: it was the main addressee of the movement and the main actor in pushing through demands made by the movement. In environmentalism, Uekötter argues, certain iconic conflicts often had an important role in sustaining movements and campaigns for many years to come. Internationalization of environmental concerns is nothing new: it was perhaps, suggests Uekötter, as intense around 1900 as it was towards the end of the twentieth century, even if the movement was not yet so interconnected. The future of environmentalism appears uncertain to Uekötter on account of the many tensions that are inherent in a concept that is as undertheorized as it is changeable.

The women's movement, in Ilse Lenz's chapter, is delineated from feminism in an attempt, first of all, to achieve some conceptual clarity about what a chapter on the women's movement in global perspective should be dealing with. Like Berger on the labour movement, Lenz struggles with the Western-centrism of the concept of women's movement with its well-known caesuras and temporalities which do not work in other non-Western contexts. Whilst global gender inequality was at the heart of women's movements everywhere, their shape and consequences depended largely on markedly local contexts that varied widely. In Europe the ideological separation of a public (for men) from a private (for women) sphere served the legitimation of the subjugation of women. Furthermore, the productive (male) sphere became separated from the reproductive (female) sphere under capitalism. These developments led to the setting up of space- and time-specific gender orders which are traced by Lenz in global perspective. However, she also points out that the transnational character of the women's movement ensured that the movement's highly time- and space-specific characteristics were blended into diverse characteristics on a global scale. Hence, Lenz speaks of a 'blended women's movement' in global perspective. Different ideological orientations characterized the women's movement, from liberalism to materialism and socialism right through to anarchism and anti-imperialism. The women's movement, like other social movements, was characterized by a strong internationalism that found expression in the setting up of many international organizations. Lenz charts the impact of the new feminism from the 1960s onwards and highlights the alliances it built, for example with the homosexual-rightsmovement—again at different times in different places. Under the impact of the new women's movement, the emphasis tended more and more to the cultural construction of gender and sexuality, with a strong rebuttal of biological explanations. There was also a significant push towards the globalization of gender issues, which now found new international platforms, raising all the conceptual problems discussed in Park's chapter. Overall, however, Lenz emphasizes the pluralization and flexibilization of gender concepts over time—something which the global women's movement had an important part in.

Similarly, Holger Nehring's chapter on peace movements does not tell a story of modernization. Instead, his chapter emphasizes the constant coexistence of different concepts of 'peace' as well as 'movements' over time. In particular, he calls attention to the importance of historicizing both the complex and often paradoxical meanings of 'peace' that the movements promoted and the forms of organization that they chose. He argues that it is possible to identify a broad shift from liberal bourgeois pressure groups organizing in the nineteenth century to a broader, network-based social movement activism after 1945. Although peace movement activists thought in terms of 'world peace' throughout the 200 years of their history, their conceptions of the world were not necessarily global and often contained particularist, if not exclusionary patterns. Nehring follows Sandi E. Cooper and others in analysing the national embeddedness of European pacifism in the nineteenth century.[84] He also highlights patterns

[84] Sandi E. Cooper, *Patriotic Pacifism. Waging War on War in Europe, 1815–1914* (New York: Oxford University Press, 1991).

of exclusion in terms of gender and race. Ultimately, the key issue that peace movements had to come to terms with in the twentieth century was the growing force of anti-colonial nationalism that sat uneasily with the peace movement's emphasis on a global universalism in a world threatened by nuclear war.

The environmental, women's and peace movements were all fundamentally affected by the student protest movements which are often referred to by '1968'. Gerd-Rainer Horn analyses 1968 as a truly global moment. He emphasizes the festival character of 1968 and sees its most important legacy in having shown the potential of a different way of organizing the social sphere. Student protests united Western and Eastern Europe in the late 1960s, even if the political contexts, ambitions, and messages were quite different in East and West, but, as Horn impressively demonstrates, 1968 was not just transatlantic and Northern, spanning also the North American continent, it made its presence felt in places such as Mexico City and Dakar. Horn relativizes the often-quoted spontaneity of 1968 protests and points to the underlying organizational networks and action groups that prepared the ground for protests that might have looked spontaneous but were grounded in social movement activities. He stresses the role of cultural nonconformity in preparing the ground for 1968 as far back as the 1950s and early 1960s, and he stresses that 1968 was at its most successful where it could build powerful alliances with the labour movement. Horn argues that there is a clear north–south divide in the way in which student protests in northern Europe remained singular and isolated, whereas in southern Europe, they managed to forge broad alliances with workers and represent a threat to the existing political system. Radical forms of political Catholicism in the south had their part to play in explaining this patterning of 1968, although Horn admits that research on the precise reasons for this interesting divide is as yet in its infancy.

One transnational phenomenon often connected to radicalized 1968ers is that of left-wing terrorism in the West during the 1970s. In his chapter on terrorism, Klaus Weinhauer seeks to analyse terrorism in conjunction with its intricate and manifold relationships with social movements, the state and the media, through which much societal communication is channelled. He distinguishes five broad time periods: a first period from the 1870s to the First World War, in which radical left-wing as well as radical nationalist terrorists were active. A second period from the end of the First World War to the 1930s dominated by right-wing paramilitary terrorism characterized by violent anti-Semitism and anti-Bolshevism. A third period from the mid-1930s to the 1980s that saw the rise of anti-imperial and anti-colonial terrorism, often in search of liberation from imperial and colonial regimes. In a fourth period from the 1960s to the early 1990s, terrorism associated with radicalized student protest and the New Left came to the fore. Finally, during a fifth period from the 1980s onwards, religiously motivated terrorism was the focus of attention. Weinhauer surveys all five periods with a view to illuminating transnational connections and patterns. It is striking to see how the anarchist terrorism of the late nineteenth century already had a global presence. Once again the main addressee of terrorist attacks was for a long time the state; however, with the internationalization of terrorism and the globalization of media, more recently, it can be argued that there has been a shift from the state to global media as the main addressee of international terrorism.

In Weinhauer's chapter on terrorism, fascist terrorism already features prominently. The next two chapters deal with fascist and extreme right-wing movements as social movements. Rucht already outlined in his conceptual chapter that social movement studies have a clear left-wing bias in that they are predominantly concerned with left-of-centre movements. However, there have always also been right-wing social movements, many of which remain seriously under-studied in social movement research. Kevin Passmore starts his chapter by situating a social movement approach to the history of fascism in a variety of different, more dominant paradigms, from the search of generic types of fascism to the political religions approach, which has gained so much attention recently. He concludes that historians of fascism, whether they have looked for structures or for ideas, have tended to focus on fascist *regimes*, seriously underestimating the movement aspect of fascism. His chapter seeks to correct this by surveying the classic cases of Italy and Germany and augmenting them by two European cases, France and Hungary and three non-European ones— Latin America, China and India. Situating the emergence of fascist movements in the context of the political violence unleashed in the aftermath of the First World War, Passmore considers the many differences and parallels in the emergence and development of fascist and far-right regimes in different parts of the world, making a convincing case to take their movement character more serious than research on fascism has hitherto done.

Fabian Virchow's chapter brings the comparison of far-right social movements closer to the present. Like many contributors, he begins his chapter conceptually, separating post-fascist right-wing social movements from right-wing political parties and single events associated with the political right. Throughout his chapter he uses the theoretical arsenal provided by social movement studies to explain the development and success of those right-wing movements across time and place. Ranging widely across European and non-European countries, Virchow looks at political mobilization, cultural representation, links of right-wing social movements to various counter-cultures, their position vis-à-vis the state and their internationalism.

The last two chapters deal with more contemporary social movements. Britta Baumgarten discusses the Global Justice Movement, which she sees characterized by diversity, decentralized horizontal networking, spectacular actions geared to achieve maximum media attention, a combination of local and global action repertoires and a radical critique of the dominant socio-economic models. She points to the deep roots of anti-globalization protests spanning several centuries, but concentrates on more recent development since the protests at the G8 meeting in Birmingham in 1998, which saw the mobilization of 70,000 anti-globalization protesters. At subsequent G8, WTO, and IMF meetings, protest gathered around economic globalization, as it was identified by a broad alliance of protesters as the root problem for a whole host of political, environmental, cultural and social problems around the world. Using mass demonstrations and the organization of counter-summits as the two major organizational protest forms, key representatives of the Global Justice Movements have been in the vanguard of shifting the discursive field on globalization and impacting on political decision-making at different territorial levels.

Finally, Nora Lafi asks whether the Arab Spring can be understood as a series of events initiated and influenced by social movements. Her search for its root causes and the reasons why it developed so differently in different parts of the Arab world uncovers a deep history to those protests, often ignored by social scientists analysing the events. Lafi points to the peculiar formation of civil societies in the Arab world, which reaches back centuries and was built against the background of the complex, rich social and cultural heritage of the region. Her analysis of the historical roots of civic mobilization in the Arab world highlights the importance of cultures and milieux rooted in city quarters and neighbourhoods and often going back to the Medieval period. She underlines the importance of professional organizations and religious communities operating in Arab societies over very long time periods. The Ottoman state had implemented traditions of petitioning and mediation which have taken root in many Arab societies and constitute a special relationship of civic society with the state. If the state is seen by civic society actors as violating those traditions, conflict is the most likely outcome. This deep history also informs Lafi's analysis of events between 2010 and 2014. Thus, she relativizes the idea that it was largely the import of Western democratic and human rights thinking which prompted and sustained the protests. Her chapter is a fitting reminder of the dangers of Western-centrism in research on social movements in the non-Western world. Giving a rich tapestry of the evolution of diverse movement in different parts of the Arab world, she analyses the many differences in the transition from old to new regimes and the reasons why such transitions failed or succeeded.

Throughout the conceptual, spatial and the thematic chapters of this book, certain themes are particularly prominent. Thus, first, many spatial differences we can observe are directly related to the history of Western imperialism. Second, the role of the state has been a powerful one for many centuries, both as addressee of social movement action and as agency providing the environment in which social movements could thrive. Thirdly, a strong internationalism of social movements has been a major theme in many of the chapters assembled here. Fourth, such internationalism has been related to the transnationalism of particular themes and issues that social movements have dealt with in different parts of the world. Social movements thus combine the global with the highly local. Fifth, many authors of chapters grapple with definitions and concepts of social movements and how to apply them to their respective cases. It seems obvious that the rich tapestry of the history of social movements that emerges out of the narratives of the following pages cannot easily be pressed into the Procrustean bed of social movement theory. Thus this volume aims to contribute to a rethinking of the relationship of historical narratives to historical theory.

PART I

Conceptual, Methodological and Theoretical Considerations

Studying Social Movements: Some Conceptual Challenges

Dieter Rucht

In acknowledging, though not stressing, my disciplinary identity as a sociologist, I will present and reflect on several challenges that we are confronted with when analysing social movements. Among the many more challenges that exist, five of these will be identified, discussed and partly illustrated in what follows: defining the subject of research, asking relevant questions, theorizing social movements, choosing adequate methods and sources, and interpreting and contextualizing findings.

Defining the Subject of Research

When talking about social movements, we should be conscious about the kind of definition we use. More recently, almost all scholars, for good reasons, are offering nominal definitions only. Unlike so-called real definitions that imply assumptions about the nature or essence (the *Wesen* in German philosophy) of the matter or object under study, a nominal definition is nothing more than a convention to delineate a phenomenon so that it can be distinguished from other ones that are similar or opposite to the defined one. While social movements are often said to be 'fuzzy' phenom-

D. Rucht (✉)
Institut für Protest- und Bewegungsforschung, Berlin, Germany

© The Author(s) 2017
S. Berger, H. Nehring (eds.), *The History of Social Movements in Global Perspective*, DOI 10.1057/978-1-137-30427-8_2

ena or 'moving targets',[1] and therefore the search for precise boundaries may be wasted energy, this did not prevent various scholars from listing some criteria that, in their view, characterize social movements.[2]

When considering the many attempts to define a social movement, a few problems can and indeed should be avoided. First, some scholars have offered extremely inclusive definitions. An example is the proposition of John McCarthy and Mayer N. Zald to define social movements as 'a set of opinions and beliefs in a population which represents preferences for changing some elements of the social structure and/or reward distribution of a society'.[3] One weakness of this definition is that it also includes those holders of the described opinions and beliefs who remain totally inactive. Should one attribute a person to a social movement when he/she just sympathizes with the movement's cause but has no social bonds with adherents of and makes no contributions to the movement? Another problem with this wide definition is that it includes also people engaged in religious congregations, private interest groups, political parties and public administrations that may act totally separate from, or even in opposition to, a given movement. Third, this definition remains silent about social movement structures although its proponents were among those who have emphasized the role of resources and organization in the emergence and survival of social movements.

A second problem with definitions of social movement arises from some scholars' strong political mission. While these scholars may have included certain structural elements in their definition, they restricted it,

[1] See Sidney Tarrow, 'Understanding Political Change in Eastern Europe. "Aiming at a Moving Target"': Social Science and the Recent Rebellions in Eastern Europe', *PS: Political Science & Politics* 24 (1991), pp. 12–19.

[2] The French term *mouvement social* was used in the eighteenth century to denote major changes in society, whatever their cause may be. Soon after, it diffused to other languages, including German and English. Roughly since the 1830s, the term also referred to groups, especially socialist groups, which deliberately sought to bring about societal changes. This dual meaning of the concept as process and a collective actor can be found, for example, in the writings of Karl Marx. Since the late nineteenth century, the second meaning took over and, still today, is no longer restricted to groups from a particular ideological strand. On the history of the concept, see Otthein Rammstedt, *Soziale Bewegung* (Frankfurt/Main: Suhrkamp, 1978); Eckart Pankoke, *Sociale Bewegung—Sociale Frage—Sociale Politik. Grundfragen der deutschen 'Socialwissenschaft' im 19. Jahrhundert* (Stuttgart: Klett, 1970).

[3] John McCarthy and Mayer N. Zald, 'Resource Mobilization and Social Movements: A Partial Theory', *American Journal of Sociology* 82 (1977), pp. 1212–1241, here pp. 1217–1218.

on the level of ideology, to the 'progressive' or 'emancipatory' spectrum only.[4] This approach is clearly guided by political sympathy and, as a nominal definition, makes clear what the authors' are referring to. However, it leaves unanswered the question of how to name those groupings that meet the structural criteria usually attributed to a social movement but cannot be categorized as 'progressive' because their major goal does not fit the dimension of conservative/progressive or because they have an anti-progressive stance.

Third, there are scholars who list a number of reasonable criteria when defining a social movement but fail to separate the concept of a distinct actor from that of the conflict in which this actor is engaged. An example of such a conflation has been presented by Charles Tilly, who, by the way, was somewhat reluctant to use the concept of social movement[5] and, moreover, changed his definitions over time. In a widely cited and acknowledged proposal, Tilly characterized a social movement as

> a sustained series of interaction between power-holders and persons successfully claiming to speak on behalf of a constituency lacking formal representation, in the course of which these persons make publicly visible claims for changes in the distribution of the exercise of power, and back those demands with public demonstrations of support.[6]

This definition of a social movement implies a fundamental logical problem because it even includes the power-holders who are, like their challengers, involved in Tilly's 'sustained series of interactions'. Probably Tilly became aware of this conceptual flaw when, in his later writings, he restricted the

[4] Theodor W. Adorno, 'Bemerkungen über Statik und Dynamik in der Gesellschaft', *Kölner Zeitschrift für Soziologie und Sozialpsychologie* 8 (1956), pp. 321–328; Werner Hofmann, *Ideengeschichte der sozialen Bewegung des 19. und 20. Jahrhunderts* (Berlin: Walter de Gruyter, 1970).

[5] Instead, he preferred terms such as 'popular collective action' and 'contentious action'. In his early work, he offered only a vague definition of social movements as a unit in the study of collective action at the intersection between populations, groups, events, beliefs and actions. See Charles Tilly, *From Mobilization to Revolution* (Reading, MA: Addison-Wesley, 1978), p. 9f.

[6] Charles Tilly, 'Social Movements and National Politics', in Charles Bright and Susan Harding (eds), *Statemaking and Social Movements* (Ann Arbor, MI: University of Michigan Press, 1984), pp. 297–317, here p. 306.

notion of social movements to one conflict party only, namely the claim-making 'ordinary people'.[7]

This understanding of social movements as a distinct conflict party, whatever the additional definitional criteria may be, is widely shared by today's social movement scholars.[8] They jointly stress that social movements engage in a publicly visible struggle about bringing (or resisting) social change.

However, it is problematic to define social movements in opposition to power-holders only, as Charles Tilly and many others have suggested.[9] First, power-holders may be sided by what is commonly understood as a social movement. This applies, for example, to the situation in Bolivia where Evo Morales' presidency rests on a range of supporting movements. Second, we can easily imagine a struggle between a social movement and a counter-movement in which power-holders play only a minor role or that of a third party.

The aim to bring about, or resist, social change is a crucial definitional element. What is meant here is not any minor change *in* society but rather fundamental change *of* society. Obviously, what 'fundamental' means in this context needs to be clarified. In a preliminary take, fundamental change refers, first, to the basic patterns of distribution of power and material resources in a given society and, second, to the values and justifications for maintaining this order. Depending on the context, social movements may promote values that are opposed to the dominating ones, as was the case when liberal bourgeois movements questioned the values

---

[7] Tilly defines a social movement as 'a series of contentious performances, displays and campaigns by which ordinary people make collective claims on others' (Charles Tilly, *Social Movements, 1768–2004* [Boulder, CO: Paradigm Publishers, 2004], p. 3). He argues that social movements include three basic elements: campaigns, a repertoire of contention and WUNC: participants' concerted public representation of worthiness, unity, numbers and commitments on the part of themselves and/or their constituencies.

[8] See, for example, Mario Diani, 'The Concept of Social Movement', *The Sociological Review* 40 (1992), pp. 1–25; Donatella della Porta and Mario Diani, *Social Movements: An Introduction*, 2nd rev. edn (Oxford: Basil Blackwell, 2006); Joachim Raschke, *Soziale Bewegungen. Ein historisch-systematischer Grundriß* (Frankfurt/New York: Campus, 1985); Dieter Rucht, *Modernisierung und neue soziale Bewegungen. Deutschland, Frankreich und USA im Vergleich* (Frankfurt/Main: Campus Verlag, 1994).

[9] Tarrow, for example, defines social movements as 'socially mobilized groups engaged in sustained contentious interaction with powerholders in which at least one actor is either a target or a participant'. Sidney Tarrow, 'Transnational Politics: Contention and Institutions in International Politics', *Annual Review of Political Science* 4 (2011), pp. 1–20, here p. 11.

that undergirded the feudal and absolutist order. In other situations, social movements insist on the values that are rhetorically upheld by the elites and/or legally enshrined but are severely violated in practice, as was the case with the US civil rights movement. Accepting reference to a fundamental societal change as a definitional element does not necessarily mean that this reference is explicitly articulated in every single protest event or campaign. Social movement groups often concentrate on, and articulate, more tangible and specific aims, for either purely tactical reasons or because the ultimate goal of fundamental change is all too obvious when minor steps into a certain direction are envisaged.

The 'social' or, preferably, the '*societal*' dimension of social movements should not be misinterpreted as being non-political. Many basic social norms and institutions are defined, shaped and enforced by political rulers and institutions. Hence an attempt to change society almost inevitably requires engagement in the *political* sphere and confronting political actors. In that sense, most social movements are also political movements, an aspect that, for example, led Craig Jenkins to propose the term 'sociopolitical movements'.[10]

Still, in purely analytical terms, it makes sense to separate comprehensive social movements from political, religious and cultural movements that predominantly act in a particular realm or sub-system of society. Also, we should separate both social and political movements from political campaigns. The latter are more limited in their thematic scope and duration when trying, for example, to modify a particular law, to prevent the deportation of asylum seekers or to get rid of a corrupt political leader.

If we take seriously the criterion of social movements as collective attempts to bring about fundamental social change, we have to conclude that social movements did not exist in pre-modern times.[11] Changing society according to human will is essentially a modern idea that has been expressed since the era of Enlightenment. Earlier struggles and rebellions, from the insurrection of slaves in the Roman Empire to the peasant revolts in the early sixteenth century, were attempts to re-establish a traditional, natural and/or divine order that, in the eyes of the insurgents, has been violated by rulers, landlords, nobles and so on. The aim of pre-modern

---

[10] Craig Jenkins, 'Sociopolitical Movements', in Samuel L. Long (ed.), *Handbook of Political Behavior*, Vol. 4 (New York and London: Plenum Press, 1981), pp. 81–153.

[11] Dieter Rucht, 'Neue soziale Bewegungen—Anwälte oder Irrläufer des Projekts der Moderne?' *Frankfurter Hefte* 11/12 (FH-extra 6) (1984), pp. 144–149.

insurrections and rebellions was to re-establish a perceived 'natural' order with 'natural' rights and obligations.[12]

In addition to the struggle about a fundamental social change, three further definitional elements should be added. First, in *structural* terms, a social movement is a network of individuals, groups and/or organizations, or, as Neidhardt has put it, a 'mobilized network of networks'.[13] A network has no top and no clear centre that could steer and control the whole of its activities. It may include organizations, even those with a highly formalized character such as a political party, but it is not an organization. As a network of groups and organizations, it has a certain size and duration. A handful of people assembling for a spontaneous protest action would definitely not qualify as a social movement, though such actions may be part of a social movement.

Second, in the perspective of *self-attribution*, a social movement is based on a kind of we-feeling, hence a collective identity that allows a line to be drawn between 'we' and 'they'. This identity is stabilized by both self-perceptions and external attributions.[14]

Third, collective public protest is a social movement's key instrument to pursue its goals. Protest is the medium to convey motives, reasons and demands, and eventually to put pressure on the movement's opponents. But collective protest also has an expressive and performative function. It may expose emotions such as anger and disenchantment; it may symbolize unity, solidarity and strength, thereby serving the creation and mainte-

---

[12] Eric J. Hobsbawm, 'Peasants and Politics', *Journal of Peasant Studies* 1 (1973), pp. 1–22; Winfried Schulze, *Europäische Bauernrevolten der frühen Neuzeit* (Frankfurt/Main: Suhrkamp, 1982); Norbert Schindler, *Widerspenstige Leute. Studien zur Volkskultur in der frühen Neuzeit* (Frankfurt/Main: Fischer, 1992); Peter Blickle, *Der Bauernkrieg. Die Revolution des Gemeinen Mannes*, 4th rev. edn (Munich: Beck, 2012); Samuel K. Cohn, Jr., *Lust for Liberty: The Politics of Social Revolt in Medieval Europe, 1200–1425* (Cambridge, MA: Harvard University Press, 2006).

[13] Friedhelm Neidhardt, 'Einige Ideen zu einer allgemeinen Theorie sozialer Bewegungen', in Stefan Hradil (ed.), *Sozialstruktur im Umbruch. Karl Martin Bolte zum 60. Geburtstag* (Opladen: Leske + Budrich, 1985), pp. 193–204, here p. 195.

[14] Alberto Melucci, 'Getting Involved. Identity and Mobilization in Social Movements', in Bert Klandermans, Hanspeter Kriesi and Sidney Tarrow (eds), *From Structure to Action: Comparing Social Movement Research Across Cultures* (Greenwich, CT: JAI Press, 1988), pp. 329–348; Dieter Rucht, 'Kollektive Identität: Konzeptionelle Überlegungen zu einem Desiderat der Bewegungsforschung', *Forschungsjournal Neue Soziale Bewegungen* 8 (1995), pp. 9–23; Francesca Polletta and James M. Jasper, 'Collective Identity and Social Movements', *Annual Review of Sociology* 27 (2001), pp. 283–303.

nance of collective identity and, by its very form, conveying a message of appeal and/or threat.[15]

If we summarize these four key elements in a formula, a social movement can be defined as *a network of individuals, groups and organizations that, based on a sense of collective identity, seek to bring about social change (or resist social change) primarily by means of collective public protest.* This broad definition encompasses different kinds of social movements that can be distinguished according to various criteria such as: societal context (e.g. industrial and post-industrial movements; movements of affluence and movements of crisis), ideological tendency (e.g. Marxist, liberal, nationalist and fascist movements), strategic orientation (e.g. reformist and revolutionary movements), social carriers (movements of peasants, workers, students, women, youth and so on) and thematic concern (civil rights, peace, environmental protection and so on).

The distinction between 'old' and 'new' social movements has been extensively discussed during the last decades. This terminology emerged in a particular historical context in Western Europe when, after the rise of the New Left, student movements gained momentum in the second half of the 1960s.[16] Partly inspired by the student movement, a plethora of movements took shape during the 1970s, focussing on issues such as environmental protection, anti-nuclear power, peace, women's rights, gay and lesbian rights and poverty in Third World countries. To some extent, these movements, similar to the New Left groups, set themselves apart from the stereotyped image of the labour movement as the prototypical 'old' movement.

From an analytical perspective, five characteristics of new social movements can be stressed: they are middle-class based, focus on the sphere of reproduction, are highly decentralized, favour a strategy of what might be coined radical reformism and promote participatory democracy. The stu-

---

[15] Ralph H. Turner, 'The Public Perception of Protest', *American Sociological Review* 34 (1969), pp. 815–831.

[16] Touraine was among the first to use the concept new social movement (in singular). See Alain Touraine, *Le mouvement de Mai ou le communisme utopique* (Paris: Seuil, 1968). He was politically disappointed by the course of the labour movement. See Alain Touraine, *Production de la société* (Paris: Seuil, 1973). He was hoping that another movement would become *the* key player in the new 'postindustrial era'. After his disenchantment with the short-lived student movement, Touraine continued his search for the new historical agent from the anti-nuclear movement to the women's movement to the Polish Solidarność, ending with disillusion again.

dent movement of the 1960s serves as a bridge between the old (labour) movement and the new social movements: It endorsed some ideas of the 'old' movements (e.g. the concept of socialist revolution) but at the same time had some characteristics in common with the subsequent new social movements (e.g. the middle-class base). Whether or not the concept of new social movements can be also applied to other periods such as the early nineteenth century, as Calhoun[17] has suggested, depends on the underlying definition: emphasis is either put on the specific historical context in which the concept emerged or on formal criteria as listed above. In the latter case, there are probably movements in the nineteenth and first half of the twentieth century that meet at least some of these criteria.

ASKING THE RELEVANT QUESTIONS

As scientists in a liberal political environment, we are basically free to pursue any research question we find interesting. Nevertheless, the 'weight' of questions, at least from the viewpoint of broader societal, political and scientific communities, varies greatly when considering admittedly debatable criteria such as relevance, timeliness, urgency, profoundness, compatibility with social norms and so on. Moreover, different types of questions represent different challenges.

Most social movement research focusses on answering *descriptive* questions. Because the activities and structures of social movements are much less documented than those of governments, political parties or large corporations, there is a wide and open field to investigate both historical and contemporary movements.

Obviously the description of movements in the past is essentially the domain of historians. By contrast, the analysis of contemporary movements is rather a matter for sociologists, political scientists and cultural anthropologists.[18] Most descriptions of today's movements, however, are delivered by journalists. While these accounts may provide useful information and, occasionally, valuable insights, they also tend to exhibit particular biases. After all, journalists are keen to unveil the latest trends, to report especially on spectacular and/or disruptive social movement actions, often

[17] Craig Calhoun, '"New Social Movements" of the Early Nineteenth Century', *Social Science History* 17 (1993), pp. 385–427.

[18] See Bert Klandermans and Conny Roggeband (eds), *Handbook of Social Movements Across Disciplines* (New York: Springer, 2007).

exaggerating the 'newness' or 'uniqueness' of what they are observing, and overestimating the role of certain 'leaders' and 'key figures' in an attempt to give their stories a 'personal spin'. The downside of these approaches is their lack of a broader comparative angle and historical background to put present phenomena into perspective. Also, by their very nature, journalistic reports usually do not provide systematic data based on sophisticated research methods as is expected from historians and social scientists.

Unlike the description, the causal explanation requires some sort of theory. While journalists tend to rely on common sense and rudimentary implicit theories, scientists put emphasis on explicit and elaborated theories that can be submitted to an empirical test. Causal explanation focussing on *why* something happened or came into place is preceded by the assumption that what is going to be explained is a matter of fact, hence based on obvious evidence or results of prior empirical research.

Ideally, the selection of a theory should not depend on any pre-existing preferences but guided by the research question at hand and the level of observation, ranging from the micro to the macro perspective. This is why, in the field of social movement studies, we should be sceptical of approaches that seek to answer rather different questions with one and the same theory, be it rational choice, resource mobilization, framing theory, exchange theory, functional theory, modernization theory, Marxist theory or something else. Rather, we can assume that different theories have different explanatory power with regard to different kinds of causal questions. Depending on the research question at hand, a theory may be more or less applicable and useful, and have more or less explanatory power. Also, it is worth considering whether or not different theories need to be combined in order to get a more comprehensive explanation.

Regarding *normative* questions, many scholars contend that they are beyond the scientific enterprise. However, a differentiated position seems to be more appropriate. Some issues are of a purely ethical nature. This, for example, applies to the question of whether or not the death penalty can be legitimated on moral grounds. While this question should not be addressed in the realm of science, it is a matter of empirical scientific research to investigate whether or not the death penalty, in statistical terms, has a prohibitive effect in reducing severe crimes.

Other normative questions, however, are a genuine concern of science. An obvious example is when we are asking which methods and indicators are best in order to test a certain hypothesis. Another example is scientific advice for non-scientific purposes. While the arguments for choosing a certain political goal are beyond the realm of science, it can be a scientific problem to answer which methods, for example in terms of a cost–benefit calculation, are best to reach the stated goal. With regard to social movements, as researchers we can, therefore, tackle questions such as: Which channels of mobilization work best under certain conditions? The answer to this empirical question, which obviously is of crucial interest for political activists, requires a causal analysis, including a comparison of both the preconditions and effects of different channels.

Broadly speaking, key subjects in social movement studies can be designated by 'the triple c': characteristics, conditions and consequences of social movements. Among the *characteristics* are social base, ideology, frames, claims, organizational structures, strategies and action repertoires. Identifying these characteristics is essentially a descriptive task.

Conditions comprise the factors for the emergence, transformation and eventually decline of social movements. Here a number of both internal (e.g. resources, leadership) and external factors (e.g. grievances, political opportunities, strategies of opponents, precipitating incidents) come into play. Identifying and analysing the effects of these potential factors is essentially an explanatory endeavour.

Consequences or outcomes of social movements cannot be identified in the same way as, for example, structural properties or action repertoires. Similar to conditions, they require the reconstruction of a causal chain which, in this case, is an extremely difficult operation.[19] After all, many factors and many actors come into play whose effects, including their interactive effects, are difficult to assess. There may also be late effects based on hardly visible diffusion processes. Finally, the very idea of consequences should be extended beyond a movement's stated goal such as introducing universal suffrage or banning nuclear weapons. Consequences also include changes of political rules and procedures (e.g. a freedom of information act as a side effect of various movements focussing on environmental protection and other issues), effects on agenda setting, public opinion, changes of daily behaviour and biographies of activities. Especially the investigation of conditions and consequences points to the need for theory.

---

[19] Marco Giugni, 'Was it Worth the Effort? The Outcomes and Consequences of Social Movements', *Annual Review of Sociology* 98 (1998), pp. 371–393; Felix Kolb, *Protest and Opportunities: The Political Outcomes of Social Movements* (Frankfurt/Main: Campus, 2007).

THEORIZING AND CONCEPTUALIZING THE PHENOMENON UNDER STUDY

Everyday communication as well as scientifically based empirical description relies on the use of concepts. While in daily life our intuition about causalities may suffice, scientifically based causal explanation and interpretation is more demanding. Besides inter-subjectively controllable methods of data production, explicit theorizing is also indispensable.

While definitions of and criteria for theories differ, there is at least a bottom line. At the very least, a theory implies assumptions about causal links, mechanisms and/or motives. These factors, in the realm of social interaction, produce regularities, probabilities and patterns as opposed to complete contingency and indeterminacy. Typical statements grounded on some sort of theory in social movement studies are, for example:

- The co-presence of factors A, B and C are likely to produce strong movements.
- Violent action tends to increase in the downswing phase of mass mobilization because this is the only way for the remaining 'hard core activists' to maintain pressure and keep momentum.
- People join social movement activities predominantly because of selective incentives.

In the field of social movement studies, theories with different explanatory tasks and different ranges from the micro to the macro level are at hand. Preferences for certain theories and paradigms change considerably over time. Rather than being a matter of taste, these preferences are strongly influenced by historical constellations, e.g. periods of crisis and practical challenges for political decision-makers, but also by internal dynamics of the sciences, e.g. the gradual undermining of an established paradigm by a growing body of counter-evidence.

In the second half of the nineteenth century, the theoretical focus was on societal structures conducive to the emergence of social movements. Around the beginning of the twentieth century, mass psychology became fashionable. In the first half of this century, a number of different approaches, ranging from social psychology to symbolic interactionism to structural functionalist and Marxist approaches, coexisted and left their traces throughout the second half of the century. After the dominance of resource mobilization theory in the 1970s and 1980s, the theoretical landscape became very diversified. Overall, a rationalist bias in interpreting movement activity prevailed, stressing the role of individual cost-benefit calculus, movement organizations, political process and political opportunities, strategic framing, relations with mass media and so on. More recently, this rationalist bias was challenged by a cultural turn emphasizing the role of symbols, emotions and collective identity.[20]

Generally speaking, broad and comprehensive theories about preconditions, functions, roles and effects of social movements, for example Marxist theory of class struggles, have moved into the background. At the same time, the field has become populated by middle range theories[21] and theories on rather specific aspects of social movements, e.g., incentives for individual participation, conditions for conflict escalation, requirements for successful framing and interaction with mass media. To some extent, these theoretical preferences are driven by an ongoing tension between basic concepts focussing on structure vs. agency, expressive vs. instrumental behaviour and micro- vs. macro-sociological explanations.

Various scholars have listed or classified the basic types of theory in social movements studies.[22] For the most part, they present a laundry list without explicit criteria of selection or an organizing principle. Instead, social movement theories can be mapped according to various dimensions. Drawing on and modifying a categorization that originally was designed to systematize the conditions for the stabilization of social movements,[23] one can locate various theories along two dimensions: first, the level on

[20] See Jeff Goodwin and James M. Jasper, 'Caught in a Winding, Snarling Vine: The Structural Bias of Political Process Theory', *Sociological Forum* 14 (1999), pp. 27–54; Francesca Polletta, 'Culture and Movements', *Annals of the American Academy of Political and Social Science* 619 (2008), pp. 78–96.

[21] These are 'theories that lie between the minor but necessary day-to-day hypotheses that evolve in abundance during day-to-day research and the all-inclusive systematic efforts to develop a unified theory that will explain all the observed uniformities of social behaviour, social organization and social change'. Robert K. Merton, 'On Sociological Theories of the Middle Range', in Robert K. Merton, *Social Theory and Social Structure* (London: The Free Press, 1968), pp. 39–72, here p. 39.

[22] Kai-Uwe Hellmann, 'Paradigmen der Bewegungsforschung. Forschungs- und Erklärungsansätze—ein Überblick', in Kai-Uwe Hellmann and Ruud Koopmans (eds), *Paradigmen der Bewegungsforschung. Entstehung und Entwicklung von Neuen Sozialen Bewegungen und Rechtsextremismus* (Opladen: Westdeutscher Verlag, 1998), pp. 9–30.

[23] Dieter Rucht and Friedhelm Neidhardt, 'Towards a "Movement Society"? On the Possibilities of Institutionalizing Social Movements' (orig. in German 1993), *Social Movement Studies* 1 (2002), pp. 7–30.

Table 2.1 Reference points for social movement theories

	Individual experience level	*Level of collective interpretation and decision*	*Structural level*
Motivation	Deprivation	Framing	Structural strains
Capacity	Motivational theory	Collective identity	Mobilizing structures
Opportunities	Removal of barriers to participate	Perception of opportunities, choice of strategies	Societal opportunity structures

which theories are situated; second, the functional or structural aspect to which theories are referring to (Table 2.1).

The level of individual experience is basically covered by social psychologists' theories of absolute and relative deprivation, rational choice and motivation. The two remaining levels are primarily the domain of sociologists, political scientists, cultural anthropologist and historians.

At the level of collective interpretation and decision-making one can situate framing theory, cultural theory and, with regard to the perception of opportunities and strategic choices, actor-centred theories of rational choice.

Finally, the structural level, especially when it comes to the macro-perspective, is the domain of general sociological theory, social history theories and organizational theories.

While these approaches cannot be presented and discussed here, I can at least exemplify the potential of one of them, namely the resource mobilization theory that, remarkably, was presented by its key protagonists John McCarthy and Mayer Zald only as a 'partial theory'. Their starting point was the observation that there is only a weak link between grievances and the emergence of social movements.[24] Social movements, these scholars argued, come only into existence when there are organizers who collect/mobilize and use resources. Inspired by economic theories, they put much emphasis on social movement entrepreneurs, social movement

---

[24] The authors 'want to move from a strong assumption about the centrality of deprivation and grievances to a weak one, which makes them a component, indeed, sometimes a secondary component in the generation of social movements'. See McCarthy and Zald, footnote 3, p. 1215.

organizations (SMOs) and social movement industries, also highlighting the aspect of competition among SMOs. This emphasis was a deliberate paradigm shift directed against what McCarthy and Zald perceived, and partly misperceived, as the dominant earlier paradigm conceiving of social movements as rather unstructured collective behaviour largely driven by emotions—retrospectively called the contagion approach.

While the resource mobilization approach was not as innovative as its promoters have claimed, still it was a well-grounded re-emphasis on the structural underpinnings of social movements.[25] However, the original promoters of the resource mobilization approach did not go very far in theorizing social movement organizations.

Other scholars adopted some basics of this approach to come up with more elaborate conceptions. As an illutration, I refer to a concept of the Swiss sociologist Hanspeter Kriesi who argued that social movement structures, once established, are exposed to two kinds of tensions: first, constituency or client orientation vs. authorities orientation and, second, political representation vs. direct participation of the constituency. During their life course, Kriesi states, social movement groups can move into four different directions, which are developing a structure geared towards

1. services ➔ commercialization
2. self-help ➔ involution
3. political representation ➔ institutionalization
4. a genuine social movement organization ➔ radicalization (Fig. 2.1).

This concept could serve as the basis of a full-blown, thus far not speci-fied, theory on the evolution and transformation of social movement structures. Accordingly, one would have to single out the internal and/or external conditions under which social movement groups move into one of these four directions. In addition, one might also hypothesize under which circumstances a group, or rather a complex organization, may com-bine two or more of these functional tasks related to each of the four pathways.

---

[25] See John D. McCarthy and Mayer N. Zald, 'The Enduring Vitality of the Resource Mobilization Theory of Social Movements', in Jonathan H. Turner (ed.), *Handbook of Sociological Theory* (New York: Springer, 2001), pp. 533–565.

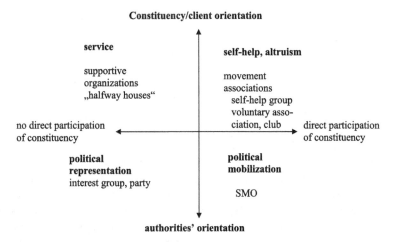

Fig. 2.1 Typology of movement-related organizations[26]

This example shows that theorizing about social movements, even within the framework of one specific approach, might become a quite specialized and ambitious enterprise. In the end, this can hardly remain an armchair reflection. It requires not only prior knowledge about the subject under study but, in order to be substantiated and tested, also systematic data collection. This brings me to the challenge of selecting the appropriate methods and sources in social movement research.

CHOOSING APPROPRIATE METHODS AND SOURCES

In principle, almost all available methods in social sciences and humanities can be valuable tools in the field of social movement studies. Accordingly, we may think about content analysis of written documents (ranging from diaries to police records to newspapers), symbolic representations of social movement groups, interviews with different degrees of standardization, oral history methods, focus groups, questionnaires, content analysis of

---

[26] Hanspeter Kriesi, 'The Organizational Structure of New Social Movements in a Political Context', in Doug McAdam, John D. McCarthy and Mayer N. Zald (eds), *Comparative Perspectives on Social Movements. Political Opportunities, Mobilizing Structures, and Cultural Framings* (Cambridge: Cambridge University Press, 1996), pp. 152–184, here p. 153.

documents, network analysis, participant observation, action research and so on.

There is no reason to assume that one of these different methods and sources is per se superior to the others. Hence an answer to the question of the appropriateness of methods and sources depends on the subject of investigation,[27] the specific research question and, of course, their availability. In research practice, the range of applicable methods and sources is often quite limited. For example, an analysis of a medieval peasant revolt may almost exclusively depend on written reports by the actual conflict parties. These reports, however, are not only biased but also unevenly distributed. While there may be documents authored by authorities and groups close to them, almost no material may exist from the side of the illiterate peasantry. Obviously, participant observation by a trained social researcher is not an option when it comes to analysing upheavals in medieval times. It may, however, be the key method of studying intra-group processes of communication and decision-making in contemporary protest groups.

Participatory observation can be applied in very different ways depending on factors such as the researcher's preferences and expertise, available resources and the groups' willingness to accept certain research procedures and tools, e.g. documentation by audio or video registration. For some researchers, participant observation may be little more than just being there and attentively watching what is going on. For others, it might include the use of standardized procedures that allow for a quantitative measurement of well-specified processes.[28]

Also, participant observation can become a demanding enterprise as soon as we want to map in some detail a complex event such as a huge mass demonstration[29] or a set of co-ordinated marches that eventually

---

[27] Theodor W. Adorno, 'Zur Logik der Sozialwissenschaften', in Theodor W. Adorno et al., *Der Positivismusstreit in der deutschen Soziologie* (Neuwied and Berlin: Luchterhand, 1969 [1957]), pp. 125–143, here p. 130.

[28] Christoph Haug, Dieter Rucht and Simon Teune, 'A Methodology for Studying Democracy and Power in Group Meetings', in Donatella della Porta and Dieter Rucht (eds), *Meeting Democracy: Power and Deliberation in Global Justice Movements* (Cambridge: Cambridge University Press, 2013), pp. 23–46.

[29] See, for example, Clark McPhail and David L. Miller, 'The Assembling Process: A Theoretical and Empirical Investigation', *American Sociological Review* 38 (1973), pp. 721–735.

converge at one central square. In such a case, one probably needs several dozen observers to document adequately this multi-facetted event. When one seeks to cover not only single events or campaigns but also the activities of big movements in large territories, primary data, created by the researchers, are simply not available. Thus we have to draw on pre-existing sources such as police archives and news agency or newspaper reports. These, as a rule, have been established for other purposes than scientific research and, therefore, are of limited value. Thus, they have to be used with much caution. Based on such sources, protest event analysis has become an established method to document and map outward-directed social movement activities.[30]

Again, while protest event analysis is an elaborated and approved method, it still has its problems as soon as one moves to the nitty-gritty details. What are adequate indicators for the 'strength' of a movement? Is it a number of events, an absolute number of participants, a number of participants relative to the size of the population, an intensity of a protest, duration of a protest or a combination of all these features? Which newspaper should be chosen? Is one newspaper enough? How do we deal with the selection bias and description biases of newspapers? What should we do with fairly unspecific reports stating, for example, that there were many local strikes during the last few months? As soon as one digs into these methodological problems, it becomes a specialist issue that is discussed by probably only a few dozen people around the globe.

With regard to other research questions, however, we can rely on standard methods that are by no means specific to social movement research. For example, quantitative surveys based on questionnaires can be applied to explore movement activists' socio-demographic characteristics, values and motives, perception of problems and chances, political leaning, past political involvements and so on.

In summary, it is safe to say that in terms of applicable methods and sources of social movement all tools are *potentially* useful. Yet as soon as we move to more specific research questions, the range of appropriate and available tools narrows drastically. Contrary to many other fields in social research, e.g. electoral behaviour, we usually lack ready-made

---

[30] Ruud Koopmans and Dieter Rucht, 'Protest Event Analysis', in Bert Klandermans and Suzanne Staggenborg (eds), *Methods in Social Movement Research* (Minneapolis/London: University of Minnesota Press, 2002), pp. 231–259.

data. Therefore, we have to produce our own primary data or rely on sources that only indirectly, or insufficiently, speak to the matter of investigation. In both regards, social movement research requires considerable resources. However, because it is hardly institutionalized in the university system in large parts of the globe, resources for research are scarce. But this also implies a chance for 'hungry' researchers: vast and multiple spaces are still 'unknown territory'.

INTERPRETING AND CONTEXTUALIZING FINDINGS

Empirical findings usually don't speak for themselves. Instead, they have to be interpreted and contextualized. In this respect, only two messages will be highlighted here.

First, it is important to be conscious about the interpreter's attitude towards his or her subject under investigation. Social movements inherently carry ideological and political baggage. This tends to affect, and even emotionalize, the interpreter, who may be tempted to highlight or downplay certain aspects according to his or her own personal stances, thereby giving the data and findings—or even worse, the production of data—a specific spin.

This danger is especially relevant when (former) movement activists begin to study, as scientists, the movement they were or are involved.[31] This danger also exists when scholars deliberately try to combine or merge the role of an activist and a researcher—a constellation that some, especially people from the radical left, praise as a 'model' for investigations.[32] The German feminist Maria Mies, in her *Methodische Postulate zur Frauenforschung*,[33] even goes as far as urging the researcher to identify with the groups under study. This advice not only risks violating well-established and sound methodological standards such as reliability of data collection but also poses practical problems: Would I have to become a

---

[31] On this aspect, see, for example, William Hoynes and Charlotte Ryan (eds), *Rhyming Hope and History: Activism, Academics, and Social Movement Scholarship* (Minneapolis: University of Minnesota Press, 2005).

[32] See, for example, Bertell Ollman, 'A Model of Activist Research: How to Study Class Consciousness ... and Why We Should'. See http://www.nyu.edu/projects/ollman/docs/class_consciousness.php (last visited 10 April 2013).

[33] Maria Mies, 'Methodische Postulate zur Frauenforschung—dargestellt am Beispiel der Gewalt gegen Frauen', *Beiträge zur feministischen Theorie und Praxis* 1 (1978), pp. 47–52.

fascist in order to study fascist movements? What should I do when the group under study splits into two rival camps? What is needed instead is a flexible balance between closeness and distance—a position that Norbert Elias (1983) has coined *Engagement und Distanzierung*.[34] On the one hand, he advocates closeness in the sense of acquiring, if possible, intimate knowledge about the subject of research and developing a sense of understanding or even empathy for the actors. On the other hand, one also needs distance in the sense of training and applying the *Tatsachenblick*,[35] a sharp and cool eye for the facts. Distance also implies separating the roles of actor and researcher, to comply with explicit and inter-subjective methodological standards, to actively seek counter-evidence for the hypothesis and to present the findings—regardless of one's attitude to the actors—as far as possible in an unbiased way.[36] In this regard, one should be sceptical not only about some feminist or other 'methodological postulates' but also about the method of 'sociological intervention' as proposed by the French sociologist Alain Touraine.[37] Besides a number of methodological problems,[38] I am also critical towards Touraine's conceptualization of social movements that, by definition, is inherently bound to what he calls 'historicité' and only allows identification of one social movement per societal stage.[39]

[34] Norbert Elias, *Engagement und Distanzierung* (Frankfurt/Main: Suhrkamp, 1983), pp. 7–71 (Chapter I).

[35] See Wolfgang Bonß, *Die Einübung des Tatsachenblicks: zur Struktur und Veränderung empirischer Sozialforschung* (Frankfurt/Main: Suhrkamp, 1982).

[36] The debate on the possibility of an 'objective' stance in scientific work is still unsettled. For many, Max Weber continues to serve as a guide. See Max Weber, 'Die "Objektivität" sozialwissenschaftlicher und sozialpolitischer Erkenntnis' (orig. 1904), in Max Weber, *Gesammelte Aufsätze zur Wissenschaftslehre* (Tübingen: J. C. B. Mohr, 1988 [1922]), pp. 146–214. Other scholars question the possibility of strict neutrality. See, for example, Pam Scott, Evelleen Richards and Brian Martin, 'Captives of Controversy: The Myth of the Neutral Social Researcher in Contemporary Scientific Controversies', *Science, Technology & Human Values* 15 (1990), pp. 474–494.

[37] Alain Touraine, *The Voice and the Eye. An Analysis of Social Movements* (Cambridge: Cambridge University Press, 1981).

[38] Dieter Rucht, 'Sociological Theory as Theory of Social Movements? A Critique of Alain Touraine', in Dieter Rucht (ed.), *Research on Social Movements: The State of the Art in Western Europe and the USA* (Frankfurt/Boulder: Campus/Westview Press 1991), pp. 355–384; Alberto Melucci, *Nomads of the Present: Social Movements and Individual Needs in Contemporary Society* (London: Hutchinson Radius, 1989).

[39] See Alain Touraine, 'L'historicité', in Edgar Morin et al., *Une nouvelle civilisation? Hommage à Georges Friedmann* (Paris: Gallimard, 1973), pp. 3–44.

The second message with regard to the task of interpreting and contextualizing data is the need for comparison. I am convinced that comparison per se is key to acquiring any practical knowledge and communicating in daily life starting from earliest childhood. Only by comparison we can identify what we tend to characterize in social and human sciences as old or new, trivial or spectacular, exceptional or frequent, typical or atypical, strong or weak, big or small, true or false—all judgments that are needed when it comes to interpreting and contextualizing scholarly claims and findings.

In social movement studies, one or more of the various axes of comparison can be applied, though obviously not all of them in one and the same piece of work. It is enlightening and rewarding to compare: (1) between events, campaigns, movements and movement sectors; (2) between core activists, movement adherents and sympathizers; and (3) to engage in thematically focussed comparisons across time and place. Cross-time comparison allows, for example, identification of waves and generations of movements, and answers the question What is new about the so-called new social movements? Regarding comparison across place, we might consider different levels of activity ranging from the local to the global. Further, we should complement the predominant focus on cross-national comparison by using other units of comparison, be they cultural spheres or local, transnational and even global coalitions of movement actors.[40] While the necessary discussion of the difficulties and fallacies of comparison is beyond the scope of this chapter, it is an important issue, especially among historians. From their methodological debate, students engaged in comparison of social movements could profit.

SUMMARY AND OUTLOOK

Among the many challenges in the field of social movements, I have selected, discussed and partly illustrated five of them. While the task of defining the subject, namely social movements, can be handled

---

[40] Stein Rokkan, 'Cross-Cultural, Cross-Societal and Cross-National Research', *Historical Social Research* 18 (1993), pp. 6–54; Erwin Scheuch, 'Society as a Context in Cross-National Comparison', *Social Science Information* 5 (1967), pp. 13–24; Joachim Matthes, 'The Operation Called "Vergleichen"', in Joachim Matthes (ed.), *Zwischen den Kulturen? Die Sozialwissenschaften vor dem Problem des Kulturvergleichs* (Göttingen: Schwartz, 1992), pp. 75–102.

pragmatically and the task of asking the relevant questions ultimately relies on an arbitrary judgement of the individual researcher, the other three challenges—choosing and/or developing adequate theories, using appropriate methods and sources, and explaining/interpreting the findings—will remain an ambitious and difficult endeavour. Regarding the last aspect, I have emphasized two lessons: (1) to keep the right balance between closeness and distance towards the subject of research; and (2) to apply, whenever possible, systematic comparison across various dimensions such as thematic issues, time and place.

I am convinced that these five challenges, in principle, also exist in other fields of research, though not necessarily always in the same form and to the same extent. With regard to the discipline of history, I have the impression that thus far little attention has been paid to the definition, conceptualization and theorization of social movements. In this respect, the social sciences can be a useful source of inspiration. On the other hand, when it comes to the use and critique of sources as well as to the ways and problems of comparison, social sciences can learn a lot from historians. The study of social movement offers plenty of opportunities for a close interdisciplinary collaboration to provide better understanding of social movements as an important but widely underestimated aspect of social reality.

FURTHER READINGS

Doug McAdam, John D. McCarthy and Mayer N. Zald (eds), *Comparative Perspectives on Social Movements: Political Opportunities, Mobilizing Structures, and Cultural Framings* (Cambridge: Cambridge University Press, 1996).

This collective volume is structured along the three concepts mentioned in the subtitle. It marks the state of the art, at least of the mainstream, in social movement studies by the mid-1990s. In the meantime, the three concepts have become more refined. Moreover, other approaches, representing the cultural turn in social movement studies, have gained importance. Apart from its conceptual focus, additional strengths of this volume are chapters in a comparative perspective, chapters on Eastern Europe and two chapters on historical movements.

Doug McAdam, Sidney Tarrow and Charles Tilly, *Dynamics of Contention* (Cambridge: Cambridge University Press, 2001).

The authors aim at broadening the field of social movements by proposing the notion of contentious politics (already earlier suggested by Tilly).
They advocate a process-oriented, dynamic perspective in which 'robust,
widely applicable causal mechanisms' play a key role. Each of these mechanisms, whose theoretical basis remains somewhat unclear, is exemplified
by of a paired comparison of cases that vary considerably in terms of their
historical and geographic background.

Donatella della Porta and Mario Diani, *Social Movements. Issues and
Problems.* Second revised edition (Oxford/Cambridge, MA: Blackwell,
1999).

A broad and systematic overview on social movement studies that provides a useful introduction for newcomers to the field but also can serve
as a guide and resource for more advanced students. The authors have
recently edited a comprehensive volume, The *Oxford Handbook on Social
Movements* (Oxford University Press 2015) that, in 53 chapters and more
than 800 pages, goes more into detail.

Mario Diani, 'The Concept of Social Movement'. *The Sociological
Review* 1 (1992), pp. 1–25.

This is a relatively early attempt to come to grips with the concept of
social movements. The author compares definitions by some of the most
influential authors in the field and offers his own 'synthetic definition' of a
social movement as 'a network of informal interactions between a plural-
ity of individuals, groups and/or organizations, engaged in a political or
cultural conflict, on the basis of a shared collective identity'.

James M. Jasper, *Protest: A Cultural Introduction to Social Movements*
(Cambridge: Polity Press, 2015).

A well-written, engaged and intriguing introduction into key dimensions and practices of social movements. Without simplifying complex
phenomena, this book is especially useful for undergraduate and graduate
students. As the subtitle suggests, the book highlights the role of cultural
aspects of movements. It provides an exemplary case of the cultural turn
in social movement studies, thereby representing a challenge to structural
analyses that prevailed from the 1970s to the early 2000s.

Hank Johnston, *What is a Social Movement?* (Cambridge: Polity Press,
2014).

This is an excellent and concise up-to-date introduction to the field of
social movement studies, including an attempt to clarify the concept of
social movement and to elaborate its social, political and cultural aspects.
In a condensed form, the author emphasises the role of culture, discourse,

identity, frames and emotions without ignoring the structural and organizational dimensions of social movements. Additional sections are devoted to political, cultural and religious movements that, seemingly, are considered as variants of social movements.

Karl-Dieter Opp, *Theories of Political Protest and Social Movements. A Multidisciplinary Introduction, Critique and Synthesis* (London: Routledge, 2009).

An attempt to integrate contemporary key approaches in social movement studies (resource mobilization, political opportunity structures, collective identity and the framing perspective) into an extended rational choice perspective. The focus is on the question why individuals engage in social movement activities. One may wonder whether the rational choice perspective is overstretched by this synthetic enterprise on the basis of a 'general theory of action'.

Otthein Rammstedt, *Soziale Bewegung* (Frankfurt am Main: Suhrkamp, 1978).

Even in the German scholarly community, this is a largely ignored but extremely valuable book. It covers the historical semantics of the term social movement as well as the evolution of the concept and theories from the early century to the 1970s. Moreover, the author offers a sophisticated ideal-type of the evolutionary stages of a social movement. Unfortunately, this book was never published in English and therefore remained largely unknown to the Anglo-Saxon scholarly community.

Sidney Tarrow, *Power in Movement: Social Movements and Contentious Politics.* Revised and Updated Third Edition (New York: Cambridge University Press, 2011).

This is one of the best known and most often cited books on social movements in the last two decades. It covers a wide range of aspects with a focus on structural patterns on the meso- and macro-levels. The third edition includes more recent developments of transnational mobilization and new material on civil wars, terrorism and guerrilla movements. Compared to the two earlier editions, the third edition strongly reflects Charles Tilly's influence on Tarrow.

Jacquelien van Stekelenburg, Conny Roggeband and Bert Klandermans (eds), *The Future of Social Movement Research: Dynamics, Mechanisms, and Processes* (Minneapolis and London: University of Minnesota Press, 2013).

Conceptual and theoretical aspects are at the fore of this volume structured around: (1) grievances and identities; (2) organizations and networks; (3) the dynamics of mobilization; and (4) the changing context of contention. Each of these four parts is closed by a single-authored 'discussion' chapter. This volume represents the cutting-edge of mainstream social movement research but neglects more marginal and radical approaches. It is attractive for specialists and researchers but too demanding for newcomers to this field.

CHAPTER 3

Subaltern Studies as a History of Social Movements in India

Rochona Majumdar

Subaltern Studies (hereafter SS, 1978–2008), a research collective and series of publications, is not typically associated with history writing on social movements in India.[1] The stated aim of the group was to document the politics of the people during the era of British colonial rule in the subcontinent. Ranajit Guha, the founder of the collective underscored the importance of popular mobilizations to the project when he wrote 'parallel to the domain of elite politics there existed throughout the colonial period another domain of Indian politics in which the principal actors were not the dominant groups of the indigenous society or the colonial authorities but the subaltern classes and groups constituting the mass of the labouring population and the intermediate strata in town and country—that is the people'.[2]

---

[1] For a history of Subaltern Studies see David Ludden, 'A Brief History of Subalternity', in David Ludden (ed.), *Reading Subaltern Studies* (New Delhi: Permanent Black, 2001), pp. 1–27. The group consisted of seven historians and was headed by Ranajit Guha who served as the editor of the first six volumes published under the same name by which the collective was known.

[2] Ranajit Guha, 'On Some Aspects of the Historiography of Colonial India', in Gayatri C. Spivak and Ranajit Guha (eds), *Selected Subaltern Studies* (New York: Oxford University Press, 1988), p. 40.

R. Majumdar (✉)
Department South Asian Languages and Civilizations, University of Chicago, Chicago, IL, USA

© The Author(s) 2017
S. Berger, H. Nehring (eds.), *The History of Social Movements in Global Perspective*, DOI 10.1057/978-1-137-30427-8_3

Compare this to a definition of social movements provided by social scientist Ghanshyam Shah. Scholarly works on social movements, Shah argues, are those 'which examine non-institutionalized legal or extra-legal collective political actions which strive to influence civil and political society for social and political change'.[3] The study of social movements understood in the terms outlined by Shah gained currency among political scientists and sociologists in India from the late 1960s onwards. Yet the historical record in India is replete with instances of mobilizations by peasants, lower castes, tribal groups, workers and women. While discrete historical studies documenting struggles by individual groups were undertaken by scholars, until the advent of SS there was no concerted effort to analyse the ways in which histories of popular mobilization, or social movements more generally, had an impact on the nature of historical inquiry and history writing in the Indian context. The historiographical intervention of SS, as will be discussed in what follows, was significantly different from the ways in which popular social movements had been earlier theorized in the 'histories from below' pioneered by Eric Hobsbawm, Christopher Hill and E. P. Thompson. The primary goal of this essay, then, is to analyse the ways in which the writing of histories of peasant movements in what may be called the *Subaltern Studies mode* have marked fundamental interventions in historiography.[4]

WHY SUBALTERN STUDIES?

The works by the SS collective deserve a re-examination from the vantage point of the historiography of social movements in colonial India. What I attempt in the following pages is not a comprehensive analysis of every monograph or article written by members of the collective. My selection pertains to those aspects of SS work that have a direct bearing on our received understanding of social movements. Excluded from this analysis are historical works by SS scholars that focussed on individual, everyday acts of insubordination and resistance against established orders of kinship and/or patriarchy. The focus instead, is on works that attempted to understand mass mobilizations to underscore the group's ideas about collective,

---

[3] Ghanshyam Shah, *Social Movements in India* (New Delhi: Sage, 2004), p. 21.

[4] While my particular case study is the work of SS, it is a well-known fact that the works of these scholars have had an impact on histories written in the context of Latin America, Eastern Europe and the United States.

insurgent subjectivity. Even as individual historians in the group focussed on histories of the Indian peasantry, religious mobilizations and working-class protests, the collective yield of their respective projects helped in outlining a 'paradigm' for popular politics in the subcontinent.

Their choice of popular mobilizations, it can be argued justifiably, adhered to a classical notion of popular unrest. What in our times are known as 'new' social movements, such as struggles for rights by sexual minorities, disabled peoples or movements against the proliferation of nuclear weapons, did not enter the ambit of their analysis.[5] One explanation for prioritizing 'older' or more 'classical' mobilizations may be found in Ranajit Guha's claim that '[p]opular mobilization in the colonial period was realized in its most comprehensive form in *peasant* uprisings. [...] in many historic instances involving large masses of working people and petty bourgeoisie in the urban areas to the figure of mobilization derived directly from the paradigm of peasant insurgency'.[6]

'The peasant', posited as the paradigmatic actor of social movements, indeed as the epitome of the mass political subject in India, derived in large measure from the different intellectual traditions from which SS scholars drew intellectual inspiration. All of these, in one way or another, dealt with the historical role of the peasantry under conditions of uneven development. These influences, recently reprised in an essay by a founding member of the collective, Partha Chatterjee, included Marxist analyses in western Europe on the inevitable dissolution of the peasantry as a result of the process of primitive accumulation of capital and the emergence of a working class, Lenin's debates in Russia with the Narodniks, Mao Zedong's writings on the peasantry in the Chinese Revolution, debates on Gandhi's ideal Indian village society that would successfully resist the vagaries of 'Western civilization'. These were mediated through critical readings of Antonio Gramsci's *Prison Notebooks* and Levi-Straussian and Roland Barthes' structuralist theories.[7] The emergence of the peasant as the paradigmatic figure of popular politics, refracted, as it was through these various intellectual currents produced an interesting and important

---

[5] On this paradigm see Dieter Rucht's Chap. 2 in this volume.

[6] Guha, 'Historiography of Colonial India', p. 41.

[7] Partha Chatterjee, 'Democracy and Economic Transition', http://kafila.org/2008/06/13/democracy-and-economic-transformation-partha-chatterjee/ (accessed on 3 June 2013).

set of displacements in the writings of SS scholars. I will have more to say about the historiographical impact of these displacements below.

Another important feature of SS that justifies studying their works under the rubric of the history of social movements is their contention that the domain of subaltern politics could not be completely subsumed into erstwhile dominant histories of nationalism or colonialism. Nor do they directly fit into conceptions of 'civil society', for their members were not primarily drawn from educated bourgeois groups who, through their associations and organizations, were able to participate in reasoned political conversations that directly impacted state policies. This is not to suggest that the domain of popular movements existed in a 'pure state'. Rather, '[t]he impact of living contradictions modified them in the course of their actualization in history'.[8] Notwithstanding this qualification, there was enough in the domain of popular movements that gave subaltern politics certain distinguishing features when compared to elite politics. A close analysis of these features is crucial for an understanding of social movements in India from a historical perspective. If the domain of popular protest was indeed different from those spearheaded by the elite, then the writings of the SS school sheds light on a critical question that any scholar of social movements must face, namely: How do we understand the 'social' in a social movement?

Related to the above is another issue. The historian of social movements in India is often faced with a persistent, if somewhat problematic dichotomy, between movements for 'political' change versus those focussed on the 'social'. Gyanendra Pandey, a founding member of the collective, emphasized the strength of such perceptions when he noted, 'it [such perception] remains dominant in the universities and among others interested in the recent history of the subcontinent, finding expression for instance, in the common equation of the Congress movement with the "political" movement and of workers' and peasants' struggles with a "social" one'.[9] Such a distinction between social movements and political ones has epistemological consequences. It produces a specious hierarchy between social and political movements by deeming the latter more important since its logical culmination is seen in the independence

---

[8] Guha, 'Historiography of Colonial India', p. 41.

[9] Gyanendra Pandey, 'Peasant Revolt and Indian Nationalism, 1919–1922', in Ranajit Guha and Gayatri C. Spivak (eds), *Selected Subaltern Studies* (New York: Oxford University Press, 1993), p. 241.

of the subcontinent from British rule. Pandey rues the fact that such positions reduced movements by 'peasants, workers, and other labouring and exploited classes' into 'sectional struggles' that were out of step with the 'primary need of the "nation" at that stage in its history—the need to advance the anti-imperialist movement'.[10]

If histories of movements composed of the most oppressed elements of Indian society cannot be subsumed into a larger narrative of nationalism, what then is the relationship between these struggles and the nation-state? What, indeed, were the issues that motivated the exploited groups of Indian society to raise their voices and arms against dominant authorities in particular local contexts? Even if a sovereign nation-state was not the desired object of these struggles, it would still be difficult to sustain the argument that it featured nowhere in the imagination of these social groups, albeit in ways that were significantly different from those of the anti-colonial elite. Teasing out the contours of these imaginaries sheds important light on social movements both in the colonial past and the post-colonial present. And this is where the work of SS scholars becomes useful to any project that seeks to find a place for peasant and working-class groups in the history of social movements in colonial India.

There is evidence in the writings of SS historians that tells us that agitating workers or peasants did not behave in ways that are commonly associated with citizenly conduct in 'modern' democracies. Nonetheless, upon the attainment of independence, peasants, workers, tribal groups and other minorities were all made citizens of the new Indian nation-state. It is incumbent upon the historian to analyse the gaps between the ideas that inform citizenly conduct versus those that motivated these disparate social groups to protest or rebel against the authority of the colonial, and subsequently the post-colonial, state. Put differently, we may ask: When we qualify or indicate the nature of a social movement by using prefixes such as women/dalit (lit. downtrodden, refers to lower caste groups of the formerly untouchable communities)/workers/peasants do we invoke collectives of citizen-subjects who take up arms, demonstrate, petition or use other means to register their particular grievances not just against the nation-state but against such other social-political institutions as patriarchy, empire, class and corporations as well? If the primary idiom of protest among these social groups is that of religion, kinship or community then does the constitutional category of the citizen-subject whose

[10] Ibid., pp. 241–242.

genealogy lies in the bourgeois liberal development of the 'West' become inadequate or restrictive to apprehend the 'social' in social movements?

Last but by no means least, the post-millennial conjuncture in India today makes this a purposeful historical exercise. Since the opening up of the Indian economy to multi-national firms from the early 1990s, the land question has assumed renewed urgency in the country. Land acquisition by the state and by foreign firms has led to a number of peasant, tribal and agrarian agitations that have been the cynosure of media and political attention in the last decade. In West Bengal, popular agitation in two areas, Singur and Nandigram respectively, around proposals to set up industry and the methods of land acquisition by the ruling Communist Party of India led to large-scale violence and anti-state mobilization not just by local cultivators and residents but also by urban civil rights groups. These two agitations were among the most important factors behind the defeat of the Left ruled government in 2011, after 34 years of uninterrupted dominance in the state and the rise to power of a party known as the Trinamool Congress (literally: Grassroots Congress).

Other states, namely Orissa, Andhra Pradesh and Maharashtra, have witnessed similar agitations. Large swathes of central India are also in the throes of Maoist insurgencies. At the forefront of these struggles are issues related to resource allocation and the rights of forest dwellers, agricultural labourers and miners to land and water resources. To what extent are present day political parties or indeed the Indian state able to genuinely represent popular grievances? Is there a gap between the sentiments and consciousness of 'the people' and the state that supposedly represents them? What, if any, is the purchase of the category of the 'subaltern' that Guha and colleagues posited 30 years ago as the paradigm for the mass political insurgent subject in contemporary India? These questions have resurfaced with urgency as land and the future of agrarian populations has come to occupy the centre-stage of political life in post-colonial, globalizing India. They make it timely to return once more to SS, to understand the collective's claims about the 'form' and 'consciousness' of popular insurgency in colonial India and their relevance, if any, to us in this era of globalization.

I will focus on three aspects of SS scholarship in the forthcoming sections. First, I will analyse the degree to which the group delivered on the aspiration articulated in its manifesto of restoring to the subaltern their rightful place in the history of India. This implies an analysis of subaltern agency on its own terms without subsuming it into the hitherto dominant narratives of colonialism and nationalism. Second, if the peasant was the paradigm for the rebellious subject, then we need to trace the ways in which the figure of the peasant formed the bedrock of other identities, namely factory workers, pre-industrial craftsmen (such as weavers), religious communities and so on. I will also look at the ways in which the claims of these disparate groups articulated with those of the nationalist elite and analyse the justification of Guha's claim that the colonial state (and later the post-colonial one) was an exercise in 'dominance without hegemony'.[11] Finally, and related to these insights will be an analysis of the intervention made by some SS historians into questions of historical method. If subaltern agency were indeed to be acknowledged on its own terms in historical works, would this not alter the basic parameters and assumptions of the discipline of history as it is practised in the academy? Acknowledging the 'small' voices of history punctures the statist discourse that has dominated history writing of all varieties in unanticipated ways.[12] Collectively, all these three aspects of subaltern mobilization have profound implications for writing histories of social movements.

'THE PEASANT' AS MASS-POLITICAL SUBJECT

Ranajit Guha's seminal volume, *Elementary Aspects of Peasant Insurgency in Colonial India* (hereafter EA), published in 1983, and a related essay 'The Prose of Counter-Insurgency' were the foundational texts of SS scholarship.[13] Both works take as their point of departure the 110 or so peasant uprisings that occurred in colonial India during the late eighteenth and nineteenth centuries. Guha's study, it is important to note, was not a close analysis of the discrete uprisings that occurred during the period covered in his texts. His goal was to outline the 'general form' of peasant insurgencies that, he argued, derived from a long history of mobilization by the peasantry and their desire to put an end to their condition of subalternity. In arguing thus for a general form, Guha drew on

[11] Ranajit Guha, *Dominance without Hegemony: History and Power in Colonial India* (Cambridge, MA: Harvard University Press, 2007).

[12] Ranajit Guha, *The Small Voice of History: Collected Essays*, edited by Partha Chatterjee (New Delhi: Permanent Black, 2009).

[13] Ranajit Guha, *Elementary Aspects of Peasant Insurgency in Colonial India* (New Delhi: Oxford University Press, 1983); Ranajit Guha 'The Prose of Counter-Insurgency', in Ranajit Guha (ed.), *Subaltern Studies. Writings on South Asian History and Society*, Vol. II (Delhi: Oxford University Press, 1983), pp. 1–42.

Marx's famous formulation about 'common forms and general ideas' that characterize class antagonisms in all past societies despite their internal differences. The idea was further refined through his engagement with Levi-Strauss and Gramsci, especially the latter's reflections about 'the first elements' that constituted 'the pillars of politics and of any collective action whatsoever'.[14]

Guha's insights were developed and carried forward in important ways by other scholars associated with SS. Where they differed from Guha was in the close attention they gave to particular local contexts and archives. Unlike Guha, whose canvas was constituted by numerous peasant uprisings sketched out in the broad brushstrokes, his colleagues focussed on particular movements that occurred during the period of high nationalism in India. Their point, however, was to highlight the autonomy of these movements, indeed their divergence from the mainstream struggle for national independence, and to delineate something like a 'peasant-communal ideology'. The collective yield of their studies was to highlight the meaning of what Guha called 'the rebel consciousness'. Animating this consciousness was a belief in the collective political authority of the community and their rights to the land that was prior to that of an individual's. '[R]eligious beliefs—origin myths, sacred histories, legends—which laid down principles of political ethics and were coded into a series of acts and symbols denoting authority and obedience, benevolence and obligation, or oppression and revolt' was the stuff that peasant consciousness was made up of.[15]

While the peasantry continued to be the subject of studies by Shahid Amin, Partha Chatterjee, Gautam Bhadra and Gyanendra Pandey, others like Dipesh Chakrabarty and Gyanendra Pandey turned their attention to other social groups such as factory workers and dominant religious and ethnic groups. David Hardiman focussed on tribal populations while David Arnold looked at the medicalized subaltern body in the context of plagues and colonial prisons.

Despite the differences between the social groups that each scholar focussed on, their works demonstrated that structuring principles of subaltern life-worlds were rooted in a rural, semi-feudal, caste and kinship

---

[14] Guha, *Elementary Aspects*, p. 12.

[15] Partha Chatterjee, 'Agrarian Relations and Communalism in Bengal, 1926–35', in Ranajit Guha (ed.), *Subaltern Studies. Writings on South Asian History and Society*, Vol. I (Delhi: Oxford University Press, 1982), pp. 12–13.

based understanding of solidarity. Since the historical period the works focus on coincides with the coming of capitalist modes of production, and of modernity in general in a colonial context it produces an important conundrum. If the subaltern mobilizations under analysis were motivated by factors that do not fit neatly into narratives of capitalist transition, or into the ways in which a liberal rights discourse complements capitalist modernity, then how do we characterize these movements? To see these as signs of persistent underdevelopment or backwardness is specious for they remain an important part of the experience of Indian modernity, from the nineteenth century to the present. Put differently, if these social movements are not pre-modern remnants in a rapidly modernizing world, studying them could lead to some fundamental questions that structure our received understandings of capitalist modernity in the colony, with implications for post-colonial developments.

Indeed, what these mobilizations draw attention to is what Dipesh Chakrabarty has called 'the presence of the archaic in the modern'. These traces are reminders that subaltern mobilizations carry 'archaeological sediments of heterogeneous time in the collective life of peasant societies' in South Asia. Analysing the fruitfulness of Guha's endeavour in shedding light on the peasant as a mass political subject, Partha Chatterjee observed that the founder of SS was 'right in insisting that it was not a case of drawing the faces in the crowd, as the radical social historians of France or Britain might have suggested' for the insurgent peasant in colonial India was not 'political in the sense of the individualized bourgeois citizen of liberal democracy'. They were, rather, 'mass political subjects whose rationality had to be sought in the collective life of the peasant community'.[16] Chatterjee also qualified that in writing about insurgent subjectivity in this manner Guha did not claim to have exhausted every aspect of individual and quotidian acts of resistance of his subjects. Citing James Scott's *Weapons of the Weak* as a counter example of the latter kind of effort, Chatterjee distinguishes Guha from Scott. Guha, unlike Scott, focussed on the structures of mass uprisings by the peasantry rather than their everyday. His claims therefore serve as a lens through which to analyse the structures of mass rebel consciousness.[17]

---

[16] Partha Chatterjee, 'After Subaltern Studies', *Economic and Political Weekly* 35 (2012), p. 46.
[17] Ibid.

Related to the above is the challenge of not casting subaltern movements under the overarching rubrics of socialism or nationalism. Likewise, although different parts of the world witnessed similar agitations by peasants, tribal groups and workers at the turn of the century, SS scholarship calls into question the validity of regarding the Indian uprisings as instantiations of global agitations. Local factors propelled these movements even when their leadership spoke a language of global or universal rights of all humanity. SS historians often demonstrated the splintering of movements among workers or peasants along particular ethnic or religious lines. In so doing, they brought to light new cases of local movements—such as agitations for cow protection or prohibition of alcohol—that often modified at the ground level what to distant observers could seem amenable to a single-category description like 'peasants' or 'workers' movements. The plethora of movements they analysed does not render the task of history writing simpler. The importance of the local may indeed justify Shahid Amin's complaint about some subaltern histories that 'do not travel well'.[18] That said, the importance of the SS project as a whole lies in the fact that local and regional differences notwithstanding, they offer certain important historiographical insights into the ways in which we might characterize the social actors who participated in these struggles.

SUBALTERN STUDIES AND ACCOUNTS OF MASS INSURGENCIES

In this section I will briefly outline some of Guha's basic claims. This will be followed by an analysis of some key works that looked at peasant mobilizations during the nationalist period in order to highlight features of peasant autonomy in movements of their own making. I will conclude with an analysis of two works on working-class and sectarian protest in order to test the hypothesis that labour as an identity in colonial India never superseded the original conditions of peasant mentality. Indeed, as mentioned above, the conditions of the Indian working classes were inextricably bound up in ties in which factors such as caste, community and religion were of paramount importance in workers' mobilizations.

A few salient points about EA are in order as we analyse the centrality of peasant insurgencies in the historiographical intervention made by SS. In the Introduction of EA, Guha makes a provocative observation

---

[18] Cited in Chatterjee, 'After Subaltern Studies', p. 49.

about the 'redundancy' of peasant insurgencies in the historiography of colonial India. What he implies is that given how commonplace peasant rebellions were in colonial India they generated a massive amount of writing by the law and order arms of the state. Hence Guha's claim that the 'historiography of peasant insurgency in colonial India is as old as colonialism itself'.[19] The documentation on insurgencies, namely law reports, police files, testimonies by rebel leaders, accounts by lower order stooges and spies of the district administration, comprise the 'sources' for the historian of subaltern life. The frequency of uprisings, however, also accounts for these events being overlooked in the grand narrative of Indian nationalism. Meticulously recorded by the colonial administration, peasant insurgencies were reduced to law and order nuisances that colonial and indigenous authorities handled expeditiously. To liberate historiography from the thraldom of nationalism and colonialism, Guha sought to find traces of rebel consciousness in the prose of officialdom. It was the task of the radical historian, he argued, to read the discourse of the state or of the indigenous elite as 'writing in reverse', thereby finding in official accounts 'the prose of counter-insurgency'. To make sense of how the insurgent turned the universe that was antagonistic to his existence, the historian perforce had to turn the documentation on insurgency upside down.[20]

Second, in EA Guha deliberately focusses on peasant movements from the period before the rise of Gandhian mass nationalism. His aim is to trace a continuum in the 'elementary aspects' of insurgencies from the earlier period into those of later day movements. This is to call into question the overwhelming tendency in nationalist histories to credit the mass mobilization of common people to a well-known leader's charisma. It is also a critique of historians of a socialist bent who regarded peasant insurgencies as harbingers of a socialist or communist type revolution on the subcontinent. Both nationalist and socialist-minded historical works were informed by a teleological perspective where the Santal uprisings, the revolt of Titu Mir, the Birsaite *ulgulan* and the hundreds of other insurgencies that Guha refers to are seen as the precursors of the socialist *Kisan Sabhas* (peasant associations), post-independence struggles in Tebhaga and Telengana, and even the Naxalite movement of the late 1960s. Examples of this kind of history writing are evident in works by Suprakash Ray,

---

[19] Guha, *Elementary Aspects*, p. 1.
[20] For an analysis of such inversions see Ranajit Guha, 'Negation', Ibid., pp. 18–76.

L. Natarajan, Abdullah Rasul and Sunil Sen. Readers will get a sense of the positions that Guha set himself up against in the following quote:

> The flames of the fire kindled by the peasant martyrs of the Santal insurrection a hundred years ago had spread to many regions all over India. Those flames could be seen in the burning in the indigo cultivators' rebellion in Bengal (1860), in the uprising of the raiyats of Pabna and Bogra (1872), in that of the Maratha peasantry of the Deccan (1875–76). The same fire was kindled again and again in the course of the Moplah peasant revolts of Malabar. The fire has not been extinguished yet, it is still burning in the hearts of the Indian peasants [...].[21]

In Guha's analysis, these historians were intent on rehabilitating peasant insurgencies from the earlier colonialist discourse. To them, the colonial state was the prime cause of peasant discontent. For many of the aforementioned scholars, the colonial administration created the power of *zamindars* (landlords) and moneylenders to sustain 'its own need for exploitation and government, and helped them directly and indirectly by offering its protection and patronage'.[22] Thus, while colonialist narratives explained peasant uprisings as a result of the failure of the paternalist state to provide adequate protection to the child-like Indian peasant, tribal and agricultural labourer, Indian historians detected the colonial state's complicity with the indigenous rural elite in the activation of processes that squeezed the peasantry. Both readings, in different ways, ended up making either the state or 'an abstraction called Worker-and-Peasant' the agent of these insurgencies. An illustration from Sunil Sen's *Agrarian Struggle in Bengal* will help clarify this point. Sen prefaces his volume by noting 'My heroes are the peasants, the unknown Indians who fought for a cause in which they believed. I think that peasant leaders should figure prominently in the story of a peasant struggle.' Lest he is accused of romanticizing the peasant, however, Sen inserts a caveat. 'It is not my purpose', he writes, 'to idealise the reality'.

> The Indian peasants are backward, mostly illiterate and extremely conscious about tangible benefits; the very system of production keeps them backward, scattered and disorganized. Here comes the crucial role of the intellectuals who went to the village, not in the Narodnik fashion, but as builders of mass

---

[21] Cited in Guha, 'The Prose', p. 76.
[22] Cited in Ibid., p. 75.

peasant movement. *Over the years the intellectual leaders trained with great patience an army of kisan cadres who emerged as local leaders.*[23]

Whatever the historical yield of these different genres of writing, they robbed insurgency of its character as a 'motivated and conscious undertaking on the part of the rural masses'.[24] On the one hand, the peasant's actions became the result of manipulation or inspiration by local leaders or an intellectual avant-garde and were converted into instances of either non-violent mass movements or socialist-type agitations. At the same time, these historical accounts failed to note the weaknesses in insurgent behaviour. So intent were they on painting an image of insurgent solidarity, either to quell it or to hail it as the harbinger of national independence, that they often missed seeing how ideas of localism, sectarianism and territoriality produced constant cracks in the ranks of the rebels.

Guha and his colleagues in SS sought to argue against both these viewpoints in order to retrieve the insurgent peasant's agency as the prime factor of these movements. Peasant insurgencies, they argued, mirrored rebel consciousness, a desire to challenge the dominant order of Indian society constituted by a triumvirate of the landlord, moneylender and colonial government. At the same time, Guha cautioned, it would be wrong to read this kind of political mobilization on the part of Indian peasant groups as the articulation of a mature politics. We shall return to this aspect at the concluding part of this section.

Ranajit Guha, Shahid Amin, Gyanendra Pandey and David Hardiman all demonstrated that the conditions of the Indian countryside during this period were largely semi-feudal and people drew their 'sustenance from pre-capitalist conditions of production and its legitimacy from a traditional culture still paramount in the superstructure'. It was a 'historic paradox' noted Guha that one of the most advanced capitalist powers in the world fused 'landlordism and usury in India so well as to impede the development of capitalism both in agriculture and in industry'.[25] Under the circumstances any attempt by the peasant to improve his conditions had to necessarily involve an attempt to overturn this structure of power. Given the risks entailed in any effort to challenge the existing order of

---

[23] Sunil Sen, *Agrarian Struggle in Bengal, 1946–47* (New Delhi: People's Publishing House, 1971), p. 10 (my emphasis).

[24] Guha, 'The Prose', p. 46.

[25] Guha, *Elementary Aspects.*

the land, SS historians were deeply critical of viewpoints that regarded insurgencies as 'spontaneous', primitive rebellions. Insurgencies were typically preceded by gatherings, demonstrations and parleys with authorities. Armed uprising was often a last resort and could never have been engaged in 'in a fit of absent-mindedness'. Such standpoints marked a clear departure from those articulated by noted historian Eric Hobsbawm in his seminal work *Primitive Rebels*.[26]

Primitive Rebels is widely acknowledged as a classic in the 'history from below' genre. In Hobsbawm's analysis the rebel peasant in traditional but modernizing societies was a 'pre-political' being because his uprisings had no 'elaborate blueprint' to replace the existing superstructure. The adjective 'pre-political' highlighted the absence of political consciousness or will. 'The bandit', wrote Hobsbawm, 'is a pre-political phenomenon and his strength is in inverse proportion to that of organized revolutionism and Socialism or Communism'.[27] Elsewhere he remarked that peasant discontent lacked any explicit articulation of 'ideology, organization or programme'. The category 'pre-political people' for Hobsbawm included those 'who have not yet found, or only begun to find, a specific language in which to express their aspirations about the world'.[28]

Guha was emphatic that the meanings conjured by the expression pre-political made no sense in the colonial Indian context. 'There was nothing in militant movements' of India's rural masses, he wrote, 'that was not political'. To see them as otherwise smacked of the historian's elitist bias where no movement was properly political unless it had a well-defined agenda, an elaborate plan on the methods that would fulfil that agenda, and a recognized leadership. In the absence of these prerequisites social uprisings could only be spontaneous upheavals. Citing Gramsci once

---

[26] Eric Hobsbawm, *Primitive Rebels: Studies in Archaic Forms of Social Movement in the 19th and 20th centuries* (New York: Praeger, 1963). For Guha's critique of Hobsbawm see *Elementary Aspects*, pp. 5–10.

[27] Cited in Guha, *Elementary Aspects*, p. 5.

[28] Guha, *Elementary Aspects*, pp. 5–6. Guha acknowledges that Hobsbawm's reading may be valid in the historical context he set out to analyse. Nonetheless, there remained some contradictions in his writing for just as he claimed that social banditry lacked in organization or ideology, he also went on to observe, 'banditry is a rather primitive form of *organized social protest*' (Guha's emphasis). Likewise, his claims about English agricultural labourers were at odds with those made by the other eminent historian of popular rebellions George Rude, who observed about these uprisings in 1830s England that 'wage-riots, machine-breaking', and the 'mobbing' of overseers and parsons 'even if erupting spontaneously, quickly developed the nucleus of a local organization'.

more, Guha argued that 'there is no room for spontaneity in politics', and it was incumbent upon the historian of radical movements to demonstrate the layers of meaning that inhered in peasants' actions that made the latter political. For Guha, insurgency 'affirmed its political character precisely by its negative and inversive procedure'.[29]

Yet to delineate the exact contours of politics in peasant struggles in India was a challenge because the actors themselves did not leave behind documentary evidence of their activities. This prompted a thornier issue of how the historian would write the peasant subaltern as the agent of his history when the latter 'looked upon his own acts of resistance as a manifestation of another's will?'[30] Peasants often invoked the power of gods, spirits and ancestors as they took up arms against their upper-class overlords. Sometimes they revolted in the name of the queen. Such examples are frequent in the works of SS historians. The history of peasant and tribal insurgencies in India were replete with 'myths, rituals, rumours, hopes for a Golden Age and fears of an imminent End of World'.[31]

Conventionally, however, these facts are rendered meaningless when historians read them as manipulation by leaders to rouse the peasantry. Or else, they are reduced to class struggles, albeit of a somewhat backward variety, given the overt marks of communal or religious strife in subaltern activity. Religion, it is clear from SS histories, was a factor that could potentially unite the rebels but also divide them. Hindu myths would no doubt sometimes alienate sections of Muslim peasantry in much the same way as lower castes could feel oppressed by the presence of upper caste gods and heroes. The desire of radical historiography in India to see in the rebel the harbinger of socialism, or the ideal liberal citizen subject whose religious beliefs were neatly privatized led scholars to elide truths about possible discord among insurgent peasants and workers. SS scholars were among the first to acknowledge superstition and religious beliefs as legitimate causes in understanding rebel consciousness, even when such beliefs defied rational explanations by social scientists.

Several of these issues are articulated in a striking fashion in Shahid Amin's account of rumours and beliefs about colonial India's most iconic political leader, M. K. Gandhi, in Gyanendra Pandey's accounts of sec-

---

[29] Guha, *Elementary Aspects*, p. 9. The chapter on negation (pp. 18–76) demonstrates the actual modalities of such inversion.
[30] Guha, *Elementary Aspects*, p. 277.
[31] Guha, 'The Prose', p. 39.

tarian movements among predominantly agrarian communities in northern India and in David Hardiman's analysis of tribal uprisings in western India under the ostensible command of a local goddess. Amin's concern in his now famous essay 'Gandhi as Mahatma' was to analyse the ways in which the Mahatma's (as Gandhi was popularly known, lit. great soul, great leader) charisma registered in peasant consciousness. In particular, he demonstrated the ways in which Gandhi's image was woven into an existing template of popular beliefs that made them feel empowered to undertake 'direct action' against the existing orders of village society. These actions were often at odds with the reigning credo of India's main nationalist party, the Indian National Congress. Amin catalogued the multiple acts of violence carried out in Gandhi's name. Their variance from Gandhian ideology might appear shocking. For example, a 'criminal tribe' called the Badhik looted a market in Gorakhpur as they chanted slogans in Gandhi's name; peasant volunteers declared 'Gandhi's swaraj' as they swept through villages and towns unleashing violence upon anyone who opposed their immediate goals; others attributed attacks on moneylenders, judges, local landlords and Englishmen—all pillars of authority in the rural hinterlands—to commands they received from Gandhi in their dreams or in miracles. In fact, the outbreak of violence in the hamlet of Chauri Chaura that led to the killing of 21 policemen and caused Gandhi to suspend the non-cooperation movement was, according to Amin's analysis, the by-product of peasants' distilling their own meanings out of nationalist slogans and expressions such as *swaraj* (self-rule).

Events during the same years, 1921–1922, that comprised the crux of Amin's analysis, but in a different region of India—the western Indian state of Gujarat—are the subject of Hardiman's work on the legend of the *devi* under whose inspiration and command *adivasis* (first-peoples) agitated against local liquor dealers and landlords. The goddess, Hardiman argues, had a continuous existence in southern Gujarat as a protector of tribals from smallpox. During this time, however, she was transformed in the tribals' perceptions from a benign divinity into a force who influenced them to change their ways of life by rising up against upper-caste moneylenders and Parsi liquor merchants. Like Amin's villagers who variously regarded Gandhi as a saint, a god, a Brahmin, so too in Gujarat the *devi* for a limited period of time emerged as a multi-headed hydra who encouraged tribals to ally with the nationalist struggle. In Gujarat, even Gandhi was seen as an extension of the *devi*. Both Amin and Hardiman relied on a variety of historical sources to craft their narratives, as did several other SS historians. They emphasized the need to read archival documents against the grain, often undertaking historical ethnography to question the depiction of peasants/tribals as mere objects of elite historiography.

Overall, their efforts succeeded in questioning the depiction of the peasantry in colonialist and nationalist writings as infantile. If Guha drew attention to the surfeit of expressions such as 'contagion', Pandey focussed on their depiction as 'fanatics', while Amin referenced 'the mythopoeic imagination of the childlike peasants' in numerous editorials and writings by Congress leaders. Following their train of thought we clearly see the ways in which nationalist leaders were bewildered by the rowdy, stick-wielding *sadharan janta* (ordinary people) that thronged to catch a glimpse of Gandhi as Hindu devotees would seek *darshan* (sighting) of their deities, or congregated as unruly mobs at Congress gathering defying all rules of modern discipline. Likewise, colonialist writers regarded peasant uprisings as the justification for carrying out 'England's work in India'. Peasant movements were the *raison d'etre* for the latter to establish *pax britanica* that would bring India under rule of law thereby rescuing the needy subaltern from the throes of landlord and moneylender exploitation. Either way, whatever their political bent, most writers found it impossible to regard peasant movements as anything other than the handiwork of agent provocateurs in the countryside or as the uncomprehending outburst of an impoverished people exploding against a causal chain of poverty, hunger and indebtedness set in motion by the dominant classes of Indian society.

The persistence of certain modes of identification rooted in a pre-industrial, agrarian social organization featured prominently in Gyan Pandey's influential essay 'Rallying Around the Cow'.[32] Pandey studied the movement for cow protection among disparate Hindu communities, of various castes, in the northern Indian state of Uttar Pradesh in an attempt to understand better the logic behind the massive riots that broke out among Hindus and Muslims around this issue. Pandey's is an interesting case of a social movement that fractured the unity of Indian nationalist politics. Given the ideological freight that the expression communalism, the name by which sectarian strife is commonly designated, carries within educated circles in India, Pandey was at pains to disprove that such strife

---

[32] Gyanendra Pandey, 'Rallying Around the Cow: Sectarian Strife in the Bhojpuri Region, c. 1888–1917', in Ranajit Guha (ed.), *Subaltern Studies. Writings on South Asian History and Society*, Vol. II (New Delhi: Oxford University Press, 1983), pp. 60–129.

was the outcome of some deep seated hatred between warring communities. He was equally critical of explanations that regarded rioting as an expression of a breakdown of harmonious dialogue between the leadership of Congress and Muslim organizations in the late nineteenth and early twentieth centuries. There was no demand for a separate Muslim state at this time, nor were Hindu–Muslim conflicts permanent. As he noted in an earlier essay, the sense of 'community' was itself ambiguous, 'straddling as it did the religious fraternity, class, quasba, and mohalla. ... It is difficult to translate this consciousness into terms that are readily comprehensible in today's social science—Muslim/Hindu, working class/rentier, urban/rural—or even to argue that a particular context would inevitably activate a particular solidarity.'[33]

Large swathes of the country witnessed such agitations that arose out of issues such as cow or pig slaughter, playing music outside mosques or the desecration of sacred shrines. One such instance in the Bhojpuri region of Uttar Pradesh is the focus of Pandey's analysis in his work on cow protection movements. Pandey emphasizes upward mobility among different peasant and agricultural groups in the region as a pre-eminent factor that forged a temporary solidarity among both Hindu and Muslim communities. Such upward mobility is testified to in politically charged actions by the community of Muslim weavers commonly known as Julahas changing their community name to *Momin* (faithful) or *Ansari* (an 'Arabic ancestor who practiced the art of weaving') in order to live down the associations of Julahas with lowly origins and manual labour. Similarly, Hindu castes such as Ahirs, Kurmis, Koeris and others that were 'middle-status agricultural castes', in an effort to forge an upwardly mobile caste status, increasingly emphasized seclusion of women, prevented them from labouring in the fields of upper castes and pushed for education for their children. Cow protection movements have to be understood against this rapidly transforming milieu in colonial India. The cow became a politically charged signifier in this period that witnessed large numbers of cattle death due to falling acreage for grazing, cattle stealing and poisoning by butchers. A symbol of Hindu pride and respectability for many different caste groups, some upwardly mobile, others threatened by such mobility, the cow became the bond of a temporary solidarity.

[33] Gyanendra Pandey, 'Encounters and Calamities: The History of a North Indian Qasba in the Nineteenth Century', in Ranajit Guha (ed.), *Subaltern Studies. Writings on South Asian History and Society*, Vol. III (Delhi: Oxford University Press, 1984), p. 269.

Pandey, however, is careful to note the pitfalls of positing anything like a 'Hindu' or 'Muslim' identity at this time. The changes in the land market, the rise in demand for cash crops, opportunities held out by plantation economies and the corresponding rise in unemployment in northern Indian plains often produced fierce rivalries among upper and lower castes. That a movement focussed on cow protection arose between 1880 and 1910 was therefore highly contingent and dependent on a range of interests felt urgently by local Hindus of the region and their rivalries with the community of Muslims. At the heart of the conflict were changes in the agrarian structure of northern India, opportunities opened up by colonial education and employment that gave many lower castes an opportunity to seek higher status for themselves. The sacrality of the cow, a seemingly primordial reflex associated with Hinduness, was heightened in an unprecedented manner under these conditions, leading to a violent, sectarian social movement demanding its protection.

To turn to the final example in this section from SS scholarship, let us take the case of factory labourers in Dipesh Chakrabarty's *Rethinking Working Class History*, a study of jute mill workers in Bengal between 1890 and 1940. Chakrabarty's central problem is to explore the contours of working class consciousness in a culture that was not quite bourgeois in the strict Marxist sense of the term. The book delves into questions of factory 'discipline', i.e. authority exercised by trade union leaders, factory bosses and 'sardars' (working-class jobbers). Chakrabarty focussed on working-class protests ranging from strikes and lock-outs to riots, and also on issues of working class solidarity and organization or the lack thereof. As in other works by SS historians here, too, we find powerful remnants of a rural culture. Kinship ties, religious bonds, community interests and filial markers were as important in the making of a workers' consciousness as trade unions. Rather than view this as a problem of India's stunted economic development due to colonial rule, however, Chakrabarty sees it as a constitutive feature of Indian modernity. As he puts it quite succinctly in the conclusion of the said work, there remains, due to powerful historical and cultural factors, an elision between the notion of 'citizen' and the 'proletarian' in the Indian context. The Indian factory worker does not adhere to the classic type of proletarian, or even to the image of an idealized citizen subject whose beliefs can be neatly privatized. Liberal values of individualism and equality before the law jostled with other competing ideas such as social hierarchy, filial piety and religious or communal solidarity in working-class protests. The roots of these rural ties hark back to peasant consciousness theorized in the works discussed above and notions of being working class had not shed these modes of being and becoming. Labour movements in colonial and post-colonial India, therefore, must be conceptualized within this complex framework.

Peasant identity formed the bedrock in most social and political activism that comprised the themes of SS histories. Collectively, the project sought to understand the nature of subaltern history and agency during a period of transition. The group was well versed in transition theories conceptualized in teleological terms, from semi-feudal to bourgeois capitalist and eventually socialist conditions. Yet, they consciously set out to undermine all projects of understanding subaltern agency that borrowed on European and teleological narratives of transition to capitalism. This awareness probably accounted for SS scholars' early sympathies towards the writings of Mao Zedong. China, like India, they believed was a society in transition without the requisite industrial framework. Within this agrarian model a kind of leftist avant-gardism made these scholars probe the issue of subaltern 'consciousness'. Seeing the peasant-subaltern as the paradigm of a revolutionary subject and attempting to understand the peasant's potential as a carrier of revolutionary consciousness was the collective's way of negotiating certain dogmatic Marxist binaries, such as those between materialism and culture, or between theory and praxis. The peasant seen as the paradigmatic mass-political subject is therefore to be understood as a manoeuvre that was simultaneously rhetorical and theoretical. The category peasant was capacious and included in its ambit tribals, forest dwellers, migrants, workers and people whose livelihoods had only partially to do with land. Understanding a plethora of labouring groups under the master sign of the peasantry was, of course, a controversial move.

By way of conclusion, I will now turn to the legacy of the SS project for our understanding of social movements, especially to the task of historicizing about such movements in a non-Western setting. Drawing on some recent writings of the SS school, which has now been officially disbanded, as well as some critical reflections on the histories written by the series from the 1980s and 1990s, I want to suggest that there is something generative in the legacy of SS for the scholarship that we produce on social movements not just in India but globally.

CONCLUSION

In a review essay on the collective's works, historian Rosalind O'Hanlon made some perceptive remarks about the conceptualization of SS's original project in its own historical context. It would be worth citing O'Hanlon at some length in order for today's reader to get a sense of the way in which historians reflected on the importance of the 'masses' in their academic endeavours some twenty years ago. Some of O'Hanlon's remarks drew their critical energies from Jean Baudrillard's provocation about the significance of the 'masses' in 'our present political culture' whereby '[T]hey are the leitmotif of every discourse; they are the obsession of every social project.' She goes on to argue that,

> At the level of our political culture, this consuming ideological imperative makes it intolerable for us to accept publicly that we cannot appropriate the masses to our projects, that there may be only silence where their own authentic voices should be raised in our support. [...] It is this same value, of course, which allows us to make the term 'elite historiography' itself into one of criticism; and which makes that undoubted majority of professional historians who remain preoccupied with elites of various kinds defend this preoccupation not with a frank disavowal of any interest in 'the people', but with the assertion that it is elites, or those in power, after all, who are most in a position to determine what happens to the people at large, and who therefore remain the best means through which we may understand the changes through which people live.[34]

O'Hanlon goes on to make some important criticisms of the way in which the SS historians undertook to write the masses back into history. Noteworthy among these was her critique about restoring the subaltern as a 'classic unitary self-constituting subject-agent of liberal humanism'. While this is an important point, O'Hanlon's remarks register the importance of the endeavour that the historians of SS undertook. Indeed, her critique was also expressed with great theoretical force by Gayatri Spivak in her essay 'Subaltern Studies: Deconstructing Historiography'.[35] Spivak characterized the endeavour to recuperate subaltern agency by the collective as 'a strate-

[34] Rosalind O'Hanlon, 'Recovering the Subject: Subaltern Studies and Histories of Resistance in Colonial South Asia', *Modern Asian Studies* 22 (1988), pp. 189–224, p. 195.
[35] Gayatri C. Spivak, 'Subaltern Studies: Deconstructing Historiography', in Gayatri C. Spivak and Ranajit Guha (eds), *Selected Subaltern Studies* (New York: Oxford University Press, 1988), pp. 3–32.

gic use of positivist essentialism in a scrupulously visible political interest'.[36] As noted by Partha Chatterjee, echoing Guha's call in the manifesto cited earlier, '[t]he task' of the subaltern historian 'is to fill up this emptiness, that is, the representation of subaltern consciousness in elitist historiography. It must be given its own specific content with its own history and development. [...] Only then can we recreate not merely a whole aspect of human history whose existence elitist historiography has hitherto denied, but also the history of the 'modern' period, the epoch of capitalism.'[37]

As noted above, this was not a simple task for under the conditions of capitalist development in India under colonial rule, capitalist and liberal values were not hegemonic in colonial Indian culture, thus producing a very specific trajectory of the peasant-subaltern who in spite of his transformation into an industrial worker remained bound up in pre-capitalist ties of loyalty, religiosity and hierarchy. Some scholars have alleged that to see the subaltern subject in this manner was also to bring him under an Orientalist gaze. Notwithstanding such criticisms one of the most important contributions of SS has been precisely to introduce the categories of religiosity, superstition and other modes of affective identification into the analysis of subaltern consciousness and politics. This was not, as some of them forcefully argued, some vestige of primitive rebelliousness in the manner analysed by earlier works of the 'history from below' genre. Rather, the presence of the 'archaic in the modern' fundamentally shaped a variety of movements that had the masses as their main actors.

The immediate conditions out of which SS grew played not a small part in the ways in which these historians sought to make room for subaltern movements within the richly documented histories of nationalism and colonialism. In retrospect, we might even detect something anachronistic in the manner in which they read their own present—the decades of the turbulent 1960s that culminated in the national emergency of 1975–77—back into the colonial past. Their collective despair with the post-colonial Indian state made them question the legacy of nationalism. Partha Chatterjee and Shahid Amin in particular questioned the capacity of the nationalist leadership to speak for the masses they claimed to represent. Chatterjee's *The Nation and its Fragments* was thus a powerful critique of

---

[36] Ibid., p. 13.
[37] Partha Chatterjee, 'Peasants, Politics and Historiography: A Response', *Social Scientist* 120 (1983), pp. 58–65, p. 62.

the state—both colonial and post-colonial.[38] However romantic the vision of recuperating subaltern agency in struggles that had little to do with a grand statist vision may appear in hindsight, the works of SS scholars serve as an important corrective to nation-state centred accounts of history. As separatist movements raged in Punjab, Kashmir, and communal rioting broke out in different parts of India in 1968, 1984 and 1989, SS historians like Gyanendra Pandey sought to analyse sectarian mobilizations from the colonial period in an effort to find structural generalities that marked such rioting.[39] In Rosalind O'Hanlon's words, Guha and some of his colleagues perhaps regarded much of their historical endeavours as 'co-terminus with the struggles of the dispossessed, feeding directly into them by making sense of them', an enterprise she calls 'fundamentally misconceived'.[40]

Without denying the critical force of O'Hanlon's critique there is something in Guha's contention about peasant insurgencies being the forerunners of a variety of struggles in both the colonial and post-colonial period that stands the test of history. This has to do with the ways in which the project offered insights into the 'genealogy of the mass-political subject in India' that remain valid in understanding contemporary insurgencies.[41]

Chatterjee identifies two broad patterns in popular movements in contemporary India. The first kind challenges the sovereignty of the Indian state. The ongoing struggles for Azad (sovereign) Kashmir, the continuing insurgencies in the forest regions of central and eastern India that have intensified in the recent spate of Maoist uprisings in these states serve as examples of such struggles. The Indian state is a complete outsider in these situations. Rather the protesting groups, the Indian state and a variety of intermediaries are involved in complex negotiations about resource allocation, militarization and governance. The everyday stuff of these negotiations involving actions such as villagers giving refuge to Maoist

---

[38] Partha Chatterjee, *The Nation and Its Fragments: Colonial and Postcolonial Histories* (Princeton: Princeton University Press, 1993); Shahid Amin, *Event, Metaphor, Memory: Chauri Chaura, 1922–1992* (Berkeley: University of California Press, 1995).

[39] Gyanendra Pandey, 'Encounters and Calamities', in Gayatri C. Spivak and Ranajit Guha (eds), *Selected Subaltern Studies* (New York: Oxford University Press, 1988), pp. 89–128; Gyanendra Pandey, *The Construction of Communalism in Colonial North India* (New Delhi: Oxford University Press, 1990); Gyanendra Pandey, *Memory, History, and the Question of Violence* (Calcutta: Center for Studies in Social Sciences, 1999).

[40] Rosalind O'Hanlon, 'Recovering the Subject', p. 219.

[41] Chatterjee is citing Dipesh Chakrabarty here. Chatterjee, 'After Subaltern Studies', p. 46.

rebels, children pelting stones at policemen, the unfurling of national flags of other countries, the blowing up of Indian army camps and transport are as Chatterjee rightly argues, reminiscent of Guha's framework of 'negation' in EA. But these examples of movements for sovereignty do not exhaust the range of social movements in India today. The latter are too multiple in Chatterjee's estimation to be fully encapsulated by the paradigm of peasant insurgency supplied by Guha. One important reason for this is that, unlike in the colonial era insurgencies where the state was an 'outsider' for the rebels, under conditions of economic liberalization the Indian state has penetrated even deeper into the lives of the Indian agriculturist. Chatterjee puts this point forcefully in his essay 'Democracy and Economic Transition' where he notes that the result of economic liberalization has not been a disappearance of the Indian peasantry but its refiguration in a completely new way where active negotiation with the Indian state has played a key role. Understanding this newness however requires a different conceptual schema and EA or the model of early SS scholarship is not adequate to that task. Chatterjee's emphasis is on the dramatically altered nature of the insurgent subject. To apprehend that subject, Guha's model of revolutionary consciousness no longer works.[42]

In thinking through the predicament of conceptualizing the revolutionary subject, or the subject of contemporary insurgencies, in India today it may be useful to turn to Dipesh Chakrabarty's essay 'Belatedness as Possibility' that offers some thoughtful reflections on the many mediations through which the mass-political subject in SS came into being. While Chatterjee elaborated on the multiple intellectual influences on Guha and his colleagues, Chakrabarty qualifies that discussion by spelling out their departures from the traditions of Marx, Lenin, Gramsci and Mao that moulded their thinking. For example, in rejecting the label 'prepolitical' to describe the peasant insurgent, Guha categorically rejected any idea of a fear of the masses. He also rejected the notion that the peasants needed a party or organization to guide their activities, as one would expect in classical Marxist or Leninist analysis. Inspired though they were by Mao's 1927 report on the peasant movement in the Hunan district

---

[42] Partha Chatterjee, 'Democracy and Economic Transition', http://kafila.org/2008/06/13/democracy-and-economic-transformation-partha-chatterjee/ (viewed on 3 June 2013). For an earlier but fuller version of Chatterjee's formulations about contemporary popular mobilizations that he puts under the rubric of 'political society' see Partha Chatterjee, *The Politics of the Governed: Reflections on Popular Politics in Most of the World* (New York: Columbia University Press, 2004).

and Gramsci's *Prison Notebooks*, 'neither Mao's references to the need for "leadership of the Party" nor Gramsci's strictures against "spontaneity" featured with any degree of prominence' in these writings.[43] Rather, EA resonated with Mao's saying during the Cultural Revolution that 'to rebel is justified'. 'Rebellion' writes Chakrabarty,

> was not a technique for achieving something; it was its own end. Indeed, from a global perspective, one might say that Subaltern Studies was the last—or the latest—instance of a long global history of the Left: the romantic-popular search for a non-industrial revolutionary subject that was initiated in Russia, among other places, in the nineteenth century. This romantic populism shaped much of Maoism in the twentieth century, and left its imprint on the antinomies and ambiguities of Antonio Gramsci's thoughts on the Party as the Modern Prince.[44]

What underwrote this academic praxis of the cult rebellion epitomised by EA was a 'once-global and inherently romantic search for a revolutionary subject outside of the industrialized West'.[45] While the political potential of that romanticism may now be well exhausted, it is important to remember it for it points to the difficulties of historically translating on to the so-called third world ideas of the revolutionary subject that Marx called the proletariat. Yet, the project of translation, despite its inadequacies, is a reminder

> that we are working at and on the limits of European political thought even as we admit an affiliation to nineteenth century European revolutionary romanticism. Recognizing the stand-in nature of categories like 'the masses', 'the subaltern' or 'the peasant' is ... the first step towards writing histories of democracies that have emerged through the mass-politics of anticolonial nationalisms.[46]

In a more recent article Chakrabarty strikes an elegiac note in his assessment of SS.[47] I invoke the elegiac here following D. N. Rodowick's

---

[43] Dipesh Chakrabarty, 'Belatedness and Possibility: Subaltern Histories Once Again', in Rosinka Chaudhuri and Elleke Boehmer (eds), *The Indian Postcolonial: A Reader* (London: Routledge, 2011), p. 170.

[44] Ibid., pp. 170–171.

[45] Ibid.

[46] Ibid., p. 172.

[47] Dipesh Chakrabarty, 'Subaltern Studies in Retrospect and Reminiscence', *Economic and Political Weekly* 48:12 (2013), pp. 23–27.

use of the term in an entirely different context. Elegy, in Rodowick's usage, derived from the French eloge, combines 'the English sense of both eulogy and elegy and something more besides, an eloge can be both praise song and funereal chant, panegyric and chaison d'adieu'.[48] Chakrabarty argues that early SS's efforts to construct a genealogy of the mass political subject in India was valuable for the way in which Guha and others saw their actions as innately political. Yet, they fall short in the contemporary context for the masses whose genealogies the project sought to historicize are not one unity. SS, he notes made an invaluable contribution to the field of historical studies for raising the question of mass politics as an autonomous domain within the discipline. But, their methods and presuppositions in defining subalternity suffered from certain limitations that were perhaps shaped by the particular historical conditions that led to the founding of the series. Reading SS works today is, in the ultimate analysis, a valuable exercise, for these works are historical documents of a post-imperial world that offer important insights into the myriad ways in which human collectives have struggled for rights and freedom without any necessary grand vision uniting different historical contexts.

FURTHER READINGS

As noted at the start of this essay, writings by the Subaltern Studies collective are not generally associated with the study of social movements. This essay presented the yields that accrue when we regard the writings of historians such as Guha from the vantage of social movements. In what follows, I want to point to a fairly large body of work that has coexisted alongside SS, but whose focus has been, more directly, on particular movements by the peasantry, caste groups, religious communities, women and tribals.

Indian peasant studies as a field developed in the late 1960s early 1970s as a response to a number of national and global mobilizations by agrarian groups in the global south. Historical and anthropological works registered this politicization of peasant masses. Books such as *Pabna Disturbances and the Politics of Rent* (New Delhi: People's Publishing House, 1974) by Kalyan Sengupta, *Agrarian Unrest in North India: The United Provinces, 1918–1922* (New Delhi: Vikas, 1978) by Majid

---

[48] David N. Rodowick, 'An Elegy for Theory', *October* 122 (2007), p. 100.

Siddiqi and *Peasant Movements in India, 1920–1950* (New Delhi: Oxford University Press, 1983) by D. N. Dhanagare are crucial in this regard. Together, they focussed on the degree of autonomy, or the lack thereof that peasant movements had from the dominant anti-imperialist politics of the Indian National Congress. Scholars such as Asok Majumdar, Sumanta Banerjee and Swasti Mitter analysed movements like Tebhaga or Naxalbari. Occurring on the cusp of colonial and post-colonial periods or in the early years of the post-colony, these movements have been studied for the ways in which rural agricultural workers protested against land policies promulgated by colonial or nationalist elites. Peasant resistance, for several of the authors mentioned above, became one of earliest articulations of protest against the injustices of the post-colonial state. Another key aspect of these works was to interrogate whether peasant mobilizations demonstrated an incipient or overt class-consciousness. As I have noted above, this was a central issue in the works of SS scholars. Likewise, Siddiqi, Dhanagare and Gyanendra Pandey also analysed whether peasants were moved to action more by considerations of community, religion or millenarianism than by class.

In the wake of studies about social movements among the peasantry came those that featured the urban working classes. The jute workers of colonial Bengal and the textile workers of colonial Bombay have been particularly rich sites of study. Samita Sen's *Women and Labor in Late Colonial India: The Bengal Jute Industry* (Cambridge, UK: Cambridge University Press, 1999), Subho Basu's *Does Class Matter? Colonial Capital and Worker's Resistance in Bengal* (New York: Oxford University Press, 2004) and Rajnarayan Chandavarkar's *The Origins of Industrial Capitalism in India: Business Strategies and the Working Classes in Bombay, 1900–1940* are some important studies in this area. Interestingly, in analysing the reasons behind workers mobilization all the historians mentioned above challenged the conclusions of SS historian Dipesh Chakrabarty whose monograph, *Rethinking Working Class History* (Princeton: Princeton University Press, 1989), made a strong case for understanding working class movements in colonial Bengal in terms that were more expansive than class consciousness alone.

Central to the study of social movements in India is the question of religion and ethnicity. There is a rich body of scholarship that focussed on nineteenth-century religious reform movements that sought to cleanse Hinduism of the encrustation of centuries old superstition and Brahminical orthodoxy. Charles Heimsath, Sumit Sarkar, Tanika Sarkar, Charu Gupta and others have analysed the ways in which movements for the purification and unification of Hinduism (*shuddhi* and *sangathana*) had an impact of the corresponding mobilization by Muslim minorities. Equally, books like *Indian Nationalism and Hindu Social Reform* (Princeton: Princeton University Press, 1964), *Hindu Wife, Hindu Nation: Community Religion and Cultural Nationalism* (New Delhi: Permanent Black, 2001), *Writing Social History* (New York: Oxford University Press, 1997) and *Sexuality, Obscenity, Community* (New Delhi: Permanent Black, 2001) by these scholars were pioneering for the ways they highlighted the links between religious reform movements and the hardening of a neo-traditionalist Hindu patriarchy.

Growth areas in the history of social movements in India are those that focus on caste mobilization and religious nationalist movements. These studies are often situated at the intersections of caste and gender, as in Charu Gupta's recent book *The Gender of Caste* (Seattle: University of Washington Press, 2016). Other important intersections are those between religion and caste politics; Rupa Viswanath's *The Pariah Problem* (2014) is an important study that links lower caste (*dalit*) politics with Christianity and Hinduism in southern India. In recent years several influential studies have emerged that probe right-wing social movements in India, particularly those that uphold the ideology of a militant Hindu nationalism. Christophe Jaffrelot's *The Hindu Nationalist Movement* in India (New York: Columbia University Press, 1996) and Thomas Blom Hansen's *The Saffron Wave: Democracy and Hindu Nationalism in Modern India* (Princeton: Princeton University Press, 1999) are two excellent instances of recent scholarship that have woven together historical and ethnographic analyses to demonstrate the rise of right-wing political forces and mass mobilization in India.

By way of closing it is important to pay attention to a small but extremely significant body of work conducted by anthropologists and sociologists with a keen historical sensibility. Nandini Sundar's 1997 book *Subalterns and Sovereigns: An Anthropological History of Bastar, 1854–2006* (New York: Oxford University Press, 1997) is among the best examples of such work. Broadly speaking, these works focus on some of the most precarious social groups on the Indian subcontinent—tribal groups that reside in the mineral rich regions such as the Bastar in central India—and chart a history of their resistance. Often broken by the might of the colonial state and then the post-colonial one, these groups continue to fight a combination of state power and multi-national corporations. Their complex association with Maoist groups increases their vulnerability. These movements are difficult to study. Together with the movements of LGBTQ groups who, among other things, have been agitating for the repeal of article 377 of the Indian constitution, they promise to shed new light on the challenges of history writing about social movements the world over.

CHAPTER 4

Transpacific Feminism: Writing Women's Movement from a Transnational Perspective

Seonjoo Park

INTRODUCTION

The women's movement might be the most successful case of a social movement becoming 'global' both in its nature and in the scope of its organization. Its newly adopted agenda, 'Women's Rights as Human Rights', played a crucial role in promoting global support and solidarity for the women's movement, mainly through UN international conferences and declarations. From the 1990s on, female activists from Asia, Africa, Latin America and the Pacific have actively contributed to global women's issues as international feminists; they have articulated perspectives from their home countries and discussed together a range of gendered human rights issues, which has successfully led to several types of women's mobilization beyond national borders. The Beijing conference held in 1995 was one of such international conferences prominent in its size and number of participants and has been regarded as an important milestone in the history of the development of the global women's movement.

However, the meaning of this success is ambiguous. It is certainly true that the globalization of the women's movement has provided a common ground to discuss different kinds of sexual inequality and discrimination and, at the same time, allowed the movement itself to achieve a wide

S. Park (✉)
Department of English Education, Inha University, Inchon, Korea

© The Author(s) 2017
S. Berger, H. Nehring (eds.), *The History of Social Movements in Global Perspective*, DOI 10.1057/978-1-137-30427-8_4

range of legitimacy and recognition as a social protest. On the other hand, it has homogenized and universalized the category of 'woman' on the global scale, thus making the movement resemble an imperialist project built on a totalizing Western concept. Tani Barlow, for example, points out that what is called 'international feminism' is an 'ideology' of the United States funded by global capital—more precisely, 'a triumph of a particularly American way of empowering women' because it is 'a series of totalizing theories that cannot admit to an outside of feminism and will not admit the tangibility of any [other] social form'.[1] Its representative agenda, 'Women's Rights as Human Rights,' is dubious as well. Considering that in many circumstances the political, social and cultural status of 'woman' has been far lower than that of 'human', and the whole history of feminism can be summarized as a series of political struggles to shorten the distance between these two, the significance of this agenda should not be underestimated. And yet, when women's rights are strongly invoked as human rights, in most cases, 'woman' tends to fall within the traditional boundaries of 'human'—the 'human' as the figure of European male bourgeois citizen modelled on the Enlightenment ideal of modernity—rather than interrogating and conceiving the category itself anew.

The irony is that, while the women's movement is most active in its attempt to move beyond national borders and presumably most radical in its defiance of the regime of the nation-state, it is at the same time the most domesticated social movement. 'Woman' is a concept around which people from different cultures, classes and ethnicities can gather and through which global connections and mobilizations might be facilitated, but sometimes it is merely a social service snugly entrenched within the normative order of nation-state, modernity and global capital.

Writing about the global history of the women's movement (or about the history of global feminism), then, is a doubly daunting task. The term 'global' would necessarily pose the challenge of a huge amount of research, a variety of experiences and perspectives, and overwhelming kind of emotional investment. And, more importantly, it is a frustrating mission because of the suspicious tendency of the signifier 'woman' to travel smoothly across borders and barriers. The more widely and broadly the slogan 'Women's Rights as Human Rights' reaches, the more abstract and repetitive the story becomes. Just as the term 'human' is ahistorical in the sense that it essentializes a particular vision of the world (that is, the West-

---

[1] Tani Barlow, 'International Feminism of the Future', *Signs* 25 (2000), pp. 1099–1105.

oriented idea of modernity) as the universal telos, 'woman' as 'supplemental' to the 'human' becomes an ahistorical tautology as well.[2] When the category of 'woman' is such an odd mixture of an active agent with global mobility and an inert concept with no alternative future, how should it be historicized? Could it be narrated differently from the celebratory writing of European national history or the global history which has traced (and confirmed) the path of modernity from the West to the Rest? Can the rich, complex and vibrant practices of protest, resistance and change by women be written outside the time-space and the regime of the 'human'?

The purpose of this chapter is to explore the possibility of tracing and narrating the history of the women's movement from a transnational perspective by problematizing the category of 'woman' and bringing it to the table of global relations where it intersects, negotiates and gets entangled with other identity formations. 'Transpacific feminism' is introduced as a way to show how this type of study and writing may be conducted. It thus highlights more generally the problems of analysing activist identities from a transnational perspective.

FORMATION OF 'WOMAN' AND POLITICAL MOVEMENT

The formation of 'woman' has always been deeply implicated in the making of other identities such as ethnicity, class or culture, and other concepts such as Enlightenment, body or citizenship.[3] Due to this complex, constitutive and contradictory dynamic, 'woman' has been fluid, unstable and constantly relational, but the regime of power has always attempted to stabilize and rigidify this category. It is not, however, just the regime of power that has been keen to the making of 'woman'; the very practice of resistance to power also has demarcated and isolated 'woman' from other identities. In other words, 'woman' has been produced and consumed both by power and resistance to it.

As many critics point out, the nation-state has most actively participated in the construction of sexual identity; the production of the naturally heterosexual, and unambiguously bi-gendered population of citizens was

---

[2] Rey Chow, 'When Whiteness Feminizes ...: Some Consequences of a Supplementary Logic', *differences: A Journal of Feminist Cultural Studies* 11 (1999), pp. 137–168.

[3] For the historical interactions and transformations of 'women' with these concepts, see Denise Riley, *Am I that Name? Feminism and the Category of Women in History* (Minneapolis: University of Minnesota, 2003).

central to the formation of nation-state because the properly heterosexual and patriarchal family was the main source of political identity in modern nation-states.[4] In fact, the nation-state has not only produced 'woman' and then subjugated it, but also effectively delegitimized all forms of non-heterosexual desire and practice. It has normalized the idea of 'sanitized' love by disciplining a variety of non-normative sexualities with legal and social interventions. The social movement for women's emancipation was inseparably linked to the project of nation-building in its emphasis on modernity; therefore, women's movement has not been able to free itself from this systemic, disciplinary, state-enforced disavowal of homosexuality and other forms of sexuality from the very beginning.[5] As Nivedita Menon says, it is 'impossible to engage with what is called "sexuality" [...] without recognizing its passage through the complexity of the practices that were homogenized under the sign of Modernity.'[6]

The women's movement, then, is not necessarily an emancipatory project as long as it is firmly grounded upon state mechanisms. It is limited at best and conservative at worst. When it deals with 'family', for example, the focus is invariably on the issue of domestic violence, and the way it solves the problem is to help families in trouble to become 'proper' and 'normal' again. In this process, the model of a heterosexual patriarchal family is reinforced and legitimized as a norm no matter how inadequate and irrelevant it may become in the actual lives of people, especially in a transnational and global setting.[7]

---

[4] For the relevant arguments, see Ann Laura Stoler, *Carnal Knowledge and Imperial Power, Race and Intimacy in Colonial Rule* (Berkeley: University of California Press, 2002); Nivedita Menon (ed.), *Sexualities* (London: Zed Books, 2008); Inderpal Grewal and Caren Kaplan, 'Global Identities: Theorizing Transnational Studies of Sexuality', *GOQ: A Journal of Lesbian and Gay Studies* 7 (2001), pp. 663–679.

[5] Afsaneh Najmabadi argues that it was the cultural encounter with Europe that produced in Iran 'the heteronormalization of love and the feminization of beauty.' She also states that the women's movement in Iran bore the 'birthmark of disavowal of male homosexuality.' *Women with Moustaches and Men without Beards: Gender and Sexual Anxieties of Iranian Modernity* (Berkeley: University of California Press, 2005), pp. 2–8.

[6] Menon, *Sexualities*, p. 11.

[7] Anannya Bhattacharjee argues that the western norm of 'family' is becoming especially irrelevant in the case of immigrant families in the U.S. Anannya Bhattacharjee, 'Mapping Home and Undomesticating Violence Work', in Jacqui M. Alexander and Chandra T. Mohanty, *Feminist Genealogies, Colonial Legacies, Democratic Futures* (London: Routledge, 1997), pp. 308–329, pp. 396–398. Avtar Brah also points out the irrelevance of the binary of home(private) vs. work(public) to South Asian women in Britain, particularly those of Muslim background, whose form of paid work is home-based. 'Global Mobilities,

The response of the women's movement to queer politics also shows how deeply it is entrenched within the nation-state's project of identity formation. Feminist activism has mostly approached homosexuality as minority rights issue, taking for granted heterosexual monogamous marriage as the unquestionable norm. While this normative framework itself remains unchallenged, people, relationships and ways of life which do not fit the dominant sexual norm are 'generously' allowed to exist outside its boundaries.[8] For similar reasons, the support that feminist groups have managed to show toward the sex workers' movement is even weaker and more inconsistent.

Considering such problematic alliances among the nation-state, the identity of 'woman', and women's movement, it is natural that women's movement gradually moves on to the global terrain attempting to liberate itself from 'the founding moment of discursive violence that both produced and predicated "the nation"'.[9] In other words, it refuses to remain state mechanism and tries to become transnational or post-national in order to practice democratic and radical social protest. But even if it reorients its theory and practice in opposition to the state hegemony, it does not become functionally counter-hegemonic; instead, it still engages with the regime of power whether it is national, global, or something of both.

In fact, this shift in women's movement also suggests that the nation-state gradually declines with the concurrent rise of globalization, and the nature of the power is going through a profound transformation. It is hard to judge whether a new global order is really emerging, as some critics claim, to replace the nation-state. What is certain, however, is that the production of sexual identity now involves more than just the state. Today, nation-states, economic formations and consumer cultures all work together to create new forms of governmentality, forming and upholding identity of subjectivities and communities. As the centralized power of the nation-state has diminished, a decentralized mode of power has emerged with a loose network of social agencies and actors and it has begun to disseminate new values and norms of identity formation. Political mobilization is not entirely free from the new matrix of power set together by the state, market operations and cultural norms. In some cases, it may oppose

Local Predicaments: Globalization and the Critical Imagination', *Feminist Review* 70 (2002), pp. 30–45.
   [8] Menon, *Sexualities*, p. 36.
   [9] Menon, *Sexualities*, p. 39.

the hegemonic power effectively, while in other cases it may cooperate with power.

Non-state agents such as NGOs, with the cooperation with other institutions such as schools or media, diffuse ideas and techniques for re-forming/re-engineering the self on the new model—a liberal, free, autonomous and self-responsible subject—in order to confront globalized insecurities and institute a neoliberal ethical regime.[10]'Woman' in this neoliberal orthodoxy is increasingly identified as 'body,' especially a 'body' vulnerable to all kinds of violence such as rape or violations of reproductive health.[11] Accordingly, the common ground of global feminism has been built on the universal grammar of this image of victimized helplessness, and its main goals have been to achieve bodily integrity, autonomy and self-determination. The 'injury identity' was powerfully invoked all over the world and transnational connections of sympathy were made based on the 'wounded attachment.'[12] Even post-colonial criticism, being particularly sensitive to universalization and emphasizing that the actual historical experiences of colonialism (and of women) have been highly varied all over the world, only manages to discuss differing 'degrees' of victimization—because the idea of 'women as victims' cannot be challenged.

The effort to articulate 'a vulnerable body' as the ground for global solidarity of women is deeply embedded to what Foucault calls 'biopower', a mode of power which tries to discipline 'body' on the biological level with various techniques and ultimately to achieve a total and direct control of life itself. The global women's movement, as long as it is centred on the totalizing idea of a vulnerable body, participates in this mode of discursive power. Moreover, the overemphasis on 'body' and 'vulnerability' not only essentializes women's experience but also marginalizes it in the political terrain. 'Body', conceptualized as what lays bare, helpless, exposed to all kinds of violence outside all the legal, political protection, is a very good example of what Giorgio Agamben embodies with the term 'bare life', whose very vulnerability constitutes the political life from the outside.[13]

[10] Aihwa Ong, 'Experiments with Freedom: Milieus of the Human', *American Literary History* 2 (2006), pp. 229–244.

[11] Charlotte Bunch, 'Transforming Human Rights from a Feminist Perspective', in Julie Peters and Andrea Wolper (eds), *Women's Rights/Human Rights: International Feminist Perspectives* (London: Routledge, 1995), pp. 11–17.

[12] Wendy Brown, *Politics Out of History* (Princeton, NJ: Princeton University Press, 2001).

[13] Giorgio Agamben, *Homo sacer: Sovereign Power and Bare Life* (Palo Alto, CA: Stanford University Press, 1998).

Thus, the 'body' concept has two contradictory effects for global feminism: while it reproduces the typical gesture of neoliberal welfare state to protect and rescue, it also manifests the inner logic of totalitarian regime to occupy the entirety of life and wield total authority over it.[14]

In other words, what global feminism, international feminism or human rights feminism claims to do with the common signifier, 'woman', actually stages the contradictory but harmonious coexistence of protection and violence from within the biopower of global discipline. It is also a different version of the imperialist myth of 'liberation and rehabilitation' in which violence and recovery are enunciated simultaneously.[15] The practices of transnational NGOs are also tightly interlocked with, and constituted by, this regime of power. In the actual practices of 'women's rights as human rights', human rights discourse usually functions as a normalizing technology to be distributed as a 'regime of truth'. A concept such as 'global civil society' operates as modes of normativity as well, and many NGOs come to see themselves 'as the saviors of women and as being above or beyond neocolonial differences of power.'[16] Certain kinds of NGOs and groups, under the name of global feminism, have exercised the hegemony of the first world on women's lives and women's groups worldwide.

The new mode of sexual normativity works closely with state-based global capital, too. For example, the Ford Foundation supported research, conferences and publications on Women's Rights as Human Rights in the 1970s and 1980s, especially on women in Arab culture, mainly in order to serve the US's national purposes.[17] Many NGOs based in Asia received funding from overseas, particularly in the 1990s, and although accepting grant money produced its own set of problems and debates, it was generally regarded as a necessary and proper means to further communications and forge closer connections with a global community of activists

---

[14] Judith Butler also proposes a 'vulnerable body' as a possible common ground for global coalition—more as a forum to talk about ethics towards others. However, her idea of 'body' challenges and questions the idea of body as an autonomous, individuated and self-determined entity; 'body', for her, is rather a 'sphere of a primary and unwilled physical proximity with others'. Judith Butler, *Precarious Life* (London: Verso, 2004), p. 48.

[15] Lisa Yoneyama, 'Traveling Memories, Contagious Justice: Americanization of Japanese War Crimes at the End of the Post-Cold War', *Journal of Asian American Studies* 1 (2003), pp. 57–93. here p. 59.

[16] Inderpal Grewal, *Transnational America: Feminisms, Diasporas, Neoliberalisms* (Durham, NC: Duke University Press, 2005), pp. 80–120.

[17] Grewal, *Transnational America*, pp. 144–145.

and organizations.[18] So, it might be argued that global solidarity or global community was in fact made possible by global capital. But of course, in some cases, competition between several NGO groups for funding undermines their solidarity.[19]

In other cases, NGO interventions are entirely about survival strategies, which reveals the irrelevance of the ideal 'human rights' to the helpless bodies, specimens of 'bare life' under total occupation in specific local contexts. As Aihwa Ong shows in her analysis of NGO activities in Southeast Asia, sometimes they make only 'on-the-ground decisions about who can or should survive, how this can be done, and how and when to make claims, depending on situated constellations of political and ethical forces'. Activists who have to cope with matters of survival do not care much about human rights, equal opportunity or access to citizenship. According to Ong, sometimes the most effective way is not to resort to the language of 'human rights', but to the language of ethics and conscience. In order to secure better working conditions for Southeast Asian maids, NGOs sometimes persuade the employer that it is in their own interest to keep its cheap labourers healthy and fit to work.[20]

Recently, increasing scepticism towards the unified category of 'woman' is causing many feminists to question the political validity of 'woman' and demand a thorough re-examination of feminist politics. There is nothing natural about 'woman'; it is one of many identities that we may put on and off for the time being like 'bourgeois', 'subaltern', 'Asian' or 'Harvard graduate'—sometimes alone and other times in conjunction with other identities. In some cases, 'woman' and 'subaltern' are not self-identical and such disjuncture intensifies the crisis in feminism's foundational identity politics.[21] But ironically, in other cases, the very gap between 'woman' and 'subaltern' is the factor that enables and enlivens the women's movement

[18] Elizabeth J. Friedman, 'The Effect of "Transnationalism Reversed" in Venezuela: Assessing the Impact of the UN Global Conferences on the Women's Movement', *International Feminist Journal of Politics* 3 (1999), pp. 357–381.

[19] Menon, *Sexualities*, p. 7.

[20] Ong, 'Experiments with Freedom', pp. 241–242.

[21] Menon mentions the Women's Reservation Bill in the Indian Parliament as a case clearly showing such disjuncture. The anti-reservation position opposing the Bill cannot be simply called 'anti-feminist' because the Bill was in fact an upper-caste strategy to stop the rising tide of lower-caste men in politics, and in fact the power of dominant castes had been strength-

because many professional activists belonging to the privileged elite class dedicate themselves to uniting and organizing women's movements. The relationship between the women's movement as a social protest and its identity politics utilizing totalizing categories might offer what Joan Scott has named in the title of her book—'only paradoxes'.[22]

Some feminist theorists suggest that in order to reorganize the women's movement as a social protest and a democratic project—in other words, to make it fight for the poor and the oppressed regardless of communal fidelities—feminist politics should be destabilized, and the emphasis on 'women' should be minimized.[23] If identities emerge not only through the regime of power but also through political mobilization, then the articulation of social movement needs to be reimagined so that it is NOT conceived in terms of a totalizing universal subject.

TRANSPACIFIC FEMINISM

I propose the term 'transpacific feminism' as a way to historicize the women's movement from a transnational perspective (which is different from writing a global history of women's movement or the history of global feminism). The term tries to articulate 'woman' in non-totalizing ways by problematizing the gender identity of 'woman' as well as the regional/national identity of '(Asia) Pacific'. It indicates a methodology to investigate the emergence and disappearance of diverse identities within the dynamics of power and resistance in a nexus of multiple political/economic regimes, economic/moral systems, discursive constructs, social movements and international relations. As Rey Chow says, the term 'woman' and its effects should be understood as 'a manner of articulating the historical—that is, mutating—relationships among various parts of culture as they have been socially institutionalized.'[24]

---

ened by women's reservations. *Recovering Subversion: Feminist Politics Beyond the Law* (Urbana: Illinois University Press, 2004), pp. 170–177.

[22] Joan Scott, *Only Paradoxes to Offer: French Feminists and the Rights of Man* (Cambridge, MA: Harvard University Press, 1996).

[23] Postmodernist feminists such as Denise Riley, Judith Butler, and Drucilla Cornell argue that 'women' should be de-essentialized to be politically effective. See Denise Riley, *Am I That Name?* (Minneapolis: Minnesota University Press, 1988), Judith Butler, *Undoing Gender* (London: Routledge, 2004), and Drucilla Cornell, *Beyond Accommodation: Ethical Feminism, Deconstruction and the Law* (London: Routledge, 1991).

[24] Chow, 'When Whiteness Feminizes ...', p. 142.

'Transpacific' also denotes a time-space for tracing the path of modernity and questioning its presumed linear, bilateral effects. In fact, the region which has been highlighted in the history of feminism is the Atlantic, not the Pacific. Anglo-American feminism on the North American model has emphasized individual agency, social reality and the achievement of equality with men, while continental European feminism—especially the French one—has been mainly concerned with language, text, signification and freedom on a symbolic level. There were active exchanges, debates and rivalry between these two parties across the ocean, and their transatlantic conversations, translations and negotiations have resulted in the so-called 'Western feminism.'

The Pacific, in contrast, has not attracted as much critical attention from feminist scholars and activists on the issue of 'woman' except in terms of 'rescue'. Women in this part of the world were categorized in Western theory as 'Third World women' and presented as an object of the male fantasy of rescue within the long-standing Western semiotic regime. This, of course, does not mean that women in the Asia-Pacific region were silent and passive while they were being presented as objects of oriental exoticism/eroticism. In fact, there have been active attempts to build indigenous feminisms, that is, autochthonous brands of feminism appropriate to local contexts. Even from the beginning of the twentieth century, many feminists in the Asian region searched for their own unique answers to the 'woman' question and self-consciously declared their 'difference' from the West.

However, 'difference', in the specific context of the Asia-Pacific region, was articulated mostly in terms of national/cultural identity, and quite naturally, was hierarchized in the global order. For example, in the pre-war era, Japanese transnational feminist groups actively participated in feminist networks in the United States and tried to be fairly represented as Japanese nationals in the international discourse. When the Second World War broke out, they turned their attention from the United States to Asia to serve the Japanese government's building of a 'Greater East Asia Co-Prosperity Sphere', and just as the American activist groups had 'generously' done with their Japanese peers, Japanese feminist groups developed their own ethnic hierarchy in relation to their Chinese 'sisters', implying their guidance as the 'elder' one.[25] Here, Naoki Sakai's argument about complicity

---

[25] Barbara Molony, 'Crossing boundaries: Transnational Feminisms in Twentieth-century Japan', in Mina Roces and Louise Edwards (eds), *Women's Movements in Asia: Feminisms and transnational activism* (London: Routledge, 2010), pp. 90–109.

between universalism and particularism—more specifically, nationalisms in the West and the Rest—applies to feminism as well. Sakai says that US imperial nationalism and Japanese nationalism might be understood as quite different and 'external' to each other, but in fact they maintain a 'compossible and internal' relationship. Japanese nationalism itself could accommodate US imperial nationalism, or even might be recognized as its essential 'organ',[26] thus demonstrating the intimacy between exclusionary nationalism and the universal spirit of integration, such as multicultural-ism and internationalism. What must be called into question about femi-nism in Asia (and in other non-Western regions), then, is the unreflective assumption of 'difference' between a Western (imperial) feminism and indigenous feminisms.

The question is, therefore, not about how different the women in Asia are from those in the United States, or those in the Pacific Rim from the North Atlantic and Europe; no matter how the differences are narrated and emphasized, 'difference' itself is in advance defined as lesser value or non-universal value. Women in the Asia-Pacific region may claim that their experiences are clearly different, but on a much deeper level, they are 'required' to be different, because within the global order of the nation/ culture, 'difference' is produced and managed as 'a liberal-pluralist collec-tion of anthropological specimens'.[27] The very language of difference may naturalize and justify the 'West' as an indispensable and normative point of comparison. Therefore, as Lydia Liu says, 'the tautology of difference as value within a structure of unequal exchange victimizes that difference.'[28] What has been irrevocably victimized in modern history is not the abstract category of 'woman', but the way 'difference' is produced, circulated and consumed.

What should be remembered here is that this victimization (of 'differ-ence') is a matter of history of modernity—the history of how moder-nity was constituted as a universal telos through global and transnational relations between cultures, ethnicity and class. It is a phenomenon that has happened in the long and complicated process of colonization and decolonization, and if we try to understand the meaning of this victim-

---

[26] Naoki Sakai, 'Imperial Nationalism and the Comparative Perspective', *positions: east asia cultures critique* 1 (2009), pp. 159–205.

[27] Petrius Liu, 'Why Does Queer Theory Need China?', *positions: east asia cultures and critique* 2 (2010), pp. 291–320, here p. 314.

[28] Lydia Liu, 'The Desire for the Sovereignty and the Logic of Reciprocity in the Family of Nations', *diacritics* 4 (1999), pp. 150–177, here p. 171.

ization on a global scale, our attention should be turned to the historical dynamics within which international relations were conceived as sexual identity and vice versa, rendering each other both unequal and universal.

The Pacific is an exemplary site to explore the interlocking relations between geopolitics and the biopolitics of sexuality because it is a problematic space conceptually and politically in the history of modernity. It shows most clearly the appropriations and re-appropriations of gender identity through unequal exchanges, unilateral coercion and the rhetoric of universal justice. At the same time, it also reveals that there have been much more complicated relationships than coercion/resistance between Asia and North America.

The Asia-Pacific, in the process of colonization and decolonization until the twentieth century, was consistently feminized by a European male sexual fantasy presenting it as an erotic paradise full of sexual pleasure.[29] Even today, the image associated with the Asia-Pacific region is dominantly feminine. The region is frequently defined as a place to go for sex tourism, to find housemaids, to buy brides and the cheap labour of female workers. The effect of such feminization is, apparently, to establish a clear demarcation between East and West, inscribing gender roles and hierarchy on international relations. According to this reading, the East is docile, submissive and in charge of the domestic/private/emotional realms, while the West makes decisions, moves around the world and governs in the public domain. The identity of each region is predetermined without any ambiguity, according to its 'biological' difference. Geopolitics and biopolitics are intertwined from the very beginning as a pre-given fact.

Arif Dirlik is a pioneering critic among many who have challenged such a reified arrangement of regions. He argues that the Pacific is 'a Euro-American invention'. According to him and several other critics,

<hr />

[29] Vilsoni Hereniko, 'Representations of Cultural Identities', in Vilsoni Hereniko and Rob Wilson (eds), *Inside Out: Literature, Cultural Politics, and Identity in the New Pacific* (New York: Rowman & Littlefield, 1994), pp. 137–166; Margaret Jolly, 'From Point Venus to Bali Ha'I : Eroticism and Exoticism in Representations of the Pacific', in Lenore Manderson and Margaretta Jolly (eds), *Sites of Desire, Economies of Pleasure: Sexualities in Asia and the Pacific* (Chicago: University of Chicago Press, 1997), pp. 99–122; Bernard Smith, *European Vision and the South Pacific, 1768–1850: A Study in the History of Art and Ideas* (Melbourne: Oxford University Press Australia, 1989); Patricia Grimshaw and Helen Morton, 'Paradoxes of the Colonial Male Gaze: European Men and Maori Women', in Emma Greenwood, Klaus Neumann and Andrew Sartori (eds) *Work in Flux* (Parkville: University of Melbourne, History Dept., 1995), pp. 144–158.

what we today regard as the Pacific region is not a geographical 'fact', but a conceptual construct formed by forces that originated outside of the region. So the relationships comprising the Pacific Rim cannot be 'understood without reference to global forces that transcend the Pacific'.[30] He also points out that there are fundamental contradictions in the Pacific because the regional formation imagined under the logic of capitalism, politics, myths, fantasies and visions—mostly of Europe—does not fit the real lives of the people who actually inhabit it.

Dirlik's purpose in this influential critique is to challenge the tendencies to fix Asia as a settled identity—as a geographical, a cultural, a gendered, or an economic entity—and to highlight its own uncontainable dynamics, fractures and contradictions. In fact, the term Asia-Pacific signifies numerous things at the same time: it could be a mode of consciousness, a sense of belonging, an institution of citizenship, a cultural identity, a territory, an ethnic group, a minority discourse or a political movement that has both capitalist and anti-capitalist implications.[31] Denying strictly territorial or nation-specific approaches to the region inevitably shifts attention to movements and interconnections, away from area studies distinctions: seas and oceans take on an active character, bringing migrations, cross-cultural contacts, shifting social organizations and ethnic diasporas into focus.[32] Such a critical shift in the Pacific studies certainly had an effect of unsettling the sexual identity of the region. Conversely, the various discursive experiments challenging the typical sexual representations of the region

[30] John Eperjesi argues that the American Pacific, as a metaphorical term, names the practices of regional articulation through which a heterogeneous or dispersed area is discursively transformed into an abstract unity. 'The American Asiatic Association and the Imperialist Imaginary of the American Pacific', *boundary 2* 1 (2001), pp. 195–219. Donald Nonini views the terms such as Asia Pacific, Pacific Rim as 'the trope for a set of economic, political, and cultural processes creating relationship within a supraregion of Asia and the United States that have been under way since approximately the mid-1970'. 'Ethnographic Grounding of the "Asia-Pacific" Imaginary', in Arif Dirlik (ed.), *What is in a Rim: Critical Perspectives on the Pacific Region Idea* (Lanham, MD: Rowman & Littlefield, 1998), p. 163.

[31] While Eperjesi and Rachel Lee see the Pacific as a subset of global capitalism, critics like Alexander Woodside and Aihwa Ong regard the idea more as a signal indicating that capitalism has been de-Westernized and the ascendancy of the East is being promoted. Rachel Lee, 'Asian American Cultural Production in Asian-Pacific Perspective', *boundary 2* 2 (1999), pp. 231–254; Alexander Woodside, 'The Asia Pacific Idea as Mobilization Myth', in Dirlik, *What is in a Rim*, pp. 37–52; Aihwa Ong, *Flexible Citizenship* (Durham, NC: Duke University Press, 1999).

[32] Matt K. Matsuda, 'The Pacific', *The American Historical Review* 3 (2006), pp. 758–780.

on the narrative level have enabled us to understand the place anew in a completely different configuration.[33] In both cases, the self-evident notion of this region as an always-present geographical/sexual unit manifesting an uncontested ahistorical given-ness is ruptured, making both regional identity and sexual identity fluid, unstable and uncertain.

Despite the achievement of these critical and artistic interventions, however, the formation of the region and the sexual politics behind it should not be romanticized as a thing to be easily overcome. The regime of the nation-state in the Asia-Pacific does not just evaporate; instead, it transforms itself into a larger formation—greater regionalism in a loose web of political, economic and cultural connections,[34] and sexualization continues to occur in parallel with this expansion in ever more complicated ways. In more advanced parts of the region, the transnational elite class, or groups of people who believe they are articulating 'alternative modernity' with moral and political superiority to the West,[35] are presented with a newly invested male power, while the less developed parts of the region, lower classes and castes, and the oppressed ethnic communities are hopelessly feminine. It is this nexus of the complicated process of geopolitics and biopolitics of sexualization that transpacific feminism has to explore to narrate the history of women's movements and the multiplicity of modernities on a transnational scale.

The political mobilization around the issue of 'comfort women' is one possible example of transpacific feminism; it shows how 'woman' have been politicized within the dynamics of the complex entanglements between national identity and sexual identity in the Asia-Pacific region. During the Pacific War from 1932 to 1945, the Japanese military comfort women system was implemented for the Japanese male soldiers through the enslavement of women from Korea, China, Japan, Taiwan, Indonesia, the Philippines and beyond. Enslaved 'comfort women' were brought to 'comfort stations' throughout the vast region which spanned East and South Asia as well as the South Pacific islands. The total number of

---

[33] Among several examples, Chen Ruoxi's novel *Paper Marriage* (1986) describes China as implicated in 'queer' desire in its relationship with the United States and it makes some significant changes on the conceptual and political borders of China by interrupting assumptions about what is Chinese and what is not. For the relevant analysis of the novel, see Petrius Liu, 'Why Does Queer Theory Need China?'

[34] Aihwa Ong views the Asia Pacific zone as a national mechanism which makes more flexible and variegated degrees of citizenship. See Ong, *Flexible Citizenship*.

[35] Ong, *Flexible Citizenship*, p. 24.

enslaved women is estimated to have been between 100,000 and 200,000, among which Koreans were the most numerous victims. The existence of the comfort women was common knowledge in Korea, but until the 1980s, no one, not even the participants themselves, publicly acknowledged what had happened because the patriarchal society of Korea has considered it a shameful part of its history which should be silenced and forgotten. The democratization movement and women's movement in Korea during the 1980s helped bring about a shift, and one of the surviving comfort women, Kim Hak-sun first testified in 1991. Since then, numerous former comfort women testified as victims, and a forgotten past was recovered for the first time as a distinct reality.

'Comfort women' has been a contested field where the signifier of 'woman' proceeds from the national terrain to the international one through various forms of translation and mediation. It is ceaselessly being appropriated and re-appropriated by several different institutions including the state, NGOs and universities in their attempts to define 'woman', 'Asia' and their relations to 'man' and 'the United States'. As a national signifier, 'woman' in 'comfort women' has been strongly identified with the collective experience of colonized Korea through the abject figure of the suffering female. Naturally, support groups in Korea have responded furiously to arguments equating the comfort women with public prostitutes. As Ueno Chizuko says, such an adamant refusal to see them as public prostitutes is due to the fact that 'comfort women' has been constructed as the national image of a 'model victim'—the 'Korean woman whose purity was violated in a forced abduction.'[36] 'Comfort women' has also become a powerful site for articulating and practising global feminism. In December 2000, the Women's International War Crimes Tribunal for the Trial of Japan's Military Sexual Slavery was held in Tokyo in order to pass judgment on the government and military of wartime Japan, which had subjected thousands of women to exploitation in the state-directed military prostitution system in the 1930s and 1940s. This event attracted over 5,000 participants, including lawyers, scholars and spectators from over 30 countries to hear the testimony of 60 survivors of the war from North and South Korea, China, Taiwan, the Philippines, the Netherlands, Indonesia, East Timor and Japan. In many ways this is indeed 'an example

---

[36] Ueno Chizuko, 'The Politics of Memory: Nation, Individual and Self', *History & Memory* 2 (1999), pp. 129–152.

of feminist advocacy on a transnational scale'.[37] The collaborative attempts to think about the issue in an international context certainly redefined the rape of the military comfort women, de-emphasizing its symbolic role as the emblem of the national shame of the 'raped nation', and highlighting the violation of fundamental human rights which should be judged 'by a single global standard'.[38]

However, the international attention to the issue and the political mobilization around it all over the world, ironically, also reinforced the image of the 'comfort women' as a national signifier reflecting the complicated and unequal power dynamics in the Asia-Pacific. Because 'comfort women' is a very convenient term to assign sexual identity to the region and to stabilize political hierarchy in the international relationship, the term has been appropriated over and over again by different political agents across the ocean for different political mappings.

Although the issue is never only about 'women' but involves several different issues such as class, ethnicity, moral/ethical economy, diaspora in the region, and the whole narrative structure interwoven by all of these elements, many accounts of the 'comfort women' focus on those elements of the women's stories that mirror pornographic themes in which female social degradation and pain is eroticized.[39] Such overly feminized narratives of their experience define Korea, Japan, the United States and other parts of the world as 'feminine' depending upon what political context is invoked. For example, the recent fascination of the academy and feminist activism in the United States with 'comfort women' shows the way the geopolitics of a United States waging war in Iraq utilizes the sexual politics of the phenomenon. 'Comfort women' can be presented to serve US nationalist ends by effectively masking US imperialism because the image of helpless Asian women subjugated to the tyrannical military power of Japan resonates with the images of crouching Afghani women wearing burqa as victims, and thus argues for US intervention.[40] This fascination can be relocated in a different context and a reversed gender representa-

---

[37] Vera Mackie, 'Shifting the Axis: Feminism and the Transnational Imaginary', in Katie Willis and Brenda S. A. Yeoh (eds), *State/Nation/Transnation: Perspectives on Transnationalism in the Asia Pacific* (London: Routledge, 2004), pp. 238–256, here p. 238.

[38] Laura Hein, 'Savage Irony: The Imaginative Power of the "Military Comfort Women" in the 1990s', *Gender & History* 2 (1999), pp. 336–372, here p. 347.

[39] Hein, 'Savage Irony', p. 343.

[40] Kandice Chuh, 'Discomforting Knowledge: Or, Korean "Comfort Women" and Asian Americanist Critical Practice', *Journal of Asian American Studies* 1 (2003), pp. 5–23, here p. 8.

tion as well: the sympathy for and identification with the comfort women (mostly by Asian American women) is supported and even promoted in the United States might be related to the country's self-fashioning as violated and violable female victim after 9/11. That is, the way the 'comfort women' are remembered and politicized as a social movement as a national as well as a global issue has been tightly interlocked with the sexualization of the national/regional identity within the power dynamics of Asia-Pacific nationalism. To understand the transnational significance of 'woman' in the 'comfort women' requires a long and multi-valent historical perspective. For it is a disarticulated experience of social disempowerment with no recourse to a single national(-ist) language or a single global standard.

CONCLUSION

We must think of more radical alternatives than simply dividing the forms of women's movement between 'national' and 'global' settings, because the actual terrain in which the politics is formed and practised needs a much more complicated analysis. The recognition of the multiple and shifting ways that identity is made and unmade with and/or against ideological power within international dynamics may help us to formulate feminist politics in a non-totalizing manner. Feminism as a social movement simultaneously should deconstruct the nationalist resistance to globalization as well as the global formulation of 'human' as the autonomous, self-enterprising and freely-choosing individual (and 'woman' as a vulnerable body which ultimately should reach that status) promoted by Human Rights discourse, global capital and neoliberal ethics. It should try to trace the different ways and processes by which 'woman' is mobilized, politicized and radicalized, and find contingent and tentative solutions to the problems of contemporary living. It also should examine the ensembles of heterogeneous elements through which the significance of 'woman' is articulated. Finally, it should disturb all-encompassing monologism of the Western epistemology of modernity. That way, 'woman' will not be entrapped within a deadlock, but new identities and new alignments will emerge around it, and the history of women's movement will be enriched—in space/time trajectories that do not mindlessly follow the dominant narrative of the nation-state.

FURTHER READINGS

Many critics have pointed out the constitutive role of the modern nation-state in the making of sexual identity and feminism. Among the most representative arguments are Ann Laura Stoler, *Carnal Knowledge and Imperial Power, Race and Intimacy in Colonial Rule* (Berkeley: University of California Press, 2002); Nivedita Menon (ed.), *Sexualities* (London: Zed Books, 2008); M.J. Alexander and C.T. Mohanty, *Feminist Genealogies, Colonial Legacies, Democratic Futures* (London: Routledge, 1997); Inderpal Grewal and Caren Kaplan, 'Global Identities: Theorizing Transnational Studies of Sexuality', *GOQ: A Journal of Lesbian and Gay Studies* 4 (2001), pp. 663–679. Inderpal Grewal and Caren Kaplan are especially important because they promoted the term 'transnational feminism' successfully in their co-authored work, *Scattered Hegemonies: Postmodernity and Transnational Feminist Practices* (Minneapolis: Minnesota University Press, 1994) and thus contributed to situating 'women' in a global context. For the feminist social critique heavily influenced by a global and post-colonial perspective, see Avtar Brah, 'Global Mobilities, Local Predicaments: Globalization and the Critical Imagination', *Feminist Review* 70 (2002), pp. 30–45; Tani Barlow, *The Question of Women in Chinese Feminism* (Durham, NC: Duke University Press, 2004); Afsaneh Najmabadi, *Women with Moustaches and Men without Beards: Gender and Sexual Anxieties of Iranian Modernity* (Berkeley: University of California Press, 2005), among many. For the remarkable survey and critique on the global feminist activism and NGO (and on its neoliberal ethics), note Aihwa Ong, 'Experiments with Freedom: Milieus of the Human', *American Literary History* 2 (2006), pp. 229–244; Inderpal Grewal, *Transnational America: Feminisms, Diasporas, Neoliberalisms* (Durham, NC: Duke University Press, 2005).

Aihwa Ong also provides valid views on the Asia Pacific zone as a national mechanism which makes more flexible and variegated degrees of citizenship. See Ong, *Flexible Citizenship* (Durham, NC: Duke University Press, 1999). For studies on the global dynamics of discursive and identitarian regimes from the location of the Asia-Pacific zone, see Arif Dirlik, *What Is in a Rim?* (Lanham, MD: Rowman & Littlefield, 1998); Naoki Sakai, 'Imperial Nationalism and the Comparative Perspective', *Positions: East Asia Cultures Critique* 1 (2009), pp. 159–205; Naoki Sakai, *Translation and Subjectivity* (Minnesota University Press, 2008); Lydia Liu, *The Clash of Empires: The Invention of China in Modern World Making* (Cambridge, MA: Harvard University Press, 2006).

For the historical interactions and transformations of 'women' in terms of geopolitics and biopolitics, postmodern feminists' insights are valuable. See Denise Riley, *Am I that Name? Feminism and the Category of Women in History* (Minneapolis: Minnesota University Press, 2003); Judith Butler, *Undoing Gender* (London: Routledge, 2004); Drucilla Cornell, *Beyond Accommodation: Ethical Feminism, Deconstruction and the Law* (London: Routledge, 1991); Wendy Brown, *Politics Out of History* (Princeton, NJ: Princeton University Press, 2001). In this regard, Giorgio Agamben is also relevant even if his argument is not exactly about women or feminism. See *Homo sacer: Sovereign Power and Bare Life* (Palo Alto, CA: Stanford University Press, 1998).

The studies on 'comfort women' from a transnational perspective are scarce; still, a lot of attempts have been done to push this issue beyond the limit of the nation-state. Ueno Chizuko and Hyunah Yang try to emancipate the (hi)story of comfort women from the official (male) narrative of national historiography. See Ueno Chizuko, 'The Politics of Memory: Nation, Individual and Self', *History & Memory* 2 (1999), pp. 129–152; Hyunah Yang, 'Revisiting the Issue of the Korean "Military Comfort Women": The Question of Truth and Positionality', *Positions: East Asia Cultures Critique*, 1 (1996), pp. 51–71. For the similar efforts to situate 'Comfort Women' in the terrain of global geopolitics, see Laura Hein, 'Savage Irony: The Imaginative Power of the "Military Comfort Women" in the 1990s', *Gender & History* 2 (1999), pp. 336–372; Kandice Chuh, 'Discomforting Knowledge: Or, Korean "Comfort Women" and Asian Americanist Critical Practice', *Journal of Asian American Studies* 1 (2003), pp. 5–23; Lisa Yonehama, 'Traveling Memories, Contagious Justice: Americanization of Japanese War Crime at the End of the Post-Cold War', *Journal of Asian American Studies* 1 (2003), pp. 57–93; Laura Hyun Yi Kang, 'Conjuring "Comfort Women": Mediated Affiliations and Disciplined Subject in Korean/American Transnationality', *Journal of Asian American Studies* 1 (2003), pp. 25–55.

PART II

Continental Perspectives on the History of Social Movements

Social Movements in Latin America: From the Nineteenth to the Twenty-First Century

Claudia Wasserman

INTRODUCTION

The multiplicity of social movements in contemporary Latin America highlights the importance of making historical and social scientific knowledge available so that we can see the genealogies of current historical developments. Activities organized by social actors—neighbourhood associations, clubs, student groups, unions, interest groups, peasants, indigenous communities or political groups—designed to produce changes in social, political, economic and intellectual structures, or aiming to prevent transformation of those threatened structures proliferate; social movements are not new in Latin American history. The analysis of social movements in Latin America between the nineteenth and the twenty-first centuries can illuminate the reasons for the propagation of the events. The difficulty in formulating theories and concepts to explain social movements is, however, proportional to the political importance of these processes in Latin American societies.

C. Wasserman (✉)
Department of History, Universidade Federal do Rio Grande do Sul,
Rio Grande do Sul, Brazil

© The Author(s) 2017
S. Berger, H. Nehring (eds.), *The History of Social Movements in Global Perspective*, DOI 10.1057/978-1-137-30427-8_5

115

Early studies of Latin American social movements appeared in the political and intellectual context marked by authoritarianism in the 1970s. These studies were substitutes for interpretations of structural dependence, which resulted in a distinctive theoretical approach to the analysis of Latin American reality that exposed the conditions of import substitution industrialization (ISI) and uncontrolled growth of the urban proletariat. The emergence of urban movements responding to economic transformations sparked the curiosity of Latin American scholars regarding protests, explosions and movements. The main studies were of an empirical–descriptive nature and were developed in universities, research centres, and postgraduate courses focussed on field research in the social sciences and humanities. In the 1970s an intense debate about class and social movements was held in Latin American academic environments. The books edited by Raul Benitez Zenteno (1977) and Bernardo Sorj (2008) are examples.[1]

In the 1980s, in a context of intensification of social movements, intellectuals saw them as strategic elements in re-democratization. Movements such as the Association of the Mothers of Plaza de Mayo in Argentina, the Landless Movement in Brazil (MST) and the Broad Front (*Frente Amplio*) in Uruguay, to name but three, though very different in membership, structure, organization and appeal, shared the same claim of working towards fuller democratic participation. The diversity and importance of these political movements challenged Latin American scholars to discuss the phenomenon theoretically.

Theoretical discussions were concerned with marking the difference from past events. Using the title 'New Social Movements'(NSM), sociologists, anthropologists and historians enumerated characteristics that differentiated the social movements of the 1980s from those in the past. Authors such as Ernesto Laclau, Maria da Gloria Gohn, Fernando Calderon and Elizabeth Jelin, Tilman Evers, Eunice Ribeiro Durham, Ruth Cardoso and others[2] engaged in a fierce debate about the nature of these NSMs. At that

---

[1] Raúl B. Zenteno (ed.), *As classes sociais na América Latina* (Rio de Janeiro: Paz e Terra, 1977); Bernardo Sorj, Fernando H. Cardoso and Maurício Font. (eds), *Economia e Movimentos Sociais na América Latina* (Rio de Janeiro: Centro Edelstein de Pesquisas Sociais, 2008); Cf. Maria da Glória Gohn, *Teoria dos movimentos sociais* (São Paulo: Edições Loyola, 1997).

[2] Cf. Ernesto Laclau, 'Os novos movimentos sociais e a pluralidade do social', *Revista Brasileira de Ciências Sociais* 1 (1986); Gohn, *Teoria*; Fernando Calderón and Elizabeth Jelin, 'Classes sociais e movimentos sociais na América Latina: Perspectivas e realidades',

time, theoretical debate prevailed in relation to empirical studies, and the studies were more frequently about urban movements, especially youth, feminist, and ecological movements. Among the NSM innovations mentioned by these scholars were a detachment from structures of domination, a fragmentation of demands, a mismatch between social sectors identified in the productive structure and the movement agents, heterogeneity of social actors within the same movement, a lack of interest regarding hierarchy and leadership, with consequent horizontal power relationships between members of the movement and, finally, a refusal to organize or align with of political parties and trade unions, and NSM multiplication outside these traditional institutions.

For Latin American scholars, the intellectual dispute surrounding the characterization of social activism in the 1980s under the NSM rubric, opposed to 'traditional' or 'classic' social movements, also referred to a certain disdain for Marxism among some of the NSM scholars; theoretical approaches inspired by Marxism emphasized the importance of structure and class action. The NSM paradigm was crucial in bringing up issues that had, until then, been forgotten in social movement studies, such as attention to the discourse of agents, formation of new social identities and a shift of the interpretational axis from economic to cultural aspects. On the other hand, the debate about the NSM paradigm encouraged the proponents of a historical–structural approach to renew their conviction through further research on the relationship between the reality of Latin American societies and the social movements spreading and presenting challenges to established interpretations.

The attribute 'new' for the social activism in Latin America during the 1970s and 1980s is, in this sense, best suited to the interpretative paradigm rather than to the nature of the movements themselves. The history of social movements in Latin America, even before the arrival of parties and trade unions on the scene, has displayed an extraordinary variety in the social composition of actors, in internal power relations, in leadership types, in the existence of central demands—whether intended to promote

Revista Brasileira de Ciências Sociais 2 (1987); Tilman Evers, 'Identidade, a face oculta dos novos movimentos sociais', *Revista Novos Estudos CEBRAP* 2 (1984); E. Durham, 'Movimentos sociais a construção da cidadania', *Revista Novos Estudos CEBRAP* 10 (1984); Ruth C. L. Cardoso, 'Movimentos sociais na América Latina', http://www.anpocs.org.br/portal/publicacoes/rbcs_00_03/rbcs03_02.htm (accessed 13 February 2012).

substantial changes or fragmented and specific demands—and in the creation of new social identities arising from participation in movements.

In this regard, this chapter aims to analyse social movements in Latin America as complex historical phenomena arising from social struggles, whose conditions of emergence are given by concrete historical, social and cultural contexts, without necessarily having a hierarchy among these aspects. It is postulated that the formation of the movements—the individuals who act in them—depends on specific needs of diverse groups whose members develop forms of struggle and strategies according to their needs and their concrete material conditions. The meaning and significance of the movements depend on the effects produced in a society's structure and in the constitution of the social identity of the subjects. We also intend to distinguish spontaneous collective behaviour—protests, confrontation, occasional uprisings and disorders—from social movements organized by a core group that provides direction and meaning to the demands in society.

Social movements have existed in Latin America since before the nineteenth century and, until their exponential multiplication in the first decade of the twenty-first century, it could have been said that they tended, over time, to establish relationships with parties, unions, Church, the state, universities or communities with varying degrees of connection. Moreover, they have had varying degrees of autonomy and social homogeneity; their demands have been connected to economic, political or cultural matters; they have questioned directly the centre of power, or they have had more specific local demands; the links with other movements have sometimes been global, sometimes transnational, often neither; and the effects on social structure and in the creation of identities have been different over time, and different for each movement.

This variety of situations does not allow us to classify social movements as new, classical, traditional, old or innovative. Instead it encourages us to analyse the meaning of each movement (or of a movement network, or of the group of autonomous movements for political struggle), the effects on participatory processes, democratization of public spaces and creation of active and conscious citizenship. Social movements—specific forms of popular mobilization, different of parties, unions or uprising and disorders—are the result of a formation of a critical view, of a negative assessment of the role of the state in relation to collective interests/demands, determined by a deficiency, material or moral.

In Latin America, these deficiencies were measured by the dimensions of the most visible and permanent reality: 'backwardness', inequality, despotism and dependence. Although there is a wide variety of economic, political, cultural and population situations, the possibility of understanding social movements in Latin America is articulated through a history common to all countries in the region. This means that it is necessary to find a balance between local specificity and the existence of broader ties that minimize diversity and allow the identification of keys that explain social movements that took place almost simultaneously in several countries.

Latin American countries have been marked by similar historical and social processes. Before the arrival of Europeans, the subcontinent was inhabited by native peoples with uneven development stages. Europeans settled in the area—particularly from the countries of the Iberian Peninsula—and subjected it to commercial monopoly. Native peoples were slaughtered or enslaved and the region became a set of large areas of monoculture, where the plantation was predominant, cultivated by slave, indigenous or African labour. The economy was directed at supplying the demands of the international market.

The achievement of independence of these countries, mostly between 1810 and 1825, was not followed by significant changes in their economic or social structures, and the new nation-states were ruled by oligarchies whose members derived their power from access to raw materials that could be exported; they despised political participation by the more general population. The economy continued to be dependent on central countries, meaning the economic demands of a metropolis determining the production of Latin American countries, and there was a delay in the development of productive forces, even in industrialized countries. The crisis of oligarchic and authoritarian governments was relatively peaceful in the southern countries—Chile, Argentina, Brazil, and Uruguay—and revolutionary in other regions. The result was a consolidation of populist governments, mostly between 1940 and 1960, or an oscillation between coups, revolutions and despotism.

Democratic rule was infrequent and inconstant across the continent. In the 1970s, South America was swept by military dictatorships of National Security Doctrine while Central America, the Caribbean and the Andean region continued to be ruled by oligarchic–authoritarian dynasties or was devastated by civil wars. In the 1980s, in the context of democratic transition, Latin America experienced a foreign debt crisis that suffocated development projects. The solution to the crisis was to accept the prescriptions of the International Monetary Fund (IMF) and the World Bank to adopt neoliberal austerity measures. Unemployment, privatization of public companies, the ostensible incoming of international capital in the productive sector and de-industrialization were the most visible results of the adoption of those measures, which accentuated economic backwardness, social inequality and dependence on hegemonic centres of capitalism in most countries in the region, and did not favour the expansion of democratic political participation.

The historical processes mentioned above resulted in the four characteristics that constitute the key to explaining social movement activism in Latin America. The periodization that structures the chapter is a response to historical analogies of Latin American countries and to the shortages triggered by similar backwardness, dependency, inequality and despotism, or to specific problems to each region of Latin America.

POST-INDEPENDENCE MOVEMENTS

The first phase of the history of Latin American social movements is the period during and immediately after liberation from metropolitan rule. It followed, by and large, similar patterns in different locations. Independence, occurring predominantly around 1810–1825, brought difficulties such as: the consolidation of the process under the eyes of the metropolis and other European countries; border disputes; economic crises as a result of wars and temporary interruption of trade ties; power disputes around the new countries; and uncertainty about the popular groups that participated in the struggle for independence.

The period from 1810 to 1870 was characterized by instability in almost every part of Latin America. The social movements of this period were, in general, movements of indigenous peasants, led by military combatants in the processes of independence.

At the time of independence nearly all rural workers (located in areas of foreign agricultural enclaves) and peasants (located in most traditional areas) were descendants of native peoples who inhabited the continent before the arrival of Europeans. In this sense, the indigenous struggle is intertwined with farmers' struggles in more traditional regions where the *haciendas* and the indigenous communities had reached a certain stability after the first century or so of colonization.[3]

---

[3] Charles Gibson, 'As Sociedades Indígenas Sob Domínio Espanhol', in Leslie Bethell (ed.), *História da América Latina. II: América Latina Colonial* (São Paulo: EDUSP; Brasília, DF: FUNAG, 1999) pp. 267–308.

Such social movements worked to oppose expansion of *haciendas* (large landed estates) on indigenous lands (deriving from the promulgation of liberal laws that abolished collective ownership of land and resulted in privatization), against the validity of the compulsory labour of indigenous peoples in the *haciendas*, and against the abandonment of traditions, languages and culture of a community as part of the drive to promote the vaunted 'national integration'. The indigenous cause was manifestly the driver for a significant number of rebellions, insurrections and revolts carried out by indigenous people from the southernmost tip of South America to Mexico, but such rebellions are not classified as social movements. To mention an example, in the Vale del Mezquital, central Mexico, in the present-day state of Hidalgo, the Nahua and Otomies Indians staged rebellions in 1850, 1854 and between 1858 and 1861. Social movements of the period had more prolonged effects, among which stands out José Artigas's in Uruguay, Hidalgo's and Morelos's in Mexico, among others. In 1810, in Mexico, a movement led by the *criollo* Miguel Hidalgo, followed by the *mulatto* José María Morelos stood out. They organized peasants' claims, followed by a mass of indigenous people. They proposed delivery of land to mulattoes to establish small properties, the maintenance of indigenous communal property and the abolition of taxes, which was done in November 1810. Both men were eventually defeated and killed.

In the Viceroyalty of Rio de la Plata, the movement led by José Artigas had an army of Guarani Indian tribe as followers and the support of the warlike Charrua tribe. Artigas promulgated a Regulation of Land in 1815, which established the division of property of the royalists among free blacks, Indians and poor whites. As in Mexico, José Artigas's movement sought to associate political independence with proposed land distribution among the poor. The project flared up across the region and attracted people in search of land and freedom from neighbouring territories of the Portuguese colonies. The agrarian movement led by Artigas was defeated in 1820 after the Portuguese–Brazilian invasion of the Oriental lands, as Uruguay's region was called. However, the democratic and distributive ideal of the movement had lasting effects on contemporary social struggles of Uruguay.

In the Altiplano (Andean plateau) of Bolivia, a movement led by the military Indian Pablo Zárate, known as 'the fearsome Willka' had a similar outcome to the movements led by Hidalgo, Morelos and Artigas. In 1899, Willka, followed by thousands of Aymara Indians, led a federal war against the southern oligarchy. He demanded the restitution of lands to its original owners and the establishment of a native government. Accused of preventing national integration, Willka was arrested and executed in 1905.

In Brazil, where the indigenous population did not survive colonization as in other countries of Latin America, an extraordinary social movement flourished between 1893 and 1897. In the hinterland of Bahia, a region dominated by unproductive landowners, whose rural population suffered from famine, drought, poverty, political violence and abandonment, emerged a popular movement of a messianic character. Its leader, Antônio Conselheiro, preached that the end of the world was near because of changes that were occurring (he was referring to civil marriage, separation of church and state, and the Republic). He advocated a primitive Christianity and believed he had been sent by God to wipe out social differences and Republican sins. With this message, he attracted *sertanejos*, the inlanders, who longed to overcome extreme poverty. In 1893, he founded a community called Belo Monte, which the elites and the state power called Canudos. Army forces destroyed the community after four assaults, but the movement represented the struggle for liberation of the poor in rural areas as well as the potential of the *sertanejo*, the folk type in the interior of north-eastern Brazil.

During the post-independence period, instability and disorganization of political structures in Latin America contrasted with the engagement of liberal elites in the constitution of the nation-states. The social movements mentioned were considered obstacles to national integration. A result of conflicts between pre-Hispanic villages and *haciendas*, the social movements of this first phase then appeared as 'archaic social movements' composed of 'pre-political people ... who followed without understanding anything and were victims of modernization'.[4] The aims of these movements were interpreted as a return to the past, the restoration of conditions before the settlement, followed by bolder proposals, such as the distribution of land to mulattoes. But in general, these social movements represented what the Argentine Domingo Faustino Sarmiento[5] called 'barbarism against civilization', to illustrate the backwardness of Latin American social formations in relation to European centres and the United States.

---

[4] Arnold Bauer, 'La Hispanoamérica rural, 1870–1930', in Leslie Bethell (ed.), *História de América Latina. América Latina: economia y sociedade, VII c. 1870–1930* (Barcelona: Crítica, 1991), pp. 133–161, p. 151.

[5] Domingo F. Sarmiento, *Facundo* (Porto Alegre: EDUFRGS, 1996).

ANTI-OLIGARCHIC SOCIAL MOVEMENTS

The second phase of social movement activism in Latin America occurred during the late nineteenth century and the first three decades of the twentieth. This was a time when anti-oligarchic movements were especially prominent. The instability of the post-independence period was followed by the consolidation of a fraction of rural elites in each region through the constitution of strongly centralized, politically exclusive states, each with an economy oriented towards export of raw materials. Economic dependence became more pronounced, while political disenfranchisement prevailed and the exploitation of workers was increased to comply with international demand. The need to enlarge productive area to meet demand for agricultural products and raw materials motivated the elites to occupy more land and resulted in large, violent expropriation processes. On the other hand, the development of the primary export sector also helped to capitalize urban-industrial development, especially in countries with wealthier primary export elites, notably Chile, Brazil, Argentina, Uruguay and Mexico. In the first decades of the twentieth century, then, social movements responded to the following context: an increase in land expropriation accompanied by uncontrolled growth of cities and incipient industries, in countries dominated by authoritarian and dependent rural oligarchies. A systematic effort would classify the social movements of this phase as labour movements, farmer movements and urban middle sector movements.

The Latin American labour movement emerged in the late nineteenth century in early-industrializing countries such as Brazil, Argentina, Mexico and, to a lesser extent, Chile and Uruguay.[6] With regard to mining, we might also include labour movements arising in countries such as Peru and Bolivia. External influences were evident in the first manifestations and organizations of workers. Spanish and Italian immigration was a determining factor for anarchist or anarcho-syndicalism inspiration. Strikes, boycotts and sabotage—instruments of direct action—became common to the workers of the slightly industrialized countries of the subcontinent. Anarcho-syndicalism was prevalent in Latin America and contributed significantly to the destabilization of oligarchic governments. In Mexico, there were 250 strikes against the Díaz government between 1876 and

---

[6]Cf. Pablo G. Casanova (ed.), *História del movimiento obrero en América Latina*, 4 volumes (México City: Siglo XXI, 1984).

1910, a general strike in Rio de Janeiro involved more than 40,000 workers in 1903, in Santiago and Valparaiso there were 65 strikes between 1905 and 1907, 231 strikes in the city of Buenos Aires in a single year, 1907, with the participation of 75,000 strikers.[7] The main claims referred to working hours, salaries and improving living conditions. The repression of strikes and uprisings was violent and the governments of Argentina, Brazil, Chile and Mexico enacted laws concerning immigrant restriction and containment of social disorder. They also widely used the expedient of the state of siege to contain protesters.

The farmer movement grew significantly in the early twentieth century. This happened in response to the forced expansion of the agricultural frontier in response to the increase in international demand for commodities and raw materials. The processes of mercantilization of property and dispossession of peasants were crucial in changing the characteristics of social movements in the countryside. Mobilizations seeking to resist the introduction of capitalism and wishing to restore the previous situation persisted. However, rural movements tied to other segments of society with the aim of social transformation became bigger and bigger.

Typical of this development is the movement led by Emiliano Zapata which emerged in the Mexican state of Morelos in 1909, a year before the beginning of the Mexican Revolution. Zapata was the leader of the village of Anenecuilco. He played a part in the defence of indigenous rights in the region and served as leader for the claims of peasants from the south of the country. He joined Francisco Madero's struggle against the dictatorship of Porfirio Díaz in March 1911, but he demanded an immediate solution for the natives' problems whose watchwords were '*Tierra y Libertad*' ('Land and Liberty'). The *Zapatistas* used guerrilla tactics, relied on 20,000 effective soldiers and managed to control several cities in the states of Morelos, Puebla, Guerrero and Oaxaca. The movement also gave rise to a parallel government, with laws and hierarchy, electing agrarian authority in each village, in order to 'representar y defender los pueblos en asuntos de tierras, montes y aguas' ('represent and defend the peoples regarding land, mountains and water'). Emiliano Zapata was assassinated in April 1919, but the survival of the political myth among the peasants of Mexico trans-

---

[7] Michael M. Hall and Hobart A. Spalding Jr., 'La clase trabajadora urbana y los primeros movimientos obreros de América Latina, 1880–1930', in Leslie Bethell (ed.), *História de América Latina. VII América Latina: economia y sociedade, c. 1870–1930* (Barcelona: Crítica, 1991), pp. 281–315.

formed the words of Porfirio Díaz about it into a contemporary prophecy: 'Madero soltou um tigre, vejamos se consegue controlá-lo' ('Madero released a tiger, let's see if he can control it').[8]

In El Salvador, Agustín Farabundo Martí led a popular movement convened by the Salvadoran Communist Party in January 1932. The masses reacted positively to the Communist Party call due to the miserable economic situation and against despotism—General Hernandez Martinez, besides perpetrating a coup d'état against the newly elected president Arturo Araújo, of the Labour Party, had cancelled legislative elections in which the Salvadoran Communist Party had some success. The uprising began in a nearly uncontrollable way: contingents of urban and rural workers occupied towns and villages and some military barracks. The movement lasted two months, when it was violently suppressed and ended with the shooting of Martí.

Between 1927 and 1933, a social movement arose and thrived in Nicaragua, headed by Augusto Cesar Sandino. Influenced by the indigenous cause present in the Mexican Revolution, and by the anarcho-syndicalism present in the oil (Tampico, Mexico) and mining areas (Segovias, Nicaragua) where he had worked as a labourer, Sandino recruited his followers with an anti-imperialist discourse and opposition to the despotism of conservative President Adolfo Díaz. He demanded the president's resignation and the cancellation of the Bryan–Chamorro Treaty that allowed the United States to build an exclusive transoceanic canal in Nicaragua. An agreement between the elites to end the Díaz dictatorship ignored the other demands of the Sandinistas and resulted in the intensification of the movement and the declaration of war against the United States. Manifestos and official reports made the movement known throughout Latin America. Despite being connected to anarchism and Communism, the movement acquired a messianic tone that evoked Judgment Day, divine justice and other aspects of restorative struggle. Sandino was betrayed and murdered in February 1934 by the National Guard, under the command of Anastácio Somoza García at the time. Almost fifty years later, in 1979, the Sandinista National Liberation Front (FSLN), a revolutionary movement inspired by the struggle of Augusto César Sandino and founded in 1961, overthrew the dictatorship of Anastácio Somoza Debayle, son of Anastácio Somoza Garcia.

---

[8] Eric R. Wolf, *Guerras camponesas do século XX* (São Paulo: Global Editora, 1984), p. 19.

The three social movements mentioned here had lasting effects on the political struggle of their countries and became examples and models of social movement activism throughout Latin America. Just like the Sandinismo movement, Zapata's and Farabundo Martí's examples had a lasting effect and reappeared after more than fifty years in movements such as the Farabundo Martí National Liberation Front (FMLN, *Frente Farabundo Martí para la Liberación Nacional*), 1980 and the Zapatista Army of National Liberation, 1994 (EZLN, *Ejército Zapatista de Liberación Nacional*).

In the early twentieth century, the workers' and the farmers' movements campaigned against social inequality and against despotism. Movements such as the Sandinistas and the Mexican labour movement, due to the geographical particularities of the region, also questioned reliance on the United States and the preference given to American workers in the distribution of better jobs. However, they prioritized very specific demands of social groups they represented, such as the land struggle of the peasants, and the struggle for better wages, better living conditions and reduced working hours for the workers.

Movements led by urban middle classes, by contrast, had more fragmented demands. They opposed despotism, the lack of parliamentary democracy and political participation, economic and cultural dependency and economic backwardness. They were more heterogeneous in composition: activists and their leaders did not necessarily belong to the same social class or to the same homogeneous professional group.

Typical for such a movement was the University Reform Movement that first emerged in Cordoba, Argentina, in 1918 as a student movement, and subsequently spread across nearly all Latin American countries. The protests that started at the University of Cordoba in 1918 affected the organization and administration of universities, higher education, and study programmes and syllabi across Latin America. More than a mere episode of student unrest, the Cordoba protest demanded internal democratization and university autonomy from the state; the students struggled against elitism at university, in teaching programmes and syllabi, and in the selection of professors. They campaigned against the university as a bastion of reactionary, Catholic and oligarchic traditions. The protests of Cordoba resonated across the country, within the organization of the Argentinean University Federation (*Federación Universitaria Argentina*), but also outside Argentina, with the creation of student federations in countries such as Peru, Cuba and Venezuela. One of the key activists of the rebellion was Deodoro Roca, son of a traditional family, and a young graduate of Cordoba University, which produced most of the documents of the revolt, and where the emphasis was on autonomy for the university, democracy and the Latin American perspective, exemplified in the slogan '*Ha llegado la hora americana*' ('The Latin-American time has come'). Another urban middle-class movement was *Tenentismo*. This was a movement that started from Brazilian officers' dissatisfaction with the low-ranking presidential succession of 1922 and, in a few years, went beyond this limit and became one of the social movements of highest impact in Brazilian history, achieving considerable popular support. The movement first emerged in a period of absence of national political parties that could channel the dissatisfaction of different regions of the country against the oligarchies and it was dismantled years after the fall of the oligarchies in 1930. In the 1920s, the lieutenants mutinied twice. The first time, on 5 July 1922, the episode of the Copacabana Fortress against the presidency of Artur Bernardes, was dismantled in two days. The second upheaval of the lieutenants occurred two years later, in 1924, and involved the uprising of several garrisons. The lieutenants came to emphasize the defence of 'national interests', the need for clean elections, nationalism and the defence of industrialization. The movement of 1924 led to the march of the 'Prestes Column', leaded by the lieutenant Luis Carlos Prestes. The key symbol of *Tenentismo*, the column travelled around various parts of the country, and ended in 1927 with the lieutenants' entry in Bolivia, to escape capture by pursuing state forces. The *Tenentismo* represented the urban middle classes in Brazil who were eager to participate in the political life of the country, advocating modernization and criticizing the dependent economy.

In Peru, the American Revolutionary Popular Alliance (APRA, *Alianza Popular Revolucionaria Americana*), founded in October 1926 by the Peruvian political and intellectual Victor Raul Haya de la Torre, was a movement that provided collective direction to the struggles of various anti-oligarchic social sectors. It emerged as a result of the student movement in Argentina in 1918, which influenced the young student Haya de la Torre. The APRA proposed actions against US imperialism, and for the political unity of Latin America, the nationalization of land and industry, the internationalization of the Panama Canal and the solidarity of all peoples and oppressed classes of the world. Haya de la Torre idealized the organization of a single front, cohesive and powerful. The protesters opposed both fascist nationalism and international socialism and were repeatedly accused of being reformists. The conflict between their ideas and the socialist José Carlos Mariátegui reflected the major contradictions within the movement. Nonetheless, the movement achieved prominence throughout Latin America. The persecution that this movement suffered throughout its history resulted in the exile of most of its members and the dissemination of their ideas throughout Latin America. In 1931, the Alliance became the Peruvian Aprista Party, an important political force in the country to this day.

These are just some of the movements of the anti-oligarchic urban middle classes that multiplied throughout Latin America in the first decades of the twentieth century. Halperin Donghi rightly described them as 'more coherent and radical in action and lacking an ideology'.[9] Another characteristic of these movements was the transposition of national boundaries. They influenced each other and were mutually stimulated. This was already the case with the labour movement and among Latin American communists. But the latter were movements with a social composition and/or similar ideology as well as with an international organization. In the case of the movement of urban middle classes, despite the similarity of the claims, social composition was diverse: students, lieutenants, professionals. The manifestos and the leaders of these movements circulated all over Latin America and diffused democratic ideas of national liberation, campaigning against economic backwardness and social inequality. The creation of networks, a characteristic of the latest Latin American social movements, would arise from those shared experiences.[10]

THE DIVERSITY OF THE NATIONALIST SOCIAL MOVEMENTS

In Latin America, the struggle for national liberation was an integral part of social movement. However, the nineteenth century's nationalism, at the time of independence processes, was weak because it had no mass support. It was led by military forces, exemplified by those following Simón Bolivar, who wished to separate Latin America from the Iberian metropoles, but it was not a genuinely national feeling.[11]

---

[9] Tulio H. Donghi, *História da América Latina* (Rio de Janeiro: Paz e Terra, 1975), p. 177.

[10] Ilse Scherer-Warren, *Redes de movimentos sociais* (São Paulo: Edições Loyola, 1993) pp. 111–123.

[11] Cf. José C. Chiaramonte, 'El problema de los orígenes de los Estados hispanoamericanos en la historiografía reciente y el caso del Rio de la Plata', Anos 90 (1993), pp. 49–83; Claudia

Two kinds of nationalist movements can be distinguished in the twentieth century: nationalist social movements inspired by national socialism or fascism, and the nationalist anti-imperialist movements that transformed the political culture of some countries of the subcontinent.

Social movements inspired by fascism and Nazism first appeared in Latin America from the 1920s onwards, but a more consistent expression surfaced at the brink of the Second World War. In Brazil, the Brazilian Integralist Action (AIB, *Ação Integralista Brasileira*), was established in 1932. In Argentina, the Patriotic League was founded in 1919. In Mexico, several movements represented fascism, among which the National League for the Defence of Religious Liberty (LNDLR, *Liga Nacional de la Defensa de la Libertad Religiosa*), responsible for the Cristero movement (1926–1929) and, later, the Mexican Revolutionary Action (AMR, *Acción Revolucionaria Mexicanista*) or Gold Shirts, created in 1935, and the National Synarchist Union in 1937. In Chile, the National Socialist Movement of Chile existed between 1932 and 1939. These are all examples of anti-liberal extreme right-wing movements, whose main beliefs were defending the quasi-feudal social order, and Catholicism; they were anti-communist and usually ultra-nationalist. Their specific emphases depended on particular national contexts. These movements had many followers; some organized themselves as parties and participated in elections, coups and insurrections. Even without taking power, these right-wing movements characterized the political culture in most Latin American countries from the 1920s to the 1940s. Even though these movements were developing between the years 1920s and 1940s, the strongest evidence of their importance occurred, in a different guise, at the time of the National Security Doctrine dictatorships in the 1970s.

However, in the years immediately following the Second World War forms of parliamentary democracy prevailed in most Latin America countries,[12] and political party and trade union organizations became stronger. The tone of the Latin American governments of that time was one of national-developmentalism, which also remained in effect in the industrialized countries of Latin America supported by populist leaders, such as Getúlio Vargas in Brazil and Juan Domingos Perón in Argentina.

Wasserman, *Nações e Nacionalismos na América Latina. (Desde quando?): a questão nacional no pensamento latino-americano* (Porto Alegre: Linus ed., 2012).

[12] Leslie Bethell and Ian Roxborough, *Entre a Segunda Guerra Mundial e a Guerra Fria* (Rio de Janeiro: Paz e Terra, 1996), p. 18.

These governments sought to contain protests and make social movements redundant by attending to some of the claims that had been incubating in Latin American societies for some time. Populist governments sought to channel popular demands for unions and parties tied to the state, legalizing and formalizing the political participation of the masses.[13] In the poorest countries of Latin America, the Andean, Central American or Caribbean countries, economically dependent and with only incipient industrialization, national-developmentalism also prevailed. In these regions, however, nationalism tended to be more intense, a product of anti-imperialist ideas. The intensity of the struggle for national liberation was proportional to the perception of voraciousness of expropriation by foreign companies in these regions.

In Bolivia, for example, the Nationalist Revolutionary Movement (MNR) emerged in 1941, founded by independent socialists, veterans of the Chaco War and youth sectors of the armed forces. The Chaco War against Paraguay, for dominance of the oil-producing region, occurred between 1932 and 1935 and resulted in the defeat of Bolivia. The defeat led young Bolivian army officers to fight against the domination of foreign interests in the country. The MNR was a movement of patriotic character, which opposed social injustice, was concerned with economic development and decrease of dependence on the international import and export markets. The MNR proposed measures designed to support social progress; it issued generic anti-imperialist pronouncements, condemned internationalist socialism, false democracy and was anti-Semitic. When the MNR rose to power in 1952 under the leadership of Victor Paz Estenssoro, a part of it defended agrarian reform, the expropriation of foreign companies and the voting rights of illiterates. The movement was divided; the more conservative fraction assumed power and cancelled the social advances almost entirely.

In Cuba, the emergence of the 26 July Movement was a response to the neo-colonial situation on the island, but also and above all, it was the result of the struggle against authoritarianism of Fulgencio Batista, the American figurehead, who staged a coup in 1952. After the coup, Cuba became for a home to the American mafia, with activities related

---

[13] Cf. Francisco Weffort, *O populismo na política brasileira* (Rio de Janeiro: Paz e Terra, 1978); Octavio Ianni, *La Formación del Estado Populista en América Latina* (Mexico City: Era ed., 1975); Ernesto Laclau, *La Razón Populista* (México City: Fondo de Cultura Económica, 2009).

to gambling, drugs and prostitution. On 26 July 1953, a group led by Fidel Castro attempted an attack to the Moncada barracks. The failure of the operation resulted in the arrest of those involved, and the revolutionary movement with perhaps the greatest impact in Latin American history took its name from the day of the attack. The 26 July Movement advocated national liberation and fought against authoritarianism, social backwardness and inequality present in Cuban society. Of all the social movements mentioned so far, from the nineteenth century to the second half of the twentieth century, the movement in Cuba was the first to be successful in terms of appropriating power and consolidating the political project of the rebels. The previous movements were repressed, or partially successful for a brief period of time or had only a few demands granted. Hence the Cuban Revolution represented a new paradigm for contemporary Latin American social movements.

SOCIAL MOVEMENTS AND REVOLUTIONARY RESISTANCE TO DICTATORSHIPS

From 1961, inspired by the Cuban Revolution, revolutionary social movements emerged in almost all Latin American countries: the National Liberation Army (ELN, *Ejército de Liberación Nacional de Bolívia*) in Bolivia, the Revolutionary Armed Forced of Colombia (FARC, *Fuerzas Armadas Revolucionarias de Colombia*) in Colombia, the Rebel Armed Forces (FAR, *Fuerzas Armadas Rebeldes*) in Guatemala, Shining Path (*Sendero Luminoso*) in Peru, the Farabundo Martí National Liberation Front (FFMLN, *El Frente Farabundo Martí para la Liberación Nacional*) in El Salvador, the Sandinista National Liberation Front (FSLN, *Frente Sadinista de Liberación Nacional*) in Nicaragua, the People's Revolutionary Army (ERP, *Ejército Revolucionario del Pueblo*) in Argentina. These movements were revolutionary and Marxist. They were classified as Trotskyites, Maoists or Leninists, according to the influences they received and according to the concrete conditions of each region. All of them worked outside institutions, some were illegal, and they organized guerrilla campaigns. They were brutally repressed by the military and a few had some success, such as the Sandinista National Liberation Front, which rose to power in Nicaragua in 1979.

Apart from revolutionary social movements, the 1970s witnessed the organization of resistance movements against the military dictatorships that derived their legitimacy from the National Security Doctrine[14] and that mainly occurred in the southern cone. Movements such as the *Montoneros* in Argentina, the *Tupamaros* in Uruguay, the Revolutionary Movement 8 October (MR8) and Popular Action (AP, *Ação Popular*) in Brazil, the Broad Front (*Frente Amplio*) in Uruguay, or the Mothers of the Plaza de Mayo in Argentina (*Asociación Madre de Plaza de Mayo*) differed from the movements inspired by the Cuban Revolution in that their organization was a product of resistance to dictatorships. Their main activities were related to claiming human rights, uniting the opposition, or developing urban guerrilla activities (such as bank robberies and kidnappings) which sought to destabilize authoritarian governments and strengthen resistance.

In the late 1970s, student movements resurfaced in several South American countries as a form of resistance to dictatorship. Once the trade unions were destroyed, a fair number of intellectual leftists were exiled, activists from leftist organizations or guerrillas were brutally repressed, but student movements resurfaced and grew stronger. The reorganization of student movements was facilitated by the continued renewal of cadres and acted as an element to destabilize dictatorships.

In this context of confronting authoritarianism there also appeared vigorous feminist and environmental movements. They were inspired by the global context, but also played a decisive role in the democratization process of the countries of the southern cone. While feminism brought to public sphere issues that in the past had been restricted to the private sphere, the ecological movements emphasized the universality of protests concerning the use of natural resources of the planet.

The experience of the feminist movement in South America during the 1970s resulted largely from the increased participation of women in the job market, but especially from the role they played in the left organizations, the guerrillas, the student movement, and the role women played in exile politics. This gave the Latin American feminist movement a more dramatic political dimension, since women had to fight against discrimination from the right and the left[15] and, simultaneously, against authoritarianism.

---

[14] Cf. José Comblin, *A Ideologia da Segurança Nacional* (Rio de Janeiro: Civilização Brasileira, 1980).

[15] Nancy S. Sternbach et al., 'Feminismo en América Latina: de Bogotá a San Bernardo', in Magdalena León, *Mujeres y participación política: avances y desafíos en América Latina* (Bogotá: Tercer Mundo ed., 1994), p. 74.

The 1970s also mark the awakening of environmental awareness in the world, evidenced by the United Nations Conference on Environment in Stockholm (1972), by the report by the Club of Rome (1972) about the limits to growth and by the proliferation of movements defending the environment. In Latin America, the combination of social inequality and environmental degradation became particularly important to the ecological movement. Initially characterized as environmentalists, the ecological movements that emerged in the 1970s in Latin America developed a model of economic development capable of overcoming social inequalities and of containing ecological imbalances. Their emergence was subtle, but their role was important—criticizing the conservative modernization proposed by elites and supported by military governments.

CURRENT SOCIAL MOVEMENTS AND THEIR CHARACTERISTICS

The 1980s were marked by the debt crisis, inflation, the lack of control of public accounts, unemployment, and de-industrialization—factors that led to the emergence of anti-systemic social movements against the new face acquired by capitalism. The movements that emerged in Latin America in the late 1980s and early 1990s were called 'new' in terms of elements that differentiated them in many ways from the previous ones. Disconnected from parties or unions, with more universal claims and independent from the production structure, free of hierarchies and without expressive leadership, contemporary social movements proclaimed that 'another world was possible', as expressed in the slogan of the World Social Forum, an event held for the first time in Porto Alegre, Brazil, in January 2001.[16]

The beginning of the twenty-first century was symbolic for these social movements. Their first appearance was in Latin America from the *Caracazo* in 1989 and from the outbreak of the Neozapatista Movement in 1994. Social movement activism increased sharply in Latin America, encouraged by democratization, by the mutual awareness of the actors and also thought networking and use of powerful media. We must, however, distinguish social movements from spontaneous protest events. Often, such spontaneous protests constituted the trigger to form consis-

---

[16] Cf. Immanuel Wallerstein, *Historia y dilemas de los movimentos antisistémicos* (México City: Contrahistorias, 2008), Chaps. 2, 3 and 4. Cf. also the chapter by Britta Baumgarten in this volume.

tent social movements. Massive and violent protests, such as the *Caracazo* in Venezuela and the *Panelazos* in Argentina, expressed the eruption of actors dissatisfied with the effects of the neoliberal economic and social policies. The *Caracazo* was a protest against an increase in bus fares that occurred in Venezuela in February 1989. In fact, the protest was a result of the harmful effects of the structural adjustment plan that the government of President Carlos Andrés Pérez, of the party *Acción Democrática* (AD), announced 11 days earlier. The *Panelazos* were street manifestations in Argentina in late 2001. Demonstrators banged pots and pans during the protests to indicate their miserable situation and to rail against the economic misfortunes that struck Argentina as a result of the disastrous implementation of neoliberal measures initiated in the military period and deepened during Carlos Menem's government (1989–1999).

The protests were carried out by parts of the population that felt socially or politically excluded from the traditional political system, in parties or trade unions. They were based around organizations of middleclass neighbourhoods and from the slums (*favelas*), representatives of the more general population, and some associations of different categories of public-sector employees. Their willingness to join protest organizations became a key factor in the processes of democratization across Latin America.

The social movements that surfaced in the late twentieth century have very diverse characteristics, but they can be divided into urban movements (homeless, workers against unfair increases in public services, respect for homosexuals, the student movement) and rural movements both of peasants and indigenous people. The latter were undoubtedly the most influential social movements in Latin America during this period. The *Via Campesina*, the Landless Workers' Movement (MST, *Movimento dos Trabalhadores Sem Terra*), the Zapatistas (EZLN, *Ejército Zapatista de Liberación Nacional*), the National Confederation of Indigenous of Ecuador (CONAIE, *Confederación de Nacionalidades Indígenas de Equador*) and the *Coordinadoras* of gas and water, organizations that expressed their wishes, aims and demands through insurrections, civil wars, marches and occupations but also through the formation of support networks, are all social movements that criticize the whole system of surplus appropriation and that require the acknowledgment of subjects who were politically and socially invisible. They fight for the maintenance of traditional and indigenous cultures, for the preservation of the environment and they grow stronger with the increasing popular empowerment.

From the point of view of their demands, these movements do not claim mere ownership of the land, as their predecessors in the nineteenth and twentieth centuries did, but they fight for the right to choose the crops and methods of cultivation, the form of surplus appropriation and the definition of strategies for environmental conservation. Moreover, contemporary social movements in Latin America are fighting for civil rights, legal recognition and preservation of the cultural and material heritage of the nation.[17] What is really novel about these movements, beyond the interpretation of social scientists, is the fact that they have acquired awareness that economic, political *and* cultural factors are important in their struggle for structural change.

Via Campesina is an international movement, founded in 1992, in Managua, by peasant leaders from Central America, North America and Europe. It gathers organizations of small and medium producers, agricultural workers, rural women and indigenous communities from Asia, Africa, America and Europe. Among its objectives are the building of solidarity and unity among organizations of small peasants fighting for equitable economic relations and social justice, land preservation, food sovereignty, sustainable agricultural production and achieving an equality based on the production of small and medium peasants. Finally, it values the strengthening of women's participation in various activities related to the struggles of the movement.

The Landless Workers' Movement (MST, *Movimento dos trabalhadores rurais Sem Terra*) is a Brazilian peasant-based movement, created in 1984 in Cascavel, whose origins date back to the path of struggle headed by the first leagues and organizations of rural workers in the 1950s. The reorganization of the peasants in the 1970s was driven by the Basic Ecclesial Communities (CEBs) and the Pastoral Land Commission (CPT). In the 1990s, the MST became a national movement. Among their goals are land reform and the settlement of families as solutions to the problem of land concentration. In the 1990s, two episodes represented the violence suffered by workers in the field: the massacre of Corumbiara in Rondônia, in 1995 and the massacre in Eldorado do Carajás, Pará, in 1996. More recently, in 2006, the movement, due to their rejection of the predatory exploitation of international capital, mobilized the women of Via Campesina against Aracruz Celulose, a Brazilian manufacturer of pulp

---

[17] Sonia E. Alvarez, Evelina Dagnino and Arturo Escobar, *Cultura e política nos movimentos sociais latino-americanos* (Belo Horizonte: UFMG, 2000), p. 16.

and paper, and destroyed its laboratory and thousands of eucalyptus seedlings, highlighting the environmentalist and anti-imperialist attitude the movement has acquired during its journey. Among the forms of protest that the MST uses àre marches, land occupations and camping, protests and occupations of public buildings. Besides the redistribution of land, the MST also proposes an autonomous project and original education and staff training, access to credit and the possibility of developing agribusinesses owned by the protesters.

The Zapatistas made their first public appearance on the same day that Mexico formalized the Free Trade Agreement (NAFTA) with the United States, in January 1994. In the first document, the Declaration of the Lacandon Jungle I, the combatants declared war on Carlos Salinas de Gortari's government and announced the struggle for democracy, freedom and justice. The document demanded the dismissal of mayors, the distribution of land and changes in the constitution concerning the recognition of the rights of indigenous peoples. With the intensification of governmental actions against the Zapatistas, various sectors of society delivered help caravans to communities at the same time that national and international human rights organizations denounced human rights violations. While the violence of the Mexican government grew, the movement acquired a global presence and impact, through the use of modern means of communication. They use the internet for news releases and with that they are able to gather international solidarity and support among teachers, artists, clergy, writers, students, NGOs and trade unions worldwide. In 1996, the Zapatistas gathered 3,000 people in the jungle, from 43 countries, for the First International Meeting for Humanity and Against Neoliberalism. At this event was created the International Network of Hope. The updating of the Zapatista Indian/peasant rebellion by the EZLN reaffirms the problems stemming from oligarchic dominance in the process of implementation and consolidation of capitalist relations in Latin America and Mexico: absolutely unequal distribution of wealth, social exclusion and political violence.[18]

In Ecuador, the indigenous movement was organized through the creation of the Confederation of Indigenous Nationalities of Ecuador (*Confederación de Nacionalidades Indígenas del Ecuador*, CONAIE), in 1986. Indigenous resistance in the country, marked by racism, has existed

---

[18] Carlos A. Aguirre Rojas, *Mandar obedeciendo: Las lecciones políticas del neozapatismo mexicano* (Mexico City: Editorial Contrahistorias, 2007), p. 125.

since the Spanish Conquest. From the 1920s onwards, the indigenous movement sought to associate the culture of the original peoples to Ecuadorian nationality with education policies intending to incorporate the native subject in society. Throughout the twentieth century, the land issue, especially in regions such as the Amazon, where ethnicity is related to a clearly delimited territory, has acquired the characteristics of an ethnic conflict. Since 1970 different confederations have been created in order to represent indigenous peoples, and CONAIE emerged as a result of those initiatives, in a context marked by the application of the neoliberal model in Ecuador. Among the goals of CONAIE have been the creation of a project for alternative development beyond Western modernization theories and neoliberalism; the implantation of participatory democracy mechanisms, keeping traditional decision-making strategies; and increasing indigenous representation in the estate structure. From March 1983, when the first national strike against the neoliberal adjustments occurred, until the indigenous–military uprising which overthrew President Lucio Gutierrez in 2005, the movement succeeded in carrying out 22 strikes, five national uprisings and overthrew two presidents, Abdala Bucaram in 1997 and Jamil Mahuad in 2000. Those strategies resulted in a series of changes. In 1988, a partnership was established between the Ministry of Education and CONAIE to implement the Intercultural Bilingual Education Program. In 1994, CONAIE took action to modify the Agrarian Reform Law, seeking to guarantee the rights of communities. In 1996, the Pachakutik Movement of Plurinational Unity—New Country was created, presenting themselves for elections that year, with some local victories.

In Bolivia, two major social movements were responsible for institutional changes and transformations in the political culture of the country. The growing process of privatization and marketization of public services and land resulted in movements articulated and directed by local organizations. They organized themselves to protest against the indiscriminate exploitation of the national heritage, involving two commodities: water and gas. In early 2000, the peasants of Cochabamba and of the Altiplano rebelled against a transnational corporation, Águas de Tunari, a consortium of Italian, Spaniard, American and Bolivian capital. The action was known as 'the water war' and intended to expel the company from the country. The peasants created the 'Co-Ordinator for the Defence of Water and Life' and blocked the roads, paralysing the region. The 'Co-Ordinator' demanded the annulment of the contract and an open dialogue with all sectors of society about the Water Resource Law and the Law of the National Institute of Agrarian Reform (INRA, *Instituto Nacional de la Reforma Agraria*), which regulated ownership and the land market. After violently repressing the protests, the Bolivian government was forced to acknowledge the strength of community feeling and will to act and started to accept changes in the law. Finally, they annulled the contract with the transnational company. Another movement surfaced in 2003, regarding gas exploitation. The Indians of Warisata and Sorata, from the Altiplano and nearby La Paz founded the 'Co-ordinator for the Defence of Gas Supplies'. The Bolivian Labourer Central (COB) and the Movement to Socialism (MAS) organized a unique manifestation to express opposition to a transnational project of partnership Pacífic LNG, which envisioned the export of Bolivian gas in raw state, through a Chilean port to Mexico and the United States. Sánchez de Lozada government's response was violent. The number of dead and wounded protesters led the international press to characterize the conflict as a real massacre. As a result, the contract was cancelled; President Sanchez de Lozada resigned and was followed by the Vice President.

The historical antecedents of both movements, water and gas, are the insurrections of Tupac Katari in the eighteenth century, and Willka in the nineteenth, in the participation of Indians in the Chaco War and their decisive action in the Revolution of 1952 when the Nationalist Revolutionary Movement (MNR) armed peasant militias. In January 2006 Evo Morales, a peasant *cocalero* (coca leaf grower), participant in the struggles against the eradication of coca crops in Chapare, in the 'water war' in 2000 and in the 'gas war' in 2003, was elected. The environmentalist content of these movements, for the dominion of natural resources, reveals that indigenous traditions have influenced current popular struggles in Bolivia.

The movement that was built through the 'Coordinadoras' encapsulates the new profile of social movements that have begun to take form in Bolivia and several other Latin American countries such as Mexico, Colombia and Peru since the 1990s. These movements are linked to popular everyday problems such as inequitable access and unsustainable use of natural resources, demands for greater participation in local administration, democratic control of decision making in what affects socio-economic conditions and quality of life for the population. These claims could articulate the needs and wishes of both rural and urban populations, considering that the exploitation of resources affects everyone. The claim for natural resource management according to 'usages and customs' questions the neoliberal program of systematic destruction of collective and community spaces.

At least two urban social movements stand out in the late twentieth and early twenty-first centuries: the *piqueteros* (street blockages) in Argentina and the Bolivarian Movement in Venezuela. In both countries, the urban movements are also related to the effects of neoliberal policies in structural adjustment. The main protagonists are the poor population in metropolitan areas of Buenos Aires and Caracas. The *piquetero* movement made a more consistent appearance during the economic crisis of 2001, but its first activities began in the 1990s as a result of impoverishment and marginalization processes in urban areas of the country, especially in Buenos Aires. At the beginning of the twenty-first century the 'Unemployed Workers' Movement' of unemployed and informal workers was created. Its organization is not hierarchical and is rooted in neighbourhood organizations. The *piqueteros* protest against unemployment and have specific demands such as building schools or hospitals. Their main strategy is to block the country's highways and draw attention of public authorities to the existence of a significant part of the population (about two-thirds) who have never had access to public services, have had no political participation and who have suffered the worst effects of neoliberalism: the growth of economic inequality and social exclusion.

The immediate antecedent of the Bolivarian movement is the episode in 1989, known as the *Caracazo*, but the movement grew stronger since 1992 under the leadership of Hugo Chávez Frías. Its origin is based in the organization of Neighbourhood Associations (*Asociaciones de Barrios*) of the capital slums (*favelas*), conditioned by impoverishment, marginalization and social and political exclusion of the residents of these areas. The Neighbourhood Associations became the social supporting base for the Bolivarian movement, which brought so many and so radical transformations to the Venezuelan society. But its first appearance is associated with social mobilizations that ended the dictatorship of Juan Vicente Gomes in 1936. According to Carla Ferreira, 'this sector of the urban working class, over-exploited or detached from industrial production, was formed in the 1980s, in a radical mass movement'.[19]

---

[19] Carla Ferreira, *A classe trabalhadora no processo bolivariano da Venezuela. Contradições e conflitos do capitalismo dependente petroleiro-rentista (1989–2010)*, Doctoral Thesis (Porto Alegre: Postgraduate Program in History UFRGS, 2012), p. 86.

Despite the great diversity among Latin American social movements between the late twentieth century and early twenty-first century, it is possible to understand the set of demands present in all Latin American societies in this period. Indigenous, peasant, slum dwellers', unemployed, neighbours', students' and women's organizations are an expression of the negative effects of neoliberal economic policies, combined with the re-democratization of Latin American countries and the history of backwardness, dependence, social inequality and authoritarianism. The struggle for democracy has provided a greater awareness for social sectors previously little or not at all incorporated into the capitalist system. These social movements contributed equally to an extensive history of struggles of the lower classes in Latin America, and their emergence often carried symbols and ideas from the past. The use of powerful media led the formation of social movement networks, reinforcement for all of them, and that resulted in a significant effect on the political culture of Latin America, either by acknowledging the merits of the claims or by the rise of governments sympathetic to these popular struggles.

CONCLUSIONS

The analysis of the trajectory of Latin American social movements throughout history indicates the persistence of problems underlying the socio-economic structure of countries that were colonized in the sixteenth century and that, from the nineteenth century onwards, joined the capitalist world system in a dependent and peripheral manner. The absence of mechanisms for social inclusion and political participation, backwardness, inequality and dependence were the central elements to trigger protests, uprisings and other spontaneous actions, but also resulted in the organization of social movements. The persistence of these harmful characteristics in Latin American societies also led to the evocation, by more contemporary activists, of social movements and leaders of the past. This inspiration resulted in the transformation of movements and characters from the past in myth and symbol, including the act of summoning them to give their names to contemporary social movements.

Throughout history, the social composition of social movements in Latin America has been extremely varied. Workers, peasants, unemployed people, urban middle classes, students, women, professionals, military officers were all persecuted for challenging the system. The repression of social movements in Latin America was brutal throughout their history, and the use of force against them was often disproportionate in relation to the danger they represented to the status quo. As a result of the repression, most social movements failed in their intentions and goals.

Repression and violence were not able, however, to make the ills of Latin American countries disappear, especially the causes of the appearance of social movements. So, for each stage of this path, struggles for a more just, more equal, more democratic, less dependent society were renewed. Over time, the aims of social movements of the past were carried out by other agents, which produced a lasting impact on the political culture of Latin American countries. One of the most extraordinary effects was the policy of democratization in this twenty-first century, evidenced by the inclusion of social actors previously little or not at all engaged with the system. The exponential multiplication of social movements in the late twentieth century indicates, on the one hand, the perverse consequences of neoliberal policies, but on the other hand, testifies to the progress in organization of movements.

In terms of periodization, it can be observed that social movements in Latin America are becoming increasingly consistent, that the ties between the various movements and formation of networks strengthen the demands and protect its participants. The movements have also become increasingly complex and, even if there is no longer a direct relationship between the claim, the social composition of a movement and the economic structure, which is usually represented as a fragmentation of a movement's demands, they end up being important to reaching a larger and more diverse portion of the population of each country.

Between the nineteenth and early twenty-first centuries, the Latin American social movements, occurring simultaneously in countries with so many important differences among them, fought to reduce dependence, authoritarianism, inequality and backwardness. This course allowed substantive changes: in the composition of social movements (they became more diversified and less consistent with the productive structure) in the relationship between movements (they formed networks and became less vulnerable); in the strategies of organization (horizontality, internal democracy and use of powerful means of mass communication), and in the organization of demands (related to the yearnings of various social groups). Despite these modifications in its trajectory, Latin American social movements have some similar characteristics that allow comparative studies.

FURTHER READINGS

The English literature about Latin American social movements mostly originates from congresses, workshops or seminars. So, most publications are collections of articles. The papers collected in those volumes are for the most part about theoretical questions or about the movements themselves. A good example is the book edited by David Slater, *New Social Movements and the State in Latin America* (Amsterdam: CEDLA, 1985). The papers collected in this volume originate from a CEDLA workshop held in October 1983. They were inspired by a belief in the importance of providing a forum for discussion and debate on the topic of new social movements and the state in Latin America. The combined analysis provides a series of theoretical points of departure and then the other papers tell us about *Sendero Luminoso* in Peru, the organization of Metalworkers in Brazil, the women's movement in Nicaragua, and so on.

The book edited by Susan Eckstein, *Power and Popular Protest. Latin American Social Movements* (Berkeley: University of California Press, 1989) is another good example of a collection. It includes case studies of Bolivian mining communities, ecclesiastic base communities in Brazil, the guerrilla peasant movement in Peru and Colombia, and also theoretical problems of the new social movement paradigm.

Carlos O. Campos, Gary Prevost and Harry Vanden, *Social Movements and Leftist Governments in Latin America: Confrontation or Co-option?* (London: Zed Books, 2012) is a book that analyses how the simultaneous development of prominent social movements and the election of left governments has radically altered the political landscape in Latin America. The cases analysed in this volume are '*piqueteros*' of Argentina, indigenous movements in Ecuador and Bolivia, neighbourhood associations in Venezuela and Landless Rural Workers movement in Brazil. The collaborative collection tries to respond to the ways in which newly elected left governments answer to the social movements that played a major role in bringing them to power.

Alain Touraine, 'An Introduction to the Study of Social Movements', *Social Research* 52 (1985), pp. 749–787 is a very important author in the theme of Latin-American social movements. He discusses the principal theoretical characteristics of the new social movements in the 1980s.

James Petras and Henry Veltmeyer, *Social Movements in Latin America: Neoliberalism and Popular Resistance* (Basingstoke: Palgrave Macmillan, 2011) discuss the social struggles in Latin America in this century: the worldwide change in social and economic relations, accompanied by a multi-dimensional global crisis and the popular uprisings led by socio-political movements in last ten years. The personages of the book are the popular sectors that have recognized themselves to be prepared to and very able to resist the machinations of imperial power and corporate elites, taking direct action as well as voting for political parties promising structural change. This book tells the story of popular resistance in its multiple forms with and against the new post-neoliberal regimes and of the changing social conditions in an era of globalization and worldwide crisis.

The most up-to-date literature about Latin American social movements appears in the Journal *La otra Mirada de Clio*, published by the collective *Contrahistoria*, two issues per year. Bolivar Echeverría, Carlos A. Aguirre Rojas, Immanuel Wallerstein, the subcommandante insurgent Marcos from Chiapas are some of the authors whose researches and articles have appeared in the volumes since 2003. Almost all articles are related to the new social movements in Latin America.

CHAPTER 6

Dissident Political History: Social Movements in North America

Felicia Kornbluh

Are humans to be denied human rights? Are members of the community to be robbed of their rights to live in the community? ... As with the black man, so with the blind. As with the Puerto Rican, so with the post-polio. As with the Indian, so with the indigent disabled.
—Dr Jacobus tenBroek, 'The Right to Live in the World', 1966.[1]

When the architects of our republic wrote the magnificent words of the Constitution and the Declaration of Independence, they were signing a promissory note to which every American was to fall heir ... Instead of honouring this sacred obligation, America has given the Negro people a bad check, a check which has come back marked 'insufficient funds'. But we refuse to believe that the bank of justice is bankrupt. We refuse to believe that there are insufficient funds in the great vaults of opportunity of this nation. So we have come to cash this check—a check that will give us upon demand the riches of freedom and the security of justice.

---

[1] Jacobus tenBroek, 'The Right to Live in the World: The Disabled in the Law of Torts', in Jacobus tenBroek and the Editors of California Law Review (eds), *The Law of the Poor* (Berkeley, CA: California Law Review, 1966), p. 527.

F. Kornbluh (✉)
College of Arts and Sciences, University of Vermont, Burlington, VT, USA

© The Author(s) 2017
S. Berger, H. Nehring (eds.), *The History of Social Movements in Global Perspective*, DOI 10.1057/978-1-137-30427-8_6

—Rev. Dr. Martin Luther King, Jr., Speech at the March on Washington
for Jobs and Freedom, 1963.[2]

These two quotations are excellent launching points for a consideration of
the history of social movements in North America. The first comes from
a late essay by the blind civil rights activist, social welfare advocate and
scholar of constitutional law, Jacobus tenBroek.[3] The second is a relatively
unfamiliar passage from perhaps the most famous rhetoric of the African
American freedom movement, Reverend Doctor Martin Luther King, Jr.'s
'I have a dream' speech, delivered at the March on Washington.[4] Both
have their origins in the United States of the 1960s, and in what scholars
often call 'new' social movements.

While the United States is not coterminous with the North American
continent, the scholarship on social movements in the modern United
States is voluminous. It is distinctive from writing about the other
countries and regions of the North American continent, Mexico,
Canada, Central America and the Caribbean. The history of North
America may some day be a common intellectual field, but it is not one
at present; only in certain areas, such as popular responses to the North
American Free Trade Agreement in the 1990s and 2000s, have scholars
of activism in North American countries taken a continental approach.
Therefore, the emphasis of this essay is upon social movements in the

[2] King in Francis L. Broderick and August Meier (eds), *Negro Protest Thought in the
Twentieth Century* (New York: Bobbs Merrill, 1966), p. 401.

[3] On tenBroek and this essay, see Anita Silvers and Leslie Frances (eds), *Americans with
Disabilities: Exploring the Implications of the Law for Individuals and Institutions* (New York:
Routledge, 2000); Felicia Kornbluh, 'Disability, Anti-Professionalism and Civil Rights: The
National Federation of the Blind and the "Right to Organize" in the Late 1950s', *Journal of
American History* 4 (2011), pp. 1023–1047 and Felicia Kornbluh, 'Turning Back the Clock:
California Constitutionalists, "Hearthstone Originalism", and *Brown v. Board of Education*',
California Legal History 7 (2012), pp. 287–318.

[4] Many historians choose the term 'freedom movement' over the narrower 'civil rights
movement' to indicate that the movement sought more than civil rights as conventionally
defined—that it started earlier than we usually think it did, was more closely tied with the
ideological left and concerned with economic issues, and ranged from the black movement
in the South to the Mexican American movement on the west coast and the multicultural
movements in large northeastern cities. See discussions and examples of scholarship in Jeanne
Theoharis and Komozi Woodard (eds), *Freedom North: Black Freedom Struggles Outside the
South, 1940–1980* (Basingstoke: Palgrave Macmillan, 2003). I share these scholars' sense of
the widened meanings of the movement, but use the terms 'civil rights movement', 'freedom
movement' and 'black' or 'African American movement' interchangeably.

United States. I include references to Canada and Mexico only to illuminate general points of similarity and difference among the three most populous states on the continent, and between North America and the European states that have been the classic sites for theorizing about social movements.

Much as the literature upon which I draw places the United States at its centre, it also centres the later part of the twentieth century and so-called new social movements, such as the movement for blind people's rights that tenBroek led and the African American movement of which King was the great symbol. Prior to the mid-twentieth century, social change campaigns in the United States were not known as social movements. After the 1960s, they were often discussed in this way—most often by scholars who identified with the movements. Scholars in the United States used the idea of social movement to distinguish the post-war initiatives they valorized, paradigmatically the African American movement, New Left opposition to the war in Vietnam, and women's liberation, from those they derided and with which they feared being associated, such as the Communist Party and the mainstream trade union movement, represented by the American Federation of Labor–Congress of Industrial Organizations (AFL-CIO). It was only after they had named and begun writing about the post-Second World War movements that historians revisited eighteenth-, nineteenth- and early-twentieth-century efforts to wield power from below and reinterpreted these along (implicitly new) social movement lines.

In what follows, I consider the model of social movement offered by Dieter Rucht's essay in this volume and its applicability to the US, Canadian and Mexican cases. While generally finding it useful, I also find that the distinction Rucht applies between old and new movements, and the very terminology of social movement, fit awkwardly with all three of the major national cases in North America. Second, I offer an overview of the major movements in the history of the United States. I end with brief thoughts on the new directions of social movement studies in the United States.

SOCIAL MOVEMENTS: NEW VERSUS OLD?

Dieter Rucht defines a social movement as 'a network of individuals, groups, and organizations that, based on a sense of collective identity, seek to bring about social change (or resist social change) primarily by means of collective public protest.'[5] The definition is intentionally flexible enough to include those seeking social change from the political right and centre as well as the left, and those who have held state power as well as those who have sought to smash the state. Rucht utilizes the common distinction between old and new social movements, and distinguishes the latter as being 'middle-class based, focus[ed] on the sphere of reproduction ... highly decentralized, favour[ing] a strategy of what might be coined radical reformism, and promot[ing] participatory democracy.'[6]

The four elements of Rucht's definition, that social movements be networks, be based in collective identity, pursue social change and engage in public protest, are all productive for describing much of the dissident political history of North America. I welcome both the breadth and narrowness of this definition. Professor Rucht echoes some of the most sophisticated reflections upon North American history when he accommodates conservative and other political tendencies not associated with the historical left. He wisely encompasses some movements associated with political parties while maintaining a distinction between movements and political campaigns. (It was precisely the failure fully to appreciate this distinction that led to terrible disappointments after self-described 'community organizer' Barack Obama assumed power in Washington, DC, in January 2009.[7])

Only one point of the four in Rucht's definition fails fully to capture the major features of social movement history in North America: Rucht writes that social movements pursue their ends 'primarily by means of collective public protest.' While it would be an error to downplay the significance of collective public protest, in the United States, law reform—both litigation in the courts and statutory law-reform campaigns that targeted legislatures—has served many social movements as a coequal strategy with public protests. Movements throughout North America have utilized media (pamphlets, newspapers, manifestos, zines, blogs) as central tools

---

[5] See Chap. 2, pp. 148.

[6] See Chap. 2, pp. 148.

[7] Felicia Kornbluh, 'Raced and Gendered Histories and the Political Turn Since Obama Took Office', panel on 'Obama's Economic Liberalism: Historical Perspectives', American Historical Association Conference, San Diego, CA, January 8, 2010.

for achieving their ends. Many, too, utilized armed struggle or the threat thereof alongside collective public protest.[8]

Beyond questions about tactics, the major challenge for Rucht's model in terms of North American history is the most basic. It is anachronistic to apply the language of social movement to most campaigns for social change in North American history. Rucht and those whose work he utilizes build upon Western and Northern European histories when they distinguish between old and new social movements. However, in the United States, the distinction is useful mainly as a reminder of the negative referent against which (new) social movement activists defined their projects. Rucht's description of new social movements does not entirely fit the US case, either. Insofar as the African American movement is the most paradigmatic of these, new social movements cannot accurately be described as 'middle-class based'.[9] Even black teachers and preachers, the backbone of some civil rights groups, were badly underpaid. African American professionals with public-sector jobs were always at risk of losing them. And many of the activist troops in the movement, such as the majority of those who were mobilized by the Student Nonviolent Coordinating Committee—for several years, the leading edge of civil rights protest—were extremely poor landless farmers, maids and day labourers.[10] Distinctions between old and new social

[8] On law, see Mark Tushnet, *The NAACP's Legal Strategy Against Segregated Education, 1925–1950* (Chapel Hill: University of North Carolina Press, 1987); Mark Tushnet, *Making Civil Rights Law: Thurgood Marshall and the Supreme Court, 1936–1961* (New York: Oxford University Press, 1994); Linda Kerber, *No Constitutional Right to be Ladies: Women and the Obligations of Citizenship* (New York: Hill & Wang, 1998); Serena Mayeri, *Reasoning from Race: Law and the Civil Rights Revolution* (Cambridge, MA: Harvard University Press, 2011); Silvers and Frances, *Americans with Disabilities*, Samuel Bagenstos, *Law and the Contradictions of the Disability Rights Movement* (New Haven: Yale University Press, 2009); and Marc Stein, *Sexual Injustice: Supreme Court Decisions from Griswold to Roe* (Chapel Hill: University of North Carolina Press, 2010). On armed struggle, see Tim Tyson, *Radio Free Dixie: Robert F. Williams and the Roots of Black Power* (Chapel Hill: University of North Carolina Press, 2000) and *Black Against Empire: The History and Politics of the Black Panther Party* (Berkeley: University of California Press, 2013).

[9] On economic vulnerability and reprisals, see Charles Payne, *I've Got the Light of Freedom: The Organizing Tradition and the Mississippi Freedom Struggle* (2nd edn, Berkeley: University of California Press, 2007), and Lawyers' Constitutional Defense Committee, *Docket* (New York: American Civil Liberties Union, 1966), Wesleyan University Library, *Collection on Legal Change* (Middletown, CT, 1999).

[10] Howard Zinn, *SNCC: The New Abolitionists* (Boston: Beacon, 1965); Payne, *I've Got the Light*, Lawyers' Constitutional Defense Committee, *Docket*. Frances Fox Piven and Richard

movements also fit poorly with the history of women's movements in the United States. To call these movements middle-class or bourgeois is to miss the signal theoretical debate of socialist feminism concerning the class status of women, even those who were married to elite men but did not hold wealth in their own names.[11] It is also to miss the movements of the later twentieth century that addressed gender-related issues such as poverty and public assistance receipt, and the need for non-coercive, publicly funded, reproductive services. Members of these movements were a combination of poor women and women from middle-class backgrounds.[12]

The new/old model of social movements in some ways fits better with the histories of Canada and Mexico than with that of the United States However, in other ways it is an awkward fit with those histories as well. The left has been far more robust and the trade union tradition more progressive in modern Canada than in the recent United States. The successes of the Canadian social democratic left grew from successive popular mobilizations especially since the 1930s. These successes include holding political power for extended periods at the provincial and national levels. They also include legislative social policy changes, such as universal health care provision, first implemented by a series of provinces and then by the national government. In some ways, the record of Canada's social movements resembles that of the most social democratic European examples. However, as labour historian Ian McKay has argued, it would be a mistake to draw distinctions between old and new social movements (or, as he puts it, tributaries of the left) too sharply. In some ways, 'old' and 'new' movement politics were more similar to each other than different from one another. Chronologically, some quintessentially 'new' movements overlapped with the period of greatest strength for dissident trade unions and an activist social democratic party. While the left-of-centre

Cloward emphasized the degree to which middle-class African Americans and women remained disproportionately employed in the public sector through the 1980s (and were therefore vulnerable to cuts in welfare state funding) in *The New Class War* (New York: Pantheon, 1982).

[11] Zillah Eisenstein (ed.), *Capitalist Patriarchy and the Case for Socialist Feminism* (New York: Monthly Review, 1979).

[12] See, for examples, Felicia Kornbluh, *The Battle for Welfare Rights: Poverty and Politics in Modern America* (Philadelphia: University of Pennsylvania Press, 2007) and Todd Gitlin, *Occupy Nation: The Roots, The Spirit, and the Promise of Occupy Wall Street* (New York: Harper Collins/It Books, 2012).

New Democratic Party (NDP), for example, might be seen as a paradigmatic old social movement organization—invested in claiming and holding state power, built in large measure upon trade union participation, and explicitly ideological in left terms—its period of strength coincided with the height of new social movement activism elsewhere in industrialized societies. It collaborated actively with a paradigmatically new movement, the socialist feminist fraction of the movement for women's liberation, which supplied key aspects of the NDP programme.[13]

In a kind of mirror image of the US scholarship, histories of modern Mexico are weighted heavily toward what theorists typically treat as 'old' social movements. Historians of modern Mexico do not usually use the language of social movement to refer to organs of the ideological left, armed mobilizations of workers and peasants and (nominally) left-of-centre political parties, which occupy most of their scholarship on social change. This is perhaps because they so rarely write about any but the 'old' movements. Or maybe it is because, as in Canada, old-style movements persisted throughout the period during which macro accounts suggest that the new succeeded the old. Many discussions of politics 'from below' in Mexico are tied to the history of the Mexican Revolution and the development since the 1920s of the oxymoronically if accurately named Institutional Revolutionary Party (*Partido Revolucionario Institucional*, PRI). The PRI, a nominal left party from which other left factions eventually broke, held state power from its founding until the end of the twentieth century, losing in 2000 its first presidential election since its formation. Trade unions were either absorbed into the state/party apparatus or outlawed for virtually all of this period. Because of the centrality of the PRI, and the colonial history that pre-dated it, the history of Mexico does not line up neatly with models based upon European history. Essayists in the most widely cited work in this area, the edited volume *Everyday Forms of State Formation: Revolution and the Negotiation of Rule in Modern Mexico*, do not employ the language of social movement. They maintain a focus on state and revolution.[14] The leading collection on gender and

---

[13] Ian McKay, *Rebels, Reds, Radicals: Rethinking Canada's Left History* (Toronto: Between the Lines, 2005), pp. 205–206.

[14] Under the entry 'social movement', the book's index refers the reader instead to 'popular movements.' Gilbert Joseph and Daniel Nugent (eds), *Everyday Forms of State Formation: Revolution and the Negotiation of Rule in Modern Mexico* (Durham, NC: Duke University Press, 1994).

feminism in modern Mexico is similarly engaged with questions of revolution, state power and official repression.[15]

The newest generation of social movement activism in the United States, Canada and Mexico, which is North American or at least tripartite in focus, seems half-familiar from Rucht's formulation and half-unfamiliar. Protests against the North American Free Trade Agreement (NAFTA) and its consequences in the 1990s and 2000s were obviously engaged with classic left issues of economic structure and the distribution of resources. Their leaders were a combination of stereotypically old and new social movement actors, trade unionists (in Canada and the United States), members of dissident parties (in Mexico and Canada), middle-class students (in all three countries) and radicalized peasants (in Mexico). NAFTA helped define the 'new' Democratic Party in the United States, a pronouncedly neoliberal party that may have owed much to labour but repaid only pennies on the dollar. In Canada, opposition to North American economic integration was carried by the Liberal Party. NAFTA and its predecessor economic agreement between Canada and the United States thus helped reverse the strong showing of the NDP in the 1990s—a period of defeat that it took a decade for the party to undo. And it inspired the Chiapas revolt in Mexico. This revolt against the central government was inspired by drastically low corn prices, consequent high levels of immigration to cities within Mexico and across the US border (both treacherous for the people making the move), and near-starvation for many left behind.[16]

[15] Jocelyn Olcott, Mary Kay Vaughan and Gabriela Cano (eds), *Sex in Revolution: Gender, Politics, and Power in Modern Mexico* (Durham, NC: Duke University Press, 2006), and Jocelyn Olcott, *Revolutionary Women in Postrevolutionary Mexico* (Durham, NC: Duke University Press, 2005).

[16] Neil Harvey, *The Chiapas Rebellion: The Struggle for Land and Democracy* (Durham, NC: Duke University Press, 1998), Tamara Kay, *NAFTA and the Politics of Labor Transnationalism* (Cambridge: Cambridge University Press, 2010), Ralph Armbruster-Sandoval, *Globalization and Cross-Border Labor Solidarity in the Americas* (New York: Routledge, 2005), and Jeff Faux, 'NAFTA at 10,' *The Nation Magazine* 2004, posted at http://www.epi.org/publication/webfeatures_viewpoints_nafta_legacy_at10/, accessed September 19, 2013.

SOCIAL MOVEMENTS IN THE UNITED STATES: AN OVERVIEW

Definitions aside, the history of popular movements in the United States is rich, long and perhaps surprisingly militant. Although left parties and trade unions have generally been weak in the United States relative to Canada, Mexico and much of Europe, powerful initiatives from the grassroots have been a constant in the country's history. What is confusing about the history of the United States is that these initiatives have often made recognizably social-democratic or revolutionary demands while avoiding or even explicitly denouncing traditional, left–right ideological labels. In addition, the history of slavery and racial subordination, and the distinctive role played in social life and social movements by the elite courts, have made social movements assume somewhat distinctive forms in the United States.

The American Revolution itself can be understood as a kind of social movement. It was based as much in the dissenting spirit and collective action of artisans (workingmen, if relatively elite ones) as in any other class. Crowds of common people gathered for 'collective public protest' (in Rucht's phrase) when they threw English tea into Boston Harbor in a challenge to the British Crown's efforts to develop a captive economy in the North American colonies. After the Revolution, farmers, debtors and war veterans facing economic recession and policies that favoured lenders over borrowers protested widely and, sometimes, by force of arms. A series of actions historians remember as Shay's Rebellion ultimately shaped the national Constitution and, therefore, the whole legal and political history of the United States. The rebellion encouraged its opponents to draft a Constitution that defined a relatively strong national government which could dampen the ability of Shay's Rebels and their ilk to operate effectively within the states. On the other hand, the anti-elitist spirit of Shay's Rebellion delayed the ratification of the Constitution until political leaders promised that one of the first acts of the new Congress would be to draft constitutional Amendments that ensured individuals and groups freedom from national governmental power. These freedoms, including the right to assemble collectively and to publish dissenting opinions, were ultimately encapsulated in the first ten Amendments to the Constitution, otherwise known as the Bill of Rights.[17]

---

[17] Alfred Young, *Liberty Tree: Ordinary People and the American Revolution* (New York: NYU, 2006) and Leonard Richards, *Shay's Rebellion: The American Revolution's Final Battle* (Philadelphia: University of Pennsylvania Press, 2002).

The major dissenting political efforts of the early nineteenth century were the push for the abolition of chattel slavery, women's rights and labour organization in the midst of early industrialization. Their histories make evident the importance of race-based subordination and agitation, and legal reform, in social change. Abolitionists organized as a militant movement on the far outskirts of respectable public opinion. But by the middle nineteenth century they also worked within mainstream political and legal institutions. Many of them at first repudiated law, believing, with Radical leader William Lloyd Garrison, that the Constitution was a 'bloody and heaven-daring arrangement ... for the continuance and protection of a system ... dripping ... with human blood'.[18] By the 1830s many had repudiated the Garrisonian interpretation of the Constitution and begun to argue instead that the country's highest law, interpreted correctly, outlawed slavery. Perhaps paradoxically, the abolitionists' moderate-seeming claims for a better reading of the most valorized legal documents led in 1861 to an outbreak of Civil War—a pronounced departure from the tradition of political stability in the United States. The war led to a constitutional revolution: in case new interpretations of old documents were not sufficient, Congress and the states passed constitutional Amendments that embodied fundamental planks in the abolitionists' platform. These Amendments ended slavery (13th); created national citizenship and promised citizens equal protection of the laws and due process of law (14th); and promised African American men access to the ballot in national elections (15th).

The women's movement, or, as it was known in the nineteenth century, the 'Woman' movement, grew with and from the movement for abolition. It, too, must be understood vis-à-vis the distinctive roles of race and law. Most of its early leaders, such as Sarah and Angelina Grimke, Lucretia Mott and Elizabeth Cady Stanton, were white abolitionists. They learned

---

[18]William Lloyd Garrison, 'On the Constitution and the Union' (excerpt from 'The Great Crisis,' The *Liberator* 52 (December 29, 1832), [http://fair-use.org/the-liberator/1832/12/29/on-the-constitution-and-the-union], accessed September 19, 2013. For change in abolitionist thought, Howard Jay Graham, 'The Purpose and Meaning of Sections One and Five of the Fourteenth Amendment: The Historical Evidence Re-examined', Memorandum in support of Supreme Court Reargument, NAACP papers, Group II, Box B 143, 'Schools—Kansas—Topeka—Brown v. Board of Education (and other cases)—2nd Reargument—Legal papers—1954', Library of Congress, Washington, DC and Jacobus ten-Broek, *The Antislavery Origins of the Fourteenth Amendment* (Berkeley: University of California Press, 1951).

to agitate and organize from their efforts to end slavery. Like other abolitionists, they, too, initially shied away from open engagement with law. They treated mainstream politics as a sphere of corruption. However, they developed a critique of sexist family and property laws as defined in state statutes and implemented by local common-law judges. This led to reform campaigns that required participation in conventional politics. In 1848, the first major women's rights convention gathered in Seneca Falls, New York State, in part because the state legislature was debating a reform in married women's property status nearby. The convention approved a 'Declaration of Sentiments', which declared any government illegitimate that excluded women from full participation in it. This document argued for a reform of laws concerning marriage, child custody and married women's property rights. More controversially, it included Elizabeth Cady Stanton's proposal for women's suffrage.[19] In the two decades that followed, the movement became increasingly—although not singularly—focused upon the vote. The vote was seen as a key to the kind of social transformation and transformation in people's intimate lives that most women in the movement agreed were their ultimate goals.

Labour agitation grew from the contradictions many perceived in a society committed to popular rule that countenanced hierarchy between those who were independent in their work and those who laboured for others on a wage basis. In addition to a range of local organizations of workers to improve their working conditions, white male workers in New York City and Philadelphia formed workingmen's parties in 1829. These parties protested against the policies of the leading parties and bid for public power. These early labour activists may have preferred to avoid legal questions, but they were drawn into statutory and courtroom struggles. In the early nineteenth century, the legal status of unions was uncertain; there were some, if not many, successful prosecutions in a variety of jurisdictions. It was only in 1842, with the case *Commonwealth v. Hunt*, that a respected

---

[19] Ellen Carol DuBois, *Feminism and Suffrage: The Emergence of an Independent Women's Movement in America 1848–1869* (Ithaca, NY: Cornell University Press, 1978), Elizabeth Clark, 'Religion and Rights Consciousness in the Antebellum Women's Movement', in Martha A. Fineman and Nancy S. Thomadsen (eds), *At The Boundaries of Law: Feminism and Legal Theory* (London: Routledge, 1991), pp. 188–208, p. 188 (arguing that the move toward mainstream politics represented a diminution of radicalism), and Lori Ginzberg, '"Moral Suasion is Moral Balderdash": Women, Politics, and Social Activism in the 1850s,' *Journal of American History* 73 (1986), pp. 601–622.

state supreme court ruled that combinations of workers to raise wages were legal and other courts treated the matter as settled.[20]

Although men and women generally organized separately (as they worked separately), women workers, too, began protesting collectively before the legality of unions had been settled. As with the workingmen's parties, the organizations of workers were segregated by race, mirroring the labour force. The *locus classicus* of early industrial development in the United States was Lowell, Massachusetts, a company town north of Boston in which entrepreneurs opened their first textile factory in 1823. The early industrial workforce in Lowell overwhelmingly comprised young, unmarried women. Their parents were small farmers whose households needed the cash daughters could earn in the mills more than they needed these daughters' labour (and many daughters preferred factory overseers' control to their fathers' control). These young women workers formed a factory-based culture, wrote their own newspaper, and, in 1834 and 1836, organized protests against wage cuts and increases in the pace of work. In New York City, too, women textile workers in the early ready-to-wear goods industry organized collectively and protested their treatment by their employers.[21]

In the Civil War era, the major pre-war movements continued in a context shaped by national economic expansion and a strengthened national government. The war had everything to do with race, in that its central question was the fate of slavery. It had everything to do with law, in that property law had for generations accommodated the demand of agricultural employers to treat certain people as property. The centrepiece of constitutional law was a central government that (almost everyone agreed) lacked the power either to outlaw slavery outright or to prosecute the war successfully. Some of the same energies that had produced workingmen's parties re-emerged in protests of a military draft, which President

[20] *Commonwealth v. Hunt*, 45 Mass. 111 (1842). Walter Licht, *Industrializing America: The Nineteenth Century* (Baltimore: Johns Hopkins University Press, 1995); Sean Wilentz, *Chants Democratic: New York City and the Rise of the American Working Class, 1788–1850* (New York: Oxford University Press, 1984), and Bruce Laurie, *Working People of Philadelphia, 1800–1850* (Philadelphia: Temple University Press, 1980).

[21] Thomas Dublin, *Women at Work: The Transformation of Work and Community in Lowel, Massachusetts 1826–1860* (New York: Columbia University Press, 1979); Benita Eisler (ed.), *The Lowell Offering: Writings by New England Mill Women* (Philadelphia: Lippincott, 1977), and Christine Stansell, *City of Women: Sex and Class in New York City, 1789–1860* (New York: Alfred A. Knopf, 1986), pp. 130–154.

Abraham Lincoln instituted despite misgivings about its legality because he believed it was necessary for the anti-slavery forces to win. White workers protested the draft in part because it was a heavy-handed exercise of national power and allowed wealthy people to buy exemptions from service. Many objected to being compelled to risk their lives in the cause of black freedom; their perspectives had been shaped by a labour movement discourse that referred to white workingmen as victims of 'wage slavery' who owed little to those who were literally and not metaphorically enslaved. In July 1863, working-class people in New York City responded to efforts to enforce the draft law with violence and rioting aimed at individual African Americans and whites who attempted to protect them, and at symbols or allies of President Lincoln's Republican Party. To a more limited degree, non-elite people protested conscription by the pro-slavery Confederacy. For small farmers who held few or no slaves, the Confederate cause appeared as a rich man's cause and not their own.[22]

The labour movement, the women's movement and the movement for African American civil rights all changed after the Civil War. The immediate post-war period was a time of major reimagining and change, during which the movements were close in ways they had never been before to a ruling national political coalition. Building upon wartime strikes and this reforming spirit, a new national labour federation began in 1869. Unlike other labour groups, the Knights of Labor built its success upon membership by less privileged workers, including African Americans, and, as of 1881, women.[23] It was active in the formerly anti-slavery North and the formerly pro-slavery South. Like the earlier workingmen's parties, the Knights protested existing political and economic relationships and tried to gain mainstream political power of their own. The abolitionists' aspirations were never entirely fulfilled. However, the movement claimed suc-

---

[22] Iver Bernstein, *The New York City Draft Riots: Their Significance for American Society and Politics in the Age of the Civil War* (New York, Oxford University Press, 1995); David Quigley, *Second Founding: New York City, Reconstruction, and the Making of American Democracy* (New York: Hill & Wang, 2004), pp. 3–10, and, on the South, Steven Hahn, *Roots of Southern Populism: Yeoman Farmers and the Transformation of the Georgia Upcountry, 1850–1890* (New York: Oxford University Press, 1983).

[23] David Montgomery, *Beyond Equality: Labor and the Radical Republicans, 1862–1872* (New York: Alfred A. Knopf, 1967); Leon Fink, *Workingmen's Democracy: The Knights of Labor and American Politics* (Urbana: University of Illinois Press, 1983) and Susan Levine, 'Labor's True Woman: Domesticity and Equal Rights in the Knights of Labor,' *Journal of American History* 70 (1983), pp. 323–339.

cess with the three post-war constitutional Amendments.[24] For organized women, a brief period of possibility after the war was followed by bitter disappointment. The abolitionists' Amendments wrote sex discrimination into the Constitution for the first time. Elizabeth Cady Stanton's faction of the women's movement responded by breaking decisively with her former abolitionist allies and with feminists who remained in alliance with advocates for black people's civil rights. This process initiated what one scholar calls an 'autonomous women's movement', committed to the cause of women's rights first and foremost.[25]

The period of promise was short-lived. African Americans were the victims of violence and attempts to reinstate slavery under other names. They organized community groups, voters' leagues and militia-style organizations committed to armed self-defence. Their allies, the national Republicans, reneged on many of their wartime promises, especially regarding economic redistribution and provision for formerly enslaved people. Still, however, African Americans tried to make the electoral and legal systems work for them; under Reconstruction governments, men voted and ran for office, and both women and men sought legal help in relationships with their employers (landowners), local officials and spouses. Out of the many organizations formed to subordinate the newly emancipated and enfranchised African Americans, the Ku Klux Klan is one that scholars sometimes identify as having qualities of a social movement. The first Klan organization was founded in 1865, just as the war was ending. Its members worked anonymously in groups to harass and intimidate black voters, property owners and community leaders—and to harm them and destroy their property. The constant pressure by organized whites against changes in the former Confederacy led to the final withdrawal of national military troops from the region in 1877—a signal that the national Republican Party was no longer the carrier of the ideals of the radical movement for abolition and civil rights. In this period, the 'autonomous' wing of the women's movement, unmoored from its abolitionist beginnings, pursued a 'search for allies' that included making temporary alliances with unsa-

---

[24] tenBroek, *Anti-Slavery Origins*; William Nelson, *The Fourteenth Amendment: From Political Principle to Judicial Doctrine* (Cambridge, MA: Harvard University Press, 1988), and Amy Dru Stanley, *From Bondage to Contract: Wage Labor, Marriage, and the Market in the Age of Slave Emancipation* (Cambridge: Cambridge University Press, 1998).
[25] DuBois, *Feminism and Suffrage*.

voury proponents of the continued subordination of African Americans and Chinese and Irish immigrants.

Much of the social movement activity that occurred at the turn of the twentieth century concerned the economy. Major economic recessions in the 1870s, 1890s, and repeatedly in the early twentieth century, and vast expansions in business and banking enterprises, spurred new forms of collective popular organizing. This organizing took new forms in part as a response to the legal and political settlement after the Civil War. One consequence of the new constitutional Amendments was a greater role for the national government, as against states and localities, and greater legitimacy for its interventions into the economy. The national courts grew in power; a leading legal historian describes the late-nineteenth-century Supreme Court as a 'man-eating tiger'.[26] In a terrible reverse of the abolitionists' intentions, this new power was expressly not used to protect African Americans from encroachments upon their freedom. Instead, the constitutional provisions for 'equal protection of the laws' and 'due process' for national citizens were increasingly used for the protection of business corporations against state and even federal regulation. In the notorious case *Plessy v. Ferguson* (1896), the Supreme Court made explicit what was already implicitly clear: that the national courts would not interfere with state-level efforts to write the subordination of African Americans into statute.[27]

Farmers, who suffered from widely varying prices for their goods and from their dependence on increasingly monopolistic or oligopolistic railroad corporations, created some of the most significant social movements of the turn of the twentieth century. As Populists and members of the Grange, they tried to regulate railroad rates, help farmers escape cycles of debt and gain control over commodity prices. This was the first nationally significant agrarian organizing to occur since Shay's Rebellion shaped the country's founding. Populists, in particular, fostered a wide-ranging anti-elitist political and social agenda. The highly decentralized movement included virulent racists and anti-Semites. It also inspired activism by

---

[26] Lawrence Friedman, *A History of American Law* (New York: Simon and Schuster, 1973), p. 302.

[27] Friedman, *American Law*, pp. 299–300. On the period generally, economic change and conflict, see Nell Irvin Painter, *Standing at Armageddon: The United States 1877–1919* (New York and London: W.W. Norton, 1987) and Alan Dawley, *Struggles for Justice: Social Responsibility and the Liberal State* (Cambridge, MA: Harvard University Press, 1991).

farmers who included African Americans in their organizing, and blamed bankers and railroad magnates, not Jews, for their troubles.[28]

The women's movement built new organizations at the turn of the twentieth century that reflected the new, national structures of politics, law and economy. After years of division and false starts after their alliance with African American civil rights activists dissolved, the white-led women's movement organized anew in the 1890s. Its leaders eventually chose as their overarching goal the reversal of the legal sexism that had been created after the Civil War by means of a new constitutional Amendment expressly granting women the right to vote in national elections. Elizabeth Cady Stanton and her colleagues joined with their former antagonists (those who had remained in alliance with black civil rights activists) to form the National American Woman Suffrage Association in 1890. Activists in the new association embarked upon aggressive attempts to gain members and build local chapters. In the absence of progress at the national level, they pushed to grant women the vote in local and state-level elections, and built an impressive record of success; by the time the US Congress passed a law in favour of women's suffrage, 15 states had already granted women the elective franchise. By arguing, as the great organizer Susan B. Anthony did, that access to the ballot represented access to better wages and working conditions, they persuaded thousands of working-class women and trade unionists to support their cause.[29]

African American women organized for suffrage, sometimes in alliance

[28] Interpretations of Populism track the political development of social movement historiography. For a highly critical view from post-Second World War consensus politics, see Richard Hofstadter, *The Age of Reform: From Bryan to F.D.R.* (New York: Alfred A., Knopf, 1955) and discussion in Robert Collins, 'The Originality Trap: Richard Hofstadter on Populism', *Journal of American History* 1 (1989), pp. 150–167. Sympathetic views from the left and New Left (or 'new social movement' synthesis) are C. Vann Woodward, *Tom Watson, Agrarian Rebel* (New York: Macmillan, 1938) and Lawrence Goodwyn, *The Populist Moment: A Short History of the Agrarian Revolt in America* (New York: Oxford University Press, 1978). The renaissance of critique in recent on the basis of race and gender appears in Stephen Kantrowitz, *Ben Tillman and the Reconstruction of White Supremacy* (Chapel Hill: University of North Carolina *Press*, 2000).

[29] Nancy Cott, *The Grounding of Modern Feminism* (New Haven, CT: Yale University Press, 1989); Ellen Carol DuBois, 'Working Women, Class Relations, and Suffrage Militance: Harriot Stanton Blatch and the New York Woman Suffrage Movement, 1894–1909', *Journal of American History* 1 (1987), pp. 34–58; Meredith Tax, *The Rising of the Women: Feminist Solidarity and Class Conflict, 1880–1917* (New York: Monthly Review Press, 1980), and Annelise Orleck, *Common Sense and a Little Fire: Women and Working-Class Politics in the United States, 1900–1965* (Chapel Hill: University of North Carolina Press, 1995).

with whites and sometimes separately. The writer, activist and political organizer, Ida B. Wells-Barnett, started her career fighting the epidemic of violence against African Americans in the South. By the early twentieth century, she had relocated to Chicago and was leading a political organization rooted in the African American community that had women's enfranchisement as one of its cornerstone demands.

The movement for African American civil and political rights, too, emerged in new forms and ultimately at new strength at the turn of the twentieth century. Ida Wells-Barnett's attempt to fight lynching in the South with her journalism helped inspire an anti-lynching movement. Like the violent practice itself, this movement peaked in the 1890s. African American women merged local self-advocacy organizations into a National Association of Colored Women (NACW) in 1896. The writer Paula Giddings has argued, persuasively, that the modern African American movement began with organizing among black women to curb extra-legal violence by whites.[30] Limited and halting coalitions between African American and white women also fought against lynching.

In the late nineteenth century, the most prominent African American male intellectual leader was the educator Booker T. Washington, who publicly renounced the fight against 'social equality' between the races (code for interracial romance and a general term for quotidian forms of integration). Washington accepted legal segregation and democratic disfranchisement, and advocated industrial education and employment for black Americans. It may not be accurate to think of him as the head of a social movement, but he was certainly popular among poor and working-class African Americans, and with white philanthropists and politicians. An interracial coalition of intellectuals who opposed Washington's message formed the movement organizations that ultimately carried the civil rights struggle in the twentieth century. The sociologist and writer W.E.B. DuBois, the key intellectual opponent of Washington's approach, joined with other highly educated, reform-minded whites and African Americans in the Niagara Movement. In 1909, they created the National Association for the Advancement of Colored People (NAACP), an

---

[30] Paula Giddings, *Ida: A Sword Among Lions—Ida B. Wells and the Campaign Against Lynching* (New York: Amistad/Harper Collins, 2008). See also Patricia Schechter, *Ida B. Wells and American Reform, 1880–1930* (Chapel Hill: University of North Carolina Press, 2001) and Mia Bay, *To Tell the Truth Freely: The Life of Ida B. Wells* (New York: Hill & Wang, 2009).

advocacy and membership organization dedicated to undoing legalized forms of segregation and subordination that were imposed upon African Americans.[31]

The arc of development of the male-led labour movement resembled that of the male wing of the African American movement. Labour, too, experienced a period of growth under conservative leadership at the end of the nineteenth century and then a burst of more radical organizing early in the twentieth century. The Knights of Labor declined at the end of the nineteenth century, and the labour movement came to be led by the American Federation of Labor (AFL) under the presidency of the Jewish cigar maker Samuel Gompers. The AFL eschewed left ideology and battles for control of the state. Unlike the Knights of Labor, its strength lay in unions of workers like Gompers, men in craft industries who were in relatively strong bargaining positions with employers. Gompers had tried in the 1880s to reform New York State law to forbid cigar manufacture in homes, thus giving members of his union an advantage over immigrant and female workers who might prefer home-based work. The state appeals court invalidated the legislation on the basis of the due process language in the state and federal constitutions (at the federal level, again, language that had been added as a result of abolitionist agitation). The judges claimed that neither workers nor property owners could be deprived of the enjoyment of their property (i.e., labour power, residential real estate, cigar company profits) without due process of law—in effect, that the relationship between capital and labour could not be regulated to this degree. Gompers and other AFL leaders learned from this experience, and from similar actions by the courts on questions of labour regulation. Unlike many of their counterparts in Europe, at the height of their strength Gompers and his brethren eschewed legislative campaigns and attempts to form political parties that would pursue labour's agenda. Instead, they favoured making material gains for skilled workers through collective bargaining, seeking economic gains for working people and at the same time, strengthening their ties to their AFL unions.[32]

---

[31] Louis Harlan, *Booker T. Washington; The Making of a Black Leader, 1856–1901* (New York: Oxford University Press, 1972) and Louis Harlan, *Booker T. Washington: The Wizard of Tuskegee* (New York: Oxford University Press, 1986); David Levering Lewis, *W.E.B. DuBois: Biography of a Race, 1868–1919* (New York: Owl Books, 1994) and Tushnet, *NAACP's Legal Strategy.*

[32] William Forbath, *Law and the Shaping of the American Labor Movement* (Cambridge, MA: Harvard University Press, 1991); Samuel Gompers, *Seventy Years of Life and Labor: An*

One disturbing exception to this general trend of avoiding legislative entanglements was the collective campaign by AFL unions to exclude Chinese citizens from California and, ultimately, from entrance into the United States. Although immigration restrictions were feeble answers to the economic uncertainty of the period, organized labour and sectors of white working-class public opinion won a national Chinese Exclusion Act in 1882. After repeated efforts at amending US immigration law, they succeeded in 1924 at provoking passage of a national law that forbade immigration by all Asians.[33]

The period just prior to and following the First World War was a time of significant radicalism and reform in the United States. The void at the social democratic centre of US politics, which was due in part to the role of the courts in stopping labour reforms, created opportunities for socialists, anarchists, communists (after 1917) and militant labour organizers as well as for 'bread and butter' trade unionists like Gompers. The Socialist Party enjoyed considerable success in urban immigrant neighbourhoods and limited success among native-born organized workers. The railway worker and union leader Eugene V. Debs ran afoul of the anti-labour courts in 1894 for coordinating a national strike in support of the employees of the Pullman Corporation, maker of luxury railroad cars. When he was released from prison, Debs declared himself a socialist and ran for President of the United States four times, beginning in 1900. In 1912, he polled one million votes, approximately 6% of the total. Debs was a cofounder of the Industrial Workers of the World (IWW), an international federation of industrial, as opposed to craft, labour organizations. The IWW and its member organizations welcomed black as well as white workers, women as well as men, the well-paid and 'skilled' as well as those whose skills were undervalued or considered easily replaceable. Although there was an historic wave of strikes immediately following the First World War, there was also a wave of repression by the government, which included jailings and expulsions from the country of left and labour leaders. This helped to destroy any popular support enjoyed by the socialists or the IWW, and to

Autobiography (New York: E.P. Dutton, 1925), and, for the critical New Left and 'new social movement' view, Paul Buhle, *Taking Care of Business: Samuel Gompers, George Meany, Lane Kirkland, and the Tragedy of American Labor* (New York: Monthly Review Press, 1999).

[33] Gwendolyn Mink, *Old Labor and New Immigrants in American Political Development: Union, Party, and State, 1875–1920* (Ithaca, NY: Cornell University Press, 1986) and Mae Ngai, *Impossible Subjects: Illegal Aliens and the Making of Modern America* (Princeton, NJ: Princeton University Press, 2004), Chapter One.

limit the number who would admit to admiring the achievements of the Soviet Revolution.[34]

Women's movements were more successful than the left wing of the labour movement at sustaining their momentum after the First World War. Some of the more long-lasting campaigns grew out of the left, but went their own way when the mainstream of US politics became so much more conservative in the 1920s. One example of this is the campaign for legal birth control that was inspired initially by the anarchist Emma Goldman and led for decades thereafter by Margaret Sanger. Sanger started advocating in the socialist press early in the twentieth century for increased sexual freedom and access to mechanical means of birth control. Her cause became a social movement in 1914–1915, when she was indicted for publishing birth control information and sending it through the federal mails. The nationwide tour on which she embarked after the government decided not to prosecute her made Sanger a celebrity and drew people into the birth control cause—a cause that separated itself increasingly from its left origins especially in the 1920s. The campaign for suffrage reached a crescendo of militancy just prior to 1917, when the United States entered the war. Scholars disagree about whether it was the retreat of a portion of the movement from militancy—and toward traditional, nationalistic support activities on behalf of troops in the field—or the continued protests of another portion of the movement that deserves greater credit for the ultimate passage of the woman suffrage Amendment to the Constitution. After women began voting in national elections, in 1920, the movement did lose momentum and change focus. Those who had not abandoned direct-action tactics or supported the war either moved left toward the Communist Party or directed their energies toward the transnational peace movement, for example, in creating the Women's International League for Peace and Freedom. Those who had moved closer to mainstream politics helped found the League of Women Voters and attempted to shape a women's voting bloc. They became active in the major political parties, choosing the Republican Party initially as their most natural allies. A small group attempted to sustain a National Woman's Party (NWP) with a

[34] Nick Salvatore, *Eugene V. Debs: Citizen and Socialist*, 2nd edn (Urbana: University of Illinois Press, 2007); Nick Salvatore et al., *The Pullman Strike and the Crisis of the 1890s: Essays on Labor and Politics* (Urbana: University of Illinois Press, 1999), and Michael Kazin, *American Dreamers: How the Left Changed a Nation* (New York: Alfred A. Knopf, 2011) Chapter Four, 'A Tale of Three Socialisms'.

combination of direct-action and legislative tactics. NWP members advocated total equality of treatment between women and men. They were the first to use the term 'feminist', and their leader, Alice Paul, drafted an Equal Rights Amendment to the Constitution, which had its first hearing in Congress in 1923.[35]

The high point of both trade-union strength and social-democratic reformism occurred in the period between the beginning of the Depression in the late 1920s and the 1940s. In this reawakening of the activist energies that had been quieted by post-war repression, explicitly left parties and movements were more visible than they had been, and the 'autonomous' movements for women's and African American rights were less visible. However, race and law continued to play determinative roles in the history of social movement success and failure. The activism of Communist Party members in response to the Depression ranged from mass (successful) efforts to keep people who had missed rent or mortgage payments from being put out of their homes, to organizing among groups the AFL did not touch, such as Mexican American cannery workers in California and African American farmers and factory workers in the Deep South. This activism earned the Communist Party new adherents and drove labour and the mainstream political parties to the left. Communists participated in a new wave of workplace militancy, characterized by unauthorized, 'wildcat', strikes and the formation in the mid-1930s of the Congress of Industrial Organizations, a rival labour federation to the AFL.

Fear of movements on the left and right led the Democratic Party to an open confrontation with the federal courts. These elite judges continued to interpret the Fourteenth Amendment as a bar to the regulation of workers' well-being. Democrats, and the left activists who supported them in a 'popular front' coalition, endorsed a variety of measures that regulated markets and ensured a modicum of economic security to ordinary people. They dared the courts to declare these measures illegal, and they won the dare. By the end of the 1930s, new government programmes had been created to build affordable housing, help families purchase homes, support prices for major agricultural commodities, sustain workers in times of unemployment and after retirement and supplement the incomes of

---

[35] Cott, *The Grounding*; Ellen Chesler, *Woman of Valor: Margaret Sanger and the Birth Control Movement in America* (New York: Simon & Schuster, 1992), and, for a more critical view, Linda Gordon, *Woman's Body, Woman's Right: A Social History of Birth Control in America* (New York: Grossman, 1976).

impoverished old and blind people and women raising children without male economic support. African Americans supported these governmental benefits, which were available at least in theory to all citizens who qualified, and participated in inter-racial party and movement politics where they were not forbidden from doing so. Many voted for the first time in elections that were organized under the Farm Security Administration, the smaller and more radical of two national agencies dedicated to agriculture. The United States Supreme Court ceased illegitimizing the victories of social movements.[36]

After a spurt of radical, popular front-style activism in the late 1940s, anti-communist and anti-welfare state politics crested to their highest point yet. The two national labour federations increasingly resembled one another. They joined to create the AFL-CIO in 1955. The federation's member unions remained fairly strong in terms of their numbers and the degree to which mainstream politicians included their representatives in deliberations. But they largely lost their social movement qualities; they purged communist members, consolidated and engrossed their organizations, elected leaders who were nearly immune from democratic challenges, and devoted too few of their resources to organize industries and people who were not yet in the labour movement. The AFL-CIO revivified Gompers' disinterest in legislative solutions to working-class economic needs (although without Gompers's legalistic justification), favouring instead privately negotiated 'fringe' benefits such as pensions and health insurance. The lack of labour support was devastating to efforts of other movement activists to create universal, public alternatives to these limited private benefits. In the face of ceaseless persecution and negative propaganda, the self-described left shrank to the point of near irrelevance.[37]

---

[36] William E. Leuchtenberg, *F.D.R. and the New Deal, 1932–1940* (New York: Harper and Row, 1963), Linda Gordon, *Pitied but Not Entitled: Single Mothers and the History of Welfare* (New York: Free Press, 1994), and William Chafe (ed.), *The Achievement of American Liberalism: The New Deal and its Legacies* (New York: Columbia University Press, 2003).

[37] One way historians have charted these changes is through the biographies of major laboUr leaders whose careers spanned the period of transition from outsider militancy to bureaucratization. See Nelson Lichtenstein, *The Most Dangerous Man in Detroit: Walter Reuther and the Fate of American Labor* (New York: Basic Books, 1995) and Steve Fraser, *Labor Will Rule: Sidney Hillman and the Rise of American Labor* (New York: Free Press, 1991). On labour's engagement with the welfare state, see Jennifer Klein, *For All These Rights: Business, Labor and the Shaping of America's Public-Private Welfare State* (Princeton, NJ: Princeton University Press, 2003) and Nelson Lichtenstein, *Labor's War at Home: The CIO in World War Two* (New York: Cambridge University Press, 1982).

The combined force of the domestic Cold War and missteps by labour and the left diminished the degree to which 'new' social movements in the 1950s through 1990s were able to pursue the multi-part agenda outlined by Martin Luther King, Jr., and Jacobus tenBroek. However, popular movements other than those explicitly identified with labour and the ideological left were strong in tactics, numbers, and the breadth of their demands. Race and law continued to be determining factors in their development. Through protest tactics and legal reformism, the movements found it easier to gain public respect for what Sir Isaiah Berlin termed 'negative', freedom-from-interference rights than their 'positive', freedom-to-act or economic rights.[38] But they had successes with both, even at height of the deepest anti-left animus in mainstream politics. In the African American movement, protesters and attorneys won a court ruling that property deeds forbidding purchase by people of colour were unconstitutional and therefore unenforceable; after decades of activism and litigation, they won *Brown v. Board of Education*, a landmark Supreme Court ruling against segregated education. These were in themselves victories for positive rights. However, when movement members demanded the financial resources that would allow African Americans to buy homes in middle-class suburbs and therefore attend the best schools, they usually lost.[39] Activist efforts to equalize spending on public schools in wealthy and poor districts have had a spotty record of success and failure over the past half-century. The civil rights movement by and for blind people, which tenBroek led, helped implement public pension programmes

[38] Robert Self utilizes this distinction extensively in his synthetic work on sex and gender in post-1960 America. I agree about the outcome of many of the political conflicts of the period but differ markedly with him on both his assessment of the social movements of the period and the causes of the difficulty they faced in implementing a more extensive programme of 'positive rights'. I do not think there was anything inevitable about US political culture, even in this period, that produced stronger negative than positive rights; rather, I see a record of claims for positive rights, some success, and failures that were the result of contingency and discrete exercises of power. Robert O. Self, *All in the Family: The Realignment of American Democracy Since the 1960s* (New York: Hill & Wang, 2012) and Felicia Kornbluh, 'Divided We Stand,' *Women's Review of Books* 30 (2013), 10–12.

[39] For the more positive view of their achievements, see Tushnet, *NAACP's Legal Strategy*, Tushnet, *Making Civil Rights Law*, and Richard Kluger, *Simple Justice: The History of Brown v. Board of Education and Black America's Struggle for Equality* (New York: Vintage, 1975). For critical views, see Herbert Hill, *Black Labor and the American Legal System* (Washington, DC: Bureau of National Affairs, 1977) and Risa Goluboff, *The Lost Promise of Civil Rights* (Cambridge, MA: Harvard University Press, 2009).

for indigent blind adults in the 1940s and succeeded at expanding these programmes during the Cold War. Advocates and activists spurred creation in the 1950s of additional public aid and insurance programmes for all disabled people—on a two-track system of indigent relief for those outside the labour force and disability insurance for those who became disabled while employed. The militant disability rights movement of the 1970s demanded independence and access, both of which had 'negative' and 'positive' dimensions. Although they scored successes in both arenas, they were more successful in eliminating overt barriers to education and employment than in gaining adequate subsidies with which to hire personal assistants or pay for all of the costs disabled students faced when they pursued higher education.[40]

A similarly complex pattern prevailed in the history of other post-Second World War movements. The early 'homophile' activism of the LGBT movement demanded health and pension benefits for lesbian and gay war veterans, and non-discriminatory access to public employment. In the early years of this effort, they had little success—although the battles themselves helped build membership in activist groups and the stigma placed upon gay veterans played a back-handed role in creating gay communities. The most explicit bars to public employment were defeated beginning in the middle 1960s and 1970s. The bar against service in the US military—a great distributor of positive benefits—was removed only in 2011. In the 1980s, members of the AIDS Coalition to Unleash Power (ACT-UP) responded to the epidemic by demanding accessible and affordable treatments from the state and from private pharmaceutical firms. A minority of activists also demanded a universal national health programme that would serve HIV-positive and -negative people alike. The movement changed the public system of drug trials, improved access to treatment, and pushed successfully for a new government assistance programme for people who were HIV-positive and poor. They did not

---

[40] Felicia Kornbluh, 'Disability, Anti-Professionalism, and Civil Rights'; Edward Berkowitz, *Disabled Policy: America's Programs for the Handicapped* (Cambridge: Cambridge University Press, 1987); Richard Scotch, *From Good Will to Civil Rights: Transforming Federal Disability Policy* (Philadelphia: Temple University Press, 1984), and Scotch and Sharon Barnett (eds), *Disability Protests: Contentious Politics, 1970–1999* (Washington, DC: Gallaudet University Press, 2001).

succeed in their most expansive positive-right or material, demands, e.g., in the battle over healthcare.[41]

The so-called 'liberal' wing of the women's movement demanded non-discriminatory access to apprenticeships, jobs and higher education. Its members argued for legal abortion as a need for low-income women, and as a support to all women's ability to plan and execute their educational and career plans. They joined with 'radical' feminists in a campaign for a new national programme of child care, which came close to fruition in the early 1970s.[42] They won dramatically expanded access to jobs and educational opportunities, which widened women's economic options and changed relations between women and men forever. They also won legal abortion. However, by the end of the 1970s, legal abortion was no longer covered by the major public medical programme for people of child-bearing age or some private insurance programmes. While a short period of 'family leave' was ensured by national law for women or men with new-born children or other care-taking responsibilities, hopes for a more meaningful parental leave policy or publicly funded child care were dim.

At the end of the twentieth and beginning of the twenty-first century, it became ever-harder for movements to fulfil the material dimensions of their

---

[41] John D'Emilio, *Sexual Politics, Sexual Communities: The Making of a Homosexual Minority in the United States, 1940–1970* (Chicago: University of Chicago Press, 1988), Allan Berube, *Coming Out Under Fire: The History of Gay Men and Women in World War Two* (New York: Free Press, 1990); Daniel Hurewitz, *Bohemian Los Angeles and the Making of Modern Politics* (Berkeley: University of California Press, 2007); Jennifer Brier, *Infectious Ideas: U.S. Political Responses to the AIDS Crisis* (Chapel Hill: University of North Carolina Press, 2009); David France, Director, 'How to Survive a Plague', Public Square Films/Ninety Thousand Words, 2012, and Sarah Schulman and Jim Hubbard, producers, 'United in Anger A History of ACT UP', 2012.

[42] In terms of abortion, my understanding of the reform campaign is informed by the memories of my parents, David Kornbluh and Beatrice K. Braun, who participated actively in it in New York State. See also Rickie Solinger, *Beggars and Choosers: How the Politics of Choice Shapes Adoption, Abortion, and Welfare in the United States* (New York: Hill & Wang, 2002); Ruth Rosen, *The World Split Open: How the Modern Women's Movement Changed America* (New York: Viking, 2000); Flora Davis, *Moving the Mountain: The Women's Movement in America Since 1960* (New York: Simon and Schuster, 1990); Sonya Michel, *Children's Interests/Mothers' Rights: The Shaping of America's Child Care Policy* (New Haven, CT: Yale University Press, 1999); Deborah Dinner, 'The Universal Child Care Debate: Rights Mobilization, Social Policy and the Dynamics of Feminist Activism, 1966–1974', *Law and History Review* 3 (2010), pp. 577–628, and discussions of these issues in Self, *All in the Family*.

agendas.[43] Race and law continued to shape the movements in distinctive ways. However, the paucity of cultural or political space for articulating economic demands did not keep movements from making them. Although the African American movement generally was fairly weak, a rejuvenated movement for welfare rights, which had been strong between the early 1960s and early 1970s, arose again in the 1990s to speak for poor people and people of colour. This was not a racially specific movement, but its aim was to counter stereotypes about social welfare that were bound to old racist, sexist and elitist assumptions—and to allow recipients of the most stigmatized forms of public aid to participate in public debate. The movement fought the draconian 'welfare reform' proposals of the middle 1990s and led a major street protest at the Republican National Convention of 2000.[44] The number of private-sector workers in labour unions dropped to an almost negligibly small number. Still, a new generation of activists sustained the movement spirit of labour. They spurred organizing campaigns in service industries that had often received short shrift from labour in the past, and which had disproportionately female, immigrant and low-wage workforces. Large national unions remained active in legislative efforts to raise minimum wages and expand social benefits for working families.[45] The disability movement scored one of the period's great victories, the Americans with Disabilities Act of 1990 (ADA), which promised greater equality at work and in education, as well as more complete access to public space, greater mobility, and therefore increased political participation. The ADA was the result of the movement's continued protests, litigation and lobbying through the 1970s and 1980s.[46]

[43] For one treatment of the reasons and ramifications for this, see Daniel T. Rodgers, *The Age of Fracture* (Cambridge, MA: Harvard University Press, 2011).

[44] Kornbluh, *Battle for Welfare Rights*; Annelise Orleck, *Storming Ceasar's Palace: How Black Mothers Fought Their Own War on Poverty* (Boston: Beacon Press, 2006), and David Zucchino, *Myth of the Welfare Queen* (New York: Touchstone, 1997).

[45] Nelson Lichtenstein, *State of the Union. A Century of American Labor*, 2nd edn (Princeton, NJ: Princeton University Press, 2013), Leon Fink and Brian Greenberg, *Upheaval in the Quiet Zone: 1199SEIU and the Politics of Health Care Unionism*, 2nd edn (Urbana: University of Illinois Press, 2009); Jennifer Klein and Eileen Boris, *Caring for America: Home Health Workers in the Shadow of the Welfare State* (New York: Oxford University Press, 2012), and, for a very critical view of recent developments, Steve Early, *The Civil Wars in U.S. Labor* (Chicago: Haymarket, 2011).

[46] Silvers and Frances, *Americans with Disabilities*; Joseph Shapiro, *No Pity: People with Disabilities Forging a New Civil Rights Movement* (New York: Times Books, 1994), and Bagenstos, *Law and the Contradictions*.

The straight-identified, majority-white and able-bodied women's movement was in abeyance from the 1980s onward. However, many feminists joined a new 'reproductive justice' movement, which wrote material concerns and racial sensitivity into advocacy for legal abortion. This movement had enjoyed a heyday in the late 1970s and 1980s, when it critiqued reproductive policy for denying women the right to raise children via welfare benefits and an end to coercive sterilization policies. Reproductive justice had a renaissance in the late 2000s and 2010s.[47]

In terms of an explicit focus upon economic (and political) structure, one of the most dramatic new developments was the emergence of a mass anti-globalization movement in the United States and internationally. In addition to its focus upon NAFTA and similar multi-state trade agreements, this movement addressed itself to the workings of global institutions such as the World Bank. It was a massive and often militant global effort to change the political conversation and redirect resources in the wake of the Cold War. US-based activists worked in parallel and sometimes in concert with counterparts in the labour and indigenous movements elsewhere in North America and around the world. However, they were not able to make major changes in either global trade policies or the workings of the global financial institutions.[48] In addition, the so-called war on terror that began in 2011, a war without a discrete enemy and avowedly without end, nearly drove to the margins all discussions about reinvesting public resources from the military and the national security surveillance apparatus.[49]

The history of social movements in North America is a complex and multi-faceted one. It is, first of all, not one hemispheric history but several histories, interpretation of which is the responsibility of separate groups of historians with diverse interests and emphases. In the United States,

---

[47] Solinger, *Beggars and Choosers*; Marlene Gerber Fried (ed.), *From Abortion Rights to Reproductive Justice: Transforming a Movement* (Boston: South End, 1990); Jael Silliman, Marlene G. Fried, Loretta Ross and Elena Gutierrez, *Undivided Rights: Women of Color Organize for Reproductive Justice* (Cambridge, MA: South End Press, 2004); Andrea Smith, 'Beyond Pro-Choice or Pro-Life', *NWSA Journal* 17 (2005), pp. 119–140, Alison Kafer, *Feminist, Queer, Crip* (Bloomington: University of Indiana Press, 2013).

[48] Harvey, *Chiapas*; Kay, *NAFTA*; Armbruster-Sandoval, *Globalization*, and Faux, 'NAFTA at 10'.

[49] For efforts to theorize politics in these political economic moments, see Michael Hardt and Antonio Negri, *Empire* (Cambridge, MA: Harvard University Press, 2000) and Michael Hardt and Antonio Negri, *Multitude: War and Democracy in the Age of Empire* (London: Penguin, 2004).

the language of 'social movement' was not widely used until after the Second World War. Even then, it referred explicitly to movements that emerged after the war, in tension with both the mainstream labour movement and left parties. Putting definitional matters aside, and focussing upon the United States, it is possible to understand social change from 1776 to the twenty-first century as the product of social movement-like forces—with the caveat that law in courts and legislatures and racial subordination played more significant roles in this history than they did in other parts of the world. Although overall there may have been as much militancy in these movements as there was elsewhere, those in the United States faced more severe challenges than movements in Europe, Canada or Australia did at translating their militancy into substantive, economically significant gains. The understanding of these movements has changed since the first generations of writing about the black, women's, anti-war and student movements. Historians have brought attention to conservative and even violently racist movements that challenge the customary evaluation of social movements, and left parties that were closer to the 'new' movements than many activists were comfortable in admitting during the Cold War era. This history now encompasses more of the quotidian political work that translated movement energy into state policy, and it illuminates the points of overlap and collaboration between and among movements. It has a subtler appreciation for the strengths and limitations of movement efforts to progress on the 'positive-rights' side of the ledger, and for the forces arrayed against such efforts. Altogether, an increasingly careful, subtle and line-crossing picture of the past can only help scholars, advocates and activists understand how social change has happened and how it might happen today.

Further Readings

The literature on social movements in North American history is vast. I will focus here on US history and the twentieth century.

The first issues in this literature concern the very definition of a social movement—as opposed to a political party, or movement committed to armed struggle, or some other formation—and the distinction between 'new' and 'old' movements. Dieter Rucht argues that one characteristic of a new social movement is its middle-class character, but I am not sure this holds for the most paradigmatic US movement groups. The class dimensions of African American struggle and of white reprisals have not received enough consideration. But they have appeared persistently in the literature, starting with the fascinating combination of first-person reflections and scholarly analysis in radical historian Howard Zinn's, *SNCC: The New Abolitionists* (Boston: Beacon, 1965). Civil rights historian Charles Payne added depth to Zinn's account with *I've Got the Light of Freedom: The Organizing Tradition and the Mississippi Freedom Struggle* (2nd edition, Berkeley: University of California, 2007), which opens with a breathtaking litany of economic and violent reprisals visited upon southern African Americans. I considered these issues, vis-à-vis public benefits to alleviate hunger and how they were manipulated by southern whites, in the essay, 'Food as a Civil Right: Hunger, Work, and Welfare in the South after the Civil Rights Act', in the journal *Labor* 1–2 (2015), pp. 135–158. I do not know of good secondary literature on the class dimensions of women's status, but a key primary document that questions whether even white women married to middle-class men can themselves be considered 'middle class' is Zillah Eisenstein (ed.), *Capitalist Patriarchy and the Case for Socialist Feminism* (New York: Monthly Review, 1979).

In the United States, the language of 'social movement' was rarely used prior to the late 1960s or to refer to labour organizations or reform within political parties. However, 'New Left' historians who identified with the movements of their era came to interpret earlier movements in social movement terms and wrote about them thus in the scholarship published in the late 1970s, 1980s and 1990s. One of the most significant works in this vein is Lawrence Goodwyn, *The Populist Moment: A Short History of the Agrarian Revolt in America* (Oxford: Oxford University Press, 1978), a book that has inspired generations of budding activists who studied US history at the college level—despite the existence of powerful alternative interpretations of populism as a dangerous movement (Richard Hofstadter, *The Age of Reform: From Bryan to F.D.R.* (New York: Knopf, 1955)), or, more recently, a fundamentally racist one (Stephen Kantrowitz, *Ben Tillman and the Reconstruction of White Supremacy* (Chapel Hill: University of North Carolina Press, 2000)).

One of the distinctive features of social movement history in the United States is the place of formal law as a factor enabling, disabling, constraining and otherwise shaping virtually every aspect of activist effort. Particularly in the middle-to-late twentieth century, the most elite legal forums were seen as places where poor and marginalized people could receive succour and support—although these same legal arenas were the centres of anti-labour and anti-civil rights action in the nineteenth and

early twentieth centuries. The positive case for law (in the form of stories of legal victories that were also significant social movement victories)
appears in Mark Tushnet, *The NAACP's Legal Strategy Against Segregated
Education, 1925–1950* (Chapel Hill: University of North Carolina Press,
1987) and eadem, *Making Civil Rights Law: Thurgood Marshall and the
Supreme Court, 1936–1961* (New York: Oxford University Press, 1994).
Concerning the women's movement(s), more measured interpretations,
which nonetheless centre the formal, legal dimensions of social movement struggle, appear in Linda Kerber's award-winning volume, *No
Constitutional Right to be Ladies: Women and the Obligations of Citizenship*
(New York: Hill & Wang, 1998) and law professor Serena Mayeri's excellent study, *Reasoning from Race: Law and the Civil Rights Revolution*
(Cambridge, MA: Harvard University Press, 2011)—as well as in the classic from the 'new social movement' era, Ellen Carol DuBois, *Feminism
and Suffrage: The Emergence of an Independent Women's Movement
in America 1848–1869* (Ithaca, NY: Cornell University Press, 1978).
Multiple interpretations of law (in this case, statutory law, the Americans
with Disabilities Act of 1990, or ADA) appear in Anita Silvers and Leslie
Frances (eds), *Americans with Disabilities Exploring the Implications of
the Law for Individuals and Institutions* (New York: Routledge, 2000),
and Samuel Bagenstos, *Law and the Contradictions of the Disability Rights
Movement* (New Haven, CT: Yale University Press, 2009), which illuminates weaknesses of the ADA and holds the disability movement itself
responsible for generating these. The scholarship on the LGBTQA movement has generally focused less on courtroom or statutory law than have
the literatures of other movements, but significant works have recently
pursued what historian Marc Stein has called 'queer legal history' and
meditated deeply upon the effects of law upon the queer movement and
vice versa. Readers may be interested in Stein's own work, *Sexual Injustice:
Supreme Court Decisions from Griswold to Roe* (Chapel Hill: University of
North Carolina Press, 2010), as well as Margot Canaday's *The Straight
State: Sexuality and Citizenship in Twentieth-Century America* (Princeton,
NJ: Princeton University Press, 2010) and my review essay, 'Queer Legal
History: A Field Grows Up and Comes Out', *Law and Social Inquiry* 2
(Spring, 2011), pp. 537–559.

CHAPTER 7

European Social Protest, 1000–2000

Marcel van der Linden

Introduction

There is no doubt that without uprisings, social movements and everyday forms of collective resistance, today's Europe would look quite different. In no small measure, guild battles, peasant wars and revolutions have helped shape our present. Despite this, historians have for many years shown little interest, or no interest at all, in the protests of the lower classes. Instead, 'riots' were seen as highly emotionally charged eruptions of confused masses, layers that historical research was unable to analyse. Only in the course of the twentieth century, and particularly since the 1960s, has this changed somewhat. Frequently, because historians had now often taken part in protests and social movements themselves, they could concretely see how forms of resistance could develop and what conditions gave them a chance of success. A new perspective was thus formed, outlined internationally in the concepts of opportunity structure, resources and framing. *Opportunity structure* describes the framework within which protests are articulated (the level of state repression, the independence of the mass media, etc.). The concept of *resources* emphasizes that protesters need means to mobilize people, such as, for example, social relationships,

M. van der Linden (✉)
International Institute of Social History, Amsterdam, Netherlands

© The Author(s) 2017
S. Berger, H. Nehring (eds.), *The History of Social Movements in Global Perspective*, DOI 10.1057/978-1-137-30427-8_7

forms of wider communication, places where they can meet and persuasive speakers. *Framing* highlights how protesters articulate their resistance through particular meaning and belief systems, which they themselves often remodify. Taken together, these three concepts make clear that protests always develop in particular political contexts independent of them; that they need a more or less explicit legitimating ideology, and that they need social and material resources for the protest to be effectively articulated. It goes without saying that all three elements undergo constant change. Repression, mass media, belief systems and the required resources vary from region to region and from period to period.[1]

In the history of Europe, three processes in particular caused long-term changes in protest behaviour: the growth of states, capitalism, and the city.[2] The process of state formation got under way slowly during the Middle Ages, but gathered pace from the middle of the millennium and was completed around 1900—although shifts have also occurred repeatedly since then. Down to the eighteenth century, European states were either very small (port cities with hinterlands) or composed of relatively independent regional segments. Down to the eighteenth and nineteenth centuries, kings and emperors were dependent on the support of local representatives for collecting taxes, recruiting soldiers and so on. The unity of the larger states was therefore very weak, something that was apparent in their wide linguistic, cultural and legal heterogeneity. However, these states gradually expanded. Circa 1500, Europe was home to roughly 500 independent political entities with an average area of 6,115 square kilometres and an average population of 124,000 people. Four hundred years later only thirty states remained, with an average area of 101,389 square kilometres and an average population of 7.7 million. This growth went hand in hand with an internal structural change. Monarchs gradually succeeded in depriving the local rulers of their power, in establishing unified tax and legal systems, state monopolies on the use of force and other measures of this sort.

At the same time there was yet another important development. At the beginning of the period under consideration, the European economy was

---

[1] See e.g., Sidney Tarrow, *Power in Movement: Social Movements and Contentious Politics*, 2nd edn (Cambridge: Cambridge University Press, 1998).

[2] I'm basing myself here on the writings of Charles Tilly. For a critical evaluation see my 'Charles Tilly's Historical Sociology', *International Review of Social History* 2 (2009), pp. 237–274.

predominantly agrarian, with handicraft adjuncts. Production was geared towards subsistence, and perhaps towards local markets, although there have always been subordinate forms of long-distance trade as well. From the fourteenth century onwards, the influence of commodity production, handicraft and trade increased significantly, a development driven further forward by the 'discovery' of America and the circumnavigation of Africa. Putting-out systems penetrated large parts of the rural areas and prepared the 'Industrial Revolution' of the late eighteenth century, with its factories and masses of workers.

State formation and emerging capitalism combined, leading to a third major trend: the growing number, and increasing size, of cities. In the year 1000, 9.7% of Europe's population lived in cities with more than 5,000 inhabitants. In 1500 this figure was 10.7%, in 1850 it was 18.9% and in 1980 it was 66.5%.

To a considerable extent, these three tendencies determined the development of the form and content of social protest. At the beginning of the period under consideration, the grievances of protesters were mostly local in nature. Their demands were aimed at regional strongmen, merchants and so on; that or they exhorted influential individuals in the region to exert pressure on the central authorities. Social movements with institutionalized movement organizations did not yet exist. However, especially since the Industrial Revolution and the consolidation of nation states between 1750 and 1850, protestors' grievances were far more often supra-regional or even national in nature, and direct appeals to the central authorities were made more regularly. Also, social movements in the contemporary sense of the term came into being. The protesters' repertoire likewise changed. Protests in the pre-Modern era were often personal in nature. They attacked their enemy's integrity through caterwauling (charivari, rough music), kangaroo courts or ridicule; or they punished him through arson, assassination and theft. In contrast, Modern-era protests tend to be instead directed against certain laws and measures, or occasionally against individuals who embody such laws and measures. They indict injustice through demonstrations, blockades, strikes and rallies.

In what follows I will concentrate on forms of public protest that are visible to all. But we should bear in mind that open protest is but one form of collective resistance. In fact, one that is rare. The much more common forms of 'evasive' resistance (whereby one does not seek to collectively confront the enemy in an open and direct fashion) are extremely diverse, including the passive violation of rules ('quitter'-behaviour, 'work to rule', etc.), or even anonymous acts such as arson or murder.[3]

I would like to distinguish two periods. The first period covers the Middle Ages and the period of transition to a fully developed capitalist society. This period was far shorter in Western Europe (especially in England and the Netherlands) than in Eastern Europe. The second period spans the years when capitalism had been consolidated (i.e. when social formation is characterized by generalized commodity production, where labour power, the means of production and the products of labour all circulate predominantly through market mechanisms) and, additionally, the 'real existing socialist' dictatorships in the Soviet Union and Eastern Europe.

PROTESTS IN PRE- AND EARLY CAPITALIST SOCIETY

Peasant Protests

Down to the eighteenth century agriculture was the main branch of the economy in Europe, although the importance of trade—and later on industry—gradually increased. Not only did the peasants produce food, they often also paid taxes in kind (labour, the products of their labour) or in money. The rights and gains of peasant groups were repeatedly infringed by the pressures of wars, epidemics (the Black Death), attempts to construct centralized state structures and the emerging profit motive—such as, for example, through the privatization of common lands and increasing tax pressure. Peasants might put up with such degradation for long periods before what might be a relatively insignificant event sparked open resistance. In peasant households, a central role was played by the 'moral economy', that is to say the idea that there are certain norms of social justice and social propriety to which everybody is subjected, even those in power. If the powers that be violate these norms, then serious massive protest was justified.[4]

---

[3] See e.g. Robin Cohen, 'Resistance and Hidden Forms of Consciousness amongst African Workers', *Review of African Political Economy* 19 (1980), pp. 8–22 [Reprinted in Cohen, *Contested Domains. Debates in International Labour Studies* (London: Zed Books, 1991), pp. 91–109]; James C. Scott, *Weapons of the Weak: Everyday Forms of Peasant Resistance* (New Haven, CT: Yale University Press, 1985).

[4] Comparative analysis in FrederikW. Hugenholtz, *Drie boerenopstanden uit de veertiende eeuw: Vlaanderen, 1323–1328, Frankrijk, 1358, Engeland, 1381: Onderzoek naar het opstan-*

EUROPEAN SOCIAL PROTEST, 1000–2000

Although there had already been peasant revolts in the high Middle Ages, such as the poorly documented peasant war in Normandy in 996 under Duke Richard II, in many European regions these revolts only gained importance from the thirteenth century. A very important resource for such protests was the existence of relatively autonomous structures, such as the supra-regional drainage systems (*wateringen*) in West Flanders, the regional popular assemblies (*ting*) in Sweden or the villages of Central Europe. As far as we know, peasant uprisings always had their origins in such social networks, which themselves were the result of historical development. Villages, for example, have not always existed. They only gained in importance with the emergence of the tributary economy. In some parts of Europe (including Central Europe) this tributary economy was based on the serf economy. In other parts of Europe (Sweden, for example) there had not been any bondage and hardly any serfdom before the emergence of the tributary economy. During this transition, group settlements of independent farmers came into existence, which presided over their own farms and gardens and collectively worked the common land (pasture and forest). Such villages developed forms of patriarchal self-administration, in which the male farmers' assembly was the centre of power. If the landlords or chatelaines threatened these village communities in any way, then the communities were equipped with a common basis for resistance.

In the course of time the peasant protests became more far-reaching. To begin with the protests were mainly of a regional nature, but in the late Middle Ages they increasingly encompassed entire regions of many villages. In all probability, the expanded horizon of protest was a reaction to the processes of state-building, which had led to comprehensive measures (including tax collection). In general, the most elementary protests with the most basic demands arose at a local level. Supra-local and supra-regional protests raised more fundamental and more general demands. However, this contradistinction is not absolute, as overarching protests could also incorporate demands that were locally specific alongside the general discontent. For the peasants, protests were always about ensuring their survival and retaining their old rights.

dig bewustzijn (Haarlem: H.D. Tjeenk Willink, 1949) [2nd edn, The Hague: Martinus Nijhoff, 1978]; Michel Mollat and Philippe Wolff, *The Popular Revolutions of the Late Middle Ages* (London: Allen & Unwin, 1973).

The first major peasant revolt took place in Flanders, and was directed against what were perceived as unjust taxes.[5] It began in the form of scattered riots in October–November 1323, but quickly escalated into a large rebellion that convulsed the whole area for five years. The peasants elected their own leaders and cleared out the officials and aristocratic allies of the Count of Flanders. They confiscated and distributed the exiles' property. They organized their own fighting forces, and in the middle of 1325 they had replaced the Count's representatives with their own functionaries, who collected taxes, held court and paid out monies. Although the movement had begun in the countryside, many city dwellers also sympathized with it. From 1325 these city dwellers also rebelled, seizing power in various cities. Only in August 1328 was there a counter-attack, when the French king, with the Pope's support, sent an army to Flanders and—following a victorious battle in which more than 3,000 peasants perished—carried out huge 'cleansing'.

Far better-known are the May 1358 peasant revolts in the north of France, which came to be known under the name of the *Jacquerie*.[6] (At that time, 'Jacques Bonhomme' was a derogatory term for a peasant.) In 1356, the English had taken the French King John II captive during the Hundred Years' War (1337–1453) and two contenders to the throne had entered the fray. There was an uprising in Oise valley to the north of Paris after the peasants, continually beset by war, plague and plundering by mercenaries, and taking advantage of the power vacuum at the top of society, finally revolted. Under the leadership of Guillaume Cale, the rebels drove out or murdered aristocratic families, setting fire to more than 150 castles. A rapidly formed army, led by King Charles the Bad of Navarre, defeated the peasant forces at the battle of Mello on 10 June 1358. Guillaume Cale and around 20,000 insurgents were killed. However, this did not entirely pacify the French peasantry. A short time later (from around 1360 to 1400), a new peasant revolt, the so-called Tuchin-movement (or *Tuchinat*), unfolded in central France. This adopted more clandestine forms and was characterized by social banditry.[7]

[5] William H. TeBrake, *A Plague of Insurrection. Popular Politics and Peasant Revolt in Flanders, 1323–1328* (Philadelphia: University of Pennsylvania Press, 1993).

[6] Siméon Luce, *Histoire de la jacquerie d'après des documents inédits* (Paris: A. Durand, 1859).

[7] Marcellin Boudet, *Documents inédits du XIVe siècle: la jacquerie des tuchins 1363–1384* (Rion: U. Jouvet, 1900); Nicholas Wright, *Knights and Peasants. The Hundred Years War in the French Countryside* (Woodbridge: The Boydell Press, 1998), esp. Chaps. 4 and 5. Idem,

The Hundred Years' War prompted peasant revolts in England too. Despite the absence of military successes, the 1370s saw new taxes imposed in the name of King Richard II, who was still a minor. The outcome was the peasant uprising of 1381. The unrest particularly targeted John of Gaunt ('Jan van Gent'), the king's most influential adviser, and Robert Hales, the head of the order of St. John, and thus a symbol of the church's wealth. An insurgent army of around 50,000 farmers was formed under the leadership of the craftsman Wat (Walter) Tyler, which initially conquered Canterbury and then moved to London, apprehending and then beheading the Archbishop Simon Sudbury in the Tower. The then 15-year-old King Richard agreed to speak with Tyler. The mayor of London was also present at this meeting. He became infuriated by Tyler's audacity and murdered him with his sword. The king subsequently convinced the insurgents that he would issue them with letters of manumission and send them home. However, he did not keep his word and had the rebel leaders killed.[8]

The French *Jacquerie* and the English peasant revolts both lasted just a few weeks. A longer conflict along the lines of the Flemish model arose in fifteenth century Scandinavia. When the rudiments of a tributary economy came into existence in Sweden, this ignited a genuine peasant war. It is likely that news of the Hussites (see below) in part acted as an inspiration for this. The war began in middle of the country on Midsummer Day 1434, when outraged farmers set fire to Borganäs fortress and then, a few days later, miners caused similar havoc at the Laglösaköping. Very quickly, the insurgents received the support of peasants from other areas. With the shield-bearer Engelbrekt Engelbrektsson at its head, a rebel army moved to Uppsala. In a speech made there, Engelbrektsson demanded that one-third of the taxes be waived, and the aristocrats present felt they had no other choice but to accept this measure. Emboldened by this success, the movement expanded. Castles and palaces soon burned in the North, and in Finland too. Throughout, Engelbrektsson and his 10,000 supporters occupied Stockholm, the most important commercial

---

'"Pillagers" and "Brigands" in the Hundred Years War', *Journal of Medieval History* 1 (1983), pp. 15–24; Samuel K. Cohn Jr. (ed.), *Popular Protest in Late Medieval Europe* (Manchester: Manchester University Press, 2004), documents pp. 61–67.

[8] Rodney Hilton, *Bond Men Made Free. Medieval Peasant Movements and the English Rising of 1381* (London: Routledge, 2005); Rodney H. Hilton and Trevor H. Aston (eds), *The English Rising of 1381* (Cambridge: Cambridge University Press, 1984); Richard B. Dobson (ed.), *The Peasants' Revolt of 1381* (London: Macmillan, 1970).

centre in Sweden, and reached a deal with the city's commandant. The uprising continued to spread. A turning point came in the autumn of 1434, when the rebels assailed the highest aristocratic body, the Imperial Assembly, in the small town of Vadstena, and forced the assembled lords to renounce their loyalty and obedience to the Danish king. From this point on, the peasants had high-aristocratic 'allies' whose interests were completely different to their own. As a result, the contradictions in the rebel camp grew. Engelbrektsson's peasants won more allies across the nation. The Norwegian peasants also rose up from 1436 onwards, while poor urban residents in Sweden also joined in. Engelbrektsson was killed by an aristocrat in May 1436, but this did not bring the peasants' war to an end. Erik Puke took Engelbrektsson's place, but he was captured and executed in 1437. The peasants' war thus ended in a defeat, but nevertheless it had achieved some successes—amongst other things, tax pressure was reduced.[9]

Perhaps the most extensive and serious agrarian protest of all took place in Catalonia in the late fifteenth century. When, as a result of a plague epidemic, the landowners severely restricted the freedoms of their peasants and imposed new taxes upon them (such as a tax for the right to marry), this produced great discontent among the rural poor. This class was exceptionally well organized and sent delegations to plead the case with the king residing in Naples. The lack of success there led to an uprising in 1462. This first wave of struggle lasted for about ten years, but did not lead to any significant results. But a second uprising, commencing in 1484, was victorious: in 1486 the king abolished serfdom and determined that peasants could henceforth only be leased in exchange for payment. The economic dynamic that resulted from this greatly promoted the growth of the Catalan economy in the centuries that followed.

From the fourteenth century through to the Reformation, peasant communities radicalized in the German Empire as well. If we divide the unrest into generations of 25 years, then from the calculations of Peter Blickle it emerges 'that in the fourteenth century there is merely one uprising per generation, in the second half of the fifteenth century this figure is already as high as six or eight per generation, and in the period between 1500 and

[9] John J. Murray, 'The Peasant Revolt of Engelbrekt Engelbrektsson and the Birth of Modern Sweden', *Journal of Modern History* 3 (1947), pp. 193–209; Kimmo Katalaja (ed.), *Northern Revolts. Medieval and Early Modern Peasant Unrest in the Nordic Countries* (Helsinki: Finish Literature Society, 2004).

1525 this figure eventually reaches 18.'[10] Simultaneously, the demands of the insurgents went further and further. While to begin with only a few privileges or measures of the rulers were challenged, by the beginning of the sixteenth century a fundamental critique of these rulers had emerged. However, the emperor was mainly exempt from this criticism.

After unsuccessful regional peasant plots in different areas of south-west Germany between 1493 and 1517, between 1525 and 1526 the so-called peasant war broke out, stretching over southern Germany, Austria and Switzerland. It formed the high point of Central European peasant protest. Tax increases were the occasion for protests here too. Three armies were formed in February and March 1525 from around 30,000 Swabian peasants armed with flails and scythes: the crowds (*Haufen*) of Leubas, of Balring in the vicinity of Biberach and of Lindau. Representatives of the three groups met in the free imperial city of Memmingen, and after intense negotiations, they adopted the so-called twelve articles on 20 March 1525. The central demands of these articles were the abolition of serfdom and certain taxes, the return of the commons to the peasants, the carrying out of labour services only in exchange for payment, and the free election of priests by parishioners. Following the example of Switzerland, an Upper Swabian Confederation was established to safeguard mutual solidarity. The twelve articles and the Federal Rules of the Confederation are documents of great historical significance: not only did they signal the beginning of the codification of peasant resistance, but they also made possible the standardization of peasant resistance and systematic propaganda in which solidarity preachers like Thomas Munzer played an important role. Both documents were printed and distributed in large numbers. In return, the nobility, financially supported by the Fuggers of Augsburg, organized its own army. Now a real war commenced, with many battles and victories for both sides at different stages. However, it was clear by June 1525 that the nobility would win. By September the old order had been completely restored. Around 100,000 peasants had been killed. Extensive repression followed.[11]

[10] Peter Blickle, *Unruhen in der ständischen Gesellschaft, 1300–1800* (Munich: Oldenbourg Verlag, 1988), p. 13.

[11] Peter Blickle, *Die Revolution von 1525* (Munich: Oldenbourg, 1981); Horst Buszello, Peter Blickle and Rudolf Endres (eds), *Der deutsche* Bauernkrieg, 2nd rev. edn, (Paderborn: Schöningh, 1984); James M. Stayer, *The German Peasants' War and the Anabaptist Community of Goods* (Montreal: McGill-Queen's University Press, 1991); Bob Scribner and Gerhard Benecke (eds), *The German Peasant War of 1525: New Viewpoints* (London: Allen

Later there were similar developments in Eastern Europe, certainly no less radical than the German revolt. In Russia, four peasant uprisings resembling civil wars occurred in the seventeenth and eighteenth centuries. They were led by Ivan Bolotnikov (1606–1607), Stepan Razin (1670–1671), Kondratii Bulavin (1707–1708) and Emelian Pugačev (1773–1774). Not only peasants and serfs took part in these, but also Cossacks, city dwellers and even some *Pomeščiki* (a type of vassal). Pugačev's uprising was part of a series of a large number of peasant revolts that occurred after 1762, and was probably the biggest of them. Pugačev, a Cossack veteran of the Seven Years' War (1756–1763) and the sixth Russo-Turkish War (1768–1774), recruited a large peasant army, and in so doing was supported by many priests, amongst others. He called himself Peter III, claiming that he was actually the legitimate ruler of Russia, not Catherine the Great. In 1773 his troops captured the cities of Samara and Kazan; for a short time, they were able to bring an extensive area between the Volga and the Urals under their control. At the end of 1774 the rebellion was crushed by Tsarist troops; Pugačev was executed in Moscow in 1775.[12]

In Romania, there was even a *jacquerie* at the beginning of the twentieth century. In this instance, the peasants' protests were aimed at the (often Jewish) intermediate tenants or *Arendators*, who extorted rent out of the rural population of rent instead of the landowners. Beginning in March 1907, the uprising rapidly spread across almost the whole of Moldavia, and partly Wallachia too. Under the slogan of 'We want land', many Arendators were killed or injured, and the landowners' properties were destroyed. The state declared a state of emergency, mobilized 140,000 troops and suppressed the rebellion with great force.[13]

& Unwin, 1979); Tom Scott and Bob Scribner (eds), *The German Peasants' War: A History in Documents* (Atlantic Highlands, NJ: Humanities Press International, 1991).

[12] Roland Mousnier, *Peasant Uprisings in Seventeenth Century France, Russia, and China* (New York: Harper & Row, 1970); Ruslan G. Skrynnikov, *Smuta v Rossii v načale XVII v.* Ivan Bolotnikov (Leningrad: Nauka, 1988); Idem, *The Time of Troubles: Russia in Crisis, 1604–1618* (Gulf Breeze, FL: Academic International Press, 1988); Philip Longworth, 'Peasant Leadership and the Pugachev Revolt', *Journal of Peasant Studies* 2 (1975), pp. 183–205; Chester Dunning, 'Crisis, Conjuncture, and the Causes of the Time of Troubles', *Harvard Ukrainian Studies* 19 (1995), pp. 97–119.

[13] Philip Gabriel Eidelberg, *The Great Rumanian Peasant Revolt of 1907. Origins of a Modern Jacquerie* (Leiden: Brill, 1974); Daniel Chirot and Charles Ragin, 'The Market, Tradition, and Peasant Rebellion: The Case of Romania in 1907', *American Sociological Review* 4 (1975), pp. 428–444.

Guild Battles

Guilds—permanent local organizations of certain professions whose main purpose is to eliminate competition, and which are recognized by the regional or central government authority—were predominantly, but certainly not exclusively, found in Western and Central European cities. The more important the cities became, the greater the significance of their guilds. City dwellers had attempted to free themselves from the guardianship of feudal and ecclesiastical rulers from the twelfth century. This trend was first visible in the most economically developed regions of Europe—Flanders and Northern Italy. But France, Switzerland and Central Europe followed fairly quickly. Guilds played a central role in these struggles for freedom, although they were often genuine struggles of the people in which all rural strata and classes joined forces. However, these struggles never resulted in genuine democracy, only in an oligarchy of a small group of influential families. In Flanders it was mainly the cloth manufacturers who held power, in Florence it was the *popolo grasso* ('the fat people'), the wealthy middle class of merchants and businessmen. The latter were often supported by less prestigious guilds, from which the unorganized lower classes were excluded.

Anti-oligarchic aspirations were articulated by different sections of the city population: by the traditional artisan guilds but also by the workers' dependent on early capitalist entrepreneurs. In 1225 the weavers and cloth manufacturers of Valenciennes unseated the city council, confiscated the possessions of the rich and proclaimed a commune. Revolts against the urban elites broke out in Liège/Luik in 1253, Dinant in 1255 and Huy in 1299. One of the weavers' and cloth manufacturers' actions provoked harsh repression and forced many insurgents to flee to nearby Brabant. In 1280 there were rebellions in almost all of the Flemish cities: here the protest might be aimed at certain tax measures, there it could target the undemocratic city administration. Since the Count of Flanders backed the insurgents on a number of occasions, the city elites called on the support of the French king, who invaded Flanders in 1300. Under the leadership of their 'King Peter', a weaver, the lower classes of Bruges formed the vanguard of resistance against the French invaders. On 11 July 1302 a battle broke out in Courtrai/Kortrijk between the French chevalier army and the insurgents, in which half of the approximately 2,000 nobles involved were killed. The victorious Flemish seized hundreds of golden spurs, which is why the skirmish has become known as the 'Battle of the Golden Spurs'—July 11 is a Belgian public holiday.

According to recent estimates, there were 210 guild battles (often erroneously deemed guild revolutions) in 105 towns in the German Empire between 1300 and 1550.[14] The results of these uprisings varied enormously. In some cases, the artisans were unable to consolidate their influence and the city administration remained in the hands of the old elite. This was particularly the case in many Hanseatic cities, such as Brunswick from 1374 to 1386 and Lübeck from 1380 to 1384.

In Strasbourg, Basel and other cities in south-west Germany the guilds were able to win several seats in the municipal councils. Strasbourg is an instructive example. In the thirteenth and early fourteenth century the city was governed by a council. Each member of the council personally appointed his successor, who usually came from the same family. The great mass of the citizens had no political influence. This produced growing discontent as Strasbourg's trade and commerce blossomed in the course of the thirteenth and fourteenth centuries and the fact of their political impotence became more and more irksome to the craftsmen and merchants. As early as 1308, 16 rebellious citizens had been killed in battles. In 1332 there was a large uprising when a conflict broke out amongst the ruling families, and in a sense a 'breach' opened for the discontented city residents, making their speedy victory possible. A new council was now installed, comprising fifty seats in total. The guilds were able to take up one half of these, the elite the other.

In other cases, the guilds were hegemonic and provided all the councillors. In 1396 in Cologne, for example, the guilds, led by the goldsmiths and weavers, seized power and decided on a new constitution (the so-called *Verbundbrief*), according to which the city was to be governed by guild representatives henceforth. Something similar happened in Ravensburg in 1346 and in Speyer in 1349.

The *communero*-revolts in Castile were the largest urban rebellion in early-modern Europe. The conflict began from 1520, when a group of cities in Castile opposed King Charles I's new tax measures (shortly afterwards he became the Emperor Charles V of the Holy Roman Empire). The oligarchic elites in these cities formed an alliance (*junta*) and demanded not just a reduction in taxes, but reform of the entire tax system as well,

---

[14] James R. Farr, *Artisans in Europe 1300–1914* (Cambridge: Cambridge University Press, 2000), p. 177.

which amounted to a reduction of royal power. The artisans supported the rebellious city governments and formulated their own demands, which aimed at significantly enlarging their political influence at a municipal level. In 1521, royal armies subjugated the rebellious cities by force.[15]

150 years later another substantial rebellion occurred in the Spanish empire, specifically in Naples, at that time one of Europe's biggest cities with 300,000 inhabitants. The occasion for this was a new tax on fruit. In 1647 the insurgents, under the leadership of a fishmonger by the name of Masaniello, looted the palaces of tax officials and called for the abolition of all taxes on staple foods such as cereals, olive oil, wine and cheese. The protests radicalized and, despite the assassination of Masaniello, soon became political. The rebels now demanded that new taxes should only be decided upon by a popular assembly, and demanded free elections to city councils. When Spanish troops laid siege to the city, the rebels declared a republic under French protection. In April 1648 the citizens opened up the gates when they were promised general amnesty and the abolition of taxes on foodstuffs and other goods.

From the late seventeenth century onwards, such violent conflicts occurred less frequently. The increasing centralization of state power gradually led to a relocation of the battle arenas. The influence of cross-city institutions such as courts and parliaments grew, while at the same time the guilds were more heavily controlled by the central authorities.

Food Riots

The continuing disintegration of the feudal natural economy resulted in ever-greater numbers of the lower classes having to acquire their food on the market. If food supply faltered or prices rose too sharply, this could lead to food riots. The earliest of these occurred in a number of English port cities in 1347. In the centuries that followed, similar riots repeatedly occurred until, in the second half of the nineteenth century, they became

---

[15] José Antonio Maravall, *Las comunidades de Castilla: Una primera revolución* moderna (Madrid: Revista de Occidente, 1963); Henry L. Seaver, *The Great Revolt in Castile: A Study of the Comunero Movement of 1520–1521* (New York: Octagon Books, 1966 [1928]); Juan I. Gutiérrez Nieto, *Las comunidades como movimiento antiseñorial: la formación del bando realista en la Guerra Civil Castellana de 1520–1521* (Barcelona: Editorial Planeta, 1973); José Luis Díez, *Los comuneros de Castilla* (Madrid: Editorial Mañana, 1977); Stephen Haliczer, *The Comuneros of Castle: The Forging of a Revolution, 1475–1521* (Madison: University of Wisconsin Press, 1981).

more sporadic. There were even isolated protests between 1916 and 1918. In France, riots occur from the 1630s to around 1854. In the German Empire, the riots begin in the second half of the eighteenth century and extend well into the twentieth century (1914–1923, 1945–1949).[16] The study of food riots in widespread parts of Europe (especially Eastern Europe) is not very advanced, and data is therefore missing.

Food riots could assume several forms. Those going hungry often prevented the shipment of food from their own region (such actions were also called *entraves*) or they extorted lower prices (*taxation populaire*). Mills, warehouses and shops were regularly attacked, or market riots broke out. Women played a disproportionally large role in such conflicts. To what extent the hunger riots were driven by popular notions of an alternative 'moral' economic order is a controversial question, as is the extent to which these revolts were actually about pragmatic emergency measures.

Workers' and Journeymen's Struggles

There were regular workers' protests as far as back as the high and late Middle Ages. This was especially the case in the textile industry, the earliest European branch of the economy to be organized along more or less capitalist lines. As early as 1345, the wool-carder Ciuto Brandini was arrested, and accused of having

> deliberated together with many others seduced by his words to form with the largest membership possible a brotherhood between the wool-carders and wool-combers and the other workers of the *Arte della Lana*, and to nominate from such new corporations, *Consoli* and Heads, and to this end had on different occasions and places assembled very many workmen of the worst reputation, and had in such assemblies proposed that each should contribute a certain sum (a matriculation tax) in order that thus it would more surely succeed.

In spite of massive strikes and riots in support of Ciuto, the authorities hung him.[17] It certainly looks like Ciuto tried to establish a trade union,

[16]Manfred Gailus and Heinrich Volkmann (eds), *Der Kampf um das tägliche Brot. Nahrungsmangel, Versorgungspolitik und Protest 1770–1990* (Opladen: Wesdeutscher Verlag, 1994).

[17]Niccolò Rodolico, 'The Struggle for the Right of Association in Fourteenth-Century Florence', *History* 27 (1922), pp. 178–190, here p. 184.

with membership dues and elected workers' representatives—as far we know, this was the first of all such attempts.

Even after this defeat, the Republic of Florence remained a centre of working-class resistance. In the 1370s, when a series of plagues, famines and wars had undermined the authority of the city administration, there was an uprising of unprecedented proportions. In June 1378, members of the lower guilds sparked a revolution; they set the palaces of the most hated big bourgeois ablaze and formed a new government. The *Ciompi*, wool-carders and other unskilled textile workers, were involved in this. Their spokesman, the wool-carder Michele di Lando, played an important role in the revolutionary administration. The unorganized workers formed three new guilds and radicalized quickly. The measures of the new government did not go far enough for them. On August 31, the Ciompi rose up against the government that they themselves had placed in the saddle, but the forces looking to uphold order, led by the butchers' guild, bloodily suppressed the uprising.

The average number of apprentices with a single master increased with advancing economic growth. But since, according to the rules of the guild, normally only one journeyman could ever become the successor of the master, a certain 'proletarianization' of the journeymen took place from the Middle Ages. They became aware of the fact that they would most likely never make it as a master, and would therefore have to remain dependent wage-workers their whole lives. They created their own journeymen's associations that not only served religious and social purposes, but quickly served as a point of departure for forms of social protest as well. If there was a conflict of interest with one, several, or even all the masters in one city, then the journeyman could boycott the master, or in the worst case, leave the city altogether.[18]

A well-documented example of an early trade union are the *Griffarins* in Lyon in south-central France, a guild of book printers formed at the beginning of the sixteenth century. The Griffarins had membership funds, secret initiation rites and an oath pledging them to complete solidarity. If a master violated the rules of the guild, for example by having an apprentice carry out the work of a journeyman, then the Griffarins gave him three warnings. If the master refused to budge, then one of the journeymen said

[18] Niccolò Rodolico, *I Ciompi: una pagina di storia del proletariato operaio*, 3rd edn (Florence: Sansoni, 1980); Istituto nazionale di studi sul Rinascimento, *Il tumulto dei ciompi* (Florence: L.S. Olschki, 1981).

the words 'tric, tric' and all members had to leave the workshop—either for a day or until the conflict had been resolved. During such a strike, none of the Griffarins could accept a job with the master. Apprentices who refused to join the strike were beaten until they did. On two occasions, in 1539 and 1570, the Griffarins organized strikes that encompassed the entire city.[19]

In some parts of Europe, strikes of this nature were actually quite common. In 1643 in the Dutch textile city of Leiden, the shearers threatened to collectively leave the city if their wages were not increased. The city administration immediately wrote a letter to other towns in the area, requesting that potential shearers from Leiden not be given any work, because they were engaged in a 'mutiny'. The city's counter-action was effective, and the strike ended in defeat.[20]

In some cases, there was even a general strike, as in Hamburg on August 23 and 24 1791, when all the craft journeymen jointly stopped work. The reason for this was a violation of the locksmith journeymen's traditional right to autonomous jurisdiction, which within a few days led to the solidarity action of all journeymen. The strikers led festive processions with musicians, 'in which the journeymen marched in double file and paraded their flags and other emblems in forms of representative publicity.'[21] On August 25 the city administration forcibly intervened; there were several deaths and the strike had to be broken off.

Millenarian Movements

The plague epidemics, the social crises of the late Middle Ages and the burgeoning of capitalist economic relations brought insecurity to large numbers of the European population. On several occasions, religious hysteria seized masses of people. This was directed against both the corruption of the Catholic Church and against the Jews. The latter not only had a different faith, but many of them—because they were excluded from agricultural activity—played an important role in trade and money

---

[19] Natalie Zemon Davis, 'A Trade Union in Sixteenth-Century France', *Economic History Review* 1 (1966), pp. 48–69.

[20] Rudolf Dekker, 'Labour Conflicts and Working-Class Culture in Early Modern Holland', *International Review of Social History* 3 (1990), pp. 377–420.

[21] Andreas Grießinger, *Das symbolische Kapital der Ehre. Streikbewegungen und kollektives Bewußtsein deutscher Handwerksgesellen im 18. Jahrhundert* (Frankfurt am Main: Ullstein, 1981), p. 115.

lending. Between the thirteenth and fifteenth century, flagellants, for example, moved in groups from city to city, whipped themselves up into a frenzy and—since they thought that the Jews poisoned wells and brought the Black Death—carried out anti-Semitic excesses. Such forms of fanaticism were mostly an expression of millenarianism, i.e. the expectation that the Thousand Year Empire predicted by John in his Revelation (Chap. 21) was imminent.[22]

There were also chiliastic influences amongst a section of the so-called Hussites.[23] This movement emerged in the fifteenth century, after the Prague theologian and reformer Jan Hus (1370–1415) had been burned at the stake on the orders of the Catholic Church. Hus had criticized the Church's wealth and benefice economy, challenged the authority of the Pope and declared the bible as the only touchstone in questions of faith. Both amongst the nobility and the lower social classes, the death of Hus led to large protests in Bohemia and Moravia, which escalated into an anti-German war directed at the Pope. A more moderate wing, the so-called *Calixtines* (the Latin term *calix* means cup), who demanded, amongst other things, that all believers should be allowed to drink from the cup of wine, were placated by the church. A radical wing, on the other hand, wanted to immediately establish the Kingdom of God, and founded a new city in South Bohemia by the name of Tabor, where many poor people from the town and country settled. These so-called *Taborites* strove for the full social equality of all men ('no one shall be the subject of another') and for the eradication of the aristocracy. The Taborites were defeated in a battle in May 1434; more than 10,000 of them were killed.

The experience of the Taborites partly inspired the Anabaptists. This tendency, which emerged in Zürich in 1525, was extremely critical of the Catholic Church and, amongst other things, demanded an end to child baptism, since only adults could consciously choose a faith. Anabaptists gained influence particularly in the Netherlands and Westphalia, and were cruelly persecuted in many places. In 1534 a number of them succeeded in conquering the city of Münster, driving out the archbishop, and creating 'communitarian' relations in their New Jerusalem by redistributing property and introducing polygamy. Following a siege lasting many months, the bishop and his allies were able to recapture the city after tough street

---

[22] Norman Cohn, *The Pursuit of the Millennium. Revolutionary Millenarians and Mystical Anarchists of the Middle Ages* (London: Essential Books, 1957).

[23] Heinz Rieder, *Die Hussiten* (Gernsbach: Katz, 1998).

battles. The 'King' of the Anabaptists, the Dutchman Jan Beukelsz, as well as two of his comrades-in-arms, were cruelly executed; their bodies were hung in baskets at the tower of a local church (the baskets are still there today).

Social Revolutions

In social revolutions, the political power of the old elite is forcibly wrested from them and transferred to another group seeking to bring about a revolution of all hitherto existing social relations. A social revolution therefore differs fundamentally from a putsch or a coup d'état, which entails one section of the elite replacing another without bringing about any fundamental socio-economic shifts. There were social revolutions, or attempts at them, as far back as the Middle Ages, as shown by the examples of the Ciompi or the Taborites. However, these early revolutions occurred at the level of the town. Large-scale social revolutions that led to upheavals in centralized states are more recent.

Many historians consider the Dutch revolt against Spain (1566–1609) to be the first 'modern' revolution in Europe. In a sense, however, it was a transitional form, because during and after the revolt there was not yet a centralized state in the Netherlands, but merely a number of independent cities that worked together. Several motives conjoined in the resistance to the Habsburgs: aversion to the strict interpretation of the Catholic faith demanded by Spanish King Philip II, opposition to tax increases which were seen as unfair, and opposition to Spanish attempts to centralize state power to the detriment of urban autonomy. The revolution began in 1566, when craftsmen and other plebeian groups led an 'iconoclastic riot'—systematically destroying statues, paintings and so on in the churches of Flanders and other parts of the Netherlands. After the Spanish army, under the leadership of the Duke of Alba, had suppressed the rebellion, a second wave of insurgent actions followed between 1572 and 1581. Again under the leadership of a few noblemen, of whom Prince William of Orange was the most important, the northern provinces of Holland and Zeeland now succeeded in freeing themselves from Spanish rule and establishing an independent federation: The United Provinces, more commonly known under the name of the Dutch Republic. In response, Philip II's troops conquered Antwerp, until then the most significant commercial city in the Low Countries, an area that was roughly the same as the territory of Belgium and the Netherlands later on. This finally shifted the economic focus of the Netherlands to the north, and Amsterdam could become a world centre of capitalist trade.[24]

The first 'modern' European revolution in the strict sense of the term was the English Revolution of 1642–1649. Religious, political and economic factors all played a role here as well. In his attempts to raise old taxes and to introduce new ones, King Charles I felt hindered by a parliament composed exclusively of representatives of the upper classes. At the same time, he felt attached to the Catholic royal houses of Western Europe, especially those of France and Spain. A section of the nobility, and the majority of traders in and around London in the south of England, had more sympathy for the Protestant opponents of the Catholic royal families, hoping that weakening these families would grant them easier access to the markets of America and East India. When, in January 1642, Charles I tried to have arrested five parliamentarians who stood in opposition to him, there ensued the 'first civil war' of the revolution (1642–1645), in which the landowner, Oliver Cromwell, became the leading figure of the insurgents. Cromwell conjured an army of a new type, the so-called New Model Army. It was composed of volunteers and was more disciplined than previous armies. Cromwell's troops defeated the king in June 1645. When Cromwell tried to dissolve the army immediately after this, the soldiers began to organize independently. The regiments elected speakers (so-called agitators) who advocated radical demands, and liaised with radical elements outside the military sphere. A radical-democratic group, the Levellers, increasingly won influence in the regiments. In the summer of 1648 the 'second civil war' broke out, in which Charles I once again tried to regain his power. Cromwell managed to discipline the rebels in his army by authorising an 'army council', in which soldiers and officers were equally represented. Thereupon, the king was defeated by this army and beheaded in January 1649.

Normally the French Revolution is regarded as *the* classical revolution.[25] In May 1789, financial problems had compelled King Louis XVI to summon the three estates (the clergy, the nobility and the 'Third Estate' of the bourgeoisie). Because the third estate, along with the non-represented peasants, put up the most in taxes (the nobility and the church were exempt) and at the same time were treated by a section of the nobility

---

[24] Pepijn Brandon, 'The Dutch Revolt: A Social Analysis', *International Socialism* 116 (2007), pp. 139–167.

[25] Albert Soboul, *Histoire de la Révolution française*, 2 vols (Paris: Editions Sociales, 1962).

in a very arrogant fashion, its representatives refused to continue to sit together with the other general estates. On June 17 they formed their own 'National Assembly', which was to deal with tax issues. Many representatives of the church and some nobles joined the new assembly. In Paris, meanwhile, the middle and lower classes' discontent with the economic and political situation grew. On July 12 an uprising began which, two days later, led to the storming of the Bastille (a redoubt and prison in the city, which, incidentally, was almost empty at the time). A wave of mob law and looting (also called *La Grande Peur*—the great fear) ensued, which very quickly spilled over into the rural areas and other cities. The new National Assembly quickly radicalized and took historic decisions in August. Serfdom was formally abolished and the now famous 'Declaration of the Human and Civil Rights' was adopted. The power of the king was weakened, so consequently he invoked the other European monarchs to support him. A war of the revolutionary forces against Prussia, Austria, and later against other countries as well, ultimately ended in victory after the French had introduced general military service (*levée en masse*) in 1793. While this war was being waged King Louis XVI was beheaded. Then, in the second half of 1794, a counter-revolution within the revolution took place (the so-called Thermidor), when Robespierre, the strong man of the revolution's first phase, was brought down and a *directoire* (consisting of five 'directors') seized power and reversed most of radical-democratic measures. This junta was able to survive until the General Napoleon Bonaparte became 'Consul' through a coup in November 1799 (he was emperor from 1804).

The Dutch, English and French revolutions had great consequences for society. New economic forces like the commercial bourgeoisie, the market-oriented landowners and the industrialists could now develop in a more uninhibited way than before. In this sense—i.e. because they aided and abetted these forces, and not because the bourgeoisie played a central role in these struggles—one can say that these revolutions were 'bourgeois' (revolutions promoting capitalism).

Several revolutions also occurred in nineteenth and twentieth century Europe. Since the French Revolution was aborted halfway, in the following decades there were several attempts to restart the process. Thus, further upheavals came about in 1830 and 1848. This latter revolt made France a republic once more, and inspired other revolutionary movements that unfolded in the German and Habsburg empires almost simultaneously. After the French army had been defeated by the Prussians, a highly symbolic rebellion took place between March and May of 1871. The residents of the capital organized the self-governing, so-called 'Commune of Paris', in which soldiers elected their own officers, night work in the bakeries was forbidden, and a significant women's movement developed. During the 'Bloody Week' (*Semaine Sanglante*) at the end of May, the French government, with Prussian support, succeeded in recapturing the city.

The First World War (1914–1918) strongly destabilized social relations in the belligerent nation states, particularly the losers in that conflict. Thus, large protest movements emerged in Russia in 1916, but also in others countries like Germany, Austria, Hungary and Italy. In Russia, which had already seen a failed revolution between 1905 and 1907, the Tsarist regime collapsed in 1917. On March 2 of that year, an uprising broke out in Petrograd in reaction to food shortages. It could not be suppressed because the soldiers refused to shoot on the masses in revolt. The tsar stepped down in favour of his brother, but even he only stayed in office for a few hours. A new, predominantly liberal, government was formed. However, it was not able to get the situation under control because, at the same time, workers' and soldiers' councils were emerging, which were under the influence of the socialist opposition. These councils held their first All-Russian Congress as early as June. The outcome was a situation of dual power, which on 7 November 1917 culminated in the opposition, under the leadership of Lenin's Bolshevik Party, seizing power and proclaiming Soviet rule. In spite of the massive use of violence on the part of its opponents, the regime was able to hold its ground, forming the Soviet Union in 1922. Shortly after the beginning of the Russian Revolution, revolutionary situations developed in Central and Southern Europe (particularly Germany and Italy). Nowhere, however, did these situations lead to a fundamental changeover of power.[26]

The Spanish Revolution of 1936–1939—usually called the Spanish Civil War—also ended in defeat. Following the electoral victory of the left-wing People's Front in 1936, conservative military officers launched an uprising under the leadership of General Francisco Franco. Sections of the left's supporters experimented with radical forms of self-government, while at the same time a war broke out with the old army. Franco won in

---

[26] Francis L. Carsten, *Revolution in Central Europe, 1918–1919* (London: Temple Smith, 1972).

1939, suppressed all democratic forces and constructed an authoritarian state.[27]

The most recent revolution in the capitalist part of Europe was the upheaval in Portugal. Since the 1960s, the fascist-ruled country had suffered ever greater economic difficulties because costly battles against the national liberation movements in the colonies of Angola, Mozambique and Guinea-Bissau had produced large foreign debts, a trade deficit, galloping inflation, capital flight and low wages. Disaffected middle-ranking officers in the army secretly joined together in a 'movement of the armed forces' and prepared a military coup. When on 25 April 1974 a church radio station broadcast the melody of the banned song 'Grandola vila Morena', this was a sign to occupy Lisbon and overthrow the government. This unleashed a tremendous social dynamic. Workers 'and soldiers' councils emerged, employees placed factories under self-management and the rural workers collectivized the *latifundia* (the great landed estates). Two counter-revolutionary coups failed in September 1974 and March 1975. The first general elections for 50 years took place on 25 April 1975; more than 90% of the electorate participated. A clear left majority emerged. Its strongest force was the moderate (social democratic) Socialist Party. Besides the SP, more radical parties retained great influence as well. The contradictions between the moderate and radical movements increased, both within the armed forces and amongst the population. On 25 November 1975 the SP leadership and a group of military officers deprived the army's radical elements of their power in a 'legal coup', and established a new 'order'. This ended the revolutionary process.

When looking at the revolutions under European capitalism, it is striking that they all occurred in relatively underdeveloped socio-economic conditions. While there have also been revolutionary situations in the most advanced capitalist countries (most recently in France in 1968, see below), these invariably ended in ultimate defeat. There is disagreement over the reasons for this. Some historians locate this failure politically, ascribing it to the influence of moderate forces (such as the Social Democrats), that act as a brake on resistance. Others suspect that structural causes are more important, especially the fact that the modern state—in contrast to agrarian society—has deeply penetrated everyday life through infrastructural subsidies.

[27] Pierre Broué and Emile Témime, *The Revolution and the Civil War in Spain* (Chicago: Haymarket, 2008).

PROTESTS UNDER DEVELOPED CAPITALISM

Since the late eighteenth century, social protest has gradually changed in Europe, beginning with the United Kingdom. A very special form of social protest now emerged: social movements. Social protest in this specific form had hitherto not existed. Distinctive features of social movements are the following:

- A social movement's power base is not firmly institutionalized. Supporters have to be mobilized over and again, and convinced of the importance of their involvement. Support is constantly sought; the movement is forced to remain in 'movement'.
- A social movement is highly diverse; it is made up of several organizations that occasionally compete with each other, and it deploys various means of exerting pressure.
- Social movements are not ephemeral. They exist for some time and are heard of for some months, sometimes even for many years.
- There is a very highly developed feeling of 'us', based on the antagonism between the movement's supporters and its opponents.
- People can participate in social movements in different ways; they can be members of official organizations involved in the movement, they can also be involved in the activities and demonstrations—or provide support—in a completely different manner.
- A social movement attempts to change, or prevent a change in a fairly specifically identified and important aspect of society.
- Social movements are often not restricted to national or regional frameworks, but are national or international in nature: they attempt to influence the authorities, businessmen, etc.

What particularly distinguishes social movements from earlier forms of protest is that they involve movement organizations (action groups, etc.) and that they mainly concentrate on specific social issues that are centrally valued. The nature of a social movement is distinguished by its dynamic, diverse and changeable form and by the fact that *nobody* fully controls it, while all sorts of organized centres are active within it simultaneously.

Social movements are generally not disorganized, but organization is not of crucial importance to them. Organization provides, amongst other things, continuity, coordination and impetus, but without the spontaneous and erratic behaviour of those who work outside the organization, not much would result from it—certainly not a social movement. The remarkable thing about a social movement is precisely the interaction between the movement's organization and its variable parts.[28]

The first social movement in this sense of the term was in all likelihood the movement against slavery that had been active in Britain since 1787. Its efforts were crowned in 1807, when King George III signed the 'Act for the Abolition of the Slave Trade'. The movement organized public meetings and was able to compel the press to report them on a regular basis. Its first large campaign (1787–1788) was a mass petition to parliament by the people of Manchester; almost 11,000 people signed the Declaration—20% of the city's male inhabitants.

In the subsequent period there have been countless social movements in Europe. For a long time, their most important manifestation was the different national workers' movements, with the result that in the nineteenth and twentieth centuries, 'workers' movement' and 'social movement' were regularly used as synonyms. There were several sources of workers' movements. In part they drew sustenance from the traditions of the older guild organizations and their notions of honour and mutual aid. In part they were inspired by socially liberal, socialist or anarchist thought. In part they were also concerned with basic democratic objectives like the right to vote (which they often understood first and foremost as the vote for adult males). Normally, workers' movements emerged locally and then, in the course of time, developed regional, national (and later international) structures.

Even before the emergence of national organizations, international connections were established between the local groups. Nineteenth-century England was the most powerful and economically advanced country in Europe (and the world) and, as a result, wages were higher there than on the continent. Thus if British workers went on strike, it was not difficult for their employers to fetch scab labour onto the island from France or Germany. As a counter-measure, the British workers strove to build an international organization which could police this strike breaking, and which would simultaneously support workers' struggles on the continent. Their attempts were successful. In mid-1864 the International

---

[28] Joachim Raschke, *Soziale Bewegungen. Ein historisch-systematischer Abriss* (Frankfurt am Main: Campus, 1985), pp. 79–80.

Workingmen's Association (IWMA) was formed, which later was called the 'First International'. The IWMA was first actively involved in stopping an attempt to break a strike in April 1866: the tailors of London had organized and demanded a wage increase of one penny per hour. The employers responded to this with a lockout, and tried to recruit strike-breakers in Germany, as they had done on several occasions in the past. The IWMA helped prevent this in Hamburg and Berlin, which contributed to the victory of the London tailors. The IWMA was only granted a short life. It was severely weakened as early as 1872 and came to a definitive end in 1876.

In the following years—during and after the 'Great Depression' (roughly between 1873 and 1895)—consolidated national trade union organizations spread in Europe, from Switzerland (1880), through Spain (1886), Germany (1890), Austria (1893), France (1895), Sweden (1898), Hungary (1898), to Serbia (1903) and Bulgaria (1904). More or less parallel to this, increasing numbers of workers' parties were established, mainly social democratic in nature. They were founded in many countries, including Germany (1875), Denmark (1876), Belgium and Spain (1879), Switzerland and Hungary (1880), Norway and Austria (1889), Britain (1893), Bulgaria (1894), Russia (1898), Finland (1899), Serbia (1903) and Romania (1910).

These developments facilitated a new phase of international cooperation. In 1889 the so-called 'Second International' was founded in Paris. Anarchists and socialists initially worked together in the international, until the former were excluded in 1896. There were also international trade union mergers around the same time. First came the so-called International Trade Union Secretariats, associations for cooperation between national trade unions of a particular occupation. It started in 1889 with the typographers and printers, the hat-makers, cigar-rollers, tobacco workers and shoemakers. And then other professional groups rapidly followed, right down to the hairdressers (1907) and the postal workers (1910). When the foundation of the International Trade Union Secretariats proved a success, the cooperation of national trade union federations also began to gather momentum. In 1903 the International Secretariat of the national trade union associations was launched, which became the International Trade Union Confederation (ITUC) in 1913.

In the two decades prior to the First World War, the workers' movement went through a big upswing. One expression of this development was a new phenomenon, the great political strike. The main goal of this kind of struggle was the right to vote for (male) members of the lower classes, as in Belgium (1891, 1893 and 1902) and Sweden (1902). This orientation towards parliamentary politics provoked oppositional forces; time and again there were strong currents opposing the efforts to influence the state and in favour of building up autonomous power. At first it was mainly the so-called revolutionary syndicalists who organized separately; they saw the general strike as the most important means of bringing about social transformation. After the Russian Revolution of 1917 it was mainly the newly formed communist parties who rejected parliamentarism. Until well into the twentieth century, the European workers' movement was to know two main opposing wings: the social democrats and the communists.

Many other social movements developed parallel to the workers' movements—the anti-militarist and the women's and youth, for example.[29] All these were able to draw on the lessons of older traditions. Thus the women's movement had existed in embryonic form as far back as the French revolution. After the Second World War there were also movements in solidarity with the 'Third World'. The most important examples of this were the groups in France, but also in other countries, who supported the Algerian insurgents' war of liberation against French colonial rule (until independence in 1962). A little later, the American war against the Vietnamese liberation movement was to have an even greater impact. In the late 1960s the rebellion reached its climax with the forces freed by the liberalization of the communist regime in Czechoslovakia (the so-called 'Prague Spring'—see below) and the uprising of workers and youth in France in May 1968. Both revolts failed, but had long-term significance as an inspiration for rebellious youth in Europe and beyond. In addition, we have also seen environmental movements since the 1970s.

Protests Under 'Actual Existing Socialism'

There have been protests under so-called 'actually existing socialism' of Eastern Europe almost from its beginnings. In the Soviet Union of the 1920s there were numerous strikes that have only recently begun to be documented. When the Soviet sphere of influence had been consolidated after the Second World War and dictatorial planned economies had been

[29] Gernot Jochheim, 'Zur Geschichte und Theorie der europäischen antimilitaristischen Bewegung 1900–1940', in Reiner Steinweg, *Schwerpunkt: Friedensbewegung* (Frankfurt am Main: Suhrkamp, 1977), pp. 27–49.

introduced, disturbances quickly came about, particularly in the more economically advanced parts of the continent. When, in May 1953, output norms were raised by 10% in the GDR, a protest movement emerged from June 16/17 onwards, in which hundreds of thousands participated. The protesters quickly became radicalized and politicized. Amongst other things, they began to free political prisoners. Only with the support of Soviet tanks were the GDR rulers able to suppress the rebellion by force.[30]

When, following the death of Soviet dictator Joseph Stalin, a process of 'destalinization' began a new situation appeared to arise in Eastern Europe, culminating in Nikita Khrushchev's secret speech in February 1956. In that speech, Khrushchev claimed, amongst other things, that Stalin had departed from the 'clear and unambiguous principles of Lenin' and had carried out 'mass terror', for which there had been 'no serious reasons'. In the more relaxed political situation which emerged after this speech, there were soon more revolts in the Soviet concentration camps, following the pattern of those that had taken place in Noril'sk, Vorkuta and Kingir in 1953–1954. These contributed to the demise of the 'Gulag Archipelago', which was largely disbanded a few years later.[31] But there were also uprisings in numerous cities. For example, in the provincial town of Novočerkassk in 1962 workers blocked a busy railway line and occupied the city centre in response to wage cuts and price increases. KGB troops struck down the rebellion. According to official figures, 26 were killed. Gradually these forms of resistance assumed an organized character. Thus in 1978 the miner Vladimir Klebanov formed an 'Association of Free Trade Unions', from which—after this association was broken up—the 'Free Inter-professional Association of Workers' emerged as its successor. Under repressive conditions, however, such an approach remained marginal.

In Poland, notably in Poznań, there was a workers' uprising. While it remained relatively small, it formed the beginning of a long chain of revolts, in which the subversive networks formed at the time repeatedly played a role. In Hungary the revolt began in late October 1956, when thousands of students—explicitly alluding to the revolution of 1848—held

[30] Roger Engelmann and Ilko S. Kowalczuk (eds), *Volkserhebung gegen den SED-Staat. Eine Bestandsaufnahme zum 17. Juni 1953* (Göttingen: Vandenhoeck & Ruprecht, 2005).

[31] Karl Schlögel, *Der renitente Held. Arbeiterprotest in der Sowjetunion 1953–1983* (Hamburg: Junius, 1984); Andrea Graziosi, 'The Great Strikes of 1953 in Soviet Labor Camps in the Accounts of Their Participants. A Review', *Cahiers du monde russe et soviétique* 4 (1992), pp. 419–445.

a demonstrative march through Budapest that led to a violent confrontation with the police. In the following days the protests spread across the entire country. The government was brought down. Councils emerged which tried to replace the administration, political prisoners were freed and prominent supporters of the Soviet regime killed. At first the new government appeared willing to make concessions to the insurgents, but then it opted for bloody repression, supported in this by Soviet troops. When the futility of resistance became evident, around 200,000 Hungarians fled to the West.[32]

From 1963 onwards there had been a certain political liberalization as a result of a crisis in the Czechoslovak Socialist Republic's (CSSR) planned economy, which eventually led to the so-called 'Prague Spring'. In March 1968 the old Party Secretary Antonín Novotný was replaced by the reformer Alexander Dubček. Censorship was abolished and the Communist Party adopted a programme of action that demanded, amongst other things, the separation of party and state, secret ballots, the right to self-determination of both nations (Czechs and Slovaks), freedom of assembly and organization, and economic reform. In the months that followed, a globally respected euphoria for political and cultural reform developed, which was drowned in August 1968 by an invasion of troops from the 'fraternal socialist countries' (the USSR, Hungary, Poland, the GDR and Bulgaria). However, the dissidents remained active underground. On 1 January 1977—in celebration of the so-called Helsinki accords of 1975, the 'universal significance of human rights and fundamental freedoms' which had also been signed by the Czechoslovak government—they founded the Charter '77 movement, which criticized abuses of human rights and was acclaimed across the country.

Poland became the focal point of resistance in the 1970s and 80s. As early as May 1968 there had been enormous student protests that were suppressed by the government; the repression was combined with an anti-Semitic hate campaign and forced thousands of Jewish intellectuals to emigrate. Price increases had caused riots, street battles and factory occupations on the Baltic coast (Gdánsk, Szczecin), which led to the downfall of the party secretary Władisław Gomułka in 1970. In June 1976 newly planned price increases were answered by strikes, demonstrations and the tearing up of railway tracks; within 24 hours the government backtracked on the measures. In that same year the Workers' Defence Committee

[32] Bill Lomax, *Hungary 1956* (London: Allison & Busby, 1976).

(KOR) was formed, which quickly developed into the core of a new independent workers' organization.

But for the state, the contraction of the Polish economy in 1979 was a reason to strengthen market forces: from 1 July 1980 improved types of meat were only available in expensive commercial shops. Workers in different cities responded to the announcement of this measure with a strike wave that lasted for six weeks. From August, various inter-plant strike committees emerged. On 17 September 1980 these formed the independent, self-governing trade union 'Solidarity' (*Solidarność*) and elected Lech Walesa as its chairman. 'Solidarity' grew explosively, and within a very short time had millions of members. Its growth increasingly infringed upon the regime's power. In December 1981 the Polish government therefore declared a state of war and criminalized 'Solidarity'. However, the weakened organization continued to exist underground.

In the late 1980s, when the economic problems of the 'socialist' countries threatened to become uncontrollable, different traditions of resistance surfaced once more. After taking office in March 1985 the Soviet party secretary Mikhail Gorbachev continually reduced levels of political repression, thus creating space for independent initiatives in the USSR and other Eastern European countries. In April 1989 'Solidarity' was made legal again and in August of the same year the Polish trade union rose to become the most important governing party. Between 1989 and 1991 there were political upheavals in other Eastern European countries as well, mainly driven by citizens' protests and workers' struggles.[33]

CONCLUSION

Social protest is an essential part of European history. Its causes and effects can vary greatly. Three driving forces repeatedly make an appearance: the longing for a minimum of social security, for adherence to certain standards of social justice, and for respect. A good number of the protest movements ended in defeat, and only a relatively small number of them were directly successful. But even defeats could be 'productive' for the rebels in the longer term; not only did they provide tactical and organizational lessons, they also warned the authorities that certain boundaries

[33] Melanie Tatur, *Solidarność als Modernisierungsbewegung. Sozialstruktur und Konflikt in Polen* (Frankfurt am Main: Campus, 1989).

were not to be crossed. Through resistance, people learn to 'walk upright' (Ernst Bloch), which is essential in democratic societies.

FURTHER READINGS

Comprehensive overviews of European social protests during the last thousand years do not exist. But there are many historical case studies and comparisons of separate cases. Works on protests in pre-capitalist and early capitalist society are numerous, but most of them have not been published in English. Very helpful is Samuel K. Cohn Jr. (ed.), *Popular Protest in Late Medieval Europe* (Manchester: Manchester University Press, 2004), a collection of translated documents covering numerous protest events in Italy, France and Flanders from 1245 until the fourteenth century. A full treatment of the Flemish peasant rebellion is given in William H. TeBrake's *A Plague of Insurrection. Popular Politics and Peasant Revolt in Flanders, 1323–1328* (Philadelphia: University of Pennsylvania Press, 1993). A classical study on the English peasant uprising is Rodney Hilton's *Bond Men Made Free. Medieval Peasant Movements and the English Rising of 1381* (originally published in 1973; now available in an updated edition, London: Routledge, 2005). Peasant rebellions of the fourteenth to eighteenth centuries in Scandinavia, Finland and Iceland are discussed in Kimmo Katalaja (ed.), *Northern Revolts. Medieval and Early Modern Peasant Unrest in the Nordic Countries* (Helsinki: Finnish Literature Society, 2004). Studies of the German peasant war of 1525 include Janos Bak (ed.), *The German Peasant War of 1525* (London: Frank Cass, 1976), and Bob Scribner and Gerhard Benecke (eds), *The German Peasant War of 1525: New Viewpoints* (London: Allen & Unwin, 1979). An interesting comparative perspective is developed in Roland Mousnier, *Peasant Uprisings in Seventeenth Century France, Russia, and China*. Trans. Brian Pearce (New York: Harper & Row, 1970). The Rumanian *jacquerie* of 1907 is reconstructed by Philip Gabriel Eidelberg in *The Great Rumanian Peasant Revolt of 1907. Origins of a Modern Jacquerie* (Leiden: Brill, 1974). A remarkable study of English rebellious farm labourers in the early 1830s is Eric J. Hobsbawm and George F. Rudé, *Captain Swing* (first edition 1968; London: Verso, 2014).

Urban rebellions between 1280 and 1435 are a major topic in Michel Mollat and Philippe Wolff, *The Popular Revolutions of the Late Middle Ages*, trans. A.L. Lytton-Sells (London: Allen & Unwin, 1973). Guy Fourquin's *The Anatomy of Popular Rebellion in the Middle Ages.*, trans. Anne Chesters

(Amsterdam and New York: North-Holland, 1978) contains some useful insights too. Specific urban struggles are studied in, for example, Henry L. Seaver's classic *The Great Revolt in Castile. A Study of the Comunero Movement of 1520–1521* (New York: Octagon Books, 1966), originally published in 1928, and in Rosario Villari's, *The Revolt of Naples*, trans. James Newell, Foreword Peter Burke (Cambridge: Polity Press, 1993), a study of the rebellion of 1647. See also Samuel K. Cohn, Jr., *Popular Protest in Late Medieval English Towns* (Cambridge: Cambridge University Press, 2013).

Closely connected with these urban struggles were workers' and journeymen's struggles. A first exploration can be found in Catharina Lis, Jan Lucassen, and Hugo Soly (eds), *Before the Unions. Wage Earners and Collective Action in Europe, 1300–1850.* Supplement to the *International Review of Social History*, 39 (1994). The trade union of the *Griffarins* is described in Natalie Zemon Davis, 'A Trade Union in Sixteenth-Century France', *Economic History Review*, 19 (1966), pp. 48–69. Rudolf Dekker gives an informative overview of Dutch developments in his 'Labour Conflicts and Working-Class Culture in Early Modern Holland', *International Review of Social History*, 25 (1990), pp. 377–420. Information on later developments in the nineteenth and twentieth centuries is offered in Dick Geary (ed.), *Labour and Socialist Movements in Europe before 1914* (Oxford: Berg, 1989), and in Stefan Berger and David Broughton (eds), *The Force of Labour. The Western European Labour Movement and the Working Class in the Twentieth Century* (Oxford: Berg, 1995). Perhaps the most important form of workers' struggle is the strike. An influential longitudinal study was Edward Shorter and Charles Tilly, *Strikes in France, 1830–1968* (London: Cambridge University Press, 1974). An international perspective is offered in Sjaak van der Velden et al. (eds), *Strikes Around the World, 1968–2005. Case studies of 15 Countries* (Amsterdam: Aksant, 2007).

Food riots and other forms of crowd action happened both in urban and rural areas. Pioneering studies include George F. Rudé, *Paris and London in the Eighteenth Century: Studies in Popular Protest* (London: Collins, 1970), and Edward P. Thompson's famous essay 'The Moral Economy of the English Crowd in the Eighteenth Century', *Past and Present* 50 (February 1971), reprinted in Thompson's *Customs in Common* (Harmondsworth: Penguin, 1993). An interesting case study (of a food riot in France 1775) is Cynthia A. Bouton, *The Flour War: Gender, Class, and Community in Late Ancien Regime French Society* (University Park,

PA: Pennsylvania State University Press, 1993). Recent studies include Buchanan Sharp, *Famine and Scarcity in Late Medieval and Early Modern England. The Regulation of Grain Marketing, 1256–1631* (Cambridge: Cambridge University Press, 2016), and Michael T. Davis (ed.), *Crowd Actions in Britain and France from the Middle Ages to the Modern World* (Basingstoke: Palgrave Macmillan, 2015).

The standard reference for millenarian movements is still Norman Cohn, *The Pursuit of the Millennium: Revolutionary Millenarians and Mystical Anarchists of the Middle Ages.* Revised and expanded edition (New York: Oxford University Press, 1970). But see also Andrew P. Roach and James R. Simpson (eds), *Heresy and the Making of European Culture: Medieval and Modern Perspectives* (Farnham: Ashgate/Variorum, 2013). Case studies include Thomas A. Fudge, *Heresy and Hussites in Late Medieval Europe* (Farnham: Ashgate/Variorum, 2014); Anthony Arthur, *Tailor-King. The Rise and Fall of the Anabaptist Kingdom of Münster* (New York: Thomas Dunne, 1999), and Sigrun Haude, *In the Shadow of 'Savage Wolves': Anabaptist Münster and the German Reformation during the 1530s* (Atlantic Highlands, NJ : Humanities Press, 2000).

The literature on social revolutions is overwhelming. Jack A. Goldstone offers a brief (sociological) introduction in his *Revolutions: A Very Short Introduction* (Oxford: Oxford University Press, 2014). Useful is also Charles Tilly's *European Revolutions, 1492–1992* (Oxford: Blackwell, 1992). Case studies include Geoffrey Parker, *The Dutch Revolt* (Ithaca, NY: Cornell University Press, 1977); Christopher Hill, *The Century of Revolution 1603–1714* (London: Routledge, 1993); Albert Soboul, *The French Revolution, 1787–1799: From the storming of the Bastille to Napoleon.* Trans. Alan Forrest and Colin Jones (New York: Random House, 1974; second edition London: Unwin Hyman, 1989); Wolfram Siemann, *The German Revolution of 1848–1849.* Trans. Christiane Banerji (New York: St Martin's Press, 1996); Francis L. Carsten, *Revolution in Central Europe, 1918–1919* (Aldershot: Wildwood House, 1988); Pierre Broué and Émile Témime, *Revolution and War in Spain,* trans. Tony White (First edn: Cambridge, MA: MIT Press; second edn: Chicago: Haymarket Books, 2008). The best-studied social revolution is undoubtedly the Russian revolution of 1917; there is even an academic journal that is completely devoted to this topic: *Revolutionary Russia,* published since 1988. An excellent introduction to the topic by a participant is Leon Trotsky, *History of the Russian Revolution,* trans. Max Eastman (1st edn New York: Simon and Schuster, 1932; Chicago: Haymarket Books, 2008). Important recent studies are Alexander Rabinowitch, *The Bolsheviks Come to Power: The Revolution of 1917 in Petrograd* (first edn New York: W.W. Norton, 1976; Chicago: Haymarket Books, 2004), and Ken Murphy, *Revolution and Counterrevolution. Class Struggle in a Moscow Metal Factory* (Oxford: Berghahn, 2005).

The invention of social movements in 'modern capitalism' is reconstructed in Charles Tilly's *The Contentious French* (Cambridge, MA: Belknap Press, 1986), and in *Popular Contention in Great Britain, 1758–1834* (Boulder, CO: Paradigm, 2005), by the same author. Craig Calhoun, *Roots of Radicalism: Tradition, the Public Sphere and Early Nineteenth-Century Social Movements* (Chicago: University of Chicago Press, 2012) explores early social movements and reveals some similarities with movements in the late-twentieth century. Interesting is Mark Traugott's *The Insurgent Barricade* (Berkeley, CA: University of California Press, 2010), which reconstructs the invention and diffusion of barricades in from the eighteenth century until 1848. Labour movements as social movements have been discussed above.

There is a substantial literature on the history of peace movements, mostly focusing on national histories. Wim H. van der Linden has written two massive studies on early peace movements: *The International Peace Movement 1815–1874* (Amsterdam: Tilleul, 1987), and *The International Peace Movement during the First World War* (Almere: Tilleul, 2006). David Cortright gives a general overview in his *Peace. A History of Movements and Ideas* (Cambridge: Cambridge University Press, 2009). The period after the Second World War is covered by April Carter, *Peace Movements. International Protest and World Politics since 1945* (London: Longman, 1992).

Another class of movement bridging the nineteenth and twentieth centuries is women's movements. Overviews are given in Janet Saltzman Chafetz and Anthony Gary Dworkin, *Female Revolt: Women's Movements in World and Historical Perspective* (Totowa, NJ: Rowman and Littlefield, 1986); Mary Fainsod Katzenstein and Carol McClurg Mueller (eds), *The Women's Movements of the United States and Western Europe: Consciousness, Political Opportunity, and Public Policy* (Philadelphia: Temple University Press, 1987); and Anna Bull, Hanna Diamond, and Rosalind Marsh (eds), *Feminisms and Women's Movements in Contemporary Europe* (New York: St Martin's Press, 2000). On women's movements in Eastern Germany, Poland, Czech Republic, Slovakia and Hungary after the collapse of state socialism, see Barbara Einhorn, *Cinderella Goes to the Market: Citizenship,*

Gender and Women's Movements in East Central Europe (London: Verso, 1993).

Social movements after 1945 are discussed in Hara Kouki and Eduardo Romanos (eds), *Protest beyond Borders. Contentious Politics in Europe since 1945* (Oxford: Berghahn, 2011), and Martin Klimke and Joachim Scharloth (eds), *1968 in Europe. A History of Protest and Activism, 1956–1977* (New York: Palgrave Macmillan, 2008). The literature on the movements of '1968' is enormous. A good, but controversial, interpretation can be found in Michael Seidman's *The Imaginary Revolution. Parisian Students and Workers in 1968* (New York and Oxford: Berghahn, 2004). Movements of the 1980s are the topic of Knud Andresen and Bart van der Steen (eds), *A European Youth Revolt: European Perspectives on Youth Protest and Social Movements in the 1980s* (Basingstoke: Palgrave Macmillan, 2015). Recent protests are at the centre of Cristina Flesher Fominaya and Laurence Cox (eds), *Understanding European Movements: New Social Movements, Global Justice Struggles, Anti-Austerity Protest* (London: Routledge, 2013).

The literature on social protest and social movements in 'actually existing socialism' focuses predominantly on Solidarność in Poland. Informative are the documents collected in Oliver MacDonald's [pseudonym of Peter Gowan] *The Polish August. Documents from the Beginnings of the Polish Workers' Rebellion* (Seattle: Left Bank Books, 1981). The dramatic events of 1980 are the topic of Michael Szporer, *Solidarity: The Great Workers' Strike of 1980* (Lanham, MD: Lexington Books, 2012). Contextual information, also covering later developments, can be found in Andrzej Rychard and Gabriel Motzkin (eds), *The Legacy of Polish Solidarity: Social Activism, Regime Collapse, and the Building of a New Society* (New York: Peter Lang, 2015), and in Jack M. Bloom, *Seeing Through the Eyes of the Polish Revolution. Solidarity and the Struggle against Communism in Poland* (Leiden: Brill, 2013).

The Hungarian workers' uprising of 1956 is at the centre of Bill Lomax, *Hungary 1956* (London: Allison & Busby, 1976), and of Paul Lendvai, *One Day that Shook the Communist World: The 1956 Uprising and Its Legacy*. Trans. Ann Major (Princeton, NJ: Princeton University Press, 2008). A well-informed and broad contextual interpretation can be found in Adam Fabry (ed.), *From the Vanguard to the Margins. Workers in Hungary, 1939 to the Present. Selected Essays by Mark Pittaway* (Leiden: Brill, 2014). A more general discussion of East European Rebellions since the 1940s is offered in Kevin McDermott and Matthew Stibbe (eds),

Revolution and Resistance in Eastern Europe: Challenges to Communist Rule (Oxford: Berg, 2006).

There is no good English-language survey of protests and protest movements in the Soviet Union. Fragments can be found in Marta Craveri, 'The strikes of Noril'sk and Vorkuta Camps and Their Role in the Breakdown of the Stalinist Forced Labour System', in Tom Brass and Marcel van der Linden (eds), *Free and Unfree Labour. The Debate Continues* (Bern: Peter Lang, 1997); Andrea Graziosi, 'The Great Strikes of 1953 in Soviet Labor Camps in the Accounts of Their Participants: A Review', *Cahiers du Monde Russe et Soviétique* 4 (1992); Robert Hornsby, *Protest, Reform and Repression in Khrushchev's Soviet Union* (Cambridge: Cambridge University Press, 2013); and William Moskoff, *Hard Times. Impoverishment and Protest in the Perestroika Years: the Soviet Union, 1985–1991* (Armonk, NY: Sharpe, 1993). An informative but too optimistic analysis of workers' struggles during the USSR's collapse can be found in David Mandel, *Perestroika and the Soviet People. Rebirth of the Labour Movement* (Montreal: Black Rose, 1991).

CHAPTER 8

Social Movements in Africa

Andreas Eckert

A NEGLECTED FIELD

The theme of 'Social Movements' does not—and never did—rank high among those issues that historians of Africa would consider crucial.[1] Already a quick glance at the relevant literature does not only confirm this impression, but also reveals that much of the quantitatively rather meagre social and cultural studies literature on social movements in Africa suffers from historical short-windedness. Thus, writing an overview about the *history* of social movements in Africa is mainly an exercise in producing whipped cream out of skimmed milk. On the other hand, there was a recent (but rather short-lived) interest in current social movements in Africa largeley fuelled by the so-called Arab Spring. The events in Northern Africa and the Arab world led to a changed perception of political resistance in these countries, but also in sub-Saharan Africa. Western media and political commentators suddenly no longer called for an almost apolitical 'civil society' meant to stabilize the state, but started to appreciate social

[1] Just note that there is no reference to 'social movements' in the index of a recently published authoritative handbook on African history (John Parker & Richard Reid (eds), *The Oxford Handbook of Modern African History*, Oxford: Oxford University Press, 2013).

A. Eckert (✉)
Department of African Studies, Humboldt University, Berlin, Germany

© The Author(s) 2017
S. Berger, H. Nehring (eds.), *The History of Social Movements in Global Perspective*, DOI 10.1057/978-1-137-30427-8_8

movements that aim at bringing down their respective governments.[2] One of the questions asked in this context was: 'Will the Arab Uprising Spread to Sub-Saharan Africa?'[3] However, those who began to take interest in social movements in Africa had to realize that the study of this topic so far is a neglected field of research in African studies and social sciences. Not only does Africa remain largely absent from social science research using a social movement perspective. Social movement theory largely focuses on socio-political movements in Europe, North and South America. 'In the absence of historically grounded empirical research', some authors recently lamented, 'social movements in these societies [of the global South] and the struggles that underpin them are not infrequently reduced to carica-ture'. Most of the research, they go on, 'denies the complexity of social formations in the South, and, ignoring any prospect of agency, portrays their members as the hapless victims of tyrannical rulers and traditional culture or the passive recipients of Northern-led actions'.[4]

In addition to that, the literature on social movement theory has so far hardly been explored within African studies, even though a growing num-ber of empirical studies are dealing with different forms of civil action and political mobilization in current African contexts. This is especially true for the case of the Republic of South Africa. Scholars have explored the struggle against apartheid as well as a broad range of movements in post-apartheid South Africa against privatization and liberalization of basic social services or discrimination related to sexual identity, for land rights or gender equality.[5] Still, especially compared to Latin American Studies where labour unions,

---

[2] See Nikolai Brandes and Bettina Engels, 'Social Movements in Africa', *Stichproben. Wiener Zeitschrift für kritische Afrikastudien*, 11 (2011), pp. 1–15, here: p. 1.

[3] This was a headline in Nairobi's *Daily Nation*, 8 September 2011, cited in ibid.

[4] Lisa Thompson and Chris Tapscott, 'Introduction: Mobilization and Social Movements in the South—The Challenges of Inclusive Governance', in idem (eds), *Citizenship and Social Movements. Perspectives from the Global South* (London: Zed Books, 2010), pp. 1–32, here: p. 1.

[5] Brandes and Engels, 'Social Movements', p. 2. Examples of this literature include Karl von Holdt, 'Social Movement Unionism: the Case of South Africa', *Work, Employment & Society* 2 (2002), pp. 283–304; Rebecca Pointer, 'Questioning the Representation of South Africa's "New Social Movements": A Case Study of the Mandela Park Anti-Eviction Campaign', *Journal of Asian and African Studies* 4 (2004), pp. 271–294; Kimberly Lanegran, 'South Africa's Civic Association Movement: ANC's Ally or Society's "Watchdog"? Shifting Social Movement–Political Party Relation', *African Studies Review* 2 (1995), pp. 101–126; Peter Alexander, 'Rebellion of the Poor: South Africa's Service Delivery Protests: a Preliminary Analysis', *Review of African Political Economy* 123 (2010), pp. 25–40.

landless workers' movements or feminist movements are central terrains of both empirical and theoretical investigation,[6] social movements in Africa, as Brandes and Engels summarize the state of the art, 'largely remain under-researched and under-theorized'[7]—and, one could add, under-historicized.

SOCIAL MOVEMENTS AS CIVIL SOCIETY?

A rough periodization of the history of social movements in post-colonial Africa would start with the first three decades of independence (1960s to 1980s) which can be seen as a period when liberation movements held state power—and then often transformed themselves into repressive and authoritarian governments that quickly established one-party states. In the early 1990s a wind of change blew through Africa, multi-party systems were introduced, and enormous democratic hopes were put on the respective 'civil societies'. A third period followed, during which numerous civil society groups were co-opted by international agencies and donors such as the World Bank. These groups then often turned into professional development agencies.[8]

Social movements in Africa are often analysed in the framework of civil society. The concept of 'civil society' appeared prominently in the field of African studies at a time when the failure of African states and their elites to deliver services regarded as essential for a 'modern' state such as health services, education and infrastructure became apparent.[9] 'Civil society' then appeared as a 'deus ex machina' that was very much inspired by North American structures and institutions. In the eyes of scholars and development practitioners, civil society not only represented spaces of political opposition and autonomy, but was also conceptualized as the most promising 'agent of modernization'. The success of civil societies in

[6] See Susan Eckstein (ed.), *Power and Popular Protests: Latin American Social Movements* (Berkeley: University of California Press, 1989); Gary Prevost et al. (eds), *Social Movements and Leftist Governments in Latin America. Confrontation or Co-optation?* (London: Zed Boooks, 2012); Richard Stahler-Sholk et al. (eds), *Latin American Social Movements in the Twenty-First Century: Resistance, Power, and Democracy* (Boulder, CO: Rowman & Littlefield, 2008).

[7] Brandes and Engels, 'Social Movements', p. 2.

[8] Ibid., p. 4. This development is apparent in Ebenezer Obadare (ed.), *The Handbook of Civil Society in Africa* (Berlin: Springer, 2014).

[9] It is crucial to note that this failure is closely linked to the effects of the oil crisis of 1973/1974 and the politics of IMF and World Bank which banked on the miracles of the market, not on the state. See Frederick Cooper, 'Writing the History of Development', *Journal of Modern European History* 1 (2010), pp. 5–23.

engaging authoritarian states in Eastern Europe even furthered the idea of African civil societies as alternatives to the apparently weak and at the same time authoritarian African states.[10] The pursuit of civil society throughout the African continent, the political scientist Crawford Young stressed in the early 1990s, is a 'drama of redemption whose potential nobility commands our admiration'.[11]

The perspective on African civil society as the *locus sine qua non* for progressive politics changed: A few years later civil society was no longer understood as an a priori space of homogenous political opposition, but as a rather unpredictable factor shaped by conflicting and even politically conservative interests based, for example, on gender, ethnic identities and class. Some authors emphasized that civil society also constituted an arena in which states and other powerful actors intervene to influence the political agendas of organized groups with the intention of defusing opposition.[12] Two dynamics between civil society and the state came to the forefront of the debate: Firstly, social services continued to be dismantled in the neo-liberal wave after 1989 while authoritarian rule did not go away even after the introduction of multi-party systems. This further motivated some political actors to digress from state institutions. Civil society became conceptualized as a shelter for disadvantaged social strata that turned away from the state instead of confronting it. Often supported by Northern NGOs, grassroots organizations started to organize their own supply with social services and thereby structurally replaced and supported the state. Secondly, the idea of participation in governance issues allowed for the conceptualization of civil society organizations as independent organs for the control of the government, as intermediate structure between the state and local populations or as multipliers of ideas of human and civil rights or

---

[10] The debates of the late 1980s and 1990s are represented by René Lemarchand, 'Uncivil States and Civil Societies. How Illusion became Reality', *Journal of Modern African Studies* 2 (1992), pp. 177–191; John W. Harbeson et al. (eds), *Civil Society and the State in Africa* (Boulder: Lynne Rienner, 1994); Robert Fatton Jr., 'Africa in the Age of Democratization. The Civil Limitations of Civil Society', *African Studies Review* 3 (1996), pp. 67–99; Maxwell Owusu, 'Domesticating Democracy: Culture, Civil Society and Constitutionalism in Africa', *Comparative Studies in Society and History* 1 (1997), pp. 120–152; Michael Bratton, 'Beyond the State: Civil Society and Associational Life in Africa', *World Politics* 3 (1989), pp. 407–430.

[11] Crawford Young, 'In Search of Civil Society', in Harbeson et al. (eds), *Civil Society*, pp. 33–50, p. 48.

[12] See Julie Hearn, 'The "Uses and Abuses" of Civil Society in Africa', *Review of African Political Economy* 28 (2001), pp. 43–53.

rule of law.[13] The focus of external donors shifting away from the state to civil societies went often hand in hand with a new emphasis on decentralization. This created unintended consequences. In order to benefit from development aid, it became crucial to stress the belonging to a specific group or locality. The effect was that in many places struggles emerged over the question of who was entitled to be 'autochthonous' and thus could profit from a development project.[14]

In short, in Africa as in other places, 'civil society' evoked for a while 'a polythetic clutch of signs. An all-purpose placeholder, it captures otherwise inchoate—as yet unnamed and unnameable—popular aspirations, moral concerns, sites and spaces of practices; likewise, it bespeaks a scholarly effort to recalibrate worn-out methodological tools, and to find a positive politics, amid conceptual confusion.'[15] From a decade or so ago, however, 'civil society' has lost its attraction both as a political saviour and as an analytical concept.

In the sparse scholarly production on social movements in Africa two central questions have emerged over the last two decades. The first addresses the ambivalent relationship of African social movements towards the colonial and post-colonial state, while the second focuses on the relation of social movements towards external actors and the related issue of the risk being controlled by donors and international NGOs. In the introduction to a volume published by the Dakar-based think tank 'Council for the Development of Social Movements and Democracy' (CODESRIA), Mahmood Mamdani warned against the conflation of social movements with civil society, and criticized most (Western) scholars for reproducing an allegedly universal idea of 'civil society' that is deeply rooted in the false dualism of tradition and modernity emerging from modernization theory.[16] This volume, rarely referred to in the European debates, remained on

---

[13] Brandes and Engels, 'Social Movements', p. 8. See Thomas Bierschenk and Jean-Pierre Olivier de Sardan, 'Local Powers and a Distant State in Rural Central African Republic', *Journal of Modern African Studies* 3 (1997), pp. 441–468; Aili Mari Tripp, *Changing the Rules. The Politics of Liberalization and the Urban Informal Economy in Tanzania* (Berkeley: University of California Press, 1997).

[14] See Peter Geschiere, *The Perils of Belonging. Autochthony, Citizenship and Exclusion in Africa and Europe* (Chicago: University of Chicago Press, 2009).

[15] John L. Comaroff/Jean Comaroff, 'Introduction', in idem (eds), *Civil Society and the Political Imagination in Africa. Critical Perspectives* (Chicago: University of Chicago Press, 1999), pp. 1–43, here: p. 3.

[16] See Mahmood Mamdani, 'Introduction', in idem and Ernest Wamba-dia-Wamba (eds), *African Studies in Social Movements and Democracy* (Dakar: CODESRIA, 1995), pp. 1–34.

its own for a long time. Two recent publications both raise the question whether social movements in Africa are to be understood as global phenomena or if these African movements differ fundamentally from those in Europe or the Americas. In other words: What is African about African social movements, and to what extent they were shaped by external actors, concepts and norms? Miles Larmer is convinced that

> social movements actually existing in Africa are unavoidably hybrid in nature, utilizing and adapting Western ideas, funding, forms or organization and methods of activism. Consequently, the enduring influence of universalist models that have their origins in the West, and the profound inequalities and power relations between Western agencies and African social movements, should be part of the analysis of social movements.[17]

There can be little doubt indeed that international, and in particular 'Western', actors, ideas and norms exercise substantial influence on African social movements and struggles. However, it is often ignored that there are social movements in Africa that reflect 'Western' ideas to a much lesser extent. Consequently, these movements are hardly recognized as social movements from a Western—neither academic nor activist—perspective. This ignorance particularly applies to Muslim organizations in Africa which often have their own media and centres of debate at their disposal, which play important roles in a variety of social movements.[18] So far, Western scholars and activists have tended to privilege Westernized intellectuals as their counterparts and objects of study for both ideological and more pragmatic reasons, such as the accessibility of the European languages in

---

[17] Miles Larmer, 'Social Movement Struggles in Africa', *Review of African Political Economy* 125 (2010) (Special issue on Social movement struggles in Africa), pp. 251–262, here: p. 257. The other volume addressing related questions is Stephen Ellis and Ineke van Kessel (eds), *Movers and Shakers: Social Movements in Africa* (Leiden: Brill, 2009).

[18] It is telling that the scholarship discussing social movements in the context of Islam and contemporary Muslim societies does not consider sub-Saharan Africa. See Quinatn Wiktorowicz (ed.), *Islam Activism: A Social Movement Theory Approach* (Bloomington: Indiana University Press, 2004). One has to add that Islam studies is still largely neglecting the theme of social movements. For one of the few case studies that employs a focus on Muslim social movements in Africa see Benjamin Soares, 'An Islamic Social Movement in Contemporary West Africa: NASFAT of Nigeria', in Ellis and Van Kessel, *Movers*, pp. 178–196.

which these intellectuals communicated.[19] Many scholars of Africa avoid a straightforward definition of social movements and opt instead for a list of different organizations and activities—NGOs, civil society organizations, self-defined social movements, strikes and riots, the mob and the crowd—in order to circumscribe the phenomenon.[20]

How do the data we have on contemporary social movements in Africa—most of these data in fact referring to South Africa—relate to the general debates that have emerged in the study of social movements? In this regard, two assertions seem to be particularly crucial:[21] first, that the central point of social struggles for a more human development has shifted from the arena of production to that of consumption; and second, that struggles concerning identity are replacing ones mainly oriented towards material issues, especially in post-industrial societies. Looking at the evidence from Africa, it is true that social struggles, again especially in South Africa, have expanded into the arena of identity politics. However, movements concerned with relations of production continue to exist and remain crucial to the sustainability of struggles concerning consumption. Thus while identity movements and struggles are increasing, material issues are as relevant to these struggles as they were to earlier social movements. Habib and Okupu-Mensah stress that the main feature of social movements in Africa is that they are 'an avenue for marginalized people and those concerned about their possibility to impact material distribution and social exclusion and to claim a certain degree of influence and power over the state itself'.[22] In this capacity, they are also vital for a functioning democracy in African states, especially in those with only one dominant political party. But it does not necessarily ensue that social movements are inherently democratic.

---

[19] There is much research on (the history of) Muslim intellectuals that is never discussed in the framework of social movements. See e.g. Benjamin Soares and René Otayek (eds), *Islam and Muslim Politics in Africa* (Basingstoke: Palgrave, 2007).

[20] Larmer, 'Social Movement Struggles', p. 252.

[21] See Adam Habib and Paul Opoku-Mensah, 'Speaking to Global Debates through a National and Continental Lens: South African and African Social Movements in Comparative Perspective', in Ellis and van Kessel, *Movers*, pp. 44–62.

[22] Ibid., p. 59. See also Ebrima Sall, 'Social Movements in the Renegotiation of the Bases for Citizenship in West Africa', *Current Sociology* 4 (2004), pp. 595–614.

THE LATE COLONIAL LABOUR MOVEMENTS

At least for historians it is a kind of truism to state that contemporary social movements in Africa—and elsewhere—can only be understood against the background of the historical and social-political surroundings they emerged from. Social movements in Africa, however, do not seem to have much of a history. This has to do with the fact that labour movements, for instance, are usually not discussed in the framework of social movements. A telling example for this observation is the rich and multi-layered historiography of the South African labour movements, which rarely refers to social movement approaches.[23] This equally applies to the history of labour movements in the decolonization period. Labour movements in Africa began to play an important role in the period immediately after the Second World War, when colonial governments in Africa were anxious to find a new basis of legitimacy and control, while social and political movements in Africa were asserting themselves with new vigour. These two processes shaped one another: while African movements sought to turn the government's need for order and economic growth into claims of entitlements and representation, officials had to rethink their policies in the face of new African challenges. The African historiography of the 1960s to 80s that developed a certain interest in labour history too easily subsumed labour movements under the nationalist question. But in fact labour movements and nationalist movements stood in—often creative—tensions to each other.[24]

When did the labour question become an important issue in colonial politics? And when did labour unrest and strikes cease to be simply local events and become issues that shaped both colony and metropolis? According to Fred Cooper, 'labour' became an important issue in colonial Africa in the 1930s. And since then, he argues, workers, and especially the more 'advanced' varieties—dock and railway workers, copper and tin miners, substantial agriculturalists such as Ghana cocoa farmers, organized in labour unions and farming co-operatives—largely forced the pace of decolonization. Cooper goes so far as to argue that colonial policy is best

[23] See Bill Freund, 'Labour Studies and Labour History in South Africa: Perspectives from the Apartheid Era and After', *International Review of Social History* 3 (2013), pp. 493–519.

[24] The key text for the history of labour and labour movements in the decolonization period is Frederick Cooper, *Decolonization and African Society: The Labor Question and French and British Africa* (Cambridge: Cambridge University Press, 1996). The following paragraphs are based on this study, which is crucial for the understanding of the central place of labour movements in Africa in the decade after the Second World War.

assessed by its relation to African labour. Key issues flow from this through their presence or absence: class, the changing economy, race and gender as socially defining categories. In its pre-war heyday, Cooper argues that colonialism, even when administered by relatively democratic governments in the home context, evaluated its African subjects essentially as primitive and ineffably 'different' tribesmen belonging to patriarchal and rural societies. The conservation of an apparently tribal Africa in combination with the extraction of unskilled seasonal or casual labour was common wisdom. The debates of the day were about the necessity for forced labour and the extent to which Africa was becoming diseased and depopulated due to the colonial demand for labour. Dynamism in this system was more or less exclusively confined to white settlers or some Levantine and Asian traders.

These assumptions began to be challenged in the 1930s, first by minority voices and then, in the years after the Second World War, on a broader front. This had various causes, not least the realization that the continuation of pre-war policies would lead to semi-stagnation in a world where development became the mantra of the day. The suddenly manifest capacity of African workers to organize and throw a spanner in the works of the extractive economy was, however, also of fundamental importance. Arguments mounted that African workers needed to be treated as workers, not as Africans: They could be permitted to form trade unions, but, critically, this was also a strategy of containment and boundedness. The colonial state also tried to conceptualize structures that would allow for a stable 'detribalized' urban working class in towns focused on a European family model. 'By the mid to late 1940s,' Cooper writes, 'influential officials wanted Africa to have a working class, to separate an identifiable group of people from the backwardness of rural Africa, attach its members to particular jobs and career ladders and over time make them into a predictable and productive collectivity.'[25] In his book, Cooper devotes much time to the careful analysis of particular strikes, conflicts and policy watersheds where these issues were repeatedly hammered out. It should be added here, that strikes in cities and mine towns between the 1930s and 1950s up to the 1970s constituted a kind of empirical centrepiece of African labour historiography. Most historians roughly distinguish three types of urban unrest: (1) general strikes which involved workers, the urban poor and, partially, other groups such as market women; (2) strikes of workers in key industries, for instance mining workers in the Zambian copper fields, or railway workers in French West Africa; (3)

[25] Cooper, *Decolonization*, p. 14.

uprisings of a 'cross-section' of the urban population, when, for example in Douala in September 1945, poor urban, workers organized in trade unions, and squatters joined in protests against the French administration.

Cooper convincingly shows that this early component of modernization theory applied to Africa was even more of a fantasy in the realm of real possibilities than the approach of the pre-war system to traditional African societies. Such change soon proved to be neither affordable nor politically manageable. Dualist policies which tried to draw a ring around a section of Africans who might prove to be able to modernize broke down rapidly. To some extent, African labour organizers turned the new discourse to their own advantage by making claims desired by their followers while African politicians found the resulting impotence of colonial administrators opportune. Colonial rulers decided that the contradictions that were increasingly apparent would best be resolved by African politicians rather than by them; the expenditures entailed by reform strategies were not worth engendering. Cooper therefore places the labour question squarely at the heart of the explanation for the precipitous character of the decolonization in Africa. He argues that major shifts in approach are especially dramatic and clear in French West Africa, where elements of destructive compulsion were still firmly in place in the 1930s but where the impulse towards modernization and assimilation quickly became so much stronger.

There is an ironic charm—but also a kind of Pyrrhic victory—in the African success in defeating European developmentalist logic. Cooper views the Europeans' decision to accept unionist demands that African labourers should be treated on the same basis as their European counterparts as a mutual failure to comprehend African social reality. It was a consequential failure, since the cost of providing European-scale wages and benefits under African economic conditions could not be borne by either colonial or post-colonial regimes. European governments were thus encouraged to withdraw from Africa, while their local successors co-opted some of the labour leadership regime but rather quickly suppressed the unions as an autonomous force. An interesting topic for future research is, in fact, the fate of trade unions and labour movements in independent Africa.[26] There are some implicit answers in the studies of Cooper and others which need

---

[26] The scholarly literature on trade unions in independent Africa is very sparse. For a recent collection see Craig Phelan (ed.), *Trade Unions in West Africa. Historical and Contemporary Perspectives* (Berne: Peter Lang, 2011). One of the few newer books on labour in post-colonial Africa (beyond South Africa) is Lynn Schler et al. (eds), *Rethinking Labour in Africa, Past and Present* (London: Routledge, 2011).

further evaluation: First, the colonial state, through its policies of registration and welfarism that were only directed towards certain sectors of the economy, succeeded in breaking the unity of the working class before the end of the colonial period. Hence independent African states inherited an already fragmented and weakened working class. Second, many workers considered 'stabilized' in fact were then able to maintain links with rural areas, and this still continues. This ensured a certain, continuously shrinking, level of security outside the job. Thus, jobs have been less crucially important for basic survival than for European or American workers and militancy has suffered. Third, the period of effective strikes in Africa in the final decades of colonialism was coterminous with a period of general economic expansion, whereas the economic contraction that independent African states have experienced, especially after the oil crisis of 1973/1974, has given workers naturally worried about their position in a faltering economy little opportunity to strike.

Another observation deriving from Cooper's work is how important the labour question in fact was for the decision of European powers to leave Africa. There is good reason to think that Cooper tends to exaggerate the significance of both the colonial authorities and African subjects in determining the stages and outcomes of the decolonization process. The decisive power over African affairs ultimately lay at higher levels of European public and private sectors, reacting to their own perceptions of Africa's role in the international economy. It was the crises of the Depression and post-Second World War eras, rather than colonialist understandings of what were still very small African urban populations and African working classes, that drove the modernization and development policies analysed by Cooper. It was also the recognition, by the mid-1950s, of Africa's irrelevance to the reinvigorated European and global economies that made the cost of misconceptions about managing newly growing African cities and African workers so unacceptable.[27]

The range of social movements in Africa is potentially huge: from loser groups such as some neighbourhood, women's or youth groups and more or less spontaneous protests to well organized and highly institutionalized forms such as trade unions. Some socially based movements such as the labour movement in French West Africa in the late 1940s and 50s, mobilization against apartheid, the campaign against blood diamonds, and the women's movement in Liberia, had a major effect on Africa's recent

---

[27] See Ralph A. Austen, Africa and Globalization: Colonialism, Decolonization and the Postcolonial Malaise, *Journal of Global History* 3 (2006), pp. 403–408.

history. Yet the most influential theories concerning social movements worldwide have paid little heed to Africa, basing themselves more often on cases drawn from other continents. Thus it would be crucial for a more global perspective on social movements to include evidence from Africa, while Africanists working on social and political activism should link their work more systematically to theories on social movements derived from the North Atlantic realm and Latin America. In Africa, as elsewhere, social movements are by no means recent phenomena, and much work is needed to historicize recent developments in the realm of politics and notions of political and social protest and integrate them into longer histories. A very promising starting point for such an endeavour could be the history of labour associations and trade unions and an analysis of their activities both in their concrete historical settings and in their global entanglements. In this context, it will be essential to look not only at the wage labour sector, but to include those activities which are usually lumped under the vast and imprecise category of the 'informal sector'.

FURTHER READINGS

This article argues that social movements have been largely neglected in the field of African studies, especially concerning their historical dimensions. Consequently, the number of relevant studies is limited. A few collective volumes and special journal issues provide useful introductions, but mainly or exclusively focus on social movements in independent Africa, with an emphasis on developments after 1990. The volume *African Studies in Social Movements and Democracy*, edited by Mahmood Mamdani and Ernest Wamba-dia Wamba and published in 1995 by the Dakar-based think tank CODESRIA, warns against the conflation of social movements with civil society, and argues that social movements in Africa may include initiatives such as NGOs that are non-governmental and formally apolitical, but may equally comprise initiatives that are explicitly anti-governmental and overtly political. The editors further argue that no distinction should be made between 'political' and 'social' movement.

It took 14 more years for the next relevant volume on social movements to see the light of day: Stephen Ellis and Ineke van Kessel (eds), *Movers and Shakers: Social Movements in Africa* (Leiden: Brill, 2009) comprises eight case studies covering a wide range of social movements and underlining their great diversity. One of the insights of the volume is that movements in Africa never did fit into the sketch of a neat chronological succession from working-class to middle-class activism, and that recently, especially in Southern Africa (South Africa and Zimbabwe), trade unions and labour movements played a crucial role. Two special journal issues further summarize the state of the art and conclude that social movements remain largely under-researched and under-theorized: Nikolai Brandes and Bettina Engels (eds), *Social Movements in Africa* (*Stichproben. Wiener Zeitschrift für kritische Afrikastudien* 20 (2011)); and Miles Larmer et al. (eds), *Social Movement Struggles in Africa* (*Review of African Political Economy* 37 (125), (2010)). One recent monograph attempts to put social movements at the centre of contemporary African history and argues with fervour that social movements—defined as popular movements of the working class, the poor, and other oppressed and marginalized sections of African society—have played a central role in shaping Africa's history since independence: Peter Dwyer and Leo Zeilig, *African Struggles Today: Social Movements since Independence* (Chicago: Haymarket, 2012).

There is a growing number of case studies on contemporary social movements in Africa, especially on South Africa. Steve Robbins, *From Revolutions to Rights in South Africa. Social Movements, NGOs & Popular Politics after Apartheid* (Woodbridge: James Currey, 2008) shows that innovative and NGO–social movement collaborations in post-Apartheid South Africa mainly developed in the political margins, beyond national organizations such as COSATU, one of the most politically influential and largest social movements in South Africa. Ercüment Celik, *Street Traders. A Bridge Between Trade Unions and Social Movements in Contemporary South Africa* (Baden Baden: Nomos, 2010) adopts a rather optimistic tone in arguing that the mobilization of street traders' struggles brought together social movements with trade unions, emphatically signalling the potential reactivation of social movement unionism in South Africa. General volumes on social movements such as Lisa Thompson and Chris Tapscott (eds), *Citizenship and Social Movements. Perspectives from the Global South* (London: Zed Books, 2010) include African examples, again mainly from South Africa. There are also some instructive comparative studies including South Africa, most notably Gay W. Seidman, *Manufacturing Militance: Workers' Movements in Brazil and South Africa, 1970–1985* (Berkeley: University of California Press, 1994). And one may refer to a number of articles that focus on specific movements in different parts of Africa, albeit usually without substantial contextualization within broader theories of social movements. See e.g. Aili Mari Tripp, 'The Politics of Autonomy and Cooptation in Africa: The Case of the Uganda Women's Movements', *Journal of Modern African Studies* 1 (2001), pp. 101–128.

Finally, some studies recently employed a longer historical perspective on social movements in Africa and included the late colonial period, but remained on a rather general level. See Miles Larmer, 'Historicizing Activism in Late Colonial and Post-Colonial Sub-Saharan Africa', *Journal of Historical Sociology* 1 (2015), pp. 67–89; Peter Dwyer et al., 'An Epoch of Uprisings: Social Movements in Africa since 1945', *Socialist History Journal* 40 (2012), pp. 1–23. There is some excellent work on labour and labour movements in late colonial Africa, most notably Frederick Cooper, *Deceolonization and African Society. The Labour Question in French and British Africa* (Cambridge: Cambridge University Press, 1996), but again there is very little systematic discussion of social movement theory and approaches. This also applies to an excellent case study of a strike in West Africa a few years after the Second World War that shows the complexity of strike activities and the various layers of workers' movements: Frederick Cooper, '"Our Strike"': Equality, Anticolonial Politics and the 1947–1948 Railway Strike in French West Africa, *Journal of African History* 1 (1996), pp. 81–118.

CHAPTER 9

Popular Movements in the Middle East and North Africa

John Chalcraft

INTRODUCTION

If it is reasonable to define popular movements as projects of networked, transgressive, collective action for transformation mobilizing subaltern social groups, then the history of such movements in the Middle East and North Africa is extraordinarily rich and varied. While countries such as the UAE and Qatar, both historically and in the present, are considerably less marked by popular movements, the history of other countries, from Morocco and Algeria in the West to Iran in the East, is unthinkable without them. This chapter uses the term 'popular' to draw attention to the subaltern, transgressive and transformative aspects of certain political, economic, cultural or social movements. The phrase popular movement (*al-haraka al-sha'biyya*) also has a longer pedigree in Arabic than the neologism 'social movement' (*al-haraka al-'ijtima'iyya*). It also maps more credibly onto the even older term '*ammiyya*', which translates as 'rising of the commoners'. The relevant historiography in English, French, Arabic,

The author wishes to thank the Economic and Social Research Council (ESRC) for funding the research project 'Popular Politics in the Making of the Modern Middle East' which made this chapter possible.

J. Chalcraft (✉)
Department of Government, London School of Economics, London, UK

© The Author(s) 2017
S. Berger, H. Nehring (eds.), *The History of Social Movements in Global Perspective*, DOI 10.1057/978-1-137-30427-8_9

225

and other languages is vast. The rush of studies appearing since the Arab uprisings of 2011, along with recent work subjecting contestation to the analytics of social movements theory and contentious politics, are very much the tip of the iceberg: historians and social scientists influenced by a wide variety of approaches from Orientalism to Marxism to post-colonialism have long-produced relevant research.[1]

The contexts for such movements are many, but it is a measure of the importance of imperialism in the Middle East and North Africa that it is hard to find five consecutive years since 1830 (when the French invaded Algeria) when a major armed or unarmed struggle against one or other version of imperialism, invasion or occupation was not being carried out. Beyond geopolitics, however, state formation and domestic politics, social and economic structures and changes, along with cultural hierarchies and mobilizing languages of all kinds have provided crucial contexts for the many and various popular movements in the region, secular or religious, violent or non-violent. This chapter aims to show how movements were situated within these dynamic contexts.

The chapter sets the region's popular movements in four major periods stretching back to the early 1800s. First, the highly diverse, but oft-slighted nineteenth century, from 1807 until 1911; second, the period of wars, invasions, and patriotism from 1911 to 1939; third, the decades of Third Worldism, national liberation, socialism and neo-colonialism, from 1939 to 1979; and finally, the epoch of Islamism, 'people power' and neoliberalism from 1979 to the present. This periodization, like any other, has merits and defects. The idea here is that it helps to capture major shifts, not only in regard to geopolitical, political and economic forms, but also in relation to cultural contexts and (border-crossing) mobilizing discourses. Inevitably, however, in such a diverse and varied region, these periods have jagged borders.

The chapter argues that popular movements in the region have not merely expressed some indigenous reaction *against* capitalism, modernization, globalization or the West—an Orientalist narrative dogged by cultural essentialism and exceptionalism. But nor did such movements find their origins in the putative contradictions *within* capitalism, modernization, or globalization, that the West somehow implanted in a region that was otherwise passive—a Modernist narrative that misses historical

---

[1] See Nora Lafi's Chapter 23 in this volume on the most recent developments in the region.

dynamics specific to the region. Instead, in a break with Orientalism and Modernism alike, but drawing eclectically on the strengths of historical sociology, cultural history, social movements theory, and postcolonial scholarship, I will emphasize the rich, inherited, diverse, and changing traditions of protest and resistance that have marked the region. The chapter underlines, furthermore, the ways in which popular movements were not purely indigenous or national affairs; they were not hermetically sealed from other parts of the region or the world: on the contrary, protests and popular movements were highly syncretic, drawing voraciously on translocal models and resources.

DEFINITIONS AND APPROACHES

Several more or less useful approaches to the history of popular movements in the Middle East and North Africa have been followed. Many historians have incorporated resistance and protest into their accounts, without paying much attention to definitions and concepts. The richest historiographical tradition has rooted questions of collective action and popular protest in capitalist development, modernization, political economy and social class. Such histories have concentrated above all on movements of workers, peasants, and 'popular masses'.[2] More recently, there has been a conscious borrowing of definitions and concepts from conventional social movements theory and revisionist theories of contentious politics.[3] In a parallel development, cultural historians and others drawing on post-colonialism, gender studies, and the linguistic turn, have refused to define finally the notion of resistance, and have instead interrogated its various apparent forms, stressing the dangers of closure, binary, and taxonomy, and discovering resistance (or the lack of it) in unexpected places.[4]

---

[2] Edmund Burke III and Ira Lapidus (eds), *Islam, Politics and Social Movements* (Berkeley: University of California Press, 1988); Joel Beinin, *Workers and Peasants in Modern Middle East* (Cambridge: Cambridge University Press, 2001).

[3] Quintan Wiktorowicz (ed.), *Islamic Activism: A Social Movement Theory Approach* (Bloomington: Indiana University Press, 2004); Joel Beinin and Frédéric Vairel (eds), *Social Movements, Mobilization, and Contestation in the Middle East and North Africa* (Palo Alto, CA: Stanford University Press, 2011).

[4] Julia Clancy-Smith, *Rebel and Saint: Muslim Notables, Populist Protest, Colonial Encounters (Algeria and Tunisia, 1800–1904)* (Berkeley: University of California Press, 1994).

There are important strengths and weaknesses in all of these approaches. Historians capture a wide range of phenomena, but definitions can seem arbitrary. Historical sociology's salient emphasis on social class and economic inequality is often hampered by teleology, determinism and materialism.[5] The conceptual robustness and comparativist strengths of social movements theory are marred by inattention to imperialism, authoritarianism, economic domination and racial, civilizational and gendered hierarchies. While conventional social movements theory suffers from objectivism and rationalism, 'contentious politics' appears subjectivist and inattentive to structural forms of power and issues of Eurocentrism. The theoretical sophistication of post-colonialism on the subtleties of domination, and its ability to open up new lines of enquiry, is dogged by the fact that definitions of resistance can therein become highly elusive: the subaltern is spectralized—she 'cannot speak'.[6] Here popular movements can become mere ciphers of elite texts.

The definition offered at the outset of this chapter aims to draw on the strengths and avoid the weaknesses of these approaches. This chapter seeks to capture, in historical mode, a wide range of phenomena, but, in order to avoid arbitrariness, it does not give up on the question of a definition. It maintains an eye on issues of labour and the economy while eschewing what Sewell criticized long ago as a 'materialist hierarchy' in labour history.[7] It borrows from theories of social movements and contentious politics in order to sharpen the analysis and to join a larger analytic conversation—but the goal here is to understand a history, not to add some new wrinkle on a social movement concept. The idea is to borrow from the sophistication of studies of gender, hegemony and discourse—but the chapter seeks to avoid subaltern spectralization by emphasizing the productivity and force of popular movements and the mobilizing projects they involve. Popular movements are not doomed to be only silently subversive; subaltern social groups are not condemned to a history in fragments and episodes. Popular mobilizing projects begin in the cracks and fissures of

---

[5] See Zachary Lockman's definitive critique in Zachary Lockman (ed.), *Workers and Working Classes in the Middle East: Struggles, Histories, Historiographies* (Albany, NY: State University of New York Press, 1994), pp. 11–31.

[6] Cf. Sumit Sarkar, 'The Decline of the Subaltern in Subaltern Studies', in Vinayak Chaturvedi (ed.), *Subaltern Studies and the Postcolonial* (London: Verso, 2000), pp. 300–322.

[7] William H. Sewell, 'Towards a Post-Materialist Rhetoric for Labour History', in Lenard Berlanstein (ed.), *Rethinking Labour History* (Urbana, IL: University of Illinois Press, 1993), pp. 15–38.

dominant formations, but can become transformative through the collective and mobilizing re-direction of capacities and agencies that challenge existing distributions of power. This approach complements that of Charles Tripp, who refuses to abandon the notion of resistance, finding it in practices that fundamentally contest whole systems of power and their exclusions and inclusions.[8] The approach followed here rejects the use of long-falsified cultural exceptionalist and essentialist stereotypes about Muslims and Arabs so familiar in neo-Orientalist scholarship.[9] On the contrary, this chapter situates popular movements within various geopolitical, political, and economic structures and processes—while attempting to weigh social construction and cultural creativity in the balance. Finally, the chapter pays attention to transnational and transregional forms, understood as involving transversal links and connections across major national and imperial boundaries between non-state actors (rather than between governments).[10] This contribution highlights in particular the ways in which mobilizing discourses are appropriated in consequential ways by popular movements in particular contexts in the service of their projects and contests.

State-Building, Invasion, Encroachment, Islamic Renewal, Patriotism, Justice, and Millenarianism, 1807–1911

During the nineteenth century, the major, polyglot, multi-national, decentralized, agrarian and trade-based polities of the Middle East and North Africa—the Ottoman empire, Qajar Iran and Alawi Morocco— lost the relative autonomy vis-à-vis Europe that they had once enjoyed. Partly in response to the changing terms of war and trade, and partly to secure their own power, rulers engaged in major projects of dynasty building and state centralization, and military, fiscal and administrative change. These structures were much more developed in the Ottoman centre and in Egypt by the First World War than they were in Qajar Iran or

---

[8] Charles Tripp, *The Power and the People: Paths of Resistance in the Middle East* (Cambridge: Cambridge University Press, 2013).

[9] See Zachary Lockman, *Contending Visions of the Middle East: the History and Politics of Orientalism*, Second Edition (Cambridge: Cambridge University Press, 2010), p. 216ff.

[10] Laleh Khalili, *Heroes and Martyrs of Palestine: The Politics of National Commemoration* (Cambridge: Cambridge University Press, 2007).

the Sultanate of Morocco. The region also underwent colonial invasion, occupation, and economic encroachment, and new political and economic forms developed. The port cities, including Tangier, Alexandria, Beirut and Izmir, once villages, grew immensely at the expense of the inland cities; merchants, landowners, usurers and other agents and entrepreneurs of the emerging colonial economy made vast gains relative to other actors in the economy, 'protected' as they were under the Capitulations in the Ottoman empire, and favoured by the Qajar shahs, and to a lesser extent late nineteenth-century Moroccan sultans. New physical infrastructures (communications, utilities, agro-processing, transport) were built, employing wage-labour. Crafts and service trades were restructured. New European-style schools trained middle classes, who staffed new professions and bureaucracies.

Historical sociologists have rightly insisted that the terms of this (geo) political economy explain much about popular movements during a century in which the problem of European domination was posed in acute form. Scores of books and articles have indicated the ways in which protests—far from being rooted in 'xenophobia', personal gain, or 'religious fanaticism' as most Europeans insisted at the time—were linked to colonialism, state centralization and socio-economic transformation.[11] The uprising in Egypt of 1798–1801 can only be understood in relation to the Napoleonic occupation that it helped to throw off.[12] The prolonged resistance against French settler colonialism in Algeria that lasted from 1830 down to even the early 1900s must be contextualized within the near-genocidal military and economic assault on the population occasioned by French settler colonialism.[13] The tobacco boycott of 1891–1892 in Iran, led by Shi'a *ulema* (religious scholars) against the vast concessions (in both senses of the term) offered to a European company by the Qajar Shah, cannot be comprehended outside of the conflicts attendant on colonial encroachment and new forms of capitalistic economy.[14] French economic and political encroachment in Morocco, especially after the defeat

---

[11] See, for example, Ervand Abrahamian, *Iran between Two Revolutions* (Princeton, NJ: Princeton University Press, 1982), pp. 72–73.

[12] Juan Cole, *Napoleon's Egypt: Invading the Middle East* (Basingstoke: Palgrave Macmillan, 2008).

[13] Peter Von Sivers, 'Arms and Alms: The Combative Saintliness of the Awlad Sidi Shaykh', *Maghreb Review* 4 (1983), pp. 113–123.

[14] Abrahamian, *Iran Between Revolutions*, p. 73ff.

of the Moroccan sultan in the Battle of Isly 1844 and subsequently was a crucial context for protests down to 1912.[15]

The protests of the townspeople, *ulema* and Janissaries that unseated Ottoman Sultan Selim III in 1807, were in many ways about resistance to centralization in the shape of a new conscript and centralized army.[16] The *'ammiyya* (rising of the common people) of 1820 in Mount Lebanon opposed a new and onerous tax.[17] The popular uprising in Fez in 1873 was in part in opposition to rising taxes especially the 'hated' *maks*—a levy on primary materials and transactions imposed by the sultan seeking revenue for centralization and 'reform'.[18] By the same token, crafts and service workers in Egypt's cities protested in the 1870s against guild shaykhs who had been co-opted by the state in taxation and regulation.[19] Under Mehmet Ali (1805–1849) but especially Ismail (1863–1879) in Egypt, peasants fought tenaciously—by desertion, evasion, dissimulation, petitioning and uprisings—against a crushing new tax burden, forced labour, and conscription.[20] On the other hand, an important new form of protest aimed at, and sought to draw in the increasingly centralized institutions of the state in order to regulate lives, and deliver desired goods and services. Peasant petitioners in Palestine, for example, 'openly adopted the government's public interpretation of the *tanzimat* and used it as a weapon against the authority and privileges of their traditional leaders'.[21]

Strikes and protests by wage-workers in Egypt's new physical infrastructure after 1882 and especially in the 1900s and in the Ottoman empire by the early twentieth century cannot be understood outside the changing relations of production and exchange as well as new relation-

---

[15] Edmund Burke III, *Prelude to Protectorate in Morocco: Precolonial Protest and Resistance, 1860–1912* (Chicago: Chicago University Press, 1976).

[16] Cemal Kafadar, 'Janissaries and Other Riffraff of Ottoman Istanbul: Rebels without a Cause?', in Baki Tezcan and Karl K. Barbir (eds), *Identity and Identity Formation in the Ottoman World* (Madison, WI: University of Wisconsin Press, 2007), pp. 113–134.

[17] Yusuf Khattar al-Hilw, *Al-'Ammiyyat Al-Sha'biyya fi Lubnan/Popular Uprisings in Lebanon* (Beirut: Dar al-Farabi, 1979).

[18] Abdallah Laroui, *Les origines sociales et culturelles de nationalisme Marocaine, 1830–1912* (Paris: Maspero, 1977), pp. 129–131.

[19] John Chalcraft, *The Striking Cabbies of Cairo and Other Stories: Crafts and Guilds in Egypt, 1863–1914* (Albany, NY: State University of New York Press, 2004), Chap. 3.

[20] Nathan J. Brown, *Peasant Politics in Modern Egypt: the Struggle against the State* (New Haven, CT: Yale University Press, 1990).

[21] Beshara Doumani, *Rediscovering Palestine: Merchants and Peasants in Jabal Nablus, 1700–1900* (Berkeley: University of California Press, 1995), p. 18.

ships with the state. Widespread strikes involving 'virtually every category of labour in the empire' followed the revolution of 1908.[22] Peasant protests including attacks on landlords, the destruction of property, and major confrontations with landowners, debt-collectors and authorities, in late nineteenth-century Egypt can readily be understood in a context of new economic pressures and exploitative relationships between rich and poor in the countryside.[23] In the face of taxes and debts, peasants were sometimes able to evict their oppressors and form self-governing communes. In Iran in the early 1900s, for instance, 'The peasants of several villages expelled the overseers, refused to pay taxes, and proceeded to form local *anjumans*—local councils—in their villages. No government officer, landlord, or overseer dared enter such villages in order to collect taxes.'[24] Doumani, echoing many others, cast peasant protests in rather teleological and modernist terms as relating in the Palestinian context to the 'slow dissolution of patronage ties between peasants and long-time ruling subdistrict chiefs, as well as the transformation of the latter into agents of urban interests'.[25]

Historical sociologists, in escaping the cultural essentialism and exceptionalism of Orientalism, have been weaker at grasping the gendered and meaning-laden contexts and dynamics informing popular movements during this period. The rise of nationalism, for example, was often treated in residual terms as an inevitable structural outgrowth of economic, political and social change, in which primordial and parochial identities were transcended, never mind that Muslim identity was continent-spanning, and far from parochial or primordial. More traditional forms of history writing, meanwhile, saw nationalism as an abstracted body of intellectual thought articulated by (mostly) Christian elites in schools and literary salons which involved an awakening to a higher state of consciousness, inspired by Europe.[26] Cultural history and post-colonialism, however, has given us

---

[22] Donald Quataert and Erik Jan Zurcher (eds), *Workers and the Working Class in the Ottoman Empire and the Turkish Republic, 1839–1950* (London: I.B. Tauris, 1995), p. 72.

[23] Alexander Schölch, *Egypt for the Egyptians! The Socio-political Crisis in Egypt 1878–1882* (London: Ithaca Press, 1981), p. 37, p. 40.

[24] Janet Afary, *The Iranian Constitutional Revolution, 1906–1911: Grassroots Democracy, Social Democracy, and the Origins of Feminism* (New York: Columbia University Press, 1996), p. 146.

[25] Doumani, *Rediscovering Palestine*, p. 172.

[26] George Antonius, *The Arab Awakening: The Story of the Arab National Movement* (London: H. Hamilton, 1938).

a stronger grasp of the unevenness of nationalism by geography, gender and social class, its diversity (where and what exactly was the Arab nation, Turkish nation etc.?), its complexity (being fed by intellectual currents such as Islamic modernism that were previously thought alien to it), and its ambiguities and occlusions (concealing other struggles around gender, ancestry, 'ethnicity' and the like).[27]

In some respects, though, recent studies, so concerned with deconstruction and contextualization, have left us without a good grasp of the potency of nationalist ideas for popular movements, which drew on and re-fashioned notions rooted in the region, appropriated ideas and models drawn from struggles taking place elsewhere, and made creative contributions to nationalism and even the formation of national-states in the region. Notions of 'homeland' (*watan*), for instance, and the 'interest of the homeland' (*maslahat al-watan*) were at play in popular movements during the nineteenth century. These ideas were appropriated and re-interpreted by popular movements during the Greek struggle for independence in the 1820s, Mount Lebanon in 1840 and again in 1858–1860, in Egypt in 1881–1882, Iran 1905–1906, and Istanbul in 1908. Colonel Ahmad 'Urabi's movement (1881–1882) raised the slogan 'Egypt for the Egyptians!' and was informed by notions of the 'welfare of the nation/ community' (*maslahat al-umma*) and the advantage of the fatherland/ homeland (*manfa'at al-watan*).[28] Or, during the session of the first *majlis* (representative assembly) 1906–1907 in Iran, deputies overwhelmingly saw their society as formed of 'a corrupt governing elite' (*dawlat*) oppressing a 'national people' (*mellat*).[29] In a context of polyglot, multinational and multi-ethnic political communities, these concepts of community, applied to politics, were potentially explosive, as they implied the need to generate a congruence between the state and a national people. These concepts were 'pirated' by popular movements from a wide variety of sources—from European movements, and from local elites. They were also re-articulations of existing, dynamic forms of popular and elite culture. The words of the resistance leader Abd al-Qadir illustrate such rootedness. In the late 1840s he invoked 'a poet', who wrote that 'The

[27] For a review see James L. Gelvin, *Divided Loyalties: Nationalism and Mass Politics in Syria at the Close of Empire* (Berkeley: University of California Press, 1998).

[28] Schölch, *Egypt for the Egyptians!*, p. 80.

[29] Abrahamian, *Iran Between Revolutions*, p. 10.

country is beloved to men/They passed their youth there/When they remember it, they remember their promises'.[30]

The region, furthermore, had long known the concept of 'Islamic community' (*umma*)—a term which underwent many nuances but was incorporated within the nationalist lexicon to mean 'nation'. It was nothing new in the mid-nineteenth century to speak in the region of Copts, Arabs, Christians, Ajami (Persians), North Africans, Muslims and so on. Osman II, Ottoman sultan from 1618 to 1622, proposed to create a 'national militia' of Muslim peasants from Anatolia and Syria; to turkify the palace and the Janissary corps; and to move the government to Bursa or Ankara.[31] The petitions of Mt Lebanon from 1820 speak of the 'interest of the country' (*maslahat al-bilad*), whereas those of 1840 speak of the interest of the 'homeland/fatherland' (*maslahat al-watan*).[32] These notions in turn were linked to the idea of the 'interests/welfare of the people' (*maslahat al-ahali*)—a common invocation in petitions in the eighteenth and nineteenth century. These ideas re-worked existing concepts—and they did not require a long sociological or political preparation through print capitalism, the colonial state, the census, the map, the museum. They imparted important dynamics to movements.

In general, before the 1910s, nationalism was by no means the lead note in popular movements in the region. For some movements, the notion of Islamic community or the Islamic world (*Dar al-Islam*) was the key. In the name of saving the *Dar al-Islam* against Christian invasion, volunteer fighters—some of them men who had been shamed into action by women—flocked from Arabia to Egypt in 1798.[33] Armed *jihad* in defence of Islam was invoked in Algeria in the 1830s, Morocco in the 1840s and 1860s, or among the Al-Sanusi against Italians in Cyrenaica in 1911.[34] In the early 1870s, the peripatetic, Iranian-born activist Jamal al-Din 'al-Afghani' attracted crowds in Istanbul as he urged the entire Muslim world to work together to oppose European imperialism—while adopting the

[30] Abd al-Qadir, *L'Emir AbdelKader Autobiographie: Ecrite en prison (France)* (Paris: Dialogues Editions, 1995).

[31] Stanford Shaw, *History of the Ottoman Empire and Modern Turkey*, Vol. I (Cambridge: Cambridge University Press, 1976), p. 192.

[32] Al-Hilw, *Al-'Ammiyyat Al-Sha'biyya/Popular Uprisings*, p. 35, p. 91.

[33] Lutf Allah Jahhaf, *Nusus Yamaniya 'an al-Hamla al-Faransiyya 'ala Misr/Yemeni Texts on the French Campaign in Egypt* (Cairo: Markaz al-Dirasat al-Yamaniyya, 1975), p. 87.

[34] Rudolf Peters, *Islam and Colonialism: The Doctrine of Jihad in Modern History* (The Hague: Mouton Publishers, 1979).

technologies of the West and insisting that Islam was compatible with civilization, science and progress. His activism struck such a chord in unofficial circles—especially at a time of atrocities against Muslims in Central Asia and the Balkans—that he was forced by the authorities to leave Istanbul in 1871.[35] Al-Afghani's influence, alongside that of other Islamic 'modernists' and pan-Islamists, played a role in Egypt in 1881–1882 as well in Iran in the early 1900s. Pan-Islam was a minor key in Morocco in the 1900s.[36] Al-Afghani's hugely influential ideas, we note, stemmed not from a technocratic or European education, but from the conclusions he drew from his visit to India following the British repression of the Indian uprising of 1857.

Many others, perhaps most, mobilized in terms more heterodox, Sufi, millenarian, Salafi or reformist. The Salafi movement of the *Al-Muwahhidun* (those proclaiming the unity of God, or *tawhid*) was the basis of three successive Saudi kingdoms from the 1740s to the 1930s. In Algeria, the *Tijaniyya* in Algeria opposed the Turks, and the *al-Qadiriyya*, and many other orders mobilized against the French. In Morocco, Sufi orders were often linked to uprisings against the central government. In what became Libya, the Al-Sanusi order was the organizational basis of the *jihad* against the Italian invasion of 1911. The heterodox al-Bab movement in Iran in the 1840s was rooted in eighteenth-century Sufism. The tremendous spread of Sufism in the eighteenth and nineteenth centuries in North Africa and the Muslim world more generally was linked not just to the decentralization and failures of the central state in the seventeenth and eighteenth centuries, but also to the cultural energies unleashed by Salafi and neo-Sufi reformist attempts at purification and renewal of the faith on the basis of the original sources of the law: orthodoxy stood accused of rigidity and blind imitation; the Ottoman 'Turks' of deviation and usurpation; the French and the English of unbelief; the central authorities of tyranny; folk religion of polytheism and superstition; and elites of excessive attachment to reason, luxury and decadence.[37]

---

[35] Stanford Shaw, *History of the Ottoman Empire and Modern Turkey*, Vol. II (Cambridge: Cambridge University Press, 1977), pp. 156–157.

[36] Edmund Burke III., 'Pan-Islam and Moroccan Resistance to French Colonial Penetration, 1900–1912', *Journal of African History* 1 (1972), pp. 97–118.

[37] John Voll, 'Muhammad Hayya al-Sindhi and Muhammad ibn 'Abd al-Wahhab: An Analysis of an Intellectual Group in Eighteenth-Century Madina', *Bulletin of the School of Oriental and African Studies* 1 (1975), pp. 32–39.

Millenarian movements hailed a rightly-guided 'deliverer' (*Mahdi*) who would abolish tyranny and usher in a reign of justice, paving the way for the second coming of the prophet Jesus and the day of reckoning. Sometimes a quietist idea, millenarianism had explosive revolutionary potential. The Mahdi of Sudan may have started out in the Sufi *Sammaniyya* order, but proclaimed in millenarian mode the abolition of all Sufi orders in the 1880s.[38] Millenarian movements appeared in 1786 and 1798, the 1820s, 1832 and 1865 in Egypt—while 'Urabi in 1881–1882 was hailed in the countryside as a deliverer on Mahdist lines. There were strong millenarian strains—this time in Christian, neo-Byzantine colours—in the Greek uprising of the 1820s.[39] Numerous Mahdist movements appeared in both Morocco and Algeria throughout the nineteenth century.[40] Would-be Mahdis crossed borders: Ahmad al-Tayyib, who led the rising in Egypt in 1865, was said to come from India.

Underestimated in the existing scholarship are the ways in which changing notions of justice, rights, custom, and of the people, informed popular movements in the region during this period. These did not express a 'nascent class consciousness',[41] an overly modernist and teleological formulation that slights as merely 'becoming' what was instead a vital, living tradition. Collective petitions and mobilizations from Vidin in Bulgaria to Nablus in Palestine to Cairo in Egypt against local exploiters, notables, landowners *inter alia* drew on and transformed rich traditions invoking the justice of the sultan, the rights of the subjects (*huquq al-ra'iyya*), the welfare of the people, and the demands of customary and ancient practice.[42] In addition, numerous groups in town and country (tribes, villages, city quarters, guilds, Sufi orders and so on) were staunch defenders of their autonomy in the face of central authorities. As a nineteenth-century 'Iraqi' tribal chant stated 'It [the government] is a flabby serpent and has no venom.'[43] A more radical tradition of 'liberty against the law' was

---

[38] P. M. Holt, *The Mahdist State in the Sudan, 1881–1898: A Study of its Origins, Development and Overthrow*, 2nd edn (Oxford: Clarendon Press, 1970).

[39] Richard Clogg, 'Aspects of the Movement for Greek Independence', in Richard Clogg (ed.), *The Struggle for Greek Independence* (London: Macmillan, 1973), pp. 1–40.

[40] Laroui, *Les origines sociales*, pp. 129–131.

[41] Doumani, *Rediscovering Palestine*, p. 180.

[42] Mark Pinson, 'Ottoman Bulgaria in the First Tanzimat Period—The Revolts in Nish (1841) and Vidin (1850)', *Middle Eastern Studies* 2 (1975), pp. 103–146.

[43] Hanna Batatu, *The Old Social Classes and the Revolutionary Movements of Iraq* (Princeton, NJ: Princeton University Press, 1978), p. 14.

bequeathed by the Celali brigands, social and otherwise, with their origins in the late sixteenth century, but continued to play important roles in popular movements (under various names—*klephts* and *levents*) down to the Greek uprising of the 1820s.[44] The popular movements involving subaltern social groups of the 1900s in both Istanbul and Iran had much less to do with middle class constitutionalism and much more to do with popular notions of justice, equality, and rights.[45]

Languages of equality, liberty, representation, republicanism, and popular sovereignty, drawn from struggles in Europe, and deployed in Mount Lebanon in 1858–1860, Egypt, 1881–1882, and during the constitutional revolutions in Iran in 1905–1906 and the Ottoman empire in 1908, were grafted onto, transformed, and were transformed by terms that existed in the region. Such terms were not as new as some have imagined. The republic of Bu Ragrag was founded by Andalusian Muslims near Rabat in the 1610s. One group 'formed a self-governing community, ruled by an elected governor who held office for a year with the assistance of a diwan of elders.'[46] Calık Ahmed, a Janissary rebel, suggested in 1703 that the Ottoman dynasty be discarded in favour of a '*çumhur çem'iyyeti*', for which the literal translation is 'popular assembly'.[47] Karim Khan, who established himself in 1765 as ruler of most of Iran, 'deliberately fostered the view that he was representative of the common people' by using the title '*vakil al-ra'aya*' which translates as 'representative of the subjects'. He also referred to himself as 'representative of ... all the people of Persia, rather than simply of the [now displaced] Safavid shah.'[48]

---

[44] Sam White, *The Climate of Rebellion in the Early Modern Ottoman Empire* (Cambridge: Cambridge University Press, 2011).

[45] Ervand Abrahamian, 'The Crowd in the Persian Revolution', in Albert Hourani, Philip S. Khoury and Mary C. Wilson (eds), *The Modern Middle East: A Reader* (London: I. B. Tauris, 1993), pp. 289–309, p. 296.

[46] These citizens also undertook piracy and apparently hated Christians. Jamil M. Abun-Nasr, *A History of the Maghrib in the Islamic Period* (Cambridge: Cambridge University Press, 1987), p. 221.

[47] Kafadar, 'Janissaries and other Riffraff', p. 133. Kafadar cautions as to the reading of the term *çumhur* in this context.

[48] Ann K. S. Lambton, 'The Tribal Resurgence and the Decline of the Bureaucracy in the Eighteenth Century', in Thomas Naff and Roger Owen (eds), *Studies in Eighteenth Century Islamic History* (Carbondale, IL: Southern Illinois University Press, 1977), pp. 108–129, p. 117.

A *Majlis al-Shura* (Consultative Assembly) was organized under Ibrahim Pasha in Egypt in August 1829.[49]

Struggles over structures of economic power were also by no means either mindless, maximizing, or simply derivative of European socialism. Communistic traditions on the Arabian Peninsula hailed back at least to the Qarmatians of the ninth century. The fifteenth and sixteenth centuries saw major movements based around the equal distribution of wealth in the Ottoman empire. Atlantic-style sugar factories based on black slave labour were broken up by an uprising in Morocco in the early seventeenth century.[50] Ascetic critiques of luxury and decadence were strongly articulated during the nineteenth century in many Sufi orders, organizations which overlapped very strongly with urban guilds, crafts, and trades.[51] After the fall of Khartoum in 1885, one of the right-hand men of the Mahdi wrote of the importance of avoiding the temptations of gold and of 'disdain for the things of this world'.[52] Such critical disdain was reinforced in a context of nineteenth-century port city wealth and 'decadence'. The Mahdi Ahmad al-Tayyib in Upper Egypt in 1865 proposed the redistribution of wealth.[53] Crowd actions over the price of bread, profiteering and exactions, sometimes led by women, and peopled neither by the wealthy nor even the *ulema*, but by the common people, were a regular occurrence in eighteenth-century Egypt,[54] in nineteenth-century Morocco and were particularly prominent in Iran.[55] The sugar carriers of the imperial refineries in eighteenth-century Egypt wanted to 'distribute guild income equally among themselves'.[56] The porters' guild of Alexandria in the early 1870s demanded a redistribution of wealth among their members

---

[49] Marsot, *Muhammad Ali*, p. 108.

[50] Roger Le Tourneau et al., 'Revolution in the Maghreb', in Panayiotis J. Vatikiotis (ed.), *Revolution in the Middle East and other Case Studies* (London: George Allen and Unwin, 1972), pp. 73–119, p. 78.

[51] André Raymond, 'Les porteurs d'eau du Caire', *Bulletin de l'Institut Français d'Archéologie Orientale* 57 (1958), pp. 183–203.

[52] Babikr Bedri, *The Memoirs of Babikr Bedri* (London: Oxford University Press, 1969), p. 32.

[53] Schölch, *Egypt for the Egyptians*, p. 37.

[54] André Raymond, 'Quartiers et Mouvements Populaires au Caire au XVIIIe Siècle', in Peter M. Holt (ed.), *Political and Social Change in Modern Egypt* (London: Oxford University Press, 1968), pp. 104–116.

[55] Raymond, 'Mouvements populaires', pp. 112–115; Abrahamian, 'The Crowd'.

[56] Pascale Ghazaleh, *Masters of the Trade: Crafts and Craftspeople in Cairo, 1750–1850* (Cairo: American University in Cairo Press, 1999), p. 64.

(*rukiyya*) as a matter of old custom.[57] On the other hand, women working in new silk-spinning factories in Mount Lebanon were dishonoured and stigmatized because of their contact with 'strange men' and putative sexual transgression.[58]

In short, the movements of the nineteenth century were not just legible through the hydraulics of (geo)political economy, but they were deeply embedded in diverse and syncretic tissues of meaning, living traditions and gender codes that could be linked to contestation. Movements drew on and transformed long-standing languages, rights, customs and beliefs, while voraciously appropriating new ideas and new organizational forms as they went.

COLONIALISM, NATIONALISM, LIBERALISM AND ISLAMIC MODERNISM, 1911–1939

Historical sociology displaced and discredited Orientalist and socio-psychological accounts of the popular movements of the inter-war period. Instead of being seen as fanatical or backward ('bandit marauders', as Tom Bowden described the protagonists of the mass uprising in Mandate Palestine in 1936–1939),[59] a large body of scholarship since the 1960s has made sense of these movements in terms of political economy and above all social and economic transformation. The emergence of new social classes—professionals (journalists, civil servants, lawyers, doctors and so on), educated women, and new forms of exploitation and dispossession among industrial workers, peasants, small-scale crafts- and service-worker and migrants, along with new forms of urban space, migration, transport infrastructure and print media, have been linked in different ways to the development of modern forms of mobilization, the rise of mass politics, the developing strength of nationalism, increasingly inflected by social and economic questions, and the weakening of the old social classes (notables, landowners, merchants, money-lenders, tribal chiefs and so on)—especially in the Mashriq and Egypt.[60] Mass politics in inter-war Syria, in

---

[57] Chalcraft, *Striking Cabbies*, pp. 97–101.

[58] Akram Fouad Khater, "House" to "Goddess of the House": Gender, Class, and Silk in 19th Century Mount Lebanon', *International Journal of Middle East Studies* 3 (1996), pp. 325–348.

[59] Tom Bowden, 'The Politics of the Arab Rebellion in Palestine 1936–39', *Middle Eastern Studies* 2 (1975), pp. 147–174.

[60] For a magisterial example, see Batatu, *The Old Social Classes*.

Gelvin's account, was permitted by a 'social and economic framework' that in turn was the fruit of 75 years of social and political transformation.[61] Al-Khafaji linked these many socio-economic changes to the crisis of the *ancien regime* in the region.[62]

This research certainly helps to capture the many ways that social and economic contexts mattered. During these decades, labour movements in most parts of the region established themselves as significant part of the social, economic and political landscape, often winning the right to organize collectively in syndicates and unions.[63] This development is hardly thinkable outside of the changing structure of the economy. The resistance of Palestinian peasants to Zionist colonization stemmed in part from the fact that their lands were bought up from under their feet by settlers, and peasants were evicted, only to face penury and unemployment, especially in new, urban slums.[64] It was, after all, in the slums of Jaffa that Izz al-Din al-Qassam, who urged armed *jihad* against Britain and Zionism in the 1920s and 1930s, recruited his followers. Khoury has shown, plausibly enough, how in inter-war Damascus, rural–urban migration, changing urban space, and the arrival of new quarters undermined the patronage networks of landowning, position-holding and merchant notables—making urban constituencies available for new kinds of mobilization.[65] Egypt's *effendiya* certainly joined the uprising of 1919—shocking their British overlords, as did women, educated and not so educated, along with workers of many kinds. There was also a wave of economic nationalism against foreign and colonial control of the economy in Egypt from the 1900s to the 1920s.[66]

The importance, however, of socio-economic change has often been pushed too far—at the expense of the role of imperialism, political contexts, and cultural dynamics. In many ways, the troughs and peaks of mobilization do not really fit a teleological chronology that expects a rising wave

---

[61] Gelvin, *Divided Loyalties,* p. 1, 20.

[62] Al-Khafaji, *Tormented Births.*

[63] Joel Beinin and Zachary Lockman, '1919: Labor Upsurge and National Revolution', in *The Modern Middle East,* pp. 395–428.

[64] Ted Swedenberg, 'The Role of the Palestinian Peasantry in the Great Revolt (1936–1939)', in *The Modern Middle East,* pp. 467–502.

[65] Philip S. Khoury, 'Syrian Urban Politics in Transition: The Quarters of Damascus During The French Mandate', *International Journal of Middle East Studies* 4 (1984), pp. 507–540.

[66] Eric Davis, *Challenging Colonialism: Bank Misr and the Egyptian Industrialization, 1920–1941* (Princeton, NJ: Princeton University Press, 1983).

of activism in response to social and economic change. Rapid social and economic change in Egypt cannot be linked to a rising wave of mobilization during 1882–1906, simply because there was no such rising wave. Or, the proliferation of armed struggles from Morocco in the West to Iraq in the East 1911–1927—and their subsequent *demobilization*—does not fit such a theory. Nor, indeed, does the fact that it was not mass mobilization that cut the Gordian knot in Egypt in 1952, but a coup d'état undertaken by a group of around 100 Free Officers. If the popular committees of 1920 in Damascus were the fruit of long social and economic change, as Gelvin argues, then this cannot explain why they then disappeared for much of the subsequent two decades. Moreover, if rapid change provokes radicalism, this cannot explain the fact that the main armed struggles in the region in the 1920s were rooted in rural areas—the Rif mountains, the Jabal Druze, northern Iraq—not urban—and that many of them were led and staffed not by urban elites, but by warlords, tribal elements, militant peasants, ex-Ottoman soldiers, neighbourhood bosses and the like. As Provence has written regarding Syria, '[c]ontrary to the expectations of the mandatory power, the uprising began in an apparently remote and supposedly backward rural region [Jabal Druze]'.[67]

Absent from—or merely supplementary to—socio-economic accounts, is the vitally important context of imperialism and geopolitics. From 1911 till the early 1920, most of the powers of Europe (Britain, France, Russia, Italy and Spain) tried (and often failed) to rule directly or partition the great majority of the region's territory for the first (and last) time. This represented a major assault on almost the entire region—compared to what had gone before. Italy invaded the Ottoman provinces that became Libya in 1911. Britain and Russia invaded Iran in 1911. France took official control of Morocco in 1912. Britain declared Egypt a protectorate in 1914, terminating the fiction of Ottoman sovereignty. The victorious powers in the First World War, which involved many privations including famine in its own right, tried to carve up the Ottoman empire (which surrendered in 1918) and its Arab provinces in the Mashriq between 1918 and 1922.

The great wave of contestation from 1911 to 1927, and in Mandate Palestine above all between 1936 and 1939, must be understood partly in the context of resistance to direct colonial rule, colonization and partition.

---

[67] Michael Provence, *The Great Syrian Revolt and the Rise of Arab Nationalism* (Austin: University of Texas Press, 2005), p. 12.

Al-Hiba's heterodox armed jihad of Mauretanian origin that briefly took Marrakech in Morocco in 1911–1912, must be linked to Sultan Abd al-Hafiz's signing over of Morocco to France. The jihad declared by Al-Sanusi in Cyrenaica in 1911 was in part a response to Italian invasion—and the return of the movement in the 1920s reflected the new, colonizing assault on Libya brought in by Italian fascism.[68] The uprising of 1919 in Egypt, and especially the involvement of the peasantry, can hardly be separated from the massive pressures that British war-time mobilization had placed on Egyptian society: conscription, requisition, inflation and so on.[69] The Turkish War of Independence began as a popular uprising in response to the attempt to partition what remained of the Ottoman empire; it drew on mass support in a way that the constitutional revolution of 1908 never did. The result was an independent, republican Turkey by 1924. Abd Al-Krim's extraordinary armed struggle in the Rif mountains (1921–1926) against first Spain and then France can hardly be disassociated from the Spanish and French attempt to rule directly the region.[70] Likewise the uprisings in Iraq (1920), Syria (July 1920 and 1925–1927) and the tide of protest in Mandate Palestine that culminated in the great revolt of 1936–1939 were in part the responses of people in the Ottoman empire and its Arab provinces to aggressive colonization and partition in places long accustomed to independence from European rule—in Palestine at the hands of Zionist colonization and the search for a state as well as British imperialism. On the other hand, encouragement to popular movements in the late 1910s came from Wilson's pronouncements on national self-determination, and in more concrete terms from the Bolshevik refusal of the imperialist politics of annexation.

Dynamics linked to state power and politics were also important. Resistance to state centralization was far less salient during this period than it had been during the nineteenth century for the simple reason that in Algeria, Tunisia, Egypt and Turkey large measures of military, legal, administrative and fiscal centralization had already largely been put in place. Here movements—especially in urban areas—increasingly

---

[68] Enzo Santarelli et al., *Omar Al-Mukhtar: the Italian Reconquest of Libya* (London: Darf Publishers, 1986).

[69] Ellis Goldberg, 'Peasants in Revolt—Egypt 1919', *International Journal of Middle East Studies* 2 (1992), pp. 261–280.

[70] David M. Hart, *The Aith Waryaghar of the Moroccan Rif* (Tucson, AZ: University of Arizona Press, 1976), pp. 369–404.

sought to capture and direct the agencies of the state, rather than to fight against state encroachment. The development of ideology—liberalism, communism, Islamism—can be understood at least partly in this context. These were bodies of thought that could be applied as programmes to the social formation as a whole by the powers of the newly centralized state. Nonetheless, in Morocco and Iran, where the state only now undertook to bring the tribes to heel by force, there was a significant and ongoing resistance (only quelled in the 1930s) to such military centralization. In Saudi Arabia, resistance to such centralization existed in regions such as 'Asir, but was more muted because the tribes were integrated into the central structures of the state—just as they were in Jordan and Iraq with British sponsorship. In Kuwait, Dubai, Qatar and Bahrain, tribal families who had attained pre-eminence during the nineteenth century by seeking protection by British imperialism actually became the state.

Cultural and political dynamics were also crucial. Heterodox, neo-Sufi, and millenarian aspects very much drop from view. Nor, unlike in South Asia, did any popular movement rally to the Caliphate, before or after its dissolution: the last Ottoman sultan-caliph had fatally compromised with the British and the French. One of the most immense structural powers and cultural icons of the Islamic world sank with barely a ripple in the Middle East and North Africa because of the dynamics of a given political situation. Wahhabism was important in what became a top-down project to unify the Saudi state—but it was hardly relevant outside of the borders of the Saudi state—especially after Ibn Saud used British machine guns to massacre the Ikhwan who had helped him unify the state, and defected from the armed struggles of the period to boot. On the other hand, Islamic revivalism or the *salafiyya* movement in Algeria and Morocco played a vital role in asserting the unity of Muslims under French rule in the 1920s and 1930s: out of such circles came the first assertions, in the 1930s, that the Algerians were a nation. And this came at a time when secular figures such as the liberal Ferhat Abbas were denying the existence of such a nation, and calling for assimilation. While in Egypt nationalism had a liberal and secular cast, the Muslim Brotherhood (founded 1928) introduced a new dynamic: neither a mosque nor a Sufi order nor a political party, but an urban society, the Muslim Brotherhood was devoted to making what it saw as a morally decadent and religiously deviant Egypt a more Islamic society, through piety, charity, persuasion and reform; by the 1940s this

society had hundreds of thousands of members and had become inextricably linked with Egyptian politics.[71]

Jihad in the cause of God helped to mobilize in northern Iraq the
tribes, rallied in part by calls from Ahmad al-Sanusi, ex-leader of the *jihad*
in Libya, who now fought with the 'Gazi' Atatürk in eastern Anatolia.[72]
Jihad was also invoked by the Shi'a *ulema* of Iraq's cities, it was important
in Morocco, and in what became Libya, Eastern Anatolia and in Syria
and Palestine. The innovation, however, of the 1920s is that the leading
note was taken in the rugged armed struggles that broke out after the
First World War, by the call to liberation, freedom and independence on
national lines. These languages were thoroughly inter-linked with various
tissues of common sense and spontaneous philosophy. In Syria, the Druze
warlord Sultan Al-Atrash, for example, rallied his tribal and peasant troops
in August 1925 with appeals to God, country, ancestry, national honour,
the will of the people and sacred hopes, and inveighed against French rule
as theft, division, and the crushing of freedom of religion, speech and
movement.[73] Fawzi al-Qawuqji, the ex-Ottoman officer who fought all
over the region in the inter-war years, was a passionate convert to Arab
nationalism. While al-Qawuqji paid little attention to the Bolshevik revolution of 1917, he was highly impressed by the contemporaneous exploits
of the 'hero Abd al-Krim' who was fighting the French and Spanish in
the Rif mountains of Morocco in the early 1920s.[74] Abd al-Krim, in turn,
sought an independent republic in the Rif mountains—a nation like any
other—a decisive break from all major movements in Morocco prior to
1914. In Mandate Palestine, popular notions of justice, rights, and custom
were at play in the protests and great uprising of the inter-war period.[75]
Gender codes and norms on sexuality were important at all points in the
mobilizations of these years.[76]

---

[71] Brynjar Lia, *The Rise of an Islamic Mass Movement, 1928–1942* (Reading: Ithaca Press, 1998).

[72] Claudia Anna Gazzini, 'Jihad in Exile: Ahmad al-Sharif Al-Sanusi, 1918–1933', Unpublished MA Thesis (Princeton University, 2004).

[73] Provence, *Great Syrian Revolt*, p. 1.

[74] Fawzi Al-Qawuqji, *Mudhakkirat Fawzi Al-Qawuqji/The Memoirs of Fawzi Al-Qawuqji* (Damascus: Dar al-Namir, 1995), p. 104.

[75] Rosemary Sayigh, *The Palestinians: from Peasants to Revoutionaries* (London: Zed Books, 1979), pp. 1–61.

[76] Ellen L. Fleischmann, 'The Other "Awakening": The Emergence of Women's Movements in the Modern Middle East, 1900–1940', in Margaret L. Meriwether and Judith

NEO-COLONIALISM, PAN-ARABISM AND SOCIALISM, 1939–1979

Assorted Orientalists and modernization theorists read the popular movements of the years from the uprising in Palestine of 1936–1939 to the Islamic revolution in Iran in terms of a series of irrational, hostile and extremist movements threatening to undermine order and stability and stemming from the psychological strains of rapid modernization. In such views, modernizing militaries and 'new middle classes' played the constructive role, especially in a Cold War context.[77] For Jacques Berque, in sharp contrast, this period involved 'the most violent, and yet deliberate, effort ever made by man to break the chains of weakness, poverty and colour'.[78] For Al-Khafaji, the three decades between the 1940s and the 1970s were *the* age of revolution in the region during modern times.[79] Revolutionary mobilization was understood by important historical sociologists in terms of capitalism, class, the sometime reassertion of traditional forces, and the politics of uneven development, whereby political development did not keep pace with socio-economic change.[80] Nonetheless, socio-economic change is not capable of explaining the diversity or the dynamics of popular movements during this period: imperialism, and especially political and ideological dynamics must be given their due: communism, pan-Arabism, Arab socialism, and popular Shi'ism, although very different, all embodied powerful ideas which mattered in under appreciated ways in the popular movements of this period.

Decolonization was hardly a linear process. Indeed, the Second World War involved a return to a more invasive direct rule. The British re-invasion of Iraq and Iran, along with the return of a more heavy-handed British rule in Egypt during the Second World War meant new privations and provoked new grievances. Meanwhile, the fact that so many Muslim Algerians had fought for France between 1939 and 1945, meant that many

E. Tucker (eds), *Social History of Women and Gender in the Modern Middle East* (Boulder, CO: Westview Press, 1999), pp. 89–140.

[77] Manfred Halpern, *The Politics of Social Change in the Middle East and North Africa* (Princeton, NJ: Princeton University Press, 1963).

[78] Jacques Berque, *Egypt: Imperialism and Revolution* (London: Faber and Faber, 1972), p. 26.

[79] Isam al-Khafaji, *Tormented Births: Passages to Modernity in Europe and the Middle East* (London: I.B. Tauris, 2004).

[80] Abrahamian, *Iran Between Revolutions*.

on the streets of the provincial town Sétif on liberation day (8 May 1945) expected that France would signal her willingness to reward them with independence. That the French provoked and then massacred thousands of civilians was a powerful impetus towards mobilization. Organized groups were proposing armed struggle by 1949, a project which was definitively launched against French colonial rule on 1 November 1954.[81] Algerian nationalism was not just provoked by imperialism, but sought to make use of the various rivalries that did exist in a Cold War context.[82] Meanwhile, volunteers (as well as regular forces) from Egypt and the Mashriq above all, flocked to Palestine in 1948 to oppose the ethnic cleansing of the Palestinians at the hands of Zionism and the establishment of Israel.[83] The irregular forces proved ineffective, and the failure of the regular forces was blamed by younger, patriotic officers on the civilian leaderships in Egypt and Iraq. In Egypt this gave the impetus to a group styling themselves Free Officers to plan for a coup designed to restore sound parliamentary life and remove imperialism in Egypt.[84] A similar group of Iraqi officers started to meet in the autumn of 1952 to set afoot plans for a repeat of Nasser's coup in the British client monarchy Iraq.[85] The loss of Palestine in 1948 was widely read not just as a defeat, but as a calamity that illuminated a crisis in the entire Arab order.

Beginning in 1965, but picking up greatly in 1968 (once the Arab states had shown themselves incapable of doing the job through their defeat in 1967), the PLO fought a revolutionary armed struggle to liberate Palestine from Israel—which only ran out of steam in 1982 with the eviction of the PLO from Lebanon following the Israeli invasion.[86] Palestinians in Lebanon found ways to survive and practice steadfastness (*sumud*) in the face of Israeli and Syrian siege and massacre.[87] All around

[81] William B. Quandt, *Revolution and Political Leadership: Algeria, 1954–1968* (Cambridge: The M.I.T. Press, 1969).

[82] Matthew Connelly, 'Rethinking the Cold War and Decolonization: the grand strategy of the Algerian war for independence', *International Journal of Middle East Studies* 2 (2001), pp. 221–245.

[83] Ilan Pappé, *The Ethnic Cleansing of Palestine* (Oxford: Oneworld Publications, 2007).

[84] Joel Gordon, *Nasser's Blessed Movement: Egypt's Free Officers and the July Revolution* (Cairo: American University in Cairo Press, 1997).

[85] Batatu, *The Old Social Classes*, pp. 764–807.

[86] Yezid Sayigh, *Armed Struggle and the Search for State: the Palestinian National Movement 1949–1993* (Oxford: Oxford University Press, 1997).

[87] Rosemary Sayigh, *Too Many Enemies: The Palestinian Experience in Lebanon* (London: Zed books, 1994).

the Arabian Peninsula there were movements, fed by labour migration, against colonial direct and indirect forms of rule from the 1950s to the 1970s—most dramatically in South Yemen, where an armed struggle launched in 1963 drove out the British in 1967.[88] The coup carried out by the Arab nationalist officers in Libya in 1969, which put Gaddafi in power, could hardly be dissociated from a larger geopolitics, in which US and British power in Libya was conceived of as intolerable.

Neither Ba'thism, pan-Arabism nor Nasserism can be grasped outside of the geopolitical context: all had as their goal the achievement of political and economic independence and Arab unity in one form or another in the face of either European, Israeli, or newly assertive US power. As Europe retreated, some of the features of the increasingly heavy-hand of US geopolitical power in the region were the CIA-sponsored coup d'état in Iran in 1953, the Eisenhower doctrine of 1957, the landing of US marines in Lebanon in 1958, and the shift to the massive support of Israel in the wake of 1967. Instead of the hope that Wilsonian pronouncements had represented to the generation of 1919, the popular movements of the post-1945 decades increasingly saw US-sponsored neo-colonialism as the enemy. Nasserism derived a tremendous impetus from its victory against the Tripartite Aggression of 1956, when France, Israel and Britain conspired: France to punish Egypt which was backing the Algerian revolutionaries; Britain to reverse the nationalization of the canal; Israel to seize the Sinai and cripple Egypt's military forces. Even Habib Bourguiba of Tunisia and King of Morocco owed much of their fate and fortunes to nationalist movements against French control. King Hussein of Jordan Morocco barely survived Arab nationalist attempts to unseat him in the mid-1950s, leading to the eviction of the long-established British advisor, Glubb Pasha. The movements in Iran between 1941 and 1953 can hardly be understood aside from the ways they challenged neo-colonialism and economic domination; likewise the protests of 1963 in Iran were in part about foreign control. The Iranian revolution of 1979 had a good deal to do with neo-colonialism. The Shah was seen as a puppet of the United States—and his authoritarian regime owed its longevity to high levels of military, diplomatic and economic support of the United States. The CIA had organized the 1953 coup which removed the liberal, aristocratic, and democratically

---

[88] Fred Halliday, *Arabia Without Sultans* (London: Penguin, 1974); Abdel Razzaq Takriti, *Monsoon Revolution: Republicans, Sultans, and Empires in Oman, 1965–1976* (Oxford: Oxford University Press, 2013).

elected politician Mossadegh and returned the Shah to power. In this context, demonstrators on the streets of Tehran in 1978–1979 shouted 'death to America' and also, in a repudiation of the great power politics of the Soviet Union, 'neither East nor West, Islamic Republic'. As Khomeini put it: 'the rulers of the world are America's serfs'.

Domestic state power and politics formed another major context for the movements of these decades. Nasserism was a republican movement: within days of coming to power the Free Officers had sent Egypt's King Farouk packing and declared a republic, ending the dynasty founded in 1805. Monarchs were then toppled in Tunisia, Iraq, North Yemen, and Libya. The movements in Lebanon in 1958, and then far more powerfully from the late 1960s until 1976, were directly against the conservative, sectarian political system, in which representation was highly unequal, above all for the Shi'a of the south—who joined Musa Sadr's movement of the dispossessed among other movements.[89] An important aspect of the Palestinian experience in Lebanon, especially in the 1980s, involved survival and steadfastness (*sumud*) in the face of state breakdown, siege, massacres, and the activities of a wide variety of militias on the local stage.[90] Shi'a movements in Saudi Arabia and Bahrain were in part in a context of political exclusion and discrimination.[91] The popular uprising in Iran— one of the most mass-based revolutions of modern times—replaced the Pahlavi monarchy with an Islamic republic. The revolution was the fruit of Islamist leadership among the clerical and other supports of Khomeini in Iran—but also the work of liberals, nationalists, socialists, feminists and the participation of many men and women from all walks of life.[92] Where military, fiscal and legislative power was in the hands of centralized states in the region, all politics became ideological, the need to capture the state was central.

Unequal relations of production and exchange, and forms of economic exploitation and scarcity were also an important context for protest movements during these years. Workers and peasants rose up to take control of land, housing and means of production left behind by departing colons

[89] Augustus R. Norton, *Amal and the Shi'a: Struggle for the Soul of Lebanon* (Austin, TX: University of Texas Press, 1987).

[90] Sayigh, *Too Many Enemies*.

[91] Toby Craig Jones, 'Rebellion on the Saudi Periphery: Modernity, Marginalization and the Shi'a Uprising of 1979', *International Journal of Middle East Studies* (2006), pp. 213–233.

[92] Abrahamian, *Iran between Revolutions*, pp. 419–529.

(and in some cases would-be new Muslim owners) in Algeria in the summer of 1962.[93] Poor peasants 'armed with forks and scythes' seized land directly from landowners and set up a popular committee to administer them amid the 'popular intifada' that swept South Yemen in 1970–1971.[94] Palestinians in camps in Lebanon were also fighting for jobs and livelihoods. Wild-cat strikes, typically opposed by the official, statist, corporatist, trade union federation, were a more or less continuous feature of the life of Egyptian industrial workers from the 1960s to the 1980s.[95] Organized labour movements, as well as massive spontaneous strike action, by paralysing the economy, especially the oil-sector, played an important role in the Iranian revolution of 1979.[96] Worker control in factories in Iran was a powerful force for a year or so after 1979 before co-option by the state[97]; others occupied housing left vacant by the departed rich.[98]

It should already be clear that the protests of these years were not simply a matter of structure and process. Relational phenomena, social construction and ideological dynamics must be given their due. The idea, for example, that 'the triumph in Syria of advanced ideas on the peasant question' resulted, at bottom, from 'the coming to the political forefront of military elements of peasant origin' seems overly determinist, and grants too little to the ideological and political context.[99] Social justice, Arab socialism, Third Worldism, communism, land reform, progressive taxation, the redistribution of wealth and feminism were all important themes in the protest movements of these years.[100] Landowners, Pashas, notables, shaykhs, merchants and usurers were in many ways seen as stooges of imperialism, political tyrants and patriarchal, economic exploiters. By the same

[93] Ian Clegg, *Workers' Self-Management in Algeria* (London: Allen Lane, 1971), esp. p. 44ff.

[94] Halliday, *Arabia without Sultans,* p. 248.

[95] Marsha Pripstein-Posusney, *Labor and the State in Egypt* (New York: Columbia University Press, 1997).

[96] Fred Halliday, *Islam and the Myth of Confrontation,* Second Edition (London: I.B. Tauris, 2003), pp. 42–75.

[97] Asef Bayat, *Workers and Revolution in Iran: A Third World Experience of Workers' Control* (London: Zed Books, 1987).

[98] Asef Bayat, *Street Politics: Poor People's Movements in Iran* (New York: Columbia University Press, 1997), p. 73.

[99] Hanna Batatu, *Syria's Peasantry, the Descendants of Its Lesser Rural Notables, and Their Politics* (Princeton, NJ: Princeton University Press, 1999), p. 38.

[100] Valentine Moghadam, *Modernizing Women: Gender and Social Change in the Middle East* (Boulder, CO: Lynne Rienner, 1993), pp. 69–97.

token, labour quiescence in the 1950s and 1960s was not only because of repression and co-optation, but also because of Nasserism's emphasis on 'the contributions made by workers and peasants to the cause of national development' which gave workers a sense of belonging.[101] While a concern with social justice could lead straight into Islamist politics,[102] the fact is that Islamism, so important in the inter-war period, was profoundly muted during these decades—'an ever dwindling activist fringe' in the words of an important scholar of the movement.[103] Indeed, Islam was drawn on by socialist politics in other ways: Mehdi Ben Barka, the most important Moroccan socialist leader, understood Islam to be a thoroughly democratic force.[104] The intellectual work behind the socialism and communism of the 1950s and 1960s involved *inter alia* Marx, Lenin, Mao, Che Guevara, Franz Fanon, Samir Amin, Anwar 'Abd Al-Malek and Albert Memmi.[105] Activist networks linked movement cadres in one location to far-flung places, channelling inspiration and training. 'When I went there [to China] I was a nationalist,' said one South Yemeni, 'Now I am a Marxist-Leninist.'[106]

NEOLIBERALISM, ISLAMISM AND PEOPLE POWER, 1979–PRESENT

Since the 1970s, geopolitical, political, economic and cultural contexts and dynamics—along with popular movements—have undergone important shifts. Among the rich and powerful countries, especially with the fall of the Soviet Union, and the non-conflictual integration of China, India, and other major states, global inter-state economic and political rivalry has greatly diminished, reducing the possibilities for popular movements and small states to exploit elite rivalries. This concentration of power may be linked to the increase of war and invasion in the region. A global economic system—justified with reference to the mantras of neoliberalism

---

[101] Alia Mossallam, *Hikayat Sha'b—Stories of Peoplehood: Nasserism, Popular Politics and Songs in Egypt, 1956–1973*, Unpublished PhD Dissertation (LSE, 2013).

[102] John Calvert, *Sayyid Qutb and the Origins of Radical Islamism* (London: Hurst, 2010).

[103] Richard Mitchell, *The Society of the Muslim Brothers* (Oxford: Oxford University Press, 1969), p. 23.

[104] Le Tourneau et al., 'Revolution in the Maghreb', p. 86ff.

[105] See, for example, Anwar Abd al-Malek (ed.), *Contemporary Arab Political Thought* (London: Zed Books, 1983).

[106] Halliday, *Arabia without Sultans*, p. 331.

and free markets—has emerged in which manufactures (mostly from Asia) are bought with cheap credit (mostly by Europe and the United States). Most states in the Middle East and North Africa have been attached to this system. The oil-rich states sell their oil to China and other countries, and spend their petro-dollars patronizing small national populations, building palaces and infrastructure with super-exploited migrant labour, and pumping money into financial centres. The formerly 'revolutionary republics' provide minor services to the international dominant bloc by paying off debts, buying arms, recycling aid money and geopolitical rents to global corporations, winning for local elites in the process opportunities for business, corruption and kleptocracy. Elites repeat global economic mantras, roll back social protections, and increasingly securitize their rule, while claiming this is necessary to counter the 'Islamic threat'. In this period, new forms of protest emerged—on the one hand tied into varieties of Islamism, on the other, varieties of people power, liberalism, and democracy.

Geopolitics, imperialism, regional war and occupation again weighed heavily in any comprehension of protest movements in the region since 1979. Indeed, in an echo of the early twentieth century, invasion, occupation and the direct deployment of military force became more significant relative to the previous period. The Soviet invasion of Afghanistan in 1979 split the Non-Aligned Movement, and inaugurated a US and Pakistan-funded *jihad* against the 'atheist' 'materialist' occupation during the 1980s. Cold War rivalry combined with a powerful social movement to produce a successful armed jihad in the name of God—one which its more zealous followers saw as bringing down a long-despised empire. While the promise of the United States had palled for popular movements after 1945, that of the Soviet Union did so especially after 1979. Armed struggle in the cause of God had been hardly relevant in the region since the early 1920s. Afghanistan, however, now provided the funding, the space, the recruiting ground, and a reference point for volunteer fighters from the (usually Sunni) Muslim parts of the Middle East and North Africa (and elsewhere).[107] Meanwhile, Israel's (US-tolerated) invasions of Lebanon, culminating in the occupation of Beirut and 10% of Lebanon from 1982 to 2000 may have exiled the secular nationalist PLO to Tunis, but they were the crucial context for the rise of Iranian-backed Hizbullah

---

[107] Madawi al-Rasheed, *Contesting the Saudi State: Islamic Voices from a New Generation* (Cambridge: Cambridge University Press, 2006).

as a disciplined guerrilla movement mobilizing Shi'a constituencies, assassinating Leftist intellectuals, and struggling as the 'Party of God' against the occupation in the south of Lebanon. Libya played a role by decapitating the major Shi'a 'movement of the dispossessed' of the 1970s—by covertly assassinating its leader, Musa Sadr, in the late 1970s. After the end of the civil war, in the 1990s, Hizbullah was morphed into a political party—with an armed wing—on the Lebanese political scene. They were to score a success in 2000, when they played a role in forcing Israel to withdraw from south Lebanon.

A third invasion was equally important. The Iraqi invasion of Iran in 1980, with at the very least a supportive tilt from the United States and its allies (with countries such as West Germany supplying chemical weapons), played an important role in greatly diminishing the pluralistic potential of the newly-minted Islamic Republic of Iran. In mobilizing for war against Iraq, and in the clash with the US, in an echo of the Jacobin Terror in the face of the crowned heads of Europe, the Islamic revolution devoured its children: 'open, collective, and audible mobilization was seriously undermined, and the disenfranchised withdrew into backstreet politics'.[108] By 1982, in the heat of a bloody regional war, much of the political pluralism of the Iranian revolution was extinguished, activists were killed, imprisoned or exiled, and real power in the state was taken by a clerical leadership under Imam Khomeini.

The wealthy renegade, and veteran of the jihad in Afghanistan, Osama Bin Laden, like Umar Makram in 1807, perhaps, wanted to organize a non-state-based defence of Saudi Arabia against the Ba'thist-Iraqi invasion of Kuwait in August 1990. His offer was rejected, and the Saudi kingdom, in spite of its own very high levels of military spending, led the other states of the Persian Gulf in requesting that the United States come to protect their regimes against the Iraqi foe. Saudi Arabia, along with Arab allies from Egypt to Syria who joined the 'coalition', thus moved decisively into the US camp, just as the Soviet Union was disappearing from the scene. The wave of revulsion and protest that followed was not only in opposition to the one of the most punitive bombing campaigns (during early 1991) against Iraq, seen as a beacon of Arabism, in the region's history, but also to the way the regimes of the region, led by Saudi Arabia, were seen as stooges of imperialism. The Arab regimes did nothing against one of the most severe sanctions regimes in the history of the UN. Much of

[108] Bayat, *Street Politics,* p. 164.

the growing Saudi opposition now operated in exile, whether in London, Sudan, Somalia or Afghanistan. The idea of striking the 'far enemy' (the United States) was born in the ranks of Osama Bin Laden's growing organization, Al-Qaeda.[109] This geopolitics was therefore a central part of the context for the attacks on the World Trade Centre in September 2001—which had nothing to do with the (neo)Orientalist fantasy that they expressed the ancient, invariant enmity and hatred of 'Islamic civilization' towards the 'Judeo-Christian West'.[110]

Israel's ongoing occupation of the Occupied Palestinian Territories, and especially its reversion to colonization after 1977, formed the context for the first *intifada* (from 1987 to 1991), involving non-violence, mass civil disobedience and self-organization in the name of national self-determination and a two-state solution.[111] The Oslo process which followed, however, failed. Instead of a state, the Palestinians found themselves fragmented in bantustans. This was the key context for the outbreak of the second intifada in September 2000, and the rise and growing popularity during the 1990s of the Islamist movement Hamas, who had always said against their local secular foes that it was pointless to negotiate with 'infidels' and 'Jews'.[112] Israeli bombing campaigns and invasions in the Occupied Palestinian Territories (Jenin 2002, Gaza 2008–2009) and in Lebanon (August 2006) gave Hizbullah a new lease of popularity in much of the region. On the other hand, hundreds of thousands of Lebanese engaged in non-violent demonstrations in March 2005 in the wake of the assassination of former PM and billionaire Rafiq Hariri. This movement successfully drove out Syrian troops that had long occupied the country.

The invasion of both Afghanistan (2001) and Iraq (2003) by the United States and its allies, and what the US called the 'War on Terror' in the wake of 9/11[113] were the context for the rise of new groups of fighters, generally rather small in number, ready to espouse the cause of armed

[109] Fawaz Gerges, *The Far Enemy: Why Jihad Went Global* (Cambridge: Cambridge University Press, 2005).

[110] Samuel Huntington, *Clash of Civilizations and the Remaking of World Order* (London: Simon and Schuster, 1997).

[111] Mazin B. Qumsiyeh, *Popular Resistance in Palestine: A History of Hope and Empowerment* (London: Pluto Books, 2011).

[112] Sara Roy, 'Why Peace Failed: An Oslo Autopsy', *Current History* 101 (2002), pp. 8–16.

[113] Laleh Khalili, *Time in the Shadows: Confinement in Counterinsurgencies* (Palo Alto, CA: Stanford University Press, 2012).

struggle against imperialism, 'Jews', 'crusaders' and 'infidels'.[114] The new imperialism, along with Israel's US-backed turn from negotiations to wall-building, siege and periodic massacre was also the background for anti-war movements and new kinds of secular protest in and outside of the region. More than 16 million marched around the world in February 2003—perhaps the largest and most global single protest event that the world had ever seen.[115] Many of the Arab states, especially Egypt, started to see protests in non-religious languages against imperialism after September 2000. The Israel re-invasion of Jenin, and the iconic impotence of Arafat at the Arab Summit in March 2002 were directly relevant to the growth from 2002 of the transnational Boycott, Divestment and Sanctions movement opposing Israeli apartheid, racism and violations of international law and human rights, spearheaded by Palestinians under occupation.[116]

We have already seen in the case of Saudi Arabia, Egypt and the Palestinian Authority, how protest did not respond only to imperialism directly, but to the weakness, capitulation and collaboration of Arab power-holders with it. When the president of the most populous Arab state, and the country that had done so much to lead the movements of the 1950s and 1960s, signed the Camp David accords in 1979, he was seen by many as selling out the Palestinians, pursuing narrow Egyptian national interests against pan-Arab ones, and capitulating to the historic enemy. It was in this context that in Egypt the long-dormant notion of armed jihad was re-discovered, and Sadat was assassinated by Islamists, while the uprising they expected failed to materialize.[117] In the 2000s, Mubarak's capitulation to the United States and Israel over Gaza was reviled as a quid pro quo for the US turning a blind eye on his attempt to install his son Gamal as his successor: this time protest was republican, constitutional and placed heavy emphasis on law and human rights.

The other major shift in the policies and structures of the state, especially in the formerly revolutionary republics, that played a vital role in

---

[114] Timothy Mitchell, 'McJihad: Islam in the US Global Order', *Social Text* 20 (2002), pp. 1–18; Fawaz Gerges, *The Rise and Fall of Al-Qaeda* (Oxford: Oxford University Press, 2011).

[115] Sidney Tarrow, *The New Transnational Activism* (Cambridge: Cambridge University Press, 2005).

[116] Omar Barghouti, *Boycott, Divestment, Sanctions: The Global Struggle for Palestinian Rights.* (Chicago: Haymarket Books, 2011).

[117] Gilles Kepel, *The Prophet and Pharaoh: Muslim Extremism in Egypt* (London: El Saqi Books, 1985).

protest movements from the 1970s to the 2010s was the retreat from statist developmentalism and social protection, and the embrace of neoliberal economics, involving structural adjustment programmes, corruption, kleptocracy, aid recycling and privatization. When subsidies on basic commodities were stripped away, protests and 'bread riots' broke out in one country after another—from the *intifada* of 18 and 19 February 1977 in Egypt to the riots and protests of October 1988 in Algeria and elsewhere in Jordan, Morocco and Tunisia.[118] Political rights had been ceded in exchange for social and economic rights, but now this 'social pact' was under radical assault from the regime.[119] The regime also became the target of labour protests and strikes when it moved to remove social protections, entitlements and the like.[120] In Egypt in the 2000s, many workers held the regime responsible for marginalizing them from the 'map of social and economic development', and for abolishing rights and protections to which they had become accustomed.[121] The corruption that accompanied interactions with international financial institutions, the award of business contracts, and the public purse was also a source of considerable public discontent. It is important to note, moreover, that the retreat of statist provision helps explain the success in Egypt in the 1970s and 1980s of reformist, non-violent Islamist movements—which concentrated not on overt protest on Leftist lines, but on providing charitable goods and services to constituencies neglected by the state.[122]

The state's failure to engage in serious political liberalization or democratization, or to uphold the rule of law, was also a context of considerable protest in many parts of the region. The dramatic cancellation of the elections that had given such a degree of popular support to the FIS in Algeria precipitated a devastating armed struggle in Algeria during the 1990s—in part as a result of the exclusion of Islamists from the political

[118] John Walton and David Seddon, *Free Markets and Food Riots: The Politics of Global Adjustment* (Oxford: Blackwell, 1994).

[119] Larbi Sadiki, 'Popular Uprisings and Arab Democratization', *International Journal of Middle East Studies* 32 (2000), pp. 71–95.

[120] Posusney, *Labor and State*, pp. 129–150.

[121] Joel Beinin, 'A Workers' Social Movement', in Beinin and Vairel, *Social Movements, Mobilization, and Contestation*.

[122] Carrie Rosefsky-Wickham, *Mobilizing Islam: Religion, Activism, and Political Change in Egypt* (New York: Columbia University Press, 2002).

process.[123] The 1990s saw a long struggle for constitutionalism and parliament against Sunni sectarianism and ruling family authoritarianism in Bahrain. The reform movement in Iran in the 1990s and 2000s opposed clerical monopoly in seeking a far more democratic and pluralistic version of the Islamic Republic than that of the 1980s.[124] The attempt to impose a dynastic succession in Egypt was the occasion for the Kifaya movement in Egypt in 2005–2007. The political parties that supported the uprising of 1977 in Egypt, or the lawyer's mobilization there in the 2000s were very much over issues of legal rights and due process. Nor could the Arab uprisings of 2010 onwards be understood outside of the condemnation of the incumbent regimes over questions of political freedom.[125]

The rise of extra-legal forces linked to the state, organized corruption and routine violence and torture within the police and security forces, the diminished role of the state itself in making and enforcing binding rules and regulations was another important context in the changing nature of resistance and survival. The pervasive role of corruption in the bureaucracy encouraged the formation of informal networks as avenues of participation.[126] For the new urban poor in slums, the state hardly existed as such, it was in 'bits and pieces', encountered in routinized humiliation and torture at the hands of the police. In this context 'contentious politics' involved a series of violent and fragmented encounters.[127] Police in Egypt were partly para-militarized because of the encounter with militant Islamism in the 1990s—and repression was always claimed as necessary to repress 'fundamentalism' and 'terrorism'. Authoritarianism, physical repression of declared opposition, the lack of multi-party democracy, were part of the context for urban poor resistance through the 'quiet encroachment of the ordinary': 'a silent, patient, protracted, and pervasive advancement of ordinary people on the propertied and powerful in order

---

[123] Mohammed M. Hafez, 'Armed Islamist Movements and Political Violence in Algeria', *Middle East Journal* 54 (2000), pp. 572–591.

[124] Asef Bayat, *Making Islam Democratic: Social Movements and the Post-Islamist Turn* (Palo Alto, CA: Stanford University Press, 2007), esp. pp. 106–135.

[125] Fawaz Gerges (ed.), *The New Middle East: Protest and Revolution in the Arab World* (Cambridge: Cambridge University Press, 2013).

[126] Diane Singerman, *Avenues of Participation: Family, Politics and Networks in Urban Quarters of Cairo* (Princeton, NJ: Princeton University Press, 1995).

[127] Salwa Ismail, *Political Life in Cairo's New Quarters* (Minneapolis: University of Minnesota Press, 2006).

to survive hardships and better their lives'.[128] The state was no longer seen as a prize to be captured for this or that programme. The rationale for the ideological capture of the state was diminished where the state itself was disaggregated.

Systems of accumulation, economic structures of power, exploitation, inflation in basic commodities and housing, and unemployment played a role throughout the period. Rising prices entailed hardship and griev-ances. Landlords hired thugs to evict peasants from their land follow-ing the land law of 1992.[129] The massive growth of slums formed the spatial context for new, violent and sometimes uncoordinated contests with police.[130] The growth of the informal sector—or what Elyachar has characterized as 'markets of dispossession'[131]—which fragmented and dis-organized workforces was part of the making of everyday modes of resis-tance.[132] Unobtrusive and survivalist forms of resistance appeared among those displaced or evicted by 'accumulation by dispossession'. In some respects, the very existence of the 'informal' (in the sense of unregulated) sector was a result of a large-scale if uncoordinated attempt to avoid the predatory features of state involvement. The failure of these economies to provide jobs for graduates and others was part of the context for move-ments of the unemployed that attempted to secure such jobs. Workers in particular plants fighting on bread and butter issues may not have been supported by the official union structure, but strike action and protests were a feature of the whole period—above all in Egypt from 2004 to the present day—when more than a million workers, civil servants and their families have been involved in strike action, and the formation of new independent unions.[133] Issues of wealth distribution, and the ostentatious wealth of the few, were very much part of the context of the uprisings of 2010–present.[134]

[128] Bayat, *Street Politics*, p. 7, 21.

[129] Reem Saad, 'State, Landlord, Parliament and Peasant: the story of the 1992 tenancy law in Egypt', in Alan Bowman and Eugene Rogan (eds), *Agriculture in Egypt from Pharaonic to Modern Times* (Oxford: Oxford University Press, 1999), pp. 387–404.

[130] Ismail, *Cairo's New Quarters*.

[131] Julie Elyachar, *Markets of Dispossession: NGOs, Economic Development, and the State in Cairo* (Durham, NC: Duke University Press, 2005).

[132] Bayat, *Street Politics*, p. 7.

[133] During the 1989 strike at Helwan Iron and Steel Plant, union leaders fled the factory and urged the authorities to storm the factory. Posusney, *Labor and State*, pp. 151–157.

[134] Gilbert Achcar, *The People Want: A Radical Exploration of the Arab Uprising* (London: Saqi Books, 2013).

As in previous periods, popular movements cannot be seen as only provoked or shaped by structures of geopolitical, political, and economic power. Interpretive contexts and mobilizing discourses dramatically shaped protest movements. As before, these were rich and various, ranging from the Gandhian repertoire of civil disobedience in the name of a national community of the first intifada through to the notion of armed struggle targeting civilians in the name of God. Interpretations were not simply the structural inheritance of the past. They involved dynamic re-interpretation on the ground, and intellectual work, sometimes of the highly abstract variety. The rise of Islamist politics—in popular Shi'a, Salafi-sectarian, or reformist-modernist mode—did not begin with the Iranian revolution or the *jihad* in Afghanistan—nor was it simply a resurgence of 'ancient hatreds'. As for the first, in Iran, probably the most popular ideologue of the revolution was a schoolteacher Ali Shariati, who engaged in an ambitious synthesis of activist Shi'ism with Marxism and Third Worldism—an intellectual work which made Shi'ism available as a language of protest to hundreds of thousands of people who might otherwise have been more inclined to see it as backward, ritualistic, irrational and arcane. Shi'a activism was increasingly evident on the ground in the 1970s: in Lebanon Musa Sadr's movement of the dispossessed; in Iraq, Muhammad Baqir al-Sadr and the *intifadat al-safar* of 1977 against the Ba'thist regime; in Bahrain a religious bloc had appeared in that country's truncated parliamentary life in the early 1970s. As for militant Sunni Islamist movements, these drew heavily on the intellectual exegesis of the Qur'an put forward by Sayyid Qutb in Nasser's prisons before his execution in 1966. Qutb argued that Muslim rulers had been so thoroughly corrupted they could be considered as having reverted to a state of pre-Islamic ignorance (*jahaliyya*).[135] More generally, new forms of Islamism drew on a major intellectual edifice of interpretation relevant to changing times.[136]

On the other hand, the proponents of non-violent resistance in secular mode, such as Edward Said, Eqbal Ahmad or Raja Shehadeh, developed extensive intellectual rationales in a re-worked democratic and humanist tradition. Educated groups who participated in Egypt's intifada of 18–19 January 1977 insisted on their law-abiding, socialist, and democratic credentials—and drew on a developed language of social class, popular

---

[135] Calvert, *Sayyid Qutb*.

[136] Ibrahim Abu-Rabi, *Intellectual Origins of Islamic Resurgence in the Modern Arab World* (Albany, NY: State University of New York Press, 1996).

struggle, and capitalist exploitation. Unions in Egypt, in the 1980s, tended to be more sympathetic to labour demands when leftists were present on their boards,[137] pointing to the dynamic role of ideology. The reform movement in Iran in the 1990s and 2000s cannot be understood without serious attention to the intellectual critique by major figures from Mohsen Kadivar to Abdulkarim Soroush, who sought to redefine the meaning of Islamic politics and the Islamic republic.[138]

The fabrics and new weaves of meaning were not always of the abstract kind. Popular traditions—such as of Shi'a mourning—were re-worked and politicized—the stuff and substance of spontaneous philosophy and proverbial wisdom now thrown into acute political struggle. A homologous form was at work in Algeria in 1988—with crowd protests being informed by a popular culture enjoining the need for leaders worthy of respect, protection from abuse, collective decision-making, and the value of justice over the arrogance of the powerful.[139] Or, it is hard to fully grasp worker sit-ins in Egypt that increased rather than halted production without a sense of the resonance of the language of 'productivity in the name of the nation'. Protests in Egypt in the 1980s over the stripping of entitlements (such as the 'riots' in Alexandria in 1984), over the demand for parity (equal wages for equal work), and protests over unmet promises were part of a moral economy, not just a system of economic power.[140]

The popular joke in Algeria that informed the riots of 1988 regarding wealthy, corrupt leaders as enjoying 'villa, honda, blonda' linked 'decadent' sexuality to those revelling in material luxury through corruption and the West.[141] Masculinist and sometime misogynistic and homophobic languages vilifying presidential wives for corruption and consumption, or corrupt leaders who bought too many Italian shoes as 'dandies' were intertwined with popular mobilization. During the first intifada, young Palestinian men who underwent beatings, detention and torture at the hands of the Israeli military and returned defiant enhanced their male

---

[137] Posusney, *Labor and the State*, p. 151.

[138] Charles Kurzman, 'Critics Within: Islamic Scholars' Protests Against the Islamic State in Iran', *International Journal of Politics, Culture, and Society* 15 (2001), pp. 341–359.

[139] Hugh Roberts, 'Moral Economy or Moral Polity? The Political Anthropology of Algerian Riots', *Crisis States Programme, Working Papers Series No. 1* (LSE, DESTIN, 2002).

[140] Marsha Pripstein-Posusney, 'The Moral Economy of Labor Protest in Egypt', *World Politics* 46 1 (1993), pp. 83–120.

[141] Martin Evans and John Phillips, *Algeria: Anger of the Dispossessed* (New Haven, CT: Yale University Press, 2007), pp. 102–142.

status, honour and leadership roles in the movement itself. Repression here begat resistance, for reasons only explicable through an understanding of gender codes.[142]

CONCLUSION

Against top-down or one-dimensional histories, this inevitably brief and generalized overview has tried to draw attention to the importance and the variety of popular movements in the Middle East and North Africa since the eighteenth century. Resistance has occurred at multiple scales, from the imperial to the domestic, and involved everyday forms as well as collective confrontations, abstract ideology and proverbial wisdom, religiosity and secularism, organization and spontaneity, and armed struggle, civil disobedience, and persuasion. The chapter has understood this rich variety of form and content in terms of historical and power-laden contexts—geopolitical, political, socio-economic, and cultural—while aiming to avoid structuralism or determinism. What stands out in this survey is the role of state-building and state centralization in provoking protests during the period 1807–1911, and the role of an unprecedented colonial assault on the region in doing likewise from 1911 to 1939. This chapter has also underlined how ideological forms seeking to capture state power mattered so much during the period 1939–1979. In the most recent period, it is the degradation of the state, in combination with neoliberalism and a return to imperialism that take the lead. More generally, while the cultural essentialism and exceptionalism of (neo)Orientalism is rejected in favour of cultural dynamism and historical specificity, the chapter has also sought to refuse the socio-economic determinism that was invoked by so many scholars to debunk (neo)Orientalism: attention has been drawn instead to the vital roles played by both (geo)politics and cultural dynamics. This chapter also rejects developmentalism and historicism: that is, the movements in this chapter are not riding a meta-historical escalator of progress and development: activism is jagged with peaks and troughs; form and content change over time; consciousness does not simply expand: ideas are lost or forgotten (sometimes the best ones) as well as re-discovered or developed anew. Moreover, rather than seeing the national context as the natural one for the history of popular movements, the chapter has illustrated some of

---

[142] Julie Peteet, 'Male Gender and Rituals of Resistance in the Palestinian 'Intifada': A Cultural Politics of Violence', *American Ethnologist* 1 (1994), pp. 31–49.

the ways in which transversal ties between non-state actors have been at play in such movements—at the transcontinental, transimperial, transnational, and regional levels. This chapter has also aimed to underline that the history of popular movements can make an important contribution by drawing attention away from sometimes overly abstracted and presentist debates about methods and explanatory concepts, and drawing attention towards the substance and meaning of popular movements themselves as rooted in dynamic and power-laden historical contexts. Finally, the aim here has been to show that popular movements cannot be reduced to a series of discursive effects. Subaltern social groups have not been entirely voiceless, shapeless, or fragmented. Popular movements instead have mattered in making, modifying and breaking socio-economic and cultural structures, regimes, states, nations and empires. It seems reasonable to view resistance and popular movements not as epiphenomenal, but as an integral part of the aggregate dynamics of the social formation as a whole in the region.

FURTHER READINGS

Comprehensive histories of social movements in the Middle East and North Africa are few and far between. The 'long version' of this chapter is to be found in John Chalcraft, *Popular Politics in the Making of the Modern Middle East.* (Cambridge: Cambridge University Press, 2016). Charles Tripp's *The Power and the People: Paths of Resistance in the Middle East* (Cambridge: Cambridge University Press, 2013) is a landmark book on themes of resistance, exclusion and power in the region, particularly with reference to the period since independence. The most important work in relation to workers and peasants is Joel Beinin's *Workers and Peasants in Modern Middle East* (Cambridge: Cambridge University Press, 2001). Edmund Burke III's introduction in Edmund Burke III and Ira Lapidus (eds), *Islam, Politics and Social Movements* (Berkeley: University of California Press, 1988) is still seminal reading for its chronological and historiographic overview. An important edited volume in the history-from-below tradition is Stephanie Cronin, *Subalterns and Social Protest: History from Below in the Middle East and North Africa* (London: Routledge, 2008). Another useful volume is Ellis Goldberg (ed.), *The Social History of Labor in the Middle East* (Boulder, CO: Westview Press, 1996). Zachary Lockman's introduction to his edited volume, *Workers and Working Classes in the Middle East: Struggles, Histories, Historiographies* (Albany,

NY: State University of New York Press, 1994) offers an overview of the historiography and critique of determinism in labour history. Also useful is Donald Quataert and Erik Jan Zürcher (eds), *Workers and the Working Class in the Ottoman Empire and the Turkish Republic, 1839–1950* (London: I.B. Tauris, 1995). Gilbert Achcar's *The People Want: A Radical Exploration of the Arab Uprising* (London: Saqi Books, 2013) is an important overview of the Arab uprisings, written under the sign of Marx.

Two outstanding examples of histories of protest in particular countries are Hanna Batatu's *The Old Social Classes and the Revolutionary Movements of Iraq* (Princeton, NJ: Princeton University Press, 1978) and Julia Clancy-Smith, *Rebel and Saint: Muslim Notables, Populist Protest, Colonial Encounters (Algeria and Tunisia, 1800–1904)* (Berkeley: University of California Press, 1994). Another is Ervand Abrahamian's *Iran between Two Revolutions.* (Princeton, NJ: Princeton University Press, 1982). Juan Cole's book on the 'Urabi movement in Egypt and its social origins is still important *Colonialism and Revolution in the Middle East.* (Princeton, NJ: Princeton University Press, 1993), as is Fred Halliday's *Arabia Without Sultans* (London: Penguin, 1974). A recent important history, paying attention to the transnational, colonialism, and armed struggle, is Abdel Razzaq Takriti's *Monsoon Revolution: Republicans, Sultans, and Empires in Oman, 1965–1976* (Oxford: Oxford University Press, 2013).

Important works with a strong thematic cast include Parvin Paidar's *Women and the Political Process in Twentieth Century Iran* (Cambridge: Cambridge University Press, 1995) useful for its analysis of gender and women in political processes in Iran. Beth Baron's *Egypt as a Woman: Nationalism, Gender, and Politics* (Berkeley: University of California Press, 2007) is a thorough history of high-status women's activism in Egypt during 1919 and after. Laleh Khalili's *Heroes and Martyrs of Palestine: The Politics of National Commemoration* (Cambridge: Cambridge University Press, 2007) explores the role of the translocal, as well as nationalist commemoration in shifting discourses of Palestinian resistance. An important article showing how culture and consciousness and the translocal can be written into historical materialism is Zachary Lockman's 'Imagining the Working Class: Culture, Nationalism and Class Formation in Egypt, 1899–1914', *Poetics Today* 15 (Summer 1994), pp. 157–190. Mazin Qumsiyeh's *Popular Resistance in Palestine: A History of Hope and Empowerment* (London: Pluto, 2011) surveys the history of non-violent resistance among Palestinians. An important article in regard to 'terrorism' is Joel Beinin, 'Is Terrorism a Useful Term in Understanding the

Middle East and the Palestinian–Israeli Conflict?', *Radical History Review* 85 (Winter 2003), pp. 12–23.

A useful edited volume bringing conventional social movement theory to bear on Islamic activism is Quintan Wiktorowicz (ed.), *Islamic Activism: A Social Movement Theory Approach* (Bloomington: Indiana University Press, 2004). Works by Wickham, Hafez, and Clark have applied social movement concepts to the rise of Islamism since the 1970s: Carrie Rosefsky-Wickham, *Mobilizing Islam: Religion, Activism, and Political Change in Egypt* (New York: Columbia University Press, 2002); Muhammad Hafez, *Why Muslims Rebel: Repression and Resistance in the Islamic World* (Boulder, CO: Lynne Rienner, 2003); Janine Clark, *Islam, Charity, and Activism: Middle Class Networks and Social Welfare in Egypt, Jordan, and Yemen* (Bloomington: Indiana University Press, 2004). A thorough application of social movement theory to the Egyptian uprising is Jeroen Gunning and Ilan Zvi Baron, *Why Occupy a Square? People, Protests and Movements in the Egyptian Revolution* (London: Hurst & Co, 2013). Joel Beinin and Frédéric Vairel (eds), *Social Movements, Mobilization, and Contestation in the Middle East and North Africa* (Palo Alto, CA: Stanford University Press, 2013) breaks new ground by drawing on relational revisionism in contentious politics. Charles Kurzman's *The Unthinkable Revolution in Iran* (Cambridge, MA: Harvard University Press, 2004) offers a striking rejection of structuralism. Asef Bayat's *Street Politics: Poor People's Movements in Iran* (New York: Columbia University Press, 1997) is important for its focus on everyday forms of resistance and 'quiet encroachment'. New and important work on the Arab uprisings, written with an eye on debates about protest, includes Neil Ketchley, 'The Army and the People are One Hand! Fraternization and the 25th January Egyptian Revolution', *Comparative Studies in Society and History* 1 (2014), pp. 155–186; Maha Abdelrahman, 'Social Movements and the Question of Organization: Egypt and Everywhere' (London: Middle East Centre, LSE, Paper Series, 2015) and Charles Tripp, 'Battlefields of the Republic: The Struggle for Public Space in Tunisia' (London: Middle East Centre, LSE, Paper Series, 2015).

CHAPTER 10

Social Movements in India, 1800 to the Present

Arvind Elangovan

INTRODUCTION

In the Indian general elections in spring/summer of 2014, candidates of a new political party called the Aam Aadmi Party (AAP, literally translated as Common Man's Party) entered the political fray, challenging candidates from established political parties such as the Indian National Congress (INC, founded in 1885 by A.O. Hume, a Scottish gentleman), and the Bharatiya Janata Party (BJP, founded in 1980), which has emerged as a political and ideological alternative to the Congress.[1] Arvind Kejriwal, a graduate of the prestigious Indian Institute of Technology and a former bureaucrat, founded the AAP in 2012 after more than a decade of social activism.[2] Serving as a civil servant in the Income Tax Department in New Delhi, India's capital, Kejriwal soon realized that bribes and kickbacks

---

[1] For a good account of the emergence of the Congress, see Sriram Mehrotra, *A History of the Indian National Congress*, Vol. I (New Delhi: Vikas Publication House, 1995). For a history of the BJP, see Yogendra K. Malik and Vijay B. Singh, *Hindu Nationalists in India: The Rise of the Bharatiya Janata Party* (Boulder, CO: Westview, 1994).

[2] The following brief description of Kejriwal's career follows the profile written by Mehboob Jelani, 'The Insurgent', *The Caravan. A Journal of Politics and Culture* 1 September (2011).

A. Elangovan (✉)
History Department, Wright State University, Dayton, OH, USA

© The Author(s) 2017
S. Berger, H. Nehring (eds.), *The History of Social Movements in Global Perspective*, DOI 10.1057/978-1-137-30427-8_10

were the norms of the department. In order to help the common citizens, Kejriwal started *Parivartan* (change), an organization designed to help the ordinary man to get his due without having to pay bribes. Following the success of Parivartan, Kejriwal involved himself in the ongoing campaign to pass legislation on the citizens' freedom of Right to Information (RTI). Touring India's countryside and villages, Kejriwal in his speeches urged people to support the RTI in order to fight the endemic corruption in the governmental and political system. By September 2010 Kejriwal was involved in drafting new anti-corruption legislation (the Janlokpal Bill). However, sensing the government's reluctance to evolve comprehensive legislation to target corruption, Kejriwal, along with another well-known activist in the western Indian state of Maharashtra, 73-year-old Anna Hazare, planned and executed one of modern post-colonial India's most famous public demonstrations, which incidentally coincided with the Arab Spring in the Middle East. Though Hazare was the face of the movement against corruption, Kejriwal was intricately involved in developing the architecture of the movement. The mass peaceful protest against the government's inaction in producing anti-corruption legislation managed to unite people in different parts of the country in an unprecedented manner. Though the movement succeeded in raising public awareness about the need to combat corruption legislatively, it did not lead to the changes desired by Kejriwal and other activists involved in the demonstrations. As a result, by the autumn of 2012 Kejriwal announced the formation of a political party, the AAP. The party's website claims that since all other courses of action, such as 'peaceful protesting, courting arrest, indefinite fasting, several rounds of negotiations with the ruling government' had failed, the resulting situation called for the founding of a political party.[3]

Kejriwal's transition from a social activist to a politician and his movement's transformation into a political party reveals both the possibilities and limits of the impact of social movements in India. On the one hand, India's democratic institutions and tradition of peaceful protest enable a vibrant culture of social movement activism; yet, the chances of a social movement assuming a political agenda or becoming an extension of a political party's ideology are increased manifold in contemporary India. For example, Kejriwal and Anna Hazare were long accused

[3] Aam Aadmi Party, 'Why are we entering Politics? Aam Aadmi Party, India', http://aamaadmiparty.org/page/why-are-we-entering-politics (accessed June 22, 2013).

by the ruling Congress Party of acting as an agent of its main opposition, the BJP, an accusation consistently denied by Kejriwal. Without delving into the merits or demerits of this conflation of the life of a social movement with political pressures, the point is that such an overlap between the social and the political did not always exist in India. As a British colony, India was subject to that unique colonial condition that separated institutional structures of governance (such as all levels of government and their associated bureaucracy) from pressures of societal structures and politics. Indeed, this did not mean that there was a complete conceptual separation between Indian society and the colonial government. Rather, because the colonial government did not necessarily depend on the Indian population for consent, the social movements that emerged during the colonial period had at least two characteristics that are important for the purposes of this essay. Firstly, the encounter with the colonial government and becoming a part of a global empire generated an era of social criticism that produced socio-religious reform movements in India, which could be considered as precursors of social movements in post-colonial India. Secondly, following this, social movements in India are therefore reflective of a history of striving to bridge this gap between society and politics, between social aims and political objectives, a gap that the colonial government effectively opened up and then maintained throughout its reign. These movements, regarded conventionally as nationalist movements, were a form of social activism that not only sought to bring about immediate changes but also aimed to align changes in society with the larger anti-colonial struggle. In other words, the movement for Indian independence itself became a leitmotif for addressing social problems in a political way. The moment of independence then, was a point of culmination, a reflection of a commitment by the founding fathers to address social problems politically, a point most elegantly argued by Uday Mehta.[4] In particular, Mehta suggests that in contrast to Hannah Arendt, who believed that the conflation of social and the political would lead to totalitarianism, India's leaders fused the social and the political to bring about radical changes in the society without becoming a totalitarian state.

---

[4] Uday Mehta, 'Indian Constitutionalism: Articulation of a Political Vision', in Dipesh Chakrabarty, Rochona Majumdar and Andrew Sartori (eds), *From the Colonial to the Postcolonial: India and Pakistan in Transition* (New Delhi: Oxford University Press, 2005), pp. 13–30.

In what follows, I present an overview of this history of social movements in three broad temporal phases of Indian history, namely the colonial, the nationalist (late colonial) and the post-colonial periods. In the process, through specific examples I will highlight the different forms of social movement activism that emerged in these three periods in order to illustrate the overarching transition of the trajectory of social movements in India from socio-religious reform movements to contemporary socio-political movements in India. Each of the examples chosen demonstrates the following main points about the broad pattern of social movements in India. Firstly, the distinction between state and society, induced by colonialism, created conditions for socio-religious reform movements in India. Secondly, social movements in the later colonial period, or the nationalist phase, witnessed movements that attempted, among other objectives, to bridge the gap between the state and society. Finally, with the dawning of post-coloniality and democracy in India, the fusion of the socio-political has meant that social movements have had to largely function within the parameters dominated by political parties. Towards this end, I describe the social reform movement led by Raja Ram Mohan Roy in early nineteenth century as an illustration for socio-religious reform movements that emerged in the colonial period. Next, I outline the socio-political movements led by Mahatma Gandhi and Bhim Rao Ambedkar as examples of contrasting responses to the increased imperative to address social questions politically. Finally, I focus on the environmental movement, Chipko, to point out the peculiar problem of the fate of social movements in contemporary Indian democracy, which not only enables activism but also constraints these movements. I conclude the essay with a brief assessment of the successes or failures of these social movements and suggestions for possible directions for future research.

Before proceeding further, a caveat is in order. This chapter by no means offers a comprehensive survey of the many and diverse forms of social movement activism that both pre-date the nineteenth century as well as populate the two centuries after. Such an enterprise would require several volumes to adequately survey the vast arena of social movements in the Indian subcontinent. Instead, this chapter outlines the broad parameters around which social movements could be usefully classified and analysed, with the recognition that there may be movements that do not fall neatly within these parameters.

HISTORIOGRAPHY

Addressing political scientists in particular in his introduction to studies of social movements in India, the eminent scholar, Ghanshyam Shah, lamented that 'the study of politics of the masses, their aspirations and demands, articulation of their problems, the modus operandi in asserting their demands outside the institutional framework and their occasional efforts at overthrowing the existing state power are, by and large, ignored by political science academia.'[5] However, Shah's complaint could easily be expanded to other disciplines, such as history. Conventionally, the three broad forms of social movement activism mentioned above, namely socio-religious reform movements, the nationalist movement, and post-colonial social movements, have always been treated separately and not considered as a long history of social movements in India. Hence, it would be useful to briefly review the major historiographical debates in each of these three areas of social movement activism.

In the existing literature, the phase of social reform movements (mostly nineteenth-but also partly twentieth-century phenomena) is usually characterized as a period of renaissance during which, through cultural transformation, native society was able to reclaim a unique identity. The recognition of such an identity, it is argued, was crucial to the later development of nationalism in India, a narrative most commonly found in nationalist accounts of Indian history.[6] However, other historians have questioned this uncritical acceptance of social reform movements as harbingers of modernity. Scholars such as Sumit and Tanika Sarkar lament the absence of a rigorous socio-economic analysis of the central figures and events involved in these social movements, which they argue would enable a better understanding of them. The Sarkars, for instance, suggest that delving into the regional, class and caste basis of social reformers could have opened a way to understand regional variation and the nature of the public sphere (including the question about what constituted the public sphere). Moreover, they point out how little discussion there is of the legislative and judicial aspects of social reform legislation, which could significantly enhance an understanding of these reform movements.[7]

---

[5] Ghanshyam Shah, *Social Movements in India: A Review of Literature* (New Delhi: Sage, 2004), p. 16.

[6] For instance see R C Majumdar, *An Advanced History of India* (Delhi: Macmillan, 1973).

[7] Sumit Sarkar and Tanika Sarkar, 'Introduction', in Sumit Sarkar and Tanika Sarkar (eds), *Women and Social Reform in Modern India: A Reader* (Ranikhet: Permanent Black, 2007), pp. 1–7.

Studies of Indian nationalism can be characterized as a process in which the Subaltern Studies collective departed from the conclusions of both the Cambridge and the nationalist schools of historiography. The Cambridge scholar, Anil Seal, in laying out the basic argument about Indian nationalism claimed that the roots of the anti-colonial movement in India have to be seen in the associations that educated elites formed in the three major cities, Calcutta, Bombay and Madras.[8] Scholars such as Christopher Bayly, David Washbrook and David Gallagher further argued this point of view.[9] By focusing almost exclusively on the elites, the Cambridge school sidelined other forms of agitations and politics in favour of institutionalized political associations. The nationalist school, on the other hand, defined by the approaches adopted by R.C. Majumdar and Bipan Chandra, for instance, focused almost exclusively on the role played by the Indian elite leaders, such as Mahatma Gandhi and Jawaharlal Nehru, and the Congress party. In their view, the charismatic leadership of these leaders was singularly responsible for the movement of Indian nationalism, with the masses largely following the leadership.[10] In contrast, the Subaltern Studies collective argued that both the Cambridge and the nationalist approaches ignored the role of the masses in organizing protests. Scholars such as Ranajit Guha, Dipesh Chakrabarty, Partha Chatterjee, David Hardiman and others argued how different social groups, such as peasants, factory workers, or women, participated in the nationalist struggle even as they remained largely out of the formal institutionalized space of politics. By viewing history from the subalterns' perspective, the collective put forward a bold intervention in larger narratives of Indian nationalism that typically marginalized the 'people'.[11]

In the post-colonial period, Ghanshyam Shah has aptly summarized that scholars have approached social movements in either a Marxist or a

---

[8] Anil Seal, *The Emergence of Indian Nationalism: Competition and Collaboration in the Later Nineteenth Century* (Cambridge: Cambridge University Press, 1968).

[9] See John Gallagher, Gordon Johnson and Anil Seal (ed.), *Locality, Province and Nation: Essays on Indian Politics, 1870–1940* (Cambridge: Cambridge University Press, 1973).

[10] Bipan Chandra, Mridula Mukherjee, Aditya Mukherjee, Sucheta Mahajan and *Kavalam* M. Panikkar, *India's Struggle for Independence, 1857–1947* (New Delhi: Viking, 1987).

[11] For a good overview of subaltern studies, see Vinayak Chaturvedi, *Mapping Subaltern Studies and the Postcolonial* (London: Verso, 2000). Also see the contribution by Rochona Majumdar in this volume.

non-Marxist paradigm.[12] There are, however, significant variations within these two broad paradigms. Subaltern Studies, for instance, even as it uses Marxism in its methodology, also departs from the core Marxist concern of economy and instead focuses attention on culture. Traditional Marxist scholars have criticized proponents of the Subaltern Studies approach for being 'Hegelian idealists' and ignoring structural factors and viewing 'consciousness independent of structural contradictions'.[13] Scholars who work outside the Marxian framework tend to focus on identities, such as caste, class, gender, tribalism, students, middle class, environmentalist and so on.[14]

The different kinds of social movement activism in India—socio-religious, nationalist, and the post-colonial social movements—clearly call for an inter-disciplinary and comparative approach that would help in combining these forms of activism in a singular narrative, as a history of social movements in India. Thus, in what follows, this survey attempts to engage with these different historiographical debates by considering these different forms of activism as a long history of social movements by emphasizing the contextual conditions under which the movements emerged and the roles played by their leaders at different points of time. This history of social movements, then, is as much a story of the elites initiating debates and changes as much as it is about the people paving their own path through these struggles. The survey will also demonstrate the need to move beyond the Marxist/non-Marxist dialectic to comprehend the history of social movements in India.

STATE VERSUS SOCIETY: SOCIAL MOVEMENTS IN THE COLONIAL PERIOD

By the middle of the nineteenth century, through a series of victories in political battles and diplomacy, the English East India Company (EIC), which had hitherto been only a commercial enterprise, transitioned to becoming a political sovereign by acquiring territories in India. The Battle of Plassey in Bengal, fought and won by the EIC in 1757, inaugurated successive waves of conquest by the EIC over the next few decades. Its

[12] Ghanshyam Shah, 'Introduction', in idem (ed.), *Social Movements and the State* (New Delhi: Sage, 2002), pp. 13–31, p. 20.
[13] Shah, *Social Movements*, p. 21.
[14] Shah, *Social Movements*.

final acquisition, the princely province of Awadh in northern India in 1856, provided the impetus for a revolt by disgruntled Indian soldiers and affected Indian royalty. Though the EIC successfully quelled the revolt, its credibility was damaged enough to prompt the British Crown to take over direct control of India in 1858.

The East India Company's rule over the subcontinent, which lasted about a hundred years, though relatively brief, nevertheless became an integral part of the changing social landscape of India. Indeed, Calcutta, the capital of the EIC in India, soon emerged as the centre of social reform movements in the region. Naturally, at least one reason (and there were several) for the emergence of socio-religious reform movements was that Bengal had become the most important meeting point between a Western culture infused with ideas of liberalism and an equally historically rich Eastern culture that included both Hinduism and Islam, among others. This cultural–colonial interaction would lead to immense social and political changes in India in the future decades and in the following century.

However, it is important to remember that this interaction did not occur in a vacuum, but rather was influenced by the politics of conquest, not only of territory but also of knowledge. After initially following a policy of patronizing India's native languages such as Sanskrit, Persian and Arabic, the EIC changed its policy in 1835, English being adopted as the language of administration. The company started promoting English language schools. This shift in language policy, combined with a keen interest displayed by some of elite sections of the native society, not only resulted in the establishment of several educational institutions but also served to provoke criticism of existing social customs and practices. Thus, for instance, in 1817 a collaborative initiative between Indians and Europeans led to the inauguration of Hindu College in Calcutta, India's first English-language educational institution. As Barbara and Thomas Metcalf note: 'by the 1830s several thousand Indians were studying English in that city alone'. Notably, these institutions became the centres of rejection of traditional Hindu customs. Some young men in these colleges, for instance were 'defiantly eating beef and drinking whiskey', and 'derided "irrational" Hindu customs; some few among them [...] converted to Christianity'.[15]

The introduction of English education and the proliferation of English thought in India was one of the important factors in the emergence of

---

[15] Barbara D. Metcalf and Thomas R. Metcalf, *A Concise History of Modern India* (Cambridge: Cambridge University Press, 2006), p. 83.

socio-religious reform movements. For many young, educated individuals certain practices of Hinduism went directly against their own sense of justice as well as against the ideals of liberalism that they now encountered through the medium of the English language. In this context, social reform movements emerged all over India to purge all Indian religions of some of their practices in a quest to redefine them in the new colonial context. Among these revivalist and reformist movements in the north were the *Tariqah-i-Muhammadiyah*, a movement to establish Islamic supremacy, and the *Deobandis*, concerned with re-establishing the role of the Ulama as 'natural leaders of the Muslims.'[16] In the Deccan, movements such as Satnamis, the Manav Dharma Sabha, the Satya Mahima Dharma and others attempted to engage with an increasingly prominent colonial presence, Christianity, critiquing the practices of orthodox Hinduism, and fighting the caste system. In southern India, because of the presence of a majority of Hindus and a minority of Christians, the conflict and movement occurred mostly along caste lines of Brahmins and non-Brahmins. Significantly, the theosophical movement took its roots in the south, inspired, as remarked by Kenneth Jones, by 'centuries of socio-religious dissent and protest within western civilization'.[17] Interestingly, however, the theosophist movement led to the strengthening of orthodoxy and the status quo, thereby undermining efforts of other movements to uplift the status of the members of the 'lower' castes.[18]

Bengal in eastern India witnessed reform movements among its Muslim population, especially in rural areas. One such significant movement was the founding of the *Fara'izis*. Concerned with religious purification, its founder, Shari'at 'Ullah, called for a return to the obligatory duties of Islam such as 'profession of faith, attending daily prayers, fasting in Ramadan, paying the poor tax and pilgrimage to Mecca'.[19] The movement, along with other allied movements, created a sense of communal identity, which was particularly fostered by the spread of the Islamic message through the vernacular language of Bengali. Significantly, unlike the Hindu reform movements, the Muslim revival movement in Bengal was not affected by the colonial environment, but instead derived inspiration

---

[16] Kenneth W. Jones, *Socio-Religious Reform Movements in British India* (Cambridge: Cambridge University Press, 1989), p. 83.

[17] Jones, *Socio-Religious Reform Movements*, p. 183.

[18] Jones, *Socio-Religious Reform Movements*, p. 183.

[19] Jones, *Socio-Religious Reform Movements*, p. 19.

from places such as Saudi Arabia. Most famously, however, Bengal was also the home of the *Bramho Samaj* movement and its founder, Raja Ram Mohan Roy.

RAJA RAM MOHAN ROY AND BRAHMO SAMAJ IN BENGAL

In the annals of histories of socio-religious reform movements, Raja Ram Mohan Roy (1772–1833) occupies a preeminent position for a number of reasons; chief among which were his successful efforts to outlaw the practice of *sati*, or widow burning on the husband's funeral pyre, and his sustained search for a Unitarian religion based on man's innate ability to reason, which led him to found what would become an influential organization in Bengal and other parts of India, the Brahmo Samaj (Assembly of God). Roy's social activism took many forms, including writing books, publishing pamphlets and forming organizations in an effort to purge Hinduism of its idolatry, superstition and polytheistic nature, and to fight against the practice of sati (which was eventually outlawed in 1829). In 1830 Roy founded Brahmo Samaj. Its purpose was to worship and adore a single, 'Eternal, Unsearchable, and Immutable Being', for the strengthening of relations between men of all religions and creeds.[20] Roy died soon after, in 1833.

Recently, scholars like Christopher Bayly, Andrew Sartori and Lynn Zastoupil have drawn our attention to the 'trans-national context of the political ideas of Rammohan' in order to situate Roy's contributions, and in their wake the legacy of the Brahmo Samaj, amidst an emerging global debate on liberalism, religious reform and the place of free trade in the British empire, whose fortunes were on the rise in the early to mid-nineteenth century. Bayly argues that Roy's reading of European debates on constitutional government influenced his approach to India's own past in addressing contemporary problems.[21] Sartori points out that Roy's arguments against the 'corrupt practices of Hindu priests' were akin to 'British liberalism's use of anticlericalism and anti-Catholicism to assert freedom of conscience and the individual right to pursue rational self-

---

[20] Cited in Jamuna Nag, *India's Great Social Reformer: Raja Ram Mohan Roy* (New Delhi: Sterling Publishers, 1972), p. 74.

[21] Christopher Bayly, 'Rammohan Roy and the Advent of Constitutional Liberalism in India', *Modern Intellectual History* 1 (2007), pp. 25–41, p. 29.

interest.'[22] Similarly, Sartori continues, Roy's agitation against *sati*, his argument for private property, the rule of law and the freedom of the press were expressions of what could be called the ideological structure of 'classical liberalism'.[23] Most significantly, Lynn Zastoupil demonstrates that the flow of ideas was not unidirectional (west to east) but in the case of Roy, the flow went from east to west as well. Towards the end of his life, in 1824, Roy had been introduced to Unitarian thought by an unknown Scottish gentleman.[24] As is well known, the Unitarians were at the 'forefront of the intellectual and political radicalism that led to the undoing of the British establishment in the early nineteenth century'.[25] Unitarianism's emphasis on simplicity tied in with Roy's own commitment to a religion independent of the hold of orthodoxy. In documenting the correspondence that Roy had with Unitarians in Britain, and Roy's own felicitous reception in England between 1831 and 1833, Zastoupil shows how Roy was invoked in debates on reforming the British society during this period.

The significance of Roy and the Brahmo Samaj lies in their profound influence over generations of social and political critics in Bengal and other parts of the subcontinent. Indeed, after Roy, under the leadership of Debendranath Tagore (1817–1905), Keshab Chandra Sen (1838–1884) and Rabindranath Tagore (1861–1941), Brahmo Samaj continued to impact the minds of young Bengalis and Indians. Roy's impulse to engage with wider transnational debates, excavate India's historical and religious past and participate in an emerging public sphere foreshadowed the public lives and work of later intellectuals and leaders such as Mahatma Gandhi, Jawaharlal Nehru and others. The Brahmo Samaj encouraged an independent critical streak amongst intellectuals who refused to bow to orthodoxy, thus becoming a platform from which they could launch a critique of existing social norms, an exercise that was largely conducted independently of the state.

[22] Andrew Sartori, *Bengal in Global Concept History: Culturalism in the Age of Capital* (Chicago: University of Chicago Press, 2008), p. 82.

[23] Sartori, *Bengal in Global Concept History*, pp. 77–89.

[24] Lynn Zastoupil, 'Defining Christians, Making Britons: Ram Mohun Roy and the Unitarians', *Victorian Studies* 2 (2002), pp. 215–243, p. 224.

[25] Zastoupil, 'Defining Christians, Making Britons', p. 220.

SOCIAL MOVEMENTS AND INDIAN NATIONALISM

The decades following the assumption of power by the British Crown from the East India Company witnessed far-reaching changes in both the colonial relationship between the metropole and the colony and Indian society in general. Administratively, the colonial relationship now pivoted around the gradual introduction of constitutional reforms, designed to incorporate Indians into higher levels of administration and eventually into the legislative and executive bodies at the provincial and the federal levels. However, this did not mean that a liberal regime of colonial governance was inaugurated in the later nineteenth century. On the contrary, these constitutional reforms went hand in hand with the colonial government's steps to restore order with brute force whenever there were incidents or threats of mass disturbance, prompting the historian Anthony Low to characterize the British government attitude as one of intrinsic 'ambiguity'.[26]

The colonial government's ambiguity was primarily in response to the vibrant and rapid growth of what can generically be termed 'Indian nationalism'. Beginning in the second half of the nineteenth century, aided by the press and the formation of a series of organizations and associations that provided a common ground for the coming together of sectional interests (among which the Indian National Congress (INC) was one), there emerged a steady growth of a public sphere that actively debated issues of national interest and the effect of colonial rule. By the end of the first decade of the twentieth century, the INC had grown to be a prominent organization with influential provincial leaders who were able to clearly envision the merits and demerits of British colonialism and sharply disagreed with one another on the way forward. The Congress soon came to stand in for ideas of Indian nationalism and in the beginning aimed to speak for all sections of the society, namely the peasants, the members of the working class, religious and linguistic minorities, women, and, *dalits* (those placed lowest in the caste hierarchy). However, the increased inability of the Congress to speak for all sections soon gave way to different groups forming their own associations in the hope of protecting their interests.

---

[26] Anthony D. Low, *Britain and Indian Nationalism: The Imprint of Ambiguity, 1929–1942* (Cambridge: Cambridge University Press, 1997).

The introduction of British constitutional reforms in India in the context of an increasingly intense and competitive collection of Indian political groups had an interesting consequence. Though the constitutional reforms appeared as concessions granted by the imperial power to satisfy the demands of the nationalists, the reforms effectively succeeded in entrenching Britain's power more firmly than before, the reason being that the political groups that emerged in opposition to the Congress had diminished faith in the ability of the Congress to act in the interests of all sections of society; instead they placed their trust in the governmental structure established by the British. As a result, the final question of decolonization in the 1940s was not whether Britain would quit India, (which was considered inevitable in the context of the Second World War), but whether there would be protection for minorities in an independent India.[27] Most prominently, the Indian Muslim League, formed in 1906, despite initially working with Congress on the question of constitutional reforms, eventually demanded partition of India and the creation of Pakistan for its Muslim inhabitants; meanwhile, members of the 'lower' castes, under the leadership of Bhim Rao Ambedkar, demanded the enshrining of affirmative action in India's new constitution. Though these demands were met, the end of colonialism in India did not lead to the beginning of a nation that had resolved its tensions amongst various groups. If anything, post-colonial India had to contend with multiple and overlapping layers of demands in the form of social movements drawn from and representing groups that felt that their demands were not met at the moment of independence. The nationalist movement then became a movement not only to evict Britain from India but also to protect the interests of fragmented minorities in a democratic nation-state that would be governed by majority rule in Britain's absence. It was in this sense that social movements that emerged during this nationalist phase increasingly became driven to attempt to resolve social questions politically, for, in the popular imagination, securing political representation effectively guaranteed the rectification of social injustice and conflict.

In the decades following the founding of the INC in 1885, several movements arose that could be broadly described as nationalist, although all the movements were not necessarily against the British colonial government. Though Mahatma Gandhi's socio-political movements against

---

[27] For an early statement on this impact of British constitutional reforms in India, see Robin J. Moore, *The Crisis of Indian Unity, 1917–1940* (Oxford: Clarendon Press, 1974).

the colonial government and Bhim Rao Ambedkar's movement for caste equality were the most popular, there were several other social and political movements at the provincial and national levels. Between 1903 and 1908, the *Swadeshi* (indigeneity) movement emerged in Bengal in response to the British decision to partition the province of Bengal, arguably to weaken the growing sense of nationalism. The movement's actions ranged from organizing protest meetings (about 500 were held in East Bengal alone in 1903) to submitting petitions against partition (numbering between 50,000 and 70,000 signatories in 1905), boycotting foreign goods and boycotting government schools and colleges and government titles.[28] Significantly, the Swadeshi movement also led to the production of a number of literary works that celebrated India's rich cultural heritage. One of the foremost cultural exponents was the leader of the Brahmo Samaj and Nobel laureate Rabindranath Tagore. The Swadeshi movement became the forerunner for similar and more vigorous nationalist movements, particularly those led by Gandhi.

In addition, between the late nineteenth and a better part of the twentieth century, several labour struggles that at times became a part of the national movement took place across the country. Industrialization, which was introduced in the early nineteenth century, grew only gradually, providing employment for less than 10% of India's workforce as late as the 1960s.[29] Yet, as Chandavarkar notes, the employment of nearly four million workers in the mines and railways, the mushrooming of manufacturing workshops across small towns and big cities, and the ready availability of crops and labour for manufacturing purposes from the villages meant that the social and political significance of the industrial workforce was far greater than statistics reveal. In such a scenario, labour struggles and movements had a visible and profound impact on the economy, culture and politics in the colonial period and indeed in the post-colonial period as well. Protest movements by industrial workers typically took the form of strikes. Though unorganized strikes began as early as the 1880s in the railway and the textile sectors, organized strikes became more numerous and influential in the second decade of the twentieth century. Notable were the famous strikes led by the Madras Labour Union representing the

[28] Chandra et al., *India's Struggle for Independence*, pp. 126–127.

[29] Rajnarayan Chandavarkar, *The Origins of Industrial Capitalism in India: Business Strategies and the Working Classes in Bombay, 1900–1940* (Cambridge: Cambridge University Press, 2002), p. 2.

textile workers in 1918, and the strike led by Ahmedabad textile workers in the (present) western Indian state of Gujarat. The period of accelerating anti-colonial struggle coincided with a steady increase in these labour struggles as well. For instance, Ghanshyam Shah, citing the works of V.V. Giri, V.B. Karnik and V.P. Joshi, notes that between 1921 and 1925 around 400,000 workers were engaged in strikes. By 1947, there were over 1,800 strikes by the industrial workforce across the country.[30]

An important aspect of these labour struggles was the growing influence of communism. Initially aligning with the mainstream nationalist movement, the left parties, forming a coalition of peasants and workers, were instrumental in the organization of these strikes. Though the communist influence would later be weakened in the face of the colonial Government's policies as well as opposition from Congress leaders such as Jawaharlal Nehru, workers' struggles continued to play an important role in mass demonstrations against the government. For instance, about 90,000 workers struck in response to Britain's unilateral decision to involve India in the Second World War. Similarly, in 1945 Calcutta port workers struck work, refusing to load British supplies meant to quell expatriate Indian guerrillas fighting Britain in Indonesia, and in 1946 industrial workers took action in solidarity with naval mutineers.[31]

In addition to movements that were explicitly against the colonial government, such as the Swadeshi movement and many of these industrial working-class movements, this period also witnessed the emergence of movements for the amelioration of socially, economically and politically marginalized groups, such as the dalits. While Ambedkar's anti-caste movement will be discussed below, mention may also be made of the anti-Brahmin movement led by Jyotirao Phule (1827–1890). As Rosalind O'Hanlon's excellent work illustrates, Phule argued that Brahmanism could be fought through education, organization and a return to pre-Brahmanic traditions, in order to skirt Brahmin superiority in the caste hierarchy. While there were several more social movements during this 'nationalist' phase, it is essential to note that the emerging public sphere in India, the implications of British constitutional reforms in splintering Indian political interests, the conflation of peasant and industrial problems with the national question, the struggle to obtain equality among castes, and such other issues around which social movements arose, were

---

[30] Shah, *Social Movements in India*, pp. 184–185.
[31] Chandra et al., *India's Struggle for Independence*, pp. 222–223.

simultaneously a manifestation of an attempt to address social questions in a political way. The distinction between state and society, which was crucial to the early colonial state, was impossible to maintain in the later colonial period in the face of the rise of nationalist interests. However, two iconic individuals, Mahatma Gandhi and Bhim Rao Ambedkar, articulated two different responses to this question of state and society through their socio-political movements, as we will now discuss.

MAHATMA GANDHI (1869–1948)

In his long and distinguished life, Gandhi led several mass political movements that criticized the British Government and sought to force the end of Britain's colonial rule in India. One of the striking features of Gandhi's mass movements was that they involved a fundamental engagement with and critique of the social order of the Indian society as a precondition to waging a political struggle, thus making these protests social movements as well. In other words, Gandhi's political movements would be empty without considering the fundamental societal changes that he sought. To be able to fight the colonial government, Gandhi demanded the denunciation and renunciation of all practices and ideologies that indirectly enabled the colonial government.[32] His first task, therefore, was to create a 'model', ethical protestor before undertaking the task of generating a social movement.[33]

Gandhi put forward his views on anti-colonialism and nationalism in his political tract *Hind Swaraj* (India's self-rule), which was published in 1909.[34] Regarding nationalism, Gandhi brusquely critiqued the factions of the INC, the Moderates and the Extremists, for clamouring for home rule, which would only result in effectively continuing colonial rule in India without the presence of colonists.[35] In this tract, Gandhi did not blame the British as much as he lamented the malaise of modern civilization with its

[32] On the political importance of this figure of a renouncer and the idea of freedom, see Mithi Mukherjee, 'Transcending Identity: Gandhi, Nonviolence, and the Pursuit of a "Different" Freedom in Modern India', *American Historical Review* 2 (2010), pp. 453–473.

[33] On this question of means and ends of politics in Gandhi, see Karuna Mantena, 'Another Realism: The Politics of Gandhian Non-Violence', *American Political Science Review* 2 (2012), pp. 455–470.

[34] Anthony J. Parel (ed.), *Gandhi: Hind Swaraj and Other Writings* (Cambridge: Cambridge University Press, 2007).

[35] Parel, *Gandhi: Hind Swaraj*, p. 28.

excessive dependence on machinery and mediating institutions like parliament, courts, lawyers and doctors, all of which fundamentally alienated man from himself and nature.[36] Colonialism, for Gandhi, was thus a part of this civilizational malaise that had afflicted not only the colonizer but also the colonized. Hence, as part of the struggle against colonialism he argued that freedom for the country could not materialize unless the protestor was able to first control himself and have complete control over his body.[37] The ideal of a nation's self- rule was predicated on first establishing mastery over one's self, which Gandhi demonstrated through his non-violent campaigns, such as the Non-cooperation Movement that he launched against the British.

THE NON-COOPERATION MOVEMENT, 1920–1922

Gandhi developed a strategy for the Non-cooperation Movement against the British government that was approved by the Indian National Congress in its 35th session, held on December 26th to 31st, 1920. It followed in large part the boycott movement launched during the Swadeshi movement.[38] Significantly, these modes of protest were not to be practised by everyone. The resisters had to be committed to the principles of abjuring foreign cloth, have knowledge of spinning cloth, believe in non-violence, support Hindu–Muslim unity, and work towards the removal of the practice of untouchability.[39]

The Non-Cooperation Movement had some success in its objectives. In different parts of the country efforts were made to convert existing colleges into national institutions by divesting colleges from government control. Similarly, several national educational institutions were established during this period, which also witnessed the gradual withdrawal of students from government-aided institutions. For instance, the geographically large provinces of Madras, Bombay, Bengal and United Provinces saw an increase in the number of national educational institutions by 92, 189, 190 and 137 respectively.[40] Similarly, the number of students in government colleges reduced from 10,402 to 7585 between

[36] Parel, *Gandhi: Hind Swaraj*, especially Chaps. 6, 9, 11, 12 and 13.

[37] Parel, *Gandhi: Hind Swaraj*, pp. 72–73.

[38] Shiri R. Bakshi, *Gandhi and Non-Cooperation Movement, 1920–22* (New Delhi: Capital Publishers, 1983), p. 68.

[39] Bakshi, *Gandhi*, p. 75.

[40] Bakshi, *Gandhi*, p. 117.

1920 and 1921. The withdrawal of students from primary and secondary schools was even more drastic—nearly 23% of students dropped out in protest.[41] Leading by example, Gandhi, Hakim Ajmal Khan and Sarojini Naidu renounced their previously awarded government titles.[42] The Congress Party also boycotted the elections called by the British Government in 1920. In many constituencies the turnout of voters was 10% or less.[43]

Despite these successes, Gandhi suspended the Non-cooperation Movement in 1922 after hearing about the violent killing of policemen by an infuriated mob in a village called Chauri Chaura.[44] Though initially shocked, the Congress Party eventually passed a resolution supporting the suspension of the movement. However, the impact of the movement was felt long afterwards in colonial and post-colonial India. Gandhi's call galvanized the masses in ways that had been unimaginable a few years earlier. Importantly, as stressed above, this political movement required societal change as a prerequisite for participation. Gandhi's ideas of discipline, order and the renunciation of government-sponsored goods would direct Gandhi's own subsequent civil disobedience movements in the later decades and inspire generations of social movement leaders in the post-colonial world.

BHIM RAO AMBEDKAR (1891–1956)

Ambedkar, born into an 'untouchable' community called the Mahars in today's Indian state of Maharashtra, personally suffered many indignities, as was typical for a member of his community. Discriminatory practices against 'untouchables' included the denial of entry into Hindu temples, the denial of access to public wells and tanks, prohibition of inter-caste dining and marriage, and other such institutional practices. Further, members of these communities were not allowed to drink water from the same vessel as others in a public place such as a school or office, nor were they allowed to use certain roads in certain villages. In many instances, even the

---

[41] Bakshi, *Gandhi*, pp. 114–115.
[42] Bakshi, *Gandhi*, p. 118.
[43] Bakshi, *Gandhi*, p. 124.
[44] For a subaltern historians' view of the events and significance of Chauri Chaura, see Shahid Amin, *Event, Metaphor, Memory: Chauri Chaura, 1922–1992* (Berkeley: University of California Press, 1995).

clothes they wore and the ingredients in their food were circumscribed by tradition.[45]

There was a distinct intellectual and practical-activist aspect to the social movements that Ambedkar led. Intellectually, Ambedkar was deeply influenced by the continental idealism of Liberty, Equality and Fraternity as well as the Marxist imperative to bring about profound social revolutionary changes in society. But Ambedkar recognized the limits of Marxism in a caste-ridden society. Gail Omvedt argues that though Ambedkar recognized that class struggle was necessary for a just society, to fight against caste discrimination, a separate struggle against Brahmanism was necessary.[46] As Ambedkar noted,

> There are in my view two enemies which the workers of this country have to deal with. The two enemies are Brahmanism and Capitalism ... By Brahmanism I do not mean the power, privileges and interests of the Brahmins as a community. By Brahmanism I mean the negation of the spirit of Liberty, Equality, and Fraternity. In that sense it is rampant in all classes and is not confined to the Brahmins alone though they have been the originators of it.[47]

In a skilful summation, Omvedt argues that Ambedkar attempted to develop a total theory that could address the peculiar problem of caste on the one hand and the economy on the other. Ambedkar identified the ending of exploitation and the achievement of the goals of liberty, equality and fraternity as central to the project. This project, he believed, could be achieved by working towards economic growth and against the social and religious practices of denial that had become the defining features of Hinduism.[48]

Most significantly, the apogee of Ambedkar's contribution to eradicating caste-based inequalities came when, as the chairman of the drafting committee of the Indian constitution, he ensured that a policy of affirmative action (reservation of certain seats in government educational

---

[45] For a good contemporary account of practices of untouchability, see the documentary *India Untouched*, directed by Stalin K., and the documentary *Jai Bhim Comrade*, directed by Anand Patwardhan.

[46] Gail Omvedt, 'Ambedkar and After: The Dalit Movement in India', in Shah (ed.), *Social Movements*, pp. 283–309, p. 296.

[47] Omvedt, 'Ambedkar and After', p. 296.

[48] Omvedt, 'Ambedkar and After', p. 298.

institutions and government employment) for the dalits were enshrined in the text of the constitution. However, in his final act, Ambedkar led several thousands of his followers to convert to Buddhism, a religion that did not recognize the hierarchy of the caste system. Ambedkar's efforts at affirmative action and his conversion to Buddhism still remain as powerful instruments for the anti-caste agitations in the post-colonial period.

Thus, in post-colonial India, Gandhi and Ambedkar were at the fore-front of social movement activism in India, though they left behind two different ways of approaching the question of society and the state. Gandhi viewed freedom as an intrinsic characteristic of the ethical protes-tor in the face of an oppressive colonial regime. Ultimately, for Gandhi, the meaning of agitation and protest stemmed from the righteous cause for discontent and righteous action to be followed. For Ambedkar, on the other hand, the discourse of rights associated with the principles of liberty, equality and fraternity was critical for the dalits to emerge from the dark abyss of caste oppression. In this sense, Ambedkar actively sought repre-sentation and protection in the debates of British constitutional reforms, a path that, for Gandhi, was inconsequential. Hence, if Ambedkar saw in the state a potential panacea for the wrongs perpetrated by the caste system, Gandhi viewed the state as representing 'violence in a concen-trated and organized form'.[49] These two contrasting views leave behind two different legacies for understanding social movements in India. On the one hand, Gandhi's critique of the state and his methods of protest-ing (peaceful, non-violent protests) are followed by contemporary social activists to create an alternative realm of public authority in the minds of the people. On the other hand, there is a firm recognition, an almost common-sense one, that progress, reform, and even addressing protes-tors, have to happen within a language defined by the state and the consti-tution. This intersection between the legacies of Gandhi and Ambedkar in post-colonial India produced interesting consequences when we consider another important structural condition of social movements in indepen-dent India—democracy.

---

[49] Cited in Karuna Mantena, 'On Gandhi's Critique of the State: Sources, Contexts, Conjunctures', *Modern Intellectual History* 3 (2012), pp. 535–563, p. 535.

DEMOCRACY: POTENTIAL AND LIMITS OF SOCIAL MOVEMENTS

In his work *India after Gandhi* Ramachandra Guha categorized social conflicts as occurring on the lines of caste, language, religion, class and gender, separate yet often overlapping sources of inequality.[50] Indeed, to these one might fruitfully add the issues of the environment, tribal populations, anti-corruption, decriminalizing homosexuality (and the LGBT movement broadly) and others. The intensity of these movements, prompted by dissatisfaction with the post-colonial state, has varied in the post-colonial era. Some of them have marked significant chapters in advancing the debates around specific interested groups. Regarding caste, for instance, the Dalit Panthers (inspired by the Black Panthers of the United States) emerged in the 1970s as a group devoted to promoting the cause of dalit emancipation by producing radical literature and attempting to craft an identity unique to the dalits.

In addition to the Panthers, a movement coalescing around caste identity, specifically aimed at non-Brahmins, emerged to protect the interests of those who were not dalits but who still did not enjoy the privileges of Brahmanism. These classes, called Other Backward Classes (OBCs), utilized their numerical majority in different parts of the country to demand a greater share of political representation as well as affirmative action in educational institutions and government jobs. As with caste, India witnessed several tribal movements, chiefly seeking access to resources and, in some cases, demanding autonomy and secession from mainland India. One of the more famous tribal struggles has been the struggle of the Nagas in north-eastern India. Claiming unique culture and tradition, the Nagas long resisted acquiescing to mainland India. Even today, the state of Nagaland enjoys a provision of exception sanctioned by the Indian constitution that allows Nagaland to maintain some of its unique cultural practices.

There have been several class struggles as well. Significantly, the Bombay textile workers' strike in 1982 extended over a year and involved about 250,000 workers demanding improvement in conditions of work,

---

[50] Ramachandra Guha, *India After Gandhi: The History of the World's Largest Democracy* (New York: Harper Collins, 2007), pp. 8–9.

including an increase in wages.[51] More recently, on September 7 2010 more than one hundred million workers went on a trade union-organized strike over deteriorating conditions of labour.[52] Peasant mobilizations and movements have occurred in different parts of the country by forming organizations such as the Tamil Nadu Agriculturists Association, the Bharatiya Kisan Union (Indian Farmer's Union) and so on.[53] Along with these caste, tribal, industrial and agrarian class movements, India has also witnessed significant environmentalist movements. While the movement to save trees and nature (Chipko) is discussed below, the 1980s also saw a movement against the building of dams that had the potential to inundate and destroy local villages.[54]

The significance of these social movements in independent India is further compounded when we consider the larger political and economic conditions under which these movements have emerged. Post-colonial India's history could be broadly categorized into three phases, the socialist-oriented Nehruvian period, the spectre of the state during Indira Gandhi's premiership, and finally the current post-liberalization regime inaugurated in 1991. Through these phases, the Nehruvian socialism that emphasized agrarian land reform and state-promoted industrialization gradually gave way to complete state control under Indira Gandhi. By the end of the decade of the 1980s, the inability of the state to propel the economy or to correct the inequities of society led to a crisis, resulting in a financial restructuring of the economy that finally opened up the Indian markets to foreign capital. The period dating from 1991 to the present has been marked by the infusion of foreign capital, reforms mandated by the International Monetary Fund and the World Bank to reduce state subsidies to farmers, suggestions to devalue the rupee, and other similar measures that experts have argued have resulted in perpetuating inequalities along already existing lines of caste, class, religion, region, language and gender, among other factors, bringing these distinctions into sharper

[51] Salim Lakha, 'Organized Labour and Militant Unionism: The Bombay Textile Workers' Strike of 1982', in Shah (ed.), *Social Movements*, p. 230.

[52] Asia Monitor Resource Centre, http://www.amrc.org.hk/node/1080 (accessed June 22, 2013).

[53] Tom Brass (ed.), *New Farmers' Movements in India* (London: Frank Cass, 1995).

[54] See Amita Baviskar, *In the Belly of the River: Tribal Conflicts Over Development in the Narmada Valley* (Delhi: Oxford University Press, 1995); John R. Wood, *The Politics of Water Resource Development in India: The Narmada Dams Controversy* (Thousand Oaks, CA: Sage Publications, 2007).

focus than ever before. Significantly, the impact of the discourse of liber-alization has been to remove the discourse of poverty from the agenda of social movements.[55]

Though democratization has enabled the vibrant presence of these protests and social movements, it has been difficult for them to acquire national prominence. Indeed, the diversity of the country and the fact that one interest group necessarily conflicts with another ensure that these movements largely remain local. Thus, curiously, even as democracy enables the proliferation of social movements, it also poses considerable limitations to them, inhibiting their chances of becoming significant at a national level.[56] I illustrate this by a brief analysis of the rise and fall of Chipko, an environmental movement to protect trees and the local economy that emerged in the 1970s.

THE CHIPKO MOVEMENT

Chipko, literally meaning 'to stick' or 'to hug', emerged as a campaign to save the trees in the forest-rich areas of the Himalayas in the northern Indian state of Uttarakhand. Though named after the physical act of hug-ging the trees in order to save them, the movement had its foundation in a long history of struggle between the native dwellers who depended on the forests for their subsistence and the beneficiaries of Government sponsored contracts awarded to private industries that took the produce of the forests for industrial purposes. This history, which stretched back to the initial awarding of contracts by the East India Company, continued in the post-colonial era, with little attention paid to the voices of the peas-ants who were directly affected by the predatory interests of the state and capital.[57]

The immediate impulse for the Chipko movement lay in the Government's decision to reject the villagers' demand for the right to fell ash trees, whose wood was used to make agricultural implements, in the village of Mandal and instead award the rights to the Simon Company, a manufacturer of sporting goods. In response, the *Dashauli Gram*

[55] See Raka Ray and Mary Fainsod Katzenstein (eds), *Social Movements in India: Poverty, Power, and Politics* (Lanham, MD: Rowman & Littlefield Publishers, 2005).

[56] For a statement on the problem of democracy in India, see Pratap Bhanu Mehta, *Burden of Democracy* (New Delhi: Penguin, 2003).

[57] For a good account of the history of the region see Thomas Weber, *Hugging the Trees: The Story of the Chipko Movement* (New Delhi: Viking, 1988), pp. 17–23.

Swarajya Sangh (DGSS, freely translated as The Freedom Association of the Village/Town of Dashauli), whose main objective was to generate local employment by using the resources of the forests, decided to protest. In a novel way, the members of the organization almost spontaneously decided that one way of preventing the felling of the trees was to hug the trees, and thus the Chipko movement was born in 1973.[58]

Though the local manifestations of the Chipko movement were phenomenal, widespread and powerful, at the heart of the struggle was a larger debate on issues of ecology, local sustenance and manufacturing use of forests, and national interest. A figure central to the movement who in a sense launched a social movement for the uplifting of dalits, poor students and the local life in the village was a charismatic member of the Congress party, Sunderlal Bahaguna. Among the many youths who were inspired by Bahaguna was Chandi Prasad Bhatt, who was later instrumental in the founding of DGSS. A brief overview of Bahaguna's career trajectory reveals the potential and limits of a social movement such as Chipko when it intersects with larger national paradigms.

Bahaguna, inspired by Gandhi and in particular by one of Gandhi's disciples, Mirabehn, began work in the Tehri district of Uttarakhand to address the local socio-economic problems of caste, employment and conservation of local resources. Between 1965 and 1971, Bahaguna and his wife also worked towards addressing the problem of alcoholism among the men of the villages.[59] Bahaguna adapted the Gandhian strategy of spreading a message by organizing long marches by road and visiting different villages. Called *Padyatras* (journey by foot), they had served as an effective way to politically mobilize hitherto secluded village populations to address emerging local, provincial and national concerns.[60] The political network that Bahaguna established in this way preceded the Chipko movement; thus, in the 1970s it became an effective network through which Bahaguna spread the word of Chipko and continued his earlier political initiatives.

Due to his extensive touring, Bahaguna by 1975 had come to the conclusion that any kind of tree felling was bound to cause enormous damage to the environment. Bahaguna's realization went directly against the views of Bhatt and the DGSS, which believed that in order to protect the local

[58] Weber, *Hugging the Trees*, p. 40.
[59] Weber, *Hugging the Trees*, p. 34.
[60] Weber, *Hugging the Trees*, pp. 37–38.

village economy from city contractors, the villagers must be allowed to use the produce of the forests. Bahaguna's shift away from economy to ecology thus started the split within the Chipko movement. It was during this time that Bahaguna shifted the message of Chipko from an exhortation to save trees for the local economy and environment to a call to 'save trees for mankind.'[61]

Thomas Weber in his book *Hugging the Trees* notes that the famed British environmentalist Richard St Barbe Baker and F.F. Schumacher's classic *Small is Beautiful* influenced Bahaguna's transition. Baker and Bahaguna not only corresponded but the two men managed to meet in 1977 and in 1980. Further, Bahaguna read Baker's autobiography, *My Life—My Trees*, during his fast in 1979. Though Bahaguna's introduction to Baker and Schumacher came late in his life, it left an indelible imprint in his mind, and he continued to use Schumacher's short film *On the Edge of the Forest* in order to make his ecology-based argument. Such a view, however, came in direct conflict with efforts for local employment and prevented any constructive cooperation with the government officials, which DGSS advocated. In January 1979, Bahaguna started an indefinite fast demanding an end to tree felling in different parts of the state. However, the implications of Bahaguna's fast took an interesting turn when the Government conceded and stopped all tree felling in the region, a step that decidedly upset DGSS and others who believed that tree felling was necessary for local agricultural and small manufacturing needs.[62] By the early 1980s it was clear that Bahaguna's desire to forge a national and international campaign to protect trees, the environment and nature in general would be undermined by the very real, local, economic interest of sustenance and commerce.

Bahaguna's career underwent a further transformation in the 1980s. Amita Baviskar has insightfully argued that though the activities associated with the Chipko movement subsided by the early 1980s, the idea that a provincial government (of Uttar Pradesh) and the central government were insensitive to the local ecological and sociological structure became an integral part of demanding a separate state in the region, which was granted in 2000 with the formation of Uttaranchal. However, as Baviskar notes, the new state government continued the old policy of felling trees and constructing dams, programmes detrimental to the local

[61] Weber, *Hugging the Trees*, p. 67.
[62] Weber, *Hugging the Trees*, pp. 70–71.

ecology. Bahaguna, who had earlier fought against such efforts, now redirected his efforts against the new state government, one that purportedly was formed to protect local ecology. Interestingly, Baviskar notes that Bahaguna formed an alliance with the right-wing Hindu fundamentalist group, the *Vishwa Hindu Parishad* (VHP, the World Hindu Committee), which was instrumental in the infamous destruction of a mosque in 1992. Bahaguna's arguments against capitalist encroachment on the ecology of the region took the form of the traditional Hindu practice of revering and worshipping the sacred rivers and mountains.[63] While this second transition of Bahaguna from being a humanitarian environmentalist to a fundamentalist religious advocate for the environment is a surprise, for the purposes of this essay it may be read as a demonstration of the inherent limits of a social movement when it intersects a transregional, national, or indeed international, idea such as environmentalism. Moreover, the formation of the state of Uttaranchal clearly demonstrates that even a successful social movement may quickly be co-opted by the larger political machinery and political process.

CONCLUSION—AN ASSESSMENT

This chapter has highlighted three broad structural changes that have occurred from around 1800 to the present, which are helpful for contextualizing the different kinds of social movement activism in India during this period. The early colonial period that engendered a porous border between the Indian subcontinent and other parts of the Empire, including the United Kingdom, enabled movements in certain parts of India to re-examine tradition and articulate an identity in the face of the new empire. The conceptual difference between institutions of the state and society enhanced the influence of these social reform movements. The nationalist phase, which was a part of the later colonial period, witnessed efforts to gradually close this gap between state and society as the movement for independence simultaneously became a movement for socio-political reforms. Finally, the post-colonial period, inaugurated by a fusion of the social and the political, a phenomenon abhorred by Hannah Arendt, became the leitmotif of social movements in India.[64] The new, demo-

---

[63] Amita Baviskar, 'Red in Tooth and Claw? Looking for Class in Struggles over Nature', in Ray and Katzenstein (eds), *Social Movements in India*, p. 166.

[64] Uday Mehta, 'Indian Constitutionalism: Articulation of a Political Vision', pp. 13–30.

cratic nation-state, which transitioned from state-sponsored socialism to a market-state in the decades following 1947, succeeded in maintaining a culture of protest and long-standing social movements even as society's diverse interests constrained provincial social movements from acquiring national prominence.

Through these broad phases of structural transition, the sources of conflict have remained similar, although the forms of protest around these sources have undergone a change. Categories identified by Guha, such as caste, class, region, religion, language and gender, remain salient in understanding the causes for social conflict and reasons for social movement in India. However, because of the structural changes from the colonial period to the national and then the post-colonial, the language in which these conflicts are addressed has changed. The largely socio-religious reform movements have given way to discourses primarily based on a language of rights and protection from the constitution and the state. Similarly, the unmistakable cosmopolitan influence that informed Raja Ram Mohan Roy's social activism has given way in contemporary India to greater international cooperation between social groups and non-governmental organizations in agitating for a particular cause. Significantly, however, India's post-colonial democracy and politics condition and shape the course of social movements. In the context of globalization, social activists increasingly feel the need to articulate their interests politically rather than simply focusing on changing social norms, as the sphere of politics is perceived as the best guarantor of social interests. Hence, Arvind Kejriwal, with whom this chapter began, formed a political party after a decade of social activism.

This survey has also attempted to demonstrate the need to go beyond the Marxist/non-Marxist and elites/people dialectics. Though class-based and identity-based social movements are important, many of the social movements employ strategies that have had to transcend their class or identity origins in order to succeed. Similarly, though emphasis has been laid on leaders of movements (who are important), it is precisely because many of the movements were adopted and appropriated by the general populace that they became iconic. Hence, it is essential to pay adequate attention to both the leaders (with their various socio-economic, educational and political backgrounds) and the people.

While it is extremely hard to speculate on the success or failures of social movements due to the shifting goals of these movements throughout their courses, India's colonial history and its post-colonial trajectory reveal an interesting aspect of social movements in India. In post-colonial India, the potential for a social movement to bring about fundamental social changes is vastly improved if the movement acquires political legitimacy. However, with the merging of the social movement with a political party, the commitment of the original social movement begins to flounder, as seen in the case of the Chipko movement. Even as these social movements are successful locally, their transregional impact is thus dependent on the wider political context.

Historical studies on social movements, then, could greatly benefit from exploring at least two areas of research. Firstly, it would be helpful to further bridge the conceptual gap between social reform movements and social movements. Social movements of the twentieth and twenty-first centuries have built on the tradition of critique that characterized the social reform movements of the nineteenth century. In this context, the role of empires in general and the British Empire in particular needs to be revisited. Secondly, the historical and conceptual relationship between social movements, nationalism, capitalism and democracy within a broader global context will be a fruitful area of research. While the presence of social movements is conventionally considered a sign of a vibrant democracy, as seen in this chapter the relationship between social movements and the state may not always be antagonistic. On the contrary, they might even share an affinity. Investigating this complex web of relations would yield a much better understanding of the functioning of a post-colonial democracy in a world that is better networked than ever before.

FURTHER READINGS

The literature on social movements in India is diverse, interdisciplinary and exegetical.

The subject of social movements have for long been of interest to historians, sociologists and political scientists, among other disciplinarians. As mentioned in the chapter, a number of historians have addressed the issue of social reform in India, particularly in the nineteenth and twentieth centuries (though they were not strictly labelled as social movements). Some of these works are extremely valuable and are a rich resource for a historical understanding of social movements in India. For a bibliographical survey of social reform movements in eighteenth and nineteenth centuries, see Sumit Sarkar, *Bibliographical Survey of Social Reforms Movements in Eighteenth and Nineteenth Centuries* (Indian Council of Historical Research, New Delhi: 1975). Rosalind O'Hanlon's *Caste, Conflict, and Ideology: Mahatma Jotirao Phule and Low Caste Protest in Nineteenth-Century Western India* (Cambridge: Cambridge University Press, 1985) was a systematic attempt to foreground the movement of the 'lower castes' in Maharashtra, which provided an alternative perspective to the elite character of the Indian national movement. In 1989, Kenneth Jones published *Socio-Religious Reform Movements in British India* (Cambridge: Cambridge University Press, 1989), an excellent analytical survey of the major socio-religious reform movements in nineteenth and twentieth centuries in India. For a different emphasis of the same time period, one has to look at Sumit and Tanika Sarkar's brilliant edited collection, *Women and Social Reform in Modern India* (Bloomington: Indiana University Press, 2008). Amiya P. Sen's edited collection, *Social and Religious Reform: The Hindus of British India* (Delhi: Oxford University Press, 2003) contains excerpts of writings by some of the major social reformers of the nineteenth and twentieth centuries along with a fine introduction on some of the conceptual challenges of writing about social movements during that period.

For historical works that links issues of social reform in late colonial and early post-colonial India with nationalism, see Charles Heimsath, *Indian Nationalism and Hindu Social Reform* (Princeton, NJ: Princeton University Press, 1964). Works by Bipan Chandra such as *Nationalism and Colonialism in Modern India* (New Delhi: Orient Longman, 1979), *Indian National Movement: The Long-term Dynamics* (New Delhi: Vikas Pub. House, 1988), *In the Name of Democracy: JP Movement and the Emergency* (New Delhi: Penguin Books, 2003) are useful. Since much of the nationalist movement was simultaneously a social movement, books on Indian nationalism would be good a reference as well. Since there are so many books around the theme of nationalism, I will limit myself to more recent works: Partha Sarathi Gupta, *Power, Politics and the people: Studies in British Imperialism and Indian Nationalism* (London: Anthem Press, 2002), Visalakshi Menon, *Indian Women and Nationalism, the U.P. Story* (New Delhi: Shakti Books, 2003), William Gould, *Hindu Nationalism and the Language of Politics in Late Colonial India* (Cambridge: Cambridge University Press, 2004), Shabnum Tejani, *Indian Secularism: A Social and Intellectual History, 1890–1950* (Bloomington: Indiana University Press, 2008).

For social movements in post-colonial and contemporary India, the work of sociologists, political scientists and historians are outstanding. Among many of Ghanshyam Shah's work on social movements his survey volumes are very useful. These are *Social Movements and the State* (New Delhi: Sage, 2002) and *Social Movements in India: A Review of Literature* (New Delhi: Sage 2004). The latter, in particular is the most comprehensive survey of literature on social movements in India. Shah analyses social movements around different social groups, such as peasants, tribals, Dalits and industrial working class to review the literature of social movements around each of these groups. Accompanied with a detailed bibliography on these movements, this is an excellent source for exploring social movements in India. Gail Omvedt's *Reinventing Revolution: New Social Movements and the Socialist Tradition in India* (New York: M.E. Sharpe, 1993) is one of the finest works on new social movements with acute theoretical insights. Omvedt also discusses the relationship between the Indian left movement and social movements, which is very valuable. The edited collection of Raka Ray and Mary Fainsod Katzenstein (eds), *Social Movements in India: Poverty, Power, and* Politics (Lanham, MD: Rowman and Littlefield, 2005) brings together authors, including Omvedt and Shah to discuss why the discourse on social movements has departed from a discourse on poverty, which is a critical point of departure for several scholars. The sociologist, T.K. Oommen's lifelong work on social change, transformation and movements are very helpful as well. Among his works, see *Protest and Changes: Studies in Social Movements* (New Delhi: Sage Publications, 1990), *State and Society in India: Studies in Nation-Building* (New Delhi: Sage Publications, 1990), and *Nation, Civil Society and Social Movements: Essays in Political Sociology* (New Delhi: Sage Publications, 2004). The edited collection of Manoranjan Mohanty, *Class, Caste, Gender* (New Delhi: Sage Publications, 2004) provides a summary account on these themes. Anupama Rao's, *The Caste Question: Dalits and the Politics of Modern India* (Berkeley: University of California Press, 2009) is a brilliant conceptual and empirical analysis of caste and caste politics in modern India. Hugo Gorringe's *Untouchable Citizens: Dalit Movements and Democratisation in Tamil Nadu* (New Delhi: Sage Publications, 2005) provides a critical overview and analysis of caste politics in the southern Indian state of Tamil Nadu. Rupa Viswanath's work on a historical account of caste discrimination is noteworthy as well; see, *The Pariah Problem: Caste, Religion and the Social in Modern India* (New York: Columbia University Press, 2014). S. M. Michael's *Dalits in Modern*

India: Vision and Values (Thousand Oaks, CA: Sage Publications, 2007) contains historical and analytical accounts of the anti-caste thought and movement in colonial and post-colonial India. For an introduction to women's movements in India, see Raka Ray, *Fields of Protest: Women's Movements in India* (Minneapolis: University of Minnesota Press, 1999). For a conceptual understanding see, Vina Mazumdar, *Political Ideology of the Women's Engagement With Law* (New Delhi: Centre for Women's Development Studies, 2000), Susanne Kranz, *Between Rhetoric and Activism: Marxism and Feminism in the Indian Women's Movement* (Zurich: Lit Verlag, 2015), and Nivedita Menon's, *Recovering Subversion: Feminist Politics Beyond the Law* (Urbana: Permanent Black/University of Illinois Press, 2004).

More recently, scholars have produced exciting new scholarship on social movements. Rochona Majumdar's essay, 'Subaltern Studies as a History of Social Movements in India', *South Asia: Journal of South Asian Studies* 1 (2015), pp. 50–68; draws attention to how we might consider the various subaltern movements in the colonial period as a history of social movements. Of course, this also opens us to viewing the entire gamut of subaltern studies literature as a way of thinking about social movements in India. Some of the prominent examples are Ranajit Guha, *Elementary Aspects of Peasant Insurgency in Colonial India* (Delhi: Oxford University Press, 1983), Dipesh Chakrabarty, *Rethinking Working Class History: Bengal, 1890–1940* (Princeton, NJ: Princeton University Press, 1989, 2000), Shahid Amin, *Event, Metaphor, Memory: Chauri Chaura, 1922–1992* (Berkeley: University of California Press, 1995). In the wake of a critical review of Subaltern Studies, Uday Chandra's recent publications are important to note. See his introduction to a special issue in *Journal of Contemporary Asia* 4 (2015), pp. 563–573. The articles in this special section rethink resistance, which was a hallmark of Subaltern Studies. Also see Uday Chandra's 'Flaming Fields and Forest Fires: Agrarian Transformations and the Making of Birsa Munda's Rebellion', *Indian Economic Social History Review* 1 (2016), pp. 69–98, for an innovative reading of both the concept 'tribal' and the meanings of rebellions as movements.

CHAPTER 11

Subjectivation and Social Movements in Post-Colonial Korea

Jung Han Kim and Jeong-Mi Park

SUBJECTIVATION AND SOCIAL MOVEMENTS

In post-colonial Korea, social movements were the main impetus for over-coming various political, economic and cultural contradictions and con-flicts triggered by the nationalization and capitalist modernization that followed the nation-state formation process. Social movements were also the means for achieving a democratic transformation of social relation-ships in a diverse number of social sectors. Yet the successive authoritar-ian regimes in post-colonial Korea had stifled freedom of assembly and association; thus social movements had to become clandestine under-ground organizations that required the individual sacrifices of committed

Translated by Michael Kim
We would like to thank Jie-Hyun Lim, the Director of Critical Global Studies Institute at Sogang University and the President of Network of Global and World History Organizations, for his advice on the overall structure and for proposing many of the key concerns of this essay. It would not be an exaggeration to consider him as another co-author. We also wish to thank Michael Kim at Yonsei University's Graduate School of International Studies for his translation and valuable comments.

J.H. Kim (✉)
Institute of Korean Studies, Korea University, Seoul, South Korea

J.-M. Park
Chungbuk National University, Cheongju, South Korea

© The Author(s) 2017
S. Berger, H. Nehring (eds.), *The History of Social Movements in Global Perspective*, DOI 10.1057/978-1-137-30427-8_11

activists. This historical background inscribed an important characteristic to the history of social movements, which is the explosive outbreak of the masses in spontaneous insurrections that subsequently triggered the formation of social movement organizations.

According to Jung Han Kim, this can be explained in the following scheme as

'mass spontaneous insurrections → collective subjectivation → organized social movements'
      rather than
'organized social movements → collective subjectivation → mass insurrections'.[1]

Mass insurrections,[2] though spontaneous, serve as a platform for the interpellation of the individual subject, and the individual subject, in turn, responds to the interpellation to become unified with the collective subject. Such a process of 'interpellation–response' builds theoretical and practical agendas that lead to organized social movements. The peculiar condition where spontaneous mass insurrections lead to organized social movements can be found in societies that restrict the freedom of assembly and association. An overview of the history of social movements in post-colonial Korea shows clearly the spontaneity of mass insurrections. Through street fights, heterogeneous people formed the masses that shared similar goals and articulated clear political messages that expressed their extraordinary agency. The masses may dissipate or disappear in a few days or weeks. However, they serve as a matrix that activates further social movements, which pose new challenges and agendas by revealing the sharp edge of conflicts and divisions immanent to Korean society. It is true that mass insurrections in their spontaneity are usually accidental, temporary and disorganized. Yet, spontaneous participation from below produces a new form of collective identification and desire to reproduce the meaning of these events among

---

[1] Kim Jung Han, *Taejung ponggiŭi minjujuŭi* [*Insurrection of the Masses and its Democracy*] (Seoul: Somyŏngch'ulp'an, 2013), pp. 6–7.

[2] Contrary to the Western tradition, the term of 'mass' in East Asian languages—*Daejung* (Korean), *Dazhong* (Chinese), *Taishu* (Japanese)—connotes the agency of people as historical actors. This article follows this usage. Jie-Hyun Lim, 'Mapping Mass Dictatorship: Towards a Transnational History of Twentieth-Century Dictatorship', in Jie-Hyun Lim and Karen Petrone (eds), *Gender Politics and Mass Dictatorship: Global Perspectives* (Basingstoke: Palgrave Macmillan, 2011), pp. 13–32.

participants. In this sense, mass insurrections also serve as the primary impetus for the subjectivation process, which forms the resistant subject. Political democratization after 1987 made it possible for labour and social movements to develop rapidly because freedom of assembly and association provided the mobility to organize labour and social movements in the public sphere. Nevertheless, the legitimate institutionalization of social movements led to inevitable compromises with the ruling order, which then led to situations where the masses criticized or even rejected the organizations and activists of social movements. The subjectivation process always has two sides: an autonomous *subjectum* and a subordinate *subjectus*. For instance, a national subject constructed in the process of nation-building may stand up against a dictatorial regime as a sovereign being, but at the same time conform to single-state nationalism. And a worker constituted through the modernization process may resist capitalist exploitation, but also act in accordance with his/her own economic–corporatist interests.

The collective subject of social movements is not a subject that expresses absolute freedom and liberation. Very often the collective subject in social movements resists the dominance and hegemony of power, while at the same time any individual subject subordinates itself to that power by internalizing its laws and orders. There is a simple truth that no pure and static subject can exist, but only impure and dynamic subjects who are caught in the ceaseless process of subjectivation. The contradictory process of subjectivation can be found throughout the history of social movements in Korea, starting from the immediate post-liberation period, in which nationalization, modernization, democratization and post-democratization became the main agendas of social movements.

NATIONALIZATION

Colonial experience in the first half of the twentieth century involved Korean social movements in the nation-state building process. After the Japanese empire surrendered to the Allied Powers on August 15, 1945, national liberation fighters immediately organized the Committee for the Preparation of Korean Independence (CPKI). The CPKI, as its name implies, pursued the establishment of an independent state. Immediately after liberation they maintained public order in the absence of government authority and replaced the colonial police, which had been the most repressive state apparatus under Japanese rule. The CPKI had nation-wide influence. By the end of August 1945, it had established 145 local branches and declared the inauguration of the Korean People's Republic (KPR) on September 6, 1945.

However, South Korea's active nation-building movements suffered a setback due to the occupation of the country by US forces. At that time, communists seized control both in South and North Korea, because they had not only led anti-Japanese movements during the colonial period but also suggested reform plans that appealed to the people after liberation.[3] US forces established a military government on September 9, 1945, and set up a pro-American, anti-communist government by means of severe suppression of leftists through mobilizing the colonial police force and right-wing terrorist groups.[4] As the Cold War accelerated, separate governments were established on either side of the 38th parallel in August and September of 1945. Left- and right-wing nationalisms, which were the two pillars of the national liberation movement in the colonial period, were respectively elevated to the official ideologies of the state of North and South Korea, and both cruelly oppressed each other's resistance within their borders. The comrades of yesterday became the enemies of today.

The establishment of separate governments not only triggered the Korean War, which was a tragic civil war, but the process itself can be viewed as a series of civil wars. For instance, the 'April 3 Cheju Uprising' in 1948, which lasted until March of 1949, and the 'Yŏsu-Sunch'ŏn Incident', which lasted from 19 to 27 October 1948 in the Yŏsu and Sunch'ŏn areas, are both examples of these successive civil wars. The April 3 Cheju Uprising was an armed struggle led by the Cheju Committee of the South Korea Labour Party to stop the elections scheduled on May 10, 1948, for the establishment of a separate South Korean government. As a result, Cheju was the only place where elections were stopped in South Korea. However, once the Syngman Rhee government was established, it implemented a 'scorched earth policy' throughout Cheju to suppress the revolt, which claimed the lives of nearly 30,000 people, one-tenth of Cheju's population. The Yŏsu and Sunch'ŏn Incident (Yŏsun Incident) was a rebellion by the Fourteenth Regiment of the Korean Army stationed in Cheju that rejected orders to suppress the Cheju Uprising. This military revolt, which disobeyed the government orders to commit fratricide and denied the legitimacy of the separate government, gained public support

---

[3] Bruce Cumings, *The Origins of the Korean War,* Vol. 1 (Seoul: Yuksabip'yungsa, 2002), p. 86.

[4] Ibid., pp. 351–381.

and thereby expanded across the Yŏsu and Sunch'ŏn area to become a mass insurrection. However, the uprising was quelled in eight days, and the Korean police and military killed almost 10,000 residents during the suppression process.

If the Cheju Uprising and Yŏsun Incident were asymmetrical civil wars between the government and the civilian militia, then the Korean War, which broke out on 25 June 1950 and lasted for nearly three years, was both a full-scale war between the North and the South and a starting point of the global Cold War. According to official statistics from South Korea, the Korean War killed 400,000 South Koreans, and destroyed 40% of its industrial facilities and 16% of its residential areas. The war did not just cause destruction. As Charles Tilly's stated, 'Wars make states'.[5] The Korean War was a period of 'primitive accumulation' for Korean politics, establishing a new political order though the dismantling of the existing political community and re-integrating society with new rules and regulations. The universal conscription system and the compulsory education system became organized as important mechanisms for nation-building, and a civil religion, composed of Cold War anti-communism, pro-Americanism and liberal democracy, was established to unify the nation.[6]

As such, two successive wars, the Second World War and the Korean War, formed the Korean nation and its citizenry. The process of 'primitive political accumulation', which creates and unifies the people, is a severely violent one.[7] It allows the complete exclusion of those unfit for the nation by the state, such as traitors and 'commies'. The series of civil wars, from the April 3 Uprising to the Korean War, was where the government used its authority to massacre communists or those suspected to be communists; the so-called 'scorched earth policy' enabled the atrocities that targeted the common people. In short, state terrorism had to accompany the 'primitive political accumulation', and the people had no

[5] Charles Tilly, *Coercion, Capital, and European states, AD 990–1992* (Oxford: Blackwell, 1992).

[6] Kang In-ch'ŏl, 'Han'gukchŏnjaenggwa sahoeŭisik mit munhwaŭi pyŏndong', in Hangu kchŏngsinmunhwayŏn'guwŏn (ed.), *Han'gukchŏnjaenggwa sahoegujoŭi pyŏnwha* ['The Korean War and the Transformation of Social Consciousness and Culture', in The Academy of Korean Studies (ed.), *The Korean War and the Changes of Social Structure*] (Seoul: Paeksansŏdang, 1999), pp. 205, 221.

[7] Kim Jung Han, 'Han'gukchŏnjaengŭi chŏngch'isahoejŏk hyogwa', *Sŏsŏk sahoegwahang nonch'ong* ['The Political and Social Effects of the Korean War', *Sŏsŏk Review of Social Science*] 3 (2010).

choice but to swear their loyalty to the state. In this sense, the Korean War created 'people for the state' rather than 'a state for the people' and the society was merely a product of the state.[8] In other words, rather than the people creating the state that they desired, the state created the people that it wanted, which was only possible because of a 'state of exception' during a full-scale war.

The Korean War is, therefore, the starting point of the Cold War, but it should also be noted as 'the cold civil war', the matrix upon which Korean social movements had to survive. This points to a conflict between people who are or are considered to be in politically or ideologically different camps within a society. The most representative example of the cold civil war is the 'red-hunt', or McCarthyism. Yet a far greater oppression took place when the cold civil war expanded to encompass everyday life and impacted not only political and ideological enemies but also those falsely accused of being communists. Generally, false accusations against neighbors may have been intended to revenge wrongs committed against family members. Yet trivial instances over petty disagreements or personal gain also turned into accusations. This kind of cold civil war not only destroyed traditional communities, it also devastated the sense of humanity itself, and eventually caused the death of the ethics that a community must maintain.

In this manner, the war united the community by excluding rebellious elements through state terrorism; in other words, the process can be viewed as nationalization through fear. As Gramsci points out, however, an authority that completely relies on coercion and violence is an unstable one that cannot last for long. Eventually, the April 19 Revolution in 1960 brought Syngman Rhee's regime to an end. However, the democratic government that emerged after the revolution collapsed as a result of the military coup led by General Park Chung Hee on May 16, 1961, and his dictatorship lasted until his assassination in December 1979.

Anti-communist state terrorism prevailed in the Park Chung Hee regime as well. Compared to the Syngman Rhee regime, Park's regime effectively utilized the desires of the majority of the people living in absolute poverty, by promising economic prosperity. In other words, while the

[8] Chŏn Sang-in, '6.25chŏnjaenggwa han'gugŭi sahoepyŏndong, kŭrigo sahoejŏk yusan', in Kim Yŏng-ho et al., *6.25chŏnjaeng' ŭi chaeinsik* ['The Korean War and the Changes of Korean Society', in Kim Yŏng-ho et al.(eds), *A New Understanding of the Korean War*] (Seoul: Kiparang, 2010), p. 436.

Syngman Rhee regime, through the application of the suppressive state apparatus represented by the police and military, devoted itself to a 'top-down nationalization', the Park Chung Hee regime took a step further by achieving 'nationalization from below'. The focus was on the idea of development, which is more universal than the idea of anti-communism. By persuading rather than suppressing, the Park regime succeeded in a 'grass-roots nationalization'. For this reason, public support for Park Chung Hee has continued until today and brought the victory of his daughter, Park Geun Hye, in the 2012 presidential election.

Some researchers suggest the concept of 'mass dictatorship' to explain the irony of prosperity's support for dictatorships that sacrificed democracy by the primary agents of democracy: the *demos*. For example, Jie-Hyun Lim points out that modern dictators, in contrast to absolute tyrants who isolate themselves from their subjects, transform the *demos* into 'active participants' in the state projects of dictatorships rather than passive spectators, by constructing and complying with their desires. Therefore, to understand modern dictatorships properly, it is important to focus on the mechanism of 'spontaneous mobilization' and the various dynamics that have been hidden under the superficial dichotomy of consent and resistance—for example, publicly expressed consent, consensus as a rationale for the system, non-compliant resistance (*resistenz*) in everyday life, and subversive political resistance (*Widerstand*).[9]

Such a perspective provides fresh viewpoints that enable us to re-examine the various Korean nationalist movements, which had been viewed as unilateral mobilizations by dictatorial governments. For instance, the *Saemaŭl undong*, also known as the New Village Movement, launched by Park Chung Hee in 1970, aimed to revive and modernize the environment of rural villages, which urban-centred industrial development had turned into desolate regions. At the same time, it was an ambitious political initiative to gain the people's consent for Park's dictatorship. Although the New Village Movement was unable to stop the rural desolation, it was successful in gaining public support for the dictatorial government. Farmers' enthusiastic participation in the New Village Movement showed their passion for improvement in their socio-economic status and their desire to become active and meaningful social actors. The government encouraged farmers' participation in the movement by creating competition among villages and rewarding the winning villages. Farmers, who had

[9] Lim Jie-Hyun, ibid., pp. 16–17.

always been isolated from centralized politics and urban-centric economic development, were given a sense of achievement and belonging to the community and ultimately, the nation through the state's recognition and praise. This recognition, in turn, pushed them to voluntarily devote themselves to the New Village Movement despite their physical exhaustion and individual sacrifice.[10]

The family planning programme can be interpreted in a similar light. This campaign was initiated by the government in 1962, to curb the national population for the sake of economic development. At the same time, however, it corresponded with a woman's agency to make rational decisions for herself and her family's future.[11] Moreover, it was also a process through which women were able to express their desire to construct sexuality that was separate from the needs of reproduction.[12] No matter how much resources and power that the government invested, without the consent and cooperation of women it would have been impossible to lower the birth-rate from 6.0% in the early 1960s to 2.8% in the late 1970s.

In this way, the authoritarian Korean state built a sophisticated mechanism to 'voluntarily' mobilize the nation. This was also a process of subjectivation by which the people were turned into a 'modern people'; in other words, modern farmers, housewives and workers who reflected on their lives and planned their present and future. However, the power of the state was not always productive and positive. Farmers were often stigmatized as communists if they did not participate in the New Village Movement,[13] and those who refused to take part in the campaign were fined or even beaten by their neighbors.[14] The family-planning programme also threatened

[10] Hwang Pyŏng-ju, 'Pak Chŏnghŭi ch'ejeŭi chibae tamnon'gwa taejungŭi kungminhwa', in Lim Jie-Hyun and Kim Yong-u (eds), *Taejungdokchae 1: kangjewa tongŭiŭi saiesŏ* ['Dominations Discourses during Park Chung Hee Regime and the Making of the Masses into National Subjects', in Lim Jie-Hyun and Kim Yong-u (eds), *Mass Dictatorship: Between Coercion and Consent*] (Seoul: Ch'aeksesang, 2004); Yun Ch'ung-no, 'Kusurŭl t'ongaebon 1970yŏndae saemaŭl undong', *Sahoewa yŏksa* ['The New Village Movement Revisited through Oral History', *Society and History*] 90 (2011).

[11] Pae Ŭn-gyŏng, *Han'guksahoe ch'ulsanjojŏrŭi yŏksajŏk kwajŏnggwa chendŏ* [A Social History of Korean Women's Birth Control] (Ph.D. thesis, Seoul National University, 2004).

[12] Cho Ŭn-ju, *In'guwa t'ongch'i: han'gugŭi kajokkyehoek saŏp* [Population and Governmentality: the Family Planning Program in South Korea] (Ph.D. thesis, Yonsei University, 2012).

[13] Hwang Pyŏng-ju, 'Pak Chŏnghŭi', pp. 494–495.

[14] Yun Chung-no, 'Kusurŭl t'ongaebon', pp. 101–102.

women's autonomy and health through its excessively demanding performance-based system and blind faith in modern medicine.[15] Furthermore, subjectivation, in a way, was another form of subjugation. As a result of the New Village Movement, the entire process of agriculture, from the purchase of seeds to the sale of crops, was absorbed into the national and international system of division of labour, and farmers became subordinated to both the state and capitalism.[16] Women's sexuality and fertility became integrated into national development through the family-planning programme, which confined women's social agency to the 'private sphere' of family life.[17]

The state's modernization project was combined with the ideology of nationalism. Modernization was repeatedly represented as 'Fatherland Modernization' and the 'Supreme National Mission'. The people were asked to sacrifice their selfhood to become unified with the larger national selfhood. Park Chung Hee, in order to legitimize his coup d'état, advocated 'National Democracy' and had a direct hand in creating the Charter of National Education in 1968 in the name of enlightening the people. The charter began with the statement: 'We were born into this land charged with the historic mission to regenerate the nation.'

The concept nation also occupied a dominant discursive position even among political dissidents against Park Chung Hee's dictatorship. Under the Park regime, reunification, which was frustrated by the global Cold War, emerged as the main agenda for social movements. In their discourse, the nation was considered to be the subject of reunification as well as the agent of resistance against a dictatorship. For instance, Kim Sang-jin, a student activist who burned himself to death at a demonstration for democracy and the liberalization of universities, stated in his will that his death was 'for the nation and for Korean history' and also 'the achievement of democracy for the fatherland'. Also, Pastor Mun Ik-hwan, the leader of a democratization movement from the 1970s throughout the 1980s, asked his family to 'pray for the country' and 'live for the nation' during his imprisonment.[18] Progressive feminists criticized the Korean

---

[15] Pae Ŭn-gyŏng, *Han'guksahoe ch'ulsanjojŏrŭi yŏksajŏk*, pp. 225–241.

[16] Hwang Pyŏng-ju, 'Saemaŭl undongŭl t'onghan nongŏp saengsan'gwajŏngŭi pyŏnhwawa nongmin p'osŏp', *Sahoewa yŏksa* ['Change in Agricultural Production Process and the Integration of Peasants', *Society and History*] 90 (2011), p. 43.

[17] Cho Ŭn-ju, *In'guwa t'ongch'i*, pp. 149–158.

[18] Kim Po-hyŏn, 'Pakchŏngŭi chŏnggwŏn'gi chŏhang ellit'ŭdŭrŭi ijungsŏnggwa yŏksŏl', *Sahoegwahagyŏn'gu* ['The Double Paradox of Resistant Elites during the Park Chung-Hee Regime', *Social Science Studies*] 13 (2005), pp. 168–171.

government for promoting sex-tourism for foreigners, in particular, for the Japanese, insisting that sex-tourism was a 'disgrace to the nation' and the women working in sex-tourism were the 'daughters of the nation' abused by the Japanese.[19] In the end, the nation stood as the 'master signifier' for not only the state's discourse but also the counter-discourse of social movements.

Nation-state building in the post-colonial period, which was triggered by the 'primitive political accumulation' after the Korean War, was a process of forming the people through the combination of top-down and bottom-up nationalization. This process produced the 'ethno-national (*minjok* 民族)' subjectivity by incorporating the people's desire for an independent nation-state, which had formed since the colonial period. The social movements against the authoritarian dictatorship were based upon this ethno-national subjectivity as well. In short, the state's efforts to transform the 'people (*inmin* 人民)' into a 'nation (*kungmin* 國民)' through nationalization, also sparked the formation of social movements, which protested against the dictatorship in the name of the nation.

MODERNIZATION

Under the global Cold War, modernization on the Korean peninsular was subject to two competing routes: American model (Rostow's model) versus Soviet model (the Stalinist model). The hegemonic competition between the US and USSR manifested itself on the Korean Peninsula through the conflict between the North and South. This phenomenon was also apparent in social movements, where the American capitalistic model of progressive liberal movements came into conflict with the Russian socialistic model of radical left-wing social movements. However, regardless of whether they were liberals or socialists, they shared the same belief: modernization was considered to be the supreme task for liberating Korean people from poverty.

---

[19] Park Jeong-Mi, *Han'guk sŏngmaemaejŏngch'aege kwanhan yŏn'gu: 'mugin-kwallich'eje' ŭi pyŏndonggwa sŏmgp'anmaeyŏsŏngŭi yŏksajŏk kusŏng, 1945–2005yŏn* [A Study on Prostitution Policies in Korea: The Transformation of 'Toleration-Regulation Regime' and the Historical Construction of 'the Prostitute', 1945–2005] (Ph.D. thesis, Seoul National University, 2011), pp. 271–281.

Due to the destruction caused by the Korean War, Korea's capitalist modernization had to depend entirely upon aid from the United States. Simultaneously, the Cold War desire to outpace the North laid the foundations for a developmental accumulation system nurturing conglomerates or *chae-bŏl* in the South, while sacrificing workers. Therefore, capitalist modernization during the 1960 and 1970s forced workers to endure long working hours for low wages under terrible working conditions, in which basic labour laws were commonly violated. The process of building up the workforce necessary to achieve rapid industrialization eliminated traditional rural communities and triggered a massive influx of rural populace into major cities, where slums began to appear. These industrial workers (especially women labourers who dominated the light industry of the 1970s) and the urban poor created a culture of mutual assistance based on the networks of traditional families and friendship in a situation where state welfare was completely absent.

Chŏn T'ae-il's death on November 13 and the Kwangju Residential Complex Incident on August 10 in 1971 triggered the beginnings of social movements that exposed the miserable condition of working poor and resisted the capitalist modernization. Chŏn T'ae-il immolated himself while demanding the preservation of the Three Primary Rights of Labourers to improve the desperate working conditions of female workers, who had been praised as the 'pillar of industrialization'. His protest became the starting point of the Democratic Labour Movement. The Kwangju Residential Complex Incident, where evictees violently expressed their anger against their destitute condition as a consequence of the Park Chung-hee government's urban migration policy and irresponsible administration, is remembered in history as the beginning of the protest for basic rights. These two incidents proved to be the catalyst for social movements in the 1970s that were usually led by the intellectuals, religious figures and opposition politicians to discover the '*minjung*' among the impoverished labourers. Afterwards, the word *minjung* gradually became synonymous with the historical agents in the Korean social movement, who protested against modernization.

The term *minjung* (民衆) in ancient China referred to those who were ruled. During the colonial period, some intellectuals used the word in a way similar to indicate the majority of the common people under subjugation in the same sense as *paeksŏng* (百姓) and *inmin* (人民). At the beginning of the post-colonial period, socialists frequently used the term *inmin*. However, after anti-communism proliferated across society and the Korean War almost cleared left-wing groups, the term *inmin* became taboo in Korean society. In this context, the rediscovery of the word *minjung* in the 1970s was a response to the political suppression of the word *inmin*.

However, in the 1970s the *minjung* of the *Minjung* Theory was not used as a common noun but rather as a proper noun.[20] Social movements created the *Minjung* Theory, where poor and neglected people emerged as agents of historical progress. In this sense, *Minjung* Theory shared the same perspective with modernization theory, which was also premised upon progressivism. Finding its origin in peasant communities of the Chosŏn dynasty, *Minjung* Theory emphasized the importance of an emotional connection with the oppressed and demanded that the ruling elite follow the bare minimum of moral standards. *Minjung* Theory, which criticized the gap between the rich and the poor caused by industrialization and urbanization, combined with liberation theology in the 1970s. It anticipated workers, farmers and the poor to become aware of their own historical consciousness through their confrontation with various social contradictions in their lives, and finally to construct a new world.[21]

However, the anticipation that the *minjung* could acquire its own historical consciousness was an ideology of social movements that were mainly led by intellectuals, religious figures and opposition politicians; in reality, the *minjung* never met the expectations of the *Minjung* Theory. Critical intellectuals were often frustrated with the *minjung*'s self-interested calculations. At the same time, they regarded female workers of the clothing industry, who played a key role in 1970s industrialization, merely as subjects of protection and assistance.[22] This shows that the progressive *minjung* with a historical consciousness was an invention of critical intellectuals rather than an actual historical entity.

The progressive *Minjung*-Theory of the 1970s then became criticized by so-called scientific class theorists and revolutionaries after the May 18 Kwangju Uprising of 1980. The assassination of Park Chung Hee on

[20] Namhee Lee, *The Making of Minjung: Democracy and the Politics of Representation in South Korea* (Ithaca, NY: Cornell University Press, 2009).

[21] Yun Kŏn-ch'a, *Hyŏndae han'gugŭi sasanghŭrŭm* [*Contemporary Korean Thoughts*] (Seoul: Tangdae, 2000), pp. 66–70.

[22] Kim Wŏn, *Yŏgong 1970, kŭnyŏdŭrŭipanyŏksa* [*Female Factory Workers' Protests in the 1970s: A Counter-History*] (Seoul: Imaejin, 2005).

October 26, 1979, was followed by the subsequent military coup d'état led by General Chun Doo Hwan on December 12, 1979. The new military authorities massacred the protestors who participated in the Kwangju Uprising, which occurred against the coup. The massacre of civilians revealed that an anti-communist liberal democracy only served as an ideology justifying military dictatorship. The citizen militia from lower class, who fought to death, revealed that the agents of a radical social movement had to be the *minjung*. Immediately after the Kwangju Uprising, the focus of social movements moved towards how to achieve an immediate revolution. For the first time since the Korean War, leftist ideologies reappeared in Korean society, including Marxism which explicitly advocated socialism as the goal of revolution.[23]

Critical intellectuals of the 1980s distinguished themselves from the *Minjung* Theorists of the 1970s, criticizing the latter as abstract and simplist. Instead, they analyzed Korean capitalism to establish a concrete theory as the basis for revolution. For example, they debated over the characteristics of Korean society focusing on contradictions of Korea's social structure and reform agendas. They attempted to overcome the limitations of the 1970s *Minjung* Theory by criticizing capitalist modernization more fundamentally.

However, the social movement against capitalist modernization began split into two groups in terms of the revolutionary agendas and pathways: the North Korean (Kim Il Sung's) model and the Soviet Union (Leninist–Stalinist) model. The former formed the National Liberalization (NL) faction, which believed that social movements should adopt the example of Kim Il Sung's *Chuch'e* ideology to advocate anti-Americanism and reunification. The latter formed the People's Democracy (PD) faction to pursue the state revolution led by the proletariat, following Leninism. The NL and PD factions were the two branches of Korean Marxism against capitalist modernization. In the 1980s, the NL faction spearheaded the anti-America movement, and the PD faction devoted itself to the revitalization of the labour movement directed against monopolistic capitalism. These two factions put great efforts into organizing *minjung* movements, while simultaneously cooperating and confronting each other.

---

[23] Kim Jung Han, *Taejung ponggiŭi minjujuŭi* [*Insurrection of the Masses and its Democracy*] (Seoul: Somyŏngch'ulp'an, 2013), pp. 191–196.

This transformation of social movements was inevitably accompanied by a reinterpretation of the *minjung* concept. The key issues of the social movements now became how to define the *minjung* and how to reform the world. While the NL faction based itself on nationalism and understood the *minjung* as the key subject of the nation, the PD faction transformed *Minjung* Theory into class theory and suggested that the working class become the core of the *minjung*. Nevertheless, the NL and PD factions both accepted the *minjung* as the subject of their social movements, the debate was in fact a repetition of the classic debate of 'nation v. class'.

The greatest achievement of the 1980s social movements was the extensive practice of 'student–labour alliances'. This activity was based on the belief that under circumstances where the *minjung* were not able to become historical agents the students and intellectuals had to join with the *minjung* to awaken and organize them. In fact, many students left their universities to secretly gain employment in factories to work and live with the workers and ultimately organize them into social movements. Although the radical students' alliances with labour were limited by the inherent elitist notion that they should be led by intellectuals, it is undeniable that this movement served as the foundation for the democratic labour unions that expanded rapidly in the late 1980s.

The 'Revolution Era' of the 1980s, which began after the Kwangju Uprising, came to an end with the fall of socialist countries in 1989–1991. Although the nationalist movements that problematized Korea's subjection to the US could gain public support, they could not bloom into mass social movements because of the presence of strong anti-communist and anti-North Korea ideologies. The class movement that problematized the exploitative structure within the production relationship could not become a political force as well, failing to move beyond economic labor unionism that focused on improving minimal working conditions.

In retrospect, the failure of Korean Marxism resulted from its inability to critique modernization itself. Instead, the movement pursued socialist modernization as an alternative to capitalist modernization and never managed to overcome the modernist ideology of continuous economic growth. For this reason, once the failure of socialist modernization became clear, Korean Marxism was unable to find critical alternatives to overcome the workers' accommodating attitudes towards the goals of national modernization and economic growth.

Though few in number, there were in fact autonomous Marxists who rejected modernization itself, but they were mostly groups of intellectuals in academia. Rather, after the fall of Marxism, new intellectual agendas surfaced in Korea during the mid-1990s through philosophical ideas such as postmodernism and poststructuralism. However, this trend has not developed into a social movement but instead remained a form of anti-Marxism among liberal intellectuals.

DEMOCRATIZATION

Democratization can be classified into three general categories: political democratization for the political rights of citizens; social and economic democratization to pursue equal distribution of wealth; and democratization of everyday life, which problematizes various forms of micro-powers rather than macro-power.

In Korea, political democratization after the liberation from Japan has its origins in the revolution of April 19, 1960. It occured against the election fraud of Syngman Rhee's Liberal Party and was led by high school and college students. Intellectuals responded to the movement to force Syngman's Rhee's resignation, toppling the first government of post-colonial Korea. However, the mass insurrection of April 19 was only possible with the assistance of the lower classes such as shoeshine boys, labourers, prostitutes and the unemployed who were described as 'rioters', 'gangs', or 'outlaws'. The April 19 Revolution energized the student and labour movement, and every level of Korean society witnessed an unprecedented wave of democratization. The number of labour unions grew rapidly to reach to 914 in 1960, compared to only 558 in 1959. Labour disputes, which had been severely suppressed by the Syngman Rhee government, grew from 95 in 1959 to 227 in 1960. The agendas of labor disputes also ranged from adopting collective agreements to wage increase to protesting the National Security Law, which hindered labour union activities. However, the new wave of labor movements was suppressed again by Park Chung Hee's coup of May 16, 1961.

Under authoritarian rule throughout the 1960s, anti-communism, modernization and developmentalism served as governing rhetoric, and the official dominant ideology of liberal democracy proved to be illusory. Moreover, in October 1972, Park Chung Hee established a developmen-

tal dictatorship through the proclamation of martial law and the dissolution of the National Assembly. Since then, the reign of terror lasted
throughout the 1970s. Although the newly revised (Yusin) Constitution
advocated 'Korean-style democracy', which was claimed to transform
liberal democracy to fit into the Korean situation, it completely ignored
fundamental liberal values and principles. College students, intellectuals,
religious leaders and opposition politicians started social movements to
protect liberal democracy and reclaim civil rights.

In this sense, liberal democracy had dual aspects in Korea: a dominant
ideology and an oppositional one. There were two reasons why political
dissidents accepted the rhetoric of liberal democracy to attack the dictatorship. First, with the predominance of anti-communist, anti-North Korean
ideology, it was very difficult, if not impossible, for dissidents to deploy
radical or socialist ideologies. In other words, because communists were
severely persecuted by the government, dissidents had to develop a strategy to criticize the dictatorship without being suspected of communists.
To advocate liberal democracy was a way of achieving this goal.[24] Second,
the government, which ostensibly claimed to support liberal democracy,
did not permit even basic rights such as the freedom of expression and
assembly. Since the gap between the ideal of liberal democracy and the
reality of Korean politics was so wide, crying for the principles of liberal
democracy gained public support.[25] These conditions of social movements
persisted throughout the 1970s. Although college students and critical
intellectuals of the 1980s started in earnest to discuss radical and revolutionary ideologies, liberal democracy remains predominant in social
movements in Korea, where the National Security Law is still operating to
suppress leftist political activities.

After 19 April 1960, the most crucial event for the institutionalization of Korean democracy was the June Democracy Movement in 1987.
This not only ended the prolonged period of authoritarianism from Park
Chung Hee to Chun Doo Hwan, but it also served as a starting point
for citizens to emerge as political subjects in Korean society. Civil insur-

---

[24] Kim Tong-ch'un, '70 yŏndae minjuhwaundong seryŏgŭi taehang ideollogi', in
Yŏksamunjeyŏn'guso (ed.), Han'gukchŏngch'iŭi chibae ideollogiwa taehang ideollogi ['The
Resistant Ideologies of Democratization Movements in the 1970s', in The Institute for
Korean Historical Studies (ed.), *Dominant Ideologies versus Resistant Ideologies in Korean
Politics*] (Seoul: Yŏksabip'yŏngsa, 1994), p. 217.

[25] Son Ho-ch'ŏl, *Hyŏndae han'guk chŏngch'i: iron'gwa yŏksa 1945–2003* [*Contemporary
Korean Politics: Theory and History*] (Seoul: Sahoep'yŏngnon, 2003), p. 161.

rection calling for constitutional revision for a direct presidential election system spread nationwide, including Seoul, Kwangju, Taegu and Pusan. Students, farmers and workers of both blue-collars and white-collars took to the streets and successfully brought about the June 29 Announcement by which the ruling party promised constitutional reform for a direct presidential election. In this way, the participants in the June Democracy Movement finally responded to Kwangju citizens' lonely battle for liberal democracy of 1980.

Similar to the April 19 Revolution of 1960, the June Democracy Movement in 1987 triggered a massive wave of democratization. During the 1970s, political dissidents lacked a solid foundation for mass social movements, and they relied on 'manifesto politics' by reading declarations or holding press conferences. In contrast, after the June Democratic Movement, grassroots democracy started to grow. For instance, immediately after the June Democracy Movement, workers across the country staged thousands of strikes, showing off the power of working class for the first time since the Korean War. From July to September in 1987, 1,316 new labor unions emerged and union membership increased from 900,000 to 1,500,000.[26] The Korean Trade Unions Conference, the most radical and combative labor union association in the country's history, was also born in 1990. Workers also attempted to replace the existing authoritarian labor unions, which had supported the dictatorship, by organizing more liberal and democratic ones. For instance, the Korean Teachers and Educational Workers' Union was newly established in 1989, to compete with the Korean Federation of Teachers' Association. Simultaneously, underground organizations that had led 'illegal protests' under the dictatorship started to reorganize themselves as 'semi-legal' ones. Universities functioned as a matrix for radical politics, in which student activists and critical intellectuals studied and discussed political theories and strategies for social transformation.

The desire for a revolutionary democracy spread throughout the nation, and the *minjung* movement established its basic organizational structure during the four years from 1987 to 1991. However, this was also a period of 'counter-attack' by the ruling classes that continuously tried to turn back the tide of democracy through 'Rule through Public Security' and the conservative alliance by 'Three Party Merger'. In this situation,

---

[26] Kim Chin-gyun, *Chŏhang, yŏndae, kiŏgŭi chŏngch'i 2 [The Politics of Resistance, Solidarity, and Memory*, vol. 2] (Seoul: Munhwagwahaksa, 2003), p. 27.

where democratic and anti-democratic forces clashed with each other, the May Struggle of 1991 served as a watershed moment that determined the direction of the Korean democracy movement.

The May Struggle of 1991, which is considered to be the second June 1987 Uprising, was ignited by the death of a university student Kang Kyŏng-dae on April 26, 1991. Kang was killed because of the police's bloody crackdown on demonstrators. Demonstrations continued for 60 days to mourn Kang's death and to demand a government apology for it. During this period, eleven people, including students and workers, committed suicide as protests; one of them was Kim Ki-sŏl. The government accused Kim's friend Kang Ki-hun of assisting suicide, arguing that he had ghost-written Kim's will. In fact, the government fabricated the incident from the very beginning to overcome the political crisis and damage the moral reputation of the social movement. In 2007, the Truth and Reconciliation Committee determined that the handwriting of the will did not match Kang Ki-hun's. However, the *minjung* movement lost considerable influence as well as moral authority after this incident.

The May Struggle of 1991 was a significant, decisive battle between the ruling classes and the *minjung* movement over the question of whether democracy should contract or expand. In the end, the *minjung* movement was defeated, and democracy retreated, leading to a limited political democracy that fell short of the Western model.[27] Simultaneously, the prospect of revolution disappeared with the collapse of the socialist nations. As the *minjung* movement was suppressed and weakened after the May Struggle of 1991, the 'civil movement' took over the leadership of the social movements. Civil movement identified itself as activism for ordinary citizens, rather than for the *minjung*. The People's Solidarity for Participatory Democracy is an exemplary case of the civil movement in the 1990s. It gained public support by advocating the rights of small shareholders to reform the financial system. It also attempted to restrict the excessive power of the conservative media and launched a campaign against corrupt politicians. However, the civil movement, led by elite intellectuals and professionals, was criticized as a 'citizens' movements without citizens'.

[27] Son Ho-chŏl, ibid.

Meanwhile, the democratic labour movement disbanded the Korean Trade Unions Conference in 1995 and founded the Korean Confederation of Trade Unions (KCTU) to develop a political basis for the labour movement. On December 26, 1996 the KCTU called a general strike against the government's undesirable amendments to the labour laws. The strike lasted until the end of January 1997, during which time 3,206 labour unions and 3,597,011 members participated. It was the first large-scale political strike since the Korean War. In 1997, the KCTU organized the Democratic Labour Party (DLP) to connect labour unions with parliamentary politics. The DLP won ten seats in the 2004 election, entering the National Assembly for the first time. However, conflicts took place between the 'self-reliance' and 'equality' factions within the party, an extension of the political factionalism between the NL and PD factions of the 1980s. The dominant 'self-reliance' faction rejected party reform attempts. As a result, the 'equality' faction left the party and founded the New Progressive Party. Weakened by this division, the leadership of both the DLP and the New Progressive Party decided to merge their parties, establishing the Unified Progressive Party in 2011. However, some members of the New Progressive Party refused to join the Unified Progressive Party.[28] These divisions within labour politics are closely related to a crisis of representation: the DLP represented permanent, full-time male employees of a few major conglomerates, and was unwilling to embrace other groups of workers such as temporary female workers in small businesses.[29]

What is paradoxical is that liberal governments after the institutional democratization deepened the crisis of democracy. The Kim Dae Jung regime and the following Roh Moo Hyun regime launched neoliberal reforms in response to the East Asian financial crisis, triggering the collapse of the middle class and social polarization. As a result, people became so frustrated and disillusioned with liberal politics that they chose conservative presidents in the following two elections. In this way, democratization from below was reversed by 'de-democratization' from above.

[28] Kim Jung Han, 'P'osŭt'ŭ Ro Muhyŏn sidaeŭi chinbojŏngch', *Chinbop'yŏngnon* ['Progressive Politics in the Post Ro Muhyŏn Era', *The Radical Review*] 50 (2011).
[29] Chang Tae-ŏp, 'Minjunoch'ongŭi taeansegyehwa inyŏm', *Marŭkŭsŭjuŭiyŏn'gu* ['The KCTU and Alter-globalization Ideology', *Marxism*] 21, 8 (2011).

POST-DEMOCRATIZATION

The social movements of the 1980s had a militant and communitarian culture that prioritized organizations, centralized leadership and the political dimension over members, individual autonomy and the cultural dimension. With the defeat of the *minjung* movement in 1991, critical introspection on such a culture ensued. While social movements of the 1980s had followed the model of the Russian Revolution in 1917, the activism of the 1990s adopted the agendas of the 1968 Revolution and the New Left, focusing on a wide variety of issues such as feminism, ecology, immigration and LGBTQ rights. The agendas of the New Left of the 1990s can be summarized with the following four points.

First, anthropology. The old left raised the issue of labour alienation based on the anthropological belief that labour forms the fundamental basis of humanity, and they believed that a change in labour relations was the most effective means to resolve this alienation. The New Left does not agree with this anthropological presumption. They prioritize communication over labour, attempting to transform the cultural area rather than the production process.

Second, subjectivity. The old left regarded the working class as the subject of revolution. By contrast, the New Left emphasizes identity politics and focuses on the ideological mechanism or discursive structure behind the subjectivity-formation process. From their perspective, it is impossible to presume a subject of revolution a priori.

Third is the issue of state and power. After Stalin advocated 'Socialism in One Country', Marx's dream of world revolution has been locked within the borders of nation-states. Accordingly, the primary goal of the old left was to seize state power (either through armed conflict or election). To this end, they support centralized party leadership to unify various forces into a single front (either radical or non-radical). On the other hand, the New Left pays more attention to various forms of micro-power. They think that power is not a thing but rather a relationship, therefore it can never be seized. To minorities, unlike traditional workers who belong to trade unions and parties approved by the state, national borders are meaningless or considered to be merely obstacles that have to be overcome. The New Left tends to be more open to international solidarity than the old left.

Fourth is the issue of post-modernism. The old left divides the premodern from the modern era on the basis of the 'mode of production'.

Capitalism is held to be the major characteristic of the modern society and changes in the capitalist production system should be the goal of a post-modern movement. In contrast, the New Left believes that cultural practices or the 'mode of subjectivation' is the core of the modern era. Therefore, changes in cultural practices should be the goal of post-modernism.

The feminist movement in Korea represents this trend of the New Left. Although feminism emerged in Korea in the early twentieth century, it reached its climax in the 1990s, challenging the gender hierarchy of the Korean society. One of the main achievements of Korean feminism was the revision of family law. The post-colonial family law that was enacted in 1958 succeeded the colonial *hoju* system, which only recognized men as the heads of households. Female activists campaigned to amend this discriminatory system as early as in the 1950s but it was only completely abolished in January 2008, after half a century of struggle. Korean feminists also redefined domestic violence as a crime by the enaction of the Domestic Violence Protection Act in 1994. Feminist agendas were not limited to family relations. They struggled against various kinds of sexual oppression and injustice taking place in the public sphere, such as sexual harassment, gender discrimination in the workplace, and prostitution. They also grappled with diverse issues such as the Second World War Japanese military's 'Comfort Women', prostitution in US military garrison towns, environmental and ecological issues and alternative globalization movements.

Even 'progressive' social movements were not immune to feminist critique. The old left in Korea prioritized national reunification and class struggle over gender equality.[30] As a result, they were insensitive to gender discrimination, sexual division of labour and sexual violence within their own organizations. In the late 1990s, female activists in social movement started to raise issues of gender democracy in everyday life. For instance, on May Day 1999, some female activists demonstrated by smashing coffee mugs that they brought from offices that they refused the role imposed on them as 'office ladies'. In 2000, 'The Committee of One Hundred

---

[30] Kim Hye-suk and Cho Sun-gyŏng, 'Minjokminju undonggwa kabujangje', in Kwangbok 50 junyŏn ginyŏmsaŏb wiwŏnhoe (ed.), *Kwangbok 50 junyŏn ginyŏm nonmunjip* ['The Democratization Movement and Patriarchy' in Commemoration Committee for the 50th Anniversary of Liberation (ed.), *Collection of Articles Commemorating the 50th Anniversary of Liberation*] (1995).

Women to Eradicate Sexual Violence within Social Movements' released the names of male activists who had committed acts of sexual violence.[31] Due to their activism, social movements started in earnest to enhance gender equality within their organizations.

More recently, Korean feminism has faced the criticism that it is not sensitive enough to differences between women. Some feminist groups newly established in the 2000s have questioned the notion of 'common interests of women' and emphasized the necessity of hearing diverse women's voices, including sexual minorities, the disabled and immigrants. Sometimes, the differences between women are expressed through dramatic conflicts. The Prostitution Prevention Acts, enacted and enforced in 2004, are an example. Mainstream feminists fought to enact more stringent laws to prohibit prostitution, insisting that prostitution is a form of sexual violence against women. However, the new legislation outlawed not only procuring but also patronizing prostitutes and acting as a prostitute. This prohibitionist legislation provoked a nationwide protest by sex workers. They demanded the government abolish the laws, and criticized feminists who had taken the lead in drafting and enacting the legislation. Although sex workers failed to achieve their goals, their activism was meaningful in that they refused to remain silent subalterns.[32]

The Korean feminist movement shares many characteristics of the New Left, in that it opposes oppression in everyday life and attempts to create new community ethics. At the same time, however, it has relied on the government to enhance gender equality and restrict male violence, and hence has been criticized as 'state feminism'. Nevertheless, it is also necessary to remember that the feminist movement was a pioneer in transnational social movement in post-colonial Korea. In the colonial period, Korean social movements actively interacted with anti-imperialism in Japan, China and the Soviet Union. However, it became isolated in the south of the Korean Peninsula after the collapse of the Japanese empire

---

[31] Park Jeong-Mi, 'Sŏngp'onglyŏkgwa yŏsŏngŭi simingwŏn: Undongsahoe sŏngp'onglyŏk ppurippopki p'aeginwiwŏnhoe sarye bunsŏk' ['Sexual Violence and Women's Citizenship: '100 Women's Committee Against Sexual Violence within Social Movement'] (M.A. thesis, Seoul National University, 2002).

[32] Park Jeong-Mi, Han'guk sŏngmaemaejŏngch'aege kwanhan yŏn'gu: 'mugin-kwallich'eje' ŭi pyŏndonggwa sŏmgp'anmaeyŏsŏngŭi yŏksajŏk kusŏng, 1945–2005 yŏn [A study on Prostitution Policies in Korea: The transformation of 'Toleration-Regulation Regime' and the Historical Construction of 'the Prostitute', 1945–2005] (Ph.D. thesis, Seoul National University, 2011), pp. 352–413.

and the division of Korea. In the early 1970s, the women's movement took the lead in building international solidarity by collaborating with Japanese women to campaign against Japanese men's sex tourism. This anti-sex tourism campaign expanded into Thailand and the Philippines in the 1980s, and the concept of 'sexual imperialism' that women activists coined became a useful concept for transnational feminist movements as well as in research on global sex commerce.[33] Moreover, this experience had a significant influence on the movement addressing the issue of Japanese military 'Comfort Women'.

Starting with a Comfort Woman survivor Kim Hak-sun's brave press interview on August 14, 1991, many survivors, who had been living with shame and stigma, began to speak about their experiences as Comfort Women. The democratization of Korean society and the dedicated support of the women's movement for victims contributed to their breaking a silence that had persisted for half a century. Arguing that such cruel war crimes should not occur again, survivors and their supporters demanded that the Japanese government recognize its historical responsibility, apologize and make legal reparation to the survivors. This campaign garnered global attention, and survivors and activists from various countries, such as Japan, the Philippines, Taiwan, Indonesia, the Netherlands, and even North Korea, joined the movement. Due to their efforts, in the 1990s the UN defined the 'Comfort Women system' as 'military sexual slavery' and called on the Japanese government to admit legal responsibility, identify and punish those responsible, compensate and apologize to the survivors and teach its students about the offence. In addition, perpetrators – including the Japanese emperor – were convicted at the Women's International War Crimes Tribunal for the Trial of Japan's Military Sexual Slavery held in Tokyo in December 2000.[34] As the movement for redress continues, a rally is held in front of the Japanese embassy in Seoul every Wednesday. On 14 August 2013, the first Memorial Day for 'Comfort Women', a chain of demonstrations was staged across 17 cities in nine countries. In this regard, the movement on behalf of Comfort Women is an exemplary case of a transnational social movement.

---

[33] Thanh-dam Truong, *Sex, Money and Morality: Prostitution and Tourism in South-East Asia* (London: Zed Books Ltd, 1990), pp. 55–56.

[34] Chŏng Chin-sŏng, *Ilbon'gun Sŏngnoyeje* [*Japanese Military Sexual Slavery*] (Seoul: Seoul National University Press, 2004).

EPILOGUE

In Korea, spontaneous mass insurrections have been catalysts for organized social movements. The history of Korean social movements can be summarized as follows: student movements in the 1960s sparked off by the April 19 Revolution; democratic labour movements in the 1970s after the death of Chŏn T'ae-il and the Kwangju Residential Complex Incident; the *minjung* movements in the 1980s triggered by the Kwangju Uprising; the massive explosion of popular movements and labour movements following the nationwide June Democracy Movement and the Grand Labour Struggle in 1987; the general strike of the KCTU in 1997, which combined party politics with labour union movement, resulting in the progressive party movements; and new civil and New Left movements after the May Struggle of 1991. It was through such insurrections that the masses experienced the collective subjectivation process, by identifying with various subject-positions: people, nation, *minjung*, citizens and minorities.

The historical characteristic of strong social momentum combined with the weak organization of social movements no longer persists in Korea, after political democratization opened the door to freedom of assembly and association. Ironically, ever since the institutionalization of democracy, social movements in Korea have been faced with a crisis of failure to represent the various interests and demands of the people. This is partly because of internal problems of the organized movements. The *minjung* movements still suffer from conflicts between the NL and PD factions, and the civil movements are suspected of accommodating to neoliberalism. Changes in Korean society are also contributing to this crisis. The advent of post-modern conditions such as labour flexibility and the emergence of new form of conflicts over gender, race and generation made it extremely difficult for any social movement to maintain organizational coherence and solidarity.

As a result, mass insurrections are still continuing to erupt, quite separately from existing social movement organizations. The exemplary cases are the candlelight rallies concerning various issues, which citizens voluntarily organize and join using new communication technologies such as the internet and mobile phones. Considering the historical lesson that the masses' spontaneous energy has always preceded new kinds of social movement, this phase is not the crisis of social movement itself but a crisis among the existing social movement organizations. In this respect, Korea may still be viewed as a laboratory for democracy.

FURTHER READINGS

A useful overview of Korean history from ancient times to the present is Bruce Cumings's *Korea's Place in the Sun: A Modern History* (New York: W.W. Norton, 2005). Joong-Seok Seo's *Contemporary History of South Korea: 60 Years* (Seoul: Korea Democracy Foundation, 2007) more specifically deals with Korea's history since its liberation from Japanese imperialism, from the perspective of social movements. Cumings also wrote an outstanding two-volume history of the Korean War: *The Origins of the Korean War, Vol. 1: Liberation and the Emergence of Separate Regimes 1945–1947* (Princeton, NJ: Princeton University Press, 1981); *The Origins of the Korean War, Volume II: The Roaring of the Cataract, 1947–1950* (Princeton, NJ: Princeton University Press, 1990). In these books, Cumings focuses on conflicts among various political organizations within Korean society, in particular, between socialism and nationalism, as a primary cause of the civil war. By contrast, Myung-Lim Park, *The Requiem for Peace, a Critical-Constructive Reflection on the Korean War* (Seoul: NANAM, 2005) rebuts Cumings's view, revealing that North Korea's leadership, supported by the Soviet Union and China, played a more important and direct role in triggering the war. Mikyoung Kim (ed.), *Routledge Handbook of Memory and Reconciliation in East Asia* (London: Routledge, 2015) covers the relationship between trauma of wars in the twentieth century, post-war nationalism, and social movements for coming to terms with the past in East Asia.

Hagen Koo, *Korean Workers: The Culture and Politics of Class Formation* (Ithaca, NY: Cornell University Press, 2001) delineates the process by which Korean workers' collective identity was formed in response to harsh suppression by the authoritarian government. T'aeil Chŏn is a symbolic figure or martyr, who heralded the emergence of progressive labour movement in Korea. The late human rights lawyer Young-rae Cho wrote a biography of Chŏn in 1991, a must-read for many intellectuals and college students in Korea, which was translated in English: *A Single Spark: The Biography of Chun Tae-il* (Seoul: Korea Democracy Foundation, 2003). Chun Soonok, *They Are Not Machines: Korean Women Workers and their Fight for Democratic Trade Unionism in the 1970s* (London: Routledge, 2003) investigates female workers' lives and struggles after Chŏn's death. Hwasook Nam, *Building Ships, Building a Nation: Korea's Democratic Unionism Under Park Chung Hee* (Seattle: University of Washington Press, 2009) explores the rise and collapse of militant labour unionism, focussing on male shipyard workers in the 1960s and 1970s. Jang-Jip Choi, *Labor and the Authoritarian State: Labor Unions in South Korean Manufacturing Industries, 1961–1980* (Honolulu: University of Hawaii Press, 1990) analyses Korean labour movements in the same period through the framework of power relations between the state, capitalists and workers.

Namhee Lee, *The Making of Minjung: Democracy and the Politics of Representation in South Korea* (Ithaca, NY: Cornell University Press, 2009) illuminates solidarities and tensions between intellectuals and 'common people', who were defined and represented as *Minjung* by the former. The Kwangju Uprising of May 18, 1980, which triggered the Minjung Movement, is outlined in detail in Sangyong Chung, *Memories of May 1980: A Documentary History of the Kwangju Uprising in Korea* (Seoul: Korea Democracy Foundation, 2003). Gi-Wook Shin and Kyung Moon Hwang (eds), *Contentious Kwangju: The May 18th Uprising in Korea's Past and Present* (Lanham, MD: Rowman & Littlefield, 2003) introduces various interpretations of this critical event. Jung-woon Choi's article in this volume 'The Formation of an Absolute Community', which is the abridged version of his book *The Social Sciences on 'May'* (Korean edition, Seoul: Pulbit, 1999), describes Kwangju citizens' loves, struggles and tragedies. Jung Han Kim, *Insurrection of the Masses and its Democracy in 1980* (Korean edition, Seoul: Somyong, 2013) sheds new light on the subjectivities of civilian militias and their pursuit of 'anti-violence'. The Kwangju Uprising and the US government's silence about it ignited anti-American sentiment, which developed into the National Liberation faction. David I. Steinberg (ed.), *Korean Attitudes Toward the United States: Changing Dynamics* (Armonk, NY: Sharpe, 2005) and Katharine H. S. Moon, *Protesting America: Democracy and the U.S.-Korea Alliance* (Berkeley, CA: Global, Area, and International Archive, 2013) deal with anti-Americanism and related social activism.

The June Democracy Movement of 1987 sparked Korea's transition from military dictatorship to institutional democracy, and Joong-Seok Seo's *The June Democracy Movement* (Korean edition, Seoul: Dolbegae, 2011) explains this process in detail, based on numerous primary sources. Jang-Jip Choi, *Democracy after Democratization: The Korean Experience* (Stanford, CA: Shorenstein Asia-Pacific Research Center, 2012) examines how democratization after 1987 ironically resulted in the political system being dominated by conservative parties. The general strike of 1997 led by the Korean Confederation of Trade Unions was a workers' reaction against neoliberalism. To understand Korean workers' struggles against neoliberal globalization, see: Hochul Sonn, 'The "Late Blooming" of the South Korean Labor Movement' (*Monthly Review* 3, 1997); Kevin Gray, *Korean Workers and Neoliberal Globalization* (London: Routledge, 2007); and Jennifer Jihye Chun, *Organizing at the Margins: The Symbolic Politics of Labor in South Korea and the United States* (Ithaca, NY: ILR Press, 2009).

Geoncha Yun's *The Trend of Thoughts in Contemporary Korea* (Korean edition, Seoul: Dang-Dae, 2000) maps Korean intellectuals' theoretical positions in the 1980s and 1990s, ranging from conservatism to socialism to postmodernism. Jinkyong Lee, *Marxism and Modernity* (Korean edition, Seoul: Munhwa Kwahak, 1997) points out the limitations of Marxism from the viewpoint of the New Left, which arose in 1990s Korea. Jie-Hyun Lim, 'Mapping Mass Dictatorship: Towards a Transnational History of Twentieth-Century Dictatorship', in Jie-Hyun Lim, Karen Petrone (eds), *Gender Politics and Mass Dictatorship: Global Perspectives*, Basingstoke: Palgrave Macmillan, 2011) criticizes Korean progressive scholars' consensus on the military dictatorship as a simple dichotomy of state dominance and people's resistance. In order to explain how ordinary people's consent and collaboration provided a hegemonic base for military dictatorship, Lim proposes a new concept of 'mass dictatorship'; Jung In Kang (ed.), *Contemporary Korean Political Thought in Search of a Post-Eurocentric Approach* (Lanham, MD: Lexington Books, 2014) reinterprets Korea's modernization and democratization from a 'Korean perspective', in an effort to escape from the Eurocentrism that permeates Korean academia.

Barbara Molony, Janet Theiss and Hyaeweol Choi, *Gender in Modern East Asia* (Boulder, CO: Westview Press, 2016) traces structural transformations in gender relations in China, Korea and Japan from ancient times to the present. The Research Institute of Asian Women at Sookmyong Women's University published two multi-volume histories of Korean women from the late nineteenth to the early twenty-first century: *A Political and Social History on Korean Women* (Korean Edition, Vols. 1, 2, 3, 2005); *A Cultural History on Korean Women* (Korean Edition, Vol. 1, 2, 3, Seoul: Sungmyong, 2005–2006). Won Kim, *Female Workers in the 1970s and Their Counter-History* (Korean edition, Seoul: Imagine, 2004) and Seung-Kyung Kim, *Class Struggle or Family Struggle? The Lives of Factory Workers in South Korea* (Cambridge: Cambridge University Press, 1997) depict the lives, struggles, and identities of female workers who played a crucial role in both the economic miracle and progressive labour movements. Korea Women's Hot Line (ed.), *A History of Korean Women's Human Rights Movements* (Korean edition, Seoul: Hanul Academy, 2015) is a useful introduction to diverse feminist movements grappling with issues ranging from sexual and domestic violence to prostitution to LGBT rights. Seung-kyung Kim and Kyounghee Kim, *The Korean Women's Movement and the State: Bargaining for Change* (New York: Routledge, 2014) examines how Korean feminists succeeded in having gender related laws enacted under progressive presidencies in the late 1990s and early 2000s.

'Comfort Women' or Japanese military sexual slavery has been considered one of the most crucial issues of women's human rights, in domestic, regional, and global contexts. Some of Korean survivors' testimonies, which sparked social movements and academic research regarding this topic, were translated into English: Korean Council for Women Drafted for Military Sexual Slavery by Japan, *True Stories of the Korean Comfort Women* (London: Cassell, 1995); Dai Sil Kim-Gibson, *Silence Broken: Korean Comfort Women* (Parkersburg, IA: Mid-Prairie Books, 2000). Against Japanese right-wing attempts to deny the historical existence of this matter, efforts to unearth historical facts based on official documents and survivors' testimonies are still going on: Yoshaki Yoshimi, *Sexual Slavery in the Japanese Military during World War II* (New York: Columbia University Press, 2000); Center for Research and Documentation on Japan's War Responsibility's periodical, *The Report on Japan's War Responsibility* (Japanese edition, 1993); Maria Rosa Henson, *Comfort Woman: A Filipina's Story of Prostitution and Slavery under the Japanese Military* (Lanham, MD: Rowman & Littlefield, 1999); Jan Ruff O'Herne, *50 Years of Silence* (North Sydney: William Heinemann, 2008); Peipei Qiu and Su Zhiliang, *Chinese Comfort Women: Testimonies from Imperial Japan's Sex Slaves* (Oxford: Oxford University Press, 2014); Caroline Norma, *The Japanese Comfort Women and Sexual Slavery during the China and Pacific Wars* (London: Bloomsbury Academic, 2015). With regard to social and artistic movements on this issue, see Margaret D. Stetz and Bonnie B. C. Oh, *Legacies of the Comfort Women of World War II* (London: Sharpe, 2001) and Chinsung Chung, *Japanese Military Sexual Slavery* (Korean edition, Seoul: Seoul National University Press, 2004).

CHAPTER 12

The History of Social Movements in Australia

Sean Scalmer

Social movements emerged as a major expression of popular politics in the late eighteenth and early nineteenth centuries. They rest upon distinctive political interactions, structures, performances and communications: first, engagement in conflict and contest; second, a practice of collective association, embodied in both formal institutions and informal networks; third, public performances that express a group's worthiness, unity, numbers and commitment; fourth, a capacity to articulate a common worldview.[1] Their appearance was a response to significant changes in modern his-

---

[1] This is an approach to social movements based on several sources. On opposition as central to the social movement: Alain Touraine, *The Voice and the Eye: An Analysis of Social Movements* (Cambridge: Cambridge University Press, 1981). For the role of institutions, see the 'resource mobilization' school, e.g., Mayer N. Zald and John D. McCarthy, *Social Movements in an Organizational Society* (New Brunswick, NJ: Transaction, 1987). For an emphasis on networks: Donatella della Porta and Mario Diani, *Social Movements: An Introduction* (Oxford: Blackwell, 1999), especially Chaps. 5 and 6. The emphasis on displays of worthiness, unity numbers and commitment is drawn from the work of Charles Tilly, e.g., Charles Tilly, *Social Movements. 1768–2004* (Boulder, CO: Paradigm Publishers, 2004). The emphasis on cultural identity is most fully expressed in the work of Alberto Melucci, *Nomads of the Present* (London: Hutchinson Radius, 1989).

S. Scalmer (✉)
School of History and Philosophical Studies, University of Melbourne, Melbourne, VIC, Australia

© The Author(s) 2017
S. Berger, H. Nehring (eds.), *The History of Social Movements in Global Perspective*, DOI 10.1057/978-1-137-30427-8_12

tory: the rise of nation-states;[2] the consolidation of industrial capitalism; the spread of the printed word.[3] But it was also a joint achievement: an expression of collective learning, as ordinary people struggled to understand their world, to draw lessons from past struggles and to challenge injustice.[4]

Modern Australia was established in 1788, more or less coincident with the birth of the social movement, and British colonists imported or established its major preconditions within a few years. But the Australian environment was distinctive: this was a settler colony and a penal colony. The state necessarily played a central and directive role; transnational relations in the context of the British Empire and beyond were always a significant presence in political life. These circumstances differed from those prevailing in the metropolis, and they helped to shape the development and the trajectory of the social movement as a political form. Australian social movements mobilized more quickly and successfully than most other societies. They were also more fully integrated and ultimately less capable of launching genuine transformation.

An historical study of Australian social movements is not simply an exploration of this fascinating trajectory, but equally an opportunity to reflect on the dynamics of contention, the key role of movement–state relations and the longevity and import of transnational ties. The pages that follow are arranged as a chronological narrative. They are also offered as a sustained investigation of these historical issues. An appreciation of Australia's unusual history, the chapter is simultaneously a broader argument concerning movement and state, mobilization and containment. In the close study of a colonial society, general forces might also be discerned.

---

[2] On the rise of the state and the national social movement, see: Charles Tilly, 'Social Movements and National Politics', in Charles Bright and Susan Hardings (eds), *Statemaking and Social Movements: Essays in History and Theory* (Ann Arbor: University of Michigan Press, 1984), pp. 297–317.

[3] On the importance of print: Sidney Tarrow, *Power in Movement* (Cambridge: Cambridge University Press, 1998), pp. 43–47.

[4] The process of collective learning and slow change is emphasized in Charles Tilly, *Popular Contention in Great Britain, 1758–1834* (Cambridge, MA: Harvard University Press, 1995).

COLONIZATION, STATE AND MOVEMENT: HISTORICAL RELATIONS

State power was fundamental to the act of British settlement. As a settler colony, modern Australia was established on the lands of indigenous people. The disruption of their lives and social arrangements provoked resistance. The state acted to establish relations with Aboriginal people; to put down Aboriginal struggles; to limit the lawless violence of settlers, usually ineffectually; and to manage the presence of peoples they considered uncivilized and threatening. Settler colonialism need not require a strong state (as the United States demonstrates), but Australia's status as a penal colony, and its great distance from Britain, made this much more likely.[5]

The European population of Australia was at first mostly based on British convicts. Between 1788 and 1868, some 160,000 convicts were sent to the Australian colonies.[6] The first governors were charged with the control and the reform of these men and women. They distributed rations; directed convict labour; planned the settlement; granted land; constructed public buildings; projected the extension of European occupation; built roads; encouraged agriculture; regulated trade. Colonists were cut off from Britain and fearful of French incursion. The soil was often inhospitable. Convicts absconded, fleeing into the bush.[7] An effective state was necessary to ensure the order of the penal population and to regulate the activity of free arrivals and emancipists. The state also became the organizer of economic development and the primary provider of infrastructure throughout the nineteenth century, under a system of growth that historians have labelled 'colonial socialism'. Its key devices were extended into the twentieth century.[8]

This context shaped the emergence and form of Australian social movements in a number of ways. A strong state became a target for political mobilization, and could therefore be considered an incitement to collective

---

[5] On settler-colonialism, see: Lorenzo Veracini, 'Introducing Settler Colonial Studies', *Settler Colonial Studies* 1 (2011), pp. 1–12.

[6] Brian Fletcher, 'Agriculture', in Graham J. Abbott and Noel B. Nairn, *Economic Growth of Australia 1788–1821* (Melbourne: Melbourne University Press, 1978), p. 191.

[7] On the earlier years of European settlement: Alan Atkinson, *The Europeans in Australia: a history* (Melbourne: Oxford University Press, 1997); John Hirst, *Convict Society and its enemies* (Sydney: Allen and Unwin, 1983).

[8] Noel G. Butlin, Alan Barnard and Jonathan J. Pincus, *Government and Capitalism: Public and Private Choice in Twentieth Century Australia* (Sydney: Allen and Unwin, 1982).

action. But the state was more than an object of appeal or demand. The capacity and form of the Australian state empowered colonial elites to repress strongly rebellious behaviour. In consequence, the early decades of European settlement were notable for the emergence and then the repression of violent collective campaigns.

Struggles for power in modern Australia originally rested upon the exertion of violent force rather than the techniques of the social movement. Indigenous people directly resisted the incursions of Europeans, and bloody altercations developed into sustained frontier wars from the last years of the eighteenth century. At times the resistance of the Aborigines was fierce and very effective.[9] The extension of European settlement incited new moments of conflict for several generations: dispossession and resistance were not singular events, but repeated cycles of desperate, sanguinary contact.[10] This was overwhelmingly a struggle waged with the spear and the musket rifle; the methods of political contention then gaining popularity in Europe were not at first deployed.

Europeans in Australia also used violence to secure their interests. From the earliest years of the colony, escaped convicts roamed the bush, robbing settlers and exploring the land.[11] Some Irish convicts plotted violent insurrection. In the largest colonial uprising, on the fringes of European settlement in 1804, some 300 convicts marched upon the centre of Sydney, attempting to overthrow their gaolers and take a ship back to their homelands[12]; the leader of the rebellion spoke of 'Death or Liberty'.[13] Only four years later, the colony was convulsed by a coup d'état. In 1808, officers and soldiers of the New South Wales Corp rose in opposition to the rule of Governor Bligh—and in defence of their economic interests in land and in

[9] John Connor, *The Australian Frontier Wars 1788–1838*, revised edn (Sydney: University of New South Wales Press, 2005).

[10] Heather Goodall, *Invasion to Embassy: Land in Aboriginal Politics in New South Wales, 1770–1972* (Sydney: Allen and Unwin, 1996).

[11] Grace Karskens, *The Colony: a History of early Sydney* (Crows Nest, NSW: Allen and Unwin, 2009), pp. 280–309.

[12] Lynette Silver, *The Battle of Vinegar Hill: Australia's Irish Rebellion, 1804* (Sydney: Doubleday, 1989).

[13] Richard Waterhouse, '"… a bastard offspring of tyranny under the guise of liberty": Liberty and Representative Government in Australia, 1788–1901', in Jack P. Greene (ed.), *Exclusionary Empire: English Liberty Overseas, 1600–1900* (Cambridge and New York: Cambridge University Press, 2010), pp. 220–247, p. 225.

the rum trade—in what would become known as the 'Rum Rebellion'.[14] Though these were perhaps the most dramatic episodes, violent affrays remained a persistent feature of public life into at least the middle years of the nineteenth century. In the decade from 1840 there were more than 30 major riots in Sydney; 20 of these were marked by explicit opposition to political authority, such as the law courts, the governor, or gatherings of the colonial elite.[15] Election rioting was also evident in other parts of colonial Australia in the 1840s and 1850s; in severe and protracted episodes, properties were sometimes destroyed and antagonists wounded and even killed.[16] European miners on the mid-century goldfields of Victoria also organized and applied violence against the Chinese community that came to share in the quest for wealth.[17]

Colonial authorities dealt harshly with most of these violent outbreaks. The majority of bushrangers were eventually caught and punished; many were hanged.[18] Irish rebels were shot, bayoneted, flogged, hanged, or transported to other settlements.[19] Indigenous resistance was suppressed, often violently; in Van Diemen's Land, European campaigns against Aboriginal people almost exterminated them completely.[20] Only the leaders of the Rum Rebellion enjoyed more gentle discipline, and even in this case one of the leaders was cashiered from the British military while the other was prevented from returning to the colony for almost a decade.[21] It has been suggested that the Australian colonies were the most policed areas in the British world until the 1870s; though the fringes of the settlement resisted

[14] Herbert V. Evatt, *Rum Rebellion: A Study of the Overthrow of Governor Bligh by John Macarthur and the New South Wales Corps* (Sydney: Angus & Robertson, 1938).

[15] See: Terry Irving, *The Southern Tree of Liberty: The Democratic Movement in New South Wales before 1856* (Annandale: Federation Press, 2006).

[16] Sean Scalmer, 'Containing Contention: A Reinterpretation of Democratic Change and Electoral Reform in the Australian Colonies', *Australian Historical Studies* 3 (2011), pp. 337–356.

[17] John Fitzgerald, *Big White Lie: Chinese Australians in White Australia* (Sydney: University of New South Wales Press, 2007), p. 38.

[18] Kirsty Reid, *Gender, Crime and Empire: Convicts, Settlers and the State in Early Colonial Australia* (Manchester: Manchester University Press, 2007).

[19] Silver, *The Battle of Vinegar Hill*.

[20] Lyndall Ryan, *The Aboriginal Tasmanians* (Sydney: Allen and Unwin, 1996); Henry Reynolds, *A History of Tasmania* (Melbourne: Cambridge University Press, 2012).

[21] Ross Fitzgerald and Mark Hearn, *Bligh, Macarthur and the Rum Rebellion* (Kenthurst, NSW: Kangaroo Press, 1988); Evatt. *Rum Rebellion*.

government control, the authorities deeply intervened into the routines of everyday life.[22]

If violent contention was vigorously repressed, then there nonetheless remained other means for the pursuit of collective interests. As a settler society, Australia was comparatively open: social mobility was conspicuous, no established church held special privileges, and the newly enriched did not command the customary deference of the English lord. Conscious of the need to reward 'unblemished' former convicts, the colony's Governors were increasingly keen to show 'no distinction' between the convict who had served his or her term (usually seven years) and the free immigrant.[23] These conditions made it possible to organize and agitate for common interests, provided that such action did not threaten the order or stability of the new colony.

Even if at first overshadowed by violence, non-violent contention was in fact evident from the foundation of European settlement. Though the officers of the NSW Corps overthrew Governor Bligh by force of arms, they issued statements of justification, framed their actions in the language of political rights, and submitted themselves to judicial processes.[24] In succeeding years, the petition became the favoured means of political intervention. Free settlers petitioned for trial by jury in 1819,[25] and added a claim for representative government ('Taxation by Representation') in a further plea, six years later.[26] From 1827, triennial petitions submitted to the British Parliament from Sydney sought the civil and political rights of British citizens.[27] Emancipated convicts also claimed the rights of 'British subjects' through petitions and in newspapers.[28] Emigrants petitioned for land grants.[29] Leaders of the Chinese community in Australia pressed legal

[22] Alistair Davidson, *The Invisible State: The Formation of the Australian State 1788–1901* (Melbourne: Cambridge University Press, 1991), p. 102, p. 106.

[23] Major General Macquarie to Earl Bathurst, 27 July 1822, in Charles M.H. Clark (ed.), *Select Documents in Australian History 1788–1850* (Sydney: Angus and Robertson, 1977), p. 310.

[24] *A Charge of Mutiny: The Court-Martial of Lieutenant Colonel George Johnston for Deposing Governor William Bligh in the Rebellion of 26 January 1808*, introduction by John Ritchie (Canberra: National Library of Australia, 1988).

[25] 'A Petition for the Redress of Grievances, 1819', in Clark (ed.), *Select Documents*, p. 311.

[26] 'A Petition for Trial by Jury and Representative Government. 1825', in Clark (ed.), *Select Documents*, pp. 321–322.

[27] Irving, *The Southern Tree*, p. 17.

[28] Waterhouse, "'… a bastard offspring'", p. 228.

[29] Irving, *The Southern Tree*, p. 28.

claims for equality of treatment,[30] composing pamphlets and petitions in this cause.[31] Aboriginal people formally requested parcels of land using similar methods.[32]

Agitation also took bolder forms. When limited representative bodies were eventually established, workingmen campaigned for their chosen candidates, won significant victories,[33] and even proclaimed their first successes as a 'birthday of Australian Democracy'.[34] Radicals anxious to win genuine self-government established formal organizations and newspapers; they convened public meetings and passed motions.[35] On occasion, they disrupted the meetings of their social betters.[36] From the early 1830s, trade societies advanced the public and industrial interests of working people; they held six large public meetings in the years 1840–1843.[37] The developing democratic agitation in Europe was a model for antipodean campaigners: leaders of the campaign for self-government and industrial rights had been educated in the Chartist campaign,[38] Irish struggles,[39] and even in continental radicalism.[40] British radicals had learnt to invoke the danger of popular commotion as a means of frightening elites into political reform;[41] Australian radicals, many of them veterans of Chartism, adopted similar techniques.[42] They created Australia's first social movement.

[30] Fitzgerald, *Big White Lie*, pp. 37–38.

[31] Fitzgerald, *Big White Lie*, pp. 114–115, p. 123.

[32] Richard Broome, *Aboriginal Australians: Black Response to White Dominance 1788–1980* (Sydney: George Allen and Unwin, 1982), pp. 70–81.

[33] E.g., the Sydney City Council Elections of 1842 returned six "practical men" from predominantly working-class backgrounds; only one-third of those elected were "gentlemen"— Irving, *The Southern Tree*, p. 87.

[34] *People's Advocate*, 10 February 1848, cited in Waterhouse, '"… a bastard offspring"', p. 235.

[35] Waterhouse, '"… a bastard offspring"', pp. 237–238.

[36] Irving, *The Southern Tree*, p. 73.

[37] Irving, *The Southern Tree*, p. 42, p. 44.

[38] Henry Parkes, democrat of the 1840s and later long-serving Premier, had been inducted into Chartism in Britain, as had the leader of the '8-hours movement', James Stephen.

[39] Charles Gavan Duffy, leader of the Young Ireland movement, later became a leading radical in Victoria.

[40] Johan Llotsky, an influential radical in Sydney in the early 1830s, had been a revolutionary in the Austro-Hungarian Empire; Raffaello Carboni, participant and historian of the Eureka Rebellion, had been a member of the Young Italy movement.

[41] Joseph Hamburger, *James Mill and the Art of Revolution* (Westport, CT: Greenwood Press, 1977).

[42] Irving, *The Southern Tree*, p. 146. On the presence of Chartists in Australian movements for democratization: Paul Pickering, '"Ripe for a Republic": British Radical Responses to the Eureka Stockade', *Australian Historical Studies* 121 (2003), pp. 69–90.

SOCIAL MOVEMENTS AND DEMOCRATIZATION

The moral force of popular agitation, combined with the threat and the outbreak of violence, served eventually to reorder the colonial polity. In the middle years of the nineteenth century the tempo of mass action increased. The discovery of gold transformed the southern colony of Victoria within a decade from a much smaller sibling of New South Wales to a thriving settlement of more than 500,000 persons.[43] Established structures failed to contain the new entrants: housing and roads were inadequate; heavy-handed and sometimes corrupt policing heightened disaffection; a costly licence imposed on all miners provoked resistance. Anxious to defend their interests, gold-seekers formed new organizations; assembled and marched in large numbers; despatched delegations to the Governor; and formulated precise demands. The words of American revolutionaries— 'No taxation without representation'—seemed to many a fair summary of their cause; a Reform League, established on the goldfields in Ballarat on 11 November 1854, echoed the major Chartist demands. But this was a cosmopolitan movement: Irish rebels, veterans of the 1848 uprisings in Europe, Chartist campaigners and North Americans numbered among the leaders of the dissent.[44]

Frustrated by the intransigence of the government, threatened and enraged in equal measure by the rapid mobilization of the military, a group of miners eventually organized themselves for combat, raised a new flag that pictured the Southern Cross above, and swore an oath of allegiance: '… to stand truly by each other and fight to defend our rights and liberties.' Though the words were powerful and enduring, the martial preparations were inadequate. A hastily erected stockade was overwhelmed by government troops on 3 December 1854; forty or so rebels were wounded, more than twenty killed. The 'Eureka rebellion' was extinguished. But if the violent suppression of armed resistance conformed to an earlier pattern, the habits of peaceful agitation now provided unaccustomed reinforcement. A public meeting in Melbourne condemned the government; civil disobedience spread to some of the other goldfields;

---

[43] Wray Vamplew, *Australians, Historical Statistics* (Broadway, NSW: Fairfax, Syme and Weldon, 1987).

[44] The best study of Victoria in this period is: Geoffrey Serle, *The Golden Age: A History of the Colony of Victoria, 1851–1861* (Carlton, Vic.: Melbourne University Press, 1963).

leading newspapers campaigned for reform; foreign radicals declared support; a jury trial of rebel leaders failed to secure a single conviction.[45]

Political reforms followed. In Victoria, the miners' licensing system was revised and political rights extended to the goldfields. Across the Australian colonies, the structures of military rule were supplanted by a version of representative democracy, organized around a bicameral legislature. A well-disposed Liberal government in London had already acknowledged colonial demands for self-government; the radicalism of the 1850s ensured that the new colonial constitutions would take on a strongly democratic form. Australian parliaments won the capacity to make laws on major issues. The suffrage for the lower house in the major colonies was broadened to include nearly all white adult males; property qualifications were removed for aspirant MPs; relatively equal electorates were designed and the secret ballot was introduced. The new democracies were hampered by significant limitations: the exclusion of Aboriginal people and European women; the continuation of upper chambers that were appointed or elected on a more restricted franchise; the entitlement of property owners to exercise plural votes. Nonetheless, the Australian order encompassed most of the major points of the constitutional programme of English radicalism, and the speed and completeness of this change variously shocked and thrilled.[46]

Historians have disputed the relative contribution of British and Australian agency, violent and non-violent contention to these changes.[47] But whether primary or subordinate, the prospect of subaltern power certainly preoccupied local parliamentarians. Proponents of a restricted franchise feared 'class legislation', 'brute majority' rule,[48] and 'tyranny'.[49]

---

[45] The leading studies of gold fields dissent is: John Molony, *Eureka* (Carlton, Vic.: Melbourne University Press, 2001). A fascinating contemporary history by a rebel leader is: Raffaello Carboni, *The Eureka Stockade* (Carlton, Vic.: Melbourne University Press, 1969). On British responses: Pickering, "'Ripe for a Republic'", pp. 69–90.

[46] Robin Gollan, *Radical and Working Class Politics* (Carlton: Melbourne University Press, 1967), p. 1.

[47] The most sceptical of Australian agency is John Hirst, *Freedom on the Fatal Shore Australia's First Colony* (Melbourne: Black Inc., 2008). The strongest recent support for local contention is evident in Irving, *The Southern Tree*, and Scalmer, 'Containing Contention'.

[48] Sequentially, Mr. Deas Thomson, cited in 'Electoral Bill', *Sydney Morning Herald*, 9 September 1853, p. 3; Mr. Murray, cited in 'Electoral Bill', *Sydney Morning Herald*, 4 June 1858, 5.

[49] Mr. Forster, cited in 'Electoral Bill', *Sydney Morning Herald*, 22 July 1858, 4.

Advocates of an expanded franchise promised that it might 'put an end for ever' to the methods of the 'Eureka Stockade'.[50] To deny reform would be 'to continue excitement and agitation',[51] it was suggested in parliamentary debate; much better to act before 'the matter had assumed a more serious importance'.[52]

Reflecting fears of further instability, the widening of the franchise was paired with important restrictions on popular assembly and speech. In Britain, the secret ballot had been embraced by the Chartist movement in order to protect the tenant from the landlord and worker from employer; in Australia, it was supported by a colonial elite for what they called 'opposite' reasons: to hold in check the 'tyranny of majority' and to protect the 'thought', 'action' and 'speech' of the educated and propertied few.[53] In Victoria, a 'Public Disturbances Act' was proposed to ensure that property-owners were compensated for any losses incurred by mass violence, aiming thereby to 'wean people from the barbarisms of broken windows and wrecked buildings'.[54] When Melbourne crowds gathered to express their dissatisfaction with parliamentarians, a further Bill was introduced to prevent 'meetings and processions of a disorderly character'.[55] Regulations policed election day.[56] In South Australia, parliamentarians sought to eliminate the 'riots and rows' of the preceding years by a new measure that restricted the direct canvassing of all candidates for elective office.[57] The 'routine' elections that followed, devoid of 'hooting', 'fighting' and 'stump oratory', were thought to vindicate the new measures.[58]

Still, this was a polity of great openness, when considered in comparative and historical terms. Charles Jardine Don, radical stonemason and former Scottish Chartist, claimed in 1859 to be the first working man elected to 'any legislature within the British empire'.[59] Victorian parliamentarians

[50] 'Representation of the Differs', *Argus*, 19 May 1855, 4.

[51] 'Parliament Bill', *South Australian Register*, 21 November 1855, pp. 2–3.

[52] Mr. Forster, cited in 'Electoral Law Amendment Bill', *Sydney Morning Herald*, 31 July 1858, pp. 5–7.

[53] 'The Ballot', *Argus*, 18 December 1855, p. 4.

[54] 'Public Disturbances Bill', *Argus*, 2 February 1855, p. 4.

[55] *Victorian Hansard*, vol. IV, Session 1858–1859, 2 November 1858, p. 185.

[56] As detailed in Scalmer, 'Containing Contention', p. 353.

[57] 'Electoral Law Bill', *South Australian Register*, 30 November 1855, p. 2.

[58] *South Australian Register*, cited in Carol Fort, *Electing Responsible Government, South Australia 1857* (Rose Park, SA: State Electoral Office, 2001), p. 24.

[59] As recalled in Charles Jardine Don, cited in 'The Late C.J. Don', *Argus*, 29 September 1866, p. 5.

soon included the leader of the violent Eureka rebellion, Peter Lalor, and a noted member of the Young Ireland movement, Charles Gavan Duffy. Across the continent, new administrations were formed promising to share land ownership more widely, and to promote the independence of the working man. Colonial liberals showed a consistent willingness to use state power to promote individual opportunity, even if this curtailed the free play of market relations.[60]

Social movements claimed an enduring if limited place in this new order. The openness of parliament to white men ensured that parliamentary politics became the major forum for the mobilization of their interests. Social movements therefore gained importance only when the interests or values of British subjects were not fully reflected in the parliamentary system. In these situations, mobilizations took on a common form: a moderate wing of the insurgent movement battled for recognition by the state and inclusion in the polity; a radical wing attempted to challenge the very form of the political system and to explore alternative ways of life. State responses also took on a regular pattern. The radical challenge was strongly repressed. Partial recognition of moderate aims was also evident: parliamentary politics was usually reorganized so as to reflect the new issues and identities; new state institutions were created to manage social movement demands. By these devices, social movements were both legitimated and incorporated.[61] The historical pattern is evident in both 'old' and 'new' social movements, across the nineteenth and twentieth centuries.

MODERN SOCIAL MOVEMENTS: LABOUR AND FEMINIST MOBILIZATION AND INCORPORATION

Workers were among the first to organize an enduring collective campaign in Australia, and as is the case elsewhere, they serve as the paradigm of the modern social movement. The growing market economy brought with it an expansion of the wage relationship and a quest to protect the collective interest of employees. Mobilization strengthened, unevenly, over several decades. Though Australian convicts included veterans of the British

---

[60] Stuart Macintyre, *A Colonial Liberalism: The Lost World of Three Victorian Visionaries* (South Melbourne: Oxford University Press, 1991).

[61] On the openness of the electoral system and the possible incorporation of social movements, see: Tarrow, *Power in Movement*, p. 84.

union movement,[62] and labour combination has been detected in the last years of the eighteenth century, skilled workers formed trade societies in substantial numbers only from the 1830s. In the years of the gold rush, newly favourable conditions incited a wider struggle. Stonemasons waged a campaign for an eight-hour day; their unprecedented success in 1856 encouraged plumbers, cabinet-makers and others to seek and win the same demand. Several strike waves convulsed the colonies in the decades afterward, then, in the 1880s, unskilled workers and women joined the aristocrats of labour in forming 'new unions' that were larger, more inclusive and sometimes more politically aggressive. National associations were formed and newspapers and educational bodies launched. Briefly, the movement exalted in its victories; unguarded labour leaders proclaimed that Australia was nothing less than a 'paradise for the working man'.[63]

Disturbed by the growing power of employees, business replicated labour's new organization and militancy. Over the early 1890s, a series of major industrial disputes tested the resources of worker and capitalist. The conflicts encompassed sea, wharves, farms, mines and cities. They commenced as the price of Australia's major exports fell, foreign debt ballooned and financial crisis engulfed the banking system. Governments sided uniformly with business. In the centres of dispute, special constables and soldiers buttressed the resources of conventional police. Artillery was despatched to one industrial town and armed force cleared the crowd of strikers in another; military reserves were instructed to fire upon 'the disturbers of law and order' in a third.[64] Magistrates punished strikers for breach of contract, or with the crimes of conspiracy and sedition. Labour's new unities could not hold, and capital won a series of bracing victories; wages fell precipitously.[65]

Still, the setback proved temporary. State repression was not so severe as to destroy the movement; it was sufficiently powerful to direct atten-

---

[62] George Rudé, *Protest and Punishment: the Story of the Social and Political Protesters Transported to Australia, 1788–1868* (Oxford: Clarendon Press, 1978).

[63] The mobilization of Australian unions is described in Sean Scalmer, *The Little History of Australian Unionism* (Carlton North: Vulgar Press, 2006), pp. 16–24. The union leader cited is H.W. O'Sullivan, President of the Sydney Trades and Labor Council, p. 22.

[64] The strikes are summarized in Scalmer, *The Little History*, pp. 28–32; the instruction was given by Colonel Price, commander of at Melbourne's Victoria Barracks, p. 30.

[65] On the major dispute, see: Stuart Svensen, *The Sinews of War Hard Cash and the 1890 Maritime Strike* (Sydney: University of New South Wales Press, 1995); declining wages, p. 229.

tion to the political realm.[66] Unionists reasoned that their defeat had been ensured by the actions of the state: 'the time has now come when Trade-unionists must use the Parliamentary machinery that has in the past used them'.[67] Freshly-fashioned labour parties stormed into parliament from 1891, first in New South Wales and then more widely. Australian Labor was the first workers' party anywhere in the world to hold major provincial or national office. Its rapid rise confirmed the durability and the signifi-cance of the labour movement.[68]

The great strikes of the 1890s elicited other enduring changes. Colonial liberals had been shocked by the breakdown of social amity, and the most visionary now contemplated fundamental reform of industrial life. Well-born and educated, often practising as lawyers, the reformers were pre-disposed to the constrained advocacy of the courtroom. From the early 1890s they proposed and then implemented wide-ranging schemes for the compulsory conciliation and arbitration of industrial disputes by new judi-cial bodies. The most influential of early judges, Henry Bourne Higgins, outlined key procedures to the *Harvard Law Review*:

> Reason is to displace force; the might of the State is to enforce peace between industrial combatants as well as other combatants; and all in the interests of the public.[69]

The new Australian Commonwealth, a federation of colonies achieved in 1901, extended the system of arbitration across the continent. In 1907 a notable judgement in the Commonwealth Court of Arbitration estab-lished the concept of a 'basic' or 'living' wage for all white, male work-ers: a floor under which wages could not fall, based on sufficient earning to support a man, his wife and three children in 'frugal comfort'. This

---

[66] A point made in Robin Archer, *Why Is There No Labor Party in the United States?* (Princeton, NJ: Princeton University Press, 2007), Chap. 5, wherein he notes the more complete repression of the American labour movement.

[67] 'Sydney Defence Committee', cited in Noel Ebbels (ed.), *The Australian Labor Movement 1850–1907* (Sydney: Australasian Book Society, 1960), p. 151.

[68] On the rapid rise of Australian Labor: Verity Burgmann, 'Premature Labour: The Maritime Strike and the Parliamentary Strategy', in Jim Hagan and Andrew Wells (eds), *The Maritime Strike. A Centennial Retrospective. Essays in Honour of E.C. Fry* (Wollongong: Five Islands Press, 1992), pp. 83–96.

[69] Judge Higgins, cited in Jack Hutson, *Penal Colony to Penal Powers*, revised edition (Sydney: Amalgamated Metals Foundry and Shipwrights' Union, 1983), p. 236.

formed the basis of what has been called a 'wage earners' welfare state'; it pre-empted most European welfare systems by some years.[70]

The Arbitration Courts afforded trade unions legal recognition and a formal process of register. Labor governments, which ruled only inter-mittently, also granted them more explicit encouragement. Thriving pro-grammes of public works enlarged opportunities for employment; new agreements extended preference to trade unionists; legislative amendments made the functioning of arbitration more commodious. Trade unionism quickly rebounded. Between 1900 and the coming of the Great War the number of labour organizations doubled and the number of members increased fivefold. At this time, Australians were more likely to combine for industrial protection than any other people in the world.[71]

Socialist visionaries had been as important to the formation of labour parties as the practical-minded;[72] the broader movement also included utopians and dreamers of many kinds.[73] The steady and unspectacular pace of reform therefore disappointed many, and radicals acted to form new organizations and to impose a more far-reaching programme upon the major party. Itinerant agitators, including North American sailors, brought with them the new gospel of the Industrial Workers of the World, and their Australian supporters briefly commanded some local support;[74] the Bolshevik revolution made communism—at first only dimly under-stood—the dominant alternative to Labor's parliamentary road. Its lead-ers rose to control major industrial unions.[75]

Communism was a subordinate presence, however. Government repres-sion was relatively persistent. Leading radicals to the left of Labour were regularly observed and sometimes arrested; a Crimes Act empowered the deportation of foreign-born strike leaders, and the Arbitration Court was

---

[70] Francis Castles, *The working Class and Welfare: Reflections on the Political Development of the Welfare State in Australia and New Zealand, 1890–1980* (Sydney: Allen and Unwin, 1985).

[71] Ross Martin, *Trade Unions in Australia*, 2nd ed. (Harmondsworth and Ringwood: Penguin Books, 1980), p. 6.

[72] Verity Burgmann, *In Our Time: Socialism and the Rise of Labor, 1885–1905* (Sydney: George Allen and Unwin, 1985).

[73] Bruce Scates, *A New Australia: Citizenship, Radicalism and the First Republic* (Melbourne: Cambridge University Press, 1997).

[74] Verity Burgmann, *Revolutionary Industrial Unionism: The Industrial Workers of the World in Australia* (Cambridge: Cambridge University Press, 1995).

[75] Stuart Macintyre, *The Reds: The Communist Party of Australia from Origins to Illegality* (St. Leonards, NSW: Allen & Unwin, 1999).

granted powers both to penalize unions for continuing strikes and to super-
vise their internal affairs.[76] The International Workers of the World (IWW)
was outlawed; the Communist Party was banned in the early years of the
Second World War and narrowly avoided suppression in the Cold War.
Anti-communist violence was sporadic but seldom punished.[77] And while
the revolutionary path was blocked, the Labor Party adopted a formal commitment to a socialist objective; this helped to preserve hopes of a peaceful
advance to a new order.[78] Even the communists who led some Australian
unions seemed Leninist in principle but reformist in practice.[79]

Government action to contain socialism was implemented by anti-
Labour parties; it was promoted by a broader movement that sometimes
achieved the dynamism and power of a genuine social movement. Anti-
socialists formed mass organizations, staged public debates, distributed
pamphlets and held public rallies. In moments of national crisis—especially war and economic depression—they mobilized under the collective
identity of 'citizens' in new organizations that commanded more than
100,000 members. Though the leaders of parliamentary parties relied
upon these groups, their energy and purpose was much greater than
periodic electoral success. From 1904, the Australian National Women's
League fought also for loyalty to the throne, the defeat of state socialism,
the purity of home life and the education of women in politics. From
1918, a series of mostly secret paramilitary groups drilled in preparation
for a socialist uprising. Defensive in character and highly conservative in
language, all of these groupings were nonetheless significant expressions
of mass politics. Movements of the right, their success is evident in the
increasingly thwarted hopes for social transformation so strongly held by
many on the left.[80]

---

[76] Frank Cain, *The Origins of Political Surveillance in Australia* (Sydney: Angus and
Robertson, 1983), p. 205; Geoffrey Sawer, *Australian Federal Politics and Law 1901–1929*
(Carlton: Melbourne University Press, 1956), pp. 268–270.

[77] Macintyre, *The Reds*, provides the most authoritative narrative until the Second World
War. The Cold War episodes are explored in Ann Curthoys and John Merritt (eds), *Australia's
First Cold War, 1945–1953* (Sydney: George Allen & Unwin, 1984).

[78] Bruce O'Meagher (ed.), *The Socialist Objective: Labor and Socialism* (Sydney: Hale &
Iremonger, 1983).

[79] Robin Gollan, *Revolutionaries and Reformists: Communism and the Australian Labour
Movement, 1920–1955* (Sydney: George Allen & Unwin, 1985).

[80] On the role of these organizations, see John Rickard, *Class and Politics: New South
Wales, Victoria and the Early Commonwealth, 1890–1910* (Canberra: Australian National
University Press, 1976) and the contributions by Sean Scalmer and Marian Quartly to Paul

The paradigm of a modern social movement, Australian labour's appearance and containment established a common trajectory: precocious arrival, rapid acceptance, ideological moderation, limited achievement. It was a pattern of advance that would be shared with the women's movement. Australian women were at first denied the political rights of their husbands and brothers, excluded from higher education and the professions, and greatly exploited on the margins of the labour market. In an insecure settler society, women were defined primarily by their capacity to populate the continent; in a pastoral economy that rewarded masculine power, the nominal protections of the home were threatened by alcohol abuse, violence and desertion.[81] As in Europe, advanced liberals spoke out in favour of women's rights;[82] like the United States, the temperance campaign served as a seed-bed of a wider movement for female emancipation.[83]

Australia's first feminists were often children of privilege, and some were able to draw upon the resources and personal contacts of the elite.[84] Their struggle to win the vote became a primary cause of the late nineteenth century, and women largely took on the forms of action so successfully deployed by Australian men.[85] Suffrage societies were established; public meetings held; letters despatched; journals founded; deputations sent; mass petitions collected; parliamentarians lobbied; institutional alliances sought. But more radical action was seldom ventured. Feminists presented themselves as the mothers of the nation and purifiers of a soiled

Strangio and Nick Dyrenfurth (eds), *Confusion: The Making of the Australian Two-Party System* (Carlton: Melbourne University Press, 2009). The best account of these groups is: Judith Brett, *Australian Liberals and the Moral Middle Class: From Alfred Deakin to John Howard* (Melbourne: Cambridge University Press, 2003). An authoritative treatment of right-wing paramilitary groups is: Andrew Moore, *The Right Road? A History of Right-Wing Politics in Australia* (Melbourne: Oxford University Press, 1995).

[81] Marilyn Lake, 'The Politics of Respectability: Identifying the Masculinist Context', *Historical Studies* 86 (1986), pp. 116–131.

[82] e.g., George Higinbotham supported the female suffrage in the Victorian parliament in 1873. See: Marian Quartly, Susan Janson and Patricia Grimshaw (eds), *Freedom Bound I: Documents on Women in Colonial Australia* (St. Leonards: Allen and Unwin, 1995), pp. 90–93.

[83] There were 57 branches of the Women's Christian Temperance Union by 1891. See: Marilyn Lake, *Getting Equal: The History of Australian Feminism* (St. Leonards: Allen & Unwin, 1999), pp. 23–24.

[84] Susan Margarey, *Passions of the First Wave Feminists* (Sydney: University of New South Wales Press, 2001), p. 52.

[85] Audrey Oldfield, *Woman Suffrage in Australia: A Gift or a Struggle?* (Melbourne: Cambridge University Press, 1992), p. 16.

polity. Though many men were resistant to any moral reform, the apparent respectability of the suffragists helped to secure prominent allies; some Liberal and Labor parliamentarians offered influential support. The provision of democratic rights to nearly all men simplified the women's objectives, while the earlier successes of liberalism had established a tradition of measured experiment. And the preoccupation with the fate of the 'white' race in the Pacific helped to justify equality among Anglo-Saxon men and women at the same time as it licensed the subordination of indigenous peoples. Victory was won first in New Zealand and then South Australia, and these accomplishments increased pressures in other parts of the mainland. All white women over 21 were extended the right to vote at the second Commonwealth election in December 1903.[86]

As with Australian labour, the success of conventional mobilization helped to temper more radical spirits. Early feminists had envisioned utopian societies and questioned the conventional paths of marriage and motherhood.[87] Entitled to the vote, they sought to use state power to address women's basic needs. Their methods varied. Whereas working-class men had formed a new party of 'labour', independent women's candidates did not enjoy electoral success. Rather, women established representative organizations and joined the political parties established by men. Though marginal in the latter, women working outside of the party system successfully pressured male leaders to bend to many of their demands. In the early years of the twentieth century a 'maternalist' welfare state provided financial support directly to mothers, restricted access to alcohol and provided greater protection from male violence. Women were appointed to special positions in the police force, schools, legal system and industrial inspection.[88] But though these achievements were important, the extent of transformation should not be overdrawn: without strong and independent means of disturbing the parliamentary system, women's claims for genuine economic and sexual equality went unrecognized. State responses to female disadvantage were less wide-ranging and supportive than the regime crafted to contain the power of employed men.

---

[86] This story is most fully outlined in Oldfield, *Woman Suffrage in Australia*. On 'whiteness' and the suffrage: Patricia Grimshaw, Marilyn Lake, Ann McGrath and Marian Quartly, *Creating a Nation* (Ringwood, Vic.: McPhee Gribble, 1994), pp. 192–193.

[87] The most prominent of the utopias was Catherine Spence's 'A Week in the Future' (1888–1889). On this and on rejections of conventional family structures see: Margarey, *Passions of the First Wave*, pp. 77–78, pp. 111–113.

[88] This argument is laid out most forcefully in Lake, *Getting Equal*, Part II.

TRANSFORMATIONS AND PLURALITY

By mid-century, the social movements of modern Australia were accepted, regulated and contained. As in North America and Western Europe, however, this was an apparent stability challenged by an unforeseen upsurge of political activism. Presiding over a boom economy in the middle 1960s, Australia's conservative government supported America's intervention in Vietnam and conscripted young men for military service abroad. This helped to trigger a remarkable 'cycle of protest'. Youthful Australian protesters were inspired by the cause of peace, but also by the fate of indigenous peoples, frustrated with the ascribed limits to gender and sexuality, and alarmed by threats to the natural world. Their inspirations were often American and French, and yet local campaigns rested also upon a sustained process of translation and reinvention.[89] A few Australian writers even attained international prominence as visionaries of the new order: Germaine Greer discovered *The Female Eunuch*; Dennis Altman helped to invent gay politics in *Homosexual: Oppression or Liberation?*; philosopher Peter Singer contemplated *Animal Liberation*; and paediatrician Helen Caldicott and historian of science Jim Falk championed the cause of nuclear disarmament.[90]

The protests that supported these ideals were more theatrical and disruptive than any in recent memory. Women's liberationists used street theatre and demonstrations to campaign for the right to sex education, birth control and safe and legal abortion; they challenged the official commemoration of Australian military service with competing protests that drew attention to the use of rape in war. From 1971 a 'Campaign Against Moral Persecution' struggled for the acceptance of same-sex desire. When a public march in Sydney in 1978 was violently set upon by police, lesbians and gay men defiantly marched again. Their repeated claiming of the city's streets was moved to summertime in 1981, and the Sydney Gay and Lesbian Mardi Gras, as it would become known, soon became a major public event. In these and other actions, previously private issues were advanced as matters of political argument and collective mobilization.

---

[89] The fullest study of the upsurge is: Sean Scalmer, *Dissent Events: Protest, the Media and the Political Gimmick in Australia* (Sydney: University of New South Wales Press, 2002). On remaking of international forms see Chaps. 1 and 2.

[90] As discussed in Sean Scalmer, 'Pressure Groups and Social Movements', in Rod A.W. Rhodes (ed.), *The Australian Study of Politics* (London: Palgrave-Macmillan, 2009), pp. 208–209.

Activists changed the culture of public life and pressured Australia's Labor Party to consider wider reforms.[91]

An influential European tradition draws a sharp division between the 'new' social movements that emerged in these years and the older radicalism of class. The newer mobilizations were allegedly inspired by fresh causes (the environment rather than distribution), values (cultural recognition rather than material goods), and actions (unconventional and network-driven).[92] Though immediately persuasive, the portrait resists empirical confirmation. Recent historical study has in fact disclosed the labour movement's equal concern with identity and recognition.[93] The subsequent fate of the 'new' movements has also established unexpected continuity with the 'old' campaigns. Certainly, the trajectory of the environmental movement contradicts dominant theoretical expectations.

Over the second half of the twentieth century, Australian cities were increasingly disfigured by the rampant pursuit of profit, as proposals for new development threatened urban parklands, architectural heritage and working-class community. Under the aegis of an unusually adventurous leadership, the Builders Labourers' Federation of New South Wales began in the early 1970s to refuse work on building projects of these kinds. Its 'green bans' saved large sections of Sydney from envelopment and inspired a wider movement of urban protection. They influenced foreign observers, and helped inspire European radicals to adopt the label 'The Greens' as a new political noun.[94] Not at all a replacement of class processes, green politics were first promoted in Australia by a venerable mass union deploying traditional industrial power.[95]

Political action to protect Australian wilderness emerged earlier, and some historians have even identified an environmental movement in campaigns to protect animals and create national parks in the late nineteenth

---

[91] On these protests: Scalmer, *Dissent Events*, pp. 92–95.

[92] Classic works of 'new social movement theory' include: Touraine, *The Post-Industrial Society*, and many later works; Claus Offe, 'New Social Movements: Challenging the Boundaries of Institutional Politics', Social Research 52 (1985), pp. 817–868; Jürgen Habermas, 'New Social Movements', *Telos* 49 (1981), pp. 33–37.

[93] E.g., Verity Burgmann, 'From Syndicalism to Seattle: Class and the Politics of Identity', *International Labor and Working Class History* 67 (2005), pp. 1–21.

[94] Bob Brown and Peter Singer, *The Greens* (Melbourne: Text Publishing, 1996), p. 65.

[95] Meredith Burgmann and Verity Burgmann, *Green Bans, Red Union: Environmental Activism and the New South Wales Builders Labourers' Federation* (Sydney: University of New South Wales Press, 1998).

and early twentieth centuries. Organizations were formed, conferences held, delegations despatched and concerned citizens assembled. The evidence for a common identity across these campaigns is less persuasive,[96] and it is only in the period around the 'green bans' that an 'ecological', 'environmental' or 'green' movement self-consciously emerged; the terms 'conservation' and 'preservation' now seemed inadequate descriptors of a more radical political challenge.[97]

Over the 1960s, conventional lobbying to protect reefs, lakes and bushland was increasingly buttressed by the techniques of social protest, evident most obviously in the campaign against the Vietnam War. It was in the island state of Tasmania that these methods were most fully and decisively employed. A Tasmanian government anxious to promote economic modernization had long been attracted to the damming of wild rivers as a means of acquiring cheap and reliable electricity; in the years after the Second World War it embraced hydroelectric schemes more repeatedly than elsewhere on the continent. One proposed dam of the early 1970s incited what has been claimed as the world's first green party, the United Tasmania Group.[98] Its failure to halt the government's plans provoked more militant tactics. When a further dam menaced the Franklin river system on the island's south-west coast, a major movement emerged in its defence. The campaign to save the Franklin encompassed mass civil disobedience on land and water; rallies in major centres of population; legal challenge; and political lobbying. Its success confirmed the significance of an abiding movement and the capacity of an enduring repertoire of contention.[99]

Threats to Australia's native forests also provoked similar campaigns in these and later years. Direct action to halt the bulldozer and the chainsaw combined with organizational bargaining and electoral calculation. The

---

[96]The argument for an 'environmental movement' stretching back to the nineteenth century is made in Drew Hutton and Libby Connors, *A History of the Australian Environmental Movement* (Melbourne: Cambridge University Press, 1999). This argument rests upon accepting that distinct campaigns or 'streams' (e.g., biological preservation, national parks, urban issues) that were not linked by a common mobilization or language should nonetheless be accepted as expressions of a single movement (see p. 86). The book is a fine contribution; this argument less persuasive.

[97]On the rejection of 'conservation' and 'preservation' as a political language: Hutton and Connors, *A History of the Australian Environmental Movement*, p. 91.

[98]Amanda Lohrey, *Groundswell: The Rise of the Greens* (Melbourne: Black Inc., 2002).

[99]*The Franklin Blockade*, by the Blockaders, Hobart: Wilderness Society, 1983; Peter Thompson, *Bob Brown of the Franklin River* (Sydney: George Allen & Unwin, 1984).

Wilderness Society and the Australian Conservation Foundation emerged as mass institutions.[100] Influenced by the popularity of the green cause, the Australian Labor Party joined the campaign to halt the Franklin dam in 1983 and pledged from the middle 1980s to expand Australia's national parks. In government, it incorporated the major green organizations in consultative bodies to support 'sustainable development'. While the most radical environmentalists chafed against such compromises, the promise of parliamentary influence exerted a strong counterweight.[101] Leaders of the movement entered parliament and in 1992 formed their own national party. In state and national politics 'The Greens' have emerged as a third force; parliamentarians have supported minority Labor governments, extracting major concessions and wielding genuine influence.[102] If European social movement theory suggests a sharp division between 'new' and 'old', Australian experience discloses a mixture of collaboration, conflict and family resemblance much more than any epochal change.

The mobilization of indigenous peoples further frustrates theoretical distinctions between the 'old' 'and 'new'. Aboriginal resistance to European incursion pre-dated the political forms of the industrial age. Native peoples acted to defend their lives, social order, and the land that gave that security and meaning. While the longevity of their struggles suggests an alternative temporal scale, the flexibility of their campaigning also traverses the customary periodization. Aboriginal people's attempts to incorporate Europeans into their own ways of managing difference were accompanied by martial conflict and, from the middle years of the nineteenth century, by modern forms of collective expression, including petitions, delegations and formal letters of request.[103] Australian governments denied Aboriginal people civil and political rights; dominant racial theories questioned their intellectual capacities; the breakdown of traditional communities undermined the possibility of collective resistance. Sympathetic white Australians offered assistance, but also sometimes unnecessary interference. Nonetheless, indigenous people developed their own political

---

[100] It has been claimed that by the late 1980s, Australian membership in environmental organizations was nearly 300,000—the highest per capita level in the Western world. See: Hutton and Connors, *A History of the Australian Environmental Movement*, p. 1.

[101] Timothy Doyle, *Green Power: the Environment Movement in Australia* (Sydney: University of New South Wales Press, 2000).

[102] Brown and Singer, *The Greens*.

[103] Bain Attwood and Andrew Markus, 'Introduction', in *The Struggle for Aboriginal Rights: A documentary history* (St. Leonards: Allen and Unwin, 1999), pp. 1–29.

campaign in the first half of the twentieth century and sometimes vigorously protested their treatment.

In the 1920s, Marcus Garvey's North American campaigns provided inspiration for the founders of the Australian Aboriginal Progressive Association;[104] in the 1950s a genuinely national organization was established: The Federal Council for Aboriginal Advancement.[105] In the 1960s civil rights campaigns in the United States spurred a new wave of local Aboriginal activism. As in the United States, renewed struggles at first drew sympathetic white support to ensure formal recognition of equality and to remove racial segregation.[106] But departing from American custom, Aboriginal people also sought to claim their distinctive rights to traditional lands. From 1966, the Gurindji people of Northern Australia conducted a long-running strike that was also an assertion of land rights;[107] in the early 1970s an 'Aboriginal Tent Embassy' outside the national parliament became a symbol of political disenfranchisement and of continuing attachment to land.[108] These and other actions brought the enduring cause a renewed attention.

Neither recognizably 'industrial' nor 'post-industrial', the movement for Aboriginal rights exerted singular demands. Its trajectory nevertheless adhered to a recognizable pattern. An initial claim for civil rights was succeeded by a more radical assertion of 'Black Power' and political independence. From the early 1970s Aboriginal people created their own community-run health and legal services; together, these helped to constitute a separate 'Indigenous Domain'.[109] State and federal governments passed limited land rights legislation from the middle 1970s, and these

[104] John Maynard, *Fight for Liberty and Freedom: The Origins of Australian Aboriginal Activism* (Canberra: Aboriginal Studies Press, 2007).

[105] Later expanded to the Federal Council of Aborigines and Torres Strait Islanders. See: Susan Taffe, *Black and White Together. FCAATSI: the Federal Council for the Advancement of Aborigines and Torres Strait Islanders, 1958–1973* (St. Lucia: University of Queensland Press, 2005).

[106] Ann Curthoys, *Freedom Ride: A Freedom Rider Remembers* (Crows Nest, NSW: Allen & Unwin, 2002).

[107] Minoru Hokari, 'From Wattie Creek to Wattie Creek: An Oral History Approach to the Gurindji Walk-Off', *Aboriginal History* 98 (2000), pp. 98–116.

[108] On the centrality of land occupation to the symbolism of the Embassy, see: Scalmer, *Dissent Events*, pp. 98–99.

[109] Geoffrey Stokes, 'Australian Democracy and Indigenous Self-determination, 1901–2001', in Geoffrey Brennan and Francis Castles (eds), *Australia Reshaped: 200 Years of Institutional Transformation* (Melbourne: Cambridge University Press, 2002), pp. 181–219.

empowered the formal return of land to some Aboriginal communities. In the early and middle 1990s the courts also recognized specific forms of Aboriginal land rights ('native title rights') as a matter of common law; these were regulated and ultimately restricted by subsequent government legislation. Native owners of ancestral lands now possessed a right to negotiate over access to their land and in some circumstances to be compensated for extinguishment or impairment of their land interests.[110] Still, the highly complicated mechanisms created to manage these issues have proved a confusing 'legal fog' for many claimants; independent indigenous action has sometimes been enveloped by the tangle of bureaucratic procedure.[111]

The management of conflicts over land was accompanied by a loss of political momentum. Persistent Aboriginal demands for a 'treaty' were rejected. Instead, governments sponsored a weaker movement for 'reconciliation' between black and white Australians. This attracted much public support and it helped to foster a wider recognition of indigenous identity and history. But the changes were overwhelmingly symbolic rather than practical, and from the later 1990s a new conservative government withdrew support; the structures of continuing Aboriginal oppression remain mostly undisturbed.[112] Overall, the renewed struggle of indigenous peoples brought marginal change, partial recognition and great disappointment: the limits of the social movement were as evident as its possibilities.

EXHAUSTION?

By the last decades of the twentieth century, the sense of containment and exhaustion was common. Like Indigenous and environmental campaigns, movements for gender and sexual equality were also rapidly constrained.

[110] The decisions of the High Court ('Mabo' and 'Wik') required legislative clarification of the means by which Aboriginal people might claim 'native title' without recourse to the courts, as well as the circumstances under which 'native title' might be extinguished. To this end, a Labor government drafted and passed a 'Native Title Act' (1993). Amendments pursued by a later conservative government, and passed in 1998, strongly restricted Aboriginal rights. Legal authorities have argued that these amendments 'may have so limited' Aboriginal rights as to 'discount the fairness of agreements reached'. See: Richard H. Bartlett, *Native Title in Australia* (Sydney: Butterworths, 2000), p. 62. On the broader conflicts and issues: Peter H. Russell, *Recognising Aboriginal Title: The Mabo Case and Indigenous Resistance to English-Settler Colonialism* (Sydney: University of New South Wales Press, 2006).

[111] Russell, *Recognising Aboriginal Title*, p. 312.

[112] Damien Short, *Reconciliation and Colonial Power: Indigenous Rights in Australia* (Aldershot: Ashgate, 2008).

In the late 1960s and early 1970s, activists sought to remake the family, reorganize the economy and reshape the meanings of gender. But these utopian visions soon gave way to close bargains over law and bureaucratic routine. The 'femocrat' became the leading figure of the feminist movement; a gay subculture was consolidated in the major cities; state programmes were established to recognize health and social needs. A precocious challenge was succeeded by an unsteady persistence.[113]

Across the social movements of modern Australia, aspirations for a new kind of life were supplanted by compromise and increasing disappointment. The state's recognition of insurgent demands also imposed a regulation and limitation that was ultimately constrictive. Partial acceptance and policing of social movements undercut much of their radical energy; over time, it threatened their independence and even their health. It thereby left victories open to diminution and even reversal.

If these tensions were undeniably long-standing, then the economic pressures of the third quarter of the twentieth century brought them to an unexpected pitch. As in many other Western societies, the novel problem of stagflation emerged at this time, and its resistance to customary responses encouraged a rejection of Keynesian orthodoxy.[114] Business and its propagandists were the first to publicize neoliberal ideas, but the major political parties and the bureaucracy soon embraced them, too.[115] Neoliberalism did not develop into a popular movement, and most Australians did not support policies of deregulation and privatization. Nonetheless, the use of state power to promote market relations rather than citizens' rights disturbed the framework of social movement campaigning.

---

[113] On the retreat from women's liberation: Jean Curthoys, *Feminist Amnesia: the wake of women's liberation* (London and New York: Routledge, 1997). On the action of 'femocrats': Anna Yeatman, *Bureaucrats, Technocrats, Femocrats: Essays on the Contemporary Australian State* (Sydney: Allen and Unwin, 1990). On gay and lesbian activism: Graham Willett, *Living Out Loud: A History of Gay and Lesbian Activism in Australia* (St. Leonards, NSW: Allen and Unwin, 2000).

[114] The broad dimensions of these shifts are wonderfully captured in Wolfgang Streeck, 'The Crises of Democratic Capitalism', *New Left Review* 71 (2011), pp. 5–29.

[115] On the work of propagandists, see: Marian Sawer and Barry Hindess (eds), *Us and Them: anti-elitism in Australia* (Perth: API Network, 2004); Nathan Hollier (ed.), *Ruling Australia: the Power, Politics and Privilege of the New Ruling Class* (Melbourne: Australian Scholarly Publishing, 2004). On the bureaucracy: Michael Pusey, *Economic Rationalism in Canberra: a Nation-Building State Changes its Mind* (Cambridge and Melbourne: Cambridge University Press, 2004).

Labor governments were the first to introduce neoliberal policies over the years 1983–1996. Labor sought to combine an extension of the market with continuing closeness with the most powerful social movement organizations, particularly the trade unions. These arrangements ensured that some social protections were retained, and that a logic of incorporation prevailed. Only the election of a succession of conservative governments from 1996 broke decisively with the past. The conservative parties were more strongly committed to the value of markets and much more hostile to the cultural recognition of gender, sexuality, race and nature. Social policies were reorganized to more strongly favour the heterosexual family; industrial rights were curtailed; the strongest opponents of the new policies faced frontal attack.[116]

Responses varied. Some social movements, including many of the leading green and welfare organizations, attempted to demonstrate their acceptance of market mechanisms, and their capacity to work with business.[117] Others, especially the trade unions, more directly confronted the government's priorities.[118] Oppositional voices did not disappear: fresh protests were launched; networks of movement education and solidarity survived. As elsewhere, a 'global justice movement' emerged to contest the apparent inevitability of the new ways.[119] And Australians were also prominent in international networks that used new technologies in the cause of social change.[120] But the capacity for widespread challenge did not recover; this was overwhelmingly a politics of fractured resistance rather than a moment of expansive mobilization.

[116] Carol Johnson, *Governing Change: From Keating to Howard* (St. Lucia University of Queensland Press, 2000).

[117] Timothy Doyle, 'Surviving the Gang Bang Theory of Nature: The Environment Movement during the Howard Years', *Social Movement Studies* 2 (2010), pp. 155–169.

[118] Kathy Muir, *Worth Fighting For Inside the Your Rights at Work Campaign* (Sydney: University of New South Wales Press, 2008).

[119] On Australian 'anti-globalization' protests of the 1990s: Verity Burgmann, *Power, Profit and Protest: Australian Social Movements and Globalisation* (St. Leonards, NSW: Allen and Unwin, 2003), Chap. 5.

[120] For example, Australians helped to develop the software used by the radical media group, indymedia, as noted in Graham Meikle, *Future Active: Media Activism and the internet* (Annandale, NSW: Pluto Press, 2002). Julian Assange was one of a series of hackers who used computing skills to attack governments and corporations, and he later turned these skills to the WikiLeaks project. See: Julian Assange, *Julian Assange: The Unauthorised Autobiography* (Melbourne: Text Publishing, 2011).

The greatest vitality and force was evident on the right. The growth of immigration from Asia and the ceding of even limited indigenous rights had disturbed many Australians. A Liberal Party candidate, subsequently disendorsed, eventually vented the unexpressed disquiet. Pauline Hanson, formerly the owner of a fish-and-chip shop, was elected to national parliament in 1996 with the largest swing in the country. Her maiden speech prophesied that Australia was in danger of being 'swamped by Asians'. Widely publicized by talk radio and tabloid newspapers, it helped to launch a political insurgency.[121] Hanson formed a new party, but the energy and controversy exceeded the bounds of routine electoral politics. The new organization was launched with a series of mass rallies across the country. These developed into sites of intense opposition, sometimes violent, and the cause of further contention.[122] It was an inversion of the patterns of earlier decades. Now a movement of the right inflamed alarm from moderates and faced legal prosecution. This was not simply an attempt to hold back the energies of the left, as evident in the anti-socialist campaigns of previous decades; it was a more ambitious attempt to reshape Australia. Though maligned by the major parties and briefly imprisoned for violation of electoral laws, Hanson's rejection of those seeking asylum soon became common policy. A strident and racialized nationalism survived her personal eclipse, too.

The change in political momentum from left to right is not the only dissonance with earlier years. A profound change is also evident in the relative prominence of social movements within the Australian polity. The colonies and the Commonwealth were unusual for the precocious mobilization of movements and for their enduring, if imperfect recognition in the political system. The antipodes were once renowned as a site of social experiment.[123] Over the twentieth century these particularities became less remarkable, and the status of social laboratory was gradually relinquished. There now appears little notable difference between the social movements of Australia and those emerging in other industrialized countries; cer-

---

[121] Sean Scalmer, 'The Production of a Founding Event: Pauline Hanson's Maiden Parliamentary Speech', *Theory and Event* 3 (1999), available at: http://muse.jhu.edu/journals/theory_and_event/toc/tae3.2.html.

[122] Sean Scalmer, 'From Contestation to Autonomy: The Staging and Framing of Anti-Hanson Contention', *Australian Journal of Politics and History* 2 (2001), pp. 209–224.

[123] New Zealand, in fact, represented the most advanced liberal experiments of these years, and they were also most fully elaborated by a New Zealander: William Pember Reeves, *State Experiments in Australia and New Zealand* (London: Grant Richards, 1902).

tainly, they exert no greater influence. Australia is a 'movement society' in which protest plays an important but mostly routine part in political life.[124] Global movements evident elsewhere also appear in the southern land. Though the product of a distinctive history, the social movement now appears to occupy an increasingly common place.

This is an historical change of still uncertain scope. Looking back over two centuries, the Australian state and the social movement shared a history of conflict and consolidation. The settler–colonial state shaped the emergence of the social movement; the mobilization of collective campaigns drove the adaptation, reform and extension of state power; government regulation both incited and constrained the social movement as a political form. But the historical expansion of state responsibilities has recently been challenged by the promotion of market relations. And highly incorporated social movements have not always responded successfully to these altered conditions. Australian history discloses the significance of a state–movement dialectic. But the current era of neoliberal globalization raises new questions of both sides of this now venerable relationship.

ACKNOWLEDGEMENTS

My thanks to Verity Burgmann, Terry Irving, Stuart Macintyre and participants at the University of Bochum conference in September 2012 for comments on an earlier draft. Deep thanks also to the editors.

FURTHER READINGS

There are good historical studies of most of the major Australian social movements. Labour's history is covered in the long-running journal, *Labour History* and many individual works. The best synthetic study is probably still: R.W. Connell and T.H. Irving, *Class Structure in Australian History* (Melbourne: Longman Cheshire, 1992). For book-length surveys of the history of the environmental movement: Drew Hutton and Libby Connors, *A History of the Australian Environmental Movement* (Melbourne: Cambridge University Press, 1999); feminism: Marilyn Lake, *Getting Equal: The history of Australian Feminism* (St. Leonards: Allen &

---

[124] On the notion of a 'movement society': David S. Meyer and Sidney G. Tarrow, *The Social Movement Society: Contentious Politics for a New Century* (Lanham, MD: Rowman & Littlefield, 1998).

Unwin, 1999). The history of the Aboriginal rights movement is examined in: John Maynard, *Fight for Liberty and Freedom: The Origins of Australian Aboriginal Activism* (Canberra: Aboriginal Studies Press, 2007) and Jennifer Clark, *Aborigines and Activism: Race, Aborigines and the Coming of the Sixties to Australia* (Crawley, WA: University of Western Australia Press, 2008), among other works. The best synoptic historical survey of contemporary movements is: Verity Burgmann, *Power, Profit and Protest: Australian social Movements and Globalisation* (St. Leonards, NSW: Allen and Unwin, 2003), but see also: Sarah Maddison and Sean Scalmer, *Activist Wisdom: Practical Knowledge and Creative Tension in Social Movements* (Sydney: University of New South Wales Press, 2006). The most sustained attempts to apply social-movement concepts to detailed historical study of protest cycles are Terry Irving's study of nineteenth century democratization: Terry Irving, *The Southern Tree of Liberty: The Democratic Movement in New South Wales before 1856* (Annandale: Federation Press, 2006) and Sean Scalmer's examination of protest movements since the 1960s: *Dissent Events: Protest, the media and the political gimmick in Australia,* (Sydney: University of New South Wales Press, 2002).

PART III

Social Movements in Transnational Historical Perspective

From Cultural Wars to the Crisis of Humanity: Moral Movements in the Modern Age

Alexandra Przyrembel

INTRODUCTION

In their *Communist Manifesto* (1848) Karl Marx and Friedrich Engels polemicized against the members of the 'bourgeoisie' who were 'desirous of redressing social grievances, in order to secure the continued existence of bourgeois society'.[1] It was these individuals—the 'economists, philanthropists, humanitarians, improvers of the condition of the working class, organizers of charity, members of societies for the prevention of cruelty to animals, temperance fanatics, hole-and-corner reformers of every imaginable kind'—who shaped global aid cultures in the Modern Age.[2] The history of these men and women, the transnational networks in which they operated, their moral agenda as well as their specific practices of aid

[1] Karl Marx and Friedrich Engels, *The Communist Manifesto.* From the English edition, ed. Friedrich Engels. Downloaded June 11, 2013: http://www.marxists.org/archive/marx/works/1848/communist-manifesto/.
[2] Ibid.

A. Przyrembel (✉)
Historical Institute, University of Hagen, Hagen, Germany

© The Author(s) 2017
S. Berger, H. Nehring (eds.), *The History of Social Movements in Global Perspective*, DOI 10.1057/978-1-137-30427-8_13

in and outside of Europe is the topic of this chapter. Although Marx and Engels accurately observed a peculiar obsession which motivated much of early humanitarian action through their social practice of providing aid, thousands of men and women implemented a new sentiment: the culture of compassion. These historical agents who belonged to the bourgeoisie or, very often, to the aristocracy founded a broad range of different organizations and associations that operated on both global and local levels: Missionary organizations, anti-slavery associations, statistical societies, as well as Societies for the Prevention of Cruelty to Animals. Ironically—at least from the perspective of Marx and Engels—humanitarian practices of these 'hole-and-corner-reformers', and not Marxism, reverberated as accepted social movements in the colours of 'development', 'aid' and 'animal rights' until the twenty-first century.

In contrast to more recent literature on humanitarianism, which understands 'moral sentiments' as an 'essential force in contemporary politics',[3] this chapter shows that moral sentiments and the *making* of social movements were intertwined since the mid-nineteenth century. In spite of a long and lasting history of moral movements from the Middle Ages through the twenty-first century,[4] the nineteenth and early twentieth centuries are of particular interest here; since it was in this period that moral organizations originated and flourished with an unprecedented intensity. From the regulation of drinking and living habits, to the organization of leisure and the control of work, these international associations addressed almost every aspect of daily life.[5]

---

[3] Didier Fassin, *Humanitarian Reason: A Moral History of the Present* (Berkeley: University of California Press, 2011), p. 1; Didier Fassin, 'Toward A Critical Moral Anthropology', in Didier Fassin (ed.), *A Companion to Moral Anthropology* (Oxford: Wiley-Blackwell, 2012), pp. 1–17.

[4] Adam J. Davis and Bertrand Taithe, 'From the Purse and the Heart: Exploring Charity, Humanitarianism and Human Rights in France', *French Historical Studies* 3 (2011), pp. 413–432.

[5] Particularly, but not exclusively Protestants targeted at those whom they perceived as 'morally depraved'. At the end of the nineteenth century members of the Swiss upper classes initiated a network of local 'Cross' associations—besides the familiar manifestations of the movement such as the temperance movement, the White Cross, for instance, aimed at combating moral depravity of the young, whereas the Green Cross movement was initiated to ban the use of tobacco. David Thomas and Janick M. Schaufelbuehl, 'Swiss Conservatives and the Struggle for the Abolition of Slavery at the End of the Nineteenth Century', *Itinerario* 2 (2010), pp. 87–103, p. 93.

This chapter argues that the bourgeois men and women who built up moral movements during the nineteenth century established lasting narratives and social practices—most notably the idea of *being* compassionate by actually practising aid work. It is this social and cultural practice of providing aid which continues to act as the driving force behind moral movements, even today. These historical protagonists articulated the immediate need for action by building up social institutions such as asylum homes, schools and medical institutions and through their actions on the streets in the urban centres of the European metropolis—whether it be in Paris, London or Berlin. This hypothesis neither implies that those historical agents—missionary organizations, national Red Cross movements and philanthropic associations which operated in the urban slums—were aware of their involvement in a larger moral movement, nor that they even shared the same moral principles. Quite the opposite seems to be true: The pejorative use of the term 'humanitarian' even at the beginning of the twentieth century indicates that this term was initially not a positive marker of social distinction.[6] These historical agents who, according to early scholarship, represented the 'social conscience of Europe' indeed followed a broad range of motives and developed distinct social practices.[7] In spite of this heterogeneity, the concept of moral uplifting did motivate the emerging social action, even if it never merged into one coherent social movement.

In the language of William Booth (1829–1912), founder of the Salvation Army, only 'crusades' would help to overcome modern decay: 'The general wreck' of humanity 'has shattered and disorganized the whole man'.[8] In short, moral organizations shared the belief that it was possible to 'revise the existing world order from within'.[9] This 'revision' is connected with a transformation of the self—expressions such as 'rescu-

---

[6] See: Anonymous, 'Humanitarians', in Cambridge University (ed.), *The Encyclopaedia Britannica: A Dictionary of Arts, Sciences, Literature and General Information*, 11th edn (Cambridge: Cambridge University Press, 1910).

[7] Francis S. L. Lyons, *Internationalism in Europe, 1815–1914* (Leydon: Sythoff, 1963), p. 264.

[8] William Booth, *In Darkest England and the Way out* (London: Funk & Wagnalls, 1890). Chapter 5 is entitled 'More Crusades' and is dedicated to slum work and the battle against drinking. See also Alexandra Przyrembel, *Verbote und Geheimnisse. Das Tabu und die Genese der europäischen Moderne* (Frankfurt/Main: Campus Verlag, 2011).

[9] Sebastian Conrad, Sebastian and Dominic Sachsenmaier, 'Introduction: Competing Visions of World Order: Global Moments and Movements, 1880s and 1930', in Sebastian Conrad and Dominic Sachsenmaier (eds), *Competing Visions of World Order. Global Moments and Movements, 1880s–1930s* (Basingstoke: Palgrave Macmillan, 2007), pp. 1–25, p. 11.

ing', 'civilizing' and 'improving' clearly indicate the necessity of an outer and inner transformation.[10] The case of the Salvation Army situated with its uniforms, brass bands and popularized Protestantism clearly on the margins of the spectrum of moral movements represents the entanglement of the attempts to 'civilize' the 'heathen' populations within and outside Europe through moral movements.

Organizations designed for moral uplift fought their battles during the nineteenth century in various *cultural wars* embedded in different national or local projects such as rescue work for wounded soldiers or efforts to improve the quality of life for the urban population—most notably in the form of improved working conditions.[11] These battles may not have generated one coherent social organization, but they did attract thousands of local activists who called for action. Their activities reso-nated in different contexts and even shaped public discourses on specific moral questions. Despite the heterogeneity of their aim, moral move-ments did consistently use the mass communication media in innovative ways.

In the first part of this chapter, I outline some of the major sites where such cultural battles were fought during the nineteenth century. Although most of the associations discussed operated within transnational networks and very often attempted to implement their agenda outside Europe, they propagated *Western* conceptions of civilization. During the twentieth cen-tury new historical agents entered the scene, connecting moral debates around a vague concept of responsibility, thus committing themselves to a general 'discourse of humanity'.[12]

---

[10] Michael Mann, '"Torchbearers upon the Path of Progress"': Britain's Ideology of a "Moral and Material Progress" in India: An Introductory Essay', in Harald Fischer-Tiné and Michael Mann (eds), *Colonialism as Civilizing Mission: Cultural Ideology in British India* (London: Anthem, 2004), pp. 1–26.

[11] Ian R. Tyrrell, *Reforming the World: The Creation of America's Moral Empire* (Princeton, NJ: Princeton University Press, 2010), p. 3.

[12] Michael N. Barnett, *Empire of Humanity: A History of Humanitarianism.* (Ithaca, NY: Cornell University Press, 2011), p. 94.

CULTURAL WARS AND INNER IMPROVEMENT: MORAL MOVEMENTS IN THE MAKING DURING THE NINETEENTH CENTURY

The nineteenth century was a period of intensified globalization, with processes of global distribution accelerating rapidly in the late century. This trend holds true for religious as much as for economic, cultural, or political movements.[13] International organizations were the most visible result of such a development. Existing transnational networks were confirmed and formalized at international conferences, exhibitions and through periodicals. The sheer number of conferences that took place is astonishing—numbering approximately 3,000 between 1840 and 1914.[14] More than 500 international organizations were created in the long nineteenth century, mainly supported by non-governmental institutions. The majority remained active until mid-twentieth century. However, the creation and activity of non-governmental organizations was particularly intense after the turn of the twentieth century—the majority being initiated before World War I.[15] In spite of manifesting a broad range of themes, the nineteenth century was deeply shaped by a 'humanitarian impulse'.[16] International organizations such as the Red Cross, local associations and individuals sought to ameliorate living conditions among populations both within and outside Europe. In short, the vast majority of civic and personal initiatives addressed moral issues as a mean of remedying 'the suffering of others', both at home and abroad.[17]

---

[13] Christopher A. Bayly, *The Birth of the Modern World, 1780–1914. Global Connections and Comparisons* (Oxford: Blackwell Publishing, 2004); Jürgen Osterhammel, *Die Verwandlung der Welt. Eine Geschichte des 19. Jahrhunderts*, 2nd edn (München: C.H. Beck, 2009); Jürgen Osterhammel, *Transformation of the World: A Global History of the Nineteenth Century* (Princeton: Princeton University Press, 2014).

[14] Lyons, *Internationalism in Europe*, p. 12.

[15] According to Lyons, 466 international non-governmental organizations were created from 1815 to 1914, 243 during the years 1905 to 1914. In the same time governments founded only 37 organizations, their activities remained stable during that time. At mid-twentieth century 191 non-governmental organizations remained active, compared with 20 governmental organizations (see the table in Lyons, *Internationalism in Europe*, pp. 263–269, 14). In spite of a recent trend among historians to analyse international institutions, the Irish historian Lyons provided a very important overview of international networks in Europe.

[16] See part IV 'The Humanitarian Impulse', in Lyons, *Internationalism in Europe*, pp. 263–308.

[17] Fassin, *Humanitarian Reason*, p. 1.

Despite the fact that claims for moral change did not foster a coherent social movement, certain aims generated the formation of associations and in some cases even the mobilization of masses. Three tropes framed a majority of the moral action undertaken by Europeans in the nineteenth century: the battle against slavery, care for victims of war and the 'improvement' of the working population. These associations developed new social practices of aid as well as new narrative strategies to promote their arguments. As a consequence of increased interest in processes of globalization, all of these fields of activity have generated a current vast literature.[18]

Slavery and the Abolition Movement

The abolition of slave trade was one of the most widely contested fields of moral intervention in the long nineteenth century.[19] The origins of the movement can be traced back to the eighteenth century. The era of Enlightenment had witnessed an explosion of the slave trade. Most continental European intellectuals did not make a strong or consistent case against slavery: in his lectures on the philosophy of history, Georg Friedrich Hegel pleaded for its 'gradual' end, asserting that man had to 'mature' to use his freedom.[20] However, in contrast to the prevailing philosophical discourse, in Great Britain anti-slavery sentiments 'became an emblem of national virtue'.[21] New actors such as the Quakers publicly campaigned against the slave trade. Throughout the British Dominions, associations such as the Society for the Abolition of the Slave Trade and the Society for the Mitigation and Gradual Abolition of Slavery (later the British and Foreign Anti-Slavery Society)—formed in 1787 and 1823

[18] Osterhammel, *Verwandlung*, pp. 1188–1213.

[19] The literature on the abolition movement and slavery is vast. For an overview see Seymour Drescher, *Abolition: A History of Slavery and Anti-Slavery* (Cambridge: Cambridge University Press, 2009); Christopher L. Brown, *Moral Capital* (Chapel Hill: University of North Carolina Press, 2006), pp. 1–30. For an overview see already Lyons, *Internationalism in Europe*, pp. 286–305.

[20] "Die Sklaverei ist an und für sich ein Unrecht, denn das Wesen des Menschen ist die Freiheit, doch zu dieser muss er erst reif werden". Georg Friedrich Hegel, *Vorlesungen über die Philosophie der Geschichte* (Berlin: Duncker & Humblot, 1837), p. 37f., see Andreas Eckert, 'Aufklärung, Sklaverei and Abolition', *Geschichte und Gesellschaft. Sonderheft Die Aufklärung und ihre Weltwirkung* 23 (2010), pp. 243–262, p. 245.

[21] Linda Colley, *Britons: Forging the Nation: 1707–1837* (New Haven, CT:Yale University. Press, 1992), p. 354.

respectively—fostered anti-slavery activities, albeit membership of the 1823 society comprised only five Lords and 14 members of the House of Commons.[22] In 1783, Quakers submitted the first public petition against the slave trade, after which more interventions followed. In 1840, a Quaker organized the world's first anti-slavery convention.[23,24] While these early activists operated independently of within networks, abolitionists continually expanded their communication channels through new types of media and discussion forums. Campaigns against slavery sought to mobilize an increasingly aware public: more than 60,000 individuals signed a petition against slavery in 1788.[25] Women also became increasingly engaged in the movement; as early as 1788, their signatures made up 10% of the total on anti-slavery resolutions.[26] Within 30 years, women had emerged as a visible factor in the abolition movement. While the aforementioned Society for the Abolition of Slave Trade had an exclusively male membership, more and more women claimed their voice in public space.[27] In contrast to Hegel's ambivalent remarks more than a decade earlier, Quaker Elizabeth Heyrick positioned herself openly against any form of slavery. As early as 1824, she called for an 'immediate, not gradual abolition'.[28] She favoured a 'temporary feudal' system as a transitional period between slave and waged labour.[29] Heyrick took responsibility both as leader of the Leicester Ladies' Anti-Slavery Society and as district treasurer of the Anti-Slavery Society of Birmingham,[30] and, in addition, produced about 20 pamphlets dealing not only with aboli-

---

[22] William A. Green, *British Slave Emancipation. The Sugar Colonies and the Great Experiment 1830–1865* (Oxford: Clarendon, 1992).

[23] Douglas Maynard, 'The World's Anti-Slavery Convention of 1840', *The Mississippi Valley Historical Review* (1960), pp. 452–471.

[24] Drescher, *Abolition*.

[25] Ibid.

[26] Peter van der Veer, *Imperial Encounters: Religion and Modernity in India and Britain* (Princeton, NJ: Princeton University Press, 2001).

[27] Clara Midgley, *Women Against Slavery. The British Campaigns, 1780–1870* (London: Routledge, 1992), p. 15.

[28] Elizabeth Heyrick, *Immediate, not Gradual Abolition: or, An Inquiry into the Shortest, Safest, and most Effectual Means of Getting Rid of West Indian Slavery* (Philadelphia: Published by the Philadelphia A. S. Society, 1837).

[29] *Report of the Sheffield Female Anti-Slavery Society* (Sheffield: J. Blackwell, 1827), here Midgley, *Women Against Slavery*, p. 108.

[30] Ibid., p. 107.

tion, but also with animal rights. She also aimed at improving living conditions for the working population.[31]

Her 1824 pamphlet *Immediate, not Gradual Abolition* circulated among British and American Quakers[32] and asserted that 'this GRADUAL ABOLITION, has been the grand marplot of human virtue and happiness; the very master-piece of satanic policy.'[33] Her manifesto condemned the 'perpetuation of Slavery' in the West Indian colonies by appealing to the conscience:

> The perpetuation of Slavery in our West India colonies, is not an abstract question, to be settled between the Government and the Planters—it is a question in which we are *all* implicated; we are all guilty, (with shame and compunction let us admit the opprobrious truth,) of supporting and perpetuating slavery.[34]

The success of the British abolition movement can be traced back to the integration of women in the movement, to the publicity of its campaigns and to the boycott of goods. It was through such strategies that British abolition movements reached the masses.

In contrast to this public outreach, French and German abolitionist movements remained tied to their religious background. Inspired by the Pères Blancs—a missionary organization founded in 1867 by cardinal Charles Martial Allemand Lavigerie (1825–1892)—the Catholic antislavery movement spread all over Europe, even in those countries without overseas colonies. In Salzburg, women of the local aristocracy founded the Austrian Movement for the Liberation of Slaves.[35] The German antislavery movement having ties to the French catholic missionary movement reached its peak in the late nineteenth century[36] and ultimately

---

[31] Jennifer Rycenga, 'A Greater Awakening: Women's Intellect as a Factor in Early Abolitionist Movements, 1824–1834', *Journal of Feminist Studies in Religion* 2 (2005), pp. 31–59.

[32] Ibid., p. 41.

[33] Heyrick, *Immediate, not Gradual Abolition*, p. 11.

[34] Ibid., p. 4.

[35] 'Österreichischer Verein zur Befreiung der Sklaven in Africa', see Horst Gründer, '"Gott will es". Eine Kreuzzugsbewegung am Ende des 19. Jahrhunderts', *Geschichte in Wissenschaft und Unterricht* 4 (1977), pp. 210–224, p. 212.

[36] Gründer, '"Gott will es"', pp. 210–224; Horst Gründer, *Christliche Heilsbotschaft und weltliche Macht. Studien zum Verhältnis von Mission und Kolonialismus. Gesammelte Aufsätze* (Münster: LIT Verlag Münster, 2004).

evolved into one of the most powerful sites of the movement. Though based in Cologne, the German movement already had 500 sub-divisions by 1889. Pamphlets entitled 'It is God's will' and 'Humanus' reached mass circulation.[37] At the same time, Protestants were debating how they could possibly intervene against Catholic anti-slavery activities, which they perceived as a threat. Protestant missionary organizations such as the Bremen-based Northern Missionary Organization intervened actively in the 1860s against slavery by buying enslaved children in Togo.[38] At a conference in 1892 aiming at building up a Protestant African association, Friedrich von Bodelschwingh—one of the leading figures of the movement—argued that 'mission, colonization, [and] humanity' were the guiding principles of any anti-slavery movement. Through participant discussions on 'colonial' and 'humanitarian' vs. 'genuine religious' arguments to end slavery, this conference emphasized the degree of scepticism articulated by religious groups towards the motives of secular anti-slavery organizations.[39]

Throughout the nineteenth century, Western debates on slavery and abolition movement were inherently paradoxical, with the controversy enduring although slavery was prohibited in a number of states. In 1807, the British parliament prohibited the trading of slaves, and British possession of slaves was outlawed entirely in 1833. A year later, the final revision of the law lead to the immediate emancipation of 800,000 slaves who were 'called from social death to life'.[40] Uruguay (1842), France (1848), Argentina (1853) and Peru (1854) followed.[41] In Germany however, anti-slavery legislation was not passed until 1895.[42] Early debates in terms of international law can be traced back to the year 1815 when the Congress of Vienna formulated a humanitarian critique of slavery, though no defini-

---

[37] Gründer, '"Gott will es"', p. 214.

[38] Martin Pabst, *Mission und Kolonialpolitik: Die Norddeutsche Missionsgesellschaft an der Goldküste und in Togo bis zum Ausbruch des Ersten Weltkrieges* (München: Verlagsgemeinschaft ANARCHE, 1988).

[39] See the confidential minutes from 20 June 1892. The speech of the Bodelschwingh is summarized by the unknown author of the Berlin Missionary Organization with some irony, see *Berliner Missionsgesellschaft*. Briefe und Manuskripte der evangelischen Mission in Ostafrika, besonders die Stationen Kisserawe, Maneromango und Daressalam, 1890–1917, BMW 1/6102, Landeskirchenarchiv Berlin, ff. 64–65.

[40] Drescher, *Abolition*, p. 265.

[41] Lyons, *Internationalism in Europe*.

[42] See "Gesetz betreffend die Bestrafung des Sklavenraubes und des Sklavenhandels" 28 July 1895 (Reichsgesetzblatt I p. 425).

tive date for its abolition was issued. The Brussels General Act of 1890, in which the major European nations as well as the Ottoman Empire participated, was one major step in a transnational solution to the slave trade. However, it placed the civilizing mission at its centre.[43] In the nineteenth century, the enduring criticism of the slave trade provoked controversies regarding the actual impact of 'moral' arguments in contrast to 'economic' factors on anti-slavery legislation.[44]

In his early study *Capitalism and Slavery* (1944), Eric Williams challenged the moral dimensions of the abolition movement by putting economic rather than ethical forces at the centre of his interpretation. He claimed that the abolitionist movement took a stand against slavery at a moment when the slave trade had lost its economic value.[45] Seymour Drescher, who published extensively on the abolition movement, emphasized in his *Econocide* (1977) that slavery was in terms of 'both capital value and of overseas trade [...] expanding not declining.'[46] In his later work, he focused on the impact of the British abolition movement in the 1830s, arguing that it had not only enforced anti-slavery legislation, but also reached a broader public.[47] The emergence of anti-slavery associations emphasized the role of religious motives in defining moral values—particularly in the British and American context, where more and more women became involved in the movement.

[43] Helmut Berding, 'Die Ächtung des Sklavenhandels auf dem Wiener Kongreß 1814/15', *Historische Zeitschrift* 219 (1974), pp. 265–289, here p. 288. Eric D. Weitz, 'From the Vienna to the Paris System: International Politics and the Entangled Histories of Human Rights, Forced Deportations and Civilizing Missions', *American Historical Review* 5 (2008), pp. 1313–1343.

[44] Joseph E. Inikori, *Africans and the Industrial Revolution in England. A Study in International Trade and Economic Development* (Cambridge: Cambridge University Press, 2002).

[45] Eric Williams, *Capitalism and Slavery* (Chapel Hill: University of North Carolina Press, 1994 [1944]). A detailed account of his argument which is related to British sugar production can be found in Eckert, 'Aufklärung, Sklaverei and Abolition', 250 and Christopher L. Brown, *Moral Capital: Foundations of British Abolitionism* (Chapel Hill: University of North Carolina Press, 2006), p. 13.

[46] Seymour Drescher, Seymour, *Econocide. British Slavery in the Age of Abolition* (Pittsburgh, PA: University of Pittsburgh Press 1977), here: Eckert, '"Aufklärung, Sklaverei and Abolition"', p. 251.

[47] See Chaps. 8 and 9, in Drescher, *Abolition*, pp. 205–266.

Battlefields and the Wounded Soldier

In 1862, Henry Dunant (1828–1910)—one of the founders of the Red Cross movement—published a widely read pamphlet entitled *Un Souvenir de Solferino*, in which he outlined the reasons why providing aid to soldiers was a moral question. Originally addressed to a narrow circle of 400 people, the text became a publishing success and was translated into many languages.[48] In his text, Dunant gives 'universal' reasons for the necessity of building up an emergency movement that assists victims of war: First, describing vividly the physical pain of wounded soldiers, the author illustrates graphically the horrors of war. Having himself witnessed the Italo–Austrian War in 1859, which claimed more than 40,000 victims, he notes that this war 'is a sheer butchery'.[49] Second, he observes the emergence of a new sentiment—that of the 'compassionate women'—whose 'quiet self-sacrifice made little of fatigue and horrors, and of their own devotion'.[50] Connecting the cruelty of war with the concept of bearing witnessing and devoted practices of aid, Dunant created a master narrative of the necessity of providing aid for soldiers as innocent victims—a sentiment that remains prominent even today.[51] However, his call for agency was by no means a general critique of war itself. For Clara Barton, *la grande dame* of the American Red Cross, the universal ethical dimension of the Red Cross movement was obvious: 'An institution of reform movement that is not selfish, must originate in the recognition of some evil that is adding to the sum of human suffering, or diminishing the sum of happiness.'[52]

The nineteenth century was an era of conflicts and battlefields resulting from European wars including the Crimean War (1853–1856), the Second Italian War of Independence (1859) and the Franco–Prussian War (1870–1871) and it resulted in the mobilization of emergency movements all over Europe. Later, Red Cross and Red Crescent movements spread

---

[48] Bertrand Thaite, 'Horror, Abjection and Compassion: From Dunant to Compassion Fatigue', *New Formations* 62 (2007), pp. 123–136, p. 135.

[49] Henry Dunant, *A Memory of Solferino* (Geneva: International Committee of the Red Cross, 1959 [1939]), p. 19.

[50] Ibid., p. 72.

[51] Thaite, 'Horror, Abjection and Compassion'.

[52] Clara Barton, *The Red Cross: a History of this Remarkable International Movement in the Interest of Humanity* (Washington, DC: American National Red Cross, [c1898]), p. 98.

outside Europe[53] and were founded in Japan (1877), the United States (1881) and China (1904).[54] In 1863 a group of philanthropists founded the International Committee of the Red Cross in Geneva. Following its establishment, mid-nineteenth century national Red Cross movements continued to increase in number and scale. Events like the Franco–Prussian War of 1870–1871 caused a notable growth in membership as well as an increase in financial resources.[55]

The global history of emergency movements has yet to be written. It is my aim to provide an overview of the movement's formative years while also concentrating on a small segment of its activities within Europe. Women played a crucial role in setting up national Red Cross movements in France, Great Britain and the German states. Due to the role they played in national wars, the role of members as *patriotic caregivers* was, in ethical and moral terms, more than ambivalent, not least because national Red Cross movements were intertwined with the imperial projects of their home states.

The German case illustrates the impact of women on the emerging organizations.[56] During the War of Liberation (1813–1815), predominantly women founded associations to aid victims of war.[57] Even though this activity would later dissolve to a great extent, women particularly belonging to the aristocracy were involved in building up Red Cross movements all over Europe. In the German states, associations exclusively for women such as the *Vaterländische Frauenverein* formed the infrastructure for Red Cross movements. Shortly after its formation, this patriotic women's organization had expanded to include 290 sub-divisions and more

---

[53] Jonathan Benthall and Jérôme Bellion-Jourdan, *The Charitable Crescent: Politics of Aid in the Muslim World* (London, New York: Palgrave Macmillan, 2009).

[54] Barton, *The Red Cross*; Marian M Jones, *The American Red Cross from Clara Barton to the New Deal* (Baltimore, MD: Johns Hopkins University Press, 2013). Julia Irwin, *Making the World Safe: The American Red Cross and a Nation's Humanitarian Awakening* (New York: Oxford University Press, 2013).

[55] For a general development of the French movement from the years 1875 to 1914 see the table 'Resources and Materials', in Rachel Chrastil, 'The French Cross, War Readiness, and Civil Society, 1866–1914', *French Historical Studies* 3 (2008), pp. 445–476, p. 446.

[56] Anonymous, *Handbuch der deutschen Frauenvereine unter dem Rothen Kreuz* (Berlin: Carl Heymann's Verlag, 1881).

[57] Dieter Riesenberger, *Das Deutsche Rote Kreuz: Eine Geschichte 1864–1990* (Paderborn: Ferdinand Schöningh Verlag, 2002), p. 11.

than 21,500 members.[58] The list of members included the *haute volée* of German aristocracy, and among the sponsors was Augusta—Queen of Prussia and later Empress of the unified German state.[59] In France, too, women belonging to conservative circles dominated the Committee of the Red Cross.[60] Although not established until 1888, the French Red Cross movement grew rapidly over the course of a few decades. By 1914, it consisted of more than 1,000 local committees, 160,000 members and 21,500 nurses.[61]

Beginning with the Moroccan crisis at the commencement of the twentieth century, the French Red Cross movement contributed to imperial projects for the first time by sending trained nurses abroad.[62] Similarly, the British Red Cross movement was also soon involved in imperial projects, the Boer War (1899–1902), for example.[63] The latter case is an interesting example of the greater involvement of national Red Cross movements in imperial wars. On both sides of the South African War, national relief organizations—such as the Boer *Het Transvaalsche Roode Kruis* (the Transvaal Red Cross Society) and *Het Oranje Vrijstaatsche Ambulance* (the Red Cross Organization in the Orange Republic)—were founded.[64] However, the war also mobilized visitors to South Africa like Gandhi and other professionals from India.[65] In addition to the recruitment of new members, the British organization also raised funding during the South African War by acquiring new donors.[66] The British Red Cross movement presented itself as the 'foremost patriotic aid society of the day' and numerous autobiographies of nurses document this patriotic spirit as well as an 'increasingly feminised identity'.[67]

---

[58] Riesenberer, *Das Deutsche Rote Kreuz*, p. 49.

[59] Ibid.

[60] Rachel Chrastil, 'The French Cross', 460.

[61] See also Table 1 and Table 2 in, ibid., p. 446.

[62] Ibid., p. 465.

[63] Rebecca Gill, 'Networks of Concern, Boundaries of Compassion: British Relief in the South African War', *The Journal of Imperial and Commonwealth History* 5 (2012), pp. 827–844, p. 833.

[64] British Red Cross Society, Report, 7, ibid., Gill, 'Networks of Concern'

[65] Ibid., p. 833.

[66] The Central British Red Cross Committee, founded in 1899, with which the NAS cooperated raised £750,000 (ibid).

[67] Ibid., p. 834.

This patriotic spirit and entanglement with the imperialist cause is also documented in various German autobiographies. Johanna Wittum's autobiographical account *Eine Heldin vom Roten Kreuz* (*A Heroine of the Red Cross*) documents the experience she gained as a nurse of the German Red Cross. This daughter of a goldware manufacturer and member of the German *Reichstag* joined the Red Cross to serve as a nurse in the hospital in the German colony of Kamerun (Cameroon), after which she was sent to assist the Boers. As was the case for many women who were mobilized by the national Red Cross movements, she intended to serve the German colonial movement as a nurse—a professional space she perceived as typically female.[68] Wittum's autobiography illustrates various motives that attracted women to the movement, ranging from the impulse to provide 'care' in a hospital to the reaffirmation of her own racial distinctiveness against the 'otherness' of the African population. A sense of patriotism, a curiosity for the colonial project and the notion of a new public space for women deeply influenced many women of this generation.[69] Moral inclinations to provide aid were often extremely partial and, as revealed by Wittum's autobiography, shaped by racial prejudices against the colonized population—both in Cameroon and South Africa.

Working Men and Heathen Souls

The idea to morally uplift the working class on a moral basis also influenced many associations. Due to the fact that such associations were initiated predominantly by local activists rather than on a transnational or even a national level, no coherent social movement was formed. Just to give some examples: Soon after its foundation in 1840, the French Catholic association *Oeuvre des pauvres malades* had visited over 10,000 families. *The Dames de la Charité*, an institution originally inspired by Vincent de Paul, was attached to the Parisian bourgeoisie.[70] The German Inner Mission Movement, originally initiated by Johann Hinrich Wichern in

---

[68] For a description of the 'black servants' see Johanna Wittum, *Eine Heldin vom Roten Kreuz*, vol. 2 (Berlin: Kameradschaft, 1912), p. 16. Johanna Wittum, *Sieben Monate im Burenkriege: Erlebnisse der ersten deutschen Ambulanz* (Freiburg: Fehsenfeld, 1901).

[69] For its meaning in the German Colonial movement see Lora Wildenthal, *German women for empire, 1884–1945* (Durham, NC: Duke University Press, 2001).

[70] From twenty founders in 1840 the association grew to 630 members in 1853, see Sarah A. Curtis, 'Charitable Ladies. Gender, Class and Religion in Mid Nineteenth-Century Paris', *Past & Present* 1 (2002), pp. 121–156, p. 129.

Hamburg, developed during the course of the nineteenth century from a small circle of awakened Protestants to a meaningful entrepreneur of social institutions.[71] Although these religious organizations did not delay processes of secularization, the associations of the German home mission movement implemented and professionalized social welfare work.[72]

In the 1830s, statistical societies developed criteria to 'measure' moral decline among the working population. The same arguments legitimized the idea of striving to morally improve working class populations, although practices to achieve such goals were not spread between organizations. A number of statistical societies throughout Britain were created in the 1830s, for instance in Manchester (1833) and in London (1834). Originally established to analyse the 'condition of mankind',[73] the statistical societies soon developed categories to morally evaluate populations. In 1837, the Manchester Statistical Society conducted a survey 'Working Population, or in a word, all those below the rank of shopkeeper', which encompassed Manchester as well as its surrounding neighbourhoods.[74] The society's agents took note of seemingly objective elements of the inhabitant lifestyle, such as the number of individuals residing in a room, their occupation and the number of children. At the same time, agents noted the number of books in the house, the quality of living conditions and whether or not a family belonged to a 'benefit society'.[75] Applying their statistical methods to other problematic issues of society like the educational system, statistical societies remained active until the end of the nineteenth century. Although they remained marginal in their local com-

---

[71] For an overview of the early Inner Mission Movement in Germany see Alexandra Przyrembel, 'The Emotional Bond of Brotherliness. Protestant Masculinity and the Local and Global Networks among Religious in the Nineteenth Century', *German History* 2 (2013), pp. 157–180.

[72] The statistic of the Inner Mission Movement (1892) gives an overview of the social activities of the Protestant associations. The appendix contains dozens of pages listing rescue homes, orphanages, asylums see Central-Ausschuß für die Innere Mission der deutschen evangelischen Kirche (eds), *Statistik der Inneren Mission der deutschen evangelischen Kirche* (Berlin: Geschäftsstelle des Central-Ausschusses für die Innere Mission, 1899), pp. 403ff.

[73] Preface *Journal of the Statistical Society of London* 1:1 (1838:5), pp. 1–5, p. 1.

[74] For the exact numbers of visited neighbourhoods see Michael J. Cullen, *The Statistical Movement in Early Victorian Britain. The Foundations of Empirical Social Research* (Hassocks: Harvester Press, 1975), p. 111.

[75] Ibid., p. 12.

munities, at least in terms of the number of members they possessed,[76] their moral arguments reverberated in seemingly different contexts. These repercussions can be traced to Friedrich Engels, the co-author of the *Communist Manifesto*.[77]

By referring to these reports in his acclaimed study *The Condition of the Working-Class in England* Engels portrays an image of constant decay that the working class has to overcome. Having investigated working class neighbourhoods, he himself witnessed seemingly unbearable living conditions. In the preface to *The Condition of the Working-Class in England,* Engels directly addresses the English working class and encourages its members to 'struggle against' their suppressors.[78] Certain elements such as housing conditions, the work ethic and an assumed sexual deviance recur in this text: 'Everywhere heaps of debris, refuse, and offal; standing pools for gutters, and a stench which alone would make it impossible for a human being in any degree civilised to live in such a district.'[79] The improvement of the working class is linked to an inner improvement, which—according to this narrative—is ultimately impossible to achieve. In spite of his outspoken plea for a revolutionary change in society, Engels perceived destitution of the working class and the 'filth' of their living conditions as almost inevitable.

Parallel to Engels' on the conditions of the working class, religious associations which aimed to ameliorate working-class conditions were being established all over Europe—in Paris, London and even Hamburg.[80] One such organization that operated on a global level was the Salvation Army. Originally founded as a grass-roots organization in London, the Salvation Army soon developed into a professional organization that established social institutions on both a global and local scale. From the 31 branches that existed in 1878, the movement grew steadily.[81] Its inter-

[76] Thirteen members initiated the Manchester Society in 1833; in 1835 40 members; and at the end of the nineteenth century 144 see Cullen, *The Statistical Movement*, p. 110, 117.

[77] Eileen Yeo, *The Contest for Social Science. Relations and Representations of Gender and Class* (London: Rivers Oram Press, 1996).

[78] The first German edition was published in 1845.

[79] Friedrich Engels, *The Condition of the Working Class in England in 1844.* With a preface written in 1892 (London: George Allen & Unwin, 1892), p. 50f.

[80] Sarah A. Curtis, *Civilizing Habits. Women Missionaries and the Revival of French Empire* (Oxford: Oxford University Press, 2010).

[81] Harald Fischer-Tiné, 'Reclaiming Savages in "Darkest England"', in Carey A. Watt and Michael Mann (eds), *Civilizing Missions in Colonial and Postcolonial South Asia. From Improvement to Development* (London and New York: Anthem Press 2011), pp. 126–164,

national expansion began in 1880 with the foundation of branches in the United States, Australia and elsewhere in Europe. In India, the Salvation Army was 'a one-man enterprise' in its initial phase, yet within twenty years, it had developed into an 'attractive partner in empire-building'.[82] In his study *In Darkest England and the Way Out* (1890) William Booth outlined programmes of social transformation. In addition to its goal of aiding the poor on a global scale, the Salvation Army set out to attack 'the evils which lie at the root of all the miseries' of modern life.[83]

The popular map found at the beginning of Colonel Booth's *In Darkest England*, portraying drowning people in the stormy sea of sin, graphically illustrates the temptations of modern life in the metropolis and beyond: among them alcohol, promiscuity and destitution. The connection of a topography of moral decay to philanthropic work is also evident in Charles Booth's famous social survey of London. In cooperation with social scientists, the entrepreneur who is not related to the cofounder of the Salvation Army categorized in the British metropolis according to the moral criteria of *Life and Labour of the People in London*. Using seven different colours—from black ('Lowest Class, vicious, semi-criminal') to yellow ('Upper-middle and upper classes')—he and his team linked the social value of the urban population to its relative income. In 1897, Booth's social investigators interviewed for example Miss Smith, a Salvation Army captain who was in charge of a slum post in Hackney Wick, London. The account of her work demonstrates graphically the impact of religious arguments on defining the urban poor: 'At Bethnal Green the people are poor because they deserve to be poor. They *do* (much emphasis) drink at B. Green. When you see them suffering you cannot help thinking it is brought on by their own sin and folly but here you think "Well poor things, they cannot help it."'[84]

Although they were figuratively fighting cultural battles in entirely different wars, the manifestations of moral movements in the nineteenth century share common key features. First, from the abolition movement to the German home mission movement, women often stood at the fore-

131, 137; Pamela J. Walker, *Pulling the Devil's Kingdom Down. The Salvation Army in Victorian Britain* (Berkeley: University of California Press, 2001).

[82] Ibid., p. 150.

[83] William Booth, *In Darkest England and the Way Out* (London: Funk&Wagnalls, 1890), p. 1.

[84] London School of Economics and Political Science (eds), Booth Collection, Book B 190, Eton Mission District, Miss Smith. Salvation Army Captain in charge of the Slum Post, 34 Mallard Street Hackney Wick (Ebd., pp. 40–47) [21.9.1897].

front of the making of a movement. Practices of aid were shaped by those female workers who used a new public space and the possibilities for professionalization. Second, in the case of the sisters of the Red Cross, as the autobiography of Joanna Wittum illustrates, this specific space was often linked to the civilizing mission.

FROM CULTURAL WARS TO MORAL CRISIS: NOTIONS OF AID AND HUMAN RIGHTS IN THE TWENTIETH CENTURY

In the twentieth century, due to the moral crisis caused by decolonization, genocides and wars, entangled conceptions of *aid* and *human rights* shaped moral action. In his book *Human Rights as Politics and Idolatry* (2001), historian and politician Michael Ignatieff argues that human rights did not become the 'lingua franca of global moral thought' until 1989.[85] The devious route of the implementation of human rights, reaching from debates at the end of the eighteenth century to their implementation in the UN charter of 1948, and intensive discussions on the topic in the second half of the twentieth century requires further exploration.[86] However, non-governmental activities concerning 'development' and human rights opened up a new dimension during the twentieth century, particularly the second half. In spite of the creation of transnational organizations like the League of Nations in 1919 and the United Nations in 1948, civic organizations remained a key factor in providing aid.[87] Again, these organizations never formed *one* coherent social movement, but in terms of their competence in using media and creating public interest, they succeeded in widely broadcasting their moral claims. Even more so than in the case of preceding moral movements, these emerging organizations operated within transnational networks and, as in the case of *Amnesty International*, emerging organizations committed themselves to a global agenda. From the broad range of organizations

[85] Michael Ignatieff, *Human Rights as Politics and Idolatry* (Princeton, NJ: Princeton University Press, 2001), p. 54.

[86] For an overview of the literature see Stefan-Ludwig Hoffmann, 'Einführung: Zur Genealogie der Menschenrechte' in Stefan-Ludwig Hoffmann (ed.), *Moralpolitik: Geschichte der Menschenrechte im 20. Jahrhundert* (Göttingen: Wallstein, 2010), pp. 7–40; Jan Eckel and Samuel Moyn (eds), *Moral für die Welt? Menschenrechtspolitik in den 1970er Jahren* (Göttingen: Vandenhoeck & Ruprecht, 2012).

[87] See Mark Mazower, *No Enchanted Palace. The End of Empire and the Ideological Origins of the United Nations* (Princeton, NJ: Princeton University Press, 2009).

that aimed to defend and extend human rights during the twentieth century, two case studies are presented here to illustrate the shift of moral arguments between the early twentieth century and the 1960s: aid efforts in the context of the Armenian Genocide and the making of Amnesty International.

Aid for Victims of Genocide: The Armenian Case in 1915 and 1916

The distribution of knowledge via new communication channels, such as the telegraph, is one of the main characteristics of processes of globalization. Surpassing transnational networks which had framed the earlier activities of the abolitionist movement, the distribution of knowledge about atrocities executed in the context of the Armenian Genocide in the years 1915 and 1916 reached a new dimension.[88] News about the atrocities against the Armenians, who resided predominantly in the territory of the Ottoman Empire, circulated from New York City to the city of Harare in Rhodesia via the channels of the news agency Reuters.[89] As moral institutions, civil organizations became visible public figures, acting as witnesses to the atrocities and as agents providing aid for Armenians attempting to flee from the acts of violence surrounding them.[90]

Missionary organizations including the American Board of Commissioners for Foreign Missions, founded in 1812, and the German Orient Mission, expressed an early fascination with missionary work in the Islamic World.[91] At the start of the twentieth century, the American Board established dozens of outposts and hundreds of smaller American repre-

---

[88] Taner Akçam, *A Shameful Act. The Armenian Genocide and the Question of Turkish Responsibility* (New York: Metropolitan Books, 2006); Donald Bloxham, *The Great Game of Genocide. Imperialism, Nationalism, and the Destruction of the Ottoman Armenians* (New York: Oxford University Press, 2005).

[89] For an overview see Donald Read, *The Power of News. The History of Reuters 1849–1989* (Oxford: Oxford University Press, 1992); J. M. Winter (ed.), *America and the Armenian Genocide of 1915* (Cambridge: Cambridge University Press, 2003).

[90] Michelle Tusan, 'Crimes against Humanity: Human Rights, the British Empire, and the Origins of the Response to the Armenian Genocide', *American Historical Review* 1 (2014), pp. 47–77.

[91] Suzanne Moranian, 'The Armenian Genocide and American Missionary Relief Effort', in J. M. Winter (ed.), *America and the Armenian Genocide of 1915* (New York: Cambridge University Press, 2003), pp. 185–213; Uwe Feigel, *Das evangelische Deutschland und Armenien. Die Armenierhilfe deutscher evangelischer Christen seit dem Ende des 19.*

sentations, located predominantly in Constantinople and administered by an estimated 150 missionaries and 800 local employees. In spite of their proclaimed goal of reaching the Muslim population first and foremost, the Christian missionary organizations were predominantly successful amongst Armenian communities due to the fact that these groups proved to already be predominantly Christian. Even after the outbreak of the First World War and later, in 1917, with the entry of the United States into the war, the American Board continued operating out of its many missionary stations. The Board not only assisted individuals seeking refuge, but also provided support to more than 150,000 survivors of the genocide in Syria.[92]

Through their proximity to the events themselves and their work in orphanages and hospitals, missionaries became crucial public witnesses to the genocide. An especially important actor in the way the Armenian Genocide was portrayed by the media was the eyewitness as a moral institution. Confronted with the radicalization of violence, missionary organizations appeared on the global stage not only as aid organizations, but also as moral voices. Members of the American Board also bore witness to crimes—as American missionary Genevieve Du Val noted in her journal, 'something terrible' and previously unimaginable lay ahead of the Armenian people.[93]

Issued in the summer of 1915 by the German Orient Mission, the 'Emergency Plea of the Orient and Islam Commission of the Evangelical Committee' clearly sought to appeal to Christian arguments. The text made an 'exceptional plea for aid needed for an indescribable hardship". It appealed to the 'compassion of the German Christians for the needs of the Armenians' and sought not to 'blame any specific party', calling the genocide 'the most terrible catastrophe known to history'. Putting it simply, the text sought 'aid for a dying people'.[94] In their monthly issue of *The Christian Orient and Mohammedan Mission*, the Orient Mission documented the events extensively. The publishers did, however, apologize to readers for their 'sporadic' reporting, claiming that this was due to

Jahrhunderts im Kontext der deutsch-türkischen Beziehungen (Göttingen: Vandenhoeck & Ruprecht, 1989).

[92] Moranian, 'The Armenian Genocide', p. 188.

[93] Ibid., p. 191.

[94] Anonym, 'Notruf der Orient- und Islam-Kommission des Deutschen Evangelischen Ausschusses. Eine außerordentliche einmalige Bitte um Hilfe für unbeschreibliches Elend', *Monatsschrift der Deutschen Orient-Mission* 4/6 (1916), pp. 9–10, p. 9.

outside censorship. Nonetheless, the paper continued to report on arrests of Armenian intellectuals, their material dispossessions and deportations.[95]

The construction of the eyewitness as a public moral figure is only one layer of the manifold dimensions of reconstructing the meaning of a moral politics of humanitarian organizations.[96] As noted by recent research on the topic, in the early 1920s, a shift took place from an early humanitarianism 'embedded in religiously driven and episodic forms of missionary activity' to more secular forms of providing aid initiated by the League of Nations.[97] However, established missionary organizations like the American Board—and, to a lesser extent, related, smaller German institutions—were able to raise funds for such aid activities.

Responsibility, Human Rights and the Making of Amnesty International

In a letter to the US branch of Amnesty International written in 1972, a member of the organization described his motivation for joining as follows: 'The world is so small and so much more interdependent today than it used to be, that it is morally right for citizens of all countries to feel responsible for possible political injustice anywhere on the globe'.[98] Amnesty International, established by lawyer Peter Benenson (1921–2005) as a one-man enterprise in 1961, had grown into a transnational organization within a few decades.[99] While it already boasted 30,000 members in 1973, more than 700,000 individuals would join in the 16 years

---

[95] Karen Jeppe, 'Das Schicksal unseres Waisenhauses im Weltkriege', *Der christliche Orient und die Muhammedaner-Mission. Monatsschrift der Deutschen Orient-Mission* 10/12 (1918), pp. 48–50.

[96] Christian Gerlach, *Extremely Violent Societies. Mass Violence in the Twentieth-century World* (Cambridge: Cambridge University Press, 2010).

[97] Keith David Watenpaugh, 'The League of Nations' Rescue of Armenian Genocide Survivors and the Making of Modern Humanitarianism. 1920–1927', *American Historical Review* 5 (2010), pp. 1315–1339.

[98] Ethel Kweskin, 'Letter to the Editor, 24 June 1972', quoted in Jan Eckel, 'Humanitarisierung der internationalen Beziehungen? Menschenrechtspolitik in den 1970er Jahren', *Geschichte und Gesellschaft* 4 (2012), pp. 603–635, p. 610.

[99] Tom Buchanan, '"The Truth Will Set You Free": The Making of Amnesty International', *Journal of Contemporary History* 4 (2002), pp. 575–597; Ann M. Clark, *Diplomacy of Conscience. Amnesty International and Changing Human Rights Norms* (Princeton, nj: Princeton University Press, 2001).

that followed.[100] Although members of the organization were predominantly female, leadership positions were not held by female members, with the exception of a few women working at Amnesty International's headquarters in London. Benenson and a group of peers comprising of lawyers, academics and social activists shaped the intellectual and organizational think-tank of Amnesty International. Like earlier moral movements, Amnesty International also carried out successful media campaigns through the use of innovative methods—one noteworthy example was their use of first-hand accounts of torture provided directly by victims.

In order to raise funds, American members of the organization hosted a variety of events—setting up musical festivals, promoting theatre performances and hosting silent vigils. Collecting accounts as well as other materials that documented torture on a global scale was a favoured strategy used to popularize Amnesty's activities. The annual reports named torture practices since the 1970s. First published in 1973, the organization's *Report on Torture* proved to be an especially successful public campaign.[101] After providing an overview of the 'Medical and Psychological Aspects of Torture' and legal practices, the booklet gave a 'world survey of torture',[102] highlighting practices carried out in sixty nations around the world. In spite of its all-embracing and fundamental approach, the *Report on Torture* clearly illustrates the limits of investigation on torture:

> It hardly needs to be said that several biases affect the availability of information. In most of the world or the famous or the wealthy are likely to be able to focus international attention on their plight once they are imprisoned and ill-treated. Only the educated—and specifically the European educated—are likely to know that an organization such as Amnesty International exists and wishes to alleviate their situation. Most important, since the prohibition of torture itself springs from a European conception of human rights, victims from other cultures may not have a realistic view of the amount of public indignation their plight could arouse.[103]

[100] The exact numbers are 30,000 in the year 1973, 100,000 (1976), 250,000 (1980), more than half a million (1985) and more than 700,000 members belonged to Amnesty International in 1989 (see Eckel, 'Humanitarisierung', 608, Fn. 15).

[101] Eckel, 'Humanitarisierung', p. 614.

[102] Amnesty International (eds), *Report On Torture*, Amnesty International Publication (London: Duckworth, 1973).

[103] Ibid., pp. 109–112.

Generally, *Report on Torture* gave an account of the specific political circumstances (such as the Apartheid regime in South Africa, for example) and described the perpetrators involved, but in some incidents witnesses of crimes were directly quoted. In its report on South Vietnam, a British television report is cited directly in which two Quaker doctors working in the City of Quang Ngai graphically describe the bodies of tortured victims: Some of these individuals were repeatedly tortured at the 'interrogation centre' of the local prison. The Quakers emphasized the limited 'trust' between the human rights activists and the victims of torture, asserting that the former were, 'after all[,] Americans', and as such, from the perspective of the Vietnamese, possibly not trustworthy[104] In its introduction, the report seeks to 'objectify' moral outrage by interpreting possible motives of the perpetrators, together with the physical and mental consequences of the experience for its victims. In the case of its report on Brazil, Amnesty International bemoaned a 'sub-culture of torture' where the 'entire ritual of torture is known as the "spiritual séance"'.[105]

Although the report occasionally mentions the necessity to 'improve' conditions, this improvement is—in contrast to assumptions of moral movements in the nineteenth century—not linked to the hope of a possible inner transformation of the individual. Through its extensive documentation of violations against humanity, Amnesty International has proven its moral legitimacy. And yet, the question of to what extent religious discourses, e.g. Christian, might have shaped the foundation and implementation of the organization remains unanswered. A convert to Catholicism himself, when asked about his participation, Benenson stated that he had been inspired by 'the idea of a movement for spiritual transformation' placing Amnesty International 'in the context of a new muscular Christianity'.[106]

CONCLUSION: MORALS AND THE MAKING OF SOCIAL MOVEMENTS IN THE MODERN AGE

Although there were many and various motives that drove moral movements in the nineteenth and twentieth centuries, four common aspects connect their emergence: First, all of the associations described in this chapter

[104] Ibid., pp. 152–159, here p. 154.
[105] Ibid, p. 61.
[106] Buchanan, 'The Truth will Set you Free', p. 582, p. 591.

act on the core belief that a stranger perceived as being in need deserves aid. Although the construction of the stranger is intertwined with specific discourses and practices of aid, one aspect seems to be crucial: the assumption that this person or group became *coincidently* victims of violence — in other words: the assumed innocence of any victim of violence or catastrophe is a precondition for any moral action. However, in the nineteenth century moral movements were more openly connected with religious aspirations or even missionary practices and conceptions of improvement seem to have overlaid discourses of innocence. This relationship of tension between moral sentiments, discourses that accompanied the making of the 'innocent' object of intervention, and an understanding of the interrelationship between religious and secular arguments need further investigation.

Second, although the cultural and political contexts in which, for instance, the abolitionist movement and Amnesty International operated differed in terms of nation-state and processes of globalization, both were driven by an inherent sense of urgency. Acknowledging Bertrand Thaite, I argue here that moral movements generally 'placed a cult of action at the centre of their philosophy'.[107] This call for action derives from the moral outrage responding to crimes against humanity. At the same time, it seems that the making of moral movements itself might have meaning that goes beyond the obvious aims of action: They also had a performative dimension. As the implementation of 'emergency movements' in the mid-nineteenth century demonstrated, the establishment of associations was often closely connected to local communities. This inter-relationship between the striving for universal claims on the one hand and the incorporation of local groups on the other needs further exploration.

Third, both the 'innocent' figure and the sense of urgency are shaped by their representation in the media. Initiating campaigns and using new genres and technologies of distribution (like the telegraph or television) were both used by different manifestations of moral movements.

Fourth, it is inarguable that all of these actions were intertwined with the political. Being at the forefront of cultural battles, moral movements developed new cultural practices to aid people in need. Following religious, very often Christian, agendas, their actions were deeply embedded in civilizing missions. However, during the first decades of the 20th cen-

---

[107] Bertrand Thaite, 'Reinventing (French) Universalism. Religion, Humanitarianism and the "'French'" Doctors', *Modern & Contemporary France* 2 (2004), pp. 147–158, p. 148.

tury, as a response to human rights violations, formerly small-scale associations turned into major businesses.

While the 'hole-and-corner reformers of every imaginable kind' which Karl Marx and Friedrich Engels attacked in their *Communist Manifesto* never formed a coherent social movement, the civic organizations that did form irrefutably shaped the making of moral sentiments in the Modern Age. From small enterprises to large-scale organizations they shaped the front lines of cultural battles—these moral interventions were entangled at all times with political interests.

FURTHER READINGS

The global history of moral movements in the Modern Age encompasses diverse historical agents, social practices and narratives across the world. Moral movements in the nineteenth and twentieth centuries emerged from different cultural, regional and political backgrounds in the Western and non-Western worlds. The heterogeneity of these movements becomes most evident, when considering the different semantic connotations associated with 'moral' actions: Most actions of social movements engaged in improving living conditions on moral terms attempted to combat 'moral decay', even 'vice'.

Very often moral organizations strived for inner improvement. The range of historical terms under which those associations sailed, indicate that the intention to morally improve society was deeply embedded in religious debates. Through their actions these associations operated within different arenas, including the improvement of animal rights, working conditions and heathen souls. In other words, their action was prevalently interwoven with religious agendas. For those historians who are interested in interdisciplinary approaches as well in contemporary debates, the *Companion to Moral Anthropology* provides a useful introduction to both, the intellectual history of morals and practice of moral anthropology. In his introduction, French anthropologist Didier Fassin critically examines key methodological approaches to the anthropology of morals (Kant, Foucault, Durkheim). Organized in five parts (Legacies, Approaches, Localities, Politics, and Dialogues), the volume also includes surveys such as Marc Edelman's essay on E.P. Thompson's moral economy or Kwame Appiah's essay on moral philosophy. Furthermore the *Companion to Moral Anthropology* contains case studies of applied moral anthropology in areas like humanitarianism or human rights (Didier Fassin (ed.), *A Companion to Moral Anthropology*, Oxford: Wiley-Blackwell, 2012).

Without explicitly referring to the term 'moral movements', historical scholarship also addressed moral issues, discourses and sets of practices within, for instance, the abolition or the labour movements. In the following remarks I concentrate on two aspects: the inter-relationship between moral and religious movements, and humanitarian activism. In his early overview of European international movements, Irish historian Francis Lyons outlines the spread of internationalism during the nineteenth century and discusses reasons why some associations survived until the twentieth century. One chapter is dedicated to the formation of an international social conscience since the 1850s, which according to the author is inherently shaped by three types of organizations: temperance, anti-slavery and Red Cross movements (Francis S. L. Lyons, *Internationalism in Europe, 1815–1914*, Leyden: Sythoff, 1963). Generally speaking, Lyons's overview is a helpful guide for anyone interested in the rise of internationalism during the nineteenth century. However, the recently edited volume *Global Anti-Vice Activism, 1890–1950* inspired by global history, moves beyond Western conceptualizations of social conscience. The collection of essays frame similar historical agents, their social practices and arguments under the umbrella term 'vice'. In their volume, the group of editors claims that anti-vice activism in the nineteenth and twentieth centuries operated so successfully in the global and local worlds, that the editors even observe a new 'turn'. This 'vicious turn' around 1900 is situated on different levels: anti-vice activism, which was targeted against prostitutes and the consumption of alcohol or drugs, 'brought together an extremely diverse set of issues, cast of characters, and assortment of debates, all centered on the habits of the body and various forms of consumption'. In contrast to earlier Euro-centred research on the topic, the editors emphasize the global dimensions of anti-vice activism. A particularly salient example is the case of Mohandas Karamchand Gandhi who turned out to be 'an ardent crusader against the unholy trinity of drugs, drink, and debauchery'. As the editors argue, Gandhi combined Indian anti-colonial nationalism with 'nationalistic puritanism' (Jessica Piley, Robert Kramm and Harald Fischer-Tiné (eds), *Global Anti-Vice Activism, 1890–1950: Fighting Drinks, Drugs, and 'Immorality'*, Cambridge: Cambridge University Press, 2016, p. 5). By identifying anti-vice activism as global endeavour, the volume breaks new ground. The idea that disentangling practices of anti-vice politics demands a profound reconstruction of genealogies of knowledge which also incorporates body practices, refers to an earlier book *Prohibitions and Secrets*. In this book I argue that the 'Western' discovery of taboo as moral system is linked with missionary agency on the one hand, and the professionalization of such systems of knowledge, on the other. Missionary action like the London Missionary Society, or the German Innere Mission, which battled decay at the home front framed moral narratives during the nineteenth century (Alexandra Przyrembel, *Verbote und Geheimnisse. Das Tabu und die Geschichte der europäischen Moderne*, Frankfurt/Main: Campus, 2011). In a more narrow sense, many moral associations (e.g. the Young Men's Christian Association, the Woman's Christian Temperance Union) emerged from religious enterprises. In light of the ongoing interest in religious vitalism in the context of global modern history (C.A. Bayly, *The Birth of the Modern World, 1780–1914: Global Connections and Comparisons*. Oxford: Blackwell, 2004), a wide range of different literature concentrated on missionary organizations, and predominantly Protestant activism. Out of this rich body of literature, two studies are recommended which both frame religious moral interventions in the context of national imperial enterprises. In his textbook *The British Missionary Enterprise* (London: Routledge, 2008), Jeffrey Cox outlines the impact of British missionary action on civilizing populations in and outside Europe. The Australian historian Ian R. Tyrrell focusses on American moral reformers of the turn of the twentieth century who aimed at morally uplifting societies. Tyrrell argues that the attempt to create a moral world based on Christian values went hand in hand with the emergence of American imperialism. Focussing on the Woman's Temperance Organization and the Young Men's Christian Association, Tyrell argues that those 'moral reformers had bequeathed to the American nation a tradition of entanglement with the wider world'. This tradition includes both, 'the urge to be part of the world and yet at the same time superior to other countries' (Ian R. Tyrrell, *Reforming the World: The Creation of America's Moral Empire*, Princeton, NJ: Princeton University Press, 2010, p. 237).

As Lyons' early observation that social conscience became a central point of reference for many associations during the nineteenth century turns out to be persuasive, one specific manifestation of 'moral' action should be included in this survey: the emergence of humanitarianism. Again, anthropologists initiated critical debates on humanitarian practices in the contemporary world (Didier Fassin, *Humanitarian Reason: A Moral History of the Present*, Berkeley: University of California Press, 2011). However, during the last decade historians of modern history have vigorously debated global practices and narratives of humanitarianism. Many studies focused on single organizations, particularly on national Red Cross movements, filling research gaps as it was not until recently that most institutions began to write their own histories (Julia Irwin, *Making the World Safe: The American Red Cross and a Nation's Humanitarian*

Awakening. Oxford: Oxford University Press, 2013; Rachel Chrastil, *Organizing for War. France 1870–1914*, Baton Rouge: Louisiana State University Press, 2010).

In the British case the inter-relationship between humanitarianism and Empire dominates in recent research: Rebecca Gill, 'Networks of Concern, Boundaries of Compassion: British Relief in the South African War', *The Journal of Imperial and Commonwealth History* 5 (2012), pp. 827–844; Matthew Hilton, 'Ken Loach and the Save the Children Film: Humanitarianism, Imperialism, and the Changing Role of Charity in Postwar Britain', *Journal of Modern History* 2 (2015), pp. 357–394. French historian Bertrand Thaite draws attention to narratives of French humanitarianism. He argues that heterogenous organizations such as the Catholic *Père Blancs* or *Médicins sans Frontières* refer to the same set of arguments. Although very different organizations, these associations referred to a 'humanitarian protocol' 'with few dramatic devices'. One of them appears to be the language of compassion which 'changed its nature and social meanings': Bertrand Thaite, 'Horror, Abjection and Compassion: From Dunant to Compassion Fatigue', *New Formations* 62 (2007), pp. 123–136, and Bertrand Thaite, 'Reinventing (French) Universalism: Religion, Humanitarianism and the "French" Doctors', *Modern & Contemporary France* 2 (2004), pp. 147–158.

Pursuing the research interest in the impact of emotions, especially compassion, on humanitarianism, another focus of recent research lies on visual representation as specific form to express and to activate humanitarian aims. Several articles in the volume *Humanitarian Photography* on humanitarian imagery discuss the meaning of particular incidents for the visual representation of atrocities on the one hand, and the proliferation of humanitarian activities following catastrophes like the Armenian Genocide or the Biafra famine in the 1970s, on the other hand. In their introduction the editors reflect the 'the morality of sight' associated with humanitarian action: Heide Fehrenbach and Davide Rodogno (eds), *Humanitarian Photography: A History* (Cambridge: Cambridge University Press, 2015).

Above all, controversy around the convoluted history of human rights since the eighteenth century, and the construction of a 'new utopia' in the second half of the twentieth century, triggered new research fields regarding agents' narratives as well as their practices. However, this research shows a clear bias toward twentieth-century human rights activism; see Samuel Moyn, *The Last Utopia: Human Rights in History* (Cambridge: Cambridge University Press, 2010); Jan Eckel, *Die Ambivalenz des Guten:*

Menschenrechte in der internationalen Politik seit den 1940ern (Göttingen: Vandenhoeck & Ruprecht, 2014). The volume *Moralpolitik* provides an overview of the contested interpretations of human rights throughout history. In his introduction, Stefan-Ludwig Hoffmann suggests a genealogical reading of human rights politics by examining its boom in the 1970s and its 'prehistory' in the nineteenth century. Instead of trying to inscribe the heterogeneous understanding of human rights into a teleological narrative, Hoffmann uses the interpretations of human rights as a starting point for understanding moments of crisis: Stefan-Ludwig Hoffmann (ed.), *Moralpolitik: Geschichte der Menschenrechte im 20. Jahrhundert* (Göttingen: Wallstein, 2010); Stefan-Ludwig Hoffmann (ed.), *Human Rights in the Twentieth Century* (Cambridge: Cambridge University Press, 2010).

In future, research will have to disentangle nineteenth- from twentieth-century humanitarian players, strategies and narratives. In her very insightful article 'Humanitarianism in Nineteenth-Century Context', Abigail Green observes the 'preoccupation with the origins of our current world-order' in recent historiography. As she argues such 'presentist' approaches fail to 'include now unfashionable nineteenth-century preoccupations like temperance, and situating humanitarian activity more clearly within a variety of religious traditions—Christian and non-Christian—may serve to demonstrate both the contingency, and the limitations, of the ways this field is currently constructed': Abigail Green, 'Humanitarianism in Nineteenth-Century Context: Religious, Gendered, National', *Historical Journal* 57 (2014/15), pp. 1157–1175. Further research will need to address 'non-Western' moral activism beyond its most famous players like Gandhi and to locate different moral concerns by analysing its religious reverberations in the local and global worlds.

CHAPTER 14

Labour Movements in Global Historical Perspective: Conceptual Eurocentrism and Its Problems

Stefan Berger

INTRODUCTION

For a long time labour historians have focussed on labour movements that emerged in the developed West during industrialization in the nineteenth century and, in their organizational and ideological concerns, homed in on the wage-earning industrial working class. The developed West also marked the space of the metropolitan centres of nineteenth-century capitalism and imperialism—with one exception, namely Japan, which formed its own 'West' in the East. The West, in the course of its imperial endeavours, exported all sorts of ideas and practices to the imperial margins, where they were rarely adopted or copied in a straightforward way. Instead they were adapted, changed and often re-exported into the metropoles, where they in turn influenced a range of developments.

With regard to labour movement historiography, the labour historians of the non-Western world initially took over the concern of their Western counterparts, concentrating on nascent wage-earning industrial working

S. Berger (✉)
Department of History, Ruhr University Bochum, Bochum, Germany

© The Author(s) 2017
S. Berger, H. Nehring (eds.), *The History of Social Movements in Global Perspective*, DOI 10.1057/978-1-137-30427-8_14

classes.[1] Undoubtedly, many colonial and post-colonial spaces in the imperial peripheries sought to industrialize, as the idea of 'catching up' and perhaps even 'overtaking' the West was widespread in developing countries after they gained independence from Western colonial powers. Yet, many colonial and post-colonial spaces retained characteristics that made them fundamentally different from 'the West', and labour historians, by concentrating on industrial wage labour and its organizations, missed many other forms of labour and many other forms of organizing labour. Over the past 20 years, the globalization of labour history has drawn attention to these insufficiencies of classical approaches to the history of labour and the history of labour movements. Labour historians are seeking to develop a more layered, ambiguous, contradictory and complex picture, both of regimes of labour and of associated social protest movements organizing labour. Any conceptualization of the history of labour movements in global perspective needs to start from these efforts.[2]

Some readers may be surprised to find a chapter on labour movements at all in a volume on the history of social movements. Political parties, trade unions and co-operatives, which form the three columns of the labour movement in the West, are all separate from social movements in that they are far more tightly organized and structured and do not resemble the loose 'network of networks' that is characteristic of social movements, according to Dieter Rucht's Chapter 2 in this volume. Yet, if we do not consider the constituent elements of labour movements but, rather, labour movements as a whole, we do find such 'network of networks'. Many activists were active in a wide variety of organizations associated with the labour movement and thereby constituted a social milieu which can indeed be understood, at least in the West, as the most powerful social

---

[1] See, for example, Rajani Kanta Das, *The Labor Movement in India* (Berlin: de Gruyter, 1923); Marjorie Ruth Clark, *Organized Labour in Mexico* (Chapel Hill: University of North Carolina Press, 1934); Guillermo Lora, *Historia del movimiento obrero boliviana*, 3 vols (La Paz: Los Amigos del Libre, 1967–1970).

[2] For excellent introductions to the new global labour history se Jan Lucassen (ed.), *Global Labour History. A State of the Art* (Berne: Peter Lang, 2006); Marcel van der Linden, *Workers of the World. Essays Toward a Global Labor History* (Leiden: Brill, 2008); Andreas Eckert, 'What is Global Labour History Good for?' in Jürgen Kocka (ed.), *Work in a Modern Society. The German Historical Experience in Comparative Perspective* (Oxford: Berghahn, 2010), pp. 169–182; Andrea Komlosy, *Arbeit: eine globalhistorische Perspektive, 13.–21. Jahrhundert* (Wien: Promedia, 2014).

movement of the nineteenth century. As such it is entirely fitting to have a chapter on the labour movement in a volume on social movements. In what follows, we shall, first of all, look at the emergence of a self-declared labour movement in the West in the course of the nineteenth century before widening our view and taking into account the development of labour movements outside the West. We shall then proceed to highlight certain global political moments in the development of the labour movement, such as the First World War, the Russian revolution, the struggle against fascism, decolonization and the Cold War, and ask whether the definition of such global moments still have a Western-centric bias and whether it is possible to escape it. We shall finish this brief survey with a summary of some of the most important challenges facing labour movements in the contemporary world.

THE EMERGENCE OF THE LABOUR MOVEMENT AS A RESPONSE TO INDUSTRIAL CAPITALISM IN THE WEST DURING THE NINETEENTH CENTURY

From the eighteenth century onwards, industrial capitalism established a range of social processes that were market-driven and aimed at the establishment of a market economy and the commodification of all social relationships. By the end of the long nineteenth century, on the eve of the First World War, serfdom was abolished everywhere in the West. The forward march of free wage labour signalled the commodification of wage labour itself. Karl Marx saw wage labour as the characteristic form of capitalist labour relations, as the workers sold their labour power to the capitalist who could make a profit from the surplus value of exploiting the labour power of workers.[3] The workers formed organizations to defend themselves against such exploitation, including friendly societies, co-operatives, trade unions and, eventually, political parties. The emergence of labour movements in the West is widely associated with craft workers, skilled labourers and journeymen trained in the artisan traditions of the Middle Ages and Early Modern Europe.[4] The introduction of mechanized forms of labour and of machines more generally brought a crisis to many

[3] Kenneth Lapides, *Marx's Wage Theory in Historical Perspective: its Origins, Development and Interpretation* (Westport, CT: Praeger, 1998).

[4] James R. Farr, *Artisans in Europe 1300–1914* (Cambridge: Cambridge University Press, 2000).

artisanal professions. Furthermore, journeymen increasingly struggled to make the step up to master artisan and so they often filled the new factories as industrial workers. However, early forms of labour organizations in the West often took root among workers working in semi-mechanized and semi-industrialized jobs. A good example are the cigar makers who formed one of the earliest trade unions, or the shoemakers, who were in the vanguard of political organization.[5] They worked in typical cottage industries and under the out-putting system. Yet they still had considerable autonomy over their workplaces and work routines and they often used their work time to have the newspapers read to them and discuss political issues of the day. The earliest working-class parties in the West, such as the German *Allgemeine Deutsche Arbeiterverein* (ADAV, General German Workers' Association), founded in 1863, were heavily dominated by artisans, journeymen and skilled workers. This also explains why many nineteenth-century labour movements in the West looked down on the '*lumpenproletariat*', i.e. those unskilled labourers, precariously employed and on the verge of dropping out of 'working-class respectability' and into total poverty or total dependency on whatever meagre welfare provisions the nineteenth-century Western state supplied.[6]

Industrialization leading to proletarianization of artisans in Europe and ultimately the rise of an industrial working class was a regional process. It had strongholds, for example, in the Genoa–Milan–Turin triangle, the Ruhr, St Petersburg, Manchester, the Pas de Calais, Asturias, Pittsburgh and many other regions of Europe and North America. It was, by and large,

---

[5] Eric Hobsbawm and Joan Wallach Scott, 'Political Shoemakers', in Eric Hobsbawm, *Worlds of Labour* (New York: Pantheon, 1984), pp. 103–130, initially published in *Past and Present* 89 (1980). Dorothee Schneider, *Trade Unions and Community. The German Working Class in New York City, 1870–1900* (Urbana: University of Illionis, 1994), Chap. 5: 'Cigar Makers and Trade Unions: Politics and the Community'; Ad Knotter, 'Transnational Cigarmakers: Cross-Border Labour Markets, Strikes, and Solidarity at the Time of the First International (1864–1873)', *International Review of Social History*, 3 (2014), pp. 409–442.

[6] For a range of surveys of the development of the European labour movement, see Jürgen Kocka (ed.), *Europäische Arbeiterbewegungen im 19. Jahrhundert* (Göttingen: Vandenhoeck & Ruprecht, 1983); Dick Geary (ed.), *Labour and Socialist Movements in Europe Before 1914* (Oxford: Berg, 1989); Stefan Berger and David Broughton (eds), *The Force of Labour: the Western European Labour Movement and the Working Class in the Twentieth Century* (Oxford: Bloomsbury, 1995).

a slow process and very uneven across Europe.[7] Later on, in the twentieth century, the highly localized/regionalized pattern of industrialization and its slow and uneven process would be confirmed at a global level. In the heavily industrializing regions of the nineteenth century, the new market-driven economies of the West produced what would be referred to in the nineteenth century as 'the social question'. It included the grinding poverty and shocking exploitation of those who only had their labour to sell. Their lives were characterized by low incomes, long working hours, lack of social insurance, dangerous working conditions, poor housing, insufficient sanitary and medical provisions and hunger. Many observers of the emerging 'social question' drew a line between the emergence of an industrial proletariat and the prospect of social conflict and revolution. And many sought to come up with solutions to the problem.

They included social conservatives, such as Otto von Bismarck, who introduced one of the earliest social insurance systems in Germany during the 1880s, partly at least to wean workers away from the nascent socialist movement which he harshly repressed through the Anti-Socialist Laws between 1878 and 1890.[8] Liberal social reformers, such as David Lloyd-George in Britain or the 'Socialists of the Chair' (*Kathedersozialisten*) in Germany, academics with a keen interest in social reform, were also very much to the fore when it came to analysing and seeking solutions to the social question. In Britain the Liberal Party sought alliances with the trade unions during the second half of the nineteenth-century in an attempt to win the 'respectable' working classes to the cause of political Liberalism. Working-class liberalism thus offered radicalism, respectability and a vision of ultimate harmony between workers and employers—a kind of social partnership, which would return in both a Catholic and a Social Democratic guise in the second half of the twentieth century. Social liberals in the nineteenth century were in favour of accepting working-class representation in parliament, legalizing 'responsible' trade unions, improving working conditions in the factories and introducing a 'fair wage'. The West had, of course, many different faces of liberalism: the Gladstonian Liberal Party in Britain, for example, was not the same as the National

---

[7] Sidney Pollard, *Peaceful Conquest: the Industrialization of Europe 1760–1970* (Oxford: Oxford University Press, 1981).

[8] Hermann Beck, *The Origins of the Authoritarian Welfare State in Prussia. Conservatives, Bureaucracy and the Social Question, 1815–1870* (Ann Arbor: University of Michigan Press, 1995).

Liberals in Germany. Yet there was a discernible social liberalism emerging across the West seeking diverse forms of partnership with working-class representatives and attempting to deal with the social question.[9]

The churches, both Catholic and Protestant, concerned themselves with the social question and sought to implement programmes aimed at helping the working classes.[10] In particular the Catholic Church organized more formal labour movements, including Catholic trade unions, cooperatives and political parties, which fought for the implementation of Catholic social teachings and a general improvement for workers. In France, Italy, Germany and Belgium they were powerful movements before 1914. The Christian principle of subsidiarity underpinned the papal encyclical *Rerum Novarum* (1891), which amounted to a powerful critique of modernity, including an indictment of both socialism and capitalism and an endorsement of the corporate state. Early trade unionism in Japan incidentally was also informed by Christian social reformism.

The socialists located the root evil of industrial labour in a new economic system that they labelled 'capitalism' and that they sought to overcome. The earliest of them, later dubbed by Karl Marx and Friedrich Engels, 'utopian socialists' included Claude Henri de Saint-Simon, François-Charles Fourier and Robert Owen.[11] A specific 'artisans' socialism' widely associated with the writings of Wilhelm Weitling, formulated the concerns of artisans under threat of proletarianization.[12] They were all concerned with finding a more just social order, in which ideas of association, cooperation and collectivism loomed large. Karl Marx and Friedrich Engels were towering nineteenth-century intellectuals who sought to analyse capitalism and who predicted its fall by the hands of a powerful labour movement who would overcome the social injustices they associated with capitalism. The industrial proletariat would be the gravedigger of capitalism. 'Scientific socialism', according to Marx and Engels, amounted to a rational and thorough economic analysis of historical developments. Their

[9] Michael Freeden, *Liberal Languages: Ideological Imaginations and Twentieth-Century Progressive Thought* (Princeton, NJ: Princeton University Press, 2005).

[10] Roger Aubert, *Catholic Social Teaching: a Historical Perspective* (Milwaukee, WI: Marquette University Press, 2003); Harry Liebersohn, *Religion and Industrial Society: The Protestant Social Congress in Wilhelmine Germany* (Philadelphia: Independence Square 1986).

[11] Keith Taylor, *The Political Ideas of the Utopian Socialists* (London: Frank Cass 1982).

[12] L. Knatz and H. A. Marsiske (eds), *Wilhelm Weitling: ein deutscher Arbeiterkommunist* (Hamburg: Ergebnisse, 1989).

historical materialism was to show that all history was the history of class struggles. Marxism inserted 'languages of class' into the labour movement that were based on the antagonism of social classes that could only be solved through violent revolution. As Karl Marx had famously stated, it was not enough for philosophers to analyse the world, they also had to contribute to changing it. And this is precisely what they did—in organizing the First International, in helping British Chartists and socialists to organize and in helping the German labour movement to come into being and to establish itself as a powerful political force in Germany.[13] From the socialist movement, the anarchist and anarcho-syndicalist movement would split in the nineteenth century. They would find in Bakunin an alternative guru to Marx and they could point to their own traditions, rooted in the political thought of Proudhon. They differed from the Marxists in their assessment of the role of the state and the role of parliaments and elections as well as in their assessment of how to best organize the industrial workers. Yet, like the Marxists they aimed at a revolution which would overcome capitalism and implement socialism. The most successful anarchist labour movement was the Spanish CNT, which, in the 1930s, had more than 2 million individual members.[14]

By the end of the long nineteenth-century the West boasted a wide array of labour movements. Some of them aimed primarily at regulating social conflict and achieving social reforms within the capitalist system, whilst others sought to revolutionize the existing economic, social and political system. Riots, machine-breaking and arson attacks were the means of 'primitive working-class rebels' and others, such as agricultural labourers and small farmers, who were unhappy with the emergence of industrial capitalism and saw in the new regime an offence to the 'moral economy' they sought to defend.[15] In the course of the nineteenth century Western labour movements increasingly found more institutionalized

[13] Stefan Berger, *Social Democracy and the Working Class in Nineteenth and Twentieth Century Germany* (London: Longman, 2000), Chap. 3.

[14] James Joll, *The Anarchists*, London: Methuen, 1968; Irving Louis Horowitz, *The Anarchists*, New York: Aldine Transaction, 2005.

[15] On 'primitive rebels' see Eric Hobsbawm, *Primitive Rebels: Studies in Archaic Forms of Social Protest* (Manchester: Manchester University Press, 1959); on the concept of 'moral economy', see E.P. Thompson, 'The Moral Economy of the English Crowd in the Eighteenth Century' (originally published in Past and Present, 1971), and 'The Moral Economy Reviewed' both, in *Customs in Common: Studies in Traditional Popular Culture*, Oxford: The New Press, 1993, pp. 185–351.

ways of battling capital. They turned to organizing and founded trade unions, co-operatives and political parties. They relied on self-help, organized strikes and sought to win political representation in national parliaments in order to influence national legislations. The more they relied on formal organizations in the states of the West, the more they became drawn into the frameworks of those states. Where they were not directly repressed and persecuted, especially in Western Europe, they became integrated into their societies in diverse ways and at least parts of the socialist labour movement lost its revolutionary edge already before 1914.[16] The possibilists in France and the revisionists in Germany as well as the progressives in Britain are examples of socialists who were keen to form alliances with middle-class parties and abandoned ideas of socialist revolution in the future in favour of social reforms in the here and now.[17]

As these short paragraphs indicate, nineteenth-century Western labour movements were incredibly diverse, organizationally and ideologically. They could build on traditions of pre-modern artisanal guild protests and millenarian religious movements that Marcel van der Linden discusses in Chap. 7 on European social movements,[18] and they organized powerful mutual aid societies. In Britain friendly societies provided both insurance and entertainment.[19] They also introduced democratic practices, such as 'one member, one vote'. London alone had around 200 friendly societies in the 1820s. By 1914 English and Welsh friendly societies organized around 7 million workers. They have often been called unpolitical, but they frequently were the germ of trade unionism in Britain. In global perspective, such forms of mutualism, including savings and loans associations, can be found in many societies around the world at widely differing times, ranging back well before the onset of capitalism and imperialism.[20]

---

[16] John Schwarzmantel, *Socialism and the Idea of the Nation* (London: Harvester Wheatsheaf, 1991); Marcel van der Linden, 'The National Integration of the European Working-Classes, 1871–1914', *International Review of Social History* 3 (1988), pp. 285–311.

[17] Manfred B. Steger, *The Quest for Evolutionary Socialism. Eduard Bernstein and Social Democracy* (Cambridge: Cambridge University Press, 2006).

[18] On social protest by wage earners before the onset of fully developed industrialization, see also: Catharina Lis, Jan Lucassen and Hugo Soly (eds), *Before the Unions: Wage Earners and Collective Action in Europe, 1300–1850* (Special Issue of the *International Review of Social History*, Cambridge, 1994).

[19] P.H.J.H. Gosden, *The Friendly Societies in England 1815–1875* (Manchester: Manchester University Press, 1961).

[20] Linden, *Global Labour*, p. 87.

Mutualism therefore can be understood as an important principle of workers' organization.

Producers' and consumers' cooperatives were also powerful attempts of self-organization by working men who sought to exclude the middlemen and abolish 'idle profit' by replacing it with the just sharing of rewards. They took up consumer protests' demands for a 'just price', and they frequently acted as savings and credit institutions for working-class families. Early socialists, such as Robert Owen, were promoting the principles of cooperation as panacea against the poverty and social misery produced by early industrialization. In 1844 the Rochdale Society of Equitable Pioneers was founded and its Rochdale Principles served as a model for cooperative societies in many places around the world. Cooperatives were rooted in local practices but they also had, from early on, a strong international orientation and formed international organizations.[21]

Trade unions were the most direct defence organizations of industrial workers against those who owned the means of production. They replaced 'collective bargaining by riot' (Eric Hobsbawm), including machine-breaking, made famous by Luddism, which had its highpoint in Britain between 1811 and 1816. The earliest formal trade unions can be found in the motherland of the Industrial Revolution, in Britain, where they were established in the 1820s and 1830s. Craft unions were initially the strongest organizations, as skilled workers were more able to protect themselves than the unskilled. The first attempts to organize the latter go back to the last third of the nineteenth century. In Britain they were associated with the 'new unionism' of the 1890s. Slowly but surely we see across the West a move to industrial unionism, where all workers of one industry, regardless of skill, are organized in one union. Before 1914 the only country in Europe with an effective and working system of collective bargaining was Britain. And even here the army was still sometimes mobilized against striking workers. In other parts of the West, employers, often in conjunction with state power, sought to repress unions ferociously. Nevertheless, in the West trade unions had become one of the most effective means of protecting wage-earning working men from the vagaries of the market and the absolutism of employers on the eve of the First World War. Within socialist circles there had been a debate surrounding the mass strike as a

---

[21] Jack Shaffer, *Historical Dictionary of the Cooperative Movement* (Lanham, MD: Scarecrow Press, 1999); Mary Hilson and Silke Neunsiger are preparing a comparative history of the cooperative movement.

political means to bring down governments or prevent war. In this mass strike debate, the majority of trade unionists remained deeply sceptical about the politicization of the primary union concern for better wages and working conditions.[22]

Working-class political parties became more important in an age of mass politics from the last third of the nineteenth century onwards, when political representation in municipal councils and national parliaments offered opportunities to improve the situation for workers. In many parts of the modern world, these parties had been suffering severe repression. In the nineteenth-century such repression was legitimized with reference to anti-socialism and the allegedly revolutionary nature of socialist parties threatening the legitimate order. Yet in many parts of Western and Central Europe, where they were allowed to act legally (despite recurring bouts of repression), they achieved increasingly impressive electoral results and built strong organizations. German Social Democracy (SPD) in particular became a model of a well-organized party before 1914. Caring for its members 'from the cradle to the grave', the wider labour movement culture of the party marked out a socialist milieu that became a cultural home, a *Heimat*, to its members, thereby also strengthening the movement character of the German labour movement. The SPD was also electorally the most successful party in the world before 1914, achieving a third of the vote in the parliamentary elections of 1912 which made them the strongest party in the national parliament. However, it remained politically isolated at national level. Whereas it could form alliances with liberals in the south-western states of Germany and in many municipal councils, it could not and would not do so at national level. Both the French and the British working-class parties, albeit much smaller, much more divided both organizationally and ideologically, found it easier to forge alliances in their respective societies and therefore were also more directly involved in politics before the First World War than was the case with the SPD.[23]

The labour movement united friendly societies, cooperatives, trade unions, political parties and, importantly, a whole range of unorganized,

[22] Geoff Eley, *Forging Democracy: The History of the Left in Europe, 1850–2000* (Oxford: Oxford University Press, 2002), p. 98.

[23] Stefan Berger and Angel Smith, 'Between Scylla and Charybdis: Nationalism, Labour and Ethnicity Across Five Continents, 1870–1939', in Stefan Berger and Angel Smith, *Nationalism, Labour and Ethnicity 1870–1939* (Manchester: Manchester University Press, 1999), pp. 1–30; for German Social Democracy see Stefan Berger, *Social Democracy and the Working Class in Nineteenth and Twentieth Century Germany* (London: Longman, 2000).

spontaneous forms of working-class protest, including food riots, factory occupations, rebellions and armed insurrection, in the labour movement milieux. These wider labour movement cultures were characterized by their emphasis on education. Education was seen as the most important tool to free the working classes from their dependency on capital and to overcome their inability to combine against the diverse forms of social and political injustice they had to face.[24] In the nineteenth century, furthermore, labour movement milieux were characterized by an intense orientation towards the future—a better future in which the ills of the present economic, social and political system would be overcome and in which humanity could fulfil all of its creative potentials.[25]

A third characteristic of the labour movement, as it emerged in the West, was its maleness. Its pioneers and key representatives as well as the overwhelming majority of its formal members were male. Female employment was often seen by the male labour movement as a means to undercut wages and dismiss male workers. Apart from rational reasons for opposing women work, representatives of the labour movement were also in good measure characterized by proletarian anti-feminism. Many trade unions did not allow any female members. Living within a patriarchal society it would have been surprising if male workers had been less patriarchal than the society surrounding them. Thus many male workers were as convinced as male capitalists that the natural place for a woman was in the home, where she should concern herself with home-making and child-rearing. Nevertheless, industrial capitalism also produced many women workers, especially in the textile industry.[26] For a long time Labour historians ignored them as they had ignored the gendered nature of labour movements. The gender politics of labour movements still needs to be explored in depth, although the proletarian women's movement has been thoroughly and

[24] For some general comments, see Stefan Berger, 'What has the Labour Movement ever Done for Us? The Impact of Labour Movements on Social and Cultural Developments in Europe', in Jürgen Mittag and David Meyer (eds), *Interventionen: soziale und kulturelle Entwicklungen durch Arbeiterbewegungen* [*Interventions: the Impact of Labour Movements on Social and Cultural Development*] (Wien: AVA, 2013), pp. 27–42; for the example of Britain, see: Kevin Manton, *Socialism and Education in Britain 1883–1902* (London: Woburn, 2001); Brian Simon, *Education and the Labour Movement, 1870–1920* (London: Lawrence and Wishart, 1965).

[25] Lucian Hölscher, *Weltgericht oder Revolution? Protestantische und sozialistische Zukunftsvorstellungen im deutschen Kaiserreich* (Stuttgart: Klett Cotta, 1989).

[26] Kathleen Canning, *Languages of Labor and Gender: Female Factory Work in Germany 1850–1914* (Ithaca, NY: Cornell University Press, 1996).

expertly examined.[27] Socialist women fighting for the rights of women could be found across the Western world by the end of the nineteenth century. Among the early socialists, Fourier and Owen had been champions of women's rights. The leader of the SPD, August Bebel, had penned a classic bestseller entitled *Woman under Socialism*, in which he also set out a vision for the emancipation of women.[28] Socialists attacked the bourgeois family as oppressive for women and fought for women's rights. Yet overall, the socialist and the feminist movements remained uneasy bedfellows. Too often, the emancipation of the male working-class from capitalism was given priority over the emancipation of women under capitalism. Too often, the patriarchal values and norms of labour movement activists dominated. Even the language and the symbolism of the Western labour movements were overwhelmingly male.

The exclusion of women from the concerns of Western labour movements was not the only exclusion. The whole informal labour sector was for a very long time similarly disregarded by labour movements, who, by and large, were focusing on the concerns of male industrial workers. As labour movement history tended to follow the object of their study, the history of forms of protest by groups of female workers, working-class families and workers working in informal labour markets are still in need of being recovered. Whilst some beginnings have been made, much still needs to be done—also for modern Western labour movement history. In a global widening of the perspective, the role of women, families and the informal sector is even more important in understanding working-class protest.

THE DEVELOPMENT OF LABOUR MOVEMENTS OUTSIDE THE WEST

Movements representing working people can also be found outside Europe. Given the widely differing forms of the commodification of labour in the non-Western world under conditions of colonialism and

---

[27] Richard J. Evans, *Comrades and Sisters: Feminism, Socialism and Pacifism in Europe, 1870–1945* (Brighton: Wheatsheaf, 1987); Jean H. Quataert (ed.), *Socialist Women: European Socialist Feminism in the Nineteenth and Early Twentieth Centuries* (New York: Elsevier, 1978); Helmut Gruber and Pamela Graves (eds), *Women and Socialism; Socialism and Women: Europe Between the Two World Wars* (Oxford: Berghahn, 1998).

[28] August Bebel, *Woman under Socialism* (New York, 1903). The German original was published in 1883.

post-colonialism, the concept of 'working class' has been replaced by the concept of 'subaltern worker'. 'Subaltern workers' were not restricted to a wage-earning industrial labour force, but were characterized by manifold internal differentiations. Yet, in increasingly globalized world markets, they also had many intimate connections with other kinds of workers in an economy that triggered vast processes of migration and produced migrant labour on a hitherto unprecedented scale.

Landless workers' movements played an important role in many non-Western regions that were dominated by agricultural production. The most recent prominent example includes the Brazilian *Movimento dos Trabalhadores Sem Terra* (MST). Issues of land grabbing, eviction of peasants and land rights were all important in producing labour movements. This, of course, was not entirely unknown in the West—as the struggle of landless labourers in the Emilia Romagna and other parts of Europe against the impact of agricultural capitalism demonstrate.[29]

Many parts of the non-Western world saw the development of large industrial enterprises in the nineteenth century which were often developed further by post-colonial post-independence regimes. The scholarship on labour movements has, for a long time, focussed on the industrial workers employed in those large enterprises, who formed the kind of organizations—trade unions, cooperatives and political parties—that were known in the West. But these workers remained, by and large, uncharacteristic of labour in the global South, where the boundaries between wage and non-wage labour and between free and unfree labour remained far more blurred than in the West.[30] A global look at the development of labour and its organizations will have to question the predominance of industrial wage labour and the evolution of capitalism as presented by Marxist or Weberian theory. Thus, for example, the 1791 revolt of Haitian slaves, which would not have been a part of traditional labour history, can now be described as the first successful working-class revolt in the world.[31] Thus, a global look at labour and labour movements will show many more

---

[29] Landless labourers figure prominently, for example, in Paul Ginsborg, *A History of Contemporary Italy: Society and Politics, 1943–1988* (Basingstoke: Palgrave Macmillan, 2003). See also: James C. Scott, *Decoding Subaltern Politics: Ideology, Disguise and Resistance in Agrarian Politics* (London: Palgrave Macmillan, 2013).

[30] Peter Linebaugh and Marcus Rediker, *The Many-Headed Hydra. The Hidden History of the Revolutionary Atlantic* (Boston: Beacon, 2000).

[31] Thomas O. Ott, *The Haitian Revolution, 1791–1804* (Knoxville: University of Tennessee Press, 1973).

interconnected, diverse labour regimes and workers' organizations in the global evolution of capitalism. Any simple differentiation between 'the West' and 'the rest' is problematized, following the powerful post-colonial critique of such binary oppositions. Dipesh Chakrabarty's *Provincialising Europe*, for example, problematized the notion, made popular by modernization theory but also Marxism, that the West's developmental path paved the way for all others, which could not be but derivative of the West. As Chakrabarty points out, many of the concepts and ideas that are used outside of the West have Western origins, but these concepts are often not sufficient to understand non-Western developments. Hence they are, in Chakrabarty's words, 'indispensable and inadequate' at the same time.[32]

This is also true for the concept of the labour movement. Insofar as it was built on notions of organizations built by a wage-earning Western industrial working class, it influenced the analysis of similar organizations in many parts of the non-Western world whose ideological and organizational set-ups have been deeply influenced by the Western concept of the labour movement, often in ambiguous, haphazard and idiosyncratic ways. The Western concept of the labour movement failed to grasp that labour regimes in non-Western world often followed different logics than the logic of wage-earning industrial labour in the West and hence produced different labour movements. A wider look at global labour regimes, therefore, will also invariably lead to a reconceptualization of the concept of labour movement and to the writing of a very different kind of labour movement history from the one that has developed in the West (and in 'the rest') from the nineteenth century to the present.

As global capitalist structures spread with the advances of colonialism and imperialism, the colonists transplanted Western categories such as private property, concepts of time and space and notions of discipline into the non-Western world. Western labour movement activists travelled to the colonial and imperial spaces seeking to encourage the building of working-class organizations along lines that looked familiar to their Western experience. In many white settler societies, labour movements were built by Western migrants who brought their own traditions and experiences to bear on the new conditions they found in their non-Western colonial habitats. In the United States, for example, the early labour movement was built, above all, by British and German migrants. However, the peculiar

<hr>

[32] Dipesh Chakrabarty, *Provincializing Europe: Postcolonial Thought and Historical Difference* (Princeton, NJ: Princeton University Press 2000).

conditions of the 'American frontier', the absence of aristocratic classes in the United States as well as the idea of basic social equality of Americans regardless of class (the 'American dream'), all contributed to major differences between European and US labour movements, as did the stronger notions of individualism and the far more powerful organizations of capital in the United States. Whilst highly class-conscious and revolutionary organizations, such as the Knights of Labor, existed in the United States, they remained relatively marginal, as did the Socialist Party. The languages of class that were so prominent in nineteenth-century Europe, were far weaker in the United States. Whilst there were still many transnational contacts and similarities between the United States and Britain in particular,[33] no powerful socialist mass party emerged in the United States and, in comparison with Europe, social democratic, socialist and communist movements had little influence on the political fortunes of the country. Instead, pro-capitalist unions, such as the American Federation of Labour (AFL), emerged which sought to improve wages and working conditions within a capitalist framework.[34]

In another white settler society, heavily influenced by British traditions, that of Australia, a powerful labour movement emerged which made Australia, together with New Zealand, a pioneer of the welfare state and had guaranteed the Australian working class an important say in the country before 1914. Their, by and large, social reformist agendas included the introduction of social insurance, unemployment benefits and workers' safety legislation. As in North America, issues of class were downplayed in the self-understanding of Australian workers, where concepts of 'mateship' and a national solidarity forged in the trenches of the First World War produced languages of class that were also quite different from those in Europe. In Australia, those languages of class could co-exist for a long time with forms of labour movement racism, such as the 'White Australia Policy' of successive twentieth-century Australian Labor governments. The Australian labour movement as a whole regarded Australia as a better, less class-ridden, version of Europe, in which white workers had the same rights and obligations as everyone else.[35] The heavy inflections of

---

[33] Neville Kirk, *Labour and Society in Britain and the USA*, 2 vols (London: Scolar, 1994).

[34] Julie Greene, *Pure and Simple Politics. The American Federation of Labor and Political Activism, 1881–1917* (Cambridge: Cambridge University Press, 1999).

[35] Terry Irving, 'Labour, State and Nation Building in Australia', in Berger and Smith (eds), *Nationalism, Labour and Ethnicity*, pp. 193ff; Greg Patmore, *Australian Labour*

languages of class by languages of race is also a phenomenon characterizing South African labour movements in the nineteenth and twentieth centuries.[36]

In the white settler societies of Latin America, once again, Europeans brought the traditions of their labour movements with them. According to Hobart Spalding's classic account of organized labour in Latin America, a first formative phase from 1850 to the outbreak of the First World War can be distinguished from a second expansive phase in the inter-war period and a third phase lasting from 1945 to the 1970s/80s.[37] By 1914, thanks to the strong economic and political influence of the US in Latin America, as epitomized in the Monroe doctrine, capital's hand vis-à-vis the labour movement was strengthened, whilst there were also many direct attempts from the north to influence the shape and form of the Latin American labour movement. Samuel Gompers, the president of the AFL, for example, created the Pan-American Federation of Labor in 1918, which was essentially a US/Mexican/Caribbean federation with the explicit aim of influencing Mexican and Caribbean trade unionism.[38] Yet many labour movements in Latin America remained influenced by strong revolutionary traditions, including Marxist and anarchist variants that continued to play a role in labour politics throughout the twentieth century up to the present day.[39]

In those parts of the world that were not settled by Europeans, the picture again is vastly varied. In Asia, Japan managed to establish itself as 'the West' in 'the East', becoming a modern industrial society and a colonizing state. Massive proletarianization followed Japan's industrial spurt, which gave rise to an industrial working class often employed in large-scale factories. It formed the organizational base for Western-style trade unionism and it was also addressed by a Japanese socialist party that had

History (Melbourne: Longman, 1991); Sean Scalmer, 'The Career of Class: Intellectuals and the Labour Movement in Australia, 1942–1956', Sydney, (PhD diss. 1996).

[36] Peter Alexander, *Workers, War and the Origins of Apartheid. Labour and Politics in South Africa, 1939–1948* (Athens, OH: Ohio University Press, 2000); Pieter van Duin, 'South Africa', in Marcel van der Linden and Jürgen Rojahn (eds), *The Formation of Labour Movements, 1870–1914: An International Perspective* (Leiden: Brill, 1990), pp. 623–652.

[37] Hobart Spalding, *Organized Labor in Latin America: Historical Case Studies of Urban Workers in Dependent Societies* (New York: New York University Press, 1977).

[38] Philip S. Foner, *U.S. Labor Movement and Latin America*, vol. 1: *1846–1919* (South Hadley, MA: Bergin Garvey, 1988).

[39] Susan Eckstein (ed.), *Power and Popular Protest: Latin American Social Movements*, updated edn (Berkeley: University of California Press, 2001).

multiple links to the West. However, the labour movement in Japan was also inflected with its own peculiarities, including the functioning of the Meji state, religion, the strong ties of Japanese workers to their agrarian origins, lasting well into the twentieth century, and feudal remnants such as the *oyakata* system used for the control of workers. After the Second World War, resurgent communist and left-wing labour organizations were repressed by the American occupiers and, under American protection, Japan began to build strongly enterprise-based labour relations based on tame company unions and a management style emphasizing harmony and partnership.[40]

If Japan had successfully transformed itself into 'the West' by systematically learning and adapting Western ideas, China for a long time refused to do the same and instead ignored the advances of Western imperialism for as long as it could—with the result that it became a semi-colonial space. In its industrial heartlands, the rise of a waged industrial working class in the inter-war period went hand in hand with the rise of the Communist Party.[41] In a huge country such as China it is not surprising to find regional variations in the development of labour movements.[42] However, there was also a powerful merger of class and national discourses within the Chinese labour movement of the inter-war period.[43] The Communist Party emerged victorious from the tumultuous period of war and civil war (1937–1949), and Maoism was to become a major influence on far-left groups in the West, especially during the 1960s and 1970s. Mao's 'great leap forward' between 1958 and 1961, and his Cultural Revolution starting in 1966 were, with hindsight, major disasters that cost the lives of millions, but its visionary politics of a completely new society brought Maoism millions of followers world-wide.[44] Communist China also made

[40] Charles Weathers: 'Business and Labor', in William M. Tsutsui (ed.), *The Blackwell Companion to Japanese History* (Oxford: Blackwell, 2009), pp. 493–510, pp. 493ff.

[41] Jean Chesneaux, *The Chinese Labour Movement 1919–1927* (Palo Alto: Stanford University Press, 1968).

[42] Elizabeth J. Perry (ed.), *Putting Class in its Place: Workers' Identities in East Asia* (Berkeley: University of California Press, 1996); Bryan Goodman, *Native Place, City and Nation: Regional Networks and Identities in Shanghai* 1853–1937 (Berkeley: University of California Press, 1995).

[43] S. A. Smith, *Like Cattle and Horses. Nationalism and Labor in Shanghai 1895–1927* (Durham, NC: Duke University Press, 2002).

[44] Michael Schoenhals (ed.), *China's Cultural Revolution: not a Dinner Party* (Armonk, NY: M. E. Sharpe); Richard Wolin, *The Wind from the East: French Intellectuals, the Cultural Revolution and the Legacy of the 1960s* (Princeton, NJ: Princeton University Press, 2010).

a major intervention in the Korean War, establishing itself as a superpower, first in alliance with the Soviet Union and later in its own right. Today the Communist Party of China is attempting to ride the tiger of turbo-capitalism and to declare it a kind of Chinese variant of communism.

Like Chinese labour history, Indian labour history for a long time concentrated on the salaried industrial work force in small industrialized pockets of the vast Indian economy. Strongly influenced by Marxism, labour historians, who often were also activists, focused on the rise of a Marxist labour movement.[45] In parallel to other colonial and post-colonial settings, the Indian labour movement also saw a powerful merger of nationalism and socialism. Thus, the Indian National Congress under Indira Gandhi was strongly socialist in orientation. Only recently have labour historians paid more attention to the huge sector of informal and unorganized labour in the Indian economy. They have begun to explore in greater depth working women and their attempts at organization.[46] And the inter-relationship between the languages of class and the languages of communalism also remains a major area of research in the Indian context, where the vastness of the subcontinent once again seems to necessitate a labour movement history that is aware of the diverse spatial contexts of the development of labour movements.

In the Islamic world, the relationship between religion and labour movements is vitally important yet often woefully under-researched. 'The Islamic world' is itself a highly problematic concept, for it brings together many different forms of Islam that should be carefully differentiated. Those labour movements that were based on a salaried industrial proletariat, once again a distinct minority among workers everywhere in the Islamic world, were mostly secular in character, i.e. hostile to Islam. Thus, socialist pan-Arabism, as represented, for example, by Nasser in Egypt, tended to repress the Islamic Brotherhood and other attempts to develop a political Islamic movement. It set up a powerful historical trajectory that to this

---

[45] Very much an older activists' perspective is provided by: Shiva Rao, *Industrial Workers in India* (London: George Allen, 1939); N. M. Joshi, *Trade Union Movement in India* (Bombay, 1927); more academic writings include R. K. Mukherjee, *The Indian Working Class* (Bombay, 1948); S. G. Panandikar, *Industrial Labour in India* (London, 1933); very much rethinking this tradition is Dipesh Chakrabarty, *Rethinking Working-Class History: Bengal 1890–1940* (Princeton, NJ: Princeton University Press, 1989).

[46] See, for example, Nirmala Banerjee, *Women Workers in the Unorganised Sector: the Calcutta Experience* (Hyerabad: Sangam, 1985); Amita Sen, *Women and Labour in Late Colonial India: the Bengal Jute Industry* (Cambridge: Cambridge University Press, 1999).

date perceives the relationship between Islam and labour movements as largely dichotomous. The rise of Islamism in Egypt and Sudan since the 1990s, for example, has left socialist and communist labour movements in those countries weak and divided. In fact, in many countries Islamist forces have become the most effective opposition against undemocratic and Western-authoritarian regimes, leaving little room for a secular left-wing labour movement to develop a popular appeal.[47]

For the late Ottoman empire Donald Quaetaert has produced over the years a steady stream of work increasing our understanding of the history of Ottoman workers and their labour movements.[48] Egypt has easily been the most industrially developed country in the Islamic world of the Middle East.[49] Hence it also has a long tradition of left-wing political activism and a strong labour movement. The development of the oil industry accelerated the rise of Egyptian wage labour after the end of the Second World War. It was accompanied by the growth of strong communist trade unions and a Communist Party that promoted strong class discourses in Egyptian society. Under Nasser, the Communist Party was under instructions from Nasser's ally, the Soviet Union, to dissolve and work within the framework of pan-Arabic nationalism represented by Nasser. It was a blow from which the party would never recover. But Egypt was not the only Islamic country in the Middle East. Strong communist labour movements could also be found in Lebanon, Syria and Iraq. The Shah, with the help of the CIA, brutally repressed such a movement in Iran in 1953. To date, few historians have focused on the masses of non-industrial workers, who often faced greater difficulties to organize, partly because of authoritarian forms of rule but partly also because of the nature of their often precarious work. A contemporary example is the army of millions of migrant workers in the oil-rich Arab states. These workers work under conditions of near-slavery and personal bondage, with no basic human rights.

In most sub-Saharan African countries, with the exception of South Africa, we can at best speak of an intermittent development of industrial

---

[47] Joel Beinin and Zachary Lockmann, *Workers on the Nile: Nationalism, Communism, Islam and the Egyptian Working-Class, 1882–1954* (Cairo: American University in Cairo Press, 1998).

[48] Donald Quataert, *Social Disintegration and Popular Resistance in the Ottoman Empire, 1881–1908* (New York: New York University Press, 1983); idem, *Workers, Peasants and Economic Change in the Ottoman Empire, 1730–1914* (Istanbul: Isis Press, 1993).

[49] Zachary Lockmann, *Workers and Working Classes in the Middle-East: Struggles, Histories, Historiographies* (Albany: State University of New York Press, 1994).

working classes and their organizations. The Western narratives of working-class formation and proletarianization make little sense here; instead, concepts of 'kinship' and 'community' as well as a highly localized sense of place seem to be far more powerful in explaining the development of labour movements here.[50] Global capitalism did not leave Africa unaffected: Of course, we also witness the emergence of trade unions and working-class parties in Africa, especially where industries and markets developed well under colonial and post-colonial regimes.[51] Mining and urban workers in black Africa belong to the best-examined groups.[52] Yet, the logic of capitalist social organization often worked rather poorly in Africa. In the Zambian copper mines and on the Nigerian railways, the promises of industrial modernization soon rang hollow to the workers employed there. And there is some evidence that in urban contexts social networks could be far more important than formal trade union organizations when it came to the organization of strikes, as exemplified by the Mombasa strikes of 1947.[53] After the Second World War, women workers also were important in overall economic activity,[54] sometimes contributing vitally to the family income. However, we know very little so far about what languages of labour signalled what working-class consciousness among the industrial workers of black Africa. And once again, it is urgently necessary

[50] Frederic Cooper, 'African Labor History', in Lucassen (ed.), *Global Labour History*, pp. 91–116.

[51] Richard Sandbrook and Robin Cohen, *The Development of an African Working-Class: Studies in Class Formation and Action* (Toronto: University of Toronto Press, 1975); Paul M. Lubeck, *Islam and Urban Labor in Northern Nigeria: the Making of a Muslim Working Class* (Cambridge: Cambridge University Press, 1986); John Higginson, *A Working Class in the Making: Belgian Colonial Labour Policy, Private Enterprise and the African Mineworker, 1907–1951* (Madison: University of Wisconsin Press, 1989).

[52] Carolyne A. Brown, *'We Were all Slaves': African Miners, Culture and Resistance at the Enugu Government Colliery* (Wesport: Greenwood, 2003); Ian R. Phimister, *Wangi Kolia: Coal, and Labour in Colonial Zimbabwe, 1894–1954* (Johannesburg: Witswatersrand University Press); Bill Freund, *Capital and Labour in the Nigerian Tin Mines* (Atlantic Highlands, NJ: Humanities Press, 1984).

[53] There are some interesting attempts to analyse data on labour conflicts and rebellions in global context. See, for example, Beverly J. Silver, 'World-Scale Patterns of Labor–Capital Conflict: Labor Unrest, Long Waves and Cycles of World Hegemony', *Review of the Fernand Braudel Center* 1 (1995), pp. 155–192; Ernesto Screpanti, 'Long Economic Cycles and Recurring Proletarian Insurgencies', *Review of the Fernand Braudel Center* 3 (1984), pp. 509–584.

[54] Aili Mari Tripp, *Changing the Rules: The Politics of Liberalization and the Urban Informal Economy in Tanzania* (Berkley: University of California Press 1997).

to start exploring the forms of resistance by those many non-industrial, non-salaried groups of workers in Africa, include slave labourers. After all, African slave labour was central to the Atlantic System, which in turn was vital for the evolution of capitalism; and in parallel to the transatlantic slave trade was a thriving intra-African slave trade.[55] Slave workers, as a considerable body of work has shown, could not easily be transformed into wage labour.[56]

GLOBAL POLITICAL MOMENTS IN THE DEVELOPMENT OF LABOUR MOVEMENTS?

If the aim is to write a new global labour movement history, the above brief glimpses have indicated the need to contextualize those labour movements carefully in highly localized regimes of labour that go far beyond the classical orientation towards a salaried industrial working class. Is the task for global labour movement history then solely one of localization, diversification and compartmentalization? I would argue that this is only one, albeit very important, side of the coin. Another one is to recognize that there continue to be universal patterns in the development of global capitalism and that there have been important political caesuras of relevance if not to all then to many labour movements in the world, struggling under conditions of diverse forms of capitalist organization of social relations. Hence the question arises whether certain global political moments can be identified which had a major impact on the development of labour movements. It may be too early to identify such global moments at present, as we simply lack the research on non-Western labour movements to produce anything other than a Western-biased list of alleged 'global moments'. And indeed, I have only been able to identify four such moments, all of which seem Western-centric: first, the caesura of the First World War; secondly, the impact of the Russian Revolution; thirdly, the struggle against fascism and right-wing authoritarianism in the inter-war

---

[55] Paul E. Lovejoy, *Transformations in Slavery: A History of Slavery in Africa*, updated edn (Cambridge: Cambridge University Press, 2011).

[56] Frederick Cooper, *From Slaves to Squatters: Plantation Labor and Agriculture in Zanzibar and Coastal Kenya, 1890–1925* (London: Pearson 1997); Anne Philipps, *The Enigma of Colonialism: British Policy in West Africa* (London: James Currey, 1989); Ahmad A. Sikainga, *Slaves into Workers: Emancipation and Labor in Colonial Sudan* (Austin: University of Texas Press, 1996).

period and beyond; and, finally, the Cold War with its accompanying histories of decolonization.

The First World War was a major caesura in the history of European labour movements, above all because it signalled the limits of labour movements' internationalism and the degree of effective nationalization of labour movements. With the exception of Russia and Ireland, no labour movement anywhere rejected the call of their respective national government to join a wartime national alliance against the nation's alleged 'enemies'. The power of the European nation-states over the allegiance of organized workers became very apparent after the summer of 1914, and the war itself furthered the integration of labour movements into national political and social systems in a major way, as is clear from the advances made in welfare regimes, the recognition of trade unions and the increase in power of working-class parties. In many parts of Western Europe, the Second World War had a similar effect, although it was in some respects only a continuation of what had started in 1914—strengthened by the impact of anti-communism in the context of the nascent Cold War. In global perspective, global labour movement history could ask whether and to what extent war, and it would not necessarily have to restrict itself to the two world wars, had facilitated the integration of labour in national states. However, the integration of labour movements in the First World War came at a price—it exacerbated differences between reformists and revolutionaries in all socialist parties, leading to formal divisions, such as in Germany in 1916, facilitating the emergence of two hostile wings of the labour movement after the end of the First World War: a communist and a social democratic wing.

In the aftermath of the Russian Revolution, Lenin used these pre-existing divisions to split the labour movement formally in most Western and some non-Western countries by forcing socialists to choose between adherence to diverse forms of social democracy and socialism and adherence to his own communist path.[57] The divide between social democrats and communists was to have a huge impact on labour movement history in many parts of the world in the period between 1917 and 1990. Whilst Leninism was transformed into Stalinism and laid the foundations for a dictatorial regime of a small group of party leaders that was replicated everywhere in the sphere influenced by the Soviet Union (at the height of

---

[57] Kevin McDermott and Jeremy Agnew, *The Comintern: a History of International Communism from Lenin to Stalin* (Basingstoke: Macmillan, 1996).

the Cold War about half of the globe), social democrats made their peace with capitalism in the post-Second World War world and sought to create a capitalism with a human face through a mixture of endorsement of a democratization of all spheres of life, social engineering from the top, the macro-economic steering of markets, welfare and educational programmes and a politics of equality of opportunities that would, above all, benefit the lower segments of society.[58] Whilst the communist and social democratic movements formed the two major wings of the labour movement in the 'short twentieth century',[59] a variety of 'third ways' and groups with distinct ideological orientations, such as the anarcho-syndicalist wing of the labour movement, continued to exist and sought to formulate positions that were independent of both communism and social democracy.[60]

In the inter-war period this global division of the labour movement was lamented by many labour movement activists, as they perceived it as vitally weakening the defences of labour against the biggest threat to the left: fascism and right-wing authoritarianism. In the economic crises of the inter-war period, many of the new democracies in Europe proved highly unstable. Eventually, Germany, Austria, Italy, Greece, Croatia, Romania, Hungary, Poland, Portugal and Spain would all fall into the hands of fascist and right-wing authoritarian regimes. Whilst communism for a long time underestimated the threat from fascism and even welcomed the destruction of democracies, arguing that after fascism it would be the turn of communism, social democracy faced a serious dilemma in most Western countries. With the exception of Britain between the 1890 and the 1950s, the industrial working class nowhere formed a majority of the population. Hence working-class parties needed alliances with other political forces and social classes to gain power through the ballot-box. Yet, there were many social democrats unwilling to compromise their positions in pursuit of electoral alliances, and, perhaps even more problematic, few 'bourgeois' political parties were willing to accept social democrats as coalition partners. For the inter-war period the Swedish example underlines starkly that

---

[58] Donald Sassoon, *Hundred Years of Socialism* (London: I.B. Tauris, 1996).

[59] Eric Hobsbawm, *Age of Extremes: The Short Twentieth Century 1914–1991* (London; Michael Joseph, 1994).

[60] Geoff Eley has pointed to the desire of labour movement historians associated with either the communist or the social democratic wing to marginalize the significance of these 'third way' positions in the overall history of the labour movement. See Geoff Eley, 'Reviewing the Socialist Tradition', in Christiane Lemke and Gary Marks (eds), *The Crisis of Socialism in Europe* (Durham, NC: Duke University Press, 1992), pp. 21–60.

social democrats were most successful where they managed to forge strong class and political alliances (in Sweden with the farmers and their party). The rise of the Scandinavian model of social democracy after 1945 had its roots in those alliances.[61] A future global history of labour movements will have to ask what kind of alliances what types of labour movement could forge, and under which specific local circumstances. Was it also a challenge from politically right-wing movements (can we call some of them fascist?) that provided the major challenge for left-of-centre labour movements outside of the West?

Where fascism and right-wing authoritarianism threatened labour movements, especially in Europe and Latin America, labour sought to build popular and united fronts—with varying success.[62] At the end of the Second World War, many labour movement activists believed that a key lesson provided by the victories of fascism in the inter-war period and the sufferings of the Second World War was the necessity for unity of the labour movement. However, the ensuing Cold War soon put a stop to those ideas and concepts, ultimately solidifying the division of the labour movement whilst at the same time globalizing the rift.

The rivalry between a global communism and a global capitalism took place in the context of an accelerating process of decolonization after 1945. Independence movements can of course often be traced back to the inter-war period and further to the pre-First World era, but the overwhelming majority of colonies only became independent during the Cold War.[63] In the inter-war period, the global communist movement had been the greatest stalwart of independence movements, so that communists often had an important influence in anti-imperial movements in the colonized world. Social democracy, by contrast, had a much more mixed record. Japanese trade unions often supported the ultra-nationalist policies pursued by Japanese right-wing governments in the 1930s and during the

[61] Klaus Misgeld, Karl Molin and Klas Åmark (eds), *Creating Social Democracy: A Century of the Social Democratic Labor Party in Sweden* (University Park, PA: Pennsylvania State University Press, 1988); in comparative perspective see also Mary Hilson, *Political Change and the Rise of Labour in Comparative Perspective: Britain and Sweden 1890–1920* (Lund: Nordic Academic Press, 2006).

[62] Gerd-Rainer Horn, *European Socialists Respond to Fascism: Ideology, Activism and Contingency in the 1930s* (Oxford: Oxford University Press, 1996).

[63] James D. LeSueur (ed.), *The Decolonisation Reader* (London : Routledge, 2003); Prasenjit Duara (ed.), *Decolonization. Perspectives Now and Then* (London : Routledge, 2004).

Second World War. British trade unions worked hand-in-hand with British governments in order to maintain British imperial rule in different parts of the world—both in the inter-war and the post-war periods. American trade unions served the interests of American foreign policy throughout the Cold War. Whilst social democrats, on balance, were in favour of decolonization, they hesitated to call the moment for such decolonization and often entertained ideas of civilizational progress as precondition for independence.[64] This also explains the greater popularity of communism in the anti-imperial movements of the colonized world, and it explains why so many post-colonial independent states became allies of the Soviet Union or at least retained sympathy for communism. The Communist International became an important forum for the meeting of post-colonial and Western communists, even if it always remained a tool in the hands of the Soviet leadership. Social democratic internationalism was also an important feature during the Cold War. Its anti-communism sought to stabilize anti-communist lefts in a range of countries in the developing world and also in Europe, where they emerged from right-wing authoritarian dictatorships, as was the case in Greece, Spain and Portugal in the 1970s.[65] The stage for a labour movement politics thus had become a truly global one during the Cold War.

However, the developmentalism promised by both communist and social democratic modernization strategies soon began to ring hollow in the post-colonial world, whose realities did not neatly fit the panaceas espoused by Marxism-Leninism or democratic socialism. Communist regimes in the developing world could not deliver on promises of economic and social development and soon retained power only through dictatorial means. Elsewhere, the global West allied itself to right-wing authoritarian dictatorships, as social democracies had little chance of establishing themselves in post-colonial states in Asia and Africa as well as in the longer established independent states of Latin America.

Disillusionment with both wings of the labour movement could not only be found in the post-colonial world. It was also coming to the fore from the 1950s in the Western metropoles. 1956 marked an important

---

[64] Eley, *Forging Democracy*, p. 353.
[65] Nuno Serveriano Teixeira (ed.), *The International Politics of Democratization: Comparative Perspectives* (London: Routledge, 2008).

starting point for a global New Left with its many national inflections.[66] The double crisis of Hungary and Suez marked double disillusionment—with communism and with Western democracies that were also supported by social democrats. An emerging first New Left now began to search for left-wing politics that was independent of both communism and social democracy, often picking up on concepts and ideas of 'third way' socialists from the inter-war period. A second New Left, associated with the student protest and anti-Vietnam movement of the 1960s, further developed those independent left-wing ideas that no longer wanted to be associated with either communism or social democracy.[67] The Vietnam War, in particular, became a global symbol for a strong anti-imperialism that united the left in the metropoles with the left in the peripheries. The New Left's often neo-Marxist ideas fed into a range of new social movements from the 1970s onwards and informed their political cultures. In international politics, the non-aligned movement, under the leadership of self-declared socialist/communist countries, such as Tito's Yugoslavia, Gandhi's India and Nasser's Egypt sought to provide leadership for those countries that did not want to associate themselves with one or the other of the dominant power blocks in the Cold War. Dependency theory and Third Worldism became important for developing new ways of thinking intent on over-coming the established ideological Cold War divisions.

The Western-centrism of these global moments in a political history of labour movements is striking. The First World War originated in Europe, although it was arguably tied up with questions of colonial rivalry and global hegemony and was also played out in non-Western spaces. The Russian revolution was a European moment, albeit one with global consequences. Fascism originated in Europe, although it again travelled to non-European spaces. And the Cold War had its origins in the rivalry between two hostile power blocks led by two Western powers—the United States and the Soviet Union, even if it eventually ended up dividing the world. Of course, there is the often-cited example of the Haitian revolution as

---

[66] Gerd-Rainer Horn, *The Spirit of 1968: Rebellion in Western Europe and North America, 1956–1976* (Oxford: Oxford University Press, 2007); specifically on Britain also: Lin Chun, *The British New Left* (Edinburgh: Edinburgh University Press, 1993); Michael Kenny, 'The First New Left in Britain, 1956–1964' (PhD diss., Manchester, 1991).

[67] See also Chap. 18 by Gerd-Rainer Horn in this volume. 1968 was another, truly global moment in the history of social movements. See, for example, on 1968 in the Senegal: Omar Gueye, 'Mai 68 au Sénégal, Senghor face au movement synodical' (University of Amsterdam PhD 2014).

the first working-class revolution of modern history, and, indeed, it might well be possible to look harder at the non-Western spaces in order to find events that might structure an alternative non-Western-centric global history of labour movements. However, even the Haitian Revolution would not have been possible without the French Revolution and the world of the European Enlightenment. With few exceptions, such as the impact of Maoism, the Vietnam War and dependentist movements in Latin America, is it the case then, and I want to leave it as an open question here, that any political history of the modern labour movement necessarily has a Western-centric perspective? It would certainly appear to be a major challenge for the future to look for non-Western events to structure global labour movement history, but looking at the moments that I chose above, it seems difficult to deny that they were genuinely global moments with an impact far beyond the Western world. Hence the West cannot be written out of global labour history; it might not even be possible, at least for the moment, to start from any other place than the West. Therefore, with all due caution, I would like to ask whether many aspects of a global labour movement and of global labour movement history will not continue to have a distinctly Western outlook?

NEW CHALLENGES FOR LABOUR IN THE POST-COLD WAR WORLD

The left had little to do with the end of the Cold War. The collapse of the communist regimes in Eastern Europe and the Soviet Union between 1989 and 1992 was celebrated in the West as a triumph of capitalism and the democratic 'free world' over communism.[68] Such triumphalism sometimes also included attempts to denounce social democrats as fifth column of Moscow during the Cold War, largely because social democrats had been in favour of policies of détente from the late 1960s onwards. But by the time the Soviet empire collapsed, Western social democracy was already in deep crisis. From the late 1970s onwards the global advances of neoliberalism had pushed social democracy onto the defensive: its strategies of social engineering, macro-economic planning and welfare expansion had all come in for devastating criticisms that proved popular at the ballot-boxes. In the post-Cold War world, when capitalism had lost its most important global enemy, it could reveal a much nastier face again, and in

[68] Francis Fukuyama, *The End of History and the Last Man* (New York: Free Press, 1992).

many parts of the world has been engaged in attempts to defeat labour movements and keep them out of government and out of businesses. Right-to-work legislation in the United States and anti-labour strategies in India are pertinent examples, as are the state-capitalist attempts in China to prevent an independent labour movement emerging. In global perspective, the memory of labour and social movements is being marginalized almost everywhere at the beginning of the twentieth century.[69]

Although the forces of neoliberalism have also made important inroads into European, Australian and Canadian social democratic societies since the 1980s, social democracy in these parts of the world, often in alliance with Christian democratic and social liberal political forces, is still attempting to formulate positions that would allow for a renewed taming of the forces of capitalism in the pursuit of solidaristic societies in which the values of social equality, equality of opportunities and democracy form the basis of social cohesion. But these societies have, for the most part, undergone processes of de-industrialization, which put structural economic change of the agenda.[70] In an increasingly post-industrial West, one of the questions for social democracy is: what constituency is there for which labour movement? The industrial working-class population has been shrinking almost everywhere. Can, therefore, the social democratic labour movement still represent the working-class? Some have argued for an 'end of social democracy',[71] whilst others have been searching for a new synthesis of liberalism and social democracy that could open up the possibility of mobilizing an electorate that increasingly does not identify itself with issues of class.[72]

In some countries of the rapidly developing global South, such as Brazil, we have witnessed over recent years the emergence of powerful and rather traditional looking lefts, often based on strong trade union movements. Especially in Latin America, scholars have observed a revival of a socialist left that presented a new version of left-wing utopian anti-capitalism

---

[69] Jürgen Mittag and Berthold Unfried (eds), *The Memory of Labour and Social Movements. A Global Perspective* (Leipzig: AVA, 2011).

[70] See, for example, Margaret Cowell, *Dealing with Deindustrialization: Adaptive Resilience in American Midwestern Regions* (London: Routledge, 2015); Stefan Goch, *Eine Region im Kampf mit dem Strukturwandel: Bewältigung von Strukturwandel und Strukturpolitik im Ruhrgebiet* (Essen: Klartext, 2002).

[71] Gerassimos Moschonas, *In the Name of Social Democracy: The Great Transformation 1945 to the Present* (London: Verso, 2002).

[72] Anthony Giddens, *The Third Way: The Renewal of Social Democracy* (Cambridge: Polity Press, 1998).

that some thought had died out with the collapse of communism. Yet in Russia, India and China, various forms of turbo-capitalism, informed by high doses of corruption, have been producing major social inequalities since the end of the Cold War. Social protest has accompanied those increases in social inequality but they have so far been controlled through a mixture of dictatorial political practices and the inability of social movements to mobilize significant support for their oppositional politics. What we might well be witnessing, as the twenty-first century progresses, is a global struggle between two different models of social organization—one that is unashamedly capitalist, based on greed and exploitation, and one that is social democratic and based on solidaristic cultures of mutualism. There are undoubtedly many shades of grey between these two models of societal organization, but the signs are that labour movements are positioning themselves to play their part in strengthening those solidaristic cultures of mutualism everywhere in the world.

Conclusion

As the formation of the subaltern worker (rather than working-class formation) came in many shapes and forms, so the labour movement took a great variety of shapes and forms in different parts of the world. In future it will be important to start labour movement history from the vantage point of the many different organizations and means of social protest developed by the much wider groups of subaltern workers, and not restrict attention to wage-earning industrial workers and their portfolios of social protest. A widening of our understanding of who is a worker also necessitates a widening of our understanding of what is a labour movement. To date we know a lot about Western labour movements and quite a bit about attempts to set up Western-looking labour movements elsewhere, but not nearly enough about alternative forms of the organization of labour that do not fit Western understandings of labour movements. In the context of the imperial subjugation of 'the rest' by 'the West' in the nineteenth century, ideas and concepts of labour and labour movements travelled from 'the West' to 'the rest' and influenced what was understood by labour movements everywhere. As this briefest of surveys has tried to indicate, such political and cultural transfers were characterized by multiple difficulties of translation. Whilst the Western concepts of labour seemed indispensable to many in understanding an increasingly globalizing world, they are also inadequate in that they failed to grasp fully the specificities of historical development in the global South. Communism and social democracy as concepts coined in the West acquired a different meaning in the South, often clashing with local traditions and forms of social organization. A global labour movement history therefore needs to pay due attention to the frictions and ambiguities produced by such conceptual imperialism and thereby take seriously Chakrabarty's call to 'provincialise Europe'. It also means paying due attention to the inter-connections between diverse labour movements in different parts of the world. Rather than compartmentalizing labour movements in nation-state frames, the new global labour history seeks to explore the transnational similarities and points of contact. However, global labour history should also be careful not to pour out the baby with the bathwater—it is, for example, undeniable that the nation-state formed an important political frame for the development of labour movements that, from the late nineteenth century onwards, often perceived the nation-state as its most importance reference point and that engaged, first and foremost, in national politics. Hence, it is unsurprising that, up to this day, labour movements remain strongly oriented towards the nation-state. What is needed, therefore, is a different conceptualization of space for different questions that are being asked by labour movement history. National framework remains important for some questions. Comparisons can be revealing for others. Transnational forms of labour history and internationalism also highlight the interconnections of labour movement struggles across the globe. What methods and strategies will be employed by labour movement historians in future depends very much on the questions they will be asking.

Further Readings

A global labour history is still very much in the making. A pathfinder on the road to a potentially global labour history was Eric Hobsbawm—see for example his *Worlds of Labour*, London: Orion, 1984. Good current surveys include Jan Lucassen (ed.), *Global Labour History. A State of the Art* (Berne: Peter Lang, 2006); Marcel van der Linden, *Workers of the World. Essays Toward a Global Labor History* (Leiden: Brill, 2008), Andreas Eckert, 'What is Global Labour History Good for?' in Jürgen Kocka (ed.), *Work in a Modern Society. The German Historical Experience in Comparative Perspective*, (Oxford: Berghahn Books, 2010), pp. 169–182, and Andrea Komlosy, *Arbeit: eine globalhistorische Perspektive*, 13.–21. Jahrhundert (Vienna: Böhlau, 2014).

Furthermore, over the last decades, a number of excellent collaborative projects with a global reach have been initiated by the International Institute for Social History in Amsterdam. They include Lex Heerma van Voss, Els Hiemstra-Kuperus, Elise van Nederveen Meerkerk (eds), *The Ashgate Companion to Textile Workers* (Aldershot: Ashgate, 2010); Sam Davies, Colin J. Davis, Lex Heerma van Voss, Lidewij Hesselink, David de Vries and Klaus Weinhauer (eds), *Dock Workers*, 2 vols, (Aldershot: Ashgate 2000). The journal of the IISG, the *International Review of Social History* (IRSH), published by Cambridge University Press, has also been in the forefront of publishing cutting-edge research on global labour history for many years. Some of its recent supplements had strong global themes, for example *Labour in Transport: Histories from the Global South, 1750–1950,* ed. by Stefano Belluci, Larissa Rosa Corea, Jan-Georg Deutsch and Chitra Joshi (2014). The turn to global labour history in IRSH is complemented by transnational and comparative work in other labour history journals, including *International Labor and Working Class History*, published by Cambridge University Press, and *Moving the Social: Journal for Social History and the History of Social Movements*, published by the Institute for Social Movements in Bochum. The latter also publishes the book series *Palgrave Studies in the History of Social Movements*, published by Palgrave Macmillan, which encourages transnational, comparative and global labour history.

Over recent years the Re:Work Centre at the Humboldt University in Berlin has also become a major hub for the promotion of global histories of work and labour. Not publishing its own journal or book series, the fellowship programme has produced much cutting-edge work in global labour history, e.g. Alice Mah, *Port Cities and Global Legacies. Urban Identity, Waterfront Work and Radicalism* (Basingstoke: Palgrave Macmillan, 2014), and Babacar Fall, Ineke Paff-Rheinberger and Andreas Eckert (eds), *Work and Culture in a Globalized World*, (Paris: Karthala, 2015).

There is also a host of networked labour archives, libraries and research institutes, the International Association of Labour History Institutions (IALHI)—mainly located in Western Europe and North as well as South America—that have been increasingly promoting transnational and global perspectives on labour history. (see http://www.ialhi.org) The so-called Linz conferences of labour historians that had been started originally as a meeting place between East and West European historians during the Cold War, has also more recently turned its attention to global and transnational themes. For a full list of their published conference proceedings see http://www.ith.or.at.

Given that the centres of labour movements have been in Europe and North America we also have a number of good surveys on those regions of the world, including Geoff Eley, *Forging Democracy: The History of the Left in Europe, 1850–2000* (Oxford: Oxford University Press, 2002) and Donald Sassoon, *Hundred Years of Socialism: The West European Left in the Twentieth-Century*, (London: I.B. Tauris, 1996), For North America there is also, in comparative perspective with Britain, Neville Kirk, *Labour and Society in Britain and the USA*, 2 vols, (Aldershot: Scolar, 1994). For South America see Susan Eckstein, *Power and Popular Protest: Latin American Social Movements*, new edn (Berkeley: University of California Press, 2001). For the Middle East see John Chalcraft, *Popular Politics in the Making of the Modern Middle East* (Cambridge: Cambridge University Press, 2016). A huge step in the direction of a global history of the communist movement has been taken by Steve A. Smith, *The Oxford Handbook of the History of Communism* (Oxford: Oxford University Press, 2014). On the anarchist movement see James Joll, *The Anarchists* (London: Eyre &Spottiswoode, 1968); Irving Louis Horowitz, *The Anarchists* (New York: Aldine Transaction, 2005).

Apart from surveys there has also been more detailed comparative and transnational work looking often at two or three, rarely more countries and comparing a variety of labour movements or looking at their inter-relationship and their exchanges. Some of the work in this category includes the book of the already mentioned Neville Kirk, and Stefan Berger, *The British Labour Party and the German Social Democrats*, 1900–1931, (Oxford: Clarendon, 1994); both, in their own ways, argue against theories of exceptionalism—in Kirk's case against an American and in Berger's case against a British, exceptionalism in labour history.

Some specific sub-themes have also been dealt with comparatively, for example the relationship between socialism and nationalism. For this see John Schwarzmantel, *Socialism and the Idea of the Nation* (London: Prentice Hall, 1991), and Stefan Berger and Angel Smith (eds), *Nationalism, Labour and Ethnicity 1870–1939* (Manchester: Manchester University Press, 1999), On migration and the labour movement see Dirk Hoerder, *Labor Migration in the Atlantic Economies: The European and North American Working Classes During the Period of Industrialization* (Westport: Greenwood Press, 1985). On labour and the women's movement see Richard J. Evans, *Comrades and Sisters: Feminism, Socialism and Pacifism in Europe, 1870–1945* (Brighton: Harvester Press, 1987); Marilyn J. Boxer and Jean H. Quataert (eds), *Socialist Women: European Socialist Feminism in the Nineteenth and Early Twentieth Centuries* (New

York: Elsevier, 1978); Helmut Gruber and Pamela Graves (eds), *Women and Socialism; Socialism and Women: Europe Between the Two World Wars* (Oxford: Berghahn, 1998).

Next to the comparative studies stand a variety of transnational studies that look more at transnational networks and connectivities than straightforward comparison. Two examples among many are Dorothee Schneider, *Trade Unions and Community. The German Working Class in New York City, 1870–1900* (Champaign: University of Illinois Press, 1994), and Ad Knotter, 'Transnational Cigarmakers: Cross-Border Labour Markets, Strikes, and Solidarity at the Time of the First International (1864–1873)', *International Review of Social History* 3 (2014), pp. 409–442; Steven Parfitt, Brotherhood From a Distance: Americanization and the Internationalism of the Knights of Labor, *International Review of Social History* 3 (2013), pp. 463–491; Frank Wolff, 'Eastern Europe Abroad: Exploring Actor-Networks in Transnational Movements and Migration History, The Case of the Bund', *International Review of Social History* 2 (2012), pp. 229–255. Whilst there has been a vociferous debate between comparativists and those more interested in questions of political and cultural transfer, there is no reason to believe that the two methods cannot and should not be integrated in a truly transnational history of labour. See the methodological remarks in Stefan Berger, 'Comparative History', in Stefan Berger, Heiko Feldner and Kevin Passmore (eds), *Writing History: Theory and Practice*, 2nd edn (London: Bloomsbury, 2010).

The overwhelming majority of all studies on labour movement history are still national in orientation, reflecting the strong nationalization of labour history from its inception in the nineteenth century. For the latter aspect see Gitta Deneckere and Thomas Welskopp, 'The "nation" and "class": European national master-narratives and their social "other"', in Stefan Berger and Chris Lorenz (eds), *The Contested Nation: Ethnicity, Class, Religion and Gender in National Histories*, Basingstoke: Palgrave Macmillan, pp. 135–170; Europe and North America are served best with those studies, and the organizational and ideological history of national labour movements has been thoroughly researched here, with a wealth of excellent studies available here. This is not really the case for the non-Western parts of the globe, where much work still remains to the done, in particular with regard to Asia and Africa. For Africa see Frederick Cooper, *Decolonization and African Society: The Labor Question in French and British Africa* (Cambridge: Cambridge University Press, 1996).

The strong organizational and history of ideas approach to the history of labour movements was challenged theoretically by the turn to cultural history. Interestingly E.P. Thompson had already stressed the importance of integrating a cultural analysis of labour in the 1960s, constructively taking up some of the ideas of Antonio Gramsci and challenging the dominant Althusserian structuralism of the times. See on the concept of 'moral economy', E.P. Thompson, 'The Moral Economy of the English Crowd in the Eighteenth Century' (originally published in *Past and Present*, 1971), and 'The Moral Economy Reviewed' both in: *Customs in Common: Studies in Traditional Popular Culture* (New York: The New Press 1993), pp. 185–351. The more recent merger between cultural and social history is holding out hope that a global labour history will also avoid the sterile attempts to play off one against the other and adopt theoretical perspectives that will be capable of integrating social and cultural perspectives.

The labour movement has also been a strongly internationalist movement almost since its inception in Europe in the last third of the nineteenth century. Hence there is also an important body of work on the institutions of the various Internationals and on internationalism more generally. For reasons of space we can here only mention two good recent examples: Kevin J. Callahan, *Demonstration Culture: European Socialism and the Second International, 1889–1914* (Leicester: Troubadour 2010), and Talbot Imlay, *The Practice of Socialist Internationalism: European Socialists and International Politics, 1914–1960* (Oxford: Oxford University Press, 2017, forthcoming).

CHAPTER 15

Myths, Big Myths and Global Environmentalism

Frank Uekötter

Few other movements have embraced globalism as enthusiastically as the environmental movement. Ever since the Apollo 8 photographs, the blue planet has served as a transnational icon from climate diplomacy to New Age fantasies. Countless activists have called for 'global awareness', to an extent that 'global' at times appeared like a synonym for 'important'. All over the world, environmentalists have attended Earth Summits, joined groups like Friends of the Earth or Earth First!, discussed James Lovelock's Gaia hypothesis and put their hopes on global environmental agreements.

But at the same time, the environmental movement provides an object lesson on the intricate problems that globalization implies for social movements. Notwithstanding globalized rhetoric and networking, environmental organizations and polities remain overwhelmingly tied to national and regional frames of reference. Issues and patterns of mobilization differ enormously around the world, and so do the styles and worldviews of the leading activists. In fact, we frequently find the interesting situation that environmentalists with international fame are marginal figures in their home countries. That holds true for Petra Kelly, probably Germany's most acclaimed international environmentalist, whose political career

F. Uekötter (✉)
Department of History, University of Birmingham, Birmingham, UK

© The Author(s) 2017
S. Berger, H. Nehring (eds.), *The History of Social Movements in Global Perspective*, DOI 10.1057/978-1-137-30427-8_15

in Germany was controversial and brief.[1] France's best-known environmentalist, Jacques-Yves Cousteau, 'became something of a pariah among French greens', as Michael Bess has argued, and Brazil's José Lutzenberger suffered a similar fate.[2] Brazil's other environmentalist of global fame, Chico Mendes, once yelled at a television feature that praised his efforts to rescue the 'lungs of the world', stating that he cared about the Amazon rainforest 'because there are thousands of people living here who depend on the forest'.[3]

With that in mind, this essay cannot depart from a generally accepted narrative. In fact, we need to raise questions about some popular clichés about environmentalism before we can move beyond the limitations of national perspectives. Half a century ago, a book of this kind surely would not have included an article on environmentalism, and neither may a volume two or three decades from now. Over the last decades, environmentalism has provided plenty of fodder for deconstruction, and the endeavour is all the easier for *global* environmentalism. Nonetheless, the notion of a global environmental movement is still lingering.

MOVEMENT IMPOSSIBLE: THE ELUSIVE CHARACTER OF ENVIRONMENTALISM

The term 'environmentalism' refers to a large variety of issues. Topics such as bird protection, pollution and efficient resource use have been embraced by distinct movements with distinctive policies until they became part of environmentalism in the post-war years. Since the 1970s, the concept of one environmental movement has been a fixture of Western politics, but it barely distracts from enormous tensions within the camp. Conflicts between environmentalists are nothing new, as the famous battle over the Hetch Hetchy valley in Yosemite National Park serves to attest, where a dam project pitted water interests and nature protection against each

---

[1] Saskia Richter, *Die Aktivistin. Das Leben der Petra Kelly* (Munich: DVA, 2010).

[2] Michael Bess, *The Light-Green Society. Ecology and Technological Modernity in France, 1960–2000* (Chicago: University of Chicago Press, 2003), p. 72; Kevin Niebauer, 'Ökologische Krise und Umweltbewegung auf der Akteursebene. Ideenwelt, Handlungsstrategie und Selbstverständnis von José A. Lutzenberger (1968 bis 1992)' (Master's thesis, Freie Universität Berlin, 2012).

[3] Quoted after Andrew Revkin, *The Burning Season. The Murder of Chico Mendes and the Fight for the Amazon Rain Forest* (Washington, DC: Island Press, 2004), p. 261.

other.[4] It is quite likely that most activists of recent decades would define themselves primarily as, for example, 'birdies' or anti-nuclear campaigners, rather than 'environmentalists'.

More importantly, the merger of divergent issues rests on a delicate theoretical footing. Ecology came across with an air of scientific reasoning when it became tantamount to the founding religion of environmentalism in the 1960s and 1970s, but the ecology of the environmentalists was quite at odds with the biological discipline of the same name. In fact, ideas about a natural equilibrium—for instance, in Frederic Clements' climax theory—went out of fashion in biology just at the time when environmentalists were embracing these notions.[5] One can write a history of environmentalism as a history of overarching concepts that came under fire and more or less fell by the wayside: ecology, wilderness, Gaia, peace with nature, no-risk. Miraculously, while critics have gnawed away the intellectual foundations of environmentalism, the building is still standing.

To be sure, the critique of environmental theory remains a contested terrain. In the 1990s, the historian William Cronon provoked an outcry from the US environmental community when he deconstructed the notion of 'wilderness'.[6] However, the passionate response could not disprove that 'wilderness', like all ideas about nature, is an intellectual concept that humans have imposed on the natural world. As such, the natural environment, in its materiality, offers no idea about what it should ideally be.

For most of the twentieth century, the nation-state was the prime arena for environmental conflicts. This made for peculiar national trajectories that are probably the greatest source of complication for charting the histories of environmental movements. Vigorous protest made Austria and New Zealand two of the few developed countries that do not produce electricity from nuclear power. However, an equally vigorous movement did not prevent Germany from becoming the fourth largest producer of nuclear electricity. There is also a peculiar perspective from the global South, where Western environmentalism frequently figures as a distraction at best and a post-colonial imposition at worst. At the 1972 UN

---

[4] Robert W. Righter, *The Battle over Hetch Hetchy. America's Most Controversial Dam and the Birth of Modern Environmentalism* (New York: Oxford University Press, 2005).

[5] Ludwig Trepl, *Geschichte der Ökologie. Vom 17. Jahrhundert bis zur Gegenwart* (Frankfurt: Athenäum, 1987).

[6] William Cronon, 'The Trouble with Wilderness; or, Getting Back to the Wrong Nature', in William Cronon (ed.), *Uncommon Ground. Rethinking the Human Place in Nature* (New York: W.W. Norton, 1996), pp. 69–90.

Conference on the Human Environment in Stockholm, Indian Prime Minister Indira Gandhi suggested a perception of environmental issues that starkly differed from that of the West. 'Are not poverty and need the greatest polluters', Gandhi wondered, thus shattering dreams of a joint planetary understanding of the environmental crisis.[7] What looked like deficient awareness from the Western viewpoint was actually a divergent agenda. Joan Martinez-Alier has coined the phrase 'environmentalism of the poor' that designates the situation of poor and disadvantaged people (particularly, though not exclusively in the global South) who seek to protect the environment because their livelihoods depend on it.[8]

We can see the consequences in a multitude of leagues and initiatives, which sets the environmental movement apart from many other social movements. Of course, there are umbrella organizations that aim for some degree of coordination such as the Green Group of Eight that focusses on EU policy in Brussels. However, these organizations are rather weak and mostly unknown to a broad public. Even among transnational organizations, we find a good deal of competition: Friends of the Earth International, Greenpeace International, WWF International, BirdLife International, Fauna & Flora International and, more recently, Attac. Ever since the first Green Party was formed in Tasmania in 1972, they have been notorious for internal conflicts and splits.

Finally, there is the perennial question of what constitutes a social movement. Some of the landmark events in the development of modern environmentalism were pamphlets. Germany's anti-nuclear protest history began with the Göttingen Manifesto of 1957, which targeted German ambitions to set up a nuclear weapons programme. In the view of its authors, peaceful uses were welcome, which fostered the illusionary idea of a firm boundary between military and civil uses.[9] Fifteen years later, the British journal *The Ecologist* published a widely acclaimed 'Blueprint for Survival'.[10] Neither group of signatories—18 for the Göttingen Manifesto, 36 for the 'Blueprint'—moved on towards organized structures. In many

[7] Indira Gandhi, *Man and his Environment* (New Delhi: Abhinav Publications, 1992), p. 10.

[8] Joan Martinez-Alier, 'The Environmentalism of the Poor: Its Origins and Spread', in John R. McNeill and Erin Stewart Mauldin (eds), *A Companion to Global Environmental History* (Oxford: Wiley-Blackwell, 2012), pp. 513–529.

[9] Robert Lorenz, *Protest der Physiker. Die 'Göttinger Erklärung' von 1957* (Bielefeld: transcript Verlag, 2011).

[10] *The Ecologist* 2 (1972).

countries, environmental issues are the province of peculiar 'one-person networks': academics or charismatic figures with connections and political clout, whose personal networks serve as functional equivalents of NGOs. Wangari Maathai and José Lutzenberger are two prominent examples.

Given this perplexing situation, it should come as no surprise that scholars are tempted to give up. 'Strictly speaking, of course, there is no green movement—rather, there is a diverse range of positions, perspectives and recipes for action', Anthony Giddens wrote.[11] Others have embraced a broad definition of environmentalism that includes people who did not see themselves as environmentalists into the narrative. Robert Gottlieb's *Forcing the Spring*, which made a point of including social reformers such as Jane Addams, is the best-known example for a history of environmentalism writ large.[12] Again others tried to turn selectivity into a virtue: those who read the two landmark books on the history of global environmentalism by Ramachandra Guha and Joachim Radkau against each other are left to wonder whether they are really dealing with the same topic.[13] In fact, Guha was honest enough to conclude the first part of his book with a chapter entitled 'Some who don't fit'.[14] A fourth way to come to terms with the field's complexity is to write about people and groups that *should* define environmentalism, thus perpetuating the eternal debate over the 'true' environmentalism—a real evergreen among activists worldwide.

This chapter takes a different approach. It discusses the topic from a number of different angles, charting the terrain while reflecting on the terms and concepts that guide our thinking. It starts with remarks on the academic discipline and the challenge of chronicling a movement that ran under different headers in the past. The article continues with a look at times and conditions that pushed towards internationalization and key issues such as the role of the state, radical environmentalism, and the broader context of environmental activism. The conclusion offers some reflections on the future of our current understanding of environmentalism.

---

[11] Anthony Giddens, *The Politics of Climate Change* (Cambridge: Polity Press, 2009), p. 50.

[12] Robert Gottlieb, *Forcing the Spring. The Transformation of the American Environmental Movement* (Washington, DC: Island Press, 1993).

[13] Ramachandra Guha, *Environmentalism. A Global History* (Harlow: Longman, 2000); Joachim Radkau, *The Age of Ecology* (Cambridge: Polity Press, 2013).

[14] Guha, *Environmentalism*, p. 59.

AN ADOLESCENT FIELD: THE DISCIPLINE
OF ENVIRONMENTAL HISTORY

Recent review essays make a point that environmental history has moved beyond the childhood stage.[15] Half a century has now passed since Roderick Nash wrote *Wilderness and the American Mind*, a broad history of American environmentalism.[16] However, it is probably not until the 1980s that we can speak of a proper scholarly field for the US, and it took even longer in many other countries. One only needs to look at related fields to note that the history of environmentalism is still a newcomer within the camp of social movement history. The gaps in our historical knowledge are still legion, and the lion's share of publications are stories of specific groups, campaigns or key figures—a genre that probably represents the embryonic state of theoretically refined social movement scholarship.

The relative youth of environmental history had another consequence that influences scholarship to this day. Unlike other social movements, environmentalism has generally flourished in the late twentieth and early twenty-first century. It was thus tempting to trace the roots of that boom, and to write the history of environmentalism as a more or less steady growth from humble beginnings to global prominence. Most overviews read this history as if there was something like a predestined rise of the green cause. We are probably beyond the point where scholars would proclaim in their title that they were dealing with 'prophets and pioneers', but the underlying teleology remains a popular one.[17] Even Radkau's monumental synthesis, in spite of many reservations and caveats, ultimately falls back into this mode.[18]

The proximity of environmentalism and environmental history has nourished these narratives of progress. The first generation of environmental

---

[15] Franz-Josef Brüggemeier and Jens I. Engels, 'Den Kinderschuhen entwachsen: Einleitende Worte zur Umweltgeschichte der zweiten Hälfte des 20. Jahrhunderts', in Franz-Josef Brüggemeier and Jens I. Engels (eds), *Natur- und Umweltschutz in Deutschland nach 1945. Konzepte, Konflikte, Kompetenzen* (Frankfurt: Campus-Verlag, 2005), pp. 10–19. Similar Nils Freytag, 'Deutsche Umweltgeschichte—Umweltgeschichte in Deutschland. Erträge und Perspektiven', *Historische Zeitschrift* 283 (2006), pp. 383–407.

[16] Roderick Nash, *Wilderness and the American Mind* (New Haven, CT: Yale University Press, 1967).

[17] Raymond H. Dominick, *The Environmental Movement in Germany. Prophets and Pioneers, 1871–1971* (Bloomington: Indiana University Press, 1992).

[18] Radkau, *Age*.

historians consisted almost entirely of self-identified environmentalists.[19] But many members of this generation are currently retiring, and younger scholars take a less emphatic view of political ecology. At the same time, recent events such as the disastrous Copenhagen climate summit have not really encouraged teleological narratives. Compared with the spectacular development from the 1970s to the 1990s, the last two decades have seen incremental progress at best—at least in the West, where environmental history is still the most vigorous.

With this in mind, one could argue that the political rationale for simple teleologies has faded away, as it is not so much a contemporary sentiment as an act of wishful thinking nowadays. However, there has also been an academic rationale for teleological models, and it has grown stronger than ever in recent years. In a field fraught with all sorts of complexities and ambiguities, suggesting a long-term trend towards the better is a convenient way to frame the narrative. After all, teleologies make history writing easy: all one has to do is follow the chronology and highlight all the things that increased. Ironically, that rationale has become more and more attractive as scholarship has grown, though certainly not more convincing.

ENVIRONMENTALISM BEFORE ENVIRONMENTALISM

Most social movements have a gestation period. People and groups are in a state of flux for a while until they come together in organizations that last, and the birth of a movement is often an act of retrospective rationalization. However, does it make sense to speak of a gestation period when it covers more than half a century? Most environmental initiatives ran under different headings before the late sixties. We even find concepts that bound different initiatives together in a way that resembles environmentalism; a prime example is the US conservation movement, which grew out of the Progressive Era and comprised expert-driven, efficiency-themed environmental campaigns. In fact, the American environmental movement initially ran under the heading 'new conservation movement'.

Some parts of what we nowadays call environmentalism are more than two centuries old, such as the animal protection movement, which has its

---

[19] However, there was also an anti-ecological strand of research. For one example, see Anna Bramwell, *The Fading of the Greens. The Decline of Environmental Politics in the West* (New Haven, CT: Yale University. Press, 1994).

intellectual and organizational roots in Early Modern England.[20] Towards the end of the nineteenth century, groups and activities multiplied, as the environmental consequences of industrialization and urban growth came into view all over the Western world. In fact, we see something like a transnational consensus emerging in the years before 1914: since that time, a country's affiliation with Western civilization hinged on some conscious efforts to preserve the natural environment. Even Japan, which had distinct traditions of nature conservation, joined the international trend after the First World War.

In terms of intensity, debates around 1900 are comparable with post-1945 environmentalism. However, the different strands that came together in the environmental movement remained strictly separate at the turn of the century, and few things pointed towards a merger over time. After all, the fragmentation of environmental initiatives mirrored the fragmentation of society. Vegetarians differed from people in nature protection, who in turn differed from the victims of pollution and so forth. In short, the concept of environmentalism is a retrospective rationalization when we move before 1970, and the only rationale for the anachronistic use of the word is our current understanding of environmentalism.

THE LURE OF THE EXOTIC: COLONIAL ENVIRONMENTALISM

It is conventional wisdom that environmental concerns do not respect national boundaries. As a result, environmentalism always comprised a transnational element, even in times of nationalist agitation. One scholar has even located the origins of environmentalism in the experiences of European imperialists on tropical islands.[21] Be that as it may, it is safe to say that the lure of the exotic was a key motif when the conservation of nature became a transnational concern in the early 1900s—fittingly illustrated in the conservation-minded American president Theodore Roosevelt, who set out to hunt big game in Africa after his time in the White House. In fact, game hunters were so important for the designa-

---

[20] Keith Thomas, *Man and the Natural World. Changing Attitudes in England 1500–1800* (London: Allen Lane, 1984); Mieke Roscher, *Ein Königreich für Tiere. Die Geschichte der britischen Tierrechtsbewegung* (Marburg: Tectum Verlag, 2009).

[21] Richard Grove, *Green Imperialism. Colonial Expansion, Tropical Island Edens and the Origins of Environmentalism, 1600–1860* (Cambridge: Cambridge University Press, 1995).

tion of protected areas in the colonial world that they nowadays run under the sobriquet 'penitent butchers'.[22] And then there were those who were simply enchanted, such as the German navy physician Augustin Friedrich Krämer, who suggested to designate the Pacific islands of Palau a nature reserve in order to save what he saw, quite literally, as a living 'fairytale' (*Märchenland*).[23]

Colonial subjects were naturally inclined to take a different view. Hunting reserves implied the expulsion of indigenous populations, limitations on land use and traditional hunting practices, and a lack of defences against dangerous animals. Many hunting reserves persist as national parks, creating a notorious source of conflicts both on the ground and in global environmental debates; critics have dubbed nature protection that seeks to keep local people out as 'fortress conservation'.[24] The record of forest conservation policies is no better: well-meaning Western efforts to preserve 'biodiversity hot spots' have come across as postcolonial intrusions as they have resulted in an unholy alliance of state administrations, conservation organizations and international donors.[25] Finding conservation policies for the global South that locals recognize as such is one of the more significant challenges of twenty-first century environmentalism.

GLOBALIZING ENVIRONMENTALISM I: 1970

The transnational consensus on the merits of nature protection is indicative of the fact that debates over environmental issues were already crossing borders in the nineteenth century. One only has to look at the concept of national parks to see lines of communication that spanned the world: starting with Yosemite and Yellowstone in the United States, national parks became a key vehicle for the preservation and celebration of natural treasures. To be sure, the concept was quite amenable to adjustments in new contexts. We can see that already in the first national park outside

[22] Jane Carruthers, *The Kruger National Park. A Social and Political History* (Pietermaritzburg: University of Natal Press, 1995), p. 29.

[23] Horst Gründer (Hrsg.), '... *da und dort ein junges Deutschland gründen'. Rassismus, Kolonien und kolonialer Gedanke vom 16. bis zum 20. Jahrhundert* (Munich: DTV, 1999), p. 147.

[24] Mark Dowie, *Conservation Refugees. The Hundred-Year Conflict between Global Conservation and Native Peoples* (Cambridge, MA: MIT Press, 2009).

[25] Thaddeus Sunseri, *Wielding the Ax. State Forestry and Social Conflict in Tanzania, 1820–2000* (Athens, Ohio: Ohio University Press, 2009), p. 165.

the United States, which was created in Australia in 1879: Royal National Park was not a remote piece of wilderness like Yosemite and Yellowstone, but merely a suburban recreational area for Sydney. In any case, the national parks idea struck a nerve internationally. As early as 1912, the British ambassador to the United States James Bryce declared, in a fine example of post-colonial humour, that national parks were 'the best idea America ever had'.[26]

Of course, some transnational initiatives were bogus. Germany saw the formation of an International Association against the Pollutions of Rivers, the Soil and the Air (*Internationaler Verein gegen Verunreinigung der Flüsse, des Bodens und der Luft*) in 1877, which generated a lot of excitement among early environmental historians until it turned out that it was little more than a one man crusade against combined sewers.[27] In 1931, a Bavarian businessman, Carl Wenglein, founded a short-lived World League for Friends of Nature and Birds (*Weltbund für Natur- und Vogelfreunde*); curiously, all board members came from the Franconian towns of Schwabach and Eschenbach.[28] Other initiatives were long on rhetoric and short on results, such as the negotiations on and around the League of Nations that Anna Wöbse chronicled in a monograph.[29] Some organizations became international by default: decolonization turned the British Society for the Preservation of the Wild Fauna of the Empire into Fauna & Flora International.[30]

However, if we consider the transnational initiatives that framed environmentalism in the long run, there is a broad scholarly consensus that the years around 1970 were particularly influential. Both national debates and global networking intensified notably, culminating in the 1972 Stockholm summit and the frantic debate over the Club of Rome's *Limits to Growth* study of the same year. However, the boom is easier to highlight than to

[26] Ney C. Landrum, *The State Park Movement in America. A Critical Review* (Columbia: University of Missouri Press, 2004), p. 4.

[27] Jürgen Büschenfeld, *Flüsse und Kloaken. Umweltfragen im Zeitalter der Industrialisierung (1870–1918)* (Stuttgart: Klett-Cotta, 1997).

[28] Johannes Mehl, *Carl Wenglein, der Weltbund und Schwabach als Zentrum des Naturschutzes. Ein Beitrag zur Geschichte des Naturschutzes 1920–1935* (Schwabach: Bund Naturschutz, 2001).

[29] Anna-Katharina Wöbse, *Weltnaturschutz. Umweltdiplomatie in Völkerbund und Vereinten Nationen 1920–1950* (Frankfurt: Campus Verlag, 2011).

[30] Richard S. R. Fitter and Peter Scott, *The Penitent Butchers. The Fauna Preservation Society, 1903–1978* (London: Fauna Preservation Society, 1978).

explain. Events of the late 1960s and early 1970s had very little to do with other civic movements of the time. In fact, it looks more like a countervailing trend. The high point of environmental activism in the United States, the Earth Day celebrations on April 22, 1970, was an emphatically bipartisan event that sought to include all Americans. After the bitter clashes over Vietnam and civil rights, it was perhaps comforting to come together in a joint celebration of the endangered planet, if only briefly. With some 12,000 individual events, Earth Day was a landmark celebration that became a global event in 1990.[31] It went along, and to some extent inspired an environmental policy offensive of the Nixon administration that created the backbone of a system of environmental regulation that lasts to this day.[32]

Negotiations at the Stockholm summit were largely inconsequential. Perhaps the greatest impact lay in the run-up to the event, as a number of countries strived to polish their environmental credentials. A Royal Commission on Environmental Pollution and a Department of the Environment were created in the United Kingdom, and in 1971, Robert Poujade became the first European Minister of the Environment in France. In Germany, the minister of the interior Hans-Dietrich Genscher pursued an aggressive policy initiative as part of the politics of reform of the coalition of social democrats and the liberal FDP since 1969. The prominence of government agents mirrors a low degree of civic organization: politicians and bureaucrats could mould environmental policy pretty much as they saw fit—in retrospect, the last time they could do so. In fact, government policy at times aimed at the *creation* of civic structures. For one, Genscher's ministry supported the formation of the *Bundesverband Bürgerinitiativen Umweltschutz* (Federation of Citizen Initiatives on the Environment) in 1972, which served as the umbrella organization for the rapidly growing number of citizen initiatives on environmental issues. The FDP's left wing had hoped to turn environmental issues into one of its proximate causes, though political radicalization thwarted these plans. The first chairman of the BBU, FDP member Hans-Helmuth Wüstenhagen, was soon embroiled in conflict and finally threw in the towel in 1977.[33]

---

[31] Adam W. Rome, *The Genius of Earth Day. How a 1970 Teach-In Unexpectedly Made the First Green Generation* (New York: Hill & Wang, 2013).

[32] J. Brooks Flippen, *Nixon and the Environment* (Albuquerque: University of New Mexico Press, 2000).

[33] Jens I. Engels, *Naturpolitik in der Bundesrepublik. Ideenwelt und politische Verhaltensstile in Naturschutz und Umweltbewegung 1950–1980* (Paderborn: Ferdinand Schöningh, 2006), pp. 332–338.

For all the importance of national and transnational networks, it is crucial to recognize the pivotal role of certain conflicts. Environmental activism clustered around specific causes in specific locales. American environmentalism would look different without the conflicts over dam projects in Echo Park and the Grand Canyon, and the same holds true for Japan and the Minamata mercury disaster or Australia and the Little Desert.[34] In fact, these early conflicts not only got things going—they defined the public image of environmentalism in the long run. For instance, the history of the struggle against nuclear power in Germany would look different if it had not been for the precedent of Wyhl, where protest remained non-violent. The charisma of Wyhl survived in spite of the civil-war-like scenes in Brokdorf and Grohnde, where violence escalated in a way that disturbed both protesters and the police.[35]

These conflicts were also important in that they brought new faces into the movement. Wyhl was a conflict that united winegrowers and university students, and these transgressions of class lines were all the more important as environmental concerns had traditionally been an elite endeavour. One of the most influential international organizations, the World Wildlife Fund of 1961, was firmly in the hand of dignitaries; from 1976 to 1981 its president was John Loudon, formerly head of Royal Dutch/Shell.[36] We do not see a transnational organization with a non-elite membership base until US environmentalist David Brower formed Friends of the Earth, which gave birth to Friends of the Earth International in 1971. Revealingly, Brower had previously been fired as managing director of the Sierra Club because his firebrand version of environmentalism was just too much for the society's more conservative board.[37] However, with activists

[34] Hal K. Rothman, *The Greening of a Nation? Environmentalism in the United States since 1945* (Fort Worth: Harcourt Brace, 1998), pp. 34–48, 75–79; Timothy S. George, *Minamata. Pollution and the Struggle for Democracy in Postwar Japan* (Cambridge, MA: Harvard University Press, 2001); Libby Robin, *Defending the Little Desert. The Rise of Ecological Consciousness in Australia* (Melbourne: Melbourne University Press, 1998).

[35] Bernd-A. Rusinek, 'Wyhl', in Etienne François and Hagen Schulze (eds), *Deutsche Erinnerungsorte II* (Munich: C.H. Beck, 2001), pp. 652–666.

[36] Alexis Schwarzenbach, *Saving the World's Wildlife. WWF—the First 50 Years* (London: Profile Books, 2011). See also the muck-raking presentation by Wilfried Huismann, *Schwarzbuch WWF. Dunkle Geschäfte im Zeichen des Panda* (Gütersloh: Gütersloher Verlagshaus, 2012).

[37] Michael P. Cohen, *The History of the Sierra Club 1892–1970* (San Francisco: Sierra Club Books, 1988); Stephen Fox, *The American Conservation Movement. John Muir and his Legacy* (Madison: University of Wisconsin Press, 1981).

from Britain, France, Sweden and the United States, Friends of the Earth was somewhat limited in its global outreach.

In short, the upswing of environmentalism around 1970 did not lead to an internationalization of environmental policy or closer cooperation of non-governmental organizations. Environmental policies remained firmly within the framework of the nation-state, and the same held true for civic groups. As a result, the fate of the green cause differed widely from country to country. Whereas the US environmental movement was under pressure during Reagan's first term, German environmentalism flourished in the early 1980S in spectacular fashion. Greenpeace International emerged as a global player of environmentalism, but the French branch collapsed in 1987. It was only towards the end of that decade that individual trajectories became more synchronous.

GLOBALIZING ENVIRONMENTALISM II: 1990

The second global boom of environmentalism around 1990 is even less researched than the first one two decades earlier. Most scholars agree that the 1992 Rio summit was a pivotal event for global environmentalism, but we do not yet have a good account of the negotiations and its significance. Furthermore, Rio was the climax of a boom of environmental issues that probably began with the Montreal Protocol on substances that deplete the ozone layer of 1987, which serves as a precedent of global environmental policy to this day.

Several trends came together in the making of this brief but momentous boom. One was the end of the Cold War, which allowed global diplomacy to flourish in the first place. Whereas Eastern European countries had not attended the Stockholm summit, with disagreements over the status of the GDR serving as the official explanation, they were now willing to agree to far-reaching commitments such as the Montreal Protocol, which reached more deeply into the sovereignty of nation-states than any previous environmental agreement. Moreover, the end of the Cold War created something of a political vacuum, and environmental issues were probably a convenient, common-sensical interlude while the lines of global policy were being redrawn. Finally, the issues had charisma. What better way to symbolize the end of Cold War tensions than a joint commitment to save planet Earth?[38] Fittingly, Mikhail Gorbachev became president of Green Cross International, an international environmental organization he helped to create when he still served as General Secretary of the Communist Party of the Soviet Union.[39]

A second impulse came from the dissident movement in Eastern Europe, which made environmental problems one of its pet themes. A lot suggests that the key reason was tactical: in socialist dictatorships, environmental issues were low-risk topics. After all, environmental mobilization in Eastern Europe had a flash-in-the-pan quality: An estimated 100,000 Lithuanians joined a demonstration against the Ignalina nuclear power plant in September 1988, and yet it was a mandate from the European Union, rather than civic protest, that led to the facility's closure more than a dozen years later.[40] Even more, the environmental community is an unstable one in most post-socialist countries, with grass-root initiatives, government-sponsored organizations, groups depending on subsidies from abroad and 'one-person networks' making for a mixture that defies Western concepts.[41]

However, the demise of environmentalism in Eastern Europe was beyond the horizon in 1990. There is little ground to doubt the vigour of environmental initiatives in the 1980s, and as the famous raid on the environmental library at East Berlin's Zionskirche on 25 November 1987 serves to attest, they were a formidable challenge in the eyes of the rulers.[42] There was even transnational coordination in the Greenway Network that activists from Poland, Yugoslavia, Czechoslovakia and Hungary formed in 1985. Headquartered in Budapest, it worked through a quarterly newsletter, personal contacts and annual meetings in Kraków, Poland (1987), Kral'ovany, Slovakia (1988), East Berlin (1989), Riga, Latvia (1990) and Mosonmagyaróvár, Hungary (1991). By 1989, Greenway had participants

---

[38] For more on this issue, see my 'The End of the Cold War: A Turning Point in Environmental History?', in John R. McNeill and Corinna Unger (eds), *Environmental Histories of the Cold War* (Cambridge: Cambridge University Press, 2010), pp. 343–351.

[39] http://www.gcint.org/our-history.

[40] Cf. http://ec.europa.eu/lietuva/documents/skelbimai/2008_08_21_frequently_asked_questions_on_inpp.pdf.

[41] Barbara A. Cellarius, *In the Land of Orpheus. Rural Livelihoods and Nature Conservation in Postsocialist Bulgaria* (Madison: University of Wisconsin Press, 2004).

[42] Michael Beleites, 'Die unabhängige Umweltbewegung in der DDR', in Hermann Behrens and Jens Hoffmann (eds), *Umweltschutz in der DDR. Analysen und Zeitzeugenberichte*, Vol. 3 (Munich: Oekom-Verlag, 2007), pp. 179–224.

from all socialist countries with the exception of Albania and Romania.[43] Needless to say, the events of 1989 bestowed the green dissidents with enormous prestige. It looked as if the global rise of environmentalism was irresistible.

A third impulse came from the discovery of environmental problems that were truly global in scope. To be sure, global contamination was a familiar trope ever since the campaigns against nuclear testing in the 1950s. Until the hole in the ozone layer and anthropogenic global warming emerged as powerful challenges in the 1980s, however, most 'global' problems were really local or national problems that occurred in many different places across the globe. At the most, pollution problems crossed national boundaries, a phenomenon that found a well-studied expression in transboundary conflicts over smelter smoke between Canada and the United States.[44] Both global warming and the ozone hole required global coordination, as pollutants did their damage no matter where they were emitted. Global warming in particular highlighted the need for international cooperation and globalized environmentalism like no other issue. While the threat to the ozone layer was on the path towards a solution ever since the 1990 London amendment to the Montreal Protocol aimed for a phase-out of all ozone-damaging substances by 2000, global warming is defying solutions to this day.[45]

To be sure, these three trends met with other developments. For one, a series of spectacular disasters supported the case for global environmentalism: the Bhopal chemical disaster in 1984, the Chernobyl nuclear explosion and the Sandoz fire in Basel, Switzerland in 1986, and the *Exxon Valdez* oil spill in Alaska in 1989. Western NGOs had also grown into a significant political force: whereas Stockholm had been a purely diplomatic event, the Rio Earth Summit drew a lot of its strength from the involvement of civil society. And yet the boom of environmentalism around 1990 remains a bit of a mystery, as it is so exceptional in social movement history. For other issues such as peace, women's emancipation or gay rights, these years were unremarkable.

[43] Carlo Jordan, 'Greenway. Das osteuropäische Grüne Netzwerk 1985–1990' *Horch und Guck* 15 (2006), pp. 31–37.

[44] John D. Wirth, *Smelter Smoke in North America. The Politics of Transborder Pollution* (Lawrence, KS: University Press of Kansas, 2000).

[45] Spencer R. Weart, *The Discovery of Global Warming* (Cambridge, MA: Harvard University Press, 2008).

Perhaps we should see environmentalism not so much as a part of a more diverse bundle of issues but as an alternative playing field that drew a lot of its attraction from the fact that it looked so disconnected from the rest of the political sphere. Douglas Weiner has explored this idea for the Soviet Union, arguing that environmental issues made for 'a little corner of freedom' in a totalitarian state.[46] In Weiner's reading, Soviet environmentalists were able to pursue their work mostly because their concern looked so little like real politics. As an alternative playing field, environmentalism allowed activists to advance when other arenas of politics were gridlocked.

THE STATE AND THE MOVEMENT

Governments have always been part of the history of environmental movements. To be sure, the appreciation of nature did not necessarily lead to state protection, as it could also find an expression in scientific and recreational interests. And yet it is symptomatic that the Isaac Walton League, founded in 1922 by a group of avid anglers, came to devote a lot of energy to the fight against water pollution in order to preserve the outdoors for recreation.[47] Almost every environmental initiative deals in one way or another with collective behaviour, and that usually brings the state into the picture.

But at the same time, the role of the state could take many different forms. In Germany, nature protection was barely born when state governments sought to co-opt the nascent cause. Organizations such as the Bavarian League for Nature Protection (*Bund Naturschutz in Bayern*) actually have their roots in government commissions. The English case is probably the other extreme, as the National Trust for Places of Historic Interest or Natural Beauty monopolized the issue for decades. Founded in 1895, the National Trust works as a charity independent from government, though the British parliament provided crucial support by declaring acquisitions of the trust inalienable in 1907. Other than that, England did not have a government policy for the protection of domestic nature until after the Second World War. However, the National Parks and Access to the Countryside Act of 1949 brought England to catch up with other

---

[46] Douglas R. Weiner, *A Little Corner of Freedom. Russian Nature Protection from Stalin to Gorbachëv* (Berkeley: University of California Press, 1999).

[47] Rome, *Genius*, p. 47.

European countries, with the first National Parks being designated in the Peak and Lake Districts in 1951. The Town and Country Planning Act of 1947 brought comprehensive land use planning and encouraged the creation of 'green belts' around major cities that proved remarkably effective in curtailing urban sprawl.[48]

Since 1970, the interplay of state and civil society has taken on a new dimension in that environmentalists served as government ministers. Yolanda Kakabadse worked for environmental NGOs before she became Minister of Environment in Ecuador and nowadays serves as president of the World Wildlife Fund. In Kenya, Nobel laureate Wangari Maathai served as deputy minister after landmark work for environmental and humanitarian groups. George Bush appointed William Reilly, who had previously been president of the Conservation Foundation and the US section of the World Wildlife Fund, as administrator of the US Environmental Protection Agency in 1989. In Germany, the former Greenpeace activist Monika Griefahn became environmental minister in Lower Saxony in 1990, the rare case of a red–green coalition without the environmental ministry in green hands.

However, there is a second type of politicians that deserves equal attention. Hans-Dietrich Genscher was the first in a series of politicians who embraced environmental issues as political entrepreneurs, advancing both environmental regulation and their own careers in the process. Scholars have been notably reluctant to discuss the careers of people like Klaus Matthiesen, Jo Leinen, Jochen Flasbarth, or Fritz Vahrenholt, not least because their role challenges a convenient myth of environmentalism. Activists liked to depict the state as a dithering leviathan that only tilted towards environmental concerns under pressure from an enraged citizenry. In reality, the state pursued its own interests in going environmental, and so did ambitious politicians: since the 1970s, environmental issues have been one of the few realms where it is possible to achieve a massive expansion of budgets and staff. In fact, we probably cannot explain the stellar rise of environmentalism in the 1970s and 1980s without consideration of these political interests, as it helps to explain a great and widely unrecog-

---

[48] Christopher Rootes, 'Environmental NGOs and the Environmental Movement in England', in Nick Crowson, Matthew Hilton and James McKay (eds), *NGOs in Contemporary Britain. Non-State Actors in Society and Politics since 1945* (Basingstoke: Palgrave Macmillan, 2009), pp. 205–207.

nized paradox: environmental policy was taking off just at the time when nation-states all over the West were facing limits.

The alliance between green activists and political entrepreneurs was crucial for the stellar rise of environmentalism in Western Germany.[49] However, synergies between activists and politicians were weaker in other countries, and some Western politicians have sought to gain credentials with anti-environmental posturing. In the global South, few activists saw the state as an ally, as environmental initiatives were often struggling with vigorous opposition and worse from authoritarian governments. Some environmentalists paid for activism with their lives. Chico Mendes and Ken Saro-Wiwa are two of the most prominent examples.

THE RIGHT GREEN

Environmental issues transcended the established lines of political conflict. A concern for public and personal health was beyond traditional left–right distinctions, and the same was true for an appreciation of nature. At best, we can identify a certain intellectual affinity: a sense of loss and a nostalgia for times past implied lines towards conservative thinking, whereas socialism had a hard time consoling its belief in scientific and technological progress with environmental sentiments. Early conservation also had a certain elitist bias, perhaps most evident in its penchant for hunting. But these were essentially resemblances of sentiment that left the door wide open for exceptions. Before 1970, we find environmentalists in all sorts of varieties: socialist, anarchist, reactionary, nationalist and so forth. By challenging anthropocentrism, green thought has tackled one of the few political convictions that were otherwise common ground from left to right. In terms of political chemistry, environmentalism before 1970 is best seen as a free radical, eager to mate wherever something fits.

This changed in the 1970s and 1980s, when environmental issues became a prime concern of the political left. To be sure, the left never achieved an undisputed hold on these issues. Elitist conservation organizations such as the World Wildlife Fund remain part of the political scene.[50] Church groups with no clear political affiliation played a signifi-

---

[49] Cf. Frank Uekötter, *The Greenest Nation? A New History of German Environmentalism* (Cambridge, MA: MIT Press, 2014).

[50] The WWF has recently come under attack for its elitist background and intransparent structures. (Huismann, *Schwarzbuch WWF.*)

cant role in environmental circles.[51] And then we have right-wing politicians such as Great Britain's National Front embracing green values in an obvious attempt to overcome their pariah status and enter the mainstream.[52] However, we can observe an overwhelming trend towards the left in Germany's Green Party, which was originally founded as a broad alliance that claimed to be 'neither left nor right but ahead'.[53] In reality, most conservatives left the Green Party after a few tumultuous months and formed a conservative environmental party in 1981, the *Ökologisch-Demokratische Partei* (Eco-Democratic Party). Characteristically, it has largely failed for lack of numbers whereas the Green Party became a fixture in the left part of the political spectrum.[54]

The turn towards the left is open to different explanation. An idealistic reading stresses the left's commitment to equality and social justice.[55] A more pragmatic view would stress the precarious situation of the post-1968 left: as Christopher Rootes has noted, environmentalism is 'the great survivor among the new social movements that arose in and since the 1960s'.[56] After failing with many other issues, the left seized on environmentalism for political gain, eventually becoming popular in a way that orthodox Marxism never was (though some were concerned that the exploitation of nature was somewhat different from the exploitation

[51] Michael Schüring, 'West German Protestants and the Campaign against Nuclear Technology', *Central European History* 4 (2012), pp. 744–762.

[52] Mike Robinson, *The Greening of British Party Politics* (Manchester: Manchester University Press, 1992), p. 2, p. 76. For obvious reasons, right-wing environmentalism has received particular attention in Germany. See Oliver Geden, *Rechte Ökologie. Umweltschutz zwischen Emanzipation und Faschismus*, 2nd edn (Berlin: Elefanten Press, 1999), and Thomas Jahn and Peter Wehling, *Ökologie von rechts. Nationalismus und Umweltschutz bei der Neuen Rechten und den 'Republikanern'* (Frankfurt: Campus Verlag, 1991).

[53] Silke Mende, *'Nicht rechts, nicht links, sondern vorn'. Eine Geschichte der Gründungsgrünen* (Munich: Oldenbourg Verlag, 2011).

[54] Cf. Raphael Mankau (ed.), *20 Jahre ödp. Anfänge, Gegenwart und Perspektiven ökologisch-demokratischer Politik* (Rimpar: dolata verlag, 1999), and Jürgen Wüst, *Konservatismus und Ökologiebewegung. Eine Untersuchung im Spannungsfeld von Partei, Bewegung und Ideologie am Beispiel der Ökologisch-Demokratischen Partei (ÖDP)* (Frankfurt: IKO-Verlag für Interkulturelle Kommunikation, 1993).

[55] See, for instance, Norberto Bobbio, *Rechts und Links. Gründe und Bedeutungen einer politische Unterscheidung* (Berlin: Klaus Wagenbach Verlag, 1994), p. 94.

[56] Christopher Rootes, 'The Transformation of Environmental Activism: An Introduction', in Christopher Rootes (ed.), *Environmental Protest in Western Europe* (Oxford: Oxford University Press, 2003), pp. 1–19, p. 1.

of workers).[57] And then there was the growing vigour of environmental demands, which drove the movement towards the left: as environmental issues gained prominence, they were bound to confront capitalists. The situation in the United States, where the right has embraced a staunchly anti-environmentalist stance due to its proximity to corporate interests, is perhaps the best case in point.[58]

RADICAL ENVIRONMENTALISM

Throughout its history, environmentalism included a number of people who took things farther than the rest. Communes and back-to-nature freaks are a significant aspect of the history of the environmental movement, and not only because they bring colour into our narratives. The tension between utopian dreams and *Realpolitik* runs through the history of environmentalism: from Arne Naess's distinction between 'shallow' environmentalism and Deep Ecology to the perennial conflict between *Fundis* and *Realos* in Germany's Green Party. In the 1980s, US environmentalists began to distinguish between mainstream groups such as the Sierra Club and radical groups such as Earth First! Textbooks and essay collections take the existence of radical ecology and radical environmentalism for granted.[59]

However, radicalism seems more convincing as a self-description than as a scholarly category in retrospect. It is quite revealing that Germany, in spite of a vibrant tradition of environmentalism, knows no popular translation for the word 'radical ecology', as people and tactics that probably would have been conceived as 'radical' elsewhere were seen as part of the overall movements. Groups such as Greenpeace have received broad popular acclaim not in spite of the fact that they practice civil disobedience, but

---

[57] A similar argument has been made for the German peace movement which showed enormous overlap with the environmental movement. See Susanne Schregel, *Der Atomkrieg vor der Wohnungstür. Eine Politikgeschichte der neuen Friedensbewegung in der Bundesrepublik 1970–1985* (Frankfurt: Campus Verlag, 2011), pp. 42–77.

[58] John Micklethwait and Adrian Wooldridge, *The Right Nation. Conservative Power in America* (New York: Penguin Press, 2004), pp. 180–182.

[59] Carolyn Merchant, *Radical Ecology. The Search for a Livable World* (New York: Routledge, 2005); Bron Taylor (ed.), *Ecological Resistance Movements. The Global Emergence of Radical and Popular Environmentalism* (Albany: State University of New York Press, 1995).

merely because of it.[60] Few people conceive the destruction of fields with genetically modified organisms as an act of extremism, though it is, technically speaking, a violation of property rights. Only violence against humans remains a taboo, as even instruction manuals for sabotage (colloquially called 'monkeywrenching') make a point of avoiding hazards to humans.[61]

In short, the distinction is hard to sustain when it comes to tactics. It has become virtually impossible with a view to goals. Environmentalism has brought radical issues into the mainstream like no other social movement; characteristically, the *New Yorker* called PETA (People for the Ethical Treatment of Animals) 'the most successful radical group in America' in 2003.[62] In the fight against global warming, demands about reforming the economy from the bottom up have become conventional wisdom, something that surely would have struck observers as extremist only a few decades ago. Of course, determination about these pending changes varies greatly among political leaders, as it surely does among activists and members of environmental organizations. However, in defining these stances, we will have to search for more refined categories and models. A simple dichotomy of 'mainstream' and 'radical' environmentalism will no longer do in the twenty-first century.

How Pure Is Green? Environmentalism and Other Causes

Environmental issues did not exist in a vacuum. When the *Heimatschutz* movement (friends of the cosy homeland) pushed nature protection in Imperial Germany, it did so in the context of a broad cultural agenda. More recently, anti-nuclear protest in France served as a vehicle for anti-elitist sentiment, with environmentalists chastising the closed network of politicians and nuclear experts as 'les nucléocrates'.[63] One of the most influential environmental NGOs, Greenpeace, combined environmental issues and peace activism in its protest against nuclear testing, though

[60] Frank S. Zelko, *Make It a Green Peace! The Rise of Counterculture Environmentalism* (New York: Oxford University Press, 2013).

[61] Dave Foreman and Bill Haywood (eds), *Ecodefense. A Field Guide to Monkeywrenching*, 2nd edn (Tucson, AZ: Ned Ludd Books 1987).

[62] Michael Specter, 'The Extremist: The Woman Behind the Most Successful Radical Group in America', *The New Yorker* April 4, 2003.

[63] Karena Kalmbach, *Tschernobyl und Frankreich. Die Debatte um die Auswirkungen des Unfalls im Kontext der französischen Atompolitik und Elitenkultur* (Frankfurt: Peter Lang, 2011).

the former eventually won the upper hand.[64] And yet the general trend since the 1970s has been to discuss environmental issues in isolation. Conventional wisdom was that environmentalism was beyond the usual lines of conflict and ultimately a concern that every human being should share. Ulrich Beck captured this sentiment nicely when he declared in his *Risk Society*, 'Poverty is hierarchic, smog is democratic.'[65]

In the United States, the environmental justice movement has challenged this conventional wisdom since the 1980s, pointing out that social and ethnic discrimination has often an environmental dimension.[66] The movement inspired a search for similar initiatives in the past, thus broadening the horizon of a field that had focussed excessively on white males.[67] However, Europe has remained a blank spot on the global map of environmental justice, though certainly not for lack of evidence. Few environmental historians have noted that Günter Wallraff's 1980s classic *Ganz unten* (*Lowest of the Low*) highlighted the excessive pollution burden of Turkish immigrants.[68]

The purity of the green cause is the most contentious issue in the exchange between the West and the global South over what environmentalism is, or should be. Generally speaking, groups in the global South see environmental issues as merely one aspect of broader social, cultural and economic grievances, a divergence that is all the more pronounced since it has roots in a different social base. In a discussion of Southeast Asia, James David Fahn put it as follows:

> whereas the green movement in the North tends to focus on the middle class, in the South not only is it centered more on the farmers and fishermen who rely on natural resources for their livelihoods but it's also concerned more with who gets to use resources, not just with how they are used.[69]

---

[64] Zelko, *Make it*.

[65] Ulrich Beck, *Risk Society. Towards a New Modernity* (London: Sage, 1992), p. 36.

[66] Martin V. Melosi, 'Environmental Justice, Political Agenda Setting, and the Myths of History,' in Martin V. Melosi (ed.), *Effluent America. Cities, Industry, Energy and the Environment* (Pittsburgh, PA: University of Pittsburgh Press, 2001), pp. 238–262.

[67] Cf. Sylvia Hood Washington, Paul C. Rosier and Heather Goodall (eds), *Echoes from the Poisoned Well. Global Memories of Environmental Injustice* (Lanham, MD: Lexington Books, 2006); Chad Montrie, *A People's History of Environmentalism in the United States* (London: Continuum, 2011). See also. Melosi, 'Environmental Justice'.

[68] Günter Wallraff, *Ganz unten* (Cologne: Kiepenheuer & Witsch, 1985).

[69] James David Fahn, *A Land on Fire. The Environmental Consequences of the Southeast Asian Boom* (Boulder, CO: Westview Press, 2003), p. 7.

It is quite likely that this rift will grow in significance; in fact, environmentalism in the pure green mode is also under pressure in the West, as
groups such as Attac stress the connections between environmental and
other issues. But be that as it may, it seems crucial to keep an eye on
ethnic, social and cultural dimensions even when—or perhaps particularly
when—environmentalists were oblivious of these implications.

ENVIRONMENTALISM IN CULTURE AND LIFE

Environmentalism was always more than a political and social movement.
It also left an imprint on culture and ways of life, though few scholars have
made that connection. We have only a few attempts at what one might call
broad cultural histories of environmentalism, with Michael Bess' study of
post-war France probably being the best-known one.[70] That is regrettable
for two reasons. First, it makes the history of environmentalism more sterile
than necessary: two huge volumes on the German Life Reform movement,
produced on the occasion of a colourful exhibition in Darmstadt, provide
an idea of how much we can gain by bringing culture back in.[71] Second, it
perpetuates the strange isolation of environmental history from general history. It will be much easier to make connections once we look at environmentalism as a force of culture and life: from such a point of view, sandals
and whole grain bread are probably as important for German environmentalism as nuclear power. In fact, green issues say a lot about a society, its
obsessions and fears, its polity and civil society, and one can only wish that
environmental historians would employ this approach more often.

THE THEORY GAP

The history of environmental movements is somewhat under-theorized.
Most scholars leave it at telling their stories, particularly those who focus on
specific campaigns, organizations or people. With the growth of research
in recent years, foci have become increasingly narrow, making it easy to
avoid large questions that require some methodological sophistication. For
a while, Inglehart's post-materialist values thesis gained some popularity
among scholars—not least because it depicted environmentalists as disin-

---

[70] Bess, *Light-Green Society.*
[71] Kai Buchholz et al. (eds), *Die Lebensreform. Entwürfe zur Neugestaltung von Leben und Kunst um 1900*, 2 vol. (Darmstadt: Häusser Verlag, 2001).

terested idealists, which nicely fitted their self-description.[72] More recently, that has given way to a benign disinterest; in Radkau's 782-page synthesis, Inglehart does not come up for discussion once.[73] Some authors even make no bones about their general disinterests in explanations. In his influential habilitation thesis, Jens Ivo Engels stated that his goal was not 'to clarify *why* the environmental movement emerged, but *how* the problem of threatened nature was dealt with in the political sphere of the federal republic'.[74]

Every student of contemporary history knows the tension between historians on the one hand and political scientists and sociologists on the other. But when it comes to environmentalism, we are really speaking of a gulf between story-tellers and model-builders, and it would seem that neither side has really benefitted from this lack of communication. In fact, one gets the impression that the issue at stake is more than a clash of academic cultures. Network approaches or resource mobilization theory force scholars to take stock of the relative strength of social movements, and that is an issue that most environmental historians tend to avoid. Maybe they sense that when we compare the membership base of German environmental NGOs with the 18 million members of the *Allgemeiner Deutscher Automobil-Club* (ADAC), the green Germany looks pretty pale. And I am not even mentioning the corporate power that global capitalism has unleashed.

A DELICATE BALANCE, OR IS ENVIRONMENTALISM AN ENDURING PARADIGM?

The Australian geographer Joe Powell once quipped that environmental history was 'like Belgium': it was 'entirely the product of a resident collective imagination.'[75] It is tempting to make a similar remark about global environmentalism. Strictly speaking, there is no such thing as global environmentalism: we merely have a huge number of environmentalisms around the globe. Nonetheless, global environmentalism made history because many people thought that there *should be* a global environmental

[72] Samuel P. Hays (in collaboration with Barbara D. Hays), *Beauty, Health, and Permanence. Environmental Politics in the United States, 1955–1985,* Cambridge: Cambridge University Press, 1989), p. 35; Raymond Dominick, 'The Roots of the Green Movement in the United States and West Germany', *Environmental Review* 5 (1988), pp. 1–30; p. 3.

[73] Radkau, *Ära.*

[74] Engels, *Naturpolitik,* p. 20. Emphasis in the original.

[75] Joseph M. Powell, 'Historical Geography and Environmental History. An Australian Interface', *Journal of Historical Geography* 3 (1996), pp. 253–273.

movement. After several decades of attempts to coordinate and harmonize environmental policies around the globe, there is no way denying that the myth of the blue planet has made history, and not just in its New Age variant.

But even then, environmentalism remains a notoriously fragile concept, one that we probably should not embrace if there were a more convincing alternative. There is no common denominator, no common foe, and not even a widely accepted philosophy that holds the environmental movement together, and we can see it as a bit of a mystery why it is so enduring. In fact, it seems as though the fissures have recently started to widen. Renewable energy projects claim precious space, energy crops reduce biodiversity, and Fukushima has merely postponed the clash between antinuclear and anti-carbon policies. All the while, pressure is mounting to link environmental and social justice more thoroughly. It is quite possible that we are currently seeing the birth of a new environmentalism, one that we have trouble to grasp for lack of words.

Obituaries for environmentalism are almost as old as environmentalism itself. And yet it helps to stimulate thinking when we imagine alternative narratives that future scholar might embrace. Given the development of life expectancies in the West, it is quite possible that scholars will once write about environmentalism in the 1970s and 1980s as a mysterious fear, not unlike that of Edna and Harry in Edward Albee's *A Delicate Balance*. On the other hand, the repercussions of global warming may make environmentalism look more prophetic than ever. Or maybe future scholars will see environmentalism as merely a precursor of a global justice movement.

More than other fields, environmental movement history is advancing on shaky ground, as most adolescents do. Environmentalism is in a state of flux, and so are narratives about its past. Both are aiming for broader context, and while that may bring all sorts of complications, it will almost certainly make both environmentalism and its history more interesting. You ain't seen nothing yet.

Further Readings

Scholarly interest in environmental movements grew in resonance with the rise of environmentalism around 1970. Roderick Nash's aforementioned *Wilderness and the American Mind* (New Haven, CT: Yale University Press, 1967) reflects the guiding intention: the book sought to describe a legacy that activists were building upon at the time. Against this background, the book took a broad and emphatic look at environmentalist traditions, with more emphasis on ideas than on organizations. Nash's monograph struck a nerve and became a bestseller, though the environmentalists' stance towards their own history was more ambiguous than that of other social movements. Many environmentalists saw history as a distraction from the exigencies of the moment.

The broad synthesis became a distinct genre of environmental movement historiography, and they were and remain all the more remarkable because they were largely based on primary sources, if only for lack of alternatives: previous scholarship was often close to non-existent. The books often blended the national histories of environmentalism with general environmental histories of the respective countries. Books of this type exist for countries as diverse as Israel: Alon Tal, *Pollution in a Promised Land: An Environmental History of Israel* (Berkeley: University of California Press, 2002) and Russia: Douglas R. Weiner, *A Little Corner of Freedom: Russian Nature Protection from Stalin to Gorbachëv* (Berkeley: University of California Press, 1999) For large countries such as Great Britain, several syntheses are available: Brian William Clapp, *An Environmental History of Britain since the Industrial Revolution* (London: Longman, 1994); David Evans, *A History of Nature Conservation in Britain* (London: Routledge, 1997); John Sheail, *An Environmental History of Twentieth-Century Britain* (Basingstoke: Palgrave Macmillan, 2002). In a reading list that focuses on English-language publications, it bears recognition that these books were written primarily for a domestic audience. For example, German readers could buy the first overview books on the history of German environmentalism in the 1980s: Rolf Peter Sieferle, *Fortschrittsfeinde? Opposition gegen Technik und Industrie von der Romantik bis zur Gegenwart* (Munich: Beck, 1984); Ulrich Linse, *Ökopax und Anarchie: Eine Geschichte der ökologischen Bewegungen in Deutschland* (Munich: dtv, 1986), years before the first English-language synthesis became available: Raymond H. Dominick, *The Environmental Movement in Germany: Prophets and Pioneers, 1871–1971* (Bloomington: Indiana University Press, 1992). Authors typically displayed a more or less pronounced sympathy towards their subjects. Anti-ecological synthesis were rare and usually less than impressive; perhaps the best-known example is Anna Bramwell, *The Fading of the Greens: The Decline of Environmental Politics in the West* (New Haven, CT: Yale University Press, 1994).

The United States was the most prolific producer of these syntheses: Stephen R. Fox, *John Muir and his Legacy: The American Conservation Movement* (Boston: Little, Brown, 1981); Hal K. Rothman, *The Greening of a Nation? Environmentalism in the United States since 1945* (Fort Worth, TX: Harcourt Brace College Publishers, 1998); Victor B. Scheffer, *The Shaping of Environmentalism in America* (Seattle: University of Washington Press, 1991); John McCormick, *Reclaiming Paradise: The Global Environmental Movement* (Bloomington: Indiana University Press, 1989), Philip Shabecoff, *A Fierce Green Fire: The American Environmental Movement* (New York: Hill and Wang, 1993; revised edition 2003), Hal K. Rothman, *Saving the Planet: The American Response to the Environment in the Twentieth Century* (Chicago: Ivan R. Dee, 2000); Thomas Raymond Wellock, *Preserving the Nation: The Conservation and Environmental Movements, 1870–2000* (Wheeling, IL: Harlan Davidson, 2007). However, the genre grew out of fashion among scholars more recently, and that is not just due to the fact that teleological tales of the irresistible rise of environmentalism have come to ring hollow in the twenty-first century. The master narrative has come under fire for being too narrow. Within the United States, Robert D. Bullard's *Dumping in Dixie: Race, Class, and Environmental Quality* (Boulder, CO: Westview Press, 1994) put the environmental activism of non-white groups into the spotlight. For the Global South, Martinez-Alier's 'environmentalism of the poor' had a similar effect: Joan Martinez-Alier, *The Environmentalism of the Poor: A Study of Ecological Conflicts and Valuation* (Cheltenham: Edward Elgar Publishing, 2002). An online Environmental Justice Atlas provides an idea of the global diversity of environmental campaigns (http://ejatlas.org).

As the understanding of environmentalism has broadened, it became more difficult to write synthetic monographs. Chad Montrie's *A People's History of Environmentalism in the United States* (London: Continuum, 2011) delivered a rather unsatisfactory solution by drawing attention to heretofore neglected groups but failing to connect their stories with existing narratives. Joachim Radkau's voluminous *The Age of Ecology* (Cambridge: Polity, 2014) seeks to outline contours of a global history of environmentalism but it ends as a diffuse patchwork of stories with a strong German accent. Michael Bess combined social movement history with a cultural history of post-war France in his *The Light-Green Society: Ecology and Technological Modernity in France, 1960–2000* (Chicago: University of Chicago Press, 2003). The present author pursued a different approach by analysing environmentalism as a set of different yet interrelated fields in the sense of Bourdieu: Frank Uekötter, *The Greenest Nation? A New History of German Environmentalism* (Cambridge, MA: MIT Press, 2014).

Recent research tends to focus on specific aspects of environmentalism. Some of the most exciting publications explore the context of the Cold War: Jacob Darwin Hamblin, *Arming Mother Nature: The Birth of Catastrophic Environmentalism* (Oxford: Oxford University Press, 2013); John R. McNeill and Corinna Unger (eds), *Environmental Histories of the Cold War* (Cambridge: Cambridge University Press, 2010); the impact of religion: Mark R. Stoll, *Inherit the Holy Mountain: Religion and the Rise of American Environmentalism* (Oxford: Oxford University Press, 2015), the population explosion trope: Thomas Robertson, *The Malthusian Moment: Global Population Growth and the Birth of American Environmentalism* (New Brunswick, NJ: Rutgers University Press, 2012), Matthew James Connelly, *Fatal Misconception: The Struggle to Control World Population* (Cambridge, MA: Belknap Press of Harvard University Press, 2008); Christopher C. Sellers, *Crabgrass Crucible: Suburban Nature and the Rise of Environmentalism in Twentieth-Century America* (Chapel Hill: University of North Carolina Press, 2012); the link between environmentalism and consumption: Thomas Jundt, *Greening the Red, White, and Blue: The Bomb, Big Business, and Consumer Resistance in Postwar America* (Oxford: Oxford University Press, 2014); and the ambiguities of activism: Kim Fortun, *Advocacy after Bhopal: Environmentalism, Disaster, New Global Orders* (Chicago: University of Chicago Press, 2001). These publications have also established links to other scholarly fields and thus challenged the intellectual isolation of research on environmentalism that had provoked some critical self-reflection, see Adam Rome, '"Give Earth a Chance": The Environmental Movement and the Sixties', *Journal of American History* 90 (2003), pp. 525–554. However, it is noteworthy that most of the aforementioned publications discuss American environmentalism, which has received by far the greatest amount of scholarly attention. While American leadership in environmental affairs has long dissipated, American scholars still retain a leading role in environmental history writing.

Several decades of research have produced a significant body of publications of highly variable quality, as ambitious scholarly efforts stand next to naive stories of activism. If one were to summarize the state of research, one might speak of a broad trend from a clear master narrative to a 10,000-piece jigsaw puzzle, with most of the pieces being only vaguely known, if at all. For all the growth in scholarship, the gaps in our knowledge about environmental movements are still legion. Compared with other fields of social movement history, research in environmental history is still lacking a certain maturity, not least because numerous scholars have focussed on telling their own stories without engaging with broader questions about environmentalism and social movements. It remains to be seen whether scholars see all this as irritant or as a tremendous opportunity for future research.

CHAPTER 16

Equality, Difference and Participation: The Women's Movements in Global Perspective

Ilse Lenz

To analyse women's movements in a long-term and global perspective constitutes a fundamental challenge indeed, but it also opens up new opportunities in analysing and understanding them.[1] These new prospects are related to basic issues of globalization research: focussing on shifting multiple power relationships beyond the national framework and theorizing the present reconfiguration of time and space, we are led to reconsider their changing relationship.[2] These aspects are highly relevant to some basic issues in researching women's movements and feminisms. Therefore, a long-term, global perspective offers prospects for reconsidering these movements' 'deep development', their regional diversity and their continuities, ruptures, innovations and transformations.

---

[1] My deep thanks go to Stefan Berger, Reinhart Kößler, Saida Ressel and Moritz Straub for their constructive comments and support. The author alone is responsible for errors.
[2] Anthony Giddens, *Sociology*, 4th edn (Cambridge: Polity Press, 2001) pp. 59–60; Sebastian Conrad, *Globalgeschichte. Eine Einführung* (Munich: Beck Verlag, 2013).

I. Lenz (✉)
Department of Social Science, University of Bochum, Bochum, Germany

© The Author(s) 2017   449
S. Berger, H. Nehring (eds.), *The History of Social Movements in Global Perspective*, DOI 10.1057/978-1-137-30427-8_16

I begin with a definition of women's movements and then consider the epistemic chances and implications of global long-term perspectives. After that I will outline women's movements and their international interchanges and networking from the late eighteenth century until the present.[3]

CONCEPTUAL ISSUES CONCERNING WOMEN'S MOVEMENTS AND FEMINISM

Social movements have been understood as mobilizing collective actors. They have been characterized as originating in response to structural contradictions and opportunity structures, as creating discourses and demands, and as forming organizations and mobilizing resources for basic continuity.[4] Whereas this definition can be modified to include women's movements, the structural contradictions of gender relations have to be considered and integrated in the conceptual modification. These considerations, again, have implications for the understanding of social movements. In modernity, gender works as a structural category of differentiation, organizing knowledge about gender definitions and differences, and of inequality in social organization; women's movements face both dimensions. Notably, as will be argued later, separation between a male-centred public sphere and a private, domestic sphere to which women were confined, and the gender division of labour have constituted different conditions for women's movements.

In a first broad working definition, women's movements can be understood as collective actors in which individuals mobilize for social change in gender relations, and in which women have decisive shares in leadership and membership. They can be understood as negotiating for gender justice and social justice as they understand and define them.[5] As they form

---

[3] In this context, however, I can only outline essential developments and long-term trajectories while paying tribute to the global and social diversity of women's movements.

[4] Edward Snow, Sarah A. Soule and Hanspeter Kriesi (eds), *The Blackwell Companion to Social Movements*, 2nd edn (Oxford: Blackwell, 2007); Doug McAdam, John D. McCarthy and Mayer N. Zald (eds), *Comparative Perspectives on Social Movements. Political Opportunities, Mobilizing Structures, and Cultural Framings* (Cambridge: Cambridge University Press, 1996).

[5] Ilse Lenz, *Die Neue Frauenbewegung in Deutschland. Abschied vom kleinen Unterschied. Eine Quellensammlung*, 2nd edn (Wiesbaden: VS Verlag, 2010); Ilse Lenz, 'Geschlechterkonflikte um die Geschlechterordnung im Übergang. Zum neuen Antifeminismus', in Erna Appelt, Brigitte Aulenbacher and Angelika Wetterer (eds), *Gesellschaft – Feministische Krisendiagnosen* (Münster: Westfälisches Dampfboot, 2013) pp. 204–227.

in different social milieux and work on a broad range of issues, they should be conceptualized in the plural and not as a homogeneous women's movement. Rather, women's movements are as diverse as working-class and middle-class women's movements, religious and secular women's associations, mothers', female migrants' or lesbian groups. They aggregate to constitute a women's (or gender) movement sector meeting in cooperation as well as in conflict.

In an already classic contribution, Myra Marx Ferree defined women's movements by their gender composition, namely by *organizing women as a constituency*.[6] However, Karen Offen (as I do myself) has pointed to the important role of men as members in or allies of women's movements, especially in socialism and in developing countries. In my working definition, emancipatory men can be seen as potential members of the women's movement.[7] This is still an open debate. But we have to consider that opting for a definition based on the constituency or on the issues underlying mobilization has important implications for the scope of research: which movements will be included in the research agenda? Which will be defined as not belonging?

I argue for a broad empirical approach based on action theory, looking at the political processes of mobilization and contention and not only at discourses. Furthermore, I aim to avoid implicitly or explicitly normative definitions using a feminist or 'progressive' yardstick. Rather I plead for an hermeneutic understanding focussing on the movements' collective action from their own interpretations of gender and social justice. The working definition outlined above seems to serve these aims and it will be applied in this article.

A long-term conceptual issue concerns the difference between women's movements and feminism. Some authors tended to conflate both, which has led to a certain ubiquity of feminisms in history. In her concise differentiation, Myra Marx Ferree defines feminism as a goal for social change in gender relations, which is different from women's movements with women as a constituency. The term 'feminism' thus can be used to characterize women's movements as well as heterosocial organizations.[8]

---

[6] Myra Marx Ferree, 'Globalization and Feminism. Opportunities and Obstacles for Activism in the Global Arena', in Myra Marx Ferree and Aili Tripp (eds), *Global Feminism. Transnational Women's Activism, Organizing and Human Rights* (New York: New York University Press, 2006) p. 6; see also Angelika Schaser, *Frauenbewegung in Deutschland 1848–1933* (Darmstadt: Wissenschaftliche Buchgesellschaft, 2006).

[7] Karen M. Offen, *European Feminisms 1700–1950. A Political History* (Palo Alto, CA: Stanford University Press, 2000) p. 21; Lenz, *Die Neue Frauenbewegung in Deutschland*.

[8] Ferree, 'Globalization and Feminism', p. 7.

This definition of feminism is broad and may be applied to diverse institutional settings. Another differentiation can be drawn when looking at
collective versus individual emancipation including both body and sexuality: women's movements mobilize for *women's collective demands* such as
the right to wage work or equal family laws. Feminism calls for *personal
autonomy or self-determination of individual women or men* over their life
decisions, sexuality or the bearing of children.[9] This definition of feminism
links it with individualization and intimate citizenship in modernity.[10]
Feminism has been both a result as well as a driving force of the processes
struggling for individual autonomy and intimate citizenship.

GLOBALIZATION AND THE RECONFIGURATION OF TIME
AND SPACE

Global long-term perspectives point to the reconfiguration of time and
space.[11] In the dimension of time, several issues are crucial for research on
women's movements: the first is taking critical distance from the explicit
or implicit narratives of progress that are abundant in the sources and
parts of literature. If we follow the definition outlined above, women's
movements are not progressive *per se*, but they mobilize for what *they see*
as gender or social justice. Sometimes, they may have proposed measures
of control and subordination whereas themselves believing in progress.
The enthusiasm of some currents for 'civilizing' colonial women or for
eugenic 'improvement' in the early twentieth century before the advent of
National Socialism are telling examples.

The second issue can be summarized as the problem of continuity, ruptures and innovations in women's movements that have beset them from
their beginnings in modernity.[12] Feminist discourses on eros, sexuality,

---

[9] Nancy Cott, *The Grounding of Modern Feminism* (New Haven, CT: Yale University
Press, 1987).

[10] Kenneth Plummer, *Intimate Citizenship. Private Decisions and Public Dialogues* (Seattle:
University of Washington Press, 2003).

[11] Giddens, *Sociology*, pp. 59–60.

[12] For the different trajectories of women's movements see the comprehensive international bibliography by Ilse Lenz, Anja Szypulski and Beate Molsich, *Frauenbewegungen
international. Eine Arbeitsbibliographie* (Opladen: Leske & Budrich, 1996); Offen, *European
Feminisms 1700–1950*; Karen Offen (ed.), *Globalizing Feminisms Before 1945* (London:
Routledge, 2010); Louise Edwards and Mina Roces (eds), *Women in Asia: Critical Concepts
in Asian Studies* (London: Routledge 2009).

work and political participation have developed in 'long waves'[13] from the Enlightenment down to the new worldwide women's movements after 1968, and they are still crucial for the twenty-first century.[14] Also, the level of organization or representation did not increase gradually over time. Characteristically, departures with intense mobilization, upheaval and innovation were followed by phases of broad organization and consolidation, then often by doldrums or latency, until the next eruptive departure.[15]

For Europe and North America, the established periodization distinguishes between the first waves from the nineteenth to the early twentieth century until attaining suffrage, democratization and formal norms of public equality after the First World War, and the second wave of the 'new women's movements' in the wake of the international student and youth movement after 1968. Sometimes, a third wave is assumed to have started from the early 1990s, in which queer, anti-racist and migration feminists and young media women raised their voice.[16]

But the periodization would be different for societies which followed different development paths within multiple modernities. In post-colonial societies like India or Korea, women's movements grew in the anti-colonial struggle and receded after independence. They then flared up again in the 1960s student and youth risings. In Eastern Europe or Russia, these movements mobilized until the Stalinist dictatorship and then re-emerged in the context of post-socialist system transformation after the mid-1980s.[17] In Japan, a basic continuity characterized the women's

[13] Ute Gerhard, 'Die "langen Wellen" der Frauenbewegung—Traditionslinien und unerledigte Anliegen', in Regina Becker-Schmidt and Gudrun-Axeli Knapp (eds), *Das Geschlechterverhältnis als Gegenstand der Sozialwissenschaften* (Frankfurt/Main: Campus, 1995), pp. 247–278.

[14] For different perspectives on the present see Nancy Fraser, *Fortunes of Feminism. From State-Managed Capitalism to Neoliberal Crisis* (London: Verso, 2013); Angela McRobbie, *The Aftermath of Feminism. Gender, Culture and Social Change* (London: SAGE, 2009); Lenz, 'Geschlechterkonflikte um die Geschlechterordnung im Übergang'; Louise Edwards and Mina Roces (eds), *Women's Movements in Asia: Feminism and Transnational Activism* (London: Routledge, 2010), Chandra Talpade Mohanty, *Feminism Without Borders. Decolonizing Theory, Practicing Solidarity*, (Durham, NC: Duke University Press, 2003).

[15] Offen is critical of the metaphor of ,waves' and pleads for metaphors of eruptions, flows and fissures; see Offen, *European Feminisms 1700–1950*, p. 25.

[16] Ute Gerhard, *Unerhört. Die Geschichte der deutschen Frauenbewegung.* (Reinbek: Rowohlt, 1990); Lenz, *Die neue Frauenbewegung in Deutschland.*

[17] Richard Stites, *The Women's Liberation Movement in Russia. Feminism, Nihilism, and Bolshevism 1860–1930* (Princeton, NJ: Princeton University Press, 1990); Bianka Pietrow-Ennker, *Russlands 'neue Menschen'. Die Entwicklung der Frauenbewegung von den Anfängen*

movements from the 1910s, when they formed, until the late 1960s. In their mainstream phase, they mobilized during the ultranationalist regime from the late 1930s supporting the war effort, but after 1945 a basic continuity in leadership and organizations can be observed until the new feminism starting in 1970. Therefore, the image of an ascending trajectory with deep ruptures is more fitting for the Japanese movements than the metaphor of the first and second waves.[18] In China, several phases are assumed, ranging from democratic anti-imperialist mobilization during the late Qing Dynasty and the early republic, communist mass organization in the People's Republic of China (PRC) and national organizations in Hong Kong and Taiwan, whereas at present one sees a new feminist mobilization after the political opening of the PRC and the global networking around and after the UN Conference at Beijing 1995.[19] These examples illustrate the range of trajectories in different regional and national contexts. However, the new feminism, which commenced from the late 1960s, became a global phenomenon when it flared up in the global youth and student movement and it was able to utilise the opening opportunity structure around the UN social conferences and women's conferences from 1975 onwards (see below). Thus, women's movements were confronted with incontemporaneity (*Ungleichzeitigkeit*) according to their social context. The constellations in which they were emerging reflected international inequality, which has been considered in the spatial turn in globalization research.

bis zur Oktoberrevolution (Frankfurt/Main: Campus, 1999); Brigitta Godel, *Auf dem Weg zur Zivilgesellschaft. Frauenbewegung und Wertewandel in Russland* (Frankfurt/Main: Campus, 2002); Barbara Einhorn, *Cinderella Goes to Market. Citizenship, Gender and Women's Movements in East Central Europe* (London: Verso, 1995).

[18] Vera Mackie, *Feminism in Modern Japan. Citizenship, Embodiment and Sexuality* (Cambridge: Cambridge University Press, 2003); Ilse Lenz, 'Differente Partizipation. Die Frauenbewegungen im modernen Japan', in Michiko Mae and Ilse Lenz (eds), *Frauenbewegung in Japan. Gleichheit, Differenz, Partizipation* (Wiesbaden: VS Verlag, forthcoming 2017).

[19] Zheng Wang, *Women in the Chinese Enlightenment. Oral and Textual Histories* (Berkeley: University of California Press, 1999); Louise Edwards, 'Chinese Feminisms in a Transnational Frame: Between Internationalism and Xenophobia', in Mina Roces and Louise Edwards (eds), *Women's Movements in Asia. Feminisms and Transnational Activism* (London: Routledge, 2010), pp. 53–74, p. 74; Dorothy Ko and Zheng Wang, *Translating Feminisms in China* (Oxford: Blackwell, 2007); Astrid Lipinsky, *Der Chinesische Frauenverband. Eine kommunistische Massenorganisation unter marktwirtschaftlichen Bedingungen* (Berlin: LIT Verlag, 2006).

The dimension of space points to the universality and diversity of women's movements in the context of multiple modernities. Women's movements are universal in the sense that they have emerged in most modern societies in response to the challenges of internal modernization and internationalization. They are highly diverse in their contexts, however, and while exchanging concepts and impulses on an international level—at least since the late eighteenth century—women's movements translated these approaches into national and local contexts.

Yet, as internationalization was driven forward by the Western nations in quest of markets, raw materials and colonies, it created structurally unequal power relationships. One main global divide consisted in the emergence of modern nations and their colonies, which form deeply interrelated processes.[20] Modern European nations did not develop within a closed contained space, as is sometimes assumed; they strove and struggled for colonial domination, subordinating large parts of Africa, Asia and Latin America. This nexus of imperialist nation-building and colonialism deeply influenced gender relations in the modernizing nations as well as in their colonies.[21] As will be shown, power relations and the gender division of labour in modern 'Western' nations were based on the ideal norm of the mother and the housewife within the domestic sphere. Simultaneously, in the name of civilization, colonial powers propagated and institutionalized the domestication of women parallel to the subordination of men under the market economy and wage labour.

These global divisions and hierarchies deeply influenced the forms and trajectories of women's movements: in industrializing nations, women's movements mobilized for access to the public sphere, from which housewives were largely excluded, and for equality in the family. Their goals, such as access to education, skilled work and autonomy over their intimate relationships and their bodies, have been summarized as a quest for embodied citizenship.[22] In anti-colonial struggles, women's movements often fought publicly for equal rights within an independent nation—in other words, they constituted themselves as public citizens in the projected post-colonial nation. In some regions, these movements also

[20] Conrad, *Globalgeschichte*.

[21] Clare Midgley, *Feminism and Empire. Women Activists in Imperial Britain 1790–1865* (London: Routledge, 2007); Vrushali Patil, 'From Patriarchy to Intersectionality. A Transnational Feminist Assessment of How Far We've Really Come', *Signs* 4 (2013), pp. 846–868.

[22] Mackie, *Feminism in Modern Japan*.

struggled against the domestication and dependence of women as prop-agated by the colonial powers including female colonialists. Even now, post-colonial power relationships constitute crucial challenges to global women's networking and research.[23]

WOMEN'S MOVEMENTS, SOCIAL STRUCTURES AND TRANSFORMATION

Women's movements change with social change. However, women's movements are not only products, but also driving powers of moderniza-tion. As they reflect on the changes they have contributed to, they develop self-reflexive ways of thinking and mobilizing. They also intervene in the globalization and flexibilization of economy, society and globalization. New approaches are desirable, which combine the consideration of struc-tural causes with the ways women's movements mobilize through the cre-ation of discourses and organizations.

In modern Western societies, three structural changes have deeply influ-enced the emergence and trajectory of women's movements. The first is the systematic separation between the male-centred public sphere embracing politics and the market and the private domestic sphere to which women were relegated. This separation was fundamental in modern liberal politi-cal thought as represented by John Locke or Jean Jacques Rousseau. As Carole Pateman has shown, the sexual contract in which men held author-ity over women and children in their household, speaking for them in polity, preceded the social contract concluded amongst those male citizens who commanded the requisite material and moral property.[24] This separa-tion, and the concomitant neopatriarchal subordination of women to the home, were then incorporated into the Code Napoléon, which influenced vast areas of Europe. This ideology also shaped the gender culture of the emerging bourgeoisie and middle classes in the enthusiastic reception of Rousseau into the literature of the late eighteenth century.

Separation of public and private and the subordination of women was legitimized by contemporary European gender knowledge: gender was now considered as dual biological category according to which all human beings are classified as either men or women with different characters,

---

[23] Mohanty, *Feminism Without Borders.*
[24] Carole Pateman, *The Sexual Contract* (Cambridge: Polity Press, 1988).

roles and tasks ordained by nature (and not by social norms).[25] In effect, when struggling for a public voice women's movements confronted first and foremost the need to break through the barriers excluding women from the public sphere: the gender stereotypes of natural mother and housewife, the exclusion of women from political participation and their marginalization in public discourse and presence. To be sure, the male-centred workers' movements also faced exclusion from political participation in their early stages, but male workers were seen as public subjects, whereas women were located in the private sphere.

A second crucial transformation was the rise of industrial capitalism, which relied on international exchange as well as regional or national forces. In the modern gender division of labour, production and reproduction were separated: men were primarily constructed as wage workers for production and women as mothers and housewives carrying out unpaid reproductive care work. In the working class, however, women combined reproductive work with wage work or informal work, mostly in unskilled and subordinate jobs.[26] Therefore, several wings of the women's movements developed from educated women in the middle class. Other wings emerged as working women's movements within socialism.[27] Different class positions influenced the emergence of diverse women's movements, yet not in any deterministic way.

In a broader sense, women's movements should be conceptualized as plural, since they form in different social milieus and around diverse issues while basically all working on issues of perceived gender and social justice. Movements of educators, mothers, Catholic, Protestant, Islamic or Buddhist women emerged next to women workers', anarchist or socialist groups during the first waves. After 1968, the movement landscape appeared even more diverse, with different socio-political currents from liberal to socialist feminism, lesbian, migrant or global feminisms and the

---

[25] Karin Hausen, 'Family and Role-Division. The Polarization of Sexual Stereotypes in the Nineteenth Century. An Aspect of Dissociation of Work and Family Life', in Richard J. Evans and W. R. Lee (eds), *Social History of the Family in Nineteenth and Twentieth Centuries Germany* (London: Weidenfeld & Nicolson, 1981), pp. 51–83; Claudia Honegger, *Die Ordnung der Geschlechter. Die Wissenschaften vom Menschen und das Weib 1750–1850* (Frankfurt/Main: Campus, 1991).

[26] See Karin Hausen, *Geschlechtergeschichte als Gesellschaftsgeschichte* (Göttingen: Vandenhoeck & Ruprecht, 2012).

[27] See Offen, *European Feminisms 1700–1950.*

constructivist or queer networks. These plural movements provide tensions as well as dynamism for the entire movement sector.[28]

The third relevant social development was the spread of education and communication linked to nation-building from the late eighteenth century. Modern schools and universities as well as mass media were established in most nation states. Even if women were excluded from public participation in politics and economy, they could participate in public communication as readers and, on occasion, as writers. In this way, leaders in and around the women's movements were able to confront modern society on its own promises of freedom, equality and solidarity, but also take stock of their own developments and the changes effected by them in reflexive ways.

Vera Mackie proposed the approach of embodied citizenship to analyse the relationship between these structural changes and the mobilization of the women's movement in Japan. This concept captures the struggle for participation and recognition in work and politics, and autonomy in relationships, sexuality and the body.[29] By focussing on women's agency and their striving for participation in modernization, it helps to overcome the classical narrow view limited to male unilateral domination.

Another approach looks at the inter-relationship between the changing modern gender order and women's movements. For post-industrial, capitalist societies, Lenz has proposed conceptualizing three stages of modern gender order as a framework for analysing gender conflicts and social movements, especially women's movements.[30] Gender orders can be defined as gendered structures and institutions which create and reproduce inequalities and social hierarchies. They are legitimated by changing hegemonic gender cultures and their norms. Gender as a structural category recreating inequalities is operating in concert or in conflict with other categories such as class, race, migration or desire.

The three stages of gender orders are conceptualized by looking at the division of power and labour: the main factors are gendered structures and institutions in the division of power and labour, and forms of capitalism and of the welfare state. Forms of dominant gender norms are also considered.

---

[28] See for Germany Lenz, *Die Neue Frauenbewegung in Deutschland*.

[29] Mackie, *Feminism in Modern Japan*, pp. 4–12

[30] Lenz, 'Geschlechterkonflikte um die Geschlechterordnung im Übergang'.

In the first stage of national modernization and capitalist consolidation, the neo-patriarchal gender order was established in many European societies: it assigned public and domestic power to men, institutionalizing a division of labour in which men were defined as breadwinners and women mainly as dependent mothers and housewives. Whereas feminist debate has become critical of a broad use of the concept of patriarchy, the term neo-patriarchal gender order is specified and contextualized: it comprises modern gender orders as they pertained in most Western societies until the early or mid-twentieth century, in which men and women are assigned different spheres of power and work and in which men are considered superior to women. Fathers had hegemonic and legal authority over their wives and children.

The difference-based gender order developed as neo-patriarchal authority somewhat receded after World War I. Formal and legal male superiority was reduced with the arrival of women's suffrage, legal reforms for women's rights to their own property and the gaining of a voice in decision-making within the family. These reforms and the change of political culture were among the achievement of the first waves of women's movements, but were also connected to the crisis of the neo-patriarchal authoritarian order during the great wars of the twentieth century. In Europe and North America, women's suffrage was mostly achieved after the First World War, and in Africa, Asia and the Caribbean after the post-Second World War struggles for decolonization. The legacy of joint struggle against colonialism, including women activists, and the UN Declaration of Human Rights 1949, with its basic norm of gender equality, supported access to women's suffrage in many post-colonial societies.

The worldwide spread of mass production in the form of Fordism or Toyotism supported the comprehensive, stable recruitment of men for wage work and women's relegation to unpaid care work or semi-skilled work before marriage. Emerging welfare states institutionalized this division of labour with the breadwinner–housewife model. Gender division or polarity (and not male superiority) was institutionalized in labour market, family, and power distribution; gender difference was the leading ideology legitimizing this gender order.

The difference-based gender order has been eroding under the combined impact of new women's movements, reflexive modernization and change towards global flexible capitalism. Globalization and global capitalism, economization and full use of human resources have advanced as well as flexibility in the labour market and irregular employment.

Therefore, it is assumed that, at present, a transformation towards flexible gender orders is under way. This transformation is promoted by a pluralization and deconstruction of gender norms: gender is widely seen as a social construction, and different forms of lifestyles from the orthodox model to homosexual or queer variations are becoming increasingly legitimate. The breadwinner–housewife model has been eroded by the flexibilization of work and the reduction of long-term employment security for men. But it has also become culturally obsolete as economic constraints pressure people into becoming dual earners, an ambivalent process linked to value changes towards gender equality: some women enter careers in wage work, and some men engage in unpaid care work.

This broad structural framework has been drawn up for currrent capitalist societies, which show important variations, of course: for example, diverse gender welfare regimes.[31] In various post-colonial societies, diverse gender orders evolved in regions such as sub Saharan Africa, India and Latin America, but research on this is still at an early stage.[32] Gender orders in socialist command states like Cuba, China or Vietnam also cannot be homogenized while they all proclaim an ideology of gender equality and mobilization of women for wage work. The same goes for the post-socialist successor states, which often propagated pre-socialist ideologies of gender difference and nationalism while continuing with high rates of education and employment of women. Gender order is a middle-range approach that can prove useful in investigating women's movements' relationship to their specific socio-cultural context.

MOBILIZATION, ORGANIZATION AND INTERNATIONALIZATION OF WOMEN'S MOVEMENTS IN THE NEOPATRIARCHAL GENDER ORDER

In Europe and the USA, women's movements formed during the mobilization phases of the struggles for freedom and democracy in the late eighteenth and the first half of the nineteenth century. In the revolutionary

---

[31] Diane Sainsbury, *Gender and Welfare State Regimes* (Oxford: Oxford University Press, 1999); for East Asia see Sirin Sung and Gillian Pascal (eds), *Gender and Welfare States in East Asia. Confucianism or Gender Equality?* (Basingstoke: Palgrave Macmillan, 2014).

[32] The former model of 'Third World patriarchies' in which Southern societies were homogenized and constructed in contrast to an idealized 'egalitarian West' has been proven Eurocentric; see Mohanty, *Feminism Without Borders*.

democratic waves around 1789, 1830 and 1848, these movements faced the complex challenge of confronting 'new' as well as pre-existing, often reorganized, forms of gender inequalities and subordination.[33]

Two interconnected dialectics operated in the formation of these women's movements: one was the interchange between the public and domestic sphere: women's movements were confronted with the challenge of intervening in public while they were excluded from politics and assigned to the domestic sphere in modern Western nation states. In this case, the articulation of critical discourses and the formation of networks and circles can be seen to be a result of their mobilization to overcome the boundaries of the domestic home to enter and intervene in the public sphere. Therefore, public protest should not be considered as main criterion for the existence or vitality of a social movement, as it usually has to rely on preceding mobilization and on networks which first have to be created by the movement.[34] By their interventions, on the other hand, women's movements brought the experiences of care, reproduction, female sexuality and bodies into the androcentric public sphere.

The other dialectic, which will be discussed in the next section, concerns the interplay between international and national thinking and organization. One variation of this dialectic developed in the context of nation-building: whereas modern Western nations had excluded women from politics, women's movements mobilized using and appropriating international approaches.[35] Discourses of gender freedom and equality circulated internationally, and local activists perceived and selected international ideas while combining them with local and national elements.

[33] Offen, *European Feminisms 1700–1950*; Offen, *Globalizing Feminisms before 1945*.

[34] This criterion has been derived from male-centred movements such as the workers' movements which, after overcoming the early sanctions could move into the public sphere; it does not apply to other mobilizing collective actors relegated to the domestic sphere such as women, who face the challenge of first creating subjectivities aiming to gain public voices and mobilize in public. Other examples for persons excluded from the public are irregular migrants or even slaves, who also first have to build up subjectivities, mobilization and networks before organizing public protest.

[35] Leila Rupp, *Worlds of Women. The Making of an International Women's Movement* (Princeton, NJ: Princeton University Press, 1997); Offen, *Globalizing Feminisms before 1945*; Susan Zimmermann, 'A Struggle over Gender, Class and the Vote. Unequal International Interactions and the Formation of the "Female International" of Socialist Women (1905–1907)', in Oliver Janz and Daniel Schönpflug (eds), *Gender History in a Transnational Perspective. Networks, Biographies, Gender Orders* (Oxford: Berghahn, 2014), pp. 101–127, for East Asia see Edwards, Roces, *Women's Movements in Asia*.

This process is not adequately described by the term 'translation' in the sense of transposing an international concept into a local frame. Local activists, rather, fused these international ideas with their own contexts, and reinterpreted traditions so that they could grow with new, blended transcultural meanings. They often showed highly creative potential and agency in these processes. Therefore, I speak of the *blended composition* of emancipatory or feminist thinking.[36]

From the late eighteenth century until the mid-nineteenth century, European and US women's movements developed different discourses on women, gender and society. Discourses were spread internationally in a unilateral way: they were received in anti-colonial and national resistance movements of women, but the blended compositions of women's movements and their intellectual leaders in the periphery were rarely noticed or appreciated in the metropolis.

One basic current called for equal rights with men, referring to liberal democratic ideas while recognizing gender difference as mothers and lovers. One example is the playwright Olympe de Gouges (1748–1793) who took up the cause of women and slaves in her dramas. She wrote the *Declaration of the Rights of Woman and the Female Citizen* in 1791, responding to the *Declaration of the Rights of Man* of 1789. In this manifesto, she stipulated equal political and social rights for women, but also their right not to name the father of their child. Thus, she introduced the issue of reproduction and mother's rights—what today is covered by the term reproductive rights—into the concept of human rights. Such an approach is characterized by *equality in difference*, and it inspired liberal and socialist women's movements until the late twentieth century. It tended to connect gender inequality to other deep inequalities, especially of slaves and of wage workers, and to seek for alliances with other emancipatory movements.[37]

The other broad current sprang from women's difference to men in their role as mothers, basing demands for rights on their different contribution to the modern state and society. In this view, women as (potential) mothers would contribute care and social work, education for girls as strong

---

[36] Lenz, 'Differente Partizipation'.

[37] For this typology of equality in difference versus difference and maternalist thinking, see, among others, Offen, *European Feminisms 1700–1950*; Ute Gerhard (ed.), *Differenz und Gleichheit. Menschenrechte haben (k)ein Geschlecht* (Frankfurt/Main: Helmer, 1990); Lenz, *Die Neue Frauenbewegung in Deutschland*.

national future mothers and a relational and communal culture beyond the rationality of the male market and politics. This approach has been called 'relational feminism' or maternalism, and it can be understood as *difference as a basis for participation*. It tended to connect difference and motherhood with the nation, especially based on liberal nationalism. Both currents grappled with the issues of gender difference: the former based its claims on rights of equal embodied citizenship irrespective of difference, as expressed in the slogan 'human rights have no gender', and the latter framed demands for rights mainly on difference and assumed female relationality. Feminist thought in the late twentieth century began questioning and deconstructing the concept of gender difference itself as a cultural representation.

The main results of early women's circles until the mid-nineteenth century consisted in establishing these discourses in politics and the media and creating social awareness about gender inequality and the 'woman question'. From these discursive circles, the movements in Europe and the USA developed into more stable organizations around the mid-nineteenth century. These national associations were linked by international umbrella councils.[38] In this way, it was possible to mobilize a broad constituency from different social milieux, mainly from rising middle classes, the working class and dissident, socially engaged Protestant sects. Around 1900, diverse religious women's organizations were formed in Catholic, Jewish and Protestant circles.

These organizations developed in six intellectual orientations. These can be systematized by considering their gender concepts, namely equality in difference or difference/maternalism on the one hand, and their views on society, which was seen as modern male, patriarchal or class society, on the other.[39]

1. One liberal current followed the approach of equality in difference outlined above, demanding equal social and political participation

---

[38] Offen, *European Feminisms 1700–1950*; Rupp, *Worlds of Women*.

[39] Due to limited space, I cannot quote the sources and literature on each current, but have to refer mainly to the comprehensive historiography of the Western women's movement by Offen, *European Feminisms 1700–1950*, the bibliography by Lenz, Szypulski and Molsich, *Frauenbewegungen international* and some monographs. An interesting contemporary account from the moderate wing's perspective is Gertrud Bäumer, 'Die Geschichte der Frauenbewegung in den Kulturländern', in Helene Lange and Gertrud Bäumer (eds), *Die Geschichte der Frauenbewegung in den Kulturländern, Handbuch der Frauenbewegung Vol. 1* (Berlin: W. Moeser Buchhandlung, 1901).

for women in what it saw as the modern authoritarian male state. Often it also called for social justice for workers or slaves. It was based mainly in the middle class.[40] One important international pioneer was the women's rights and suffrage movement in the United States. Its leaders came from the international anti-slavery movement. Working and black women, such as the former slave Sojourner Truth, were attracted to its claims for equality in difference and social justice.[41]

This thinking was also appropriated by liberal women's activists in other world regions in democratic and anti-imperialist contexts. For example, in the Japanese movement for Freedom and People's Rights (1874–1889), Kishida Toshiko called for full political participation of women, pointing to the models of political women in Chinese history as well as to Western suffragists.[42]

2. Later, moderate middle-class women's movements changed their thinking towards gender difference and relational maternalism. They focussed on the heteronormative family and mothers' contribution to state and society. They also increasingly emphasized the importance of social motherhood or care as the foundation of women's participation in the nation state, which was seen as a male-rationalized or bureaucratic state. Based on this maternalism, women were proclaimed as educators, social workers and sometimes peace-keepers of the nation. The religious women's movements—Catholic as well as Protestant associations—widely shared this maternalism. But this current also paved the way for the support of the nation during the First World War, when it extended and nationalized the relational maternal norms into engaging for and controlling public provision of food at the home front, organizing care for wounded soldiers etc. The support of women's movements for the nation at

---

[40] For a critical revision of the dualism of bourgeois and proletarian women's movements, see Marilyn Boxer, 'Rethinking the Socialist Construction and International Career of the Concept "Bourgeois Feminism"', in Offen, *Globalizing Feminisms before 1945*, pp. 296–302.

[41] Ellen Carol DuBois, *Woman Suffrage and Women's Rights* (New York: New York University Press, 1998); Steven M. Buechler, *Women's Movements in the United States. Woman Suffrage, Equal Rights, and Beyond* (New Brunswick, NJ: Rutgers University Press, 1990); Gerda Lerner, *Black Women in White America. A Documentary History* (New York: Pantheon Books, 1972).

[42] Lenz, 'Differente Partizipation'.

war was instrumental in gaining the vote after 1918 in Great Britain, Germany and the United States.

3. Radical middle-class currents argued for equality and difference inspired by the image of originally powerful and presently subordinated mothers and women, and they aimed to change what they saw as male-dominated state and society with its capitalist-rationalized norms, sexual double standards, war and violence. They developed in contention with both moderate national and socialist women's movements and called for universal equality, non-violence and individual autonomy. These strands took up class issues, such as the exploitation of female servants and mass prostitution, but emphasized autonomous feminist perspectives and criticized the socialist concepts arguing the identity of class and gender oppression. These radical groups formed the pioneers and pillars of women's internationalism for social justice: they fought for peace and international understanding, e.g. in the Women's International League for Peace and Freedom (WILPF, 1915), forming alliances with the cosmopolitan peace movements and the emerging League of Nations.[43] Some of them, like Sylvia Pankhurst, engaged for socialism and anti-colonialism. Also, they took up issues of sexuality and self-determination over women's bodies and reproduction, attacking discrimination against single mothers, the prohibition of abortion and state control of prostitution. These groups gained new ideas and charisma by international networking, but in their national contexts they mostly remained radical minorities opposing the mainstream and forming a hotbed for educating radical younger generations.

4. Socialist women's movements struggled against modern neo-patriarchy and capitalism, expressing the position of equality and difference. It held up a triple image of women which was somewhat contradictory: In this view, women constituted equal human beings with citizenship rights to work and vote, but they also formed the female part of a (socialist) couple, supporting their male comrade and standing behind him, and they were seen as natural mothers caring for children and family. Thus, the focus on gender equality was tempered by heteronormative and maternalist norms. Following the analysis of Friedrich Engels, August Bebel and Clara Zetkin, the

---

[43] Rupp, *Worlds of Women.*

class structure of society and social gender, were seen as the cause of women's subordination: its origins were located in the development of class society and the state as its political instrument. Thus, the socialist revolution—which would abolish the class system—would also end women's oppression: women would be integrated as workers into public production; housework would be socialized by public kindergartens and kitchens, though care for family and children remained the 'natural domain' of mothers. Therefore, socialist women's movements emphasized equality in wage work in combination with maternal norms of women as natural mothers.

The integration of women into socialist movements under men's leadership provided political and leadership training as well as access to resources like communication and meeting spaces, publications and education. But it also could legitimize general control of women's groups by male as well as by female leaders. For example, Clara Zetkin played a crucial role in prioritizing class struggle, refusing all cooperation with 'bourgeois women righters'. Thus, socialist women's movements developed in tension between gender solidarity and male dominance.

Pointing to the integration into socialism and control by male party leaders, some feminist historians tended to exclude socialist women from women's movements and feminism[44] or to focus on trends towards ignorance and sex discrimination in the socialist and workers' movements. This interpretation is based on the understanding that women's movements are defined by their constituency of women and therefore cannot exist as part of or close alliance with androcentric parties or organizations.[45] Such an approach risks reproducing a middle-class perspective by excluding the struggles of working women. Furthermore, it ignores the essential contributions of socialist women's movements to the organization and empowerment of working women towards equality at work, and suffrage at the local, national and international level.[46]

[44] Schaser, *Frauenbewegung in Deutschland*.

[45] In contrast, religious women's groups which are also part of androcentric organizations tend to be classified as part of women's movements.

[46] Silke Neunsinger, 'Creating the International Spirit of Socialist Women. Women in the Labour and Socialist International 1923–1939', in Pernilla Jonsson, Silke Neunsinger and Joan Sangster (eds), *Crossing Boundaries. Women's Organizing in Europe and the Americas, 1880s–1940s* (Uppsala: Uppsala University Press, 2007), pp. 117–156; Zimmermann, 'A

5. From the nineteenth century onwards, women's movements in anarchism developed from utopian communities and discourses on autonomy, free association and eros.[47] They were based on gender concepts of eros, autonomous motherhood and care, and on the idea of individual freedom and responsibility without a controlling state. Therefore, their contribution towards political thinking and women's movements consisted in ideas of free love and marriage from a women's perspective, free education and autonomous and equal individuals. Anarchist feminism was strongly opposed by moderate middle-class women leaders, who repudiated ideas of free love and marriage as sexual anarchism, instead propagating legal marriage and children from views of morality and women's economic security. While this concept of free love and eros was clearly a minority position, in the long term it became highly influential in the new women's movements after 1965.[48]

6. Anti-colonial and anti-imperialist women's movements developed in the context of independence movements in various regions in Africa, Latin America and Asia. Unfortunately, the state of research is still elementary here. These movements demanded national independence and citizenship, which opened up the opportunity for women to work, suffrage and more egalitarian and secular marriage laws. Such women's movements often worked in alliance with independence movements, especially their socialist wings.[49] They often became the nucleus of women's mass organizations and provided their leaders at both national and UN level after independence.

In the context of colonial dominance and anticolonial women's mobilization, the fundamental international inequality and incontemporane-

Struggle over Gender, Class and the Vote'; for Japan Vera Mackie, *Creating Socialist Women in Japan. Gender, Labour and Activism, 1900–1937* (Cambridge: Cambridge University Press, 1997).

[47] Martha A. Ackelsberg, *Free Women of Spain. Anarchism and the Struggle for the Emancipation of Women* (Bloomington: Indiana University Press, 1991); for Japan Andrea Germer, *Historische Frauenforschung in Japan. Die Rekonstruktion der Vergangenheit in Takamure Itsues 'Geschichte einer Frau' (Josei no rekishi)* (München: Iudicium, 2003).

[48] For Germany, see Lenz, *Die Neue Frauenbewegung in Deutschland*; for Japan Mae and Lenz, *Frauenbewegung in Japan*.

[49] *Kumari Jayawardena, Feminism and Nationalism in the Third World* (London: Zed Press, 1986); for the communist women's league in Indonesia, see Saskia Wieringa, *Sexual Politics in Indonesia* (The Hague: Institute of Social Studies, 2002).

ity of women's movements is striking: middle-class moderate or rightist women's movements of the colonial ruling nations supported colonialism in self-proclaimed roles as 'educators' or 'civilizers' of 'native gender relations'. Nationalist women's organizations recruited women for the colonies or procured wives and brides for the white masters from their fatherland. Only some radical or socialist women's activists engaged in international solidarity with anti-colonial struggles.

These diverse currents of women's organization were aware of their distinct programmatic, discursive, and organizational approaches, and they interacted in debates, in some communication, but mostly in contention. This was acerbated by ideological and moral demarcations between their organizations, in particular between moderate middle-class movements and socialist or anarchist groups. Fundamental divisions arose on issues which concerned the image of the pure woman and the mother of the nation: sexuality versus morality (for example, the abolition of the regulation of prostitution) and support for national war versus an international struggle for peace from the First World War onwards. Moderate currents campaigned for national morality as well as for war support, and radical and some socialist activists strove for a new morality and new sexual norms as well as international peace.

Women's activists developed networks, everyday meetings and rituals in their life world,[50] but this shared movement culture tended to be confined to each particular group. Personal friendships, however, could bridge cleavages between contending camps, thus enabling some exchange and even strategic accords.

These movements also built up alliances with men, political parties and civil society organizations which followed or sympathized with their sociopolitical convictions: liberal activists tended to cooperate with liberal leaders and parties the same way as socialist ones gravitated towards socialist groups.

After the deep crisis of the First World War and the support of moderate groups for national war, women achieved suffrage in many Western nations.[51] After 1900, they also gained access to higher education, to lower white collar positions as nurses, telephone workers or secretaries, and to professions in the

---

[50] Mineke Bosch and Annemarie Klostermann (eds), *Politics and Friendship: Letters from the International Woman Suffrage Alliance, 1902–1942* (Columbus: Ohio State University Press, 1990); Ulla Wischermann, *Frauenbewegungen und Öffentlichkeiten um 1900. Netzwerke—Gegenöffentlichkeiten—Protestinszenierungen* (Königstein: Helmer, 2003).

[51] For European women's movements from the 1920s, see Offen, *European Feminisms 1700–1950*, pp. 277–379; Ute Gerhard (ed.), *Feminismus und Demokratie. Europäische Frauenbewegungen der 1920er Jahre* (Königstein: Helmer, 2001).

field of medicine and law. But even if political participation was achieved, the gender division of labour and the laws, which upheld domestic inequality and women's obligation for unpaid housework, were widely maintained. Gradually, difference-based gender order was established in the industrial capitalist societies in which gender inequality had been based on concepts of biological gender dualism, difference and gender division of labour. Women's movements in the West dropped into the doldrums,[52] while they kept mobilizing in other regions, in anticolonial struggles, as in India or Korea, or in national democratization movements, as in Japan from 1920 to 1938.

INTERNATIONAL ORGANIZING AND THE RISE OF INTERNATIONAL INSTITUTIONS

The dialectic of the international and national can also be observed in the field of organization. During the intermittent mobilization waves from 1848 onwards, border-crossing communication networks were formed between leaders and activists by meetings, letters or exchanges and translations of publications. French activists had organized the first international women's rights congress during the World Exposition in 1878. The International Council of Women (ICW) was then established in 1888 at the second international conference called by the US national Suffrage Women's Association in Washington. Most of its members came from Western, Northern and Central Europe, but Australia (1899), New Zealand (1900), South Africa (1913), India (1925) and some Latin American nations (1923–1927) joined later.[53] The ICW was an elite and rather gender-conservative organization following maternalist ideas, but it also campaigned for suffrage and women's work, and against traffic in women.

The internationalization of women's movements promoted national organization processes, whereas national groups provided expertise, exchange and legitimacy for international associations. For example, the Federation of German Women's Associations was formed in 1890 out of several national groups in response to the formation of the ICW.[54] In

[52] Leila Rupp and Verta Taylor: *Survival in the Doldrums. The American Women's Rights Movement, 1945 to the 1960s* (New York: Oxford University Press, 1987).

[53] Rupp, *Worlds of Women*, p. 14, pp. 16–18.

[54] Gertrud Bäumer, 'Die Geschichte der Frauenbewegung in Deutschland', in Helene Lange and Gertrud Bäumer (eds), *Die Geschichte der Frauenbewegung in den Kulturländern, Handbuch der Frauenbewegung Vol. 1* (Berlin: W. Moeser Buchhandlung, 1901), p. 131ff.

times of rising nation states, the international was more or less understood as multiplication of the national.[55] The ICW, as an international umbrella association, was an aggregation of national groups whereby each group functioned as representative of its nation. Decisions were made on the principle of consensus so that action was not possible in disputed issues such as domestic workers' rights, abortion or single mothers.

Thus, internal debates and conflicts on both national and international levels encouraged the formation of diverse international organizations. The International Woman Suffrage Alliance (IWSA; later the International Alliance of Women, IAW) was organized by radical and suffrage activists advocating an equality-in-difference position at the 1904 conference of the ICW in Berlin. Committed to action for equality, political participation and peace, it brought together members from East Asia, Latin America, the Near East and Southern Africa.[56] When both the ICW and the IAW reduced their activities during the First World War due to national war support of its member organizations, radical and peace activists called for an international women's peace conference in The Hague in April 1915, where the Women's International League for Peace and Freedom (WILPF) was organized. The WILPF mobilized for international peace and social justice and against fascism.[57]

These three leading organizations continued discussions and somewhat coordinated their activities. They aimed to cooperate with the League of Nations and ran a campaign to appoint more women to their executive offices in 1925. While changing their actual issues and programmes, they have continued their work as an important NGO until the present day, cooperating with the UN on gender equality and peace.

Another trajectory of the international and national dialectic is the socialist women's movements. They aimed to participate in the international socialist debate on gender equality in theory and strategy, which then deeply influenced the orientation of socialist parties at the national level.

---

[55] Susan Zimmermann, 'The Challenge of Multinational Empire for the International Women's Movement: The Habsburg Monarchy and The Development of Feminist Inter/National Politics', in Offen, *Globalizing Feminisms 1700–1950*, p. 154.

[56] Rupp, *Worlds of Women*, pp. 15–18.

[57] Ibid., pp. 26–32.

CHANGES AND CONTINUITIES IN THE NEW WOMEN'S MOVEMENTS AFTER 1965

The student and youth movements of the late 1960s stimulated women's mobilizations on a global scale.[58] In this context of anti-authoritarian discourses, new ideas and groups emerged. Striving for collective and personal liberation, they questioned Western capitalism as well as Eastern dictatorial socialism. Feminists developed visions of collective social eros and individual liberation and autonomy, mostly calling for social transformation. Whereas the former waves had demanded equality in difference for *women as a group* in core institutions as the family, work and nation, the new women's movements combined the call for horizontal social equality and justice for all persons with the desire for *individual* liberation and autonomy as embodied subjects. Such aims implied fundamental criticism of these unequal institutions, especially unequal family relations and job segregation as well as hierarchical and bureaucratic organizations. In their critique they firmly distanced themselves from these organizations differing from women's moderate middle-class movements and tendencies. Also, their autonomous wings developed new network organizations: promoting horizontal structures and consciousness-raising, they mobilized and empowered those actors who formerly had been denied a voice.[59]

Thus, new women's movements contributed towards shaking and eroding the core structures of the modern neo-patriarchal *and* difference-based gender order. Firstly, by claiming that 'the personal is political', they transcended the demarcation of public and private which up to then had structured unequal gender relations in modernity. This claim was based on the understanding that 'domesticated' or 'privatized' forms of subordination structured women's marginalization in the public sphere. Their main forms were assignation of unpaid care work to women as their 'biological

---

[58] Lenz, Szypulski and Molsich, *Frauenbewegungen international*; an in-depth qualitative study for the United States is Ruth Rosen, *The World Split Open. How the Modern Women's Movement Changed America* (New York: Viking, 2000).

[59] Myra Marx Ferree and Beth Hess, *Controversy and Coalition. The New Feminist Movement Across Three Decades of Change.* (New York: Twaine Publ., 1994); Ilse Lenz, 'Changing Agents of Change? Anmerkungen zur Transformation sozialer Bewegungen am Beispiel der Neuen Frauenbewegung', in Jürgen Mittag and Heike Stadtland (eds), *Theoretische Ansätze und Konzepte in der Forschung über soziale Bewegungen in der Geschichtswissenschaft* (Essen: Klartext, 2014), pp. 359–378.

role', the refusal of self-determination over their sexuality and birth giving potential and widespread gender violence.[60] New feminisms linked this claim to the right to women's self-determination over their sexuality and bodies. Human and women's rights now gained an individual and embodied shape. In this, they met with homosexual movements. Concepts of embodied subjects and intimate citizenship[61] reflect this call for individual and collective autonomy. These demands for sexual and reproductive rights were taken up by global women's health networks at the UN Conferences on women as well as at the Cairo UN Conference on population in 1993 and the Fourth UN Conference of Women in Beijing.[62]

The main currents of new women's movements can again be systematized by looking at their concept of gender and of society.[63] Now, in

[60] Hausen, *Geschlechtergeschichte als Gesellschaftsgeschichte*; Lenz, 'Geschlechterkonflikte um die Geschlechterordnung im Übergang'.

[61] Kenneth Plummer, *Intimate Citizenship*; compare the fascinating case study of the global reception and rewriting of a feminist sexual health reader first published in the United States Kathy Davis, *The Making of Our Bodies, Ourselves. How Feminism Travels Across Borders* (Durham, NC: Duke University Press, 2007).

[62] Hilkka Pietilä, *The Unfinished Story of Women and the United Nations* (Genf: United Nations, 2007) http://www.un-ngls.org/pdf/UnfinishedStory.pdf; United Nations, *Report on the Fourth World Conference on Women* (Beijing, September 1995); Rosalind Petchesky and Karen Judd (eds), *Negotiating Reproductive Right. Women's Perspectives Across Countries and Cultures* (London and New York: Zed Books, 1998); Rosalind Petchesky, *Global Prescriptions. Gendering Health and Human Rights* (London: Zed Books, 2003); see also the critical analysis in Susanne Schultz, *Hegemonie—Gouvernementalität—Biomacht. Reproduktive Risiken und die Transformation internationaler Bevölkerungspolitik* (Münster: Westfälisches Dampfboot, 2006).

[63] A vast literature of feminist international discourses has evolved since the mid-1960s which cannot be cited here due to limitations of space; see Lenz, Szypulski and Molsich, *Frauenbewegungen international*. I can only refer to some outstanding collections and monographs. Some collections have been edited on European and US feminisms; see, among others, Carole McCann and Seung-kyung Kim (eds), *Feminist Theory Reader. Local and Global Perspectives* (London: Routledge, 2013) including some texts of migrant feminists in the United States and global texts; for Germany, see Lenz, *Die Neue Frauenbewegung in Deutschland* and for Japan Mae and Lenz, *Frauenbewegung in Japan*. For a groundbreaking comparative overview of the basic currents in Europe and the United States, see Judith Lorber, *Gender Inequality. Feminist Theories and Politics* (Oxford: Oxford University Press, 2012). For East Asia, see Asian Center for Women's Studies, *Women's Studies in Asia Series*. 8 vols. (Seoul: Ewha Womans University Press, 2005). For Africa Obioma Nnaemeka, *Sisterhood, Feminisms and Power. From Africa to the Diaspora* (Trenton, NJ: Africa World Press, 1998).

contrast to the first waves, its main currents integrated the basic idea of autonomy and self-determination on one's personal life and sexuality into its sets of demands. Therefore, following the definition outlined above, these currents represent diverse wings of feminism: Liberal feminism argued for gender equality and individual autonomy in democratic capitalist society. Socialist feminism saw the origins of women's subordination in the combination of capitalism and patriarchy as social systems and therefore mobilized for system reforms and transformation. Some men became active in socialist feminism, mobilizing for the abolition of the unequal division of labour and of gender violence, and analysing hegemonial and subordinated masculinities in patriarchy. In contrast, radical feminism[64] and radical lesbianism considered patriarchy as main structure of dominance over women.

In a reflexive turn, the differences between women resulting from race, ethnicity or desire were emphasized from the mid-1970s. Black feminism contested the concepts of white feminism and elaborated the triple oppression of black women by gender, class and race. Lesbian and gay feminism criticized heteronormativity by which they understood a set of compulsory naturalized norms oppressing queer as well as heterosexual desires.

On a global level, ecological feminism criticized the subordination and exploitation of women and nature by global patriarchy and capitalism. Developmental feminism criticized global and gender inequality. Postcolonial feminism focussed on the neo-colonial continuity in international inequality from structural and cultural perspectives.

Eventually, these feminist debates achieved a fundamental transformation of the meaning of gender: it changed from a biologistic concept legitimating collective norms of marriage and motherhood for all women (and of hegemonial masculinity for all men) to a category of social differentiation and inequality.[65] Feminists refused established definitions of women, femininity and gender and engaged to gain autonomous power of definition. From the 1970s, the debate on *equality in difference* versus *difference for participation* was revived under new terms of social (and

---

[64] For radical feminism in the United States, see Alice Echols, *Daring to Be Bad. Radical Feminism in America 1967–1975* (Minneapolis: University of Minnesota Press, 1997) and in Japan Setsu Shigematsu, *Scream From the Shadows. The Women's Liberation Movement in Japan* (Minneapolis: University of Minnesota Press, 2012).

[65] Judith Lorber, *Gender Inequality*, Lorber, *Paradoxes of Gender* (New Haven, CT: Yale Univ. Press, 1994); Judith Butler, *Gender Trouble. Feminism and the Subversion of Identity* (London: Routledge, 1990).

not biological) interpretations of gender. In the United Kingdom and the United States, liberal feminists tended to argue for individual equality and non-discrimination. Socialist and Marxist feminists developed structural approaches based on gender divisions of labour, including wage and unpaid work in patriarchal capitalism. They argued for equality and difference. Radical feminists tended to focus on gender difference in global patriarchy. In the global South, covering the nations of Africa, Central and Latin America and most of Asia, feminism struggled for development and peace as well as against social and domestic violence, which was important for mobilization and growing local roots.[66] These different semantics converged in the claim that gender is socially constructed, refuting biologistic and fundamentalist religious determinism.

From the 1970s onwards, the new women's movements became pluralized, embracing sub-movements of workers, migrant and black women, mothers, lesbians, and certain professions like teachers, lawyers or artists. They also reached out to men, who formed their own networks, often starting from the issue of fathering or working against gender violence. Gay groups formed coalitions with lesbian and heterosexual feminists. This pluralization of gender categories was again reflected in new intersectional understandings of gender looking at the interchange with other forms of inequality as class, ethnicity or desire.

In the 1970s, women's studies were formed in the context of the new movement. From the 1980s onwards, this new academic branch has already evolved into gender studies around the world, developing international and transnational communication and exchange.[67] Now the demand for power of definition, which included women's experiences and contributions, could be substantiated by scientific knowledge systems. From innovative approaches in philosophy, biology and sociology the constructivist paradigm of gender emerged.[68] This approach considered gender as an effect of culture which is institutionalized in language and knowledge

[66] Ferree and Tripp, *Global Feminism*. For East Asia, see Asian Center for Women's Studies, *Women's Studies in Asia Series*.

[67] Ilse Lenz, 'Contemporary Challenges for Gender Research in the Context of Globalisation', in Birgit Riegraf, Brigitte Aulenbacher, Edit Kirsch-Auwärter and Ursula Müller (eds), *Gender Change in Academia. Remapping the Fields of Work, Knowledge and Politics from a Gender Perspective* (Wiesbaden: VS-Verlag, 2006), pp. 203–216.

[68] Regine Gildemeister and Katja Hericks, *Geschlechtersoziologie. Theoretische Zugänge zu einer vertrackten Kategorie des Sozialen* (München: Oldenbourg, 2012); Butler, *Gender Trouble*.

systems and which has to be performed in everyday interaction according to hegemonial gender norms. The constructivist approach to gender and the critique of biologistic gender dualism has been appropriated in different international settings in Asia, Africa, Latin America, Europe and North America. For example, in East Asia, the constructivist approach was related to gender flexibility in Taoism, in which male and female blend and interchange. In Japan, feminists coined the term *gender-free* for a society in which persons can realize their individual life perspectives unburdened from the constraint of hegemonic gender norms.[69] The new paradigm of gender diversity has been accepted by many actors and institutions. Thus, in the early twenty-first century, gender is increasingly considered as social construct to be integrated into an intersectional perspective with class, ethnicity and desire. Gender has become more flexible, plural and individual in the context of international mobilization, whereas hegemonial gender norms are still powerful.[70]

WOMEN'S MOBILIZATIONS AND THE EMERGING GLOBAL MULTI-LEVEL SYSTEM

The new women's movements seized the opening international opportunity structures and arenas in the wake of globalization. In its aims and discourses as well as in its organizations and networks, they have increasingly been transcending the nation and its hegemonic gender norms. The movements cooperated with the UN, the EU and other regional supranational organizations. Step by step, an equality-oriented global gender regime was established and accepted by the great majority of nations around the UN World Conferences of Women (1975–1995).[71] Gender equality is one of the showcases for soft regulation of equality, peace and development in the debates on globalization, which is often reduced to process of deregulation only.

---

[69] Lenz, 'Differente Partizipation'.

[70] Raewyn Connell, *Short Introductions. Gender*, 2nd edn (Cambridge: Polity Press, 2009).

[71] Pietilä, *The Unfinished Story of Women and the United Nations*; Devaki Jain, *Women, Development, and the UN. A Sixty-Year Quest for Equality and Justice* (Bloomington: Indiana University Press, 2005); Gülay Caglar, Elisabeth Prügl and Susanne Zwingel (eds), *Feminist Strategies in International Governance* (London: Routledge, 2012). The emergence of the global gender regime also comprised the establishment of gender regulations for equality in several supranational organizations i.a. the EU; Sylvia Walby, *The Future of Feminism* (Cambridge: Polity Press, 2011).

The UN Decade of Women was initiated by the First UN World Conference of Women in Mexico in 1975, in which activists from the 'North', the 'South' and the 'East' were engaged in lively and contentious debates concerning political and emancipatory strategies. The Fourth UN World Conference in Beijing 1995 agreed on the World Action Platform, which can be considered an international charter of women's and human rights endorsed by governments and women's movements of most countries.[72] The implementation of its principles was carried out and monitored after 1995 in a number of other conferences taking place at the UN headquarters at intervals of five years. Thus, the entire UN process of institutional and international mobilization extended all the way from the 1970s to the new millennium. In its course, an international gender regime became established under the auspices of the UN.

The main goals of the UN Decade of Women were 'equality, development and peace', thus providing a wide framework for discussing differences and convergences. At the Beijing conference of 1995, the empowerment of women, i.e. the formation of power and autonomous participation as well as gender mainstreaming were defined as further aims. Gender mainstreaming is understood as the aim of achieving gender equality in all organizations and institutions, a process in which both men and women are actively engaged, and with both genders equally participating in making decisions. Currently, this is largely being replaced by diversity concepts, according to which women, migrants and elderly people, among other sections, should participate equally. After the initial focus on gender differences, other differences resulting from culture, race or desire, for example, have been recognized and are now being integrated into equality concepts.

The UN decade and its conferences on gender have yielded three outstanding results which are still vital and effective. The first was the creation of a common language and semantics for gender equality. This enabled global feminist movements to negotiate and process international differences and power relations and to develop shared aims and demands. In particular, international women's networks were successful in recognizing cultural and social differences, while they were defining equality in new ways at the same time. The women's and human rights approach provided a core concept for bridging cultural differences as it allowed the articulation of different experiences within specific socio-cultural contexts

---

[72] United Nations, *Report on the Fourth World Conference on Women*.

and then sought common grounds based on universal rights.[73] Thus, women's rights gained a universal and global meaning which is appropriated in blended compositions in diverse local and national contexts. These debates basically created and substantiated *reflexive universalism* in which Eurocentric gender discourses are criticized and different regional or cultural perspectives converge.[74]

The second result was the setting-up of international conventions and subsequent establishment of norms on gender equality agreed upon by the large majority of UN member states. These conventions established global equality norms while also respecting cultural differences. The most important of these are the Convention for Eliminating all Forms of Discrimination Against Women (CEDAW) of 1979[75] and the World Action Platform of the Fourth UN World Conference on Women in Beijing in 1995.

The third important result is the establishment of women's departments (now mostly gender departments) in political, social and economic organizations. At the First World Women's Conference of 1975 and in CEDAW, all ratifying governments committed themselves to establishing departments for equal opportunities or women's desks. Consequently, in political, social or economic organizations, equal opportunities sections were formed that often cooperated with civil society as well as the women's movement.

In this context, transnational women's networks and organizations were formed which created reflexive universal discourses and mobilized in a global multi-level system: They appealed to the UN, regional organizations and nation states and could achieve global norms for equality and non-violence while building up projects and support at the local level.[76] In

[73] Sally Engle Merry, *Human Rights and Gender Violence. Translating International Law into Local Justice* (Chicago: University of Chicago Press, 2006); Valentine Moghadam, *Globalizing Women. Transnational Feminist Networks* (Baltimore, MD: Johns Hopkins University Press, 2005).

[74] Ilse Lenz, 'Differences of Humanity from the Perspective of Gender Research', in Jörn Rüsen (ed.), *Approaching Humankind. Towards an Intercultural Humanism* (Göttingen: V&R Unipress), pp. 185–200.

[75] Susanne Zwingel, *Translating International Women's Rights. The CEDAW Convention in Context* (Basingstoke: Palgrave MacMillan, 2016); Hannah B. Schöpp-Schilling and Cees Flintermann (eds), *The Circle of Empowerment. Twenty-Five Years of the UN Committee on the Elimination of Discrimination Against Women* (New York: Feminist Press, 2007).

[76] Moghadam, *Globalizing Women*; for Latin America, see Yin-Zu Chen, *Transnationale Bewegungsnetzwerke und lokale Mobilisierungen in Lateinamerika und der Karibik.*

the first waves, international women's organizations had been established which were formed as a multiplication of nations. In contrast, some new leading networks worked in transnational ways: feminists from the South formed the network DAWN (Development Awareness with Women for a New Era) in 1985 which worked as an epistemic community creating knowledge and strategies for equality, development and peace from a global Southern perspective. Mainly Southern feminists organized the global network Women Living under Muslim Law (WLUML) which provided innovative research and support for gender equality in Islamic societies.[77] Networks for women's health and reproductive rights, for peace and against gender violence coordinated regional and global groups.

Sexual and reproductive rights such as contraception, abortion and homosexuality remain a contested terrain and counter-coalitions of Catholic and Islamic states and organizations either aimed to block global women's rights conventions or to establish culturalist exemptions to them. The issue of prostitution brought about a deep split between one global network that argued for a sex work perspective and another that called for abolition and prohibition of prostitution.[78] Counter-movements such as anti-feminism and fundamentalism have strongly mobilized, in many cases including gender-conservative women. Militarization and the trend to bilateralism in international relations has worked against effective global governance, not only in the field of gender.

WOMEN'S MOVEMENTS IN LONG-TERM PERSPECTIVE: ISSUES AND IMPACT

This chapter has analysed women's movements and feminism from a social movement perspective as mobilizing collective actors rather than from a study of their discourses and texts. The relegation of women to the domestic or private sphere in modernity had complex consequences for

---

Organisationen—Strategien—Einflüsse. Das Beispiel des Frauenbewegungsnetzwerkes RSMLAC und seine Bedeutung für die peruanische Frauengesundheitspolitik 1985–2000 (PhD Ruhr-University Bochum 2005) www-brs.ub.ruhr-uni-bochum.de/netahtml/HSS/ Diss/ChenYinZu; for Japan Hiromi Tanaka, *Japanische Frauennetzwerke und Geschlechterpolitik im Zeitalter der Globalisierung* (München: Iudicium, 2009).

[77] Moghadam, *Globalizing Women.*

[78] Joyce Outshoorn (ed.), *The Politics of Prostitution. Women's Movements, Democratic States and the Globalisation of Sex Commerce* (Cambridge: Cambridge University Press, 2004).

women's movements. Firstly, they have had to overcome high institutional and cultural barriers to raise their voice and mobilize. Therefore, protest should not be the decisive criterion for the existence of a social movement in the case of groups that are excluded from the public, such as women, slaves or irregular migrants. If we want to broaden the understanding of social movements and not measure them by the yardstick of public political contention, mobilization of discourses and networks should also be considered as criteria for the existence and vitality of social movements.

Secondly, women's movements—in the plural—mobilize in cross-cutting and inter-changing ways between production and reproduction, between politics, work, family and sexuality. Therefore, they have contributed wide and diverse perspectives of equality in difference, of care and of the meaning of eros and equal personal relationships.

In a long-term global perspective, women's movements first formed in times of broad social mobilization and sometimes in revolutionary waves. But once they established critical discourses and networks, they initiated long waves of their issues and discourses. Thus, women's movements are not new social movements limited to the West, as is sometimes assumed. As shown in the dialectics of the international and the national, women's discourses and issues were selected and appropriated around the world from the nineteenth century, and international umbrella organizations established international cooperation within the movement sector and with the League of Nations. Until the 1970s, the international organizations worked as multiplication of the nation to which at least the moderate middle-class movements gave priority. With the rise of political and cultural globalization, and supported by information and communication technology, transnational and global women's networks emerged which aimed to intervene along the global multi-level system for gender equality. As a result of global and national commitment, with marked impact from global women's groups, a global gender regime with the norms of equality, peace, non-violence and development has been established based on soft regulation.

Gender has been pluralized and flexibilized. Feminist thinking has been appropriated and advanced by women's groups worldwide. Queer approaches are travelling globally while being contested by gender-conservative, nationalist and fundamentalist forces. Under the double impact of global capitalism and feminism, women in many societies have entered the public spheres of the labour market and politics and have gained some power, though still in minority positions. Whereas modern gender inequalities are being contested, the flexibilization of the gender order implies new challenges for women's and emancipatory movements and their reflexivity.

FURTHER READINGS

Since the 1970s, research on women's movements and feminisms has rapidly increased. The present wealth of theoretical approaches and empirical studies cannot be discussed fully here, meaning the omission of many excellent studies. Research on women's movements worldwide up to the mid-1990s is included in Lenz et al., *Frauenbewegungen international. Eine Arbeitsbibliographie (International Women's Movements. A Working Bibliography*; Opladen: Leske+Budrich, 1996; accessible in English). I will first discuss works on the diverse currents of women's movements, then touch on their internationalization and introduce some studies on their effects.

Women's movements developed in the context of such *diverse sociopolitical currents* as liberalism, maternalism, socialism, anarchism, nationalism and anti-colonialism. Karen Offen traced liberal, maternalist and socialist in Europe in her seminal *European Feminisms 1700–1950: A Political History* (Palo Alto, CA: Stanford University Press, 2000). Gerda Lerner described the genealogies of feminist thinking in Europe in *The Creation of Feminist Consciousness. From the Middle Ages to 1870* (Oxford: Oxford University Press, 1994). Ann Taylor Allen, *Feminism and Motherhood in Western Europe, 1890–1970: The Maternal Dilemma* (Basingstoke: Palgrave Macmillan, 2005) focused on maternalism which emphasized gender difference and women's potential as social mothers. Socialist women's movements are still under-studied after a first series of publications from about 1975 to 1995. The heyday of anarchist feminism has been described by Martha A. Ackelsberg in Free *Women of Spain: Anarchism and the Struggle for the Emancipation of Women* (Bloomington: Indiana University Press, 1991). Patricia Hill Collins, *Black Feminist Thought: Knowledge, Consciousness and the Politics of Empowerment* (New York, London: Routledge, 2nd edn, 2000) is a classic of US black feminism.

While anti-colonial and national democratic women's movements have been researched in diverse world regions, due to restrictions of space I can refer only to East Asia: Wang Zheng, *Women in the Chinese Enlightenment. Oral and Textual Histories* (Berkeley: University of California Press, 1999),

Louise Edwards, *Women Politics and Democracy: Women's Suffrage in China* (Palo Alto, CA: Stanford University Press, 2008) or Vera Mackie's long-term study (1880–2000) on *Feminism in Modern Japan: Citizenship, Embodiment and Sexuality* (Cambridge: Cambridge University Press, 2003).

Several collections cover the scope and diversity of feminist thinking from the 1960s, mainly in Western Europe and the United States (including black feminism and women of colour): Barbara A. Crow, *Radical Feminism. A Documentary Reader* (New York: New York University Press, 2000) focuses on the radical feminist and lesbian texts in the 1970s and 1908s in the United States. Diana Tietjens Meyers, *Feminist Social Thought. A Reader* (London: Routledge, 1997) contains main feminist debates on the construction of gender, care, difference and equality. Leslie H. Heywood, *The Women's Movement Today: An Encyclopedia of Third Wave Feminism* (2 vols., Westport, CT: Greenwood, 2006) introduces the third wave's key issues mainly from the United States. Carole McCann and Seung-kyung Kim (eds), *Feminist Theory Reader: Local and Global Perspectives* (New York: Routledge, 2013) collect US, European and global texts. Donald Hall and Annamarie Jagose, *The Routledge Queer Studies Reader* (London: Routledge, 2013) trace the emergence and development of Queer Studies. Lisa Disch and Mary Hawkesworth (eds), *The Oxford Handbook of Feminist Theory* (Oxford: Oxford University Press, 2016) discuss the genealogy of key feminist topics and treat the development and actual state of main debates. The Asian Center for Women's Studies, *Women's Studies in Asia Series* (Seoul: Ewha Womans University Press, 8 vols., 2005) is an excellent compendium on feminisms and gender studies in eight East Asian societies including issues of global and local influences on framing theories. Judith Lorber, *Gender Inequality. Feminist Theories and Politics* (Oxford: Oxford University Press, 2012) gives a brilliant comparative overview of the basic feminist currents in Europe and the United States. Regina Becker-Schmidt and Gudrun Axeli Knapp, *Feministische Theorie zur Einführung* (Hamburg: Junius, 2000) sum up feminist critical theory between subject constitution and changing social structure.

Source collections of the movement discourses and practices are Ilse Lenz, *Die Neue Frauenbewegung in Deutschland. Abschied vom kleinen Unterschied. Eine Quellensammlung. (The New Women's Movement in Germany.* Wiesbaden: VS Verlag, 2nd edn, 2010) for Germany with comprehensive introductions and annotations. For Japan Michiko Mae and

Ilse Lenz, *Frauenbewegung in Japan* (*The Women's Movement in Japan*. Wiesbaden: VS Verlag, 2017).

Internationalization and, later, globalization were fundamental for women's movements from their emergence in the eighteenth century until the present. The internationalization of liberal and maternalist currents and their organizations until about 1945 is treated by Leila J. Rupp, *Worlds of Women. The Making of an International Women's Movement* (Princeton, NJ: Princeton University Press, 1997). Clare Midgley, *Feminism and Empire. Women Activists in Imperial Britain 1790–1865* (London: Routledge, 2007) explores connections between early metropolitan feminisms, colonialism and imperialism. Karen Offen (ed.), *Globalising Feminism 1789–1945* (London: Routledge, 2009) looks at internationalization, for instance, of religious or suffrage movements and of the socialist concept of 'Bourgeois feminism'.

The globalization of women's movements and their outstanding effects in the context of the UN decades of women after 1975 stimulated important research. Gülay Caglar et al. (eds), *Feminist Strategies in international Governance* (London: Routledge, 2013) and Myra Marx Ferree and Aili Mari Tripp, *Global Feminism. Transnational Women's Activism, Organizing and Human Rights* (New York: New York University Press, 2006) analyse crucial processes and strategies of feminisms in global governance. Susanne Zwingel, *Translating International Women's Rights: The CEDAW Convention in Context* (Basingstoke: Palgrave Macmillan, 2016) studies the multilateral framing and the efficiency of this first obligatory global norm for gender equality. Valentine Moghadam, *Globalizing Women. Transnational Feminist Networks* (Baltimore, MD: Johns Hopkins University Press, 2005) analyses leading global feminist networks working against global inequalities for gender justice. She also co-edited an important volume on *Making Globalization Work for Women. The Role of Social Rights and Trade Union Leadership* (Albany: State University of New York Press, 2011). Kathy Davis, *The Making of Our Bodies, Ourselves. How Feminism Travels Across Borders* (Durham, NC: Duke University Press, 2007) traces the global reception and local rewriting of a feminist sexual health reader first published in the United States in a brilliant case study of transcultural change.

The Research Network on Gender Politics and the State (RNGS, 1995–2012) cooperated in comparative studies on institutional and policy effects of the New Women's movements after 1970: Joni Lovenduski (ed.), *State Feminism and Political Representation* (Cambridge: Cambridge

University Press, 2005); Dorothy McBride Stetson (ed.), *Abortion Politics, Women's Movements and the Democratic State: A Comparative Study of State Feminism* (Oxford: Oxford University Press, 2001); Joyce Outshoorn (ed.), *The Politics of Prostitution: Women's Movements, Democratic States and the Globalisation of Sex Commerce* (Cambridge: Cambridge University Press, 2004); Joyce Outshoorn et al. (eds), *European Women's Movements and Body Politics. The Struggle for Autonomy* (Basingstoke: Palgrave Macmillan, 2015). Aili M. Tripp, *African Women's Movements: Transforming Political Landscapes: Changing Political Landscapes* (Cambridge: Cambridge University Press, 2009) compares the political and social changes effected by women's movements in African societies. Seung-kyung Kim, *The Korean Women's Movement and the State. Bargaining for Change* (London, New York, Routledge, 2014) analyses the impact of feminism on legislation on gender equality in the family and prostitution.

Looking at the societal impact, Nancy Fraser, *Fortunes of Feminism: From State-Managed Capitalism to Neoliberal Crisis* (London: Verso, 2013) criticizes the cooption of mainstream feminism by neoliberalism. Sylvia Walby *The Future of Feminism* (Cambridge: Polity Press, 2011) rather sees advances in EU gender policy as well as contradictions between precarization and increasing female autonomy.

CHAPTER 17

Peace Movements

Holger Nehring

The terms 'peace movements' and 'pacifism' describe a broad spectrum of positions, ranging from the absolute refusal to condone violence and force in personal, social and international relations over the rejection of the use of force in international affairs to more moderate demands for reforms of the international system. The term 'pacifism' was first coined, as a normative concept, by the Frenchman Émile Arnaud in 1901 in order to establish a common ideological denomination for the various bourgeois movements that campaigned across Europe for a federation of states, for disarmament or for international arbitration, and to put it on par with the other big-ism of the time: socialism. It was thus itself the product of growing transnational convergence and cooperation amongst European and North Atlantic peace movements. Ideologically speaking, the very concept of 'peace' is directly related to transcending borders and establishing some kind of 'global community', either, as in Christian (especially Methodist and Quaker), Hindu and Buddhist thinking as part of a cosmos, however

H. Nehring (✉)
Division of History and Politics, University of Stirling, Stirling, UK

© The Author(s) 2017
S. Berger, H. Nehring (eds.), *The History of Social Movements in Global Perspective*, DOI 10.1057/978-1-137-30427-8_17

defined, or as a corollary of Enlightenment ideas of a world unified by reason.[1]

It is, therefore, not surprising that peace movements have been amongst the most active transnational and global actors, and that pacifism is often seen as the paradigmatic representative of internationalism. Yet the history of peace movements as global social movements was far from straightforward. Connections beyond borders might take place at different levels: organization, direct contacts, as well as communication and observation about aims and forms of protest between countries and regions. And addressing local and national audiences might be at odds with demands for transnational or even global cooperation.

Analysing peace movements as global social movements implies two things: first, it means that peace movements are analysed as a sub-set of social movements, as opposed to pressure groups, non-governmental organizations or other civil society actors. If, as Dieter Rucht points out, social movements are engaged in promoting or preventing change, then 'peace' becomes the *specific* issue of social change that these movements seek to address.[2] Thus, while it acknowledges an overlap with peace activities within labour and women's movements,[3] the main focus in this chapter is on movements that explicitly campaigned for 'peace' as a social and political utopia. This is distinct from, say, socialist anti-militarism, for example, whose main emphasis lies on a critique of the role of the military within society, culture and politics. The focus of this chapter, therefore, comes to lie on the strands that Martin Ceadel has called pacifism, the complete rejection of violent means of conflict resolution in international and domestic affairs, and 'pacific-ism', a more pragmatic approach that allows for the use of violence under specific circumstances, especially in the context of ending violence.[4]

The second issue that requires conceptualization is the global nature of peace movements. This will involve two aspects: a discussion of to what extent peace movements framed 'peace' as a global issue and a discussion of the ways in which peace activists formed networks and links of

[1] This chapter is a significantly and substantially expanded, updated and amended version of my chapter on pacifism in Akira Iriye and Pierre-Yves Saunier (eds), *Palgrave Dictionary of Transnational History* (New York: Palgrave Macmillan, 2009); Wilhelm Janssen, 'Friede', in Otto Brunner, Werner Conze and Reinhart Koselleck (eds), *Geschichtliche Grundbegriffe. Historisches Lexikon zur politisch-sozialen Sprache in Deutschland*, vol. 2 (Stuttgart: Klett Cotta, 1975), pp. 543–591.

[2] See Dieter Rucht's chapter in this volume.

[3] See the chapters by Stefan Berger and Ilse Lenz in this volume.

[4] Martin Ceadel, *Thinking about Peace and War* (Oxford: Oxford University Press, 1987).

a global nature, both geographically and in terms of their membership and organizations. Importantly, none of these aspects—the meanings of 'movement', 'peace' and 'the global'—was historically stable. Analysing peace movements historically as global social movements, therefore, means historicizing these three elements, as the meanings and practices that surrounded these concepts developed through a process of significant change and transformation. This transformation was not, however, simply a process of modernization where new forms replaced old, for example where old modes of middle-class associationalism were replaced by more network-based forms of organization; or liberal ideas of peace got replaced by socialist ones. Instead, we can see a process whereby older forms and ideas entered new relationships in novel contexts, often leading to para-doxical fusions that a simple notion of modernization cannot capture.

This paradoxical nature of historical developments in the context of peace movements brings to light especially well one of the key challenges of a global history of social movements: an argument can be made that most peace activism is, in its very nature and substance, linked directly and inextricably to the concepts of the European Enlightenment and political liberalism. Globalizing the history of peace movements over the course of the past two centuries in order to counter such Eurocentric views and to, in Dipesh Chakrabarty's terminology, 'provincialise Europe' is therefore particularly difficult.[5] Notwithstanding the fact that we are now in a posi-tion to write the global history of the Enlightenment and the movements attached to it,[6] the arguments about 'peace' come with especially large blind spots.[7] This does not, of course, mean that a non-European global history of peace movements cannot be written and that peace activism beyond Europe and the transatlantic world is always a project derivative of developments in Europe, so that developments outside 'the West' would, by definition, lack agency and therefore history.[8] But it does imply that the globality of the history of peace movements always has to reflect both the

[5] Dipesh Chakrabarty, *Provincializing Europe. Postcolonial Thought and Historical Difference* (Princeton: Princeton University Press, new edn, 2007).

[6] Sebastian Conrad, 'Enlightenment in Global History: A Historiographical Critique', *American Historical Review*, 4 (2012), pp. 999–1027.

[7] Cf. in a similar vein Stefan Berger's and Andrea Eckert's chapters in this volume. For a perceptive analysis of ideas of international relations see John M. Hobson, *The Eurocentric Conception of World Politics. Western International Theory, 1760–2010* (Cambridge: Cambridge University Press, 2012).

[8] Cf. the points made by Partha Chatterjee, *The Nation and its Fragments: Colonial and Postcolonial Histories* (Princeton: Princeton University Press, 1993), p. 5.

potentially limitless utopia of a global world peace and the very limits and challenges that these utopias faced in practice.

'Peace' meant different things to different people at different places at different times. But nonetheless, it managed 'to bridge differences and to achieve transnational solidarities'.⁹ It is also important to bear in mind that 'a social-movement approach cannot be pushed too far without implying that peace activism was an obliquely expressed form of introspection about social conditions rather than a sincere attempt to tackle the problem of international war'.¹⁰ Analysing peace movements as global social movements therefore always has to involve attention to the cognitive or ideological contents of the campaigns. In order to achieve at least somewhat of a global context, this chapter will, first, provide an overview of peace activism since circa 1800 around the world. It will then focus on a number of conceptual issues to bring out some of the key issues that require further discussion.

Concepts of 'Peace', Movement and European Modernity

With a conceptual history going back to antiquity, 'peace' is also one of the foundational or key concepts of modernity and terms of movement included in Otto Brunner, Werner Conze and Reinhart Koselleck's monumental dictionary of key terms of modernity that gained novel meanings around 1800.¹¹ During this period, 'peace' and the prevention of war became feasible.¹² Concepts of 'peace' accrued new meanings that went beyond early-modern meanings of stasis, stability and justice.¹³ Older conceptions of 'peace' that interpreted 'peace' as a result of a balance of

---

⁹ Nico Slate, *Colored Cosmopolitanism. The Shared Struggle for Freedom in the United States and India* (Cambridge, MA: Harvard University Press, 2012), p. 2.

¹⁰ Martin Ceadel, *Semi-Detached Idealists. The British Peace Movement and International Relations, 1854–1945* (Oxford: Oxford University Press, 2000), p. 9.

¹¹ Janssen, 'Friede'.

¹² Martin Ceadel, *The Origins of War Prevention. The British Peace Movement and International Relations, 1730–1854* (Oxford: Oxford University Press, 1996), especially pp. 27–98.

¹³ On the variety of meanings cf. Miloš Vec, 'From Invisible Peace to Legitimation of War. Paradoxes of a Concept in Nineteenth Century International Law Doctrine', in Thomas Hippler and Miloš Vec (eds), *Paradoxes of Peace in Nineteenth-Century Europe* (Oxford: Oxford University Press, 2015), pp. 19–36.

power, as vested in interstate coordination through congresses, as based in the international economy of free trade, as based upon the legitimacy of monarchies, as a project promoted and made possible by international lawyers, or peace as a result of the solidarity of the labouring classes continued to sit side by side through a plethora of different local and national campaigns during the nineteenth century; and some are still in place today.[14]

Nonetheless, interpretations of peace increasingly encompassed the constantly dynamic nature of 'peace' as a 'continuous process of conflict resolution'.[15] As such, concepts of 'peace' expressed by peace movements were, therefore, often connected to their interpretations of warfare and specific wars. 'Peace' thus developed into a utopia, very much in the original sense of a 'non-place', it became a 'project rather than an ongoing experience'.[16] Since around 1800, 'peace' formed a 'horizon of expectation' against the 'space of experiences' of war.[17] 'Peace' came to lie in the future and, as such, part of a sub-set of more general projects of social and political change, anchored directly to developments in Europe in the wake of the French Revolution. As such, it has a potential global dimension, almost by default—the emergence of 'peace' as a concept and of peace movements becomes the natural corollary of processes of modernization. Peace, therefore, always contains the idea of 'world peace'.[18]

Within this conceptualization, the world was not necessarily conceived of as 'global'. In terms of their origins and genealogy, concepts of peace, as well as peace campaigns, were linked directly to the emergence of liberalism across Europe and in the transatlantic sphere in the context of the French Revolution around 1800. As such, 'peace' is inextricably tied to the concept of European modernity and liberalism. It therefore shares liberalism's character as 'self-consciously universal as a political, ethical and

---

[14] Thomas Hippler and Milos Vec, 'Peace as a Polemic Concept. Writing the History of Peace in Nineteenth Century Europe', in idem (eds), *Paradoxes of Peace*, pp. 3–16, here p. 9.

[15] Benjamin Ziemann, 'The Code of Protest. Images of Peace in the West German Peace Movements, 1945–1990', *Contemporary European History* 2 (2008), pp. 237–261, here pp. 240–241 (quote), also for the following summary.

[16] Ziemann, 'Code of Protest', p. 241.

[17] For a brief exposition in English see Reinhart Koselleck, 'The Temporalization of Concepts', *Finnish Yearbook* (1997) available at http://www.jyu.fi/yhtfil/redescriptions/ Yearbook%201997/Koselleck%201997.pdf (accessed 6 September 2016).

[18] Thorsten Bonacker, 'Frieden in der globalisierten Moderne. Neue und alte Antinomien', *Mittelweg 36* 2 (2006), pp. 49–60.

epistemological creed'.[19] Concepts of peace have, therefore, been in their very nature unifying concepts that have bridged boundaries. But, as such, they have also had problems in addressing the question of difference.[20] Writing the history of peace movements as global social movements always needs to bear this context in mind: 'peace' might have been 'cosmopolitan in its imagination and potential reach', but it relied on languages that were often anchored in specific local contexts.[21] This also meant that 'peace' has been a contested concept, both within the context of European modernity and beyond. 'Peace' and 'pacification' have often served to justify impe- rial and 'domestic domination'. But even within these contexts, 'peace' has meant different things to different people and groups, ranging from the balance of power to the establishment of rights of participation and citizenship to national self-determination or the establishment of interna- tional law.[22]

Accordingly, peace movements since the nineteenth century have con- ceptualized 'peace' as a global issue, although they have defined global differently. In the nineteenth century, 'global' referred primarily to the Eurocentric notion of the international system of European states that had emerged in the wake of the Congress of Vienna. After 1945, the global search for peace was predominantly framed by the global nature of the Cold War and the nuclear arms race. This optic has been reflected in most of the research on peace movements. Most research has focussed primarily on Western peace movements, those in the USA, Europe and a sprinkling in Japan, but here mainly for the post-1945 period.

From a systematic perspective, one reason for this might be that non- European conceptions of 'peace' rely on different conceptualizations. The Chinese *heping*, for example, signifies social and psychological states of peace, whereas *wu* refers to 'a peace treaty or ceasefire'. These ideas are also directly linked to the ideal of imperial rule, whereby the Emperor cre- ates peace through his authority.[23] Within the Islamic tradition, concepts of peace are conceptualized from the vantage point of war. 'War' in the Western sense is conceptualized as *harb*, which also carries connotations of

---

[19] Uday Singh Mehta, *Liberalism and Empire. A Study in Nineteenth-Century British Liberal Thought* (University of Chicago Press, 1999), p. 1.

[20] On this aspect of liberalism see Mehta, *Liberalism*, p. 24–25 as well as the contributions in Hippler and Vec (eds), *Paradoxes of Peace*.

[21] Mehta, *Liberalism*, p. 36.

[22] Hippler and Vec, 'Peace', p. 6 (quote) and p. 9.

[23] Hippler and Vec, 'Peace', p. 11.

dispossession, anger and enmity. The second concept of war *jihad*, however, does not merely denote war in the Western sense. It also embraces notions of 'an ethical struggle against the passions of the soul' and thus 'comprises what other traditions would understand as being part of the semantic of peace rather than of war'. The Arab word for 'peace', by contrast, refers to the fact of 'submission to political and religious authority'.[24] In Japan, peace and peace activism (*heiwa shugi*, 'peace' 'ism') has been understood as a 'personal moral commitment and a social-political position'.[25] In various African settings, 'peace' has connoted 'order, harmony, and equilibrium, not merely preventing war' and is often connected to ideas of social justice and the belonging to a community.[26] These differences in conceptualization make it difficult to use 'peace movements' in the European sense of the word from within the same framework of analysis for global developments.

HISTORICAL OVERVIEW

Peace movements first emerged in Europe and North America in the early nineteenth century, with an increasing involvement of the bourgeois women's movement from the late nineteenth century onwards. They had much in common with regard to their homogeneous male bourgeois appearance, their organization and their means of communication through learned journals and pressure-group activity, as well as the 'education' of the general public. Their main forms of campaigning were the advocacy of education for peace through national and international congresses and the petitioning of governments. This social homogeneity contributed to transnational communications via a broad spectrum of transnational peace literature and, in the wake of the 1848 Revolutions, via international congresses (e.g. Brussels, 1848; Paris, 1849; Manchester, 1852) at which European peace movements delivered calls for a European peace order to their rulers.

The first peace societies of these 'friends of peace' or 'peace workers' were founded in North America and Britain in the mid-1810s in the wake

---

[24] Hippler and Vec, 'Peace', p. 12. Cf. also Makram Abbès, 'Guerre et paix en islam: naissance et evolution d'une "théorie"', *Mots: Les langages du politique* 73 (2003), pp. 43–58.

[25] David Cortright, *Peace. A History of Movements and Ideas* (Cambridge: Cambridge University Press, 2008), p. 12.

[26] Cortright, *Peace*, p. 13.

of the mass experience of war following the French Revolution in 1789. They were closely linked to religious revivalism and came with a strong desire for social and personal moral reform. One of the first peace societies was established as the New York Peace Society by the Connecticut teacher David Low Dodge together with a group of evangelical clergy and merchants. By that time, 'friends of peace' had already existed in Britain: they had been set up to protest against William Pitt the Younger's intervention in the revolutionary wars and had close links to the revivalist William Wilberforce as well as to the Quakers. The first formal organization of peace activism in Britain came with the foundation of the British Society for the Promotion of Permanent and Universal Peace.[27]

These societies grew substantially over the coming years and also began to establish national organizations, most prominently with the American Peace Society founded by William Ladd, which increasingly emphasized the role of reason (as opposed to Christian religious belief) in resolving conflicts. This form of organizing spread by example and through conscious translation to continental Europe over the course of the 1820s and 1830s, with the French *Société de la morale chrétienne* (founded in 1821) and the *Société de la paix de Génève* being the most prominent ones. Like the peace societies that sprung up elsewhere, though with a slightly different emphasis from Anglo-American peace societies, they emphasized popular participation and liberalism in particular, campaigned for free trade as an insurance against the abuse of political and governmental power and thus became part of the broader campaign against the restoration that followed the Congress of Vienna. They organized a number of 'International' (1843–1879) or 'Universal Peace Congresses' (1889–1939, except for the period of the First World War). A key juncture for the growth of peace campaigning followed the European revolutions of 1848/1849. In their campaigns, the 'friends of peace' opposed the principles on which the system of states had been founded in 1815, namely the legitimacy of established monarchies and the silencing of political protests. Instead, they claimed that the basis of any 'peace' came to lie in civil society rather than governmental power. At the same time, however, the peace congresses themselves emulated, in their choreography, the 'scenic performance' of the Holy Alliance.[28]

[27] Cortright, *Peace*, p. 27.
[28] Thomas Hippler, 'From Nationalist Peace to Democratic War. The Peace Congresses in Paris (1849) and Geneva (1867)', in idem and Vec (eds), *Paradoxes*, pp. 170–188, here pp. 171–173, quote p. 171.

A second phase of peace activism emerged across continental Europe in the context of the nation-building wars of the 1860s, 1870s and 1880s as well as the rise of the organized labour movement. In 1870, W. Randal Cremer founded the Workman's Peace Association, a pioneer amongst groups that stressed the dangers of excessive governmental military spending for social justice and domestic or social peace. On one side of the more liberal spectrum was the *Ligue internationale et permanente de la paix*, founded in Paris by the liberal economist Frédéric Passy, which emphasized the importance of political participation and liberal economic policies for the creation of peace: they would curb governmental corruption and thus allow for the international arbitration of conflicts.[29]

The *Ligue internationale de la paix and de la liberté*, by contrast, which was founded in Geneva in 1867 and remained in existence until 1939, did not merely emphasize nationally specific policies. It also campaigned for national liberation and self-determination as a solution to what it regarded as universal peace. Under the leadership of Charles Lemonnier and Edmond Potonié-Pierre, the *Ligue* took its cues from the radical Italian nationalist Giuseppe Garibaldi and the French writer Victor Hugo. For them, national liberation and 'democracy' were linked, and they also came to support early forms of humanitarian intervention: wars that were supposed to create peace by bringing popular political participation and national self-determination. The name of the *Ligue*'s journal, *Les États-Unis d'Europe*, sums up the paradoxical nature of the universalism embodied in its campaigns for peace: it wanted to unite Europe by means of creating European nation-states as 'democracies', still mostly conceptualized as limited to male and middle-class voters.

The key theme of the vast majority of these peace proposals was not to create a world state or a world federation. Rather, the peace campaigners wanted to establish a form of 'internationalism' that was carried by the belief in the importance of international law and the belief in the power of reason to lead to sound proposals for international arbitration. Although there was a large variety of different internationalist proposals for peace, each with its own national context and resonance, they relied on norms of 'civilization' and 'rationality' which linked individual and governmental

[29] Cortright, *Peace*, p. 16.

morality directly to the advancement of civilization and thereby excluded many countries, especially outside Europe, from serious consideration.[30]

Following these examples, a series of peace societies was founded across continental Europe from the 1870s onwards.[31] In 1870, the first Dutch peace society (the Dutch Peace League) was founded, gaining a mass following after its merger with the Dutch section of the Women's International League for International Disarmament to become the new organization *Vrede door Recht*, which campaigned for the establishment of international legal norms and was inspired by the Dutch early-modern philosopher of international law Hugo Grotius.[32] In Milan, 1887 saw the foundation of the *Unione lombarda per la pace*, leading to the creation of a national Italian association in 1889. In 1891, Bertha von Suttner founded the Austrian peace society. Her efforts inspired the revival of German peace campaigns, which had emerged in various German states over the course of the 1850s, but which had been faced with constant censorship and intimidation. In 1892, Alfred Hermann Fried helped found the German Peace Society (*Deutsche Friedensgesellschaft*), as a federal umbrella organization for German peace campaigns.[33]

The cohesion of this nationally organized transnational community was further strengthened by the foundation of the International Peace Bureau in Bern (Switzerland) in 1892, which remained intact until the First World War.[34] While some early pacifists advocated linking social concerns to demands for a peaceful international order, this linkage remained on the sidelines of nineteenth-century transnational peace organizations, despite the contribution of socialists and anarchists within the International League of Peace and Liberty. Although their remit was much narrower, organizations such as the Inter-Parliamentary Union (founded in Paris in 1888) and the Conciliation International (founded in 1905) also belonged to the spectrum of transnational pacifist activities.

---

[30] The variety of these proposals and their links to liberal imperialism are brought out especially well by Caspar Sylvest, 'Continuity and Change in British Liberal Internationalism, c. 1900–1930', *Review of International Studies*, 2 (2005), pp. 263–283.

[31] The following overview follows Cortright, *Peace*, pp. 39–40.

[32] Cf. Sandi E. Cooper (ed.), *Peace Activities in Belgium and the Netherlands* (New York: Garland, 1974).

[33] Roger Chickering, *Imperial Germany and a World without War. The Peace Movement and German Society* (Princeton, NJ: Princeton University Press, 1976).

[34] Helmut Mauermann, *Das internationale Friedensbüro 1892 bis 1950* (Stuttgart: Silberburg, 1990).

These efforts to establish arbitration and international law as the key components of liberal peace campaigns highlighted the ambiguities of such positions, particularly when The Hague Conferences of 1899 and 1907 established international norms for conflict resolution through the establishment of an International Court of Arbitration and by establishing rules for warfare. European peace campaigns, and the international lawyers and politicians involved in them, played an important role in bringing the ideas for these conferences about and in propagating the aims and objectives.[35] But peace campaigners had strange bedfellows: Russian Czar Nicholas II, by no means an epitome of liberal government and often condemned by peace campaigners for his 'autocratic and militaristic policies', was the sponsor of the 1899 conference and used its proceedings for the purposes of Russian public diplomacy.[36]

During this period, peace campaigning also began to emerge outside the European and trans-Atlantic core, mostly in connection with imperial reform efforts or with the growth of liberalism and other agendas of modernization in these countries. In Japan, for example, lectures by William Jones of the British Peace Society provided the impetus for the foundation of the first Japanese peace society, *Nihon heiwa-kai*, in 1889. Christian peace campaigning also existed in Japan. Most famous perhaps was Uchimura Kanzō. He had been a supporter of the war against China in 1894/1895, but became an absolute non-violent pacifist in reaction to the violence and brutality he had seen there.[37]

What Sandi Cooper has termed 'patriotic pacifism', a belief in nationhood and patriotism with the expectation that nation states should fit into the international legal system, sat uneasily with pacifists' transnational aims and forms of organization well into the twentieth century; and it also sat uneasily with their campaigns for peace. With the exception of a minority of absolute pacifists, peace campaigners at the time were willing to tolerate war and violence under specific circumstances, specifically when it furthered what they regarded as national interests and national self-determination.[38] Towards the last third of the nineteenth century, the emphasis of peace campaigners shifted from an advocacy of

---

[35] Jost Dülffer, *Regeln gegen den Krieg? Die Haager Friedenskonferenzen 1899 und 1907 in der internationalen Politik* (Frankfurt/Main: Ullstein, 1981).

[36] Cortright, *Peace*, p. 40.

[37] Cortright, *Peace*, p. 29.

[38] James Hinton, *Protests and Visions. Peace Politics in Twentieth-Century Britain* (London: Radius, 1989).

the establishment of nationally organized polities towards campaigning for the establishment of 'contract-based popular sovereignty' within the context of nation states.[39]

As with the socialist anti-militarism within the context of the Socialist International, this paradoxical structure of campaigns against war did not emerge as a result of the First World War. It was deeply embedded in the ideas and practices of 'peace' that the movements developed from the 1860s onwards.[40] This also meant that many Western pacifists were often susceptible to the imperialist *zeitgeist* at the beginning of the twentieth century, thus alienating the few non-Western participants at transnational peace congresses.

Exclusionary processes did not only operate along national lines. Ideas of 'peace' and transnational organization were also shot through with inequalities of gender and political representation. We can see this especially clearly when considering the campaigns for peace within the International Council of Women (ICW). This 'most influential women's organization' had, in 1899, included peace as one of the key components of its internationalism. Like other peace groups, its main focus was on campaigning for international arbitration, relying on the essentialized conceptualization of women as especially suited for peace work. But in doing so, peace campaigners within the ICW took little notice of the fact that their emphasis on 'taming interstate relations within the Western world' and their aim to minimize 'inter-imperial rivalry' stabilized 'a world order based [upon] ongoing violence and systematic privilege of some actors over others' and tried to push aside the question of national self-determination, an issue that almost tore the organization apart during the split of Norway from Sweden in 1905. And despite its emphasis on the universal reach of its ideals, many of its national groups opposed plans to transfer authority within the organization towards the international level. Likewise, there was a heated debate about how to conceptualize popular sovereignty in the context of a politics of peace domestically: as a compromise solution the question of women's suffrage was simply taken as a separate matter from the debate about restrictive forms of political representations more generally. Increasingly, then, many within the ICW began to focus no lon-

---

[39] Hippler, 'From Nationalist Peace to Democratic War', p. 187.
[40] Marc Mulholland, '"Marxists of Strict Observance"? The Second International, National Defence, and the Question of War', *Historical Journal* 2 (2015), pp. 615–640, with references to the older literature.

ger on a politics of peace, but campaigned for concrete policies to protect women as victims of war within the context of humanitarianism.[41] This was a view that gave rise to a specific form of more generalized humanitarian pacifism in Europe in the wake of the First World War, which forms part of the complex pre-history of the United Nations' Universal Declaration of Human Rights of 1948.[42]

These ambiguities and paradoxes also meant that most of the traditional transnational peace organizations did not survive the First World War unscathed. This reconfiguration of peace campaigning away from the bourgeois associationalism that had characterized most of the nineteenth century was, however, not caused by the war, as has often been argued. The war merely accelerated a process of reflection that was already underway, especially on the fringes of the absolute pacifist movements as well as the socialist anti-militarists. The war merely brought the tensions within the peace movements, which claimed universal ideas of peace for themselves but embedded them in local and specifically national ideas of 'civilization', into sharper relief. In particular, the emphasis that philanthropists such as Andrew Carnegie and peace campaigners had placed on the importance of international arbitration, culminating in the opening of the Palace of Peace in The Hague in 1913, just one year before the war, now seemed hollow:[43] the First World War had begun with a flagrant breach of international law with the German invasion and occupation of Belgium, and it saw a number of other breaches of the conventions of the war of law by Germany as well as the entente powers in Europe and beyond, such as the use of naval blockades, chemical warfare and forced labour.[44]

The period after the First World War was characterized by a break-up of the homogeneous peace movements and the rise of novel forms of transnational peace organizations. After the First World War had set in motion

[41] Susan Zimmerman, 'The Politics of Exclusionary Inclusion. Peace Activism and the Struggle on International and Domestic Political Order in the International Council of Women, 1899–1914', in Hippler and Vec (eds), *Paradoxes of Peace*, pp. 189–215, quotes p. 189, p. 195. On women's peace politics during the First World War see: Annika Wilmers, *Pazifismus in der internationalen Frauenbewegung (1914–1920). Handlungsspielräume, politische Konzeptionen und gesellschaftliche Auseinandersetzungen* (Essen: Klartext, 2008).

[42] Jay Winter and Antoine Prost, *René Cassin and Human Rights. From the Great War to the Universal Declaration* (Cambridge: Cambridge University Press, 2013).

[43] Cortright, *Peace*, p. 43.

[44] Isabel V. Hull. *A Scrap of Paper. Breaking and Making International Law during the Great War* (Ithaca, NY: Cornell University Press, 2014).

the process of decolonization, the transnational pacifist organizations faced new challenges. They added members and national sections in Latin America, Asia, the Middle East and Africa, yet they did not shed their Eurocentric mindset and were hesitant to accept their non-European colleagues' notion that national liberation was the precondition for a stable international order. At the same time, they continued to campaign for the strengthening of international organizations, such as the recently established League of Nations. Prompted by the experience of mass combat during the First World War, a growing number of activists came to regard the nation state no longer as the basis of peace work. They instead began to search for alternative forms of international organization by linking proposals for domestic political reform and the reorganization of international politics in order to overcome the dilemmas of 'patriotic pacifism'.[45]

These views began to congeal around a more solid base for transnational links. A congress of women pacifists held in The Hague in 1915 led to the foundation of the International Women's League for Peace and Freedom in Zurich in 1919. Most typical for the transnational organization of the new peace movement was the foundation of the War Resisters' International (WRI), which was originally founded under the name of 'Paco' ('peace' in Esperanto) by the Dutch activist Kees Boeke in 1921. The WRI entertained close links with the burgeoning peace and anti-colonial movements in Africa and Asia, as well as with transnational socialist and religious bodies, such as the anarchist Anti-Militarist Bureau and the Christian International Fellowship of Reconciliation (FOR).[46]

These new transnational organizations had national, regional and local branches across the world and thus created unique transnational clearing houses for pacifist ideas and forms of action, which were discussed in the organizations' journals and during personal visits and applied in the transnational campaigns against rearmament and fascism during the 1920s and 1930s. The WRI and the FOR were crucial for acquainting European and North-American pacifists with Mohandas K. Gandhi's strategy of non-violent action in the Indian struggle for independence. Gandhi's vision of a non-violent society and non-violence as a form of

[45] Sandi E. Cooper, *Patriotic Pacifism. Waging War on War in Europe, 1815–1914* (New York: Oxford University Press, 1991).

[46] Peter Brock and Nigel Young, *Pacifism in the Twentieth Century* (Toronto: University of Toronto Press, 1999), pp. 102–105.

protest was itself the result of transnational diffusion.[47] Engaging with the work of the American writer Henry David Thoreau and the Russian novelist Tolstoy, Gandhi first linked their arguments for a non-violent life with demands for direct action in his campaign against the military draft in British-ruled South Africa in the early 1900s, building on the arguments of the Muslim spokesman Sheth Haji Habib. Gandhi modified the strategy as 'satyagraha', a non-violent personal and national battle, after his return to India in 1915 and practised it most famously in his 1930/1931 salt march campaigns.[48]

The Labour and Socialist International (LSI), established in 1919 in the Swiss city of Berne, supported the kind of liberal internationalism, often linked to imperialist ideas of 'governing the world', embodied in the League of Nations. But they tried to fill what they regarded as the socialist ideal of a League of Nations with new life by engaging with the movements for national self-determination around the world and by engaging actively with the Indian National Congress and Egyptian and Latin American nationalists at their conferences from the 1930s onwards. They aimed to achieve, towards the late 1930s as part of the Communist popular front campaigns, some form of 'democratization of international relations', 'striking 'a balance between the ideas of Marx, Mazzini and Wilson', yet still restricted by the limits that 'nationhood' posed to 'transnational action'.[49] Similarly, the liberal societies that campaigned in favour of the authority of the League of Nations in international affairs created the experience of 'Internationalism in a divided world'.[50] Such concepts appealed to many Western pacifists within the WRI and the FOR well into the 1950s and 1960s. Thus, while the following years saw the

---

[47] Devi Prasad, *War is a Crime against Humanity. The Story of the War Resisters' International* (London: War Resisters' International, 2005). For the United States see Scott H. Bennett, *Radical Pacifism: The War Resisters League and Gandhian Nonviolence in America, 1915–1945* (Syracuse, NY: Syracuse University Press, 2003).

[48] Sean Chabot and Jan Willem Duyvendak, 'Globalization and Transnational Diffusion between Social Movements: Reconceptualizing the Dissemination of the Gandhian Repertoire and the "Coming Out" Routine', *Theory and Society* 6 (2002), pp. 697–740.

[49] Daniel Laqua, 'Democratic Politics and the League of Nations: The Labour and Socialist International as a Protagonist of Interwar Internationalism', *Contemporary European History* 2 (2015), pp. 175–192, quotes p. 192.

[50] Thomas Richard Davies, 'Internationalism in a Divided World: The Experience of the International Federation of the League of Nations Societies, 1919–1939', *Peace & Change* 2 (2012), pp. 227–252; idem, *The Possibilities of Transnational Activism: The Campaign for Disarmament between the World Wars* (Leiden: Martinus Nijhoff, 2007).

demise of this brand of pacifist nationalism in India, ideas of non-violent civil disobedience gained currency amongst Western radical pacifists, such as the Americans Richard Gregg, Gene Sharp and Bayard Rustin, who visited India and introduced the strategy into transnational debates in both Europe and North America. This formed the basis for Martin Luther King's civil rights campaign, beginning in Montgomery, Alabama, in 1955/1956, and for discussions about non-violence among European activists in the 1950s and 1960s.

At the same time, these developments in the wake of the revolutions of 1918/1919 accentuated a division among peace activists further. One strand followed a broadly liberal persuasion and focussed on pressure group activities. It found its organizational form, for example, in the British League of Nations Union or the liberal wing of the German Peace Society around Ludwig Quidde. Especially in Scandinavia, such interpretations fed into versions of national identity that highlighted the importance of 'peace' and 'peaceful conflict resolution' as a key feature of political culture and foreign policy making, often crowding out the dark side of these policies, so that ideas that had remained within the realm of civil society could now also be found within governments.[51]

More radical socialist groups included the French *Ligue internationale des combattants de la paix* or the British Peace Pledge Union which organized a peace ballot in Britain in 1935. Christian peace groups often cut across these boundaries, engaging with both liberal and socialist strands.[52] The flagrant breaches of international law that occurred with the Italian invasion of Abyssinia (1935), National Socialist and Japanese expansion and remilitarization, and in the context of the Spanish Civil War between 1936 and 1939 disrupted both the practical campaigning and the moral-political foundations of European peace movements. German and Austrian pacifists faced prosecution, and peace campaigners in countries under threat from German invasion had to decide whether they wanted to oppose National Socialism with violence, or whether they continued in their advocacy of non-violent means of conflict resolution.[53]

---

[51] See the research report by Helge Pharo, 'Den norske fredstradisjonen—et forskningsprosjekt', *Historisk Tidsskrift* 2 (2005), pp. 239–255; Jon Lawrence, 'Forging a Peaceable Kingdom: War, Violence and the Fear of Brutalisation in Post-First World War Britain', *Journal of Modern History* 3 (2003), pp. 557–589.

[52] Gearóid Barry, *The Disarmament of Hatred. Marc Sagnier, French Catholicism and the Legacy of the First World War* (Basingstoke: Palgrave, 2012).

[53] Brock and Young, *Pacifism*, pp. 121–130 and pp. 151–220.

In the period after the Second World War, peace movements had to cope with two major challenges. First, they had to confront the threat of global destruction posed by nuclear weapons in an international system characterized by the nuclear-arms race between the Soviet Union and the United States. Second, 'pacifism' had become discredited as a political ideology in the West. Many now blamed the rise of aggressive nationalism and racism in Italy, Germany and Japan on the predominance of 'pacifist' feelings during the 1930s, and as the Soviet Union converted advocacy of 'peace' into one of its main propaganda tools in the Cold War. This had begun in the 1930s with the peace campaigns organized by the Communist International in the context of the popular front and the launch of an International Peace Campaign in that context in March 1936.[54] If the nineteenth century saw the 'origins of war prevention', as Martin Ceadel has argued,[55] the period after the Second World War might well have seen its end: whereas earlier peace movements could be said to have had clearly recognizable aims and tried to implement them as pressure groups trying to sway public opinion and thereby influence governments, peace campaigns after 1945 had less clearly defined aims and primarily took the form of loosely organized networks, as social movements in the way that we know them today.

Most peace activists were no longer concerned with preventing war as such. They tied their ideas to broader ideas of security and participatory citizenship that were borne by a fundamental distrust of governments to wage wars, which derived its powerful force from the experiences and memories of the bombing wars between 1939 and 1945, especially in Britain, West Germany and Japan.[56] Despite the continued significance of the WRI and the FOR in the transfer of non-violent direct action from India to Europe and North America, the relative importance of organized transnational peace efforts declined. For historians of peace movements as global social movements, it might be most helpful to analyse 'pacifism' after the Second World War not in organizational or ideological terms, but as social movements, loose networks of activists who framed the prob-

[54] Thomas Richard Davies, *NGOs. A New History of Transnational Civil Society* (London: Hurst, 2013), pp. 116–117.

[55] Ceadel, *The Origins of War Prevention.*

[56] Cf. Holger Nehring, *Politics of Security. The British and West German Protests against Nuclear Weapons and the Early Cold War, 1945–c. 1970* (Oxford: Oxford University Press, 2013); Mari Yamamoto, *Grassroots Pacifism in Post-war Japan: The Rebirth of a Nation* (London: Routledge, 2004).

lem of armaments in peculiar ways and who campaigned for very specific issues, such as for nuclear disarmament and against the American war in Vietnam.[57] Recent research has highlighted that, despite the importance of communist concepts of peace for the movements of the 1950s and 1960s, their influence was denied by mainstream campaigners fearful of facing even more recriminations in the anti-communist climate at the time.[58] Such exclusions also affected the peace campaigns by women: the gendering of the critique of peace activism often overlapped with anti-communism.[59]

The rifts caused by Cold War polarization become evident when examining the decline of the Japanese World Conferences against Atomic and Hydrogen Bombs (*Gensuikyō*), which began to gain ground as a focal point for a non-aligned global anti-nuclear-weapons movement in 1955, but rapidly lost its transnational cachet when it appeared to be hi-jacked by communists for propaganda purposes in the early 1960s.[60] In some contexts outside the European setting, peace campaigning did not take the form of social movement activism, but focussed primarily on the language as a means of overcoming enmity and creating 'peace'. Sandwiched between the demands of Japanese hegemonic foreign policy discourse and US imperialism, peace activism against the US presence on the Japanese island of Okinawa sought to highlight the power of subversive language and laughter to undermine the authority of those in power, rather than direct political organizing.[61]

[57] See Charles DeBenedetti and Charles Chatfield, *An American Ordeal: Antiwar Movement of the Vietnam Era* (Syracuse, NY: Syracuse University Press, 1990) and Alice Echols '"Women Power" and Women's Liberation: Exploring the Relationship between the Antiwar Movement and the Women's Liberation Movement', in Melvin Small and William Hoover (eds), *Give Peace a Chance: Exploring the Vietnam Antiwar Movement* (Syracuse, NY: Syracuse University Press, 1992), pp. 171–181.

[58] Robbie Lieberman, *The Strangest Dream: Communism, Anticommunism and the U.S. Peace Movement 1945–1963* (Syracuse, NY: Syracuse University Press, 2000).

[59] See, for example, Belinda Davis, 'Political Participation and Gender: Lessons from the Cold War', in Joanna Regulska and Bonnie Smith (eds), *Women and Gender in Postwar Europe: From Cold War to European Union* (New York: Routledge, 2012), pp. 139–155.

[60] Cf. Volker Fuhrt, 'Pazifismus in Japan—ein Auslaufmodell?', *Mitteilungsblatt des Instituts für soziale Bewegungen* 32 (2004), pp. 159–173; Yamamoto, *Grassroots Pacifism*.

[61] Yoshinobu Ota, 'Appropriating Media, Resisting Power. Representations of hybrid identities in Okinawan popular culture', in Richard G. Fox and Orin Starn (eds), *Between Resistance and Revolution. Cultural Politics and Social Protest* (New York: Rutgers University Press, 1997), pp. 145–170.

Although such peace movements established links with pre-existing pacifist organizations and related campaigns, such as the civil rights movement in the United States, their global connections were primarily characterized by intensified mutual observation, aided by the rising importance of the mass media in the political process in both Western and non-Western societies and bolstered by their common concerns for a world community. On the one hand, these efforts were less sustained than those of previous transnational organizations. On the other hand, however, the movements' loose and often spontaneous character made it much easier to translate global issues into local concerns and to transfer protest forms which were successful elsewhere.

The most important exceptions to this trend away from a politics of peace towards a politics of security were the communist-dominated World Peace Council (WPC), founded in the late 1940s as part of the Soviet Union's efforts at cultural diplomacy, and the Pugwash Conferences on Science and World Affairs which, following an initiative by the physicist Albert Schweitzer and the philosopher Bertrand Russell in 1955, brought together scientists across the blocs to tackle the issue of arms control from the late 1950s onwards. Pugwash played a major role in reinforcing reformist trends within the fledgling Soviet Union during the 1980s.[62]

By contrast, the campaigns against nuclear weapons in Europe during the 1950s and 1960s and again during heightened Cold War tensions in the early 1980s rarely established transnational campaign organizations and continued to frame their demands in terms of national and even local concerns. While there were some transnational organizations, their geographical scope remained restricted to Europe, such as European Nuclear Disarmament co-founded by the British social historian E. P. Thompson.[63]

The first campaigns did not emerge on a large scale until the late 1950s and they followed heightened concerns across the world about the dangers of radioactivity coming from nuclear testing, following a number of accidents and campaigns by scientists. The American campaign SANE

---

[62] Cf. Günter Wernicke, 'The Communist-Led World Peace Council and the Western Peace Movements: The Fetters of Bipolarity and Some Attempts to Break Them in the Fifties and Early Sixties', *Peace & Change* 3 (1998), pp. 265–311; Alison Kraft, Holger Nehring and Carola Sachse, 'The Pugwash Movement and the Global Cold War', Theme Issue, *Journal of Cold War Studies* (2016) (forthcoming).

[63] Patrick D. M. Burke, 'European Nuclear Disarmament: A Study of Transnational Social Movement Strategy' (PhD University of Westminster, 2004).

was founded in 1957 by a number of writers and public intellectuals.[64] Likewise, the British Campaign for Nuclear Disarmament (CND) was founded in 1958 by an Anglican clergyman, a journalist and a number of public intellectuals. In West Germany, anti-nuclear weapons protests started as party-political campaigns organized by the social-democratic party, but soon took on a life of their own in the Easter March movement.[65] In Japan, the only country in the world who experienced the dropping of two atomic bombs in the cities of Hiroshima and Nagasaki in August 1945, 'peace' had been enshrined in the constitution of the new democratic country, so that the anti-nuclear weapons protests focussed primarily on the nature of Japan's relationship with the United States and were tied up with a fundamental critique of the Japanese political system.[66] The key theme, supported by many local governments, was Japan's unique historical experience that endowed the country with a special mission to create world peace.[67]

Hence, although nuclear weapons encouraged peace campaigners to link their local and national campaigns to global concerns, following the slogan 'One World or None' that some American arms control advocates had coined immediately after the Second World War,[68] the differences between communism and anti-communism remained divisive. Moreover, the images of war from which most peace activists developed their ideas of peace were still essentially based on experiences and memories of the bombing wars of 1939–1945, rather than a global nuclear confrontation, which was hard to imagine without any concrete empirical evidence.

Similarly, the legacy of imperialism and colonialism made global cooperation difficult and prevented more effective forms of collaboration. Whereas British activists saw themselves as the natural neutral mediators between Europe and the post-colonial world, linking US peace activists with those from Ghana and other African states in the late 1950s and early 1960s, this proved very difficult in practice. The suggestion by African

[64] Milton S. Katz, *Ban the Bomb. A History of SANE, the Committee for a Sane Nuclear Policy, 1957–1985* (New York: Greenwood, 1986).

[65] Nehring, *Politics of Security.*

[66] Yamamoto, *Grassroots Pacifism* and Jennifer M. Miller, 'Fractured Alliance: Anti-Base Protests and Postwar U.S.–Japanese Relations', *Diplomatic History* 5 (2014), pp. 953–986.

[67] Lisa Yoneyama, *Hiroshima Traces: Time, Space, and the Dialectics of Memory* (Berkeley, CA: University of California Press, 1999).

[68] Cf. Fritz Bartel, 'Surviving the Years of Grace: The Atomic Bomb and the Specter of World Government, 1945–1950', *Diplomatic History* 2 (2015), pp. 275–302.

activists to tie what they regarded as the 'nuclear imperialism' of France's testing in the Sahara desert with developments in Algeria, and link this to a message of pan-African nationalism, proved extremely divisive. Thus, while both African, US and European peace activists drew on similar languages of peace and justice, and while they managed to form some links, the geopolitics of the Cold War and the reality of post-colonial nationalism and state-building worked against a more sustained cooperation, as different versions of modernity clashed, especially as the reality of statehood worked against the dream of pan-African union that the Ghanaian President Kwame Nkrumah had wished to achieve by linking peace campaigns with pan-Africanism. So, while these campaigns created new forms of links and participation, they also gave rise to new divisions.[69]

While direct and organized transnational contacts and protest events remained the exception from the 1960s onwards, movement activists continued to frame their campaigns more pronouncedly and explicitly as ones that transcended national borders and continued to engage with the campaign strategies of non-Western movements in particular. The protests against the American intervention in Vietnam which swept the Western world and Japan from the mid-1960s to the early 1970s increasingly engaged with strategies first developed by Latin American socialists, such as Fidel Castro and Che Guevara, and with Maoism, most famously at the Berlin International Vietnam Congress in 1968. Quite controversially, advocates of such strategies argued that violence might be necessary for the creation of a durable peace.[70]

In the period since the 1960s, the nation lost much of its importance as an identity space for peace protesters, especially in the Western world. Thus, transnational communication, especially mediated through the ecumenical bodies of the Christian Churches such as the Catholic Pax Christi and the All-Christian Peace Assemblies, helped bridge the Iron Curtain in the late 1970s and provided crucial support and communication networks for the emergence of an independent (that is: non-communist) peace movement in Eastern Europe during the 1980s. Given the impor-

---

[69] Rob Skinner, 'Bombs and Border Crossings: Peace Activist Networks and the Post-Colonial State in Africa, 1959–1962', *Journal of Contemporary History* 3 (2015), pp. 418–438; Jean Allman, 'Nuclear Imperialism and the Pan-African Struggle for Peace and Freedom. Ghana, 1959–1962', *Souls* 2 (2008), pp. 83–102.

[70] Cf., for example, the case of Italy sketched out by Massimo di Giuseppe and Giorgio Vecchio, 'Die Friedensbewegungen in Italien', *Mitteilungsblatt des Instituts für soziale Bewegungen* 32 (2004), pp. 131–157.

tance of Hindu, Buddhist and, more specifically, Gandhian ideas about peace and social action for Western peace movements since 1945, it is striking that indigenous transnational campaigns in non-Western settings remained rather weak, as nationalism, anti-imperialism and state-building efforts continued to influence the ways in which 'peace' was conceptualized there.

THE 'IMAGINARY WAR' AND THE POLITICS OF SPACE

It was only over the course of the 1970s and 1980s that the anti-nuclear weapons movements began to discover the dynamics of the Cold War as an 'imaginary war' that had potentially global reach and that worked by putting people on a constant state of alert.[71] Together with a new awareness of the transnational nature of environmental threats and the dangers of civilian uses of nuclear energy, such novel conceptualizations led to a renewed emphasis on global frames of analysis within the peace movements in Europe, Japan and the northern Atlantic world. In this context, 'peace' was also able to become an oppositional category of protest in the Soviet sphere of influence. Here, peace campaigners drew on official languages of peace within socialism to subvert the sclerotic state socialist systems and challenge the authority of the World Peace Council. Merging increasingly with the issue of human rights and political representations, peace campaigns therefore played an important role in bringing about the collapse of communism.[72]

During this period, ironically at a time when the nation-state was an identity space, peace campaigners also became more self-conscious about the politics of space they engaged in. By challenging the state in a key area of its existence, security and defence policy, which are often conducted in secret, peace movements have always engaged in a politics of space: by placing authority in associations or movements, they directly challenged the spatial authority vested in governments and parliament. By contesting such territorial claims of political sovereignty, peace movements also contested notions of statehood more generally. We can see this symbolic assertion of the politics of space in the opening of peace camps over the

[71] Mary Kaldor, *The Imaginary War: Understanding the East–West Conflict* (Oxford: Blackwell, 1990).

[72] Matthew Evangelista, *Unarmed Forces. The Transnational Movement to End the Cold War* (Ithaca, NY: Cornell University Press, 2002).

course of the 1970s and 1980s.[73] As such, the spread of nuclear-weapons free zones was also a process that occurred as part of a global trend.[74] Such practices have, in turn, often led to the exclusion of peace activists from more formal politics—peace activism is often viewed as fundamentally 'female' and thus also as 'emotional', not rational.

The Nature of Global Connections

Apart from the politics of space, another issue that deserves more systematic attention is the nature of global connections. Current models often discuss these in terms of a transfer of ideas of diffusion of knowledge and practices. But such metaphors, which stem from the world of Newtonian physics, often do not do justice to the historical complexity of these processes. Sean Scalmer has highlighted the importance of translation as 'a complex and uneven process' in the context of the appropriation of 'Ghandian' non-violent tactics by US and British peace movements.[75] He argues that the idea of what 'non-violent resistance' consisted of first had to be created by those who wished to appropriate it—they first had to show an interest in Gandhi and also make their ideas plausible. Then, they had to try these ideas out in specific political and social contexts. Finally, they had to appropriate it and redevelop it. All these steps were historically contingent and incredibly complex—it was never the case that discrete packages of ideas and practices were shifted across borders, as some transfer historians have assumed. Specifically, the knowledge of Gandhi's teaching in the *satyagraha* first had to be removed from its original context within a specific brand of Hinduism and be Christianized in order to be legible for the British and US peace activists. Once this had happened, British and US campaigners discussed how these forms of protest might be adapted. Through a number of experiments in the 1950s within the networks of the British Peace Pledge Union (which had been set up in

---

[73] Susanne Schregel, *Der Atomkrieg vor der Wohnungstür. Eine Politikgeschichte der neuen Friedensbewegung in der Bundesrepublik, 1970–1985* (Frankfurt/Main: Campus, 2012).

[74] Susanne Schregel, 'Global Micropolitics. Towards a Transnational History of Nuclear Free Zones', in Eckart Conze, Martin Klimke and Jeremy Varon (eds), *Nuclear Threats, Nuclear Fear and the Cold War of the 1980s* (New York: Cambridge University Press, 2016) and Maire Leadbeater, *Peace, Power & Politics. How New Zealand became Nuclear Free* (Dunedin: Otago University Press, 2013).

[75] Sean Scalmer, 'Translating Contention: Culture, History, and the Circulation of Collective Action', *Alternatives: Global, Local, Political* 4 (2000), pp. 491–514, here p. 509.

1934 to campaign against rearmament), advocates came up with the idea of a march between London and the nuclear-weapons research establishment in Aldermaston, around 80 miles away, as a quintessential form of non-violent protest: Gandhian direct action had become domesticated within the context of organizing a protest march whose form was quite similar to previous marches, but whose specific meaning and resonance derived from an engagement with the global legacy of Gandhian non-violence. None of these developments were straightforward. They were frequently and controversially discussed.[76]

This also implies that there is no one authentic model of Gandhian non-violent resistance: Gandhi's own non-violent practices were grounded in the translation and reinvention of specific protests in the context of the British Empire in the first two decades of the twentieth century, specifically in a Southern African context and in London, where he had been able to observe anti-imperial hunger strikes and the campaigns by the suffragettes. He developed them into specifically Indian notions of 'freedom' and 'peace'.[77]

The practice of non-violence and its label 'Gandhian' were, therefore, not merely out there to be transferred. They were the very products of the process of translation, where the products of 'Western' translations were presented as 'Eastern' inventions. Richard Fox has discussed these processes in the context of the tension between imaginations 'hyper-difference' and 'over-likeness' that enabled the translation process at different junctures.[78]

CONCLUSIONS

Today, peace movements are part of a burgeoning social movement sector and are often linked to campaigns for social justice and against global poverty. While some of the traditional organizations from the nineteenth century still exist in new guises, such as the German Peace Society, and some of the anti-nuclear weapons movements, such as CND and the

---

[76] Sean Scalmer, *Gandhi in the West. The Mahatma and the Rise of Radical Protest* (Cambridge: Cambridge University Press, 2011).

[77] Mithi Mukherjee, 'Transcending Identity: Gandhi, Nonviolence, and the Pursuit of a "Different" Freedom in Modern India', *American Historical Review* 2 (2010), pp. 453–473.

[78] Richard G. Fox, 'Passage from India', in idem and Orin Starn (eds), *Between Resistance and Revolution. Cultural Politics and Social Protest* (New York: Rutgers University Press, 1997), pp. 65–82, quote on p. 67.

Easter Marches, are still campaigning, their activism has moved away from broader messages of global peace, to more specific, often highly localized, campaigns against specific wars.

Overall, then, we can see five main developments in the history of peace movements as global social movements. First, we have observed the transformation of the organizational *forms* of peace campaigning: from primarily middle-class organizations that sought to create ideal types of Habermas' public sphere in order to further rational dialogue and thus create the preconditions for the creation of peace in the international arena, through rational negotiations amongst rational enlightened actors, to peace activism as social movement activism in the period after 1945, with social movements being networks of activists that do have some form or organization in terms of an address in society, but are much more dynamic and loosely organized social formations.

Second, this transformation of forms was accompanied by a *transformation of the meaning* of cross-border exchanges: from a form of cross-border exchanges in a time period in which national boundaries were still by and large in flux and where internationalism was essentially a fiction of a peaceful order that would be peaceful precisely because it was organized along clearly delineated nation-state lines; towards internationalism that focussed on the relationship between nation-states once this order had been created around the 1880s; towards transnational exchanges that were characterized, if we follow the influential definition by Patricia Clavin who, in turn, follows Robert Keohane and Joseph Nye, primarily non-governmental and societal actors that communicated, protested or otherwise acted across boundaries.[79]

Third, in terms of the *framing* of peace, we find a gradual shift from an emphasis on regulating international relations and creating norms of international law as the precondition of peace defined as international stability towards more inclusive, but also more expansive, framing of 'peace' that highlight peace as a mode of societal transformation and of movement.[80]

Fourth, there has been a growing emphasis on the transformation of the individual and the self for the creation of a sustained peace. 'Peace' came to be seen increasingly as a non-violent practice and action starting with *individual*, as opposed to policy, changes in thought and action. Peace

---

[79] Patricia Clavin, 'Defining Transnationalism', *Contemporary European History* 4 (2005), pp. 421–439.

[80] See Ziemann, 'Code of Protest', pp. 252–256 for Germany.

movements were the spaces in which these transformations could occur: peace itself came to be seen as movement, and the movement was the prefiguration of a future peace.[81] This definition made a direct reflection upon trans- and international as well as global approaches to peace campaigning obsolescent. Peace movements now directly represented global interests; the connection went directly from local to global. This transformation has, however, never been complete or teleological. The most recent peace campaigns, against the US-led interventions in the former Yugoslavia in the 1990s as well as in Afghanistan and Iraq after 9/11 have revived traditional pacifist interests in international law and legal regulation of international affairs, as the more recent debates about non-enemy combatants and the role of the United Nations in legitimizing military interventions have demonstrated.

Fifth, in terms of *context*, this chapter suggests that one of the main driving influences behind peace movements' internationalism was their assessment or framing of the kind of war and the kind of violence they opposed. Pacifists in the early twentieth century relied on an understanding of war rooted in the cabinet wars of the nineteenth century; the experiences of violence in the First World War made such views implausible and led to a more direct engagement with military violence and personal and national victimhood. This framing survived the Second World War and continued into the 1970s. It was only then that peace movement activists reframed their activities as being concerned with making visible the otherwise invisible threat of a war that had not yet happened and an arms race that was *potentially* lethal. They therefore did not stress the existing physical violence of the arms race, but the structural violence of fears of war. The globalism or internationalism of peace movements was, therefore, always dialectically connected to broader societal debates about war and violence. It is this dialectic to which historians of peace movements as social movements that crossed borders might pay more attention to in the future.

It is important to bear in mind, however, that these transformations were never complete and did not simply occur as a process of one-dimensional modernization, but that they primarily added new dimensions to pre-existing structures while never dissolving them. Peace movements continue to be primarily affairs of the educated middle class, and some

---

[81] Ziemann, 'Code of Protest', pp. 257–259.

elements of the traditional emphasis on exclusionary norms of civility and bourgeois associationalism remain to the present day.[82]

Instead of taking the 'global' and ideas of 'peace' in peace movement activism over the last two centuries for granted, this chapter has argued for the need of historicization in the vein of what the sociologist Peggy Somers has called the 'historical sociology of concept formation'.[83] It is not only through the constant reflection on the changing nature of peace campaigning in its ideologies, forms and goals, but also in the continuous historicization of the very concepts we use to describe these processes that we will be able to see the blind spots that the use of practices and languages of globality created over the course of nineteenth- and twentieth-century history within the context of peace activism. Using the concept of 'the global' cannot replace insights into how it resonated locally and nationally—in other words: we cannot merely shed national categories when we write the history of peace movements as part of a history of global social movements. Instead, this chapter makes the case for using global and transnational perspectives to combine the study of networks, transfers and protests across borders with the comparative analysis of resonances and political repercussions to uncover the national internationalism of the peace activism in different settings.[84] The same would apply for peace activism in imperial contexts: especially British peace campaigning, while explicitly global and transnational in its framings of the problem of peace, was a movement embedded in the country's imperial history. It more or less translated one-to-one British imperial discourses of moral superiority and civility into messages for world peace.[85]

The conceptual focus on analysing peace movements as global social movements should be on the ambiguities, ruptures and disjunctures in the interplay between activists' agency and the structures in which they were

---

[82] See Steve Breyman, 'Were the 1980s' Anti-Nuclear Weapons Movements New Social Movements?', *Peace & Change* 3 (1997), pp. 303–329; Lars Schmitt, 'Kritische Wissenschaft und Friedensbewegung. Soziologische Selbstreflexion zur Stärkung der Bewegung', *Wissenschaft und Frieden* 3 (2004), http://www.wissenschaft-und-frieden.de/seite.php?artikelID=0330 (accessed 6 September 2016).

[83] Margaret R. Somers, *Genealogies of Citizenship: Markets, Statelessness, and the Right to Have Rights* (Cambridge: Cambridge University Press, 2008), p. 175.

[84] Holger Nehring, 'National Internationalists. British and West German Protests against Nuclear Weapons, the Politics of Transnational Communications and the Social History of the Cold War, 1957–1964', *Contemporary European History* 4 (2005), pp. 558–582.

[85] Jodi Burkett, *Constructing Post-imperial Britain: Britishness, 'Race' and the Radical Left in the 1960s* (Basingstoke: Palgrave, 2013).

placed. It is thus that we might creatively engage with some of the social scientific work on social movements, while harnessing what historians do best: not merely apply the theories, but highlight their specific historical contexts and meanings.

FURTHER READING

There is no one book that summarizes the developments sketched out here. By far the best short overview of developments in the nineteenth century and around the First World War is provided by Martin Ceadel's chapter 'Pacifism' in Jay Winter (ed.), *The Cambridge History of the First World War* (Cambridge: Cambridge University Press, 2014), vol. II, pp. 576–605 which contains references to further readings, the most important of which are Sandi E. Cooper's *Patriotic Pacifism. Waging War on War in Europe, 1815–1914* (New York: Oxford University Press, 1991), W. H. van der Linden's, *The International Peace Movement 1815–1874* (Amsterdam: Tilleul, 1987) and Verdiana Grossi's *Le Pacifisme Européen 1889–1914* (Brussels: Bruylant, 1994), as well as Martin Ceadel's own work. A good overall summary is also provided by David Cortright in *Peace. A History of Movements and Ideas* (Cambridge: Cambridge University Press, 2008). The *Oxford Encyclopaedia of Peace* (New York: Oxford University Press, 2010), 4 vols, edited by Nigel Young, offers an unsurpassed compendium.

For the inter-war period, the best summary of the state of play is probably provided by Cecelia Lynch's *Beyond Appeasement: Interpreting Interwar Peace Movements in World Politics* (Ithaca, NY: Cornell University Press, 1999) as well as Catherine Foster's book *Women for All Seasons: The Story of the Women's International League for Peace and Freedom* (Athens, GA: University of Georgia Press, 1989). For France, Norman Ingram, *The Politics of Dissent. Pacifism in France 1919–1939* (Oxford: Clarendon, 1991) is the key work.

For the period of the Cold War, Lawrence S. Wittner's magisterial trilogy *The Struggle against the Bomb* (Stanford: Stanford University Press, 1993–2003), summarized in one volume *Confronting the Bomb: A Short History of the World Nuclear Disarmament Movemen* (Stanford: Stanford University Press, 2009). April Carter's *Peace Movements: International Protest and World Politics since 1945* (Harlow: Longman, 1992) is also useful. A good inroad into Japanese peace activism is offered by the mainly biographical studies in Nobuya Bamba and John F. Howes (eds),

Pacifism in Japan: The Christian and Socialist Traditions (Vancouver: The University of British Columbia Press, 1978). A superb analysis for the processes of translation involved in peace movements as global social movements is Sean Scalmer, *Gandhi in the West. The Mahatma and the Rise of Radical Protest* (Cambridge: Cambridge University Press, 2011).

CHAPTER 18

1968: A Social Movement *Sui Generis*

Gerd-Rainer Horn

The concept of 'social movement' is notoriously difficult to define. When, for instance, does a spontaneous strike in a single factory become a movement rather than retaining the characteristics of a momentary event? Most observers would argue that a brief militant action of any sort is likely to take on characteristics of a movement at the point when it persists over a period of time and inspires similar incidents elsewhere. But how long? And in how many hotspots? On the other end of the scale, a similar open-ended debate addresses the differences between a social movement and a societal revolt. When does a social movement undergoing a radicalizing dynamic become a social rebellion? Clearly there is a need for analytical precision and an intelligent and rational use of relevant and distinct categories of analysis.

Yet, surely, it would be counter-intuitive to restrict the label 'social movement' solely to social processes short of open challenges to the societal (political, cultural, etc.) status quo. If one followed a strict division between 'social movement' and 'social rebellion', any major social movement would then lose this label precisely at the moment when it obtained a measurable amount of success or, at the very least, a societal echo of some relevance. Thus, a flexible and pragmatic understanding of 'social

G.-R. Horn (✉)
Centre d'Histoire, Sciencespo, Paris, Frankreich

© The Author(s) 2017   515
S. Berger, H. Nehring (eds.), *The History of Social Movements in Global Perspective*, DOI 10.1057/978-1-137-30427-8_18

movement' will have little difficulty in subsuming a societal upheaval on the order of '1968' into a catch-all category comprising single-issue campaigns side-by-side with open challenges to the 'dominant paradigm', as was the case in 1968. All the more so, as the moment of '1968' took on truly international proportions, and in fact I will argue below that it became the very first trans*continental* revolt—thus sui generis, at least compared to what had come before.

As is often the case with social movements, however defined, it is easier to justify the inclusion of '1968' within the hall of fame of social movements with enormous echoes than it is to pinpoint what exactly it may have achieved. Though in the short-to-medium-term successful in obtaining significant concessions in the educational sector as well as on the factory or office floor, looked at from the vantage point of almost half a century later, most concrete gains appear to have faded beyond recognition. Thus, with virtually no one left to deny that the frontal political challenges of 1968 mostly failed, in recent years the reading public is told with increasing frequency that 1968 was probably entirely unnecessary; had May 1968 not taken place, post-1968 European and world history would essentially have taken a very similar route to the one it did take. 1968 has, in plain language, in the wake of tireless efforts by a growing fleet of commentators, been made largely redundant. It is therefore high time to redraw attention to the system-transcending dimension of 1968. For, despite Hegel, not everything that is real is rational. The most truly radical potential of 1968 lay precisely in its highlighting of the *possibilities* of a different organization of social life. 1968 pointed the finger at the existence of historical alternatives to dominant patterns of politics, the organization of production and the shaping of modern culture across the world.[1]

A FESTIVAL OF THE OPPRESSED

The calendar year of 1968 saw a variety of social movements suddenly erupting in a number of locations around the world. To mention a few highlights on European soil: January 1968 witnessed the highpoint of

---

[1] This paragraph takes up issues first raised in a commentary originally published for a symposium, 'Il 1968 nella storia europea', in an Italian journal: Gerd-Rainer Horn, 'Non tutto quel che è reale è razionale. L'eredità del 1968', *Contemporanea. Rivista di storia dell'800 e del '900* 11 (2008), pp. 477–481; the English-language original can be consulted in 'The Legacy of 1968', *Against the Current* 136 (September–October 2008).

a wave of university and high school student protests that had begun in May 1966 throughout the Flemish half of Belgium, initially focussing on the fate of the Catholic University of Leuven, but soon mutating into a region-wide mobilization to democratize education tout court.[2] March 1968 found Italy's vast network of universities from Sicily to Südtirol shut down by angry students, the high point of a mobilization cycle that reached back, once again, to 1966.[3] April 1968 saw West German university towns explode in anger in reaction to the assassination attempt on Rudi Dutschke.[4] May 1968, of course, witnessed the crown jewel in this selective highlighting of flashpoints of (thus far largely) Western European student battles, when French university students, almost literally overnight, changed the face of French and European politics. What gave the French May pride of place in this chronology of sudden radical outbursts across Europe and the wider world, however, was the positive reaction by French blue- and white-collar workers to the enthusiasm displayed by

---

[2] The historian—and erstwhile participant-observer—Louis Vos has now assembled his various article-length contributions to the history of the Leuven student movement in his *Idealisme en engagement: De roeping van de katholieke studerende jeugd in Vlaanderen (1920–1990)* (Leuven: Acco, 2011); for 'the spirit of '1968' operating at the Catholic University of Leuven, see in particular pp. 251–416. Twenty-five years ago already, he was notably involved in constructing what remains the most solid overview of Belgian student politics in the 1960s: Louis Vos et al., *De stoute jaren: studentenprotest in de jaren zestig* (Tielt: Lannoo, 1988); but notice must be taken too of Ludo Martens and Kris Merckx, *Dat was 1968* (Berchem: EPO, 1978). The most charismatic figure of the Leuven student body at that time, Paul Goossens, published his memoirs as *Leuven 1968 of het geloof in de hemel* (Zellik: Roularta, 1993). On '1968' in the capital city of Belgium, see Serge Govaert, *Mai 68: C'était au temps où Bruxelles contestait* (Brussels: Politique et Histoire, 1990).

[3] The two best contemporaneous accounts of the remarkable upsurge of student struggles throughout Italy are Rossana Rossanda, *L'anno degli student* (Bari: De Donato, 1968), and Carlo Oliva and Aloisio Rendi, *Il movimento studentesco e le sue lotte* (Milan: Feltrinelli, 1969). The most comprehensive recent secondary work on this exemplary student movement remains Jan Kurz, *Die Universität auf der Piazza: Entstehung und Zerfall der Studentenbewegung in Italien 1966–1968* (Cologne: SH-Verlag, 2001).

[4] Still the best account of the seemingly unstoppable rise of the German student movement to national prominence remains Siegward Lönnendonker, Bernd Rabehl and Jochen Staadt, *Die antiautoritäre Revolte: Der Sozialistische Deutsche Studentenbund nach der Trennung von der SPD*, vol. 1: *1960–1967* (Wiesbaden: Westdeutscher Verlag, 2002). On the charismatic leader of SDS, note, amongst a wealth of often rather tendentious publications, Michaela Karl, *Rudi Dutschke—Revolutionär ohne Revolution* (Frankfurt: Verlag Neue Kritik, 2003), Ulrich Chaussy, *Die drei Leben des Rudi Dutschke. Eine Biographie* (Frankfurt: Fischer, 1989), but also Dutschke's diary entries: Rudi Dutschke, *Jeder hat sein Leben ganz zu leben: Die Tagebücher 1963–1979* (Cologne: Kiepenheuer & Witsch, 2003).

students on the barricades and in the streets. The gigantic protest march on 13 May in central Paris and the subsequent seemingly spontaneous wave of wildcat strikes and factory occupations, radiating out from Nantes in south-western France, put workers—and their trade unions—finally back on the map of social movements operating in the golden age of late capitalism.[5] Of course, '1968' also stands as a cipher for social movements operating just before and, more frequently, for some years following the calendar year of 1968, as will become apparent in the subsequent pages.

While Western Europe appeared to stage a re-enactment of the heady spring and early summer of 1936,[6] but now with students linking arms with workers, across the Iron Curtain a separate social movement—second to none—became headline news. Here too students often played a vanguard role. The decision to cut short the planned months-long run of a the-atre play by the nineteenth-century Polish playwright Adam Mickiewicz at the National Theatre in Warsaw, Poland, deemed to contain an 'anti-Soviet' message, led to protest demonstrations attended by 300 persons after the curtain call of the final performance on the evening of 30 January in downtown Warsaw. This spontaneous protest was brutally repressed, with 35 people arrested; two supposed ringleaders amongst the student crowd were expelled from the University of Warsaw on 6 March. The dis-proportionate response by state authorities in turn led to further protest actions on 8 March, which spread throughout the city centre. Despite the mobilization of special anti-riot units, the grassroots movement against censorship and for the democratization of the Polish state now spread to other university towns. Yet, in the end, the (mostly) student protest suf-fered total defeat, with further expulsions and forced emigration putting an end to this first post-1956 democratic revolt in the most populous state of Communist Eastern Europe.[7]

---

[5] Still the superior English-language accounts of the tumultuous events of the French 'May' are: Daniel Singer, *Prelude to Revolution: France in May 1968* (Cambridge, MA: South End Press, 2002), and Patrick Seale and Maureen McConville, *French Revolution 1968* (Harmondsworth: Penguin, 1968). The most comprehensive and convincing study of the working class dimension of the French May is now Xavier Vigna, *L'insubordination ouvrière dans les années 68. Essai d'histoire politique des usines* (Rennes: Presses Universitaires de Rennes, 2007).

[6] In the course of 1935, Popular Fronts emerged as challenges to the seemingly irresistible rise of fascism across Europe, with Popular Front alliances victorious at the ballot box, first in Spain and then in France, in the course of the first half of 1936.

[7] There exists to date no book-length study of the Polish March Unrest in any Western European language. The standard monographs in Polish are Jerzy Eisler, *Marcek 1968*

The Yugoslav June and Spring in Prague

Amongst the many international solidarity actions with the students in Warsaw was the effort by students at the University of Belgrade in Yugoslavia who, within very few days, collected 1,500 signatures in support of their Polish comrades-in-arms. By the late 1960s, Yugoslav civil society had obtained a certain degree of autonomy and freedom of manoeuvre. In early June 1968, the spark of protest action in East-Central Europe transferred to the Titoist state. The trigger event for the actions was, once again—as in Warsaw and, as we will see, elsewhere—relatively incidental and circumstantial. On the evening of 2 June 1968, a concert by several musicians then touring the Yugoslav state had been scheduled to take place in open air in the student district of Belgrade. The occasion was the celebration of volunteer efforts by young workers and students then constructing the motorway from Zagreb to Belgrade. Bad weather had forced the organizers to move the concert indoors. Free tickets to the concert were then distributed to blue-collar workers only, a decision students were not informed about. When far more individuals demanded entry to the cinema where the concert was to take place than was possible to accommodate, it came to altercations between students and police. Things got out of hand, and police reinforcements aggressively beat back insurgent students. Soon the issue was no longer the denial of access to the concert hall, but police brutality in the supposedly self-managed state.

Efforts by protesters to carry their revolt into the centre of Belgrade were stymied by police. Students then returned to their neighbourhood and, some time after midnight, spontaneously organized general assemblies lasting to daybreak. By mid-morning, 3 June 1968, students once more unsuccessfully attempted to break out of their campus ghetto to

(Warsaw: Wydawnictwa Szkolne i Pedagogiczne, 1995), and Jerzy Eisler, *Polski rok 1968* (Warsaw: *Instytut Pamięci Narodowej*, 2006), which I myself, unable to read Slavic languages, did not consult. Stimulating article-length studies of aspects of the March events are Andrea Genest, 'Zwischen Anteilnahme und Ablehnung—die Rollen der Arbeiter in den Märzereignissen 1968 in Polen', in Bernd Gehrke and Gerd-Rainer Horn (eds), *1968 und die Arbeiter: Studien zum 'proletarischen Mai' in Europa* (Hamburg: VSA, 2007), pp. 184–209, as well as Martha Kirszenbaum, 'De Varsovie à Paris: Réceptions, influences et occurrences du mouvement étudiant polonais dans la contestation universitaire parisienne', in Justine Faure and Denis Rolland (eds), *1968 hors de France: Histoire et constructions historiographiques* (Paris: L'Harmattan, 2009), pp. 211–224, and Martha Kirszenbaum, '1968 entre Varsovie et Paris: un cas de transfert culturel de contestation', *Histoire@Politique. Politique, culture, société*, N° 6, septembre-décembre 2008 (<www.histoire-politique.fr>).

reach the centre of Belgrade, once again brutally clubbed back by the forces of order. Students now pronounced 'their' university the 'Red Karl Marx University', demanding an end to all privileges, democratization, freedom of speech, freedom of assembly and the right to demonstrate. In the days that followed, the occupied university turned into a centre for open debate, similar to the Odéon National Theatre in Paris or the Fine Arts Centre in Brussels at the same time. The movement spread to Zagreb, Sarajevo and Ljubljana. Yet, as was to be expected, soon the tide turned against the protesters, and the Yugoslav state and party bureaucracy used the events of early June 1968 to turn back the clock. The relative freedoms which students, intellectuals and others had benefited from in earlier years were gradually removed, and Yugoslav exceptionalism became a thing of the past.[8]

While Warsaw and Belgrade witnessed short-lived but intense flash-points of hope, the key event in East-Central Europe in the course of 1968 was the rapid and seemingly irreversible democratization of an entire society. In Czechoslovakia the relatively well-known events associated with the 'Prague Spring' soon became a laboratory par excellence of the radical dynamic of seemingly unfettered social movements, a society suddenly on the move, similar to the heady atmosphere ensuing after the Parisian Night of the Barricades on 10 May. And, unlike what occurred 20 years later in the Eastern Bloc, here, just like in Belgrade and Warsaw, the dissident social actors were then still powered by visions of 'socialism with a human face'. For a brief moment it appeared possible that the demand for radical social change in Eastern and Western Europe would find a common language and blaze a joint path to construct a better world. In the late winter and early spring of 1968, censorship disappeared in Czechoslovakia, and experimentation in all walks of life proceeded unhindered. In the spring and summer of 1968, Czechoslovakia became arguably one of the freest countries in the world.[9]

---

[8] See, above all, Boris Kanzleiter and Krunoslav Stojaković (eds), *1968 in Jugoslawien: Studentenproteste und kulturelle Avantgarde zwischen 1960 und 1975* (Bonn: Dietz, 2008), and Boris Kanzleiter, *'Rote Universität': Studentenbewegung und Linksopposition in Belgrad 1964–1975* (Hamburg: VSA, 2011).

[9] On the Prague Spring, a stimulating contemporaneous account is Zbyněk A. B. Zeman, *Prague Spring: A Report on Czechoslovakia 1968* (Harmondsworth: Penguin, 1968). Three informative secondary works in English are Galia Golan, *Reform Rule in Czechoslovakia* (Cambridge: Cambridge University Press, 1973), Gordon H. Skilling, *Czechoslovakia's Interrupted Revolution* (Princeton: Princeton University Press, 1976) and Kieran Williams,

North America and Mexico City

In a process that is still largely under investigated, the extra-European world experienced similar outbursts of anti-hierarchical and anti-bureaucratic enthusiasm. In North America, long-simmering unrest had openly erupted already in prior years. Leaving aside the little-known cauldron of Quebec, then undergoing a cycle of cross-class radical political movements similar to Mediterranean Europe,[10] the key flashpoint of social movement action was the United States. The Civil Rights Movement having prepared the terrain since the mid-1950s, social justice and political activism had transferred onto university campuses by the autumn of 1964, with the Berkeley Free Speech Movement inaugurating a cycle of more than six years' worth of protest actions centred on largely white middle-class university towns. If the year 1968 stood out amongst those years of rage, it was initially largely due to the series of assassinations of leading protagonists: Martin Luther King Jr. on 4 April and Robert Kennedy on 6 June. But from 24 to 29 August 1968, the Democratic Party Convention in Chicago became headline news, not because of the usual circus performances inside the Convention Hall, but rather due to the multiple protest actions organized outside the Hall—and the heavy-handed response to these actions on the part of the Chicago Police. Last but not least, one of the symbolic acts par excellence of 'the spirit of 1968' in general occurred on 16 October 1968 in Mexico City, site of the Summer Olympics in that fateful year. The gold medal winner in the 200 metre dash, Tommie Smith, and the bronze medal winner, John Carlos, both black US citizens, stepped up to the podium to the sounds of 'God Bless America', each raising one hand clad with a black glove symbolizing Black Power.[11] The

The Prague Spring and its Aftermath: Czechoslovak Politics, 1968–1970 (Cambridge: Cambridge University Press, 1997). On '1968' in Eastern Europe as a whole, note now also Angelika Ebbinghaus (ed.), *Die letzte Chance? 1968 in Osteuropa* (Hamburg: VSA, 2008).

[10] Good places to start to get to know this piece of Mediterranean Europe in Eastern Canada are Léon Dion, *La révolution déroutée, 1960–1976* (Montréal: Les Éditions du Boréal, 1998), and Sheilagh Hodgins Milner and Henry Milner, *The Decolonization of Quebec: An Analysis of Left-wing Nationalism* (Toronto: McClelland and Stewart, 1973).

[11] On the Chicago Democratic Party Convention, the superior account remains to this day Norman Mailer, *Miami and the Siege of Chicago: An Informal History of the American Political Conventions of 1968* (Harmondsworth: Penguin, 1968). On the Black Power salute in Mexico City, note the autobiographical account by Tommie Smith, *Silent Gesture* (Philadelphia: Temple University Press, 2007). It might be of more than passing interest in this context that the White Australian sprinter, Peter Norman, the silver medalist, in solidarity

action by the three medallists in the 200 metre dash in Mexico City's Olympic Stadium took on a heightened relevance within global politics, as Mexico itself had earlier on that same calendar year become an extraordinary hot spot of radical activism, with the most brutal repressive act by state authorities in all of 1968 taking place only kilometres away from the Olympic Stadium precisely two weeks earlier.

On 22 July 1968 in Mexico City, a football match between two school teams had triggered a brawl which stretched into a second day of violent altercations, with supporters of the team representing two polytechnic institutes receiving the brunt of police 'attention'. A protest action supported by the National Federation of Technical Students was then called for 26 July, by coincidence occurring at the same time and in the same neighbourhood as a demonstration led by the student association close to the Mexican Communist Party celebrating the Cuban Revolution. Police attacks on both contingents led to violent scenes, with makeshift barricades thrown up throughout the area. By next morning five students were dead. On 27 July, virtually all technical schools in Mexico City came out on strike, while barricade fighting continued to rent the city apart for several days. On 28 July negotiations began between representatives of student organizations in the polytechnic institutes and the giant National Autonomous University of Mexico (UNAM) in view of broadening the strike movement. These were heated discussions that continued until the early morning hours of 30 July, when the Mexican government decided on a course of action which, finally, sent Mexico City up in flames. Regular army units invaded the UNAM campus, putting a forced and bloody end to the student assembly. On that day, 30 July, the UNAM, which had thus far only seen solidarity actions by its most politicized segments, witnessed general assemblies in all schools and faculties.

An open-air protest was called for 31 July, to be addressed by the UNAM's president, to which 20,000 students and faculty members turned up. One day later, 100,000 demonstrators assembled, for the first time in Mexican history, angry students and teachers from all branches of the far-flung network of post-secondary institutions of the capital city. On 2 August, a National Strike Committee (CNH) was formed to coordinate subsequent actions. Democratically constituted, based on elected repre-

with his American comrades sported a badge expressing his solidarity with their action when on the podium. All three medal winners suffered vicious persecution in response to the bold statement of support to the radical causes of their day.

sentatives from strike committees of each school, the CNH had no formal hierarchy, and all decisions were taken by this body of, roughly, 300 delegates. On 5 August, a further mass demonstration occurred, organized by the student CNH but directed at the inhabitants of Mexico City who had no links to post-secondary institutions as such. One hundred thousand demonstrators filled the streets of Mexico City. From then on thousands of students and faculty members frequented the streets, markets, cafés and cinemas of the city day after day in order to publicize their demands, which had long outgrown 'mere' opposition to police brutality and begun to attack the foundations of the clientelist Mexican political and social order. Meanwhile, the UNAM campus literally became a centre for open exchange of opinion for anyone wishing to participate. Musicians, painters and artists invested the campus with an atmosphere usually described as that of a 'popular festival'. On 13 August, 250,000 Mexicans marched onto the giant central square of the city, the Zócalo, in open defiance of the Mexican state. On 27 August, the mother of all protest demonstrations in this 'Mexican May' took place with more than 500,000 demonstrators once again converging on the Zócalo. By then the insurgent movement had spread to other university towns throughout the Mexican state, from Baja California to Yucatán and from Nuevo León to Oaxaca.

From late August 1968 onwards, however, the movement slowly began to lose its inner dynamic. The repressive tactics by the Mexican state eventually broke the back of this social movement par excellence. On 13 September 1968, an impressive 300,000 demonstrators still marched in—ominous—total silence to the National Palace. But then the events associated with a mass meeting called for 2 October in the Plaza de las Tres Culturas turned out to mark the definitive end of the movement. Tens of thousands of mostly students filled the square. Suddenly, in a premeditated action, helicopters and tanks arrived at the square, with machine-gun-toting soldiers and government snipers from surrounding rooftops opening fire on the unarmed and helplessly exposed crowd. The best estimates of the casualty count suggest that more than 700 protesters were murdered in cold blood.[12]

---

[12] Two article-length contributions are excellent points of departures to comprehend the overall contours and the individual flashpoints of the Mexican student revolt: Salvador Martínez Della Rocca, 'El movimiento estudiantil-popular de 1968', and Ignacio Carrillo Prieto, 'Hechos ocurridos el 2 de octubre de 1968 en la Plaza de las Tres Culturas en Nonoalco, Tlatelolco', in Salvador Martínez Della Rocca (ed.), *Voces y ecos del 68* (México: Porrúa, 2009), pp. 27–62 and pp. 117–138, here especially pp. 117–131. An able survey of

May 1968 in Dakar, Senegal

Earlier on in 1968, another largely spontaneous protest action of—comparatively—even larger proportions had shook up the neo-colonial Senegalese state, then headed by Prime Minister Léopold Sédar Senghor, one of the internationally most well-known black intellectuals and an ambassador of *négritude*.[13] In the autumn of 1967, the government had decided on a series of major cutbacks in the funding of university student fellowships, which led to a number of protest actions in the winter and early spring of 1967/1968, gradually heating up the campus atmosphere. A first warning strike on 18 May 1968 was followed by a call for an unlimited general strike and a boycott of exams by the Democratic Union of Senegalese Students (UDES) starting on 27 May. Negotiations with the government failed to produce results, and on 28 May a meeting of several thousand protesters on the campus of the University of Dakar, which then counted no more than a total of 1,480 students, further upped the ante. On the morning of 29 May, a combined force of police and army units occupied the campus; 600 Senegalese students suffered arrest and internment in a prison camp; countless non-Senegalese students were summarily expelled from their host country. One dead and 700 injured were counted amongst the demonstrators.

Starting on 27 May 1968, high school students began to mobilize throughout the state, and on 29–30 May thousands of youth from the university, high schools as well as the city at large began to construct barricades in Dakar. On the evening of 30 May 1968, in a further qualitative escalation, the National Union of Senegalese Workers (UNTS), after leading an unsuccessful mediation attempt between government and students, launched a call for an unlimited general strike for democratic liberties and

the state of historical research on this event can be consulted in Frédéric Johansson, 'Le mouvement étudiant mexicain de 1968: de la tragédie au mythe. Bilan d'une recherché inachevée', in Faure and Rolland (eds), *1968 hors de France*, pp. 283–293. The most evocative reconstruction of the atmosphere and significance of the Mexican revolt remains, in the eyes of this historian, Paco Ignacio Taibo, *68* (New York: Seven Stories Press, 2003).

[13] *Négritude* emerged as a concept amongst francophone black intellectuals and writers in the course of the 1930s. It sought to create a common front against French colonialism on the basis of a common black identity of French colonial subjects. Perhaps the most famous representatives of this transnational literary and political movement were Léopold Sédar Senghor and the Martinican poet Aimé Césaire. In some respects, *négritude* can be regarded as a precursor of subsequent movements emphasizing 'Black Power' in opposition to White colonial or neo-colonial oppression.

a decent standard of living for all Senegalese citizens. Within the space of several days, then, significant sections of Senegalese civil society had come out in open defiance of a government which, outside Senegal, was often celebrated as a notable success story of African independence. 'From 29 May to 9 June, the city of Dakar and its hinterland experienced an atmosphere of insurrection never before witnessed in the country.' To be sure, after about a week of uncertainty, the situation began to de-escalate. First, on 12 June, the UNTS concluded an agreement with the government, raising the minimum wage by 15% and leading to other material improvements. Students had to wait till 13 September to reach tangible results in negotiations, which rescinded many of the counter-reforms that had sparked the protest wave in the first place.[14]

Still, though largely forgotten in the literature on global 1968, the insurrection of Dakar in late May and early June 1968 showcased in no uncertain terms that '1968' was not just a First World affair and was by no means limited to radicalized university and high school students. The relatively well-known student movements in Mexico and the even more widely supported protest movement in Senegal were only the tip of the iceberg in what remains largely uncharted terrain almost half a century after 1968. In a rare confluence of radical democratic energies and ideologies, then, radical progressive social movements with a variety of social agents—though, indeed, often with students in the forefront of battles—occurred almost simultaneously in countries belonging to the 'First', 'Second' and 'Third World'.

THE PREPARATION OF REVOLT

Wherever such protests erupted, however, without some degree of 'preparation' none of these social movements would have developed so suddenly and seemingly spontaneously, as is often asserted in memoirs and the relevant literature and as was—on the epiphenomenal level—indeed quite often the case. To take the French May as a test case: the unplanned and seemingly instinctively occurring Night of the Barricades would have

[14] Abdoulaye Bathily, *Mai 1968 à Dakar ou la révolte universitaire et la démocratie* (Paris: Chaka, 1982), citation on p. 85. Informative recent articles on this topic are Patrick Dramé, 'Le Palais, la Rue et l'Université en Mai 1968 au Sénégal', and Samy Mesli, 'La grève de mai-juin 1968 à l'université de Dakar', in Patrick Dramé and Jean Lamarre (eds), *1968, des sociétés en crise: Une perspective globale* (Québec: Presses de l'Université Laval, 2009), pp. 81–100 and pp. 101–119.

been impossible to 'construct' without a whole series of prior developments which made such a key event possible. In reverse chronology and solely focussing on some of the more important elements, the existence of the *Mouvement du 22 Mars*, the contestations at Nanterre University from 1967 onwards, the development of a dynamic dissident, quasi-Luxemburgist current within the youth wing of the French Communist Party, the concurrent lure of Maoism as an alternative to the presumed 'reformism' of traditional French communism and—perhaps most importantly—the exemplary earlier experience of the movement in opposition to the Algerian War, a movement which singularly helped shape French politics after 1956; without such powerful political developments and learning processes, the French May 1968 would never have taken on the explosive dimension which it did.[15]

The unpredictable and unexpected wave of solidarity actions in blue- and white-collar communities across France after 13 May 1968 would likewise never have reached such a level of volatility without prior ground work having been laid in patient, sometimes decades-long and ceaseless activities. A case in point is the catalyst for the wave of strikes and occupations: the airplane factory of Sud-Aviation on the outskirts of Nantes. The social movement cultures in the Loire-Atlantique and particularly the city of Nantes had been shaped by an unusually combative mix of political and counter-cultural ingredients. The most well-known and respected local trade union activist was the anarcho-syndicalist Alexandre Hébert who, along with unorthodox Trotskyist currents, operated within the (elsewhere in France rather moderate) *Force Ouvrière*. Student politics at the regionally important University of Nantes had been, for some time, shaped by a combative mix of Trotskyist and Situationist currents. Last but not least, the Loire-Atlantique in particular, and the Bretagne in general, was home to the most radical movement of small farmers in all of France at that time, fuelled in part by the radical instincts of a regionally important

---

[15] Martin Evans, *The Memory of Resistance: French Opposition to the Algerian War 1954–1962* (Oxford: Berg, 2004), is an excellent assessment and overview of the Algerian solidarity movement in France. Still unsurpassed in its evocative reconstruction of the genesis of the French student revolt is Hervé Hamon and Patrick Rotman's two volume collective biography of a generation: *Génération*, Vol. I: *Les Années de rêves*, Vol. II: *Les Années de poudre* (Paris: Seuil, 1988). For a quasi-literary celebration of the spirit of the French May, see Angelo Quatrocchi's contribution to Tom Nairn and Angelo Quatrocchi, *The Beginning of the End: France, May 1968* (London: Verso, 1998).

Left Catholicism, and operating in close alliance with radicalized industrial trade union federations for some years prior to 1968.[16]

Small wonder, then, that Nantes not only 'happened to' provide the trigger event for a three-week-long general strike in a leading industrial nation, but likewise witnessed the most outstanding example of counter-power in all of France in May/June 1968. For the duration of the general strike, effective rule and administration of Nantes and the Loire-Atlantique was in the hands of a strike committee headquartered in the *Mairie de Nantes*, with the nominal mayor playing a supporting role. To be sure, the peculiar political conditions of Nantes and the Loire-Atlantique were replicated nowhere else in France where, generally, the more traditional forces of the Left were only beginning to be challenged by a more radical and unorthodox Left. But the signal event of the factory occupation at Sud-Aviation enabled other activists elsewhere to initiate copycat actions, which spread throughout France like wildfire.[17]

In short, the seeming spontaneity of the explosive social movements of 1968 can only be explained by the pre-existence of patient preparatory work by creative and often 'non-mainstream' forces on the Left. The latter, to be sure, did not *create* the May events in France, but they created a sufficiently developed culture of dissent which, given the right circumstances, merely needed a spark to set a city or a region or an entire country alight. '1968', then, dates back at least to 1966 and, in some important ways, all the way to 1956.

[16] Note here, above all, François Le Madec, *L'aubepine de mai: Chronique d'une usine occupée. Sud-Aviation Nantes 1968* (Nantes: Centre de Documentation du Mouvement et du Travail, 1988), but also the contemporaneous text by Yannick Guin, *La Commune de Nantes* (Paris: Maspero, 1969), which remains an indispensable source of information despite the author's tendency to ascribe openly revolutionary intentions to many of the actors. The classic literary expression of the radical farmers' movement in the Loire-Atlantique is Bernard Lambert, *Les paysans dans la lutte des classes* (Nantes: Centre d'Histoire du travail, 2003). On Breton (progressive) Catholicism, note Brigitte Waché, *Militants catholiques de l'Ouest* (Rennes: Presses Universitaires de Rennes, 2004), above all pp. 67–196, but also Anne Tristan and Médard Lebot, *Au-delà des haies: Visite aux paysans de l'Ouest* (Paris: Descartes, 1995).

[17] A marvellous pictorial history of May 1968 in Nantes is Sarah Guilbaud, *Mai 68 Nantes* (Nantes: Coiffard, 2004).

THE ROLE OF CULTURAL NON-CONFORMITY

Organizational footwork by dynamic contenders in the world of local, regional and national politics in prior years and decades cannot alone explain the outbursts of 1968. Especially in moments of political stasis, in years when radical social change appears far removed from actual political reality, *cultural* non-conformity can play a crucial role in setting the stage for dissident behaviours and potential conflicts in otherwise relatively quiet circumstances.

To a growing body of social theorists the years and decades up to 1968 appeared to herald the end of all ideologies in Western Europe and North America. Modernization theorists in the West viewed late capitalist societies as the sole—and thus desirable—models to strive for and, where already deemed to be present, to perfect. Soviet ideologists twisted and distorted Marxist precepts to predict a similar conflict-less future in the socialist East. To be sure, the prominence of Third World liberation movements precisely in the heyday of 'The American Century' and 'Goulash Communism', with revolutions and revolts from Algeria to Vietnam disturbing daydreams of classless societies in both the East and the West, made it difficult to apply the consensual model of development to all corners of the globe, though not for want of trying.

Within First World countries, precisely at this nadir of critical thinking and radical social action between, say, 1948 and 1968, cultural nonconformity performed a singularly important role in keeping alive the flame of refusal and rebellion. Though frequently blissfully unaware and uninterested in radical politics or societal changes, cultural rebels continued to provide a glimpse at the possibility of a different world for successive generations of (often) youthful dissenters who had—unlike, for example, during the inter-war time period—no attractive radical political role models and milieus to fashion themselves after or to join. In fact, as it so happened, it was precisely the non-political nature of cultural revolt in the 1950s and early-to-mid-1960s, which made it possible for such cultural non-conformity to gain influence over growing numbers of disaffected denizens of the modern First World. Had Jack Kerouac been a member of the Socialist Workers Party, he would have never obtained cult status, and he would have never even dreamed—unless in a nightmare—of writing a novel like *On the Road*. Had John Lennon been consorting with the likes of Robin Blackburn and Tariq Ali already in 1964 rather than in 1971, the Beatles would never have entered the Rock 'n' Roll Hall of Fame.[18]

In Soviet societies, the role of non-conformist artists and writers in shaping dissident movements is perhaps less controversial than in the late industrial West. The rise of Václav Havel from theatre playwright to president of a nation may stand as only the most prominent symbol of the power of the word in preparing movements of revolt in the East. That, in 1968, the performance of an early nineteenth century play by Adam Mickiewicz in Warsaw, Poland, and issues surrounding a concert performance in Belgrade, Yugoslavia, could trigger student riots further proves this point. Of course, the political dimension of Eastern European artistic dissent was usually ever-present, pointing to a significant difference in the trajectories of cultural non-conformity on either side of the Iron Curtain. Yet, outside the peculiar lifeworld of Stalinist dictatorships, prior to the reawakening of political consciousness, it were non-conformist cultural rebels who promoted dissident behaviours which, eventually, in turn, helped spawn the first shoots of radical political dissent. In Western Europe, one had to wait for the comet-like rise (and decline) of movements like the Dutch Provos or the Italian Mondo Beat in the mid-to-the-late 1960s, to see a similar process of cultural rebellion taking on the clear overtones of political revolt.[19] To the best of my (limited) knowledge, the role of cultural productions in stimulating sentiments of dissent in Third World countries has not received the attention it may well deserve. Were Carlos Fuentes, Gabriel García Márquez, Ousmane Sembène and Ngũgĩ wa Thiong'o merely products of already present communities of revolt, or did they help shape them?

THE WORKING CLASS DIMENSION

Students were in the thick of the struggle in literally all instances of rebellion in 1968, and that is one qualitative difference between 1968 and all previous outbursts of social and political revolt. Yet had students remained

---

[18] See my first chapter, 'Outcasts, Dropouts, and Provocateurs: Nonconformists Prepare the Terrain', in *The Spirit of 1968: Rebellion in Western Europe and North America, 1956–1976* (Oxford: Oxford University Press, 2007), pp. 5–53.

[19] Niek Pas, *Imaazje! De verbeelding van Provo 1965–1967* (Amsterdam: Wereldbibliotheek, 2003) and Gianni De Martino and Marco Grispigni, *I Capelloni: Mondo Beat, 1966–1967: storia, immagini, documenti* (Rome: Castelvecchi, 1997).

the sole key agents in the course of 1968, it would likely have retained far less ongoing attention in the subsequent 45 years. What accounts for the particular volatility and combustive power of 1968 is the intercalation, the creative mixture and merger of student power with other social forces on the scene.

The fame and international significance of May 1968 in Paris and throughout France lies in the successful insertion of—and sustained engagement by—workers as key social actors moving in the direction of radical social change; but this truism applies not merely to France. In Italy, for instance, workers had by no means been quiescent in the course of the calendar year of 1968. Yet, in part inspired by student activism, the big breakthrough for Italian labour arrived in 1969. The Hot Autumn of sustained working class action in the second half of 1969 changed the atmosphere on Italian factory floors and office suites in previously unimaginable ways. From 1969 to 1976, Italian factories became nearly unmanageable for foremen and the managerial elite alike. Italy's social legislation changed in dramatic fashion, reshaping production relations and related issues for several decades. In combination with other centres of social unrest, for about half a dozen crucial years, Italy became a laboratory for emancipatory action in a multitude of milieus—and an inspiration for countless social movement activists elsewhere.[20]

Due to the reappearance of working class action as a major radical force in contemporary societies, in the wake of 1968 the threat to the social and political status quo took on serious dimensions. For that reason, it is merely stating the obvious to contend that the true potential of 1968 was really only reached in the course of the first half of the 1970s. The Sixties, then, really took place in the Seventies. Where traditional trade unions proved to be imaginative and flexible enough to accommodate radical grass-roots sentiments, as in Italy, the dynamic thrust of working-class action took organizational shelter largely within existing institutional structures, though adding important innovations. In France, where the Communist-led CGT refused to conform to the new winds blowing, it was the CFDT which, on 16 May 1968, declared in the midst of the rap-

---

[20] Leaving aside the wealth of Italian sources, the best book in English on the overall dimension of social movement cultures in Italy at that time remains Robert Lumley, *States of Emergency: Cultures of Revolt from 1968 to 1978* (London: Verso, 1990). The most informative and stimulating English-language study of the working class dimension of the Italian 'Creeping May'—despite its confusing title—is Miriam Golden, *Labor Divided: Austerity and Working-Class Politics in Contemporary Italy* (Ithaca, NY: Cornell University Press, 1988).

idly widening national strike wave: 'To civil liberties and rights within universities must correspond the same liberties and rights within enterprises; in this demand the struggles of university students meet up with those which workers have fought for since the origins of the labour movement. We must replace industrial and administrative monarchy with democratic structures based on workers' self-management.'[21]

Where unions were too slow to adapt to the winds of change as, at least for a time, in Belgium or in West Germany, wildcat strikes ensued. In countries with no firmly established trade union tradition, such as Spain or Portugal, the degree of volatility was the most visible. In these countries struggling to overcome long-standing dictatorships in the middle of the 'Free World', anti-dictatorial revolts rapidly turned into even more deep-going social explosions based, to a significant extent, on working-class energies. No European country practised the spirit of 1968 more thoroughly and contentiously than Portugal in its 19 short months of the Revolution of the Carnations, though the amazing growth and extension of a far-flung network of workers' commission in underground Czechoslovakia following the Soviet invasion could have, under different circumstances, played a similar role in the East.[22]

In Latin America, one of the most famous working-class engagements in the wake of 1968, threatening the foundations of the social order, was the *Cordobazo* of May 1969, a civil uprising against the Argentinian military dictatorship, once again showcasing the potential powers of an alliance of workers and students.[23] Yet, for the most part, outside of Europe the

---

[21] Cited in Albert Detraz, 'Le mouvement ouvrier, la CFDT, et l'idée de l'autogestion', in Edmond Maire, Alfred Krumnow and Albert Detraz, *La CFDT et l'autogestion* (Paris: Cerf, 1975), p. 77.

[22] On the Belgian wave of wildcat action, note Rik Hemmerijckx, 'Mai'1968 und die Welt der Arbeiter in Belgien', in Bernd Gehrke and Gerd-Rainer Horn (eds), *1968 und die Arbeiter*, pp. 231–251; on West Germany, note above all Peter Birke, *Wilde Streiks im Wirtschaftswunder. Arbeitskämpfe, Gewerkschaften und soziale Bewegungen in der Bundesrepublik und Dänemark* (Frankfurt: Campus, 2007). A good introduction to the turbulent world of Spanish labour relations is David Ruiz (ed.), *Historia de Comisiones Obreras (1958–1988)* (Madrid: Siglo XXI, 1994). In my view still the superior reconstruction of the Portuguese Revolution is Gérard Filoche, *Printemps portugais* (Paris: Actéon, 1984); for the role of workers in the Prague Spring and its aftermath, see Vladimir Fišera, *Workers' Councils in Czechoslovakia, 1968–1969: Documents and Essays* (London: Allison and Busby, 1978).

[23] Note here Juan Carlos Cena (ed.), *El cordobazo: una rebelión popular* (Buenos Aires: La Rosa Blindada, 2000), as well as Beba C. Balvé and Beatriz S. Balvé, *El 1969: huelga política de masas: rosariazo, cordobazo, rosariazo* (Buenos Aires: RyR, 2005).

most obvious and significant challenges to the respective established elites came from national liberation movements, which had followed a mobilization cycle unto their own, beginning with the Quit India Movement (1942–1944) and the Indonesian Revolution (1945–1949), reaching a first highpoint in the second half of the 1950s with the Algerian revolt and the January 1959 Cuban Revolution, ultimately culminating in 'Vietnam'.

In sum, when student radicalism managed to forge alliances with other radical forces that had an impact far beyond the university milieu, the systemic crisis to existing power elites, and the promises of social movements as harbingers of a new morning, was most pronounced. Consequently, '1968' not only began in 1956, but it lasted until, roughly, 1976.

TWO PATTERNS OF RADICALIZATION

The presence or absence of working-class radicalism in the course of 1968 in Western Europe followed an age-old geographic divide. In Romance language countries workers were key to giving social movements a decidedly promising inflection. North of an imaginary line from Antwerp via Aachen, Strasbourg, Geneva and Venice, on the whole, blue- and white-collar workers tended to remain rather passive onlookers in the social movements of their day, if not actual opponents of what activists deemed progressive changes. In these Northern European lands, university towns constituted radical islands, where mostly middle-class students could act out their dreams in splendid isolation from the rest of their respective country, providing a spectacle on television screens, with onlookers regarding student demonstrators like visitors gazing at exotic animals in a zoo.

The United States and English-speaking Canada fit the Northern European model exceedingly well, leaving Québec and a few pockets of radical union activism in the mainland United States—notably the United Farm Workers in the rural southwest and the League of Revolutionary Black Workers in Detroit's satanic automobile mills[24]—as examples of

---

[24] On the United Farm Worker experience, the recent study by Frank Bardacke, *Trampling Out the Vintage: Cesar Chavez and the Two Souls of the United Farm Workers* (London: Verso, 2011), is likely to remain the key reference work for some years to come. On the role of Black workers in late 1960s Detroit, see above all Dan Georgakas and Marvin Surkin, *Detroit: I Do Mind Dying: A Study in Urban Revolution* (Cambridge, MA: South End Press, 1998) and Heather Ann Thompson, *Whose Detroit? Politics, Labor, and Race in a Modern American City* (Ithaca, NY: Cornell University Press, 2001).

'otherness' confirming the general rule of working-class quiescence and conservatism north of the Rio Grande. It is surely not a coincidence that relatively marginalized ethnic minorities accounted for much of the fuel of the few existing radical working-class fires in North America, a role fulfilled in Northern European states by immigrant labourers from Southern Europe, North Africa and the Near East.

In Northern Europe and North America, for the most part, university (and, later, high school) students formed the core of radical forces (along with ethnic minorities), accounting for some exemplary and spectacular actions, but rendering dreams of systemic social changes mere ghost lights (*Irrlichter*) of utopian longings. In Mediterranean Europe, the stakes were qualitatively higher, the struggles more protracted and bitter, polarization more painful and threatening, and the outcome (at least initially) less certain. Serious analysis of the precise factors which may explain this age-old pattern of European social movements 'north' and 'south' is still in its infancy, though the reality of this twofold pattern has nonetheless been a powerful factor in twentieth-century European history. Relevant background factors include the predominance of vastly different political regimes in the two halves of Europe, including the relative historical strength and presence of social democracy in the North versus the far greater implantation of communism and anarchism in the South, as well as the stronger tradition of trade union cooperation in Northern Europe compared to Romance-language syndicalism.[25]

THE CHRISTIAN CONTRIBUTION

One additional important factor in rendering Mediterranean Europe a more volatile tinderbox than 'Northern' Europe was the social and cultural weight of Catholicism in these lands. (And it remains to be determined to what extent this factor played a role in the centrality of Latin America as revolutionary hotbed in the key decades of the 1960s and 1970s.) Protestant Europeans were just as much engaged on both sides of the barricades in all instances of social and political contestations as were Catholics. Yet Protestants were eminently more prepared to face up to and engage with terrestrial realities and the controversial issues of their time than were Catholics. Up to Vatican II (1962–1965), the Catholic Church had more

---

[25] For a somewhat more detailed engagement with this phenomenon of a dual Europe, note my subchapter 'A Tale of Two Europes' in my *Spirit of 1968*, pp. 228–231.

or less successfully managed to orient itself to the presumed advantages of pre-modern societal models, rather than to look to the future for solutions to contemporary problems. The Second Vatican Council suddenly effected an almost 180 degree change of course. An engagement with the present (rather than the adulation of the past) was now called for, as well as an opening to the world as it was. The option for the poor and the condemnation of war as a measure of conflict resolution in all cases on both sides of all fronts was no longer a mere ideological cover for actual regime support and the blessing of arms on both sides of the trenches, but became meaningful policy. Catholic social theory and political practice was turned upside down. A shockwave swept through the Catholic world.

Prior to Vatican II by no means all Catholics had silently followed the guidelines provided by their usually rather conservative spiritual leaders. Dissident left-wing Catholicism had first emerged in the course of a wave of radicalization towards the end and in the immediate aftermath of the Second World War. Yet, throughout the ensuing 1950s, the dwindling number of supporters of a new theological approach were pushed to the sidelines and shunted aside. In the course and aftermath of Vatican II, then, progressive Catholicism obtained the green light. Long-suppressed energies suddenly burst free. In Catholic Europe, above all in the predominantly Catholic European South, a wave of Catholic-inspired social movements caught the imagination of countless practising Catholics, precisely in the run-up to the crucial year of 1968.

A dense network of base communities began to arise, combining ecclesial with social action. The 'Mediterranean' New Left was often strongly influenced by this sudden appearance of a Catholic Left, most notably so in underground Spain, where radical Catholic currents had already played a major role in the creation of the Spanish underground New Left since 1956. Catholic trade unions were consistently in the forefront of radical action up to and beyond the watershed year of 1968. It is no accident that, in France, it was the CFDT, which had only very recently cut its official ties to the Catholic Church but which was, for quite some time, still heavily suffused with the precepts of Catholic social theory, which proved to be far more open to the spirit of 1968 than the seemingly more radical but hard-line Stalinist CGT. Student struggles in Catholic Europe likewise cannot be adequately explained without the prominent role played by radical Catholic students in the forefront of their ranks.[26]

---

[26] For an assessment of progressive Catholicism in Western Europe prior to Vatican II, see my *Western European Liberation Theology: The First Wave (1924–1959)* (Oxford: Oxford

In sum, 1968 in Mediterranean Europe (and possibly in Latin America too) took on its particular dynamism and radical direction in part as a result of the prominent role of radical Catholic activists, whose social engagements helped create a virtuous cycle in the course of their interactions with their secular allies, both aiming to change the world in conformity with their rapidly rising expectations. Of course, the inspiring role of progressive Catholic currents could be noted in Northern Europe as well; but north of the Alps Protestant traditions were frequently more important than their Roman Catholic counterparts. Thus, before ending this brief excursion onto the role of Catholic progressive currents in the social movements of 1968, particularly in Romance-language Europe, I wish to re-emphasize that Protestant Christianity was likewise often equally profoundly affected by the atmosphere of those times, and thus social movements in Northern Europe were, correspondingly, in part propelled by progressive Protestant concerns and motivations, similar to the mechanisms involving Catholicism in South Europe.[27]

THE INSPIRATIONAL DYNAMICS OF SOCIAL MOVEMENTS

The year of 1968 constituted one of those rare transnational moments of crisis and opportunity, which periodically, though unpredictably, occur in a series of states. Perhaps the sole rough equivalents in modern his-

---

University Press, 2008). For a transnational study of the phenomenon of European Left Catholicism in '1968' see my *The Spirit of Vatican II: Western European Progressive Catholicism in the Long Sixties* (Oxford: Oxford University Press, 2015). Notice should also be taken, however, of a stimulating series of reflections on 'global 1968' and the role of religion which covers both Catholicism and Protestantism: Kuno Füssel and Michael Ramminger (eds), *Zwischen Medellín und Paris: 1968 und die Theologie* (Luzern: Exodus, 2009). One of the very few recent studies of this phenomenon in English is Rebecca Clifford and Nigel Townson, 'The Church in Crisis: Catholic Activism in "1968"', *Cultural and Social History* 4 (2011), pp. 531–550.

[27] Three references on the impact of 'the spirit of 1968' on Protestant Christians in West Germany may suffice in this context: Klaus Fitschen et al. (eds), *Die Politisierung des Protestantismus: Entwicklungen in der Bundesrepublik Deutschland während der 1960er und 1970er Jahre* (Göttingen: Vandenhoeck & Ruprecht, 2011), and Siegfried Hermle, Claudia Lepp and Harry Oelke (eds), *Umbrüche: Der deutsche Protestantismus und die sozialen Bewegungen in den 1960er und 1970er Jahren* (Göttingen: Vandenhoeck & Ruprecht, 2012); Bernd Hey and Volkmar Wittmütz (eds), *1968 und die Kirchen* (Bielefeld: Verlag für Regionalgeschichte, 2008), also covers Catholicism, but the bulk of the contributions pertain to Protestant milieus.

tory took place in and around 1848, 1918, 1944 or 1989, although the truly trans*continental* dimension of 1968 made it a case *sui generis*. What characterizes transnational moments of change is a rare and virtuous creative confluence of an intense mobilization cycle of more than one social movement operating continuously and (at least temporarily) successfully at roughly the same time.[28]

A frequent by-product of such capstone experiences, further heating up an atmosphere already witnessing creative bouts of social unrest, is the inspirational effect of dynamic social movements on previously marginalized and powerless groupings. Without the events of 1968, second wave feminism would have taken much longer to become a key social agent in the late twentieth century. Just like the contentious and open-ended atmosphere of the Civil Rights Movement in the southern United States inadvertently but unequivocally forged the American women's liberation movement by the mid-to-late 1960s, becoming a much-admired model for European feminists in subsequent years, the turbulences and provocations of 1968 helped give rise to European second wave feminist movements as a concrete reality. It is surely no accident that the breakthrough events for second wave feminism in a series of Western European states occurred shortly *after* 1968, in 1969 and, most frequently, in 1970. Gay liberation movements, prisoners' rights movements, anti-psychiatry and other new social movements likewise profited from the breakthrough of social movement cultures in and around 1968.

It was an extraordinary process of individual and collective liberation which the French anthropologist and Left Catholic activist Michel de Certeau termed 'the capture of speech'. 'Last May', he wrote towards the end of 1968, 'speech was taken the way, in 1789, the Bastille was taken'. 'At the same time that previously self-assured discourses [by the elites] faded away and the "authorities" were reduced to silence, frozen existences melted and suddenly awoke into a prolific morning.'[29]

---

[28] For a discussion of the concept of 'transnational moments of crisis and opportunity' or 'transnational moments of change' as well as a series of historical examples, see Gerd-Rainer Horn and Padraic Kenney (eds), *Transnational Moments of Change: Europe 1945, 1968, 1989* (Lanham: Rowman & Littlefield, 2004).

[29] Michel de Certeau, *La prise de parole et autres écrits politiques* (Paris: Seuil, 1994), pp. 40–41.

THE CONFLUENCE OF A TRIPARTITE REVOLT

What creates a *national* moment of opportunity and crisis is the simultaneity of such pressures in 'merely' one country. Transnational moments of change are, on one level, mere multiplications of such currents across national frontiers, benefiting from a whole host of transmission mechanisms, which differ significantly depending on the individual cases studied. The particularly vibrant and truly global event of 1968, however, is a result of three different mobilization cycles operating for the most part independently of each other, but coinciding in time and thus influencing each other: student and workers power in First World countries; anti-bureaucratic dissident currents in the Second World; and national liberation movements and associated ideologies in the Third World.

In real life, of course, none of those three sectors of anti-elite systemic revolt operated completely independently from each other. Second-wave feminism and homosexual rights activists, for instance, often labelled their movements 'liberation movements' in a clear reference to their identification with Third World liberation movements. Contacts between Western and Eastern European dissidents went back at least as far as 1956, under the auspices of the burgeoning international New Left, when frequent personal exchanges of ideas were facilitated, given symbolic and practical expression in the Korčula Summer Schools of 1963–1974. One of the texts found in Che Guevara's belongings at the moment of his murder in 1967 was Leon Trotsky's *History of the Russian Revolution*.

Still, to a significant extent, the inner dynamics of the batch of social movements operating side-by-side in the three sectors of the world were qualitatively different. After 1968, however, the incidents of overlap began to increase. As the first truly transcontinental social movement, 1968 may well have changed the rules of the game and altered the parameters of world politics. Henceforth, social movements in all corners of the world had an easier time overcoming their international isolation, though this by no means assured greater success. The recent prominence of global justice or alter-globalization movements is an eloquent expression of this important change. The outbreak of the Zapatista revolt in the tropical rainforests of Chiapas was planned to occur precisely on the day the neoliberal North American Free Trade Agreement took effect: 1 January 1994. The 'Five Days that Shook the World' in late November 1999, radiating outward from the epicentre of Seattle, Washington, further consolidated the globalization of anti-globalization protest. As the world systems theorists Giovanni Arrighi, Terence K. Hopkins and Immanuel Wallerstein noted in the following five short sentences: 'There have only been two world revolutions. One took place in 1848. The second took place in 1968. Both were historical failures. Both transformed the world.'[30]

FURTHER READING

Serious attention to the Long Sixties has only become a mainstream historiographical concern since, roughly, the thirtieth anniversary of '1968'. Two attempts at an overall survey, both published in 1998, set new standards for investigation: Arthur Marwick, *The Sixties. Cultural Revolution in Britain, France, Italy and the United States* (Oxford: Oxford University Press, 1998), and the ambitious project edited by Philipp Gassert and Detlef Junker, *1968. The World Transformed* (Cambridge: Cambridge University Press, 1998). Also in 1998 appeared the still today superior pictorial history of global 1968, Tariq Ali and Susan Watkins (eds), *1968. Marching in the Streets* (New York: Free Press, 1998). The only major English-language analyses with a transnational remit to emerge from the fortieth anniversary celebrations have been Gerd-Rainer Horn, *The Spirit of 1968. Rebellion in Western Europe and North America, 1956–1976* (Oxford: Oxford University Press, 2007), and the edited volume by Martin Klimke and Joachim Scharloth, *1968 in Europe. A History of Protest and Activism, 1956–1977* (New York: Palgrave, 2008). New standards for a global vision may be established by Samantha Christiansen & Zachary A. Scarlett (eds), *The Third World in the Global 1960s* (Oxford: Berghahn, 2012). Until 1998, autobiographical testimonials were the key literary products casting light on the background to the societal upheavals under discussion here. Rather than listing them separately, I will mention the few truly noteworthy English-language (auto-)biographies in the relevant paragraphs below. An early and enormously useful and evocative series of interview excerpts with activists of the sixties generation from around the world was Ronald Fraser, *1968. A Student Generation in Revolt* (New York: Pantheon, 1988). A recent study based on similar oral history techniques is Robert Gildea, James Mark and Anette Warring (eds), *Europe's 1968. Voices of Revolt* (Oxford: Oxford University Press, 2013).

---

[30] Giovanni Arrighi, Terence K. Hopkins and Immanuel Wallerstein, *Antisystemic Movements* (London: Verso, 1989), p. 97.

For 'The Belgian Contribution to Global 1968', see my article with this title in the *Revue belge d'Histoire contemporaine/Belgisch Tijdschrift voor Nieuwste Geschiedenis* 35 2005), pp. 597–635. Still the superior English-language study of the Italian Sixties is Robert Lumley, *States of Emergency: Cultures of Revolt from 1968 to 1978* (London: Verso, 1990). There exists no truly satisfactory English-language monograph of the Sixties in Germany; perhaps the most fruitful key to West and East Germany realities is now Susanne Rinner, *The German Student Movement and the Literary Imagination* (Oxford: Berghahn, 2013). On the French May, the standard reference work remains Daniel Singer, *Prelude to Revolution: France in May 1968* (Cambridge, MA: South End Press, 2002), first published in 1970. For a very recent stimulating survey of the British dimension of 1968, see Celia Hughes, *Young Lives on the Left. Sixties Activism and the Liberation of the Self* (Manchester: Manchester University Press, 2015). Greece has now been covered in two first-rate English-language studies: Kostis Kornetis, *Children of the Dictatorship. Student Resistance, Cultural Politics, and the 'Long 1960s' in Greece* (Oxford: Berghahn, 2013), and Nikolaos Papadogiannis, *Militant Around the Clock? Left-Wing Youth Politics, Leisure, and Sexuality in Post-Dictatorship Greece, 1974–1981* (Oxford: Berghahn, 2015). No English-language monographs exist on 1968 in Poland or Yugoslavia. On the Prague Spring, Z. A. B. Zeman, *Prague Spring: A Report on Czechoslovakia 1968* (Harmondsworth: Penguin, 1968) is still the optimal introduction.

A wealth of publications covers the American Sixties. An inevitably highly selective list of recommended titles includes Steven Watson, *The Birth of the Beat Generation. Visionaries, Rebels, and Hipsters, 1944–1960* (New York: Pantheon, 1995), for the crucial prehistory; Morris Dickstein, *Gates of Eden. American Culture in the Sixties* (Cambridge, MA: Harvard University Press, 1997), first published in 1977; still the best insider account of the anti-Vietnam War movement, the much neglected Fred Halstead, *Out Now! A Participant's Account of the American Movement Against the Vietnam War* (New York: Monad, 1978); Sara Evans, *Personal Politics: The Roots of Women's Liberation in the Civil Rights Movement and the New Left* (New York: Vintage, 1980); and, last but not least, the two gems penned by Norman Mailer, *The Armies of the Night. History as Novel—The Novel as History* (New York: Plume, 1994), first published in 1968, and *Miami and the Siege of Chicago: An Informal History of the American Political Conventions of 1968* (Harmondsworth: Penguin, 1968). The Asturian-Mexican historian and journalist, Paco Ignacio Taibo, has written what is probably the very best of the large number of autobiographical accounts to emerge from any national context, his memoirs of the Mexican student movement, translated as *1968* (New York: Seven Stories Press, 2003). The best English-language compendium volume to Taibo's literary narrative is now Jaime M. Pensado, *Rebel Mexico. Student Unrest and Authoritarian Political Culture During the Long Sixties* (Stanford: Stanford University Press, 2013).

Some essential English-language volumes on the important but much-misunderstood phenomenon of cultural non-conformity in the run-up to 1968, as well as its aftermath, are: Dennis McNally, *Desolate Angel. Jack Kerouac, the Beat Generation, and America* (New York: McGraw-Hill, 1979); Theodore Roszak, *The Making of a Counter Culture. Reflections on the Technocratic Society and its Youthful Opposition* (London: Faber & Faber, 1971); Dark Star (ed.), *Beneath the Paving Stones. Situationists and the Beach, May 1968* (Edinburgh: AK Press, 2001); Mike Marqusee, *Wicked Messenger: Bob Dylan and the 1960s—Chimes of Freedom* (New York: Seven Stories Press, 2006); John Tytell, *The Living Theatre. Art, Exile and Outrage* (London: Methuen Drama, 1995); Jon Wiener, *Come Together. John Lennon in His Time* (Champaign, IL: University of Illinois Press, 1984); Tom Behan, *Dario Fo. Revolutionary Theatre* (London: Pluto, 2000); Jonathon Green, *All Dressed Up. The Sixties and the Counterculture* (London: Pimlico, 1998); Sheila Rowbotham, *Promise of a Dream: Remembering the Sixties* (London: Verso, 2000); and the sole English-language study of the enormously influential Dutch Provo revolt, Richard Kempton, *Provo. Amsterdam's Anarchist Revolt* (Edinburgh: AK Press, 2007).

There exists only one truly transnational survey of the much-neglected working-class dimension of 1968 in English, Colin Crouch and Alessandro Pizzorno (eds), *The Resurgence of Class Conflict in Western Europe since 1968* (London: Macmillan, 1978). For some excellent local, regional or national studies, note the outstanding Dan Georgakas and Marvin Surkin, *Detroit. I do Mind Dying. A Study in Urban Revolution* (Cambridge, MA: South End Press, 1998), first published in 1975; Ralph Darlington and Dave Lyddon, *Glorious Summer. Class Struggle in Britain, 1972* (London: Bookmarks, 2001); and a key work on the today almost completely forgotten highlight of post-1968 radical protest culture in Europe, Nancy Bermeo, *The Revolution Within the Revolution. Workers' Control in Rural Portugal* (Princeton: Princeton University Press, 1986). A marvellous reconstruction of the much-neglected working-class dimension of the Prague Spring remains Vladimir Fišera, *Workers' Councils in*

Czechoslovakia, 1968–1969: Documents and Essays (London: Allison and Busby, 1978). Last but not least, the recent study by Frank Bardacke, *Trampling Out the Vintage: Cesar Chavez and the Two Souls of the United Farm Workers* (London: Verso, 2011), a pathbreaking monograph on a formative labour movement in the global Sixties, is likely to become a key reference work for some years to come.

There exist preciously few English-language book-length studies on the central contribution by Christian activists to the spirit of 1968. As there are virtually no such monographs on continental Europe to date, I take the liberty of listing my *The Spirit of Vatican II: Western European Progressive Catholicism in the Long Sixties* (Oxford: Oxford University Press, 2015). There are, by contrast, a number of solid studies of radical Christian activism in the United States, notably James J. Farrell, *The Spirit of the Sixties. The Making of Postwar Radicalism* (New York: Routledge, 1997); Sara M. Evans (ed.), *Journeys That Opened up the World. Women, Student Christian Movements, and Social Justice, 1955–1975* (New Brunswick, NJ: Rutgers University Press, 2003); and the recent study by Mark S. Massa S. J. with the optimistic title *The American Catholic Revolution. How the 1960s Changed the Church Forever* (New York: Oxford University Press, 2010).

Last but not least, I wish to note a series of interviews with the leading post-Second World War Marxist intellectual and activist Ernest Mandel, *Revolutionary Marxism Today* (London: NLB, 1979). This long out-of-print paperback provides an excellent point of entry into the mindset of a generation of far left activists which accounted for a crucial portion of the volatility, promise and inner drive behind the social movements of 'global 1968'. My own assessment of '1968' as a virtuous interactive cycle of three different sectors of global anti-elite revolt owes much to the closely related analysis put forth by this Flemish Trotskyist.

CHAPTER 19

Terrorism between Social Movements, the State and Media Societies

Klaus Weinhauer

INTRODUCTION

Terrorism is a highly disputed term. In 2004 Charles Tilly postulated:

> The terms terror, terrorism and terrorist do not identify causally coherent and distinct social phenomena but strategies that recur across a wide variety of actors and political situations (…). Terrorism is not a single causally coherent phenomenon.[1]

Research on terrorism and on social movements both mainly originate in the turbulent 1960s, when social movements, student protests, urban riots and acts of political violence gained massive public attention.[2] The point

[1] Charles Tilly, 'Terror, Terrorism, Terrorists', *Sociological Theory* 1 (2004), pp. 5–13.
[2] See on terrorism research: Jacob L. Stump and Priya Dixit, *Critical Terrorism Studies. An Introduction to Research Methods* (London: Routledge, 2013); Alex P. Schmid (eds), *The Routledge Handbook of Terrorism Research* (London: Routledge, 2013); Marie Breen-Smyth (ed.), *The Ashgate Research Companion to Political Violence* (Burlington: Ashgate, 2012); Jonathan A. Matusitz, *Terrorism and Communication. A Critical Introduction* (Thousand

K. Weinhauer (✉)
Department of Germany, University of Bielefeld, Bielefeld, Germany

© The Author(s) 2017
S. Berger, H. Nehring (eds.), *The History of Social Movements in Global Perspective*, DOI 10.1057/978-1-137-30427-8_19

543

of departure of these two scholarly fields was, however, very different. 1970s terrorism research, mostly originating in the United States, analysed militant organizations in Latin America and in Cuba, as these areas were deemed to be the regions of origin of terrorism. Especially after 11 September 2001 many terrorism studies tended to have close ties to the state and to governmental policy. Today we also find 'critical terrorism studies', often written from the background of surveillance studies, whose authors criticize blind spots of terrorism research that is too uncritically related to governmental politics. Meanwhile we also find media science studies following discursive approaches. Although during the 1970s and early 1980s considerable scholarship emerged on the history of nineteenth-century anarchism in Europe and also on leading anarchists (Bakunin, Kropotkin, Malatesta, Most). Works on terrorism written by professional historians, however, still are not abundant.[3]

This is not the place to outline broadly how social movement research developed.[4] When compared to mainstream terrorism research the bulk of social movement research has taken a more critical stance toward official politics at least since the 1970s. Some authors had close personal ties to some of these movements, and this fostered critical reflection about the

---

Oaks, CA: Sage, 2013); Louise Richardson (ed.), *The Roots of Terrorism* (London: Routledge, 2006); Louise Richardson, *What Terrorists Want: Understanding the Terrorist Threat* (London: Murray, 2006).

[3] See as early historical studies Walter Laqueur, *Terrorismus* (Kronberg: Athenäum, 1977); Wolfgang J. Mommsen and Gerhard Hirschfeld (eds), *Sozialprotest, Gewalt, Terror: Gewaltanwendung durch politische und gesellschaftliche Randgruppen im 19. und 20. Jahrhundert* (Stuttgart: Klett-Cotta, 1982); Peter H. Merkl (ed.), *Political Violence and Terror: Motifs and Motivation* (Berkeley: University of California Press, 1986). See as latest research Sylvia Schraut and Klaus Weinhauer (eds), *Terrorism, Gender, and History: State of Research, Concepts, Case Studies* (Special issue of *Historical Social Research* 3, 2014); Beatrice de Graaf, *Evaluating Counterterrorism Performance. A Comparative Study* (London: Routledge, 2011); Donald Bloxham and Robert Gerwarth (eds), *Political Violence in Twentieth Century Europe* (Cambridge: Cambridge University Press, 2011); Klaus Weinhauer and Jörg Requate (eds), *Gewalt ohne Ausweg? Terrorismus als Kommunikationsprozess in Europa seit dem 19. Jahrhundert* (Frankfurt am Main: Campus, 2012); Robert Gerwarth and Heinz-Gerhard Haupt (eds), *Terrorism in Twentieth-Century Europe. Transnational and Comparative Perspectives* (Special Edition of *European Review of History* 14, 2007).

[4] On social movement research see the introduction of this volume, and: Donatella Della Porta, 'Social Movement Studies and Political Violence', in Breen-Smyth, *Political Violence*, pp. 243–260; as an outstanding comparative sociological study idem., *Social Movements, Political Violence, and the State. A Comparative Analysis of Italy and Germany* (Cambridge: Cambridge University Press, 1995).

relationship between scholarly research and movement activities. Many studies on social movements aimed to demonstrate that collective public protest was not born out of an irrational rage of misled masses but could contribute to the modernization of society and the political system. Social movement approaches contributed in several important ways to enhancing the analytic capacities of terrorism research. These studies reminded us that terrorism is not mainly the act of mentally disturbed personalities; rather, social milieux are highly important for militant activists. Moreover, it has also been stressed that terrorist militants originated in social movements. This led to the insight that state actions were instrumental in politically radicalizing movement activists. If their protests were mainly met with police or military repression, they could become convinced that they could reach their aims only by resorting to more militant actions and even by going underground. Moreover, security forces and terrorist groups can easily become trapped in processes of mutual escalation in which each side claims it is reacting to the opponent's violence.[5]

Terrorist groups quite easily can become locked into a dynamic of radicalization and social isolation that is reinforced by living an isolated, clandestine existence in the underground. De-individualization often goes hand in hand with a growing dependence on other group members, and strong internal emotional ties develop. The social isolation of the illegal group contributes to a growing radicalization of actions and of thinking. In these situations, ideology, or in some cases religion, can function as media of compensation. This process is often accompanied by the invention of particular rituals and symbols. The underground lifestyle helps foster images of heroic-elites or martyrdom (often with pre-modern resonances) and makes the group immune to social realities. Thinking and acting follows only black and white terms, leaving no space for differentiation. A hermetic culture develops in which ideology and religion can serve to support the recruitment and mobilization of new activists.

To study terrorism solely with reference to social movement approaches would raise some problems, among which the most important are definitions and terminology. Over the years a definition of social movements promoted by Dieter Rucht has gained prominence: Social movements are 'a network of individuals, groups and organizations that, based on a sense of collective identity, seek to bring about social change (or resist social change)

---

[5] See Peter Waldmann, *Terrorismus: Provokationen der Macht* (Munich: Gierling, 1998), pp. 163–177; see also Richardson, *Terrorists*, pp. 69ff.

primarily be means of collective protest' (see his Chap. 2 in this volume). It is this last phrase, with its focus on collective protest (not explicitly on violence), which makes the inclusion of terrorism problematic. To overcome this problem the few social movement studies interested in the analysis of terrorism have focused on political violence.[6] But even they are confronted with the problem that terrorist acts are often labelled as criminal and not as political actions. Thus, these studies can either choose to ignore these labelling processes or try to find a 'real' definition of political violence, which, however, comes close to the task of finding the last number.

To overcome these and other problems I would again underline that terrorism is not a coherent movement or entity. Rather, the label 'terrorist/terrorism' aims to delegitimize social movements, political groups, individuals and so on. Important heuristic clarifications on defining terrorism have been provided by the sociologist Peter Waldmann and the political scientist Louise Richardson.[7] They see terrorism as a specific form of political violence carried out by sub-state groups that plan and execute their politically motivated violent actions from a semi-legal or illegal milieu against civilians and against state institutions. The choice of victims and the type of terrorist act are of symbolic importance and aim to spread insecurity and win sympathy.[8]

Against the background of this definition, recent historical studies have fruitfully employed an approach that puts the communicative aspects of terrorism at the forefront: terrorism is a pattern of communication. This, however, must not be interpreted in a way that the media are to blame for ongoing terrorist attacks, rather, the main message is to integrate terrorism into a complex process of communication of different actors. Decoding these processes of communication helps in the analysis of the political, social and cultural repercussions terrorism has. Among these communication-based entanglements of terrorism, interactions with the state (and the perception of the state and its actions) and with media societies are of highest importance.

First, among the potential addressees of terrorist communication, the state is of key importance. Although terrorist actions also communicate

---

[6] Della Porta, 'Social Movements'.

[7] See Waldmann, *Terrorismus*, p. 10 and 13; Richardson, *Terrorists*. In this paper the terms 'militants', 'activists', and 'terrorists' are used synonymously.

[8] Waldmann, *Terrorismus*, p. 19; on milieus see Stefan Malthaner and Peter Waldmann (eds), *Radikale Milieus. Das soziale Umfeld terroristischer Gruppen* (Frankfurt am Main: Campus, 2012).

to sympathizers, supportive milieux or even competing groups, the state cannot avoid taking action, as its monopoly of physical violence is challenged. These state (re)actions, in turn, are integrated into broader social processes of communication and are telling examples of how state actions are socially perceived. Second, the agenda-setting qualities of terrorism are not confined to some news headlines or the mere production of front-page images. The fact that actions of terrorists are publicly discussed is a consequence of media societies developing in Western societies since the late nineteenth century. While early in that century it was important for political militants to choose high-ranking personalities (politicians, state officials, kings) as targets, by the later decades of the nineteenth century media coverage could generate a great deal of public attention even if only formerly unknown persons or buildings were attacked. To put it briefly: terrorism not only interacts with some media, but with media societies. In media societies, social processes and media communication are closely interwoven. Media do not just passively transmit information: they also set agendas by presenting, interpreting and discussing terrorist acts and related state actions. Media can generate wide public attention by communicating terrorists' messages. We must recognize, however, that media at the same time generate follow-up communication: terrorists are thus challenged by the media coverage of their actions. In this setting, militants have to ask themselves: what do we really want to achieve besides simply gaining public attention? Are we willing and able to communicate our aims to the public and thus stand the test of a public debate?

Since the nineteenth century a modus of communication has dominated public discourses on terrorism, where nearly all parties involved have been using binary codes of Them versus Us. In recent years, however, a new branch of historically oriented research has focussed on victims of state terror and of terrorist attacks.[9] These studies are not only about individual victims but also about their abilities to build social movements in urban

---

[9] Peter Lambert, 'National identity, Conflict and Political Violence. Experiences in Latin America', in Breen-Smyth, *Research*, pp. 281–300; Francesca Lessa and Vincent Druliolle (eds), *The Memory of State Terrorism in the Southern Cone. Argentina, Chile, and Uruguay* (Basingstoke: Palgrave Macmillan, 2011); Birgit Schwelling (ed.), *Reconciliation, Civil Society, and the Politics of Memory. Transnational Initiatives in the twentieth century* (Bielefeld: Transcript, 2012); Tanja Zimmermann (ed.), *Balkan Memories. Media Constructions of National and Transnational History* (Bielefeld: Transcript, 2012); Ernst Halbmayer and Sylvia Karl (eds), *Die erinnerte Gewalt. Postkonfliktdynamiken in Lateinamerika* (Bielefeld: Transcript, 2012).

civil societies. These publications draw our attention to two important questions: How could a third player emerge in this formerly extremely polarized setting and what was specifically urban about terrorism?

There are more challenging questions for future terrorism and social movement research. On the one hand it seems analytically fruitful to employ a communication-based approach which gives high priority to interaction with the state and with media societies and to the analysis of social movements. This would include an understanding of political violence which explicitly realizes that in a communication-based process all violent actions can be labelled as political—whether the original activists intended this or not. Second, although some studies of social movements have integrated emotional aspects, it would be very promising to integrate the findings of authors like Randall Collins who has convincingly demonstrated that it is not easy for most people to actively employ physical violence.[10] Studying these emotion-based micro-processes could help to better understand the dynamics of radicalization, the problems of group cohesion and also the emotional processes leading to terrorist acts.

As historical studies do not dominate in terrorism research, periodization of terrorism still is an important issue. Focusing on the interaction of terrorism, social movements, the state and the media five overlapping phases from the mid-nineteenth until the early twenty-first century can be discerned.[11] The first phase of terrorism began in the final quarter of the

---

[10] Randall Collins, *Violence. A Micro-Sociological Theory* (Princeton, NJ: Princeton University Press, 2008).

[11] More details are given in Klaus Weinhauer and Jörg Requate, 'Terrorismus als Kommunikationsprozess: Eskalation und Deeskalation politischer Gewalt in Europa seit dem 19. Jahrhundert', in Weinhauer andRequate, *Gewalt*, pp. 11–47; Heinz-Gerhard Haupt and Klaus Weinhauer, 'Terrorism and the State', in Bloxham and Gerwarth, *Political Violence*, pp. 176–209: My study does not follow David Rapport's classification of terrorism into four waves; see David C. Rapoport, 'The Four Waves of Modern Terrorism', in idem. (ed.), *Terrorism. Critical Concepts in Political Science*, 4 vols (London: Routledge, 2006), vol 4: pp. 3–30: The first or anarchist wave of terrorism started in the second half of the nineteenth century and lasted until the First World War. The anti-colonial terrorist wave began in the 1920s and peaked in the 1940s and 1950s. The New Left wave of terrorism mainly stretched from the 1960s until the 1980s, and the wave of religious terrorism started in the 1980s and intensified during the next decade. Rapoport's model has some analytical problems: it does not give clear criteria of how to precisely define the four phases; it also has little to say about the social roots/social milieu of terrorists; it omits the communicative elements of terrorism; and it has problems with integrating ethno-nationalist terrorism—the IRA is discussed in the anti-colonial as well as in the New Left phase of terrorism, while the Basque ETA is completely neglected.

nineteenth century. This period was shaped by militant actors who either had close ties to the labour movement or to radical intellectual milieux. Moreover, global militant nationalist movements were active in this period (Africa, India, Ottoman Empire, Balkans). The second, right-wing phase of terrorism was mainly a European phenomenon which began after the First World War and stretched well into the 1930s. When compared to post-1914 nationalist violence, inter-war right-wing terrorism developed a strong paramilitary culture, which was not only inspired by nationalism but also by anti-bolshevism and anti-Semitism. A third phase of terrorist violence, with a strong anti-colonial focus, emerged in the mid-1930s and continued through the Second World War until the 1980s. In the colonies, fears of nationalist and bolshevist revolutions fostered violent confrontations between colonial rulers and anti-colonial militants as self-appointed 'freedom fighters' (a term invented during the period). This chapter also analyses the militant actions of European ethno-nationalist activists against their perceived oppressors. A fourth phase of terrorism, associated with the New Left, globally emerged during the manifold cultural and political upheavals since the 1960s and stretched until the demise of the socialist states in the late-1980s and early-1990s.

In the fifth phase, religiously-motivated terrorism of the post-1980s period is analysed. Given the many problems inherent in this term, four qualifications need to be made.[12] First, religious convictions do not lead per se to terrorism. Religious communities resort to violent means when experiencing political and social isolation and when feeling under threat. Second, acts of religious terrorism are not only committed by Islamist groups but also by Christian fundamentalists such as Timothy McVeigh in 1995 or (in an earlier period) Jewish militants such as the Irgun. Third, religious, political, nationalist and even local concerns are often very closely related and are thus hard to separate. Anti-colonial violence had a religious character, as nationalism was articulated through local religions. Fourth, the motivations of religious terrorists stem from at least two sources: from individual religious beliefs and from an imagined transnational religious community, such as the global Islamist *Umma*. Recent patterns have led

---

[12] Overviews on religious terrorism are given by Richardson, *Terrorists*; Mark Juergensmeyer, *Terror in the Mind of God: The Global Rise of Religious Violence*, 3rd rev. and updated edition (Berkeley: University of California Press, 2007); Mark Sageman, *Leaderless Jihad. Terrors Networks in the Twenty-First Century* (Philadelphia: University of Pennsylvania Press, 2008); Bruce Hoffman, *Terrorismus—der unerklärte Krieg. Neue Gefahren politischer Gewalt* (Frankfurt am Main: Reclam, 2001).

some authors to speak of 'transnational terrorism'. This term, however, tends to neglect the local roots (the radical milieu) as well as individual belief systems of (religious) terrorists. A religious terrorist does not solely act as a 'homeless ... modern nomad' who is only symbolically connected with like-minded individuals. He or she inevitably has connections with certain social milieu.[13]

The following overview focuses on sub-state terrorism and its repertoires (Tilly) of violent action since the late nineteenth century in its relation to social movements, to the state and to media-based communication. Moreover, it will investigate how terrorists communicated with supportive social milieux, how urban terrorist militants became radicalized and how terrorism might be pacified. The geographical focus of this article will mainly be on Europe, Africa, Latin America and the United States.

ANARCHIST AND NATIONALIST TERRORISM (C. 1870–1914)

Until the mid-nineteenth century the term terror/terrorism mainly referred to the state-induced terror of the French revolution.[14] Since then, however, liberal elites have become more and more integrated into parliamentary politics and institutions, and started to perceive the organized lower classes and their collective actions, rather than an unrestrained state, as the principal threat to peaceful order. During the nineteenth century the label 'terrorism' was not widely used; 'anarchism' was often used as a substitute. Both terms came to be associated principally with social revolutionary movements (anarchist, anarcho-syndicalist) and struggles for national independence. Since the second half of the nineteenth century terrorism has been closely related to two major developments[15]: the emergence of the modern state, which at least in Europe effectively claimed a monopoly over physical force, and the rise of mass media societies.

Anarchist violence evolved across different countries and under a variety of conditions. Violent actions later labelled as terroristic/anarchistic grew

---

[13] Ulrich Schneckener, *Transnationaler Terrorismus: Charakter und Hintergründe des 'neuen' Terrorismus* (Frankfurt am Main: Suhrkamp, 2006), p. 49f.

[14] Rudolf Walther, 'Terror, Terrorismus', in Otto Brunner, Werner Conze, Reinhart Koenselleck (eds), *Geschichtliche Grundbegriffe. Historisches Lexikon zur politisch-sozialen Sprache in Deutschland*, Vol. 6 (Stuttgart: Klett-Cotta, 1990), pp. 323–444.

[15] See Weinhauer and Requate, 'Einleitung'.

out of labour disputes and strikes. Moreover, there also were many gendered cycles of revenge: a male anarchist threw a bomb, he was punished, and another male anarchist took revenge for that through another violent action.[16] Militants also explicitly attacked the ruling classes and their supporters and aimed to destabilize the existing political order. Terrorist actions sought to mobilize exploited rural and urban classes, sometimes using the famous 'propaganda of the deed'. The latter pattern was an important consequence of the European state's ability after the 1870s to establish its monopoly of physical violence against riots and strikes. Thus, a new pattern of violent action had to be invented: the propaganda of the deed, which was, however, a tactic not generally accepted even in the radical factions of the labour movement.[17] Anarchist violence was also used in countries where the legal means of defending popular interests were non-existent or dysfunctional.[18] In Western Europe, anarchists usually remained a small minority inside the wider labour movement. Parallel to the militant actions of anarchists and revolutionary syndicalists there also was global nationalist terrorism. In order to obtain political autonomy or independence national minorities in the Africa, India, the Balkans and across the Ottoman Empire used violence to sway European public opinion and promote social and political reforms.[19]

As the plentiful, high-quality research underlines, in the late nineteenth and early twentieth century anarchism and the campaigns to fight it could be found in Europe, the United States, Africa, Asia, China and Latin America.[20] This global presence of anarchism and syndicalism was

[16] Jörg Requate, 'Die Faszination anarchistischer Attentate im Frankreich des ausgehenden 19. Jahrhunderts', in Weinhauer and Requate, *Gewalt*, pp. 99–119.

[17] Ibid.; Alexander Sedlmaier, 'The Consuming Visions of Late Nineteenth-and Early Twentieth-century Anarchists: Actualising Political Violence Transnationally', *European Review of History* 3 (2007), pp. 283–301.

[18] For the different styles of labour movement mobilization see Geoff Eley, *Forging Democracy: the History of the Left in Europe, 1850–2000* (Oxford: Oxford University Press, 2002).

[19] Christopher A. Bayly, *Die Geburt der modernen Welt. Eine Globalgeschichte 1780–1914* (Frankfurt am Main: Campus, 2008), p. 576.

[20] Steven Hirsch and Lucien van der Walt, 'Rethinking anarchism and syndicalism. The colonial and postcolonial experience, 1870–1940', in Steven Hirsch and Lucien van der Walt (eds), *Anarchism and Syndicalism in the Colonial and Postcolonial World, 1870–1940. The Praxis of National Liberation, Internationalism, and Social Revolution* (Leiden: Brill 2010), pp. 31–74; see also Benedict Anderson, *Under three Flags: Anarchism and Anti-Colonial Imagination* (London: Verso, 2005).

rooted in the dense international networks upheld by a highly mobile anarchist elite and sustained by labour migration and forced migration due to political persecution, and transnational flows of money from anarchist communities dispersed all over the world.[21] Another highly important factor was that anarchists all over the world imagined themselves as being part of an international movement, a belief fuelled by the numerous anarchist newspapers that meticulously reported on activities of anarchists and syndicalists all over the world. These newspapers and anarchist clubs were widespread, but especially prominent in urban settings—often in port cities and state capitals, as here many networks overlapped and formed nodes of intense communication. Moreover, working and living conditions in some branches fostered the anarcho-syndicalist tendencies that were especially strong among highly mobile workers with no explicit craft traditions, among whom were many workers associated with the transport trade, such as seamen and dock workers, but also lumberjacks, and casually employed building, mining, shipyard and agrarian labourers.[22]

When looking at the self-conscious violent actions anarchists undertook in public spaces of Latin American cities—in early twentieth century Sao Paulo (Brasil) the police 'promoted the equation anarchism = terrorism'[23]—two special reasons must be taken into consideration. First, the strong presence of anarchism and syndicalism and their militant patterns

[21] José C. Moya, *Cousins and strangers. Spanish Immigrants in Buenos Aires, 1850–1930* (Berkeley: California University Press, 1998); Davide Turcato, 'Italian Anarchism as a Transnational Movement, 1885–1915', *International Review of Social History* 3 (2007), pp. 407–444; Kirwin R. Shaffer, 'By Dynamite, Sabotage, Revolution, and the Pen: Violence in Caribbean Anarchist Fiction, 1890s–1920s', *New West Indian Guide* 83 (2009), pp. 5–39, pp. 1–2; Kirwin R. Shaffer, 'Havana Hub: Cuban Anarchism, Radical Media and the Trans-Caribbean Anarchist Network, 1902–1915', *Caribbean Studies* 2 (2010), pp. 45–82; Kirk Shaffer, 'Tropical Libertarians. Anarchist Movements and Networks in the Carribean, Southern United States, and Mexico 1980s–1920s', in Steven Hirsch and Lucien van der Walt (eds), *Anarchism*, pp. 273–320.

[22] See Marcel van der Linden and Wayne Thorpe (eds), *Revolutionary Syndicalism. An International Perspective* (Aldershot: Scolar Press, 1990); Hirsch and Van der Walt, *Anarchism*; with case studies by Stefan Berger; Andy Croll and Norman Laporte (eds), *Towards a Comparative History of Coalfield Societies* (Aldershot: Ashgate, 2005); Klaus Weinhauer, 'Labour Market, Work Mentality and Syndicalism : Dock Labour in the United States and Hamburg 1900–1950s', *International Review of Social History* 2 (1997), pp. 219–252.

[23] Edilene Toledo and Luigi Biondi, 'Constructing Syndicalism and Anarchism Globally. The Transnational Making of the Syndicalist Movement in Sao Paulo', in Hirsch and Van der Walt, *Anarchism*, p. 387.

of action in the Caribbean and in Latin America have much to do with the use of public space. In these regions public space was open to a broad spectrum of communicative practices, including violent *and* peaceful protests. Thus, even in times of fierce repression, public space still was (well into the second half of the twentieth century) a resource that protestors could licitly resort to.[24] This use of public space marks a difference to the situation in Europe, where urban space became more and more regulated and the police suppressed demonstrations by the necessity to allow road traffic to flow undisturbed. Second, when compared to European countries like Germany and France, where the state more or less successfully maintained its monopoly of physical violence, in Latin America violent actions committed by anarchists in public spaces were less an expression of their fight against an abstract state than a manifestation of socially deeply rooted militant self-help tendencies.[25]

From the late nineteenth century onwards, states took up the fight against this new enemy, employing police forces, paramilitary organizations and in many cases the military. Police activities, however, should not automatically be interpreted as always being an effective machine of repression. In the Ottoman Empire, for example, the weakness of the army and police were proverbial. Even in Russia, where repression is seen to be very harsh, a closer look reveals that it 'was less efficiently policed' than its European neighbours.[26] Capital punishment was less frequent than in other European countries. Russia sent a smaller portion of its population to Siberia than Britain shipped overseas and the French labour colonies had more victims per year than the ones in Siberia. Moreover, the police were also consciously used by local people to meet the challenges of everyday life.[27]

On a general level, the social movements and anarchist actions that sought to reveal the state's weaknesses and shake its legitimacy ultimately

---

[24] Anton Rosenthal, 'Spectacle, Fear, and Protest: A Guide to the History of Urban Public Space in Latin America', *Social Science History* 1 (2000), pp. 33–74.

[25] Peter Waldmann, 'Nachahmung mit begrenztem Erfolg. Zur Transformation des europäischen Staatsmodells in Lateinamerika', in Michael Riekenberg and Wolfgang Höpken (eds), *Politische und ethnische Gewalt in Südosteuropa und Lateinamerika* (Köln: Böhlau, 2001), pp. 19–35; Wolfgang Knöbl, 'Imperiale Herrschaft und Gewalt', *Mittelweg 36* 2 (2012), pp. 19–44.

[26] Jane Burbank, 'Securing Peasant Society', in Alf Lüdtke and Michael Wildt (eds), *Staats-Gewalt: Ausnahmezustand und Sicherheitsregimes. Historische Perspektiven* (Göttingen: Wallstein, 2008), p. 95.

[27] Ibid., p. 96ff.

contributed to its reinforcement. European police forces were successfully modernized and de-militarized, and national governments, assisted by the media, succeeded in transforming the image of the terrorist from a kind of social and political Robin Hood to a criminal.[28] Terrorist actions also motivated different European states to initiate international cooperation to look for common procedures and agreements to prosecute terrorists across borders, to exchange information regarding violent organizations and to apply international laws and regulations to control them.[29] At the 1898 anti-anarchist conference in Rome, however, the dangers posed by dynamite and political murder were not sufficiently strong to overcome nationalist tendencies and encourage long-lasting international agreements.

Anarchist violence was declining in countries where the legalistic and parliamentary strategies employed by socialists and Social Democrats prevailed, thus opening up political space and mechanisms of political participation. As the case of French urban terrorism of the last third of the nineteenth century demonstrates, the strong public attention generated by terrorist attacks or court performances of anarchists like Ravachol was usually short-lived: This media coverage put the anarchists under pressure to explicitly communicate what, beyond simple public attention, they wanted to achieve with their violent actions. After the 1890s their answers were interpreted as being unconvincing and the attention paid to their actions diminished.[30]

RIGHT-WING (EUROPEAN) TERRORISM OF THE INTERWAR YEARS

In a global perspective classical 'anarchist' terrorism decreased in the inter-war years.[31] This was a consequence of economic improvement, but also of the fact that in most European countries the labour movement could now function under improved legal conditions. After the First World War, the Bolsheviks gained massive media attention and took on the anarchist terrorist's mantle as Public Enemy Number 1. These com-

[28] Richard Bach Jensen, 'The International Campaign Against Anarchist Terrorism, 1880–1930s', *Terrorism and Political Violence* 1 (2009), pp. 89–109, p. 100.

[29] Ibid., passim; Heinz-Gerhard Haupt, 'Gewalt als Praxis und Herrschaftsmittel. Das Deutsche Kaiserreich und die Dritte Republik im Vergleich', in Cornelius Torp and Sven Oliver Müller (eds), *Das deutsche Kaiserreich in der Kontroverse* (Göttingen: Vandenhoeck & Ruprecht, 2009), p. 154ff.

[30] Requate, 'Faszination'.

[31] A brief summary is given by Jensen, 'Campaign', p. 101ff.

munists, however, had a disciplined attitude towards terrorism. Loyal to its notion of a more coordinated strategy of revolutionary action, the acts of violence committed by communist activists tended to be more organized, formalized and goal-oriented than the sometimes individualistic and symbol-laden 'propaganda of the deed'.[32] Nonetheless, during the depression years violence in working-class neighbourhoods was labelled as terroristic. These actions grew out of militant milieux that were only loosely connected to communist parties and organizations.[33] Moreover, during the inter-war years terrorism in Europe was overshadowed by other kinds of political violence—civil war and revolution. These violent actions absorbed media attention leaving little room for discourses on anarchism.

After 1918, however, terrorist attacks did still occur in several world regions like Latin America, the United States and Europe. In Spain and Italy but also in Latin America and the United States the militancy of pre-war labour relations remained relatively unchanged and anarchism or anarcho-syndicalism had strong footholds in the labour movement, at least until the late 1920s [34] In such countries where the monopoly of physical violence had eroded and was temporarily not accepted by sections of the working class there was frequent use of violence from all sides, especially between 1919 and 1923. In Catalonia, violent conflicts between government and employers on the one side and syndicalists and anarchists on the other led to 'conditions of quasi-civil war'.[35] This violence was not only exercised by social movements, but also by the government, employers and hired gunmen, who were employed on all sides. In Italy, anarchists exploded bombs in Milan (1920 and 1923) and Turin (1921). In France, Prime Minister Clemenceau was wounded by an anarchist in 1919. In the United States, labour-related terrorist violence featured letter-bombs to high officials, but also spectacular explosions such as the one at Wall Street

---

[32] Dirk Schumann, *Politische Gewalt in der Weimarer Republik 1918–1933: Kampf um die Straße und Furcht vor dem Bürgerkrieg* (Essen: Klartext, 2001); Thomas Lindenberger and Alf Lüdtke (eds), *Physische Gewalt. Studien zur Geschichte der Neuzeit* (Frankfurt am Main: Suhrkamp, 1995).

[33] See the recent volume Klaus Weinhauer, Anthony McElligott and Kirsten Heinsohn (eds), *Germany 1916–23. A Revolution in Context* (Bielefeld: transcript and New York: Columbia University Press, 2015); but also Eve Rosenhaft, *Beating the Fascists. The German Communists and Political Violence, 1929–1933* (Cambridge: Cambridge University Press, 1983).

[34] For these remarks see Jensen, 'Campaign'; for Barcelona see Chris Ealham, *Class, Culture and Conflict in Barcelona 1898–1937* (London: Routledge, 2005).

[35] Jensen, 'Campaign', 101.

in September 1920. In Latin America many strikes culminated in violent action which in turn led to brutal police reaction.

A 'new' type of nationalist political violence, a unique European form of right-wing or fascist terrorism, occurred in countries like Italy, Austria and Germany, and also in Spain after the First World War.[36] In contrast to the pre-war years these groups did not base their actions only on nationalism; European nationalist militants were strongly influenced by anti-communist and anti-bolshevist ideas, very often imbued with anti-Semitism. The violent actions of these European right-wing groups occurred mainly in countries which had lost the war or had lost large parts of their territory as a consequence of the war. They initiated massive acts of violence in order to destabilize these states. Post-war nationalists also struggled to win the media-based prerogative of interpretation of national memory especially when it came to the commemoration of the First World War and its consequences. As recent research has elaborated, right-wing militant activists constructed an efficient transnational network.

Political murder and attempted murder in Europe after the First World War was no longer motivated by purely political motives or acts of mere revenge. Multiple motives for assassination can be found, including personal interests and jealousies.[37] As Eric Hobsbawm has observed, there was a widespread belief that 'one's own cause is so just and the adversary's so terrible that all means to achieve victory or avoid defeat are not only legitimate but necessary.'[38] In Italy, opposition to the Fascist government led to the attempted assassination of Mussolini in the Diana Theatre in Milan in 1923.[39] In Bulgaria Petko Petkov (member of the agrarian party) was murdered in 1924. In Austria there was an attempt on the life of Chancellor Ignaz Seipel (1924) and on the mayor of Vienna, Karl Seitz (1927). In Romania the fascist Iron Guard killed a police prefect (1926). In Weimar Germany several leading politicians were killed by right-wing organizations (Rosa Luxemburg and Karl Liebknecht in January 1919,

---

[36] Robert Gerwarth and John Horne, 'The Great War and Paramilitarism in Europe, 1917–1923', *Contemporary European History* 19 (2010), pp. 267–273.

[37] See for the following Steven W. Sowards, *Moderne Geschichte des Balkans* (Seuzach: private print, 2004), p. 382f; Jensen, 'Campaign', p. 101ff; Gerhard Botz, *Krisenzonen der Demokratie. Gewalt, Streik und Konfliktunterdrückung in Österreich seit 1918* (Frankfurt am Main: Campus, 1987).

[38] Eric Hobsbawm, 'Terror', in idem., *Globalisation, Democracy and Terrorism* (London: Little, Brown, 2007), pp. 121–137, p. 127.

[39] Jensen, 'Campaign', p. 102.

Matthias Erzberger in August 1921 and Walther Rathenau in June 1922).[40] In Berlin in 1921–22 Turkish politicians were assassinated by Armenian nationalists.[41] In October 1934 three Croatian nationalists killed the king of Yugoslavia, Alexander, in Marseille.[42]

As the Turkish, Russian, German and many other cases demonstrate, the political murders of the Post-First World War years were part of a new culture of paramilitarism.[43] When compared with nineteenth-century anarchism, where not only men but also women were active, right-wing terrorism after the Great War was principally a male affair. In Germany, right-wing militants comprised former First World War veterans and younger men (among them many students) who had not participated in the war but instead mythologized a collective front-line experience. Many members of these militias later joined national socialist organizations. Public reaction towards right-wing murder in the Weimar Republic was characterized by degrees of sympathy and apologism, but there were also labour strikes and public proclamations defending the democratic republic. This ambivalence also held for the Law for the Protection of the Republic, which was passed in July 1922 by the Reichstag, though the federal states decided how it would be put into practice.[44] The attacks of right-wing activists of the 1920s were only the prelude for the terror practised by fascist regimes practised when they came to power.

ANTI-COLONIAL TERRORISM (C. 1920S–1990S)

Anti-colonial terrorism of national liberation movements emerged after the First World War and gained further momentum in the aftermath of the Second World War. In the 1920s, it is hard to disentangle anti-

[40] See for Germany Martin Sabrow, *Die verdrängte Verschwörung: der Rathenau-Mord und die deutsche Gegenrevolution* (Frankfurt am Main: Fischer, 1999); Klaus Gietinger, *Der Konterrevolutionär: Waldemar Pabst—ein deutsche Karriere* (Hamburg: Nautilus: 2009); still important is Emil Julius Gumbel, *Verschwörer. Zur Geschichte und Soziologie der deutschen nationalistischen Geheimbünde 1918–1924* (Frankfurt am Main: Fischer 1984, Orig: 1924).

[41] Rolf Hosfeld, *Operation Nemesis: die Türkei, Deutschland und der Völkermord an den Armeniern* (Cologne: Kiepenheuer & Witsch, 2005).

[42] Jensen, 'Campaign', p. 103.

[43] Gerwarth and Horne, 'Paramilitarism'; see on Anatolia: Ryan Gingeras, *Sorrowful Shores. Violence, Ethnicity, and the End of the Ottoman Empire, 1912–1923* (Oxford: Oxford University Press, 2009).

[44] See Dirk Schumann, *Politische Gewalt in der Weimarer Republik 1918–1933. Kampf um die Straße und Furcht vor dem Bürgerkrieg* (Essen: Klartext, 2001), pp. 170 and 310; Sabrow, Rathenau.

colonial terrorism from other forms of political violence.[45] National liberation movements came into being in the colonized regions in Africa and Asia but also in Europe. Some of these movements achieved their aims of building national states,[46] among them were the Irish Republican Army, the Jewish *Irgun Zwai Le'umi* (Irgun),[47] the Cypriot EOKA (National Organization of Cypriot Fighters) and the Algerian *Front de Libération Nationale* (FLN). Many of their militants had earlier participated in anti-colonial social movements, ranging from religious, nationalist to communist orientation. Anti-terrorist policies of the colonial states—be they bloody counter-insurgency tactics, or trials of alleged terrorists—played an important role in radicalizing these activists. In this context it must not be forgotten that the fierce police and military repression in European colonies did not come out of the blue. Often there were, even at the personal level, continuities to the brutal and oppressive labour conditions in the colonies. As Martin Thomas has put it in his analysis of the African, Southeast Asian and Caribbean colonial contexts, most of these protests 'were more industrial than national'.[48] In Europe after 1918 newly established states like Czechoslovakia and Poland, but also Germany, Italy, Spain and Portugal, struggled hard to establish police forces which were independent of armies (the latter often strongly anti-republican) and were willing and able to defend democracy against political enemies from left and right.[49] In the colonies, however, the police forces, as an institution of

---

[45] Ulrike Lindner, *Koloniale Begegnungen. Deutschland und Großbritannien als Imperialmächte in Afrika 1880–1914* (Frankfurt am Main: Campus, 2011).

[46] See David Rapoport, 'General Introduction',in idem, *Terrorism*, Vol 1, pp. 27–37, p. 31; Hoffman, *Terrorismus*, p. 61ff.

[47] See Abraham Askenasi, 'Social-Ethnic Conflict and Paramilitary Organization in the Near East', in Merkl, *Political Violence*, pp. 311–334; J. Bowyer Bell, *On Revolt. Strategies of national liberation* (Cambridge, MA: Harvard University Press, 1976), pp. 33–70. The Irgun in July 1946 bombed the King David Hotel in Jerusalem killing 91 people and thus gaining transnational attention; see Clarke Thurston, *By Blood and Fire. The Attack on the King David Hotel* (New York: Putnam, 1981).

[48] Martin Thomas, *Violence and Colonial Order. Police, Workers and Protest in the European Colonial Empires, 1918–1940* (Cambridge: Cambridge University Press, 2012), p. 325.

[49] See Gerald Blaney (ed.), *Policing Interwar Europe. Continuity, Change and Crisis* (Basingstoke: Palgrave Macmillan, 2007); Hsi-Huey Liang, *The Rise of Modern Police and the European State System from Metternich to the Second World War* (Cambridge: Cambridge University Press, 1992).

the 'gatekeeper state',[50] had a different task: here, policing was 'less about restoring colonial control than about imposing it.'[51]

Resistance to Nazism and to the policies of the Third Reich as an occupying power drew large numbers of Europeans, in the Soviet Union, the Balkans, Greece, France and Italy to name only a few, into acts of violence which were labelled as terrorist.[52] These activists, who can be characterized as anti-colonial militants, not only aimed at winning sympathy or spreading fear (especially among those who collaborated with the occupiers), but also wished to free territories from occupying forces using guerrilla tactics. Almost everywhere in German-occupied Europe cycles of violence and repression became a dominant feature of the final years of the war. Terror of the German regime blurred the dividing line between civilians and combatants to unprecedented degrees. As a consequence, terrorists in the post-1945 period were more prepared to kill not only members of the political elites, but also innocent parties, which in turn provoked harsh state reactions.

Urban settings, where large numbers of civilians of the enemy's camp were concentrated, made an ideal setting for (post-colonial) terrorist attacks, as news of the attack and about the aims of the militants could spread quickly.[53] In colonial Algeria over a million French and other ethnically European civilians lived close to each other when Arab and Berber Muslims rebelled against French rule in 1954. Thousands of terrorist attacks were launched, with more than 10,000 casualties during the nearly eight years of the rebellion. The attacks included the explosion of bombs hidden in restaurants and other European gathering places and also the killing and mutilation of European families surprised in their homes.

The post-1945 success of worldwide anti-colonial terrorism was due to several factors. Although many of these movements originated in the 1920 or 1930s,[54] the foundations for success were facilitated by the fact that the international community—most recently with the establishment of the United Nations—embraced the principle of self-determination. Diaspora groups and foreign states supported anti-colonial actions in ways unseen before. Anti-colonial militants portrayed themselves as freedom fighters,

---

[50] Frederick Cooper, *Decolonization and African Society. The Labor Question in French and British Africa* (Cambridge: Cambridge University Press, 1996).

[51] Thomas, *Violence*, p. 332.

[52] See Haupt and Weinhauer, 'Terrorism', p. 193f.

[53] Donald Black, 'The Geometry of Terrorism', *Sociological Theory* 22 (2004), pp. 14–25, p. 21f.

[54] See Haupt and Weinhauer, 'Terrorism'.

while states and mass media continued to describe them as terrorists. Further, anti-colonial terrorists eventually largely abandoned the tactics of killing representative members of the elites, and instead targeted members of police forces and bystanders. This forced colonial powers to reinforce the military, which did not solve the conflict but through its brutality mobilized many Algerians, for example, into the ranks of anti-colonial movements.[55] In addition, anti-colonial terrorists did not employ violence alone, but endeavoured to build effective political organizations that were well-structured and sensitive to social and political change. Finally, harnessing the rapidly growing media, anti-colonial militants were able to communicate their goals beyond local regions to transnational audiences.

This transnational media communication about anti-colonial movements, their actions and aims became quite intense. As the Kenyan Mau Mau between 1952 and 1956 'took up their weapons, the world press took up its pens.'[56] With all its ambivalence of describing the rebels as terrorists and primitive, this transnational media coverage heightened attention towards their aims. Simultaneously, US-based African Americans had become more aware of liberation struggles in South Africa, Kenya and Ghana, and newspaper reports increased the breadth and depth of feeling that change was possible. Thus the Mau-Mau rebellion also had strong impacts on African American freedom struggles in the United States. These fights against British troops became a 'powerful symbol of resistance'.[57] Simultaneously, the 'terrorism' of the white settlers and white government became known. Although the use of violence by Mau Mau freedom fighters was a contested issue among African Americans, their aim of ending white supremacy was widely shared. In the United States, African Americans had to fine-tune their solidarity campaigns for the Mau Mau carefully in a climate of Cold War paranoid fantasy with a strong

---

[55] See Alistair Horne, *A Savage War of Peace. Algeria 1954–1962* (New York: New York Review Books, 2006, Orig: London, 1977); Raphaelle Branche, 'The French State Faced with the Algerian Nationalists (1954–1962): A War against Terrorism', in Samy Cohen (ed.), *Democracies at War against Terrorism. A Comparative Perspective* (Basingstoke: Palgrave Macmillan, 2008), pp. 59–75; Paul Silverstein, *Algeria in France: Transpolitics, Race, and Nation* (Urbana: University of Illinois Press, 2004).

[56] James H. Meriwether, 'African Americans and the Mau Mau Rebellion: Militancy, Violence, and the Struggle for Freedom', *Journal of American Ethnic History* 4 (1998), pp. 63–86, p. 68.

[57] Ibid., 64.

anti-communist orientation in which supporting anti-colonial struggles could be easily equated with promoting communism.

The hijacking of airliners by the Palestine Liberation Organization (PLO) made terrorism a truly international phenomenon.[58] These actions, again communicated worldwide through the media, started in July 1968 with the hijacking of an Israeli El Al aeroplane travelling from Rome to Tel Aviv. Because El Al was state-owned, the hijacking forced the Israeli state to communicate directly with the terrorists who, in this case, demanded the release of imprisoned Palestinians. Moreover, this action illustrated that these terrorists did not hesitate to choose victims from any third-party state. During the 1972 Munich Olympics, the Israeli team was held hostage by the Palestine Group Black September. The move ended in bloodshed, with nine Israeli hostages, five terrorists and one policeman losing their lives. Although Black September did not achieve their immediate aims, the situation in Palestine moved to the centre of international media attention.

Ethno-nationalist struggles in 1960s Europe (in the Basque Country and in Northern Ireland) were a special case of anti-colonial activism. In Europe these movements shared three features: They often had a working-class background; their actions were less oriented towards left-wing social-ist revolutions than aimed at defending their ethnically homogenous local territories against states which were seen as colonial rulers; their activities often involved fighting against enemies living next door—sometimes in the same neighbourhood. These militants where no social outcasts but could benefit from their tight integration into ethnically homogenous quarters.

In the Basque Country, ETA (*Euskadi ta Askatasuna*) was founded in 1959 and fought against the cultural repression initiated by the Franco regime. ETA leaders viewed their country as a colony, occupied by a for-eign imperialist power, and emulated the guerrilla tactics employed in Latin American countries.[59] The Northern Irish case once again under-lines that fierce state repression can be instrumental in forging terrorism. In 1968–1969, a peaceful social movement of mostly Catholic groups from the middle classes met harsh repression by the police, which led to massive political radicalization among its followers.[60] Close-knit networks

---

[58] Hoffman, *Terrorismus*, p. 85f.

[59] Peter Waldmann, *Ethnischer Radikalismus. Ursachen und Folgen gewaltsamer Minderheitenkonflikte* (Opladen: Westdt. Verl, 1984), p. 119 and p. 125.

[60] See Niall ó Dochartaigh, 'Northern Ireland', in Martin Klimke and Joachim Scharloth (eds), *1968 in Europe. A History of Protest and Activism, 1956–1977* (Basingstoke: Palgrave

ranging from the family ties to the local neighbourhood set the stage for these bloody and long-enduring conflicts. Nationalism, violence and ethnicity together with myths, symbols and memories of the past were deeply entrenched in Basque as well as in Northern Irish societies, all these tools were mobilized to legitimize violent politics.

The example of the ETA draws our attention to gendered aspects of radical terrorist communities. Families could help bridge the gap between the private (traditional family culture) and the political (with its often harsh police repression)—and vice versa. Against the background of social and political transformations in Spain during the 1960s, which allowed women to take up factory jobs and also to take part in covert cultural and political activities in radical youth organizations, by the 1970s women began to join ETA on a larger scale.[61] A decade later, female membership of ETA had reached 10–15%, and roughly 8% of ETA prisoners were women. In joining the ranks of the militants, these women gained temporary access to ETA's male-dominated power structures. The life-histories of these early female activists underline the importance of their families, father and mother alike, in the process of radicalization. Many of the early female militants remembered their fathers as strong, politically active figures, which influenced their own politically inclined rebelliousness. The Basque nationalist discourse about the role of the family also influenced radicalization. In contrast to Italian female activists of 1968, who often distanced themselves from their mothers, the early female militants of ETA did not portray their mothers' roles as being confined to (passive) domestic duties and by male chauvinism. Against the background of intensified social change in the 1960s, motherhood in the Basque country came to signify the potential for future political rebellion.

Like their Basque colleagues, for militants in Northern Ireland, whether the Catholic-nationalist Irish Republican Army (IRA) or the Protestant-loyalist Ulster Volunteer Force (UVF) and Ulster Defence Association (UDA) paramilitary organizations, the interaction with the surrounding social milieu (the community, the neighbourhood) with its traditions, myths

Macmillan, 2008), pp. 137–152; Simon Prince, 'The Global Revolt of 1968 and Northern Ireland', *The Historical Journal* 3 (2006), pp. 851–875.

[61] The following is based on: Carrie Hamilton, 'Re-membering the Basque Nationalist Family: Daughters, Fathers and the Reproduction of the Radical Nationalist Community', *Journal of Spanish Cultural Studies* 1 (2000), pp. 153–171. These arguments are fully developed in Carrie Hamilton, *Women and ETA: The Gender Politics of Radical Basque Nationalism* (Manchester: Manchester University Press, 2007).

(especially about the 1916 Easter Rising) and imagined or real threats, was also highly important.[62] Spatial components were instrumental in influencing the conflict: it was about defending communities or neighbourhoods against perceived threats from the other side. Especially in post-1969 Northern Ireland, the official monopoly over physical violence was contested by the different paramilitary organizations that sought to undermine the legitimacy of the British Army and the RUC (Royal Ulster Constabulary). Moreover, the media landscape was even more fragmented, with each party in the conflict editing numerous newspapers, while the British press was distrusted and rumours became important in the internal communication processes.

The 1998 Good Friday Agreement was negotiated in an atmosphere of an extinguished Cold War and against the background of a positive international setting provided by the Blair and Clinton administrations. Moreover, since the mid/late 1980s, three changes on the local and on the global level interacted: the narrow local political spaces broadened. First, on the local level, channels of everyday communication between members of the opposing camps (including local state actors) were successfully established. Second, through this processes of local cooperation and communication and against the background of the growing importance given to the voices of the victims of political violence, the once-hermetic local cultures of remembrance eroded. This paved the way to put these local conflicts into perspective of a worldwide anti-colonial struggle and its transnational and translocal symbols. Third, the image of the enemy, the British state changed—it was normalized: the state and its institutions lost its authority as a mighty colonial ruler.[63] As a consequence of these three processes, political parties such as *Sinn Fein,* could successfully demonstrate the peace-building potential of inter-community cooperation and dialogue.

NEW LEFT TERRORISM (C. 1960S–1980S)

New Left terrorism was a form of terrorism that in its initial phase aimed at gaining the support of the working class. It developed out of a near-global feeling of societal dissatisfaction, which saw the existing consumer

---

[62] See Jeffrey A. Sluka, *Hearts and Minds, Water and Fish: Support for the IRA and INLA in a Northern Irish Ghetto* (Greenwich: JAI Press, 1989), p. 228f.

[63] See on the broader context of contemporary processes of de-constructing the nation Stefan Berger, Linas Eriksonas and Andrew Mycock (eds), *Narrating the Nation. Representations in History, Media and the Arts* (Oxford: Berghahn, 2011).

society, state structures and political order as inherently repressive and alienating. The social profile of New Left terrorism was mainly middle class (often students) with—depending on the country—a tiny percentage of working-class members. The militants were often in their mid-twenties and in some cases the proportion of female terrorists reached up to 30%.[64]

In Latin America the stage was set for the upsurge of New Left terrorism. In this region, since the late 1950s, especially after Fidel Castro's victory over the old Cuban regime, a long series of left-wing social revolutionary militant actions had been taking place. Some were committed by (rural) guerrillas, which, unlike terrorists, mostly aimed at occupying a physical territory—terrorists aimed at occupying the imagination (*'das Denken besetzen'*).[65] The anti-imperialist, social revolutionary aspirations of the bulk of Latin American militants planned to establish a social order based on the Cuban example. They found sympathies among the educated urban middle-classes, where critiques were voiced against the established social and political autocratic order with its immobility and ineffectiveness. The improved conditions for global communication and also expectations of an emerging mass consumer society led to growing expectations of economic and industrial restructuring. In this setting, radical change oriented on technological and organizational progress, even revolution, became imaginable.

In Latin America after the Cuban revolution rural guerrilla and terrorist actions became widespread. In Uruguay in 1965 the famous *Movimiento de Liberaciòn National Tupamaros (Tupamaros)* was founded.[66] The Tupamaros were mainly in their mid-twenties, among them 10–12% female activists.[67] Their members saw themselves in the tradition of Latin American anti-imperialist resistance, naming themselves after the last king of the Incas, Tupac Amaru. They created over a couple of years

[64] Klaus Weinhauer, 'Linksterrorismus der 1970er Jahre. Ein Literaturbericht zur Bundesrepublik Deutschland und zu Italien', in Johannes Hürter and Gian Enrico Rusconi (eds), *Die bleiernen Jahre. Staat und Terrorismus in der Bundesrepublik Deutschland und in Italien* (Munich: Oldenbourg, 2010), pp. 117–125; Tobias Hof, *Staat und Terrorismus in Italien: 1916–1982* (Munich: Oldenbourg, 2011); Della Porta, 'Social Movements', pp. 136–149; Ernst Halperin, *Terrorism in Latin America* (Beverly Hills, CA: Sage, 1976), p. 17, p. 41f.

[65] Waldmann, *Terrorismus*, p. 17.

[66] Thomas Fischer, 'Die Tupamaros in Uruguay. Das Modell der Stadtguerilla', in Wolfgang Kraushaar (ed.), *Die RAF und der linke Terrorismus* (Hamburg: Hamburger Edition, 2006), pp. 736–750.

[67] Halperin, *Terrorism*, p. 42.

a small community in Montevideo with an independent counter-public (*Gegenöffentlichkeit*). They also cultivated a Robin Hood-like image of helping the poor against their oppressors. Being aware of the importance of media communication, the political elites in Uruguay curtailed freedom of the press and sought to depoliticize the Tupamaros, obliging the media always to describe them as criminals. Being object of massive state repression, especially after 1969 when they openly challenged state authority in what they called a general war of insurrection, the Tupamaros were destroyed by a military well-versed in extreme torture practices. After 1972 the Tupamaros rapidly lost influence; the urban base of Latin American terrorism shifted to Argentina and Brazil, where the main actions took place in Rio de Janeiro and São Paulo.

The famous 1971 *Minimanual* by the Brazilian militant Carlos Marighella summarized the main tactics of Latin American terrorists. They preferred decentralized attacks against members of the business or political elites, practised 'kidnapping and revolutionary incarceration' (in these actions military guards were to be saved, as it was hoped to win them over on the sides of the militants); carried out bank robberies; undertook housebreaking and robberies in the homes of the elite; and seized of radio and TV stations for 'armed propaganda'.[68] In Argentina, large-scale terrorist operations started in 1970. In 1973 there were some 178 kidnappings of foreign and Argentinean businessmen; as a result, millions of dollars were paid for their release.[69]

In the late 1960s, New Left terrorism emerged in Europe and in the United States. These organizations grew out of the social movements of the New Left. The activities of these movements, which had predecessors dating back into the late-1950s,[70] were characterized by a mix of formal political actions associated with the New Left and countercultural elements such as consumption of drugs, rock music, new dress codes and street theatre. Among the terrorist groups that emerged from these social movements were the *Brigate Rosse* (BR) and *Prima Linea* (PL) in Italy, the *Rote Armee Fraktion* (RAF) and *Bewegung 2. Juni* in Germany, the *Gauche Proletarienne* (GP) and the *Action Directe* (AD) in France, the

---

[68] Robert Moss, 'Urban Guerilla Warfare', *Adelphi paper* 79 (1971), pp.1–17; Carlos Marighella, 'Minimanual of the Urban Guerrilla', *Adelphi paper* 79 (1971), pp. 19–42, pp. 17–19.

[69] Halperin, *Terrorism*, p. 44.

[70] Holger Nehring, *Politics of Security. British and West German Protest Movements and the early Cold War, 1945–1970* (Oxford: Oxford University Press, 2013).

Grupo de Resistencia Antifascista Primero de Octubre (GRAPO) in Spain and the *Revolutionary Organization 17 November* in Greece.[71] The general development of 1960s–1980s New Left terrorism in Western Europe can be divided into two phases: from 1968 until the early 1970s and from the mid-1970s until the 1990s. The militants of the first phase of New Left terrorism were strongly influenced by the powerful social protest movements around 1968, which were initially based in universities and protested against the Vietnam War in an environment of Cold War-inspired anti-communism.[72] They were also influenced by the legacies of the past. These social movements (and the militants within them) not only established tight international networks of communication but also recognized the importance of media (especially television) for their aims. Many women became active in these terrorist organizations, which rejected traditional gender roles and accepted active female participation. The New Left terrorists mixed Marxism, Maoism and the ideologies of Third World liberation movements. Like Latin American militants, West European terrorist groups attacked buildings of symbolic importance such as press offices, police stations or US army headquarters, but they also resorted to hijacking or even killing members of the political and economic elites and police officers.[73]

---

[71] On these organizations see Yonah Alexander and Dennis A. Pluchinsky, *Europe's Red Terrorists: The Fighting Communist Organizations* (London: Frank Cass, 1992); Ignacio Sánchez-Cuenca, 'The Causes of Revolutionary Terrorism', in Richardson, *Roots*, pp. 71–82. On 17 November 1973 during the occupation of the Polytechnic University in Athens 34 students were killed by the police.

[72] See Belinda Davis et al. (eds), *Changing the World, Changing Oneself. Political Protest and Collective Identities in West-Germany and in the US in the 1960s and 1970s* (Oxford: Berghahn, 2010); Samantha Christiansen and Zachary A. Scarlett (eds), *The Third World in the Global 1960s* (Oxford: Berghahn, 2013); Klimke and Scharloth, 1968; Ingrid Gilcher-Holtey, *Die 1968er Bewegung. Deutschland, Westeuropa, USA* (Munich: Beck, 2001).

[73] On German left-wing terrorism see Klaus Weinhauer and Joerg Requate (eds), *Terrorismus in der Bundesrepublik. Medien, Staat und Subkulturen in den 1970er Jahren* (Frankfurt am Main: Campus, 2006); Heinz Steinert, 'Sozialstrukturelle Bedingungen des "linken Terrorismus" der 1970er Jahre', in Bundesministerium des Innern (eds), *Analysen zum Terrorismus*, Vol. 4(2) (Opladen: Westdeutscher Verlag, 1984), pp. 387–603; Heinz Steinert, 'Erinnerung an den "linken Terrorismus"', in Henner Hess et al. (eds), *Angriff auf das Herz des Staates. Soziale Entwicklung und Terrorismus*, Vol 1, pp. 15–54; Kraushaar, *RAF*; on the milieus see Jakko Pekelder, 'The RAF and the Left in West Germany. Communication Processes between Terrorists and their Constituency in the early 1970s', in Weinhauer and Requate, *Gewalt*, pp. 203–222.

Mobilizing supportive milieux was crucial for the numerically weak terrorist organizations of the European New Left. Only in Italy and France did coalitions with unskilled and migrant workers exist in the early years. As the German working class only responded negatively, West German terrorists were forced to establish contacts with international terrorist organizations. In 1969 the *Bewegung 2. Juni* established contacts with Palestinian militants from the Popular Front for the Liberation of Palestine (PFLP). International cooperation continued when members of the RAF met with Palestinian and Japanese terrorists in May 1972.[74] The hijacking of a Lufthansa plane in October 1977 in support of the RAF was also an example of cooperation with militant Palestinian groups.[75]

In the second phase (mid 1970s until 1990s) European militants of the New Left had a more diffuse social profile. In Germany, Italy and France they emerged from the decentralized social movements of the 1970s: ecological groups, women's movement, anti-prison, autonomous and squatting movements, and anti-nuclear power organizations. These activists had almost no first-hand experience of the 1968 movements. In Western Germany they were radicalized by three events: the trials of the early terrorists (Baader, Meinhof, Ensslin), by organizing support campaigns against the conditions of imprisonment of political prisoners, and by participating in militant squatting actions.[76] These mid-1970s terrorists concentrated on planning how to free their colleagues from prison, which culminated in the kidnapping and killing of the employers' representative Hanns-Martin Schleyer in 1977.[77] By late-1977 German left-wing terrorism was in retreat, although there were still occasional assassinations and killings. In April 1998 the RAF declared its dissolution.

In Italy some activists of the youth protests of 1977 joined terrorist organizations such as *Prima Linea* and *Formazioni Comuniste Combattenti*.[78] They introduced a stronger hedonist and countercultural element into

---

[74] Nick Thomas, *Protest Movements in 1960s West Germany. A Social History of Dissent and Democracy* (Oxford: Berghahn, 2003), p. 211.

[75] Ariel Merai, 'Attacks on Civil Aviation. Trends and Lessons', in Rapoport, *Terrorism*, Vol 3, pp. 289–305.

[76] See Klaus Weinhauer, 'Terrorismus in der Bundesrepublik der Siebzigerjahre: Aspekte einer Sozial- und Kulturgeschichte der Inneren Sicherheit', *Archiv für Sozialgeschichte* 44 (2004), pp. 219–242.

[77] Steinert, 'Sozialstrukturelle Bedingungen', p. 553.

[78] Hess, 'Italien', in idem et al., *Angriff*, p. 118.

Italian terrorism.[79] Police repression and the flexible responses of the judiciary contributed to their demise. In 1986, leading activists Mario Moretti and Renato Curcio declared the end of militant actions.[80] In France a new terrorist organization *Action Directe* (AD) was formed out of the ranks of the autonomous movement and took shape in the summer of 1977.[81] AD's members committed violent acts similar to the RAF, killing two policemen in 1983. Its ranks consisted of anarchists, anti-Franco immigrants and former activists of the autonomous movement. Action Directe was outlawed in August 1982 and its leaders were arrested in February 1987.

In both phases of European New Left terrorism, be it in Germany, France, or Italy, the approach that state institutions (mainly the police) adopted against political violence was instrumental in pushing activists to join the political underground.[82] We should not forget, however, that it was not only violent repression per se that radicalized activists: it was important how these experiences were interpreted according to histories of subjugation or injustice. In Germany, being subjected to police brutality was interpreted against the history of national socialism. For protestors it was indisputable that policemen were former fascists out to re-establish a fascist order. This perception was bolstered by the fact that, parallel to the high tide of youth protests in German cities, numerous policemen were put on trial for involvement in mass murder during the Nazi regime.[83] Many German policemen were convinced that youthful protesters wished to destroy the Federal Republic in order to establish communism. Similarly, politicians feared that the demise of the Weimar Republic would be repeated. In the eyes of protestors, however, the Federal Republic was unquestionably linked to fascism as well as US imperialism.[84] These extreme bipolar discourses and perceptions were intensified by the fact that in West Germany no strong leftist milieu existed to integrate social

---

[79] Hess, 'Italien', p. 108.

[80] Hess, 'Italien', p. 133.

[81] Dieter Paas: 'Frankreich. Der integrierte Linksradikalismus', in Hess et al., *Angriff*, p. 247, p. 266f.; see Alain Touraine et al., *Anti-Nuclear Protest* (Cambridge: Cambridge University Press, 1983); and for a more thorough treatment of the AD Michael Y. Dartnell, *Action Directe: Ultra-left Terrorism in France 1979–1987* (London: Frank Cass, 2001).

[82] Waldmann, *Terrorismus*.

[83] Klaus Weinhauer, *Schutzpolizei in der Bundesrepublik Deutschland zwischen Bürgerkrieg und Innerer Sicherheit: die turbulenten sechziger Jahre* (Paderborn: Schoeningh, 2003), p. 135.

[84] Steinert, 'Sozialstrukturelle Bedingungen', p. 540.

protest movements. All in all, in Western Germany there was no serious dialogue about how to solve the problems associated with violent behaviour. Fears of social exclusion and a loss of legitimacy curtailed political discourse.

In comparison to Germany, the dichotomization of perception was not so extreme in Italy and France. Moreover, terrorists could refer positively to national traditions of militancy. In France, the symbolism of street fighting at the barricades, violent strike traditions and the expectation of mass support from the working classes prevented early 1970s militants from developing radical strategies of individual terror such as killing members of the political or economic elites or civilians.[85] In addition, at least during the early 1970s, their social isolation was diminished due to support from intellectuals like Jean-Paul Sartre. Moreover, leading French policemen and politicians alike realized the spontaneous character of most of the student protests and were not preoccupied by the idea that they were orchestrated by foreign powers, as was the case in German ruling circles.[86] In Italy the strategy of tension initiated by right-wing institutions and terrorists during the intense bombing campaigns between 1969 and 1974 was one of the factors that served to legitimize revolutionary violence as a defence against the re-emergence of fascism.[87] Overall, the threat of fascist pasts and presents was mitigated by other influences. As the name 'Brigade' demonstrated, there were strong mental links to the communist partisan movements of the *Resistenza* during the Second World War.[88] The myth of the Resistenza—however distorted it may have been—reassured Italian militants of shared traditions and of the efficacy of violence. Additional links were perceived with the rural banditry of the nineteenth century. A socially accepted tradition of violent protests—be it during strikes or demonstrations—meant that the use of violence by policemen or demonstrators was not considered to be exceptional. Moreover, the public

---

[85] Steinert, 'Sozialstrukturelle Bedingungen', p. 486.

[86] Steinert, 'Sozialstrukturelle Bedingungen', p. 487f. Police brutality is described by Ingrid Gilcher Holtey, *'Die Phantasie an die Macht'. Mai 68 in Frankreich* (Frankfurt am Main: Suhrkamp, 1995), p. 182ff. and p. 203ff. The positive image of the French police has been challenged by Kristin Ross, *May '68 and its Afterlives* (Chicago: University of Chicago Press, 2002).

[87] Steinert, 'Sozialstrukturelle Bedingungen', p. 474.

[88] See Alexandra Locher, 'Der Weg in die Isolation. Kommunikative Strategien der Roten Brigaden im Italien der 1970er Jahre', in Weinhauer and Requate, *Gewalt*, pp. 241–260; Hess, 'Italien', pp. 59–63.

image of the state was not that of an efficient and powerful institution, while the police were believed to be corrupt, ineffective and pervaded by rivalries.

Although powerful social movements developed in both Britain and the Netherlands during the 1960s, no New-Left terrorism emerged comparable to Germany, Italy or France.[89] Young protestors in the former countries remained integrated into the social and political system, where both sides—governments and protestors—upheld networks of mutual reciprocal communication. In England, there were violent confrontations between the police and student protestors in 1967–1968, but both sides acted on the assumption that the other side would show restraint when using force. Under these circumstances the myth of the English Bobby able to handle all situations without using lethal violence was an important factor in preventing violence from getting out of hand. Moreover, neither policemen nor politicians felt that youth protests threatened the stability of the state. In the 1980s, this mutual trust was eroded and the police began to act violently, notably during the miners' strike and against black urban youth. Matters were very different in Northern Ireland, where the Royal Ulster Constabulary showed little restraint. In the Netherlands, even the late anti-colonial activism of the South Moluccans in 1975–1977 did not lead to major political or social disruption.[90]

Similar integrative processes prevented late 1960s and early 1970s US terrorist organizations like the members of the Weather Underground or the George Jackson Brigade from cutting all ties to counter cultural milieus and to civil society in general.[91] The importance of this connection is also mirrored in their name, Weathermen, derived from a song by Bob Dylan. For many of their militants the caesura to proceed to militant actions came

[89] See Martin Moerings, 'Niederlande: Der subventionierte Protest', in Hess et al., *Angriff*, pp. 281–342; Jacco Pekelder, 'Dynamiken des Terrorismus in Deutschland und den Niederlanden', *Geschichte und Gesellschaft* 3 (2009), pp. 402–428; Nick Thomas, 'Challenging the Myths of the 1960s: The Case of Student Protest in Britain', *Twentieth Century British History* 3 (2002), pp. 277–297; Klaus Weinhauer, 'Polizeikultur und Polizeipraxis in den 1960er und 1970er Jahren: Ein (bundes-)deutsch-englischer Vergleich', in Christina Benninghaus et al. (eds), *Unterwegs in Europa. Beiträge zu einer vergleichenden Sozial- und Kulturgeschichte* (Frankfurt am Main: Campus, 2008), pp. 201–218.
[90] De Graaf, *Evaluating*, pp. 33–45.
[91] Jeremy Varon, *Bringing the War Home. The Weather Underground, the Red Army Faction, and Revolutionary Violence in the Sixties and Seventies* (Berkeley: University of California Press, 2004); Nico Slate (ed.), *Black Power beyond Borders. The Global Dimensions of the Black Power Movement* (Basingstoke: Palgrave, 2012).

with the fierce confrontation at the Chicago national convention of the Democratic Party in August 1968, where protesters were confronted with massive police presence and the National Guard mobilized and armed. In the end, however, the public master narrative of a heroic and always victorious USA reassured the government and media to see the Weathermen as an atypical exception whose members surely would find their way back to the American way of life.

With the end of the Cold War came an erosion of the established binary coding (them vs. us) of New Left terrorism. Even West Germany in the late 1980s witnessed a shrinking of the entrenched lack of communication between its hermetic binary political codes. This went hand in hand with the splintering of the memories of 1970s West German left-wing terrorism.[92] This double process saw its breakthrough in the early twenty-first century. At that time, remembering 1970s terrorism was mainly characterized by victim-based communication and by individualized, often non-political narratives. Even the temporal resurfacing of old dichotomous 'frontline' arguments, such as in the debates about the Berlin RAF exhibition of 2005, could not conceal that there was no longer any nostagia or hope for the highly polarized atmosphere of the 1970s and 1980s.

RELIGIOUSLY-INSPIRED TERRORISM (SINCE C. 1980s)

Manifestations of terrorism rooted in religious cultures took shape as a global phenomenon in the late 1970s. The terrorism was triggered by Western interventions in the Middle East and North Africa, by the Israeli–Palestinian conflict, by the general rejection of a Western-dominated international order and by the Soviet invasion of Afghanistan. This pattern of terrorism became more decentralized after the collapse of the Soviet Union, when the numbers of terrorist groups with religious motivations, Islamist as well as Christian, increased. We must not forget, however, two points: it is hard to discern religious motives from political ones, and religion does not cause terrorism but serves to legitimize it. Religiously motivated terrorism like other forms of terrorism has social origins, where social milieus and cohesive in-groups are of crucial importance. In the 1990s the Islamist Al Qaeda emerged as the most formidable transnational terrorist organization.[93] Networks, peer-groups and middle-class social milieu were

---

[92] See Weinhauer and Requate, 'Einleitung', p. 31ff.

[93] On religious terrorism see Mark Juergensmeyer, *Terror in the Mind of God. The Global Rise of Religious Violence* (Berkeley: University of California Press, 2003); Marc Sageman,

highly important for this process, through which Al Qaeda became at the same time a social movement and an organization: It developed from a late 1980s territory-based to a de-territorialized transnational network in the years after 9/11.

September 11, 2001 was not the birth of suicide bombings. They emerged in the early 1980s in the Near East.[94] In April 1983 militant Islamists attacked the US embassy in Beirut, in October the headquarters of the US Marines and French paratroopers were attacked, and in November Israeli administrative buildings in South Lebanon were bombed. These attacks led to the death of nearly 500 people. In the 1990s, the Kurdish PKK was responsible for 15 suicide bombs that targeted politicians and the police. These actions were motivated less by religion than Marxist-Leninist ideology. As political scientist Robert Pape stresses '(T)he principal cause of suicide terrorism is resistance to foreign military occupation, not Islamist fundamentalism'.[95] Thus, between 2004 and 2006, 98.5% of 1,830 suicide attacks counted by Pape were targeted against military occupation.

When compared to kidnapping or hijacking planes, suicide bombers receive a great attention with relatively little effort. Women suicide bombings caused particular public interest. But it would be inaccurate to view females as mere agents following orders. Many of these militants gained a degree of status and developed a political and social consciousness that, if only temporarily, gave them independence from the machismo of their male counterparts.[96] Their use of violence, however, was bound to traditional codes and did not represent any form of progressive gender relations. As with previous terrorist movements, motivations lay less in strictly ideological issues, than in a wider social and cultural sense of marginalization and rebellion. Frequently among many Islamist militants 'social bonds came before any ideological commitment'.[97] Motivations for

---

Leaderless Jihad: Terror Networks in the Twenty-First Century (Philadelphia: University of Pennsylvania Press, 2008); Marc Sageman, 'Ripples in the Waves. Fantasies and Fashions', in Jean Elizabeth Rosenfeld (ed.), *Terrorism, Identity, and Legitimacy. The Four Waves Theory and Political Violence* (London: Routledge, 2011), pp. 87–92.

[94] See for the following Richardson, *Terrorists*, p. 143 and p. 138.

[95] Robert A. Pape and James A. Feldman, *Cutting the Fuse. The Explosion of Global Suicide Terrorism and How to Stop it* (Chicago: Chicago University Press, 2010), p. 20.

[96] See for the following Cindy D. Ness, 'In the Name of the Cause: Woman's Work in Secular and Religious Terrorism', idem (ed.), *Female Terrorism and Militancy. Agency, Utility, and Organization* (London: Routledge, 2008, pp. 1136, p. 29f.

[97] See for the following Sageman, *Leaderless*, pp. 71–88.

acts of violence rooted in moral outrage, interpretations of Western military actions and the linkage of these two factors with every day personal experiences (of discrimination) in diaspora society. In the 1990s, half of the Islamist militants arrested in France grew up together in Oran, Algeria. Emigration was regularly based on networks of family or friendship. These social bonds in the host country fostered the formation of in-groups with strong internal cohesion, mutual loyalty and sometimes a hatred for the outside world. Since the early 2000s, virtual groups interacting on the internet have also become important.

The suicide bombings on 7 July 2005 in London can demonstrate how a social movement's milieu, relationship to the state and its institutions, and media attention interacted in radicalizing young Muslims in diaspora communities.[98] The four London suicide bombers were born and raised in England. They lived in typical British Muslim neighbourhoods that were extensions of rural Pakistan communities and where many young men were without regular employment. They witnessed or suffered racial prejudice or even racist attacks, especially in the wake of September 11, 2001. Their family life was characterized by deep inter-generational tensions between their immigrant parents and themselves as young adolescents struggling against over-controlling parents and South Asian patriarchy. The dominant pattern of masculinity among these young men imposed a 'burden of responsibility' to protect others against suffering'.[99] The four were actively involved in local community affairs and had engaged in voluntary work. In addition, they also organized a street gang, which typically carried out strong-arm social policies like removing drug dealers or enforcing publicly rigid sexual norms.

In their view no social movements existed which sufficiently addressed their concerns.[100] As a result, they built a highly cohesive group[101] in which they planned and executed acts of violence. Step by step the four became

[98] See for the following: *Milan Rai, 7/7. The London Bombings, Islam and the Iraq War* (London/Ann Arbor: Pluto, 2006); Victor Jelenviewski Seidler, *Urban Fears and Global Terrors. Citizenship, Multicultures and Belongings after 7/7* (London: Routledge, 2007), Aidan Kirby, 'The London Bombers as "Self-Starters": A Case Study in Indigenous Radicalization and the Emergence of Autonomous Cliques', *Studies in Conflict and Terrorism* 5 (2007), pp. 415–428; Klaus Weinhauer, 'Religiös motivierter Terrorismus in der europäischen Diaspora zwischen transnationalen Netzwerken, lokalen Kleingruppen und Medienkommunikation', in Weinhauer and Requate, *Gewalt*, pp. 301–316.

[99] Seidler, *Urban*, p. 182.

[100] Rai, 7/7, p. 160.

[101] Marc Sageman, *Understanding Terror Networks* (Philadelphia: University of Pennsylvania Press, 2004), pp. 73–82.

involved in a Jihadist network that communicated to them 'an intensified and politicized rendition of global Muslim suffering, a theological justification, and a strategic rationale for revenge attacks, and a fundamentalist world view that removed all moral inhibitions'.[102] Islam had become for them the doorway to a transnational fellowship in a globally politicized community, which was disconnected from concrete social relations and shaped by binary codes and images.[103]

Although these 'unaffiliated terrorists' were attracted to Al Qaeda, they were not led by a supreme leader, nor were they the brainwashed instruments of terrorist masterminds.[104] Television and internet images of hundreds of dead civilians in Afghanistan and Iraq made them feel powerless against mass murder. As with the Madrid train bombers of 11 March 2004, the political aspirations of the London group were less influenced by a national identity or the aspiration to establish a sovereign nation state than by an imagined worldwide Muslim community, the *Umma*. This concept of a political Islam, dominant among young British Muslims, rested on dichotomies of good versus evil, the Umma versus the West.

CONCLUSIONS

In looking back at the 150-year period of terrorism under scrutiny here, this chapter has focused on sub-state terrorism in five phases, demonstrating that there is no continuous or unitary history of terrorism. Political violence labelled as terrorism is a phenomenon that is inseparable from a complex process of communication between the terrorist militants, state institutions and media (societies). Moreover, terrorist violence is rarely the tool of fully developed social movements but something which emerges at a time when the strategies and aims of these movements remain vague or when these movements are in demise.

Since the last two decades of the twentieth century communication about terrorism has changed on a global level: The polarized narrative of 'them versus us' (terrorists vs. state/society) eroded. 'New global cultures of transitional justice'[105] appeared, where victims and their organizations could establish themselves as a third player in this formerly binary setting.

---

[102] Rai, *7/7*, p. 160.
[103] Rai, *7/7*, p. 108.
[104] See for the following Rai, *7/7*, p. 156f.
[105] Birgit Schwelling, 'Transnational Civil Society's Contribution to Reconciliation. An Introduction', in idem, *Reconciliation*, p. 20.

Three factors led to this crucial change. First, the importance of the end of the Cold War with its binary coded anti-communism and fear of revolution has already been mentioned. Second, in terrorism discourses the state lost its image as an all-powerful suppressor, it became less an enemy worthwhile fighting against. It still is true that even today states are forced to act immediately against terrorist attacks, as their monopoly of physical violence is challenged. Sending political messages to the state, however, has become a much more contested issue. Third, in urban consumer societies of the late twentieth century it became hard for any terrorist to communicate messages primarily to the state. In the age of digital media this message could easily get lost. The actions of urban suicide bombers almost instantly generated tremendous public attention: their acts became news commodities which were structured around victim-based discourses on trauma and suffering. These messages were not primarily addressed to the state but rather to consumers and their needs for identity formation in a highly competitive 'society of consumers' (Z. Baumann). As a growing percentage of the world population lives in cities, where networks of communication are tightly knit and news commodities circulate extremely fast, at the end of this article the question arises: Will such urban settings (not the state) one day become the main addressee of terrorist attacks?

FURTHER READING

Research in social movements and in terrorism is mostly motivated by contemporary problems. Thus, unsurprisingly, political science and sociological studies dominate. Since the early 2000s, however, terrorism and social movements have begun to be studied by professional historians. As the state of social movement research is discussed in the Chaps. 1 and 2 I will give only a brief historically focused overview of publications on the interaction of social movements, terrorism/political violence and the state in (Western) Europe, the United States and Latin America.

For a quick English language overview some handbooks, although mostly lacking thorough historical perspectives, are good starting points, among them are Donatella della Porta and Mario Diani (eds), *The Oxford Handbook of Social Movements* (Oxford: Oxford University Press, 2015); Jacob L. Stump and Priya Dixit, *Critical Terrorism Studies. An Introduction to Research Methods* (London: Routledge, 2013); Marie Breen-Smyth (ed.), *The Ashgate Research Companion to Political Violence* (Aldershot: Ashgate, 2012). Methodologically broader perspectives are offered by Erich Goode (eds), *Handbook of Deviance* (Oxford: Wiley-Blackwell, 2015), and Paul Knepper and Anja Johansen (eds), *The Oxford Handbook of the History of Crime and Criminal Justice* (Oxford: Oxford University Press, 2016). A historically focussed and interdisciplinary overview is given by Sylvia Schraut and Klaus Weinhauer (eds), *Terrorism, Gender, and History: State of Research, Concepts, Case Studies* (Special issue of *Historical Social Research* 3, 2014); also a good starting point is Donald Bloxham and Robert Gerwarth (eds), *Political Violence in Twentieth Century Europe* (Cambridge: Cambridge University Press, 2011).

As most terrorism studies focus on non-state violence, it is important to include the state's counter-insurgency actions here. A solid historical study is Richard Bach Jensen, *The Battle against Terrorism. An International History* (Cambridge: Cambridge University Press, 2014). For the long history of US involvement in counter-insurgency see Russell Crandall, *America's Dirty Wars. Irregular Warfare from 1776 to the War on Terror* (Cambridge: Cambridge University Press, 2014). Latin American cases are studied in David M. K. Sheinin, *Consent of the Damned. Ordinary Argentinians in the Dirty War* (Gainesville: University of Florida Press, 2012); Fernando Herrera Calderón and Adela Cedillo (eds), *Challenging Authoritarianism in Mexico. Revolutionary Struggles and the Dirty War, 1964–1982* (London: Routledge, 2012). For a geographical perspective see Joe Bryan and Denis Wood, *Weaponizing Maps. Indigenous Peoples and Counterinsurgency in the Americas* (New York: The Guilford Press, 2015). A fine edited volume on an often-overlooked country is Bart Luttikhuis and A. Dirk Moses (eds), *Colonial Counterinsurgency and Mass Violence. The Dutch Empire in Indonesia* (London: Routledge, 2014). Transnational perspectives and challenging interpretations are given in Patricia Owen's groundbreaking book with case studies on Philippines, Malaya, Kenya, Vietnam, Afghanistan and Iraq: *Economy of Force. Counterinsurgency and the Historical Rise of the Social* (Cambridge: Cambridge University Press, 2015).

Still neglected is the question of how political violence is socially remembered: Eugenia Allier-Montaño and Emilio Crenzel (eds), *The Struggle for Memory in Latin America. Recent History and Political Violence* (Basingstoke: Palgrave Macmillan, 2015); Francesca Lessa and Vincent Druliolle (eds), *The Memory of State Terrorism in the Southern Cone. Argentina, Chile, and Uruguay* (Basingstoke: Palgrave Macmillan, 2011); Bill Kissane (ed), *After Civil War. Division, Reconstruction, and Reconciliation in Contemporary Europe* (Philadelphia: Pennsylvania University Press, 2015).

For the often-underestimated urban aspects of social movements and political violence, see Pedro Ramos Pinto, *Lisbon Rising. Urban Social Movements in the Portuguese Revolution, 1974–1975* (Manchester: Manchester University Press, 2013); Chris Ealham, *Anarchism and the City. Revolution and Counter-Revolution in Barcelona, 1898–1937* (Edinburgh: AK Press 2010); Javier Auyero and María Fernanda Berti, *In Harm's Way. The Dynamics of Urban Violence* (Princeton, NJ: Princeton University Press, 2015), Carl Smith, *Urban Disorder. The Great Chicago Fire, the Haymarket Bomb, and the Model Town of Pullman* (Chicago: Chicago University Press, 2007).

Historical studies on anarchism and syndicalism, which are also often labelled as terrorism, have recently included transnational and global aspects: Constance Bantman, *The French Anarchists in London, 1880–1914. Exile and Transnationalism in the First Globalization* (Liverpool: Liverpool University Press, 2013); Constance Bantman and Bert Altena (eds), *Reassessing the Transnational Turn. Scales of Analysis in Anarchist and Syndicalist Studies* (London: Routledge, 2015); Steven Hirsch; Lucien Van der Walt (eds), *Anarchism and Syndicalism in the colonial and Postcolonial World, 1870–1940. The Praxis of National Liberation, Internationalism, and Social Revolution* (Leiden: Brill, 2014); Geoffroy de Laforcade and Kirwin Shaffer (eds), *In Defiance of Boundaries. Anarchism in Latin American History* (Gainesville: University of Florida Press, 2015).

From the wealth of historical studies on political violence, some can give terrorism research stimulating impulses, especially when it comes to analyse the integration of political violence into certain milieu and subcultures, among them are Dirk Schumann, *Political Violence in the Weimar Republic, 1918–1933. Fight for the Streets and Fear of Civil War* (Oxford: Berghahn, 2009); Mark Doyle, *Fighting Like the Devil for the Sake of God. Protestants, Catholics and the Origins of Violence in Victorian Belfast* (Manchester: Manchester University Press, 2009). Still relevant is James P. Brennan, *The Labor Wars in Córdoba, 1955–1976. Ideology, Work, and Labor Politics in an Argentine Industrial City* (Cambridge, MA: Harvard University Press, 1994). European and US case studies are put together in Klaus Weinhauer, Anthony McElligott and Kirsten Heinsohn (eds); *Germany 1916–23. A Revolution in Context* (Bielefeld and New York: Transcript and Columbia University Press, 2015).

CHAPTER 20

Fascism as a Social Movement in a Transnational Context

Kevin Passmore

To treat fascism[1] as a social movement in a transnational context is to buck the trend in studies of so-called 'generic fascism'. The purpose of the latter is to derive a 'model', 'definition', or 'ideal-type' of fascism from observation of its primary 'case', the Fascist movement in Italy, perhaps supplemented with features of German National Socialism. This model would capture the essence of the phenomenon and its dynamic and permit us to recognize 'cases' of fascism even where protagonists rejected the label. Theories of generic fascism suffer from general and specific problems. Generally, they exaggerate the explanatory power of models of any type and they take for granted that 'cases' of fascism are national variants of the same essence. They also harden concepts that were contested and fluid in practical politics. Specifically, and directly relevant to this essay, models of generic fascism rely unwittingly on understandings of social action derived from late nineteenth-century crowd psychology, from which social movement theory has—in principle—liberated itself.

---

[1] I use 'Fascism' to designate the Italian movement and regime and 'fascism' to refer to the generic concept.

I should like to thank Holger Nehring and Garthine Walker for their comments on the article and Federica Ferlanti for help with the section on China.

K. Passmore (✉)
Department of History, Cardiff University, Cardiff, UK

© The Author(s) 2017
S. Berger, H. Nehring (eds.), *The History of Social Movements in Global Perspective*, DOI 10.1057/978-1-137-30427-8_20

The fashionable political religions approach to generic fascism is espe-cially dependent upon this reworking of crowd psychology, transmitted via Parsonian social science, concepts of mass society and totalitarianism theory.[2] For theorists of totalitarianism, fascism was a product of the clas-sic strain–breakdown–disorientation–reintegration sequence: upheaval provokes disorientation (anomie) in the mass, making it vulnerable to a messianic, authoritarian movement that promises to restore meaning to the disrupted world. As Leonard Schapiro put it, a totalitarian movement entails leadership of an elite equipped with an impossibly utopian plan for revolutionary reorganization of society and an ideology able to appeal to the implicitly irrational 'mass' through its innate nationalism, 'the pre-dominant and most primitive mass emotion'.[3]

When Schapiro wrote, totalitarian theorists were preoccupied with structures of rule. Then from the late 1980s, they embraced the scholarly fashion for the study of ideas. Roger Griffin depicted fascism as an ideology of national rebirth (palingenesis) after a period of crisis and decline.[4] In parallel, Emilio Gentile's political religions theory maintained that sacral-ization of the state and/or party provided the ideological and emotional re-integration that the mass craved; the agency of the 'mass' is limited to expressing the desire for charismatic leadership and political religion—it is 'disposed' to fascism.[5] The 'brutalization thesis' is another cousin of these theories.[6] According to this view, the trauma of war awoke a latent disposi-tion to violence in the political culture (or mentality) of societies that had not fully modernized. Here too we see the debt to crowd psychology and the assumption of a unitary national character.[7]

[2] Kevin Passmore, 'The Gendered Genealogy of Political Religions Theory', *Gender & History* 3 (2008), pp. 644–668.

[3] Leonard Schapiro, *Totalitarianism* (Westport, CT: Praeger, 1972), pp. 45–58.

[4] Roger Griffin, *The Nature of Fascism* (London: Pinter, 1991).

[5] Roger Griffin, '"Consensus ? Quel Consensus ?" Perspectives pour une meilleure entente entre spécialistes francophones et anglophones du fascisme', *Vingtieme Siècle: Revue d'histoire* 108 (2010), pp. 53–69; Emilio Gentile, *The Sacralisation of Politics: Definitions, Interpretations and Reflections on the Question of Secular Religion and Totalitarianism* (London: Frank Cass, 2000).

[6] Annette Becker and Stéphane Audoin-Rouzeau, *14–18, retrouver la guerre* (Paris: Gallimard, 2000).

[7] Georg Mosse, *De la grande guerre au totalitarisme. La brutalisation des sociétés europée-nnes* (Paris: Hachette, 1999); Antoine Prost, 'TheImpact of War on French and German Political Cultures', *Historical Journal* 1 (1994), pp. 209–217; for a critique see Benjamin Ziemann, 'Germany after the First World War—A Violent Society? Results and Implications

Another development has reinforced top-down tendencies in the aforementioned approaches to fascism. Influenced by Michel Foucault's concept of 'governmentality', researchers have been focussing on fascist regimes' social and racial projects. This approach emphasizes the way that fascist regimes infiltrate commercialized leisure, sport and cinema, and thus service and channel the 'utopian longings' of ordinary people, and ensure that people colluded in their own oppression.[8] There are clear parallels with crowd psychology and its avatars.[9]

Taken together, these trends have shifted scholarly attention away from fascist movements towards regimes, to their rituals, cultures, and, for Foucauldians, to their 'techniques of rule'. Even some of those who do study fascist movements select those aspects of them that prefigure the political religion of the regime, or they use a version of the brutalization thesis.[10] These theories are not entirely without value. They highlight the emotional component of fascism and potentially of social movements generally, which had been neglected in some earlier social interpretations. However, they reduce fascism to these aspects, essentialize it, fail to see its internal conflicts, and rule out legitimate alternative perspectives.

Fascism theories share a weakness of models in general. They assume that the 'properties' of the model can explain the actual history of the movement. Thus, Dieter Rucht contends that a 'real definition' includes a theory about the 'coming into existence, the consequences, and/or the "nature" ... of the phenomenon'.[11] A practical illustration is the commonplace in the historiography of fascism and Nazism that their dependence on charismatic authority necessitated the continual performance of miracles and made self-destruction inevitable. In fact, definitions cannot explain the actual history of a movement because they involve selection among the many features of a given movement, and elements not included in the definition will always influence the movement's history. Moreover,

---

of Recent Research on Weimar Germany', *Journal of Modern European History* 1 (2003), pp. 80–86.

[8] Geoff Eley, *Nazism as Fascism: Violence, Ideology, and the Ground of Consent in Germany 1930–1945* (London: Routledge, 2013), pp. 212–213.

[9] There is no space here to explore the complex relationship between Foucauldian theory and modernization narratives.

[10] For example, Christopher Duggan, *Fascist Voices: An Intimate History of Mussolini's Italy* (New York: Oxford University Press, 2012), p. 22, pp. 47–52.

[11] see Dieter Rucht, 'Social Movements—Some Conceptual Challenges', Chap. 2 in this volume.

those who joined fascist movements rarely saw themselves simply as fascists. Most often, they brought with them multiple agendas and visions of what fascism was or should be, their degrees of commitment carried, as did their sympathies for other movements. Of course, some activists were fanatics, but even fanaticism requires historicization.

Another difficulty with the generic approach is the assumption that the world is really divided into entities, even 'fuzzy' ones, that await modelling. It is perfectly legitimate to make a conceptual distinction between social and political movements, but we must remember that reality itself is not divided in that way. The example of fascism demonstrates the point well, since depending on perspective one could see it as a political or social movement or both. One cannot solve the problem by dividing fascist organizations into social and political components either, or indeed by distinguishing between fascism-movement and fascism-regime. To be useful, definitions must be open and potentially compatible with other definitions, and we must be precise about what they show and what they do not show.

The French school of political sociology develops social movement theory in ways that is useful to the study of fascism. Like totalitarian and political religion theorists, its leading exponent, Michel Dobry, situates fascism in relation to crisis and the mobilization of groups outside the political system. However, the resemblance ends there, for social breakdown is not total, and although circumstances and options are harder to read, people do not become irrational, and they do not necessarily abandon old objectives.[12] Therefore Dobry focuses on the actions of protagonists, on the available ideas that they use and adapt to understand the situation, and on the strategies that they use to achieve their objectives and anticipate the responses of rivals and opponents.[13] Dobry's method shifts attention to the 'constructed rationality' of protagonists. His concept is open in that is does not pretend to identify necessary causes of crises or predict outcomes. It does not attempt to find a common denominator among the activists in a social movement, and does not believe it possible to establish *the* model of fascism or of a social movement.

---

[12] Crisis occurred in France in May 1968 without prior economic catastrophe or de-legitimation of the system.

[13] Michel Dobry, *Sociologie des crises politiques : la dynamique des mobilisations multisectorielles*, 3rd edn (Paris: Science Po, 2009), pp. 170–171; Michel Dobry, 'La thèse immunitaire face aux fascismes', in Michel Dobry (ed.), *Le mythe de l'allergie française du fascisme* (Paris: Albin Michel, 2003), pp. 17–67.

Notwithstanding, we cannot abandon definitions—this approach has nothing to do with the postmodern claim that historical writing is merely linguistic emplotment. First, we must define the limits of study—our *explicandum*—without pretending that the movements included within its scope share something essential. My choice is to discuss aspects of Italian Fascism, Nazism, Hungarian movements, the French leagues, and the reception of fascism in India, China and South America. While these countries conventionally figure in discussions of generic fascism, I do not enter into the (irresolvable) debate about whether or not they actually were fascist or indeed whether or not they were social movements.

Secondly, I ask instead what treating fascism as a social movement can tell us. I use Dieter Rucht's definition: 'a network of individuals, groups and organizations that, based on a sense of collective identity, seek[s] to bring about social change (or resist it) primarily by means of collective public protest'.[14] I qualify the definition with a stress on conflict concerning the movement's nature and objectives. Indeed, social movement concepts are most revealing when they allow for the convergence of multiple mobilizations in a heterogeneous movement. My definition is therefore open, and is compatible with other perspectives. Only an open concept allows for the fact that the movements I consider both share the major features of social movements (as *I* have defined them) and were dedicated to winning political power (along with other objectives), often through participation in the political system. I shall therefore discuss and compare the place of movements in the quest for power.

Thirdly, following Michel Dobry, we may ask how protagonists used their own concepts and categories in specific contexts. However sceptical we might be about fixed concepts, protagonists believed fascism to have precise characteristics, and so we may ask how the term figured in the systems of classification of the period, what was at stake in its use, and how it related to the disposition of social power. The history of fascism involved sometimes lethal conflicts about the 'true meaning' of the word, which were sometimes folded into disputes about whether fascism was a movement or a party. The same considerations apply to crowd psychology, for it too was essential to the way that protagonists understood collective behaviour, classified and recognized allies and enemies and defined strategies.

Tracing the history of categories also implies following them transnationally. Whereas generic fascism theorists see discrete national move-

---

[14] Rucht, 'Social Movements—Some Conceptual Challenges', Chap. 2 in this volume.

ments as variations of a core, a transnational approach recognizes that protagonists used and transformed ideologies in quite different contexts for different purposes. That is not to deny the importance of the national framework. Nations were another essential part of the classificatory systems that protagonists used, and were very important to the distribution of social power. Fascists privileged the nation (though inconsistently and never unproblematically) and sought power in territorial states. Moreover, transnational exchanges were as likely to reinforce boundaries as dissolve them.[15] For instance, fascists proselytized internationally to advance the cause of their own nation, and this nationalism created barriers to the diffusion of fascism. The history of fascism, though beyond the scope of this essay, is incomprehensible if we forget that fascists endeavoured to use the immense power of the nation-state to re-structure a world that was stubbornly transnational. I also suggest that the social movement aspect of fascism was important in the way that Italian Fascism was received internationally. The groups that I consider were 'entangled' as social movements.

WAR, POLITICAL CRISIS AND SOCIAL MOVEMENTS

One can hardly deny that the Great War was a traumatic experience. The contention that the war permanently brutalized all veterans or caused individuals to surrender to anomie and yearning for political religion is more contestable.[16] As well as anxiety and isolation and loss, the war provoked enthusiastic engagement in civil society organizations, charities and trade unions.[17] These groups were largely committed to winning the war (at least because they saw winning it as better than losing it), but they were politically heterogeneous and pursued multiple objectives. The more right-wing of these groups often glorified violence and adopted a Manichean view of the conflict as one between civilization and barbarism. But not all of those who espoused such ideas engaged in practical violence after the war or became fascists.

In 1919, the strains of war provoked political crisis and social mobilization even in the victorious countries, while defeat brought down the Empires of Central Europe. Bourgeois self-defence organizations, often paramilitary, emerged in many countries. They were strongest in the ethnically diverse borderlands of Eastern Europe from the German frontier

---

[15] Patricia Clavin, 'Defining Transnationalism', *Contemporary European History* 4 (2005), pp. 421–440, p. 431.

[16] Ziemann, 'Germany after the First World War', pp. 80–86.

[17] Peter Fritzsche, *Germans into Nazis* (Cambridge, MA: Harvard University Press, 1998), pp. 39–82.

with the Baltic States through the Hungarian borderlands, to the Italian frontier with Yugoslavia, where the Central Powers had lost territory and state authority had collapsed. Frontier conflicts folded into the fight against domestic socialism. Paramilitaries fought Béla Kun's revolution in Hungary, the socialists in Germany, and rural strikes and factory occupations in Italy. Violence was particularly serious in western Hungary, where Jews and allegedly politicized women were targeted.[18] Significantly, in October 1921 one paramilitary group, the Hungarian National Defence Union (MOVE) led by Gyula Gömbös helped the reactionary Miklos Horthy regime to fend off an attempt by the deposed Habsburg king to reclaim his throne—thus revealing political divisions within the counter-revolution, for the Protestant Gömbös despised the Catholic royal family. The reaction was politically heterogeneous everywhere; true, every group opposed communism, but not necessarily for the same reasons.

There was no direct line between this paramilitary counter-revolution and fascism. First, fascism did not win power where paramilitary violence was most unrestrained, i.e. in Hungary. Secondly, fascism would develop from the whole range of veteran, religious and charitable groups, bourgeois clubs, women's groups, *et cetera* that had developed during and after the war. While many of them were very right wing, they were not necessarily committed in practice to the use of violence for political purposes. There was, after all, more to fascism than physical violence. Thirdly, fascism enjoyed some support from senior functionaries, business and generals, who shared enemies, and who had become fascinated with the manipulation of massive numbers of soldiers and workers, and thus with projects for economic, social, and eugenic engineering. These networks, which were not distinct in practice, would battle to define fascism.

Following Michel Dobry's schema the post-war years witnessed a 'multi-sector mobilization', producing a 'fluid situation', as the new forces described above took the political initiative. Disruption of routine meant that circumstances were harder to read, but far from becoming irrational, protagonists continued to act rationally in the light of their inherited ways of understanding their circumstances.[19] The groups involved were often mutually antipathetic, but they could also coalesce into broader movements. Either way they disrupted existing political alignments and rou-

[18] Robert Gerwarth, 'The Central European Counter-Revolution: Paramilitary Violence in Germany, Austria and Hungary after the Great War', *Past & Present* 1 (2008), pp. 175–209; Robert Gerwarth and John Horne, 'Vectors of Violence: Paramilitarism in Europe after the Great War, 1917–1923', *The Journal of Modern History* 3 (2011), pp. 489–512.

[19] Dobry, *Sociologie des crises politiques*, p. 140, pp. 150–158.

tines, and shifted politics away from the state and parliament towards the streets and villages. Multi-sector mobilization also potentially undermined the usual solidarity between the sectors of the state, as economic and military powers were tempted or constrained to deal with the popular mobilization. These developments were especially dangerous where important sections of the population did not accept existing regimes.

ITALY

In 1919, Benito Mussolini was looking for a new place in the political landscape. Since 1914, his advocacy of intervention in the Great War had cut him off from the left while his calls for revolution had alienated the right. He also faced competition from the more prestigious interventionist leader, the poet and auto-proclaimed Nietzschean superman, Gabriele D'Annunzio. The term *fascio* was attractive because it meant 'close union' in a popular movement and because its first political use, by Sicilian peasant socialists in the 1890s, lent it an air of radicalism. In 1915, dissident leftists, including Mussolini, formed the *Fasci d'azione interventista* to persuade the proletariat that only intervention in the war could bring revolution. Interventionists nevertheless possessed friends in high places. In December 1917, around 150 parliamentarians formed the *Fascio parlementare di difesa nazionale*. This group was largely conservative, but it won the backing of most interventionists, including the syndicalists (revolutionary trade unionists) and the inevitable Mussolini. Local *fasci* also appeared, and by 1919, the term was an interventionist commonplace, used by Futurists (a modernist art movement) and veterans in particular.[20]

Mussolini owed his eventual primacy partly to events that were beyond his control, and which had little to do with his charisma or the programme or actions of Fascist leaders. In 1920, the movement expanded rapidly as an anti-socialist force in the countryside, thus provoking the Fascists to modify their programme in a more antisocialist direction. Meanwhile, an attempt by D'Annunzio's 'legions' to seize the border city of Fiume fizzled out. And just as the poet was restoring his reputation, he fell from a window while high on cocaine. Mussolini benefited also from his dual position as a figure of national stature and leader of the fascist movement. He established his credentials nationally by confining his journalistic output to foreign policy

[20] Adrian Lyttelton, *The Seizure of Power: Fascism in Italy, 1919–1929*, 2nd edn (London: Weidenfeld and Nicolson, 1987), p. 28, p. 42; Richard J. B. Bosworth, *The Italian Dictatorship. Mussolini and Fascism* (London: Arnold, 1999), p. 38.

matters, and by negotiation with conservatives, notably in the parliamentary elections of 1921.[21] But he did not abandon Fascism to his conservative allies. On the contrary, he feared that the unrestrained anti-socialist violence of the squads would reduce his movement to a reactionary force. He continued to stress social radicalism and even revolution, and negotiated a 'Pacification Pact' with the moderate socialist Prime Minister. The regional leaders of the squads, the ras, saw that as an affront to their own idea of revolution, which entailed elimination of socialism from a regenerated national community, led by an elite purged of 'bourgeois values' (but not the bourgeoisie). Faced with the ras' opposition, Mussolini staged his resignation in the summer of 1922. Then in November, he triumphantly returned at the inaugural congress of the Partito Nazionale Fascista (PNF), which set about disciplining what had hitherto seen itself as a 'movement'. Some activists feared that this strategy would replace the 'youth and poetry' of the movement with the 'paunch, moustache and beard' of Roman politics.[22] However, the ras recognized that if they wanted power, Mussolini alone possessed necessary national leverage. Anyway, the movement continued to matter. The November deal dropped the Pacification Pact, and so long as the squads were loyal to Mussolini, they could continue their violence against socialists and national minorities.

The Fascist movement was essential to Mussolini's capture of power. The March on Rome was not a charade; it threatened to displace the police, army, and liberal political class, and Mussolini approved, for he knew that disorder was a weapon with which to blackmail the government. He came to power because he was indispensable in both parliamentary majorities and of the conflicts in town and countryside. As such, Fascism was a product of diverse constituencies, which disagreed fundamentally on the nature of their movement. It was not clear what had won in October 1922: a movement or a party?

Closer examination of the Fascist movement in the light of the concepts of social movements, combining the characteristics of Dieter Rucht and Bert Klandermans—instrumentalism, solidarity and action frames—underlines both the relative usefulness of the concept and the point that Fascism has no 'core'.[23]

---

[21] Richard J. B. Bosworth, *Mussolini* (London: Arnold, 2002), pp. 154–166.

[22] Duggan, *Fascist Voices*, pp. 46–47.

[23] Bert Klandermans, 'The Demand and Supply of Participation: Social-Psychological Correlates of Participation in Social Movements', in David A. Snow, Sarah A. Soule and

INSTRUMENTALISM

Instrumentalism is a weak point for political religions theory. It sees fascism as a response to diffuse anomie and so cannot explain why some groups were so much more inclined to join the Fascist movement than others. Neither can it understand the specific relationships between religious motifs and other priorities. And because political religions theory sees fascism as 'revolutionary', it dismisses the support of large landowners, capitalists and the authorities for fascism as tactical or instrumental and not therefore as part of the core. Social movement theory is stronger because it allows for the eclecticism of fascism.

The same activists who used religious language to express their fascism also referred to it as a bourgeois movement. One squad member boasted that fascists had forced down wages at a time when the 'peasants were dressing like me and the cowherd's daughter was more elegant than my sister'.[24] Since 1920, the fasci had carried out a reign of terror. In the Po Valley, they attacked and destroyed socialist organizations; in the Venezia Giulia, they assaulted the Slavic population, the southernmost extent of the space of conflict opened by the collapse of the Habsburg Empire. By 1922, in towns such as Ferrara, Fascists had already imposed their rule. Often, the administration, police, army, and landowners indicated the targets, provided lorries and paid for the petrol.[25] But many activists also attacked the bourgeoisie. Often that meant criticizing it only for allowing democratic values to impede the crushing of socialism, but it could also express generational, political and social conflicts. Also, the fascist desire to reincorporate workers and peasants into the nation could mean addressing their 'legitimate grievances' against capitalism.

To that end, Fascists set up labour unions to compete with Catholic and Socialist organizations, and they may have had half a million members by 1922. These unions depended on employers' complicity, but that was not all there was to them. Fascism appealed to poor sharecroppers and peasant landholders, who had initially backed the socialists, but soon resented attempts to force them to hire union labour on their farms. The

Hanspeter Kriesi (eds), *The Blackwell Companion to Social Movements* (Oxford: Blackwell, 2006), pp. 360–379.

[24] Duggan, *Fascist Voices*, p. 37, p. 42, p. 52.

[25] Sven Reichardt, 'Fascist Marches in Italy and Germany: Squadre and SA before the Seizure of Power', in Matthias Reiss (ed.), *The Street as Stage: Protest Marches and Public Rallies Since the Nineteenth Century* (Oxford: Oxford University Press, 2007), pp. 169–193.

Fascists offered peasants and labourers selective incentives to join their own unions, promising to protect the gains won in 1919–1920 while destroying socialism. Paul Corner shows a clear sequence in Ferrara: 'violence to neutralise the socialist movement, propaganda and a carefully considered agrarian policy to initiate desertion of the [socialist] leagues and which then relied on the mechanism of the labour market in order to complete that process'. Fascism offered a relative benefit to landowners, but at the price of concessions to 'socialism' in the form of job security and land. Paradoxically, the result was to import class conflict into the Fascist movement and regime, while advantaging the powerful in this struggle even more than in democratic society.[26]

The place of women's groups in the Fascist movement was analogous. Male Fascists allied anti-feminism to treatment of women as sex objects and idealization of motherhood. Veterans were particularly resentful of female employment. Yet women still joined the movement. Some came via D'Annunzio, whose womanizing did not prevent him from promising political equality, or from Futurism, which preached the freedom of women from the domination of any single man. Other women were socialist comrades of Mussolini; a few even joined the *squadristi*, and most were more committed to gender equality than were male activists. Like trade unionists, women discovered that they were in a weaker position in the Fascist movement than in democratic society, and the cost of participation in the squads was ridicule. The January 1922 regulations for the *Fasci femminili in principle* confined women to charitable work and propaganda. Women did however have male indifference on their side, and so the unequal struggle between feminists and their opponents continued within the regime.[27]

[26] Paul Corner, *Fascism in Ferrara, 1915–1925* (Oxford: Oxford University Press, 1975); Frank M. Snowden, *The Fascist Revolution in Tuscany, 1919–1922* (Cambridge: Cambridge University Press, 1989); Frank M. Snowden, *Violence and Great Estates in the South of Italy: Apulia, 1900–1922* (Cambridge: Cambridge University Press, 1986); Frank M. Snowden, 'On the Social Origins of Agrarian Fascism in Italy', *European Journal of Sociology* 2 (1972), pp. 268–295.

[27] Victoria De Grazia, *How Fascism Ruled Women: Italy, 1922–1945* (Berkeley: University of California Press, 1993), pp. 30–34; Perry Willson, 'Italy', in Kevin Passmore (ed.), *Women, Gender and the Extreme Right in Europe (1919–1945)* (Manchester: Manchester University Press, 2002), pp. 11–32, here pp. 12–15.

SOLIDARITY

Incentives alone cannot explain participation in a social movement, for people may enjoy its fruits without participating. People were also attracted to Fascism by the kudos of membership in a prestigious group. In some cases, activism represented an extension of exclusive bourgeois social networks, from Ancona's *circolo cittadino*, via the largely upper-class student movement, to the charitable networks of wealthy women.[28] Also important were the veterans, with whom the Fascists systematically associated themselves. In his 1920 election campaign, Mussolini sang the anthem of the Arditi, the most prestigious veterans of all.[29] Soldiers, from generals to conscripts, resented the material difficulties of demobilization and agreed that their sacrifice had been wasted by politicians. Those too young to have served in the war shared the veterans' glory through participation in the squads, and for some of them activism provided a status that they otherwise lacked. Participation in punitive expeditions to Socialist towns and triumphal marches of heroes reinforced solidarity in a community of violence.[30]

Militarism reinforced hierarchy within the movement insofar as it preserved a chain of command reflecting the broader class structure. Most members were bourgeois, and most leaders were junior officers. But militarism also imported conflict into the movement. The army could not be relied on to obey orders and some generals plotted against the state. Moreover, war service reinforced the solidarity on which agricultural trade unionism depended, and so potentially hardened antagonism to bosses, including pro-fascist bosses.

Some of those who attended the first meeting of the Fasci swore their readiness to die for Italy over a dagger. Subsequently, the squads incorporated much of the lifestyle of soldiers and D'Annunzio's expedition—cocaine, drunken debauchery, abuse of women, brutality, histrionic speeches, and parades.[31] Political religions theory rightly stresses that demonstrations and rituals were intended to unite the movement and prefigure regenerated Italy. Moreover, Fascists believed that Le Bon had understood the need for an ideology that would bind followers to the leader. Emotional commitment was probably strongest among those who joined before the movement had won any successes. Yet emotional and

---

[28] Bosworth, *Mussolini*, p. 138; Grazia, *How Fascism Ruled Women*, pp. 31–32.
[29] Bosworth, *Mussolini*, p. 136.
[30] Reichardt, 'Fascist Marches', pp. 169–189.
[31] Duggan, *Fascist Voices*, pp. 22–25.

instrumental dimensions were inseparable in practice, for the power of the inner core depended on using its proximity to Mussolini. We have also seen that the breakthrough of Fascism happened quite independently of Mussolini's charismatic presence. Subsequently, Fascists rationalized their support as a response to Mussolini's qualities, and Mussolini's need to maintain his prestige consequently constrained him. It would have been hard for him to become just another Italian Prime Minister. Fascist rituals had purchase partly because they were invented within the movement: the black shirts, appeal to the fallen, the use of trucks to transport squads and the castor oil punishment. The party anthem originated with the Arditi.[32] Political religions theory cannot account for the coexistence of rituals and conflict within the fascist movement.

FRAMES

Political religions theory is on safer ground in relation to 'action frames'. Undeniably, many Fascists were emotionally committed to national rebirth, and the movement offered an outlet for outrage at Italy's treatment by the Allies. Through the press and speeches Fascist leaders disseminated their definition of the situation.[33] It defined the problem (national decline and disunity, class conflict), designated the guilty (the British, socialists, Slavs, bourgeoisie), and the solution (the advent to power of a new national elite drawn from the veterans and youth). Attacks on the socialists were legitimated by stories—too ubiquitous to be taken literally in every case—of socialists abusing veterans in the streets.

In practice, Fascist ideologies were complex. The aforementioned action frame was combined with many other motivations, perceptions and ideas. Like all social movements, in unprecedented crisis situations, Fascists used well-established ideas to understand the new situation. These ideas had histories, controversies and stakes of their own, and they resonated differently in the heterogeneous fascist constituency. Ideological debate within the movement represented a particular spin on old controversies about the nature of the political system, the relative importance of state and private initiative in social reform, the role of trade unions, the rights of women and much more, which were not specific to Fascism, out of which came new ideas and projects.

---

[32] Bosworth, *Mussolini*, p. 145.
[33] Bert Klandermans, *The Social Psychology of Protest* (Oxford: Blackwell, 1997).

Likewise, we must historicize the religious language and rituals of Fascism, for they demonstrate not the correctness of Le Bon's theories or its avatars, but the *use* of crowd psychology to shape political action. Crowd psychology provided an incontrovertible (and unfalsifiable) explanation for political conflict; it taught that the mass was potentially dangerous and vulnerable to 'demagogues', but could be a force for good if led by a genuine elite. The latter must be close enough to the mass to understand the national psychology, but distant enough from the materialist and irrational crowd to provide disinterested national leadership. Besides his debt to Le Bon, Mussolini drew on Georges Sorel, Vilfredo Pareto, Gaetano Mosca and Robert Michels, all of whom owed something to crowd psychology.[34] He held that the elite must structure the mass: 'The mass is a flock of sheep until it is organized'.[35] He saw fascist marches as restoring the colourful and picturesque in the mass mind.[36]

Treating Fascism as a social movement shows that protagonists put crowd psychology to very different uses. It could justify harnessing the nationalism of the mass to the creation of a new society. Division of the world into elites and demagogues also led Fascists to overestimate the power and dangerousness of their opponents, so that gains by socialist trade unions appeared to threaten the whole social system and legitimated Fascist violence. Violence was important to Fascist practice both in the sense that the movement viewed it as a form of propaganda and because success depended on intimidation of opposing organizations (cast as anti-national demagogues) as much as on ritual adoration of the leader.

Moreover, crowd psychology did not necessarily lead in radical directions. It also taught that the elite should pursue 'realistic' policies, in conformity with the psychology of the people and the possibilities for action. Therefore, it potentially reinforced Mussolini's willingness to compromise in the interests of winning power. Similarly, while many Fascists depicted the elite as a macho warrior caste, women portrayed themselves as an elite capable of regenerating the mass through social work—a notion with a long history in Italy and elsewhere.[37] Mussolini's appointment as Prime Minister on 29 October 1922 won him many admirers outside Italy, but

[34] Robert Nye, *The Anti-Democratic Sources of Elite Theory: Pareto, Mosca, Michels* (London: Sage, 1977).
[35] Tracy H. Koon, *Believe, Obey, Fight: Political Socialization of Youth in Fascist Italy, 1922–1943* (Chapel Hill, NC: University of North Carolina Press, 1985), p. 5.
[36] Reichardt, 'Fascist Marches', p. 180.
[37] Grazia, *How Fascism Ruled Women*, pp. 236–237.

it is not surprising that foreign observers of Fascism could not pin down its essence.

TRANSNATIONAL FASCISM

In 1919, several movements emerged that looked similar to Fascism, quite independently of it. That happened because economies, religions and ideas had always transcended frontiers, and for the purpose of analysis we may take that as given. Likewise, war was a transcontinental experience; belligerents drew on a common pool of ideas and precedents, and there had been much international exchange concerning military strategy and the organization of society for war. Afterwards, unrest affected most countries in some degree. As we have seen, the movements that most resembled Fascist paramilitarism developed in defeated Germany, Austria and Hungary, in the disputed borderlands of Eastern Europe, and there were many contacts between far-right activists in these areas. Demobilized officers keen to compensate for defeat and students wishing to prove themselves in battle were prominent, and they endeavoured to kill the Jews and Bolsheviks whom they held responsible for defeat.[38] As in Italy, future activists recounted having been spurred to action by having their decorations stripped by reds, and everywhere the far-right was divided politically and socially. In Germany, a veteran claimed to have come home to 'hysterical' crowds, composed of disease-ridden 'rats'.[39]

Italy was not initially central to the diffusion and exchange of far-right ideas and practice. The Central European far-right had little interest in a country that had benefited from the peace treaties and which some saw as racially inferior. The Western far-right did not view Italy much more positively. Indeed, it was Mussolini who borrowed from the French thinkers, Le Bon and Sorel. Yet the actions of the fascist squads in ethnic conflicts on the Yugoslav border were contiguous with the Central European space of conflict described above, and as such it represented a transitional space between eastern and western Europe. The style and methods of D'Annunzio's Fiume expedition were transferred to the class conflicts of the Po Valley and then beyond. And since the Fascist movement amounted to more than just paramilitary violence there were potential convergences with a whole range of foreign movements in terms of ideology and practice.

---

[38] Gerwarth, 'The Central European Counter-revolution'; Gerwarth and Horne, 'Vectors of Violence', pp. 493–495.
[39] Gerwarth, 'The Central European Counter-revolution', pp. 190–191.

Fascism's success turned it into a prestigious label. By 1925, movements in no less than 45 states had designated themselves as 'fascist', encouraged also by the Italian regime's efforts to spread its ideology.[40] However, the question of imitation is complex, especially if we try to separate out perceptions of fascism as a movement according to our definition. On the Italian side, the nature of Fascism remained uncertain, all the more so imitators looked both to the Fascist movement and the regime. Major disputes continued within the Fascist regime concerning the status of trade unions and Church and the relationship of state and party. Since Fascists were not sure what fascism was, it is no surprise that foreigners, not to speak of present-day scholars, could not agree what it was either. Some observers stressed authoritarianism, and did not differentiate between the Spanish and Italian dictatorships. Moreover, dislike of the Italian regime's nationalism and imperialism stymied attempts to build a 'Fascist International', and Italian Fascism was not the only model towards which foreign movements looked. Another complicating factor was that anti-fascists from Antonio Gramsci to Ernst Bloch swallowed Fascists' claim that they had found the secret of moving the mass, and so thought that analogous techniques must be used to fight fascism.[41]

NATIONAL SOCIALISM

The Great War and November Revolution had convinced many ordinary Germans that they should be involved in national politics and provoked the emergence of a network of movements in a multi-sector mobilization. This activism was not homogeneous. Socialists were part of it but so was the explicitly bourgeois and nationalist reaction against the Revolution and Versailles Treaty. The reactionaries hesitated between nostalgia for the monarchy and the conviction that the racially defined people (*Volk) rep-resented the nation. Among them, the Freikorps assembled demobilized veterans to fight socialists, communists and Slavs in the borderlands and in Germany itself. In March 1920, the Pan-German Wolfgang Kapp led

[40] For a fine survey of the issues, see Arnd Bauerkämper, 'Transnational Fascism: Cross-border Relations between Regimes and Movements in Europe, 1922–1939', *East Central Europe* 2–3 (2010), pp. 214–246, here p. 216.

[41] Dante L. Germino, *Antonio Gramsci: Architect of a New Politics* (Louisiana State University Press, 1990), p. 120; Mark Meyers, 'Feminizing Fascist Men: Crowd Psychology, Gender, and Sexuality in French Antifascism, 1929–1945', *French Historical Studies* 1 (2006), pp. 109–142.

the *Freikorps Marinebrigade Ehrhardt* (Erhardt Naval Brigade) into Berlin to carry out a coup. The Freikorps resembled Fascism in obvious respects. Yet they differed in lacking a syndicalist and trade-union wing, while anti-Semitism was far more important to them than it was to the Italian Fascists. In the 1920s, movements such as the Home Guard provided a refuge for former paramilitary activists, but it was also part of small-town associational networks. These groups lacked political ambitions of their own, but Nazism would draw something from them.[42]

Mussolini's appointment provoked excitement among opponents of the new Weimar Republic.[43] Subsequently, movements from the right-wing veterans' movement, the *Stalhelm* (Steel Helmet), to the Catholic Centre Party adopted elements of fascism, understood selectively and in the light of their own ideas. The Stahlhelm emphasized the compromise between the conservatives, perhaps including the monarchy, and Fascism. Some were especially impressed by Mussolini's seizure of power, for it seemed to prove that history was not on the side of 'progress', and that nationalists could compete with socialists in the streets. They also described themselves as a movement (*Bewegung*), but they also looked to the Italian regime, especially to the notion of the absolute leader of party and nation. To understand the resulting complexities, I shall return to the concepts used to understand Fascism as a social movement.

ACTION FRAMES

Fascist influence on Nazi ideology requires careful specification, for activists selectively incorporated the Italian model into an already well-established extreme-right tradition. However, defeat and revolution had discredited the older authoritarian, elitist, nationalism of the monarchy and pan-Germans. Hitherto marginal groups profited, and developed a new nationalism based on the racially defined people rather than the Kaiser, and blamed 'Judeo-Bolshevik' influence for Germany's misfortunes. The notion of an ethnic *Volk* including Alsace, Austria and Germans in Eastern Europe and the Baltic constituted a rejection both of old-style *kleindeutsch* nationalism (i.e. of Germany within its pre-1914 borders) and of the Versailles Treaty. The belief that Germany was engaged in a war

---

[42] Peter Fritzsche, *Germans into Nazis*, pp. 85–136.
[43] Christian Goeschel, 'Italia Docet? The Relationship between Italian Fascism and Nazism revisited', *European History Quarterly* 3 (2012), pp. 480–492.

to the death against a 'Judeo-Bolshevik' enemy and that German success in the struggle for life depended on the conquest of living space in the East was already important in *völkische* groups.[44] The discredit of established nationalism may also have made Germans receptive to Mussolini's example. But when Hitler praised Fascism for its attacks on the three weapons of international Jewry—freemasons, the international press and Marxism—he interpreted Italian Fascism in his own way, in the service of his own strategies, as did his followers.[45]

INSTRUMENTALISM

Were it not for the homogenizing effect of interpretations based on anomie, the desire for charismatic leadership and/or the need for a political religion, there would be no need to rehearse the vast scholarly literature showing the variable appeal of the Nazis. Electoral studies show that the Nazi appeal was diverse, appealed relatively more to groups such as Protestant farmers who were suffering from falling prices and to the urban middle classes alarmed by loss of savings and status.[46] These groups initially embraced Nazism for complex reasons, often quite independently of any attempt by the party to mobilize them. In the 1928 elections, with little success, the party had directed socialistic propaganda at urban constituencies. However, the party had done unexpectedly well in rural areas. Schleswig-Holstein especially had witnessed a rural social movement, the *Landvolk*, which had organized tax strikes and even engaged in terrorism. Rural voters had used the Nazi message in ways not intended by the leadership. Quickly learning the lessons, the party re-designed its message and regional organizations and saturated rural areas with permanent propaganda. A social movement had unintentionally re-shaped the party.[47]

---

[44] Peter Longerich, *Holocaust: The Nazi Persecution and Murder of the Jews* (Oxford: Oxford University Press, 2010), pp. 11–15.

[45] Goeschel, 'Italia Docet?', p. 487.

[46] Richard F. Hamilton, *Who Voted for Hitler?* (Princeton, NJ: Princeton University Press, 1982); Thomas Childers, *The Nazi Voter: The Social Foundations of Fascism in Germany, 1919–1933* (Chapel Hill: University of North Carolina Press, 1983).

[47] Michel Dobry, 'Hitler, Charisma and Structure: Reflections on Historical Methodology', in António Costa Pinto, Roger Eatwell and Stein Ugelvik Larsen (eds), *Charisma and Fascism in Interwar Europe* (London: Routledge, 2006), pp. 19–33, here pp. 28–31.

The diversity of Nazi support imported conflict into the movement. For instance, Otto Strasser advocated the socialization of big business, while Hitler retorted that he would only 'socialise enterprises that are prejudicial to the interests of the nation'.[48] Likewise, women played a complex role in the movement. As in Italy, the ethos of the Brownshirts mixed masculinism, contempt for women and idealization of mothers. Yet Hitler's refusal to allow women to occupy positions of political responsibility enabled them to organize separately. They evoked their own version of *Lebensraum* (living space), meaning the promotion of a harmonious society modelled on the home, and they propagandized for their version of National Socialism in public meetings—not just through charity work. Tensions between male and female activists remained largely subterranean until after the seizure of power. That women usually came off second best in conflicts with men was the result of differential power resources rather than acceptance of a subordinate position in a political religion.[49]

SOLIDARITY

Peter Merkl's study of some 500 autobiographies of pre-1933 members shows that nearly a third of them were attracted primarily by the social solidarity of the national community.[50] Sven Reichardt's micro-study of Berlin storm-troopers shows that the violence of the SA reinforced solidarity—for Goebbels, bloodshed for the party was 'cement'—bringing together friendship groups, workmates and practitioners of sports.[51] Furthermore, although from 1930, the Nazis toned anti-Semitism down, activists continued to attack Jews in the streets, and from 1931 to 1932, local groups intensified boycotts of Jewish businesses. The boycott campaign was not a mass phenomenon, but it too reinforced the solidarity of the movement.[52]

Rituals and demonstrations also mattered. The party took some of them from Italy, notably the use of flags, the Roman salute and the leader

---

[48] Jeremy Noakes and Geoffrey Pridham (eds), *The Rise to Power 1919–1934*, Documents on Nazism, 1919–1945 (London: Cape, 1974), pp. 66–67.

[49] Matthew Stibbe, *Women in the Third Reich* (London: Bloomsbury, 2003).

[50] Peter H. Merkl, *Political Violence under the Swastika* (Princeton, NJ: Princeton University Press, 1975), p. 12.

[51] Reichardt, 'Fascist Marches', p. 185; Sven Reichardt, 'Violence and Community: a Micro-Study on Nazi Storm Troopers', *Central European History* 2 (2013), pp. 275–297, here p. 280.

[52] Longerich, *Holocaust*, pp. 18–25.

cult.[53] However, Nazism was not a simple copy. The *Führer* cult combined the Italian example with the old conservative critique of 'leaderless democracy' which was common to several European countries, the longstanding cult of Bismarck, the idea of a people's Kaiser, and the veterans' belief in leadership combined with equality of sacrifice.[54] There was a quasi-religious dimension to these rituals. Merkl's autobiographies show that some saw Hitler, as a man who had risen from humble origins, as the only hope for Germany; others expressed their willingness to die for him. Even the worldly and egotistical Hermann Göring spoke of 'the beloved leader of the German freedom movement'.[55] A journalist encouraged readers to set up shrines to Hitler in their homes.[56]

We must beware of taking literally the Nazi's explanations of how solidarity worked, for they were derived from crowd theory and are too easily recycled in the Weberian concept of charisma or in political religions theory. The place of charismatic authority in the movement must be carefully specified, and the term must be historicized. For instance, the belief of SA leaders that they must embody the group as a whole while remaining removed from the mass was compatible with routine crowd psychology, and doubtless it shaped their subjectivity and guided their action. Blind faith in Hitler may have been strongest in those who joined the party early, before there were any successes to confirm Hitler's genius. These people were most likely to stick with Hitler to the bitter end, when facts had manifestly falsified his prophesies. Their emotional commitment may also explain why they were willing to accept radical changes of political direction, such as the alliance with the nationalist right in the 1929 campaign against the Young Plan. The many unemployed young men who joined the SA may also have been especially open to its offer of comradeship, especially as many of them had broken with their families, and had perhaps lived in SA hostels. But the SA was never characterized by the sort of solidarity about which the Nazis fantasized; many activists did have outside employment and families, and even the aforementioned unemployed

[53] Ian Kershaw, *The 'Hitler Myth': Image and Reality in the Third Reich* (Oxford: Oxford University Press, 1989).

[54] Kershaw, *The 'Hitler Myth'*, pp. 14–47; Sven Reichardt, *Faschistische Kampfbünde: Gewalt und Gemeinschaft im Italienischen Squadrismus und in der deutschen SA* (Köln: Böhlau, 2002).

[55] Merkl, *Political Violence under the Swastika*, pp. 539–553; Ian Kershaw, *Hitler: 1889–1936: Hubris* (London: Allen Lane, 1998), p. 193.

[56] Kershaw, *The 'Hitler Myth'*, p. 39.

young men could feel rivalry towards other SA groups.[57] Many young SA men were too young to have fought in the war, and identified with the front generation also because it was a socially valuable to do so. That is not to deny the strength of the emotional commitment, only to avoid essentializing it.[58] A glance at the wider Nazi constituency confirms that emotion and instrumentalism could go together. As in Italy, the Nazi's initial advance in the countryside in the 1928 elections owed little to Hitler's charisma or tactical nous. After the elections, the party attributed these gains to Hitler's genius, which became both emotional commitment and weapon in internal struggles.

Even in the inner core of the early movement, when the NSDAP remained marginal, instrumentalization and emotion were hard to separate. The limits of Hitler's charismatic leadership provoked him to instrumentalize Mussolini's leader cult. In the mid-1920s, the *Duce*'s establishment of a dictatorship helped to convince Hitler that he might himself be Germany's *Führer*, even if publicly he still deferred to other potential leaders.[59] Indeed, one of his chief opponents, Otto Strasser, claimed that activists must obey the idea rather than the 'merely human' leader, and he was more likely to refer to National Socialism as a movement than as a party.[60] A bust of Mussolini in his Munich office legitimated Hitler's pretensions.

THE ROLE OF THE MOVEMENT IN THE SEIZURE OF POWER

The Italian model particularly influenced the way in which the National Socialists read the tactical possibilities. Initially, Hitler was most impressed by the belief that movement had seized power, and wittingly or unwittingly he played down the importance of parliamentary manoeuvres. He commented, 'We only have to have the courage to act. Without struggle, no victory!'[61] Then, reflecting on the failure of his 1923 Munich coup, Hitler re-read Italian events and placed more emphasis on the combination of legality and violence. Moreover, Hitler consulted personally with Mussolini's envoy in Germany, Major Guiseppe Renzetti at least 39

[57] Reichardt, 'Violence and Community', pp. 286–289.
[58] Ziemann, 'Germany after the First World War', p. 93.
[59] Kershaw, *The 'Hitler Myth'*, p. 20–23.
[60] Otto Strasser, *Hitler and I* (Boston: Haugthon & Miflin, 1946), p. 146, cited in Noakes and Pridham, *The Rise to Power 1919–1934*.
[61] Kershaw, *Hitler*, pp. 182183.

times between 1929 and 1934. The two leaders had a common interest in attacking the Versailles Treaty, but some Nazis saw Italians as a weak race that had betrayed Germany in 1914. Renzetti consistently encouraged Hitler to ally with conservative forces, to take power legally and to join the government only as senior member.[62]

In fact, while the Nazi movement benefitted from the connivance of the judiciary, press and conservative politicians, it could not count on the police to the extent that Italian Fascists could. Consequently, Brownshirt violence was more restrained. Threats were rarely carried out and there was no attempt to destroy the left prior to a March on Berlin. Amongst other things, SA mobilizations were part of an electoral strategy, designed to demonstrate that the movement represented the nation better than the government did. Nevertheless, bourgeois opinion does seem to have approved a violent practice that respectable values forbade them to indulge in themselves.[63] Moreover, deal a deal with the conservatives brought Nazism to power. As in Italy, the conflict between National Socialists and Communists in the streets complicated the usual mechanisms of parliamentary majority formation, turned the army against the republic, and ultimately obliging the appointment of Hitler as Chancellor in order to break the parliamentary deadlock.[64]

On the night of Hitler's appointment as Chancellor, the new cabinet gathered in the Reich Chancellery to view a massive torch-lit march of SA fighters. The participation of the Stalhelm demonstrated the breadth of Hitler's coalition and confirmed the Nazis' roots in a broad social movement. Analogies with Italy were obvious to contemporaries: a journalist allegedly remarked that they were witnessing the 'March on Rome in German form'. Perhaps he knew that Renzetti was the only foreign guest invited to join the official party. During the night, attacks on socialists and communists underlined the parallel with Italy, but aggression towards persons of 'Jewish appearance' suggested something different to the Italian regime.[65]

The rise of Nazism complicated the reception of fascism, for Hitler soon eclipsed Mussolini on the international stage. One by one, movements

[62] Goeschel, 'Italia Docet?', p. 486.

[63] Bernd Weisbrod, 'The Crisis of Bourgeois Society in Interwar Germany', in Richard Bessel (ed.), *Fascist Italy and Nazi Germany* (Cambridge: Cambridge University Press, 1996), pp. 23–39.

[64] Reichardt, 'Fascist Marches', pp. 172–174, p. 184.

[65] Peter Fritzsche, *Germans into Nazis*, pp. 139–143.

that had been allied to the Italians shifted their allegiance to Germany. Mussolini responded by redoubling promotion of fascism abroad, and rivalry continued even after Italy and Germany joined the Axis Pact. To compete with the Nazis and satisfy pro-Nazis in his own party, Mussolini adopted anti-Semitism. He also depicted Fascism as 'Latin', a strategy that would have implications for fascism internationally.[66] There is no space to trace all the ramifications of the fascism on its worldwide journey. I shall concentrate on a few illustrations.

HUNGARY

Paradoxically, while Hungary had been a major theatre of paramilitary conflicts in the aftermath of the war, extreme right-wing social movements were relatively weak in the 1920s. Gyula Gömbös, on the more radical wing of the White Terror, had backed the regent, Admiral Miklós Horthy. That had ensured that agrarian and business elites remained in control of a semi-authoritarian system under Prime Minister István Bethlen. Popular mobilization was restricted by the defeat of the left in 1919 and the manipulation of elections, in which the open ballot was the norm. Soon, Gömbös was disillusioned with the conservatism of the Bethlen government. His small group of followers, the remnants of the paramilitaries and secret societies with links to the army, went into opposition. Gradually, they adopted more of the characteristics of a political movement, but remained unusual for another reason. Besides admiring Mussolini, they established links with Hitler, partly through German minorities in Hungarian towns. Hungarians were attracted to National Socialism's extreme hostility to the peace treaties and by its anti-Semitism, for they held Jewish universalism responsible for undermining the ethnic Hungarian nation. This message resonated with the officer class and bureaucrats who had recently governed a great empire.

The world economic crisis permitted the revival of Gömbös's fortunes, even though there was not a great mobilization of social movements. Deals at the peak of the state mattered more. In 1932, Horthy made Gömbös Prime Minister on condition that he renounced anti-Semitism. Gömbös complied, and anyway he had long admired Mussolini. But in June 1933, he was among the first heads of state to visit Hitler, attracted by the promise of treaty revision and by German economic power. Gömbös also attempted to build a genuine power base in the form of

---

[66] Bauerkämper, 'Transnational Fascism', p. 234.

mass party, and secured the election of 100 favourable parliamentarians in 1935. However, the absence of a threat from left-wing social movements and the conservative grip on elections meant that his success was limited. Conservatives were alarmed by Gömbös's anti-Semitism, establishment of economic ties with Germany and placing of pro-Germans in key positions in the army and governing party. Conservatives feared that these measures would undermine ties with Italy, and thus weaken opposition to the unification of Austria and Germany. In October 1936, Gömbös died and the conservatives returned to power, but conservatives were not strong enough to reverse the pro-German alignment.

Paradoxically, the defeat of fascism in the state marked the beginning of fascism as a significant social movement, the absence of which had weakened Gömbös's premiership. After his death, many of Gömbös's followers turned to a new pro-Nazi Party of National Will led by Ferenc Szàlasi, which was quickly banned but re-emerged in 1938 as the Arrow Cross. The party was more genuinely a social movement than earlier far-right groups had been, possessing perhaps 100,000 members by 1940, and it was notable for its popular appeal. Urban workers were sympathetic to attacks on Jewish employers. Poor agricultural labourers in Western Hungary were attracted by promises of land reform, ultranationalism and anti-Semitism. National Socialism also appealed because many seasonal rural workers had earned high wages in Germany. Fascist groups in Hungary did not become sufficiently strong as social movements to entirely disrupt politics at the state level, but thanks to the presence in them of so many pro-Nazi officers, they did ensure that the regime became increasingly anti-Semitic. The Arrow Cross quickly declined once Hungary had entered the war, and even more so after it became clear that Germany would not win, but in the final days of the war the remaining fascists won power. Those who now occupied governing positions issued from the 'charismatic community' within the fascist leadership, but the logic of the situation in which they found themselves, the product of earlier unwise choices, meant that their actions were not entirely irrational.[67]

---

[67] Gabriella Ilonszki, 'Hungary: Crisis and Pseudodemocratic Compromise', in Dirk Berg-Schlosser and Jeremy Mitchell (ed.), *Conditions of Democracy in Europe, 1919–1939 Systematic Case Studies* (Basingstoke: Palgrave, 2000), pp. 242–262; J. Erös, 'Hungary', in Stuart J. Woolf (ed.), *Fascism in Europe* (London: Methuen, 1968), pp. 118–150; Mark Pittaway, 'Hungary', in Richard Bosworth (ed.), *The Oxford Handbook of Fascism* (Oxford: Oxford University Press, 2009), pp. 380–397.

FRANCE

In Hungary, fascism initially lacked a social base. In France, in contrast, the social movement suffered from a lack of allies among the elites. In 1919, France too experienced an upsurge of activism on the part of veteran associations, bourgeois self-defence groups, women's groups, conservative white-collar and peasant unions. Often they were politicized, but moderate conservatives predominated. Unlike their German and Italian counterparts, French conservatives had for decades been excluded from power, and so they were better placed to capture hopes of renewal. The parliamentary right, as the *Bloc national*, won the elections of 1919.

The Bloc was dominated by informally organized elitist parties and civil society groups largely lined up behind them, notably the '1919 Movement' for reform of the constitution. But the creation of the *Démocratie nouvelle* (The New Democracy), however insignificant numerically it was, demonstrated that France was capable of generating something resembling Fascism quite independently of the Italian example.[68] Well before the March on Rome, conservatives explicitly evoked the lessons of Italy. Among the first to do so were the *Unions civiques*, local groups that had been formed to break a general strike of 1 May 1920, affiliated to which were nationalist, student and veterans' groups. One activist urged imitation of the methods of Italy and Spain which he saw as a 'bourgeois rebellion' against Socialist anti-patriots. However, the Unions did not envisage an autonomous political role, and allowed themselves to be directed by the government.[69]

By the time that Mussolini seized power, the Bloc's political capital had declined, for it failed to translate expectation into concrete legislation. Now, the discontented right wing of the Bloc evoked the successes of Mussolini, which they assimilated to Catholic authoritarian conservatism, often grouped with Primo de Rivera's Spanish military dictatorship. These admirers also made some concessions to Fascism as a social movement, calling for a French Mussolini to embody popular discontent

---

[68] Kevin Passmore, *The Right in France from the Third Republic to Vichy* (Oxford: Oxford University Press, 2013), pp. 208–209.

[69] Théodore Aubert, *Une forme de défense sociale. Les Unions civiques* (Paris: Marx Texier, 1921); Maurice Moissonnier and André Boulmier, 'La bourgeoisie lyonnaise aux origines de l'Union civique de 1920?', *Cahiers d'histoire de L'institut de recherches marxistes* 4 (1980), pp. 106–131; Andreas Wirsching, 'Political Violence in France and Italy after 1918', *Journal of Modern European History* 1 (2003), pp. 60–79.

with politicians.[70] The neo-royalist *Action française* also began to liken itself to Fascism, which it claimed derived from French ideas. According to Dieter Rucht's definition Action française was not a social movement, for its leaders aspired only to mobilize disciplined elites for a coup d'état. However, it contained a syndicalist wing, led by Georges Valois, who shared Mussolini's interest in Georges Sorel, and attempted to mobilize business and workers' groups.[71]

In 1924, the electoral victory of the *Cartel des gauches* (Left Cartel) provoked fear of revolution and completed discredit of the Bloc national. There ensued a multi-sector mobilization of Catholics and veterans. Two new extreme right-wing leagues emerged, the *Jeunesses patriotes* (JP) and the *Faisceau*. The JP ambiguously combined anti-parliamentarianism with alliance with the parliamentary conservatives, while the Faisceau rejected democracy and electoralism. Both attracted large memberships, were connected to civil society groups and were social movements in our sense. They often evoked fascism, identified with the young war generation, and embraced mass politics, paramilitarism and the leader cult. The new leagues denounced not only the Bloc and its failure to regenerate the nation and fight communism, but Action française, which it saw as timidly elitist.

From an *instrumental* perspective, the Faisceau and JP advocated or created organizations designed to constitute the kernel of a future corporatist system, thus providing selective incentives to join the movement in the form of access to employment in the present. The two leagues also offered *solidarity* through participation in tightly knit organizations identified with the veterans, and used rituals and regalia that were directly inspired by Fascism. The JP refused to adopt the 'axe or the fasces of the old Roman lictors as their badge', but their shock troops were organized in 'centuries', wore a uniform of blue raincoats and berets and used the roman salute. Faisceau members wore dark blue shirts and held military-style mobilizations with grandiose *mise en scène*, borrowed as much from the Fascist regime as from Fascist movement.

---

[70] *La République française*, 12 October 1922. See also, *L'Indépendent* (cantons of Pont-a-Mousson, Nomeny and Thiaucourt), 13 September 1923; *Bulletin de l'ALP*, 1 January, 15 April, 1 August, 15 October 1923; *Action nationale républicaine*, 3 May 1923.

[71] Eugen Weber, *Action Française: Royalism and Reaction in Twentieth-Century France* (Palo Alto, CA: Stanford University Press, 1962), pp. 155–159; Joel Blatt, 'Relatives and Rivals: the Responses of Action française to Italian Fascism, 1919–1926', *European Studies Review* 3 (1981), pp. 263–292.

Ideologically these movements were heterogeneous. Both drew on diverse French traditions and networks, but combined them with Italian ideas. Pierre Taittinger, the Jeunesses patriote leader, combined Bonapartism with Catholic conservatism and influences from outside the political sphere, such as management science. The Faisceau was divided between a Catholic conservative strand that distrusted the league's social movement dimension and Georges Valois' own syndicalism.

As we have seen in Italy and Germany, none of these aspects could be separated in the cut and thrust of practical politics, as the leagues' use of the label 'fascism' reveals. They saw in Fascism a means to renew French anti-republicanism, and initially, few expressed reservations about what they saw in Italy. However, given the diversity of the extreme-right tradition, the question of labels was potentially divisive. The JP preferred the label 'France' because reference to Bonapartism, royalism, or republicanism was potentially divisive.[72] Valois, in contrast, used the fascist label. He claimed that fascism was an international force that took different forms in different countries and like AF argued that Fascism's roots were French.[73] As Valois monopolized the Fascist label, AF and even the JP dropped it. Nevertheless, the use of fascist symbols and paraphernalia, even without use of the label, was inevitably taken as a challenge to the regime. The leagues used what Bruno Goyet calls 'the grammar of the March on Rome'. Using the language of war, the Faisceau predicted the imminence of 'H-Hour', and the JP joined in their paramilitary style mobilizations.[74] They did not imitate the systematic violence of the Italians, but used paramilitary display to portray themselves as stronger and more national than the government.

These rhetorical manoeuvres did not enable the leagues to monopolize right-wing opinion, and still less to win power. Although protests against the Cartel des gauches had created a fluid situation, and the leagues had disrupted routine political calculations, they struggled to convert street power into state power. The government retreated on its religious reforms and raised veterans' pensions. The leagues enjoyed the backing of many parliamentary conservatives, but had few deputies of their own, for there

---

[72] *Le Drapeau*, 20 April 1924.

[73] *Le Nouveau siècle*, 28 January 1926.

[74] Bruno Goyet, 'La "Marche sur Rome " : Version originale sous-titrée. la réception du Fascisme en France dans les années 20', in Michel Dobry (ed.), *Le mythe de l'allergie française du fascisme* (Paris: Albin Michel, 2003), p. 100ff.

had been no elections. In any case the strength of anti-parliamentarianism made the leagues reluctant to participate in elections.[75] Consequently, it was easier in France than in Italy to form parliamentary coalitions. In 1926, the centre-left Radical-Socialist Party switched support to the right, permitting the establishment of a new government that defused the crisis. The Faisceau quickly declined, while the JP survived only because it transferred its activist energy to regeneration of the parliamentary right.

In the 1930s, the leagues reappeared. On 6 February 1934, Action française, the JP and a new league, the *Croix de feu* (Cross of fire), demonstrated against the allegedly corrupt government on the Place de la Concorde in Paris. Again, a fluid situation developed as the initiative passed to the streets. The army, police and judiciary proved reluctant to defend the government, which resigned. Again the leagues proved unable to profit from their victory. A parliamentary national unity government under Gaston Doumergue took over, with token representation in the cabinet to 'cover' the leagues.

Certainly, it proved harder for parliamentarians to master events, for there followed years of confrontation between left and right in the streets, while divisions in parliament meant that the government could not implement promised reforms. The Doumergue government was discredited, leaving space for the most untainted league, the Croix de feu. The latter developed a complex network of specialist organizations, integrated into a broad social movement, and in terms of membership it soon became the largest political organization France had ever seen. It expanded even more from 1936, when, thanks to dissolution ordered by a left-wing government, it reformed as a political party, the Parti social français (PSF).[76]

Whether the Croix de feu was fascist remains controversial, for the answer depends entirely upon definition. It resembled Fascism and Nazism in some respects, but not others. Some members regarded themselves as fascist, notably in Montpellier, where royalists had long admired Mussolini.[77] Most rejected the fascist label and denied any affinity at all with Nazism, which it saw as an extreme form of Pan-German expansion-

[75] Michel Dobry, 'France: an Ambiguous Survival', in Dirk Berg-Schlosser and Jeremy Mitchell (eds), *Conditions of Democracy in Europe, 1919–1939 Systematic Case Studies* (Basingstoke: Palgrave Macmillan, 2000), pp. 157–183.

[76] Brian Jenkins, 'The Six Fevrier 1934 and the "Survival" of the French Republic', *French History* 3 (2006), pp. 333–351; Passmore, *The Right in France*, pp. 292–297.

[77] Philippe Secondy, *La Persistance Du Midi Blanc. L'Hérault (1789–1962)* (Perpignan: Presses Universitaires de Perpignan, 2006), pp. 237–238.

ism. Moreover, 'fascism' had become just one more reference point in the divided far right, and so as one of its leaders put it, it determined to avoid proclaiming itself 'Bonapartist, royalist, republican or fascist, and never pronounce these words that sow discord'.[78]

Nevertheless, the Croix de feu showed much interest in the Nazi and Fascist regimes (and others), which it understood in the light of French radical-right traditions (which actually were not exclusively French) and of its own priorities. Above all, the movement was open to the notion of a 'Latin' alliance with Italy and Spain. Turning to the instrumentalist dimension of the league as a social movement, debates within the Croix de feu and PSF concerning the rights of unions (syndicates) in the proposed corporatist state were part of an international exchange dating back decades, but which now had concrete realizations in Italy to discuss. Croix de feu sympathizers were among the many that visited Italy to investigate its corporatist system. Usually, they preferred Guiseppe Bottai's syndicalism and distrusted Alfredo Roccca's statist corporatism.[79] Ironically, they invoked Italian radicals to legitimate a syndicalist programme that was considered conservative in France (and by French scholars of fascism).

The Croix de feu figured in the international circulation of ideas, notably in its debt to crowd psychology. It claimed to unite its members in the 'mystique Croix de feu', that is behind a mobilizing myth that united the mass behind a regenerated veteran elite.[80] In this sense, the Croix de feu sought to create a political religion, for it assigned sacred status to its objective, borrowed the paraphernalia of traditional religion and subsumed Catholicism into the mystique.[81] To propagate the mystique, La Rocque urged the repetition of a few 'master ideas', thus revealing the assumption that mass action was non-reflective.[82] But if the Croix de feu leadership saw itself as a male elite leading a feminized mass, female activists reworked the same categories to buttress their own claim to elite status. They claimed to be technicians possessed of a vocation for social work that was unique to women and thus to be perfectly placed to propagate

---

[78] Didier Leschi, 'L'étrange cas La Rocque', in Michel Dobry (ed.), *Le Mythe de L'allergie Française Du Fascisme*, (Paris: Albin Michel, 2003), pp. 155–194.

[79] *La Petite Gironde*, 27 October 1935.

[80] *La Petite Gironde*, 27 October 1935.

[81] Gentile, *The Sacralisation of Politics*; François de La Rocque, *Service Public* (Paris: Grasset, 1934), p. 19.

[82] La Rocque, *Service Public*, pp. 14–19; *Le Flambeau*, 1 April 1934; AN 451, 5 February 1934.

the Croix de Feu mystique in the mass. Their social conception of politics set them against male activists.[83]

Turning to solidarity, Croix de feu members wore armbands, not uniforms, and the Roman salute was only used unofficially. They identified with the veterans rather than with foreign fascist movements, and association with this prestigious group was important for women too, some of whom invoked service as war nurses. However, the league's structure and paramilitary methods closely resembled those of the Faisceau. In response to secret orders, members travelled in columns of motor vehicles to locations revealed en route—sometimes to left-wing strongholds. Although violence often ensued, the purpose was more one of display and threat and to reinforce the solidarity of the movement. There was none of the systematic destruction of socialist movements that the Italian Fascists engaged in. But inevitably the practice provoked fears that the league was inspired by fascism, and we can safely assume that its leaders knowingly took that risk.[84] With hindsight, we know that Croix de feu mobilizations were remarkably similar to those in Germany, in that they were symbolic instruments meant to demonstrate the movement's fitness for office, and threats were rarely carried out.[85]

The Croix de feu proved unable to emulate the National Socialists in winning power. La Rocque privately recognized that in a large Western country, a movement could not 'rely exclusively on a romantic coup de force to get into power'. He added that 'despite the extreme nature of their doctrines, neither Mussolini nor Hitler made that mistake'; Hitler especially owed his success to elections. In Germany, La Rocque said, proportional representation and repeated dissolutions favoured Hitler, but that did not 'make the precedent any the less impressive'. In France, he argued, the problem was that while the mass of the population was accustomed to democracy, 'many members [of the Croix de feu] feel a real repugnance for elections', and they joined us because 'they no longer believed in universal suffrage'. Caught between these two stools, La Rocque resolved to give secret support to the best candidates of other parties in the coming elections. However, when the league became a party in 1936, most of

[83] Kevin Passmore, '"Planting the Rricolor in the Citadels of Communism": Women's Social Service in the Croix de Feu and Parti social français', *Journal of Modern History* 4 (1999), pp. 814–851, here p. 820.

[84] Kevin Passmore, 'Boy-scouting for Grown-ups? Paramilitarism in the Croix de Feu and PSF', *French Historical Studies* 2 (1995), pp. 527–557.

[85] Reichardt, 'Fascist Marches', pp. 175–176, pp. 177–179, pp. 181–182.

those deputies refused to join.[86] Like its 1920s precursors, neither the Croix de feu nor the PSF could convert their power as movements into leverage in parliament. In this, the movement was quite typical of admirers of fascism elsewhere in Europe, with the partial exception of the short-lived Gyula Gömbös government in Hungary (1932–1936). Elsewhere in Europe, fascist movements depended either on German invasion or, in the case of Spain, on a military rising.

FASCISM OUTSIDE EUROPE

Definitions of generic fascism take Europe as exemplary, and ask whether or not movements outside Europe match them. Not surprisingly, historians of non-European states object that this method implies the transmission from advanced to backward regions on which modernization theory assumes. If transnational approaches emphasize diffusion, they risk reproducing the same error, but they are acceptable if they allow for selective appropria-tion (and for transfer in the other direction). For non-European admirers, Fascism and Nazism seemed to provide a model for the regeneration of nations, but they potentially rejected fascism where it favoured its own eth-nic minorities abroad and harboured imperialist and racist designs. Only in Palestine did Nazi anti-Semitism have some appeal. Moreover, fascism was not the only reference for non-European nationalists.

Some Indian nationalists saw fascism as a precedent for and reinforce-ment of the independence movement. For instance, the radical Indian nationalist, Subhas Chandra Bose, made several visits to Italy and Germany in the 1930s, and was initially attracted to Fascism as a strong form of nationalism, the heir of the *Risorgimento*. In 1926 claimed that Italy would realize a new synthesis of fascism and communism. Under pressure from anti-fascists in Congress he drew back from that position, not least because Hitler justified British rule in India on racial grounds. Bose looked instead to the socialist authoritarianism of Kemal Atatürk. But he never gave up hope that Britain's enemies would help India achieve independence. In 1941 he escaped to Berlin (with the help of the USSR), where he helped to form an Indian Legion recruited from POWs, before transferring his hopes to the Indian National Army, formed from Japan's POWs.[87]

---

[86] Archives nationales, Fonds François de La Rocque, 193, 2 January 1936.
[87] Leonard A. Gordon, *Brothers against the Raj: A Biography of Indian Nationalists Sarat and Subhas Chandra Bose* (Calcutta: Rupa, 2008).

In China, the Blueshirt movement (*Laniyshe*) had greater similarities to Fascism and Nazism, or at least to some strands of them, but the social movement dimension was weak. The Blueshirts originated as part of a patriotic movement that wished the government to resist more strongly the Japanese invaders. Very quickly, they were absorbed into the governing Kuomintang Party. They became one of several groups linked to a secret military freemasonry (the *Lizingshe*) that had been formed in 1932 as a vehicle for the return to power of Chiang Kai-shek, who had recently resigned as head of the Kuomintang government. Some members had attended military schools in Italy and Germany, and the movement was formed at a time when Hitler's advent to power had provoked much interest in fascism. Some activists described themselves as fascists, and some copied the paramilitarism and ritual of European movements. Other members criticized pro-fascists for 'misunderstanding' the purpose of the Blueshirts, and some disliked the Nazis' Aryan supremacism. Historians cannot settle these rival claims to authenticity; one can only say that the Blueshirts read (or misread) fascism selectively, as means to regenerate the Kuomintang and the Chinese nation, just as it had supposedly saved Italy and Germany. This fascism meant totalitarian control, economic planning and unconditional loyalty to the Chiang Kai-shek, who was likened to Mussolini, but also to Stalin. Indeed, fascism was not the only reference point—in July 1933, Chiang identified China with the three developing nations of Germany, Italy and Turkey, in which the people allegedly worked together with the army to create a new nation. This authoritarian fascism was combined with Confucian ideas of community hierarchy, filial piety and duty. The Blueshirts founded the New Life Movement (NLM) to transmit appropriate manners to the masses (such as washing and not spitting), again combining Confucianism with the supposed orderliness of the Japanese and Germans. In sum, the movement possessed some of the characteristics of social movements, there was little independent or oppositional activism.[88]

The Brazilian *Ação Integralista Brasileira* (AIB) had more in common with fascism than the Chinese movements did, and it was a social movement in Dieter Rucht's sense, for it was one element of a network of

[88] Lloyd E. Eastman, 'Fascism in Kuomintang China: The Blue Shirts', *The China Quarterly* 49 (1972), pp. 1–31; Frederic Wakeman, 'A Revisionist View of the Nanjing Decade: Confucian Fascism', *The China Quarterly* 150 (1997), pp. 395–432; Federica Ferlanti, 'The New Life Movement in Jiangxi Province, 1934–1938', *Modern Asian Studies* 5 (2010), pp. 961–1000.

groups that sought to bring about a 'change of society'. The Revolution of 1930 had put an end to the Old Republic, an oligarchic regime based on limited franchise and dominated by coffee growers, and established a provisional regime under Getúlio Vargas. Some elements of the revolutionary coalition were the 'outs' of the old order, including regionalists from Brazil's powerful provinces, and army backing was essential to the success of the rebellion. But the Revolution also witnessed something new—a social movement based on middle-class groups in the cities of São Paulo and Rio de Janeiro and some rural areas, linked loosely to young military officers (the Tenentes—lieutenants). The middle-class groups were involved in professional groups, churches and associations of German and Italian immigrants. The revolutionaries all opposed corruption and wanted regeneration, but did not agree what that meant.

In different ways, the revolutionaries all took something from Fascism and/or Nazism. Brazilian nationalists saw fascism as the model for a strong nation, and saw assimilation of immigrants as essential to national power. But Italians and especially Germans, who were numerous in southern farming areas and in the city of São Paulo, wanted to preserve their languages and cultures. From the mid-1930s, both the Fascist and National Socialist regimes increasingly took an interest in these emigrants, competing with each other for influence in the AIB. The Nazis encouraged Germans to consider themselves 'Germans abroad' rather than Brazilians.[89]

The social question also divided the revolutionaries. The revolution had been made in the name of 'the people', but it provoked the rise of communism and independent trade unions. Paternalist liberals opposed any concessions to the workers, but some Tenentes favoured social reform in the name of universal justice. Another Tenentes spokesman wished the middle-class to lead the people—hitherto, they said, the middle class had been crushed by oligarchs who were able to exploit the 'fickle multitude'. Consequently, they rejected the liberals' demand for a constitution and free elections.[90]

By the mid-1930s the revolutionary coalition was divided between extreme left and right, both of which competed with Vargas to lead 'the

---

[89] Frank D. McCann, 'Vargas and the Destruction of the Brazilian Integralista and Nazi Parties', *The Americas* 1 (1969), pp. 15–28; Ricardo Silva Seitenfus, 'Ideology and Diplomacy: Italian Fascism and Brazil (1935–1938)', *The Hispanic American Historical Review* 3 (1984), pp. 503–534.

[90] Brian Owensby, *Intimate Ironies: Modernity and the Making of Middle-Class Lives in Brazil* (Palo Alto, CA: Stanford University Press, 2001), pp. 136–137.

people'. Some middle-class people backed the National Liberation Alliance (ANL), formed in March 1935. The ANL was an anti-fascist popular front movement, which by May 35, possessed 1600 branches. It called for can-celation of foreign debts, rights for trade unions, and breaking up the latifundia. By the end of the year it was under communist control, but initially it had been moderate and envisaged middle-class leadership of the people, and in that sense at least it resembled the AIB, even though it dismissed the latter as fascist.

In the AIB it is hard to disentangle Catholicism, nationalism, Tenentismo, Fascism and Nazism. The AIB condemned politicians, capi-talism and communism; activists wore green shirts, engaged in street violence and staged mass rallies. It was part of a network of courts, clin-ics, dispensaries, schools, women's groups and commercial enterprises, and won some support from German associations, but more joined the National Socialist Party itself.[91] The AIB defined itself in classic crowd psychology terms. It was a moral elite, ethically superior to corrupt, cos-mopolitan capitalism. It was better qualified to lead the people, which was incapable of governing itself and vulnerable to the dark mirage of com-munism, but which might serve as a source of the ideal. The AIB's mysti-cal and ethical view of the nation resembled a political religion, but it was harnessed to quite specific interests.[92]

Vargas tried to steer clear of the extremes and established a compromise constitution. In late 1935, backed by a vote of special powers in Congress and by the Integralista in the streets, his government stamped out the communist movement. Since the constitution forbade Vargas to stand for a second term, the Integralistas expected either that their leader, Plínio Salgado, would win the presidential election, or that they would provide the core of a Vargas dictatorship. In the event, Vargas assumed dictatorial powers in 1937. Soon after, he suppressed the AIB, and on 10/11 May 1938, easily snuffed out an attempted rising. In April 1938 he outlawed the National Socialist Party in Brazil. The left depicted Vargas's New State as fascist, and it did indeed have much in common with the statist, nation-alist and Catholic elements of Fascism. But the Vargas regime had sup-

---

[91] Owensby, *Intimate Ironies*, pp. 130–158.

[92] Owensby, *Intimate Ironies*, pp. 138–139. Le Bon's *La psychologie des foules* had been translated into Portuguese in 1941, but doubtless analogous categories were circulating in the Portuguese language well before that.

pressed the mass party, and with it the social movement dimension of fascism.

Like most of the admirers of fascism, the AIB failed to win power, and failed to convert its strength as a social movement into political leverage. The AIB had been inspired by the German and Italian example of combining street agitation with electoralism. However, access to political power depended ultimately on winning the presidency, and while the AIB initially thought victory in the scheduled election to be possible, Salgado soon withdrew from the campaign, doubtless aware that in the unlikely event of victory, Vargas would launch a coup. Perhaps in keeping with the unspoken rules of Brazilian politics, the AIB had focussed on regional legislatures, so had no leverage in Congress either. When Vargas carried out his coup, the AIB hoped to become a regime party. But for the new dictator, the AIB's links (real and imagined) to the Fascist and Nazi regimes made it a dangerous rival and an obstacle to his desire for US support. When the AIB attempted to seize power, it found that it had few friends in high places.

As for the Italian and German governments, they were torn between backing the AIB in order to counter each other within the movement and American influence in Brazil, and fear of alienating the Vargas government. In the end, the Germans held aloof from the AIB's attempted coup. The Italian ambassador urged the AIB to act and accused it of too great a respect for democracy, but his government overruled him. Ironically, Vargas and the press blamed the Germans, not the Italians, for the AIB's attempted coup. The government banned the use of foreign languages in schools, churches and even in public, but enforced the law only against the Germans, partly because the Fascists' emphasis of Latin solidarity had some purchase.[93] The establishment of the Vargas regime and suppression of the ANL and AIB dissipated the middle-class movement, permitting Vargas to redefine the people around the working class and to embrace a policy of social reform.[94]

---

[93] McCann, 'Vargas and the Destruction of the Brazilian Integralista', pp. 28–34; Seitenfus, 'Ideology and Diplomacy', p. 529.
[94] Owensby, *Intimate Ironies*, pp. 157–158.

CONCLUSION

The organizations considered above, or at least elements of them, conform to Dieter Rucht's definitions of a social movement. They sought to reorder society and/or resist fundamental change, in diverse and contested ways— from destruction of the left to the re-making relations between men and women. They were part of a network of networks, in that they emerged from, and competed with others to capture, a politically nebulous upsurge of collective activity, whether in the wake of the Great War, following the Japanese invasion of China or the Brazilian Revolution of 1930. They possessed a group identity, even if they disagreed on what that identity was or interpreted it differently, and they defined themselves against enemies, if not necessarily the same ones. Members joined for instrumental reasons, which often set them against other members.

In one way or another all the movements in question looked to Italian Fascism and later Nazism as a model. They admired Fascism as an example of the regeneration or actualization of a decadent or oppressed nation; they copied specific family and social programmes, and they used Mussolini's leader cult as a weapon in intra-movement conflicts. Particularly relevant is that all the organizations that I have considered (with the exception of the Indian Nationalists) meditated the Italian success in converting an anti-political street movement into a party and a regime, through the combination of agitation in the streets and political manoeuvring, while applying the lessons in different ways. Thus, the organizations that I have considered were entangled, both with fascism and as social movements, on a transnational scale.

That does not mean that they essentially *were* fascist or social movements, only that our definitions reveal particular aspects. In the case of fascism, social movements always had political ambitions, and in respects not highlighted here they acted as political parties. By the same token there was in practice no absolute distinction between movement and regime, for the practices of the movement could be detected in regimes, in spite of the purges of the Blackshirts and murder of leading Brownshirts in 1926 and 1934 respectively. In Italy, the victims of purges were described as 'anti-fascists', revealing again the importance of following definitions in action. In spite of the purges, in Italy, the violence of ex-squad members remained essential to the practice of the regime, as officials, prison guards and as soldiers in Ethiopia and in the civil war that followed Mussolini's fall. Doubtless the same could be said of Germany, but of course there were many other logics at play in both regimes.[95]

FURTHER READING

Studies of fascism as a category have not especially emphasized its social movement dimension, because their primary objective is to develop an abstract theory of the origins and development of fascism, and/or because they consider social movements to be primarily left wing. Nevertheless, some of these theories do share certain assumptions with older social movements theory, notably in the assumption that fascism is a response to rapid change, anomie, and the search for a messianic ideology. This theory is present in Roger Griffin, *The Nature of Fascism* (London: Pinter, 1991). Studies of Fascism as a political religion make similar assumptions, notably Emilio Gentile, *The Sacralisation of Politics: Definitions, Interpretations and Reflections on the Question of Secular Religion and Totalitarianism* (London: Frank Cass, 2000). The most useful empirical work to use political religion theory to study fascism as a social movement is Christopher Duggan, *Fascist Voices: An Intimate History of Mussolini's Italy* (New York: Oxford University Press, 2012).

Michel Dobry has advanced the most important critique of the strain-breakdown approach to social movements, as applied to fascism, but little of his work is available in English. Some of his ideas may be found in Michel Dobry, 'France: An Ambiguous Survival', in Dirk Berg-Schlosser and Jeremy Mitchell (eds), *Conditions of Democracy in Europe, 1919–1939. Systematic Case Studies* (Basingstoke: Palgrave, 2000), pp. 157–183 and in Kevin Passmore, *Fascism: A Very Short Introduction* (Oxford: Oxford University Press, 2nd edn, 2014).

Of studies that have approached Fascism and Nazism from a more explicitly social movement perspective. Peter Fritzsche, *Germans into Nazis* (Cambridge, Mass: Harvard University Press, 1998) remains essential. Alf Lüdkte, *The History of Everyday Life: Reconstructing Historical Experiences and Ways of Life* (Cambridge, Mass.: Princeton University Press, 1995) presents in English some of key essays considering popular support for Nazism. Benjamin Ziemann, 'Germany after the First World

---

[95] Matteo Millan, 'The Institutionalisation of Squadrismo: Disciplining Paramilitary Violence in the Italian Fascist Dictatorship', *Contemporary European History* 4 (2013), pp. 551–573.

War—A Violent Society? Results and Implications of Recent Research on Weimar Germany', *Journal of Modern European History* 1 (2003), pp. 80–86, takes issue with the view of post-war Germany as 'brutalized'. An enormous number of local studies of Fascism and Nazism that had been published since the 1960s, and some of the older examples remain useful. While these studies often treated fascism as reactionary, they rooted it in local conditions and more or less popular mobilizations. The best local studies on Italy are, Paul Corner, *Fascism in Ferrara, 1915–1925* (Oxford: Oxford University Press, 1975); Frank M. Snowden, *The Fascist Revolution in Tuscany, 1919–1922* (Cambridge: Cambridge University Press, 1989); Frank M. Snowden, *Violence and Great Estates in the South of Italy: Apulia, 1900–1922* (Cambridge: Cambridge University Press, 1986). On Germany, see the classic, William Sheridan Allen. *The Nazi Seizure of Power: The Experience of a Single German Town, 1922–1945* (New York: Echo Point Books & Media, revised edn 2014, first published 1966); Claus-Christian W. Szejnmann, *Nazism in Central Germany: The Brownshirts in 'Red Saxony'* (New York, Oxford: Berghahn, 1999). Local studies inform Richard J. Evans, *The Coming of the Third Reich* (London: Allen Lane, 2003) and Roderick Stackelberg, *The Routledge Companion to Nazi Germany* (London: Routledge, 2007), summarizes recent research on Nazism.

For fascism outside Europe, the most interesting book from a social movement perspective is Stein Ugelvik Larsen (ed.), *Fascism Outside Europe: The European Impulse Against Domestic Conditions in the Diffusion of Global Fascism* (New York: Columbia University Press, 2001).

Women's history provides important insights into fascism as a social movement. Two classics are Claudia Koonz, *Mothers in the Fatherland: Women, the Family and Nazi Politics* (New York: St. Martin's Press, 1988); Victoria De Grazia, *How Fascism Ruled Women: Italy, 1922–1945* (Berkeley: University of California Press, 1993); Kevin Passmore (ed.), *Women, Gender and the Extreme Right in Europe (1919–1945)* (Manchester: Manchester University Press, 2002), includes chapters on the role of women in far right movements in most European countries.

Some of the most interesting recent works on fascism focus on its culture of violence. The best work is Sven Richardt's comparing Italy and Germany. The following are available in English: Sven Reichardt, 'Fascist Marches in Italy and Germany: Squadre and SA before the Seizure of Power', in Matthias Reiss (ed.), *The Street as Stage: Protest Marches and Public Rallies Since the Nineteenth Century* (Oxford: Oxford University

Press, 2007), pp. 169–193; Sven Reichardt, 'Violence and Community: A Micro-Study on Nazi Storm Troopers', *Central European History* 2 (2013), pp. 275–297; Sven Reichardt, 'Violence, Body, Politics: Paradoxes in Interwar Germany', in Chris Millington and Kevin Passmore (eds), *Political Violence and Democracy in Interwar Europe, 1918–1940* (Basingstoke: Palgrave, 2015).

Other works are more explicitly transnational in focus. For instance, Robert Gerwarth, 'The Central European Counter-Revolution: Paramilitary Violence in Germany, Austria and Hungary after the Great War', *Past & Present* 1 (2008), pp. 175–209, defines a space of violence in Germany and Hungary; Robert Gerwarth and John Horne, 'Vectors of Violence: Paramilitarism in Europe after the Great War, 1917–1923', *The Journal of Modern History* 3 (2011), pp. 489–512.

CHAPTER 21

Post-Fascist Right-Wing Social Movements

Fabian Virchow

For quite a long time it seemed evident in social movement research that the subjects of research are movements aiming at progressive and demo-cratic social and political change. This was the case because most aca-demic definitions of social movements excluded reactionary, racist and right-wing social movements from the area of application, either explic-itly or implicitly.[1] Now, there is at least some academic work on these phenomena. However, a systematic and multi-disciplinary investigation of historical dimensions, current manifestations, modes of performance and ideological profiles of right-wing movements is still missing. I intend this essay to bring together main insights and trajectories of social move-ment research with real-world examples of racist and right-wing social movements from different parts of the world. The object of my analysis is limited to more recent right-wing movements, since the period of fascist regimes in Europe is over (post-fascist).

[1] Nelson Pichardo, 'New Social Movements: A Critical Review', *Annual Review of Sociology* 23 (1997), pp. 411–430.

F. Virchow (✉)
Department of Social Sciences and Cultural Studies, University of Applied Sciences Düsseldorf, Düsseldorf, Germany

© The Author(s) 2017   619
S. Berger, H. Nehring (eds.), *The History of Social Movements in Global Perspective*, DOI 10.1057/978-1-137-30427-8_21

The first section outlines briefly what kind of movements are subsumed under the term 'right-wing' in this essay and discusses the demarcation of right-wing social movements from both far-right parties and single protest events. In the following sections, relevant approaches and issues of social movement research are the starting point for a closer look at the respective approach and its importance for studying and understanding right-wing social movements. The approaches and issues include, amongst others, the role of social strains, the status of political opportunity structures, the relevance of resources and framing, the creation and maintenance of collective identities, the interaction with state agencies and counter-movements, the impact of right-wing movements and, finally, cases of transnational interaction.[2] The final section provides a brief conclusion with implications for future research.

RIGHT-WING SOCIAL MOVEMENTS—WHAT THEY ARE AND WHAT THEY ARE NOT

In their article, Kathleen Blee and Kimberly A. Creasap recalled the diversity of terminology used to label and define a broad political spectrum covering conservative and right-wing movements, political parties and individuals.[3] While they decided to use the term right wing for 'movements that focus specifically on race/ethnicity and/or that promote violence as a primary tactic or goal',[4] according to Italian philosopher Norberto Bobbio the profound difference between 'left' and 'right' is the different attitude with regard to the ideal of equality of human beings.[5] While the left is principally considered as being egalitarian, working actively to ensure that the ideal of equality becomes the guideline for political decisions, the right is non-egalitarian emphasizing the inevitability of and the need for inequality for societies to work. In consequence, political rightists defend inequality regarding race relations, gender arrangements and social issues and they deny equal rights by referring to alleged biological or immutable cultural characteristics of members of the particular group.

---

[2] For reasons of space, dimensions such as gender, body and emotions remain unconsidered in this chapter.

[3] Kathleen M. Blee and Kimberly A. Creasap, 'Conservative and Right-Wing Movements', *Annual Review of Sociology* 36 (2010), pp. 269–286.

[4] Blee and Creasap, 'Conservative and Right-Wing', pp. 270–271.

[5] Norberto Bobbio, *Left and Right. The Significance of a Political Distinction* (Chicago: The University of Chicago Press, 1996).

Regularly, right-wing social movements refer to the idea of a homogeneous national community. The political right can be further divided into the conservative right, the reactionary right and the fascist right, whereby the degree of rigidity of the intended or practised exclusion is crucial for this distinction. In this sense, a relevant distinction has to be made between a conservative right which, for example, denies equal political participation of migrants and a fascist right which goes far beyond that and campaigns for a racially purified country. Right-wing social movements range from more single-issue-focussed actors, like the anti-abortion movement[6] and anti-immigrant movements,[7] to others with a more complex agenda like the *Tea Party* movement[8] or post-war fascist movements. Right-wing social movements often have anti-feminist traits. Sivan Hirsch-Hoefler and Cas Muddehave suggested a typology of right-wing movements.[9] While they exclude mainstream political right movements from their list, they enumerate religious right-wing movements like the US *Christian Right* or the Israeli settler movement, intellectual movements like the French *Nouvelle Droite* (New Right) and leaderless movements. The latter includes such phenomena as the Tea Party in the United States and neo-Nazi networks in many countries. In addition, there are national movements like the *English Defence League* (EDL) or the *Russian Movement against Illegal Immigration* (DPNI) whose main campaign issues are migration, multi-culturalism and

---

[6] Leslie King and Ginna Husting, 'Anti-Abortion Activism in the U.S. and France: Comparing Opportunity Environments of Rescue Tactics', *Mobilization: An International Journal* 3 (2003), pp. 297–312; David S. Meyer and Suzanne Staggenborg, 'Opposing Movement Strategies in U.S. Abortion Politics', *Research in Social Movements, Conflicts and Change* 28 (2008), pp. 207–238.

[7] Nikolay Zakharov, 'The Social Movement Against Immigration as the Vehicle and the Agent of Racialization in Russia', in Kerstin Jacobsson and Steven Saxonberg (eds), *Beyond NGO-ization. The Development of Social Movements in Central and Eastern Europe* (Farnham: Ashgate, 2013), pp. 169–189.

[8] Edward Ashbee, 'Bewitched—The Tea Party Movement: Ideas, Interests and Institutions', *The Political Quarterly* 2 (2011), pp. 157–164; Henrik Gast and Alexander Kühne, '"Tea-Party"—Time in den USA? Zu Profil und Einfluss einer heterogenen Bewegung', *Zeitschrift für Parlamentsfragen* 2 (2011), pp. 247–269.

[9] Sivan Hirsch-Hoefler and Cas Mudde, 'Right-Wing Movements', in David A. Snow, Donatella Della Porta, Bert Klandermans and Doug McAdam (eds), *The Wiley-Blackwell Encyclopedia of Social & Political Movements*, 3: Pe-Z (Oxford: Wiley-Blackwell, 2013), pp. 1116–1124.

Islam. Undoubtedly, racist movements belong to any typology of right-wing movements.

Right-wing social movements utilize a wide range of articulation and mobilization modes. They act as media protagonists, organize rallies and cultural performances, collect signatures for petitions, occupy buildings, refuse to pay taxes as an expression of distrust of the central government and turn to acts of sabotage and political violence. In a number of cases, there are even heavily armed right-wing movements. Leigh A. Payne has assessed the 1980s paramilitary Nicaraguan *Contra* as a prototype of 'uncivil movement'.[10] The leitmotifs of the respective social movement are reflected in public actions, but they also find their way into the activists' everyday life. Taking the typology introduced by David F. Aberle into account, one can also differentiate right-wing social movements along the vectors of who the movement is attempting to change and to what extent change is being advocated.[11]

Several researchers have tried to understand historical fascism as a social movement.[12] For example, it was important for the leadership of the Nazi Party to call it a movement because the concept of 'party' was associated with particular interests dividing German people. The concept of 'movement' was used to emphasize the idea of a unified national community. Therefore, Klaus Eder's suggested use of self-designation as a main criterion for labelling a political or social collective actor as social movement should be treated with caution;[13] any self-designation of a particular political actor as 'party' or as 'movement' needs to be contextualized. As the case of the Portuguese *Movimento de Acção Nacional (MAN)* shows, not every political protagonist using the term 'movement' should be termed like that from a scholarly perspective.[14]

[10] Leigh A. Payne, *Uncivil Movements. The Armed Right Wing and Democracy in Latin America* (Baltimore, MD: Johns Hopkins University Press, 2000).

[11] David F. Aberle, *The Peyote Religion Among the Navaho* (Chicago: Aldine, 1966).

[12] Wolfgang Schieder (ed.), *Faschismus als soziale Bewegung* (Göttingen: Vandenhoeck & Ruprecht, 1983); Maurizio Bach and Stefan Breuer, *Faschismus als Bewegung und Regime* (Wiesbaden: Verlag für Sozialwissenschaften, 2010), Till Kössler, 'Gelegenheiten und Gewalt. Der spanische Faschismus als soziale Bewegung', in Jürgen Mittag and Helke Stadtland (eds), *Theoretische Ansätze und Konzepte der Forschung über soziale Bewegungen in der Geschichtswissenschaft* (Essen: Klartext, 2014), pp. 109–125.

[13] Klaus Eder, *Kollektive Akteure zwischen Identitätssuche und Mobilisierungsindustrie* (Hamburg: HIS, 1990), pp. 33–34.

[14] Riccardo Marchi, 'At the Roots of the New Right-Wing Extremism in Portugal: The National Action Movement (1985–1991)', *Totalitarian Movements and Political Religions* 1 (2010), pp. 47–66.

However, not every protest is an expression of social movement. According to the definition of Joachim Raschke who named a 'certain continuity' as a necessary feature of social movements,[15] I do not count isolated acts of protest as a social movement. For example, the self-immolation of 75-year-old Second World War veteran Reinhold Elstner was an individual protest event against—in his view—unfair representation of the German Wehrmacht. The anniversary of this action, however, is used by neo-Nazis to perform demonstrations.

Some researchers refer to a country's political extreme right as an extreme right social movement.[16] However, it is not obligatory to define even parties which are heavily focussed on elections and parliamentary representation as social movements. In fact, there are parties of the extreme right that are independent from and at the same time interact with a particular right-wing social movement. It might also be stimulating to think of different right-wing social movements existing at the same time in a given historical situation. Researchers should also be open to the concept of movement parties as described by Herbert Kitschelt; one such hybrid is the *National Democratic Party of Germany* (NPD) from the mid-1990s onwards.[17]

Right-wing movements also should be distinguished from right-wing lobby groups, since the latter have closer relationships to power holders and routine access to political decision-makers. They aim at influencing politicians by bargaining with the provision of information or financial contributions or even threaten political parties by withdrawing electoral support. It becomes clear that lobby groups can collaborate very closely with social movements.

Several right-wing movements have a religiously embossed profile. Recent examples are the *Christian Identity* movement in the United States[18] as well as the *Hindutva* movement—with the *Rashtriya*

---

[15] Joachim Raschke, *Soziale Bewegungen. Ein historisch-systematischer Grundriß* (Frankfurt am Main: Campus, 1985), p. 77.

[16] Bert Klandermans and Nonna Mayer (eds), *Extreme Right Activists in Europe* (London: Routledge, 2006).

[17] Herbert Kitschelt, 'Movement Parties', in Richard S. Katz and William Crotty (eds), *Handbook of Party Politics* (London: Sage, 2006), pp. 278–289; Herbert Kitschelt, 'Movement Parties'. *SAGE Handbook of Party Politics* (London: Sage, 2006), pp. 278–289.

[18] Michael Barkun, *Religion and the Racist Right: The Origins of the Christian Identity Movement* (Chapel Hill: University of North Carolina Press, 1994); Betty A. Dobratz, 'The

Swayamsevak Sangh (RSS) as its core— in India, which follows an ethno-religious nationalism and often targets non-Hindu Indians, most notably the sizable number of Muslim minority.[19] In post-civil war Serbia, the extreme right *Srpski otačastveni pokret Obraz* (Serbian Patriotic Movement Obraz) strongly refers to the Serbian Orthodox Church.[20]

In the United States, in some cases even groups like *Wotansvolk*, which is closely associated with violent neo-Nazism, are legally recognized as a church.[21] Although the above definition of right-wing movements also fits several Islamist movements, which justify the denial of equal rights under recourse to religious scriptures, the analysis of such movements had to be omitted from further examination for reasons of space.

RIGHT-WING SOCIAL MOVEMENTS AND SOCIAL MOVEMENT THEORY

Classical structural-strain theory has argued that social movements necessarily emerge in situations of social cleavages and problems which lead to a feeling of deprivation amongst particular social groups. The emergence of a social movement is then regarded as a reaction by a group of disaffected individuals to that situation. Even if it has to be admitted that social movements do not always arise as a consequence of social problems, it is clear that right-wing movements often find fertile ground in social developments which deeply affect social structures. This holds true in regard to growing immigration and increasing religious diversity as well as to the extension of civil rights and to gender mainstreaming and LGBTQI rights. These are some examples being of special importance in the context of post-war right-wing movements.

As stated by the political opportunity structure approach, the characteristics of the external environment—including amongst others the political system, the territorial and functional distribution of institutional power, the

Role of Religion in the Collective Identity of the White Racialist Movement', *Journal for the Scientific Study of Religion* 2 (2002), pp. 287–301.

[19] Peggy Froerer, 'Emphasizing "Others": The Emergence of Hindu Nationalism in a Central Indian Tribal Community', *Journal of the Royal Anthropological Institute* 1 (2006), pp. 39–59.

[20] Đorđe Tomić, 'On the "Right" Side? The Radical Right in the Post-Yugoslav Area and the Serbian Case', *Fascism* 1 (2013), pp. 94–114.

[21] George Michael, 'David Lane and the Fourteen Words', *Totalitarian Movements and Political Religions* 1 (2009), pp. 43–61, p. 53.

media, strategies of inclusion and exclusion, and political opponents—are important dimensions influencing the evolution of a social movement. This approach also revises the notion that social movements belong to civil society only. Instead, there may be multi-fold connections to the political system.[22] For example, the receptivity and vulnerability of the *Republican Party* allowed the current Tea Party movement relevant inroads. However, windows of opportunity come and go. In Germany of the early 1990s, a growing number of asylum seekers from countries torn by civil war not only led to a wave of racist violence and terror in a climate that was hostile to migrants, but the months-long campaign on the part of the Conservatives also led to a substantial restriction of the right to asylum.[23] The political opportunity structure of 2000s Germany has changed recognizably. Although there were still acts of racist violence and hateful campaigns by right-wing movements, political elites *grosso modo* agree that immigration is beneficial for Germany. The situation changed again with the rising numbers of refugees seeking shelter in Germany from the 2014 onwards and the rise of the Alternative for Germany (AfD) as a nativist and nationalist party.

Theoretical approaches with a strong focus on individual involvement, commitment to collective behaviour or macro-structural determinants should be complemented by resource mobilization theory. In this perspective, access to resources such as moral resources including legitimacy, solidarity, celebrity endorsement and integrity are discussed. This covers both financial resources, which can also be converted into resources such as property, office space and equipment, and social-organizational resources, including social networks. Support from or alliances with influential non-movement actors are crucial to social movements. Of course, human resources like experience, skills, knowledge, labour and key figures acting as movement pioneers, conflict mediators, martyrs and movement veterans are included, as well as cultural resources of how to enact protest events and produce movements. Issue-relevant literature, posters, stickers

---

[22] Charles Tilly, *From Mobilization to Revolution* (New York: Random House, 1978); Sidney G. Tarrow, *Democracy and Disorder. Protest and Politics in Italy. 1965–1975* (Oxford: Oxford University Press, 1989); Hanspeter Kriesi, Ruud Koopmans, Jan Willem Duyvendak and Marco G. Giugni (eds), *New Social Movements in Western Europe. A Comparative Analysis* (London: UCL Press, 1995).

[23] Roger Karapin, 'Antiminority Riots in Unified Germany: Cultural Conflicts and Mischanneled Political Participation', *Comparative Politics* 2 (2002), pp. 147–167.

or other media products have a relevant impact too.[24] Cultural practices of movements like *Casa Pound Italy* (CPI), whose name refers to US poet and long-time admirer of Italian fascism Ezra Pound, heavily rely on both resources for the creation, production and distribution of large quantities of posters and the organization of meetings that merge pop-cultural elements with extreme right-wing ideology. They use references to events, protagonists and political messages of historical fascism to portray modern fascism as a kind of live-style.[25]

Resources do not necessarily have to be an integral part of the movement itself. That is the case with Washington, DC, based right-wing lobby group *Freedom Works*. The group trains volunteers on issues like fundraising and web activism providing support for campaigns and giving financial support for the Tea Party movement.[26] Aside from patronage and co-option, there are additional mechanisms of resource access like the self-production of movement-related items and the development of cadres and leaders. The aggregation of constituents is of further importance.

Framing theory has played an important role in social movement research. 'Frames are cognitive and cultural schemata that organize perception and interpretation, ways of describing and analysing events or telling stories and thus identifying facts, problems, solutions and responses.'[27] Framing activities by social movements include three basic components: diagnostic framing of the problem, prognostic framing of the target state and motivational framing encouraging people to take action to solve the problem identified before and offering options of intervention.[28] The framing of the movement itself is also part of framing activities which rivals with framing the movement by other political or societal actors such as counter-movements, state agencies or the media.[29] As a constant activity,

[24] Bob Edwards and Patrick F. Gillham, 'Resource Mobilization Theory', in Snow, Della Porta, Klandermans and McAdam (eds), *Encyclopedia* 3, pp. 1096–1101; Fabian Virchow, 'Führer und Schlüsselfiguren in extrem rechten Bewegungen', *Forschungsjournal Soziale Bewegungen* 4 (2013), pp. 52–58.

[25] Heiko Koch, *Casa Pound Italia* (Münster: Unrast, 2013).

[26] Gast and Kühne, '"Tea-Party"', p. 259.

[27] John W. P. Veugelers, 'Dissenting Families and Social Movement abeyance. The Transmission of Neo-Fascist Frames in Postwar Italy', *The British Journal of Sociology* 2 (2011), pp. 241–261, p. 244.

[28] Robert D. Benford and David A. Snow, 'Framing Processes and Social Movements: An Overview and Assessment', *Annual Review of Sociology* 26 (2000), pp. 611–639.

[29] Jules Boykoff and Eulalie Laschever, 'The Tea Party Movement, Framing, and the US Media', *Social Movement Studies* 4 (2011), pp. 341–366; Matt Guardino and Dean Snyder,

framing is a significant part of identity work in a social movement integrating individuals into the collective. The juxtaposition of 'Us' versus 'Them' is a core feature of collective identity.

Right-wing movements have framed the social problems they are dealing with as well as the solutions they offer and the particular movement itself in very different ways. Declarations of the Tea Party movement surfaced in early 2009 portraying the movement, for example, as 'constitutionally conservative'. This opposes the very idea of a 'living constitution' and advocates a return to the 'original' ideas and spirit of the Founding Fathers. While these concepts may not have been that homogeneous, as the Tea Party movement declares, strong reference to the constitution is very powerful due to the fact that people in the United States hold the Constitution in high esteem.[30] The movement's programmatic core focusses on reducing taxation, inclosing federal government's spending, opposing government involvement in health care and related social activities and opposing (illegal) immigration. A relevant share of the Tea Party movement's followers are 'birthers' claiming that 'Barack Obama was not born in the US, making him ineligible to be president; some also believe, despite his claims to the contrary, that Obama is a Muslim'.[31] Obama's presidency is regarded as the latest attack on American values resulting in his characterization as 'anti-American'. The Tea Party's rhetoric follows the general pattern which was identified by scholars as forming the central rhetorical element of most nationalist movements. This pattern includes the celebration of the glorious past with the narrative of the nation as a pure, unified and harmonious community followed by a description of the degraded present with the marking of the people responsible for this development. In a third step, one can find the promise of the utopian future.[32] The Tea Party refers to a mixture of creedal and ethno-cultural nationalism in its framing. 'The former view is that Americans are bound together by a common creed, found in documents such as the Constitution and

'The Tea Party and the Crisis of Neoliberalism: Mainstreaming New Right Populism in the Corporate News Media', *New Political Science* 4 (2012), pp. 527–548.

[30] Gast and Kühne, "'Tea-Party'", p. 255.

[31] Amanda Pullum, 'The Tea Party movement (United States)', in Snow, Della Porta, Klandermans and McAdam (eds), *Encyclopedia* 3, p.1328.

[32] Jared A. Goldstein, 'The Tea Party Movement and the Perils of Popular Originalism', *Arizona Law Review* 3 (2011), pp. 827–866, pp. 835–836.

the Declaration of Independence.'[33] The other perspective declares language, faith, culture, history, soil and blood to be the ingredients making a people.

The discourse of dispossession shared by many right-wing movements in the United States is in line with the view that Obama represents the ousting from power of formerly dominant groups, which made Whites the new victims of racial discrimination. Albeit, the former is different in the degree of radicalism regarding the diagnosis, prognosis and action orientation. Most 'white nationalists placed this phenomenon in the post-World War Two period, after the fall of Hitler and Hitlerism and at the time of the advent of the black freedom movement. Some noted the decolonization of Africa and Asia as part of the loss of world-wide white supremacy. All considered this supposed dispossession in terms of race and nation, as opposed to losses that a single individual might endure.'[34]

The *White Power* movement in the United States brings together right-wing groups such as the *Ku Klux Klan* (KKK), neo-Nazis, Christian Identity sects and White Power skinheads. Although differing in their history and ideological roots—for example, the 1920s Klan with its anti-Catholic, anti-immigrant, social purity ideals[35] and the Christian identity groups with their reference to nineteenth-century British Israelism, which claimed that the 'true' Israelites were Anglo-Saxons and that Anglo Christians are God's chosen race[36]—they strongly share the idea of a 'race war' taking place. In line with framing the present situation as 'genocide against the white race', a diagnosis that is much more radical than dispossession, they strongly advocate White Power including restored racial hierarchy in the future. Statements like '14 words' ('We must secure the existence of our people and a future for white children')[37] summarize related visions. White Power and neo-Nazi groups use them as 'masterframe' all over the world. White Power movement entrepreneurs envision

[33] Leonard Zeskind, 'A Nation Dispossessed. The Tea Party Movement and Race', *Critical Sociology* 4 (2011), pp. 495–509.
[34] Zeskind, 'A Nation Dispossessed', p. 503; Ashbee, 'Bewitched—The Tea Party Movement'.
[35] Rory McVeigh, Daniel J. Myers and David Sikkink, 'Corn, Klansmen, and Coolidge. Structure and Framing in Social Movements', *Social Forces* 2 (2004, pp. 653–690, pp. 660–666.
[36] Robert Futrell and Peter Simi, 'Free Spaces, Collective Identity, and the Persistence of U.S. White Power Activism', *Social Problems* 1 (2004), pp. 16–42, p. 18.
[37] Michael, 'David Lane and the Fourteen Words'.

a racially exclusive world regarding 'non-Whites' at least subordinated to Aryan authority. As part of the White Power movement, Christian identity activists disproportionately tend to acts of violence and terrorism in order to achieve the movement's goal framing, such acts as self-defence.[38]

Casa Pound Italy (CPI) was established in Rome with the squatting of a building near the main railway station 'Termini' right in the heart of Rome's Chinatown. CPI describes itself as being beyond left–right dichotomy and its self-designation as 'non-conform' is meant to characterize the movement. The leaders of CPI 'have argued that the movement was not born on a purely ideological basis, but rather as a result of a social need […] Casa Pound, in other words, wants to represent itself as "being forced" to take political action to provide an answer to the social needs of our society.'[39] Diagnostic framing of CPI analyses 'usury' as the core problem of neo-liberal politics being held responsible for social problems like eviction orders. The issue of 'usury' already played an important role in the work of Ezra Pound. The 'social doctrine' of Italian fascism has strongly influenced CPI. Therefore, CPI pursues a strong state following an anti-immigrant, nationalistic ideology. It emphasizes the idea of economic self-sufficiency and portrays the Italian nation—instead of referring to a particular social group or class—as being the victim of foreign international powers.

The *Hindu National Volunteer Organization* (Rashtriya Swayamsevak Sangh, RSS) was founded in 1925 and has played an increasingly important role since the late 1980s. The ideological basis of the movement is the assumption that India has always been fundamentally Hindu. The equation of religious and national identity is at the very core of 'Hindutva' calling for a united community based on geographical origin, racial connection and religious belief. Accordingly, those who do not belong to the community—according to markers such as religion, origin or culture—are defined as the 'threatening Other'.[40] RSS frames historical traditions in a way that 'the political and social trajectories of the Sultanate and Mughal periods, as well as the time of British rule, are not only constructed as a

---

[38] Tanya Telfair Sharpe, 'The Identity Christian Movement. Ideology of Domestic Terrorism', *Journal of Black Studies* 4 (2000), pp. 604–623.

[39] Pietro Castelli Gattinara, Caterina Froio and Matteo Albanese, 'The Appeal of Neo-Fascism in Times of Crisis. The Experience of Casa Pound Italia', *Fascism* 2 (2013), pp. 234–258, p. 247.

[40] Christophe Jaffrelot, *The Hindu Nationalist Movement and Indian Politics. 1925 to the 1990s* (London: Hurst & Co., 1993).

fall from an original state of purity, but the citizens who today belong to the Muslim and Christian faiths are reduced to standing in for the Invader, the Plunderer, the Desecrator, and are positioned as treasonable subjects to be disciplined and suborned within the nation-state'.[41] Muscular Hindu nationalism draws on the idea of hegemonic masculinity to animate its national vision propagating the two models of virile Hinduism—Hindu soldier and warrior monk.[42] A core activity of RSS volunteers is physical training consisting of 'military drill, calisthenics, and instruction in the use of non-mechanical weapons'.[43] In addition, training courses on Indian history are held which argue that the mythical Hindu era came to an abrupt end by the violence of 'invading Muslims'. The Hindu nationalist movement's frame, according to which the Hindu community is under constant attack from its enemies—although being a numerical majority in India today—includes a strong discourse on Hindu women threatened by Muslim men. Accordingly, the Hindu nationalist movement offers paramilitary training as a mode of Hindu women's empowerment. Yet, sexual violence perpetrated by Hindu was anathema to the movement.[44]

The *Identitarian Movement*, which has its strongholds in France and Austria while it is mainly based online in Germany and other European countries up until 2015, offers another framing of victimization and contention. The French *Bloc Identitaire* (BI) was founded in 2003 as a successor organization of a group banned one year earlier due to the involvement of one of its members in an assassination attempt against President Jacques Chirac. On 20 October 2012 more than 80 members of *Génération Identitaire* (GI), the youth group of BI, made the Identitarian Movement known to a wider public with the spectacular occupation of the roof of the mosque under construction in the city of Poitiers. The implementation of the action—place, date and framing—represents both basic ideology and aims of the movement. It referred to the anniversary of the Battle of

---

[41] Parita Mukta, 'The Public Face of Hindu Nationalism', *Ethnic and Racial Studies* 3 (2000), pp. 442–466, p. 443.

[42] Sikata Banerjee, 'Armed Masculinity, Hindu Nationalism and Female Political Participation in India', *International Feminist Journal of Politics* 1 (2006), pp. 62–83.

[43] Arafaat A. Valiani, 'Physical Training, Ethical Discipline, and Creative Violence: Zones of Self-Mastery in the Hindu Nationalist Movement', *Cultural Anthropology* 1 (2010), pp. 73–99, p. 73.

[44] Meera Sehgal, 'Manufacturing a Feminized Siege Mentality. Hindu Nationalist Paramilitary Camps for Women in India', *Journal of Contemporary Ethnography* 2 (2007), pp. 165–183.

Tours and Poitiers in 732 in which Charles Martel repulsed the troops of the Umayyad Caliphate. The banner used by the Identitarian Movement's activists showed the date and the lambda symbol painted in yellow on a black background and it became the international shared icon of the movement.[45] The symbol refers to the ancient Spartan Hoplites who were armed with particular spears and shields and fought against the Persian Army led by Xerxes I in the Battle of Thermopylae. In October 2012, GI also published a YouTube video called 'Déclaration de Guerre' in which they introduced themselves as part of a generation living in social insecurity and being one of the losers of global capitalism. This self-positioning was associated with a sharp rejection of immigration and multi-culturalism. Part of the claims-making rhetoric of the Identitarian Movement is the frequent use of the term '*Reconquista*' as a formula for their demand for a spiritual and cultural revival based upon a so-called 'ethno-cultural identity' in order to fight against the alleged Islamization of Europe.

According to Dennis Zuev, the Russian Movement Against Illegal Immigration (*Dvizheniye Protiv Nelegalnoy Immigrazii*, DPNI) 'has its own "niche" rhetoric, where the main targets are residents from the former Soviet Union'.[46] Nikolay Zakharov has pointed out that framing by the DPNI makes use of visual differences of some groups of migrants to extend 'racial meaning to a previously racially-unclassified relationship, social practice, or group'.[47] Like many other racist or nativist social movements, a frame goes along with the act of racialization which describes the majority group as suffering and being hurt while the minority, in this case refugees and migrants, live a much better life. Culturally racist groups like the EDL also carry out a process of 'Othering' in which they 'distribute privilege and laid blame along a hierarchical line through the construction of opposing and irreconcilable subjects: Muslims, who were blamed for society's ills and required to radically reform their religion,

---

[45] Julian Bruns, Kathrin Glösel and Natascha Strobl, *Die Identitären. Handbuch zur Jugendbewegung der Neuen Rechten in Europa* (Münster: Unrast, 2014), p. 62.

[46] Dennis Zuev, 'The Movement Against Illegal Immigration: Analysis of the Central Node in the Russian Extreme-Right Movement', *Nations and Nationalism* 2 (2010), pp. 261–284, p. 270.

[47] Nikolay Zakharov, 'The Social Movement Against Immigration as the Vehicle and the Agent of Racialization in Russia', in Kerstin Jacobsson and Steven Saxonberg (eds), *Beyond NGO-ization. The Development of Social Movements in Central and Eastern Europe* (Farnham: Ashgate, 2013), pp. 169–191, p. 170.

and non-Muslims, who were considered the blameless victims of "Islamic extremism".[48]

In principle, right-wing social movements also have to make a strategic decision regarding their performance and framing of whether they want to be, in James Jasper's words, 'naughty or nice'.[49] Such operational decisions are often very controversial since social movements 'that come to be perceived in negative terms may lose credibility, crucial material resources, and access to power holders. Their effectiveness and even their survival may be impacted.'[50] On the other hand, too much softening rhetoric may create the impression that the movement is neither willing nor able to put forward the necessary pressure to achieve the proclaimed goals.

Of course, many right-wing social movements are also applying the tactics of niche marketing and softening rhetoric to different audiences in order to direct religious and political messages and avoid accusations of over-reaching and extremism.[51] Mitch Berbier revealed a strategy of the US White Power movement to avoid crude racist bigotry by employing a master frame of cultural pluralism instead, according to which Whites are an oppressed minority that strives for equal cultural rights.[52]

A condition for frames to be successful is that they bring up a sense of injustice, identity and collective potency. Framing by right-wing movements intensively emphasizes the representation of one's own collective defined as exclusionary national, religious or ethnic. As 'victims' they are at the mercy of other collectives like foreign interest groups or a societal

[48] George Kassimeris and Leonie Jackson, 'The Ideology and Discourse of the English Defence League: "Not Racist, Not Violent, Just No Longer Silent"', *The British Journal of Politics and International Relations* pre-print online version 1 (2014), pp. 171–188. See also Chris Allen, 'Opposing Islamification or promoting Islamophobia? Understanding the English Defence League', *Patterns of Prejudice* 4 (2011), pp. 279–294; Joel J. Busher, 'Grassroots Activism in the English Defence League: Discourse and Public (dis)Order', in Max Taylor, P. M. Currie and Donald Holbrooke (eds), *Extreme Right-Wing Political Violence and Terrorism* (London: Bloomsbury, 2013), pp. 65–83.

[49] James Jasper, 'A Strategic Approach to Collective Action', *Mobilization* 1 (2004), pp. 1–16.

[50] Herbert H. Haines, 'Dangerous Issues and Public Identities: The Negotiation of Controversy in Two Movement Organizations', *Sociological Inquiry* 2 (2006), pp. 231–263, p. 231.

[51] Ann Burlein, *Lift High the Cross: Where White Supremacy and the Christian Right Converge* (Durham, NC: Duke University Press, 2002), pp. 147–148.

[52] Mitch Berbrier, '"Half the Battle": Cultural Resonance, Framing Processes, and Ethnic Affectations in Contemporary White Separatist Rhetoric', *Social Problems* 4 (1998), pp. 431–450.

development characterized by a decline of moral and religious values.[53] The particular social movement, even if weak and small, presents itself as the only credible and potent player, probably as the avant-garde, both willing and able to eliminate what it frames as the (historical) injustice. Yet, for the most part the contention of such reactive movements is about the defence or recovery of a privileged status.[54]

DIMENSIONS OF RIGHT-WING SOCIAL MOVEMENTS

This section covers several dimensions that are important for the overall understanding of right-wing social movements. The first paragraphs outline the diversity of political activities and cultural performances organized by right-wing social movements. The dimension of violence is also included, followed by dimensions like space and narration. After that, interactions of right-wing social movements with state agencies and counter-movements are covered. Finally, transnational dimensions of right-wing movements and the issue of impact are discussed.

Right-wing social movements offer a broad range of political protest activities and cultural performances, both 'low-risk' and 'high-risk',[55] in order to present their analysis and their suggestions for societal changes to a broader public, but also to create and stabilize collective identity via participation in political action or cultural practices. Such activities include, amongst others, petitions, rallies, graffiti, squatting, hacktivism, music festivals, folk dance gatherings and different kinds of acts of violence that inflict material and economic damage and loss of life.[56] Due to the huge importance of contentious interactive performance or protest events for social movements and their analysis, a selection of political activities and cultural performances, which are highly significant for right-wing social

---

[53] McVeigh, Myers and Sikkink, 'Corn, Klansmen, and Coolidge', p. 673; Cynthia Burack, 'Getting What "We" Deserve: Terrorism, Tolerance, Sexuality, and the Christian Right', *New Political Science* 3 (2003), pp. 329–349.

[54] Phil Hubbard, 'Accommodating Otherness: Anti-Asylum Centre Protest and the Maintenance of White Privilege', *Transactions of the Institute of British Geographers, New Series* 1 (2005), pp. 52–65.

[55] Doug McAdam, 'Recruitment to High-Risk Activism: The Case of Freedom Summer', *American Journal of Sociology* 1 (1986), pp. 64–90.

[56] Martha McCaughey and Michael D. Ayers (eds), *Cyberactivism: Online Activism in Theory and Practice* (London: Routledge, 2003).

movements, are presented in the subsequent section.[57] Following Sidney Tarrow's differentiation of protest actions between conventional, disruptive and violent, issues of rallies and public manifestations are discussed as an example of conventional political action, as well as occupation and squatting as disruptive tactics.[58] Various forms of threat or the use of violence by right-wing social movements are also covered.

The street is a major arena of political action by right-wing social movements. They organize campaigns, run information booths, hold public manifestations and organize rallies and marches. Street politics aim at serving internal purposes as well as sending messages to a wider public. By organizing rallies, movement entrepreneurs intend to contribute to the coherence, growth, ideological and habitual education and performance of the movement. Often, movement entrepreneurs aim to create a temporary emotional collective which helps to recruit new followers contributing to the stabilization of the collective identity of the movement. It also helps to select cadres and to secure the formation of ideological worldviews and attitudes. The external functions of demonstrations include the evidence that an effective social movement exists, even in the face of repression and stigmatization, one that is in control of space at least temporarily.[59] In accordance with the considerations of Charles Tilly— according to whom one of the major elements to a social movement is the participants' concerted public representation of worthiness, unity, numbers and commitments (WUNC) on the part of themselves and/or their constituencies[60]—right-wing movements are fully aware of these aspects and discuss them explicitly.[61] In Poland, the annual march of far-right and nationalist groups on the occasion of National Independence Day has recorded an increasing number of participants, with some thousands

[57] Charles Tilly, 'From Interactions to Outcomes in Social Movements', in Marco Giugni, Doug McAdam, and Charles Tilly (eds), *How Social Movements Matter* (Minneapolis: University of Minnesota Press, 1999), pp. 253–270.

[58] Sidney Tarrow, *Power in Movement: Social Movements and Contentious Politics* (Cambridge Cambridge University Press, 1998).

[59] Fabian Virchow, 'Performance, Emotion and Ideology—on the Creation of "Collectives of Emotion" and World View in the Contemporary German Far Right', *Journal of Contemporary Ethnography* 2 (2007), pp. 147–164.

[60] Charles Tilly, *Social Movements, 1768–2004* (Boulder, CO: Paradigm, 2004), p. 53.

[61] Fabian Virchow, 'Capturing the Streets'—Marches as a Political Instrument of the Extreme Right in Contemporary Germany', in Matthias Reiss (ed.), *'The Street as Stage': Protest Marches and Public Rallies since the Nineteenth Century* (Oxford: Oxford University Press, 2007), p. 295–310, p. 306.

in 2010 up to 50,000 in 2013. Not only does this development reflect the soaring numerical relevance of the movement, but it also reflects the growing self-confidence of the movement with its growing willingness to risk confrontation with the police.[62]

There are numerous elements in the design and implementation of demonstrations and public meetings underlining the political messages of the particular right-wing movement. The chanting of hateful slogans and building a 'black bloc' at neo-Nazi rallies as well as robed and helmeted Ku Klux Klan followers at periodic street walks are aimed at intimidating political opponents and (members of) the group designated as a threat. At many Tea Party events, observers can easily find tri-cornered caps, Gadsden flags and Revolutionary War costumes. 'The colonial era dress is of a piece with the ubiquitous presence of copies of the Constitution at Tea Party events, and all are signs of a particular form of nationalism inhabiting this movement, as is the exaggerated assertion of American exceptionalism.'[63]

Public manifestations and interventions of right-wing movements vary widely in style and content. Music sometimes plays an important role. Music groups, for example, were performing live at German neo-Nazi rallies for a while in order to attract young people and to circumvent the ban on White Power concerts by taking advantage of the right of assembly enshrined constitutionally. Activists of the Identitarian Movement have organized so called Hardbass revolts at well-attended public places. This form of action combines public dancing with costumes, mostly facemasks, and electro music with fast bass lines. Originating from the Netherlands, far-rightists from Eastern Europe adopted this for propaganda purposes. The most popular track is 'We Bring Hard Bass to Your Home 1488',[64] whereby number '14' refers to a racist slogan[65] and the number '88' is a coded abbreviation for 'Heil Hitler'.

Occupation and squatting by right-wing movements can serve different purposes and take different forms. On 20 April 1989, a group of German neo-Nazis occupied the office of the German Press Agency (dpa) in Essen to draw attention to the hundredth birthday of Adolf Hitler and to show

---

[62] Eva Spanka and Andreas Kahrs, 'Die Bewegung marschiert. Ruch Narodowy und Polens extreme Rechte', *Osteuropa* 1 (2014), pp. 129–140.

[63] Zeskind, 'A Nation Dispossessed', 504.

[64] http://www.youtube.com/watch?v=my5KyAuGOOQ (accessed 8 August 2014); http://www.youtube.com/watch?v=GpH2gU-VHPA (accessed 8 August 2014).

[65] Michael, 'David Lane and the Fourteen Words'.

the public that there are still followers of his belief. Police ended this action quickly. In Italy, CPI organized a symbolic occupation of a centre of the car company FIAT in order to protest against the planned restructuring and relocating of production in February 2010. Two years before, *Blocco Studentesco*, the youth wing of CPI, had occupied several school buildings when taking part in larger protests against the plans of the former education minister. He intended to equate the private schools with public schools and, in doing so, to reduce the budget of the public school system by around 8 billion euros. Squatting has played an important role in CPI politics from the very beginning. Not only did they occupy a centrally located four-story building as their headquarter in 2003, but they were also running a campaign called *Occupazioni a Scopo Abitativo* (OSA; Occupations for the purpose of housing). Although actual terms only list a few Casa Pound's OSA in the whole of Italy, 'these experiences are exploited by the group to increase its visibility and originality and as a viaticum for its political discourse on the crisis'.[66] In Vienna, the Identitarian Movement temporarily occupied a church in which refugees protested against the rigid asylum and deportation politics of the Austrian government. Obviously, the occupation of buildings takes different lengths of time and serves several purposes. This reaches from raising attention to a particular issue and presenting oneself as a dedicated political actor—willing to follow a non-legalist/disruptive line of action through the escalation of a dispute and the symbolic staging of solidarity with those who are portrayed as being hurt by the 'Others'—up to the seizure of infrastructure for the permanent use by the movement itself.

Violence plays an important role for right-wing social movements, albeit the relationship is complex and therefore generalizing statements should not be made. Firstly, of course, not every right-wing social movement exercises acts of political violence. Some do so for reasons of principle, but many regard it as a question of strategy and tactics which includes, for example, the assessment that violence perpetrated by members of right-wing movements can be framed as legitimate success. In order to do so, activists of right-wing movements often make use of a 'narrative of self-defence' to justify their own violence as a response to the behaviour of others which is framed as a betrayal of the people and the nation. In the United States, for example, 'anti-abortion activists, organized hate groups, and patriot and militia groups have bombed abortion clinics,

---

[66] Gattinara, Froio and Albanese, 'The Appeal of Neo-Fascism', p. 254.

black churches, and federal buildings, and have lynched and assassinated perceived enemies in an attempt to influence public opinion and public policy'.[67] Secondly, the decision of right-wing movements to radicalize or de-radicalize regarding exercising acts of political violence is influenced by different factors varying in relevance during a protest cycle. Respective factors include the level of repression by state agencies, the level of success when using conventional forms of protest, but also 'competition for members and media attention between different movement organizations'.[68]

The militia movement in the United States is strongly opposed to gun control and taxation by the Federal government. It is also strongly influenced by claims of concealed foreign troops and concentration camps on US territory as part of plans by the Federal government or the UN with the aim to impose a New World order.[69] The militias can serve as a fascinating example of potentiality of violence in right-wing movements.[70] As US militias suspect the Federal government of plotting against the American people, they also insinuate that the government wants to ensure 'that American citizens will be deprived of the means to combat the foreign onslaught which will be masterminded by the U.N.'[71] or the US Federal government. Two events have encouraged the faith of militias in this interpretation. In August 1992, US marshals and FBI agents besieged the compound of a Christian Identity believer in Ruby Ridge, Idaho, who had sold two illegally shortened shotguns. During the siege, his son and wife were shot dead. A raid by ATF agents at the compound of the religious sect Branch Davidians at Waco in 1993 resulted in a shootout followed by a 51-day standoff that ended with a fire in which 76 Branch Davidians died. These events were like catalysts, drawing people into the movement, even from the political mainstream, and creating an upsurge of

---

[67] Verta Taylor and Nella van Dyke, '"Get up, Stand up": Tactical Repertoires of Social Movements', in David A. Snow, Sarah A. Soule and Hanspeter Kriesi (eds), *The Blackwell Companion to Social Movements* (Oxford: Blackwell, 2004), pp. 262–293, p. 265.

[68] Taylor and van Dyke, '"Get up, Stand up"', 274.

[69] Joshua D. Freilich, Jeremy A. Pienik and Gregory J. Howard, 'Toward Comparative Studies of the U.S. Militia Movement', *International Journal of Comparative Sociology* 1–2 (2001), pp. 163–201.

[70] Some scholars refer to it as the 'new militia movement'. See Stan C. Weeber and Daniel G. Rodehaever, 'Militias at the Millenium', *The Sociological Quarterly* 2 (2003), pp. 181–204.

[71] Freilich, Pienik and Howard, 'Toward Comparative Studies', p. 170; see also David C. Williams, 'The Militia Movement and Second Amendment Revolution: Conjuring with the People', *Cornell Law Review* 81 (1996), pp. 879–952.

the number of militias.[72] The level of militancy and violent action increased coming to a peak with the Oklahoma bombing in 1995.[73] After that, due to repression against the movement by state authorities, the movement declined in numbers but also went underground, propagating models of 'leaderless resistance'.[74] On programmatic terms, large segments of the militia movement transformed itself into a more explicitly racist and anti-Semitic movement, firmly rooted in the vision of reinforcing white male superiority.[75]

Regarding cultural practices and products, right-wing movements offer a wide repertoire by which they approach adherents with the aim of integrating them into the movement.[76] Music plays a central role in the White Power movement.[77] Militias gather their members regularly to do weapons training and engage in education.[78] In the US neo-Nazi movement, being tattooed with White Power insignias is not only an important means of initiation and commitment by new members, but also a symbol of intensifying identification with the movement if repeated.[79] Casa Pound Italy runs more than a dozen bookstores and offers a wide range of cultural events like film screenings, readings, exhibitions and theatre performances. Rightly, Verta Taylor and Nella van Dyke have emphasized that such cultural performances 'that meld politics with entertainment may have a range of cultural effects, including transformation in beliefs, identities, and ideologies'.[80]

[72] Mark Pitcavage, 'Camouflage and Conspiracy. The Militia Movement from Ruby Ridge to Y2K', *American Behavioral Scientist* 6 (2001), pp. 957–981.

[73] Martin Durham, 'Preparing for Armageddon: Citizen Militias, the Patriot Movement and the Oklahoma City Bombing', *Terrorism and Political Violence* 1 (1996), pp. 65–79.

[74] Betty A. Dobratz and Lisa K. Waldner, 'Repertoires of Contention: White Separatist Views on the Use of Violence and Leaderless Resistance', *Mobilization* 1 (2012), pp. 49–66.

[75] Rebecca S. Katz and Joey Bailey, 'The Militia, a Legal and Social Movement Analysis: Will the Real Militia Please Stand Up? Militia Hate Group or the Constitutional Militia?', *Sociological Focus* 2 (2000), pp. 133–151.

[76] Thomas Welskopp, 'Anti-Sallon-League und Ku Klux Klan', in Jürgen Mittag and Helke Stadtland (eds), *Theoretische Ansätze und Konzepte der Forschung über soziale Bewegungen in der Geschichtswissenschaft* (Essen: Klartext, 2014), pp. 259–260.

[77] Robert Futrell, Peter Simi and Simon Gottschalk, 'Understanding Music in Movements: The White Power Music Scene', *The Sociological Quarterly* 2 (2006), pp. 275–304.

[78] Lane Crothers, 'The Cultural Foundations of the Modern Militia Movement', *New Political Science* 2 (2002), pp. 221–234.

[79] Robert Futrell and Peter Simi, 'Free Spaces, Collective Identity, and the Persistence of U.S. White Power Activism', *Social Problems* 1 (2004), pp. 16–42, p. 30–31.

[80] Taylor and van Dyke, '"Get up, Stand up"', p. 279.

Space is a constituent aspect of contentious politics by right-wing social movements in a number of ways. For example, it is relevant in the sense that the 'Other' is denied access to public space. Physical attacks organized by far-right movements in Eastern European countries against public manifestations of LGBTQI communities can be given as a recent example.[81] Another issue is the racialization of space as a relevant implementation of nimbyism in order to keep the 'Other' completely out of a particular space.[82] As the example of the 1960s KKK in North Carolina demonstrates, spatial diffusion of right-wing movements rests on 'the presence of opportunities for connections within and across counties, through which information about the Klan could spread to other aggrieved individuals'[83] to a certain extent. It also interacts with social processes, especially threat and competition dynamics resulting from the dynamics of Civil Rights Movement's activities within localized settings.

Finally, right-wing movements have different types of 'free spaces', understood as (mostly) small-scale settings providing autonomy and shelter from dominant or hostile groups to activists in order to be able to nurture oppositional movement identities. Robert Futrell and Pete Simi have further developed the typology suggested by Francesca Polletta identifying several types of free spaces, taking the US White Power movement as an example.[84] According to the authors, families and small informal domestic gatherings count as 'indigenous-prefigurative spaces'. They allow the open expression of radical racist worldviews as they are exclusive, intimate and rooted in enduring relationships. The pre-figurative dimension is exercised by cultural practices like naming children (with symbols of Aryan or Nordic ideology), charging birthday celebrations with White Power symbolism (e.g. cakes decorated with swastikas) and home schooling in order not to hand over the kids to the 'ZOG' ('Zionist Occupation Government'). While such practices mainly serve the movement's inter-generational

---

[81] Đorđe Tomić, 'On the "Right" Side? The Radical Right in the Post-Yugoslav Area and the Serbian Case', *Fascism* 1 (2013), pp. 94–114.

[82] Phil Hubbard, 'Accommodating Otherness: Anti-Asylum Centre Protest and the Maintenance of White Privilege', *Transactions of the Institute of British Geographers, New Series* 1 (2005), pp. 52–65.

[83] David Cunningham and Benjamin T. Phillips, 'Contexts for Mobilization: Spatial Settings and Klan Presence in North Carolina, 1964–1966', *American Journal of Sociology* 3 (2007), pp. 781–814, p. 781.

[84] Francesca Polletta, '"Free Spaces" in Collective Action', *Theory and Society* 1 (1999), pp. 1–38; Futrell and Simi, 'Free Spaces', p. 18.

socialization, boundary making and fostering commitment to the movement are at the very centre of small informal gatherings in which identity
talk contributes to the definition of racial boundaries and configuration
of White Power lifestyles. In addition, 'transmovement-prefigurative
spaces' bring together members of different sections of the movement and
encourage them, through the experience of being part of a much larger
community. This is probably a more vibrant movement than the small
group they belong to on a daily basis. Such events like the *Aryan Nations*
congresses or, in the German context, the *Deutsche Stimme Pressefest* (press
festivals) are often organized on remote territory that is privately owned.[85]
Cyberspace offers another type of free space since the manifold options
for real-time communication contribute to the creation and sustaining of
virtual White Power communities. However, real world and virtual world
spaces are not separated spheres but closely intertwined.[86]

Transnational activism by right-wing movements is not a completely
new phenomenon but has rapidly advanced through developments like
'cheap airline tickets, more widely available telephone and Internet access,
expanding use of English as a global working language, and a globalized mass media'.[87] In addition, many right-wing movements assume that
a change in current developments, such as immigration to the Global
North, gender mainstreaming or increasing religious diversity in formerly
predominantly Christian societies, cannot be stopped or reversed in an
isolated nation-state context only.

Accordingly, neo-Nazis have developed a vibrant transnational demonstration practice for some time and mobilize their demonstrations with
calls in multiple languages.[88] The Internet also provides activists with
access to information on what the different movements do. The DPNI,
for example, has integrated a multi-language online translation facility on

---

[85] Virchow, 'Performance, Emotion and Ideology', p. 147–148.

[86] Pete Simi and Robert Futrell, 'Cyberculture and the Endurance of White Power
Activism', *Journal of Political and Military Sociology* 1 (2006), pp. 115–142.

[87] Jackie Smith, 'Transnational Social Movements', in Snow, Della Porta, Klandermans and
McAdam (eds), *Encyclopedia* 3, pp. 1347–1351. See also Byron Miller, 'Spaces of
Mobilization. Transnational Social Movements', in Clive Barnett and Murray Low (eds),
Spaces of Democracy: Geographical Perspectives on Citizenship, Participation and Representation
(London: Sage, 2004), pp. 223–247.

[88] Fabian Virchow, 'Creating a European Movement by Joint Political Action?', in Andrea
Mammone, Emmanuel Godin and Brian Jenkins (eds), *Varieties of Right-Wing Extremism in
Europe* (London: Routledge, 2013), pp. 197–213.

their website. The Hungarian neo-fascist movement *Hatvannégy Vármegye Ifjúsági Mozgalom* (64 Counties Youth Movement) operates a cross-border campaign in order to mobilize young members of the Hungarian minorities living in Serbia, Romania and Slovakia.[89] Actions like the first striking public appearance of the *Identitarian Movement* in France, the occupation in Poitiers and the subsequent release of a YouTube video called 'Déclaration de Guerre' led to the formation of Identitarian groups in many countries. A couple of books and meetings effective on an international level aim to give the still loosely organized movement a programmatic basis and structure.

Of course, right-wing social movements have their narratives, too. Narratives contribute to the identity building and meaning-making of a particular movement as a vital form of movement discourse. They are also an important resource for recruiting members and for aligning the heterogeneous group of followers on a strategy and on modes of action. Narratives might also give an idea of successful outcomes of one movement's struggle.

One of the many possible forms in which social movements bring forth stories of change is the novel. Right-wing social movements have spawned several novels of great importance.[90] By far the most important have been the Turner Diaries written by the leader of the National Alliance, Dr William L. Pierce (1933–2002). The novel, which has been translated into several languages, shows a violent revolution to nuclear war in the United States which leads to the overthrow of the Federal government and to race war resulting in the extermination of all groups deemed by Pierce as sinful such as Jews, homosexuals and non-Whites. By the year 2000 it was reported to have sold some 500,000 copies. Actually, the novel has been linked to several real-life acts of political violence by White supremacists the most terrible being the Oklahoma City bombing in 1995.

Casa Pound Italy has its novel too, titled 'Nessun Dolore' ('No pain') and it was written by the lawyer of the movement, Domenico di Tullio. The author's aim is to create a founding myth of Casa Pound and to draw a picture of an uncompromising movement well beyond an established bourgeois world. Right-wing movements such as CPI also make use of cultural products such as the US fantasy action film '300' based on a comic series. The narrative of the film, which was a box office success

---

[89] Tomić, 'On the "Right" Side?', p. 112.
[90] George Michael, 'Blueprints and Fantasies: A Review and Analysis of Extremist Fiction', *Studies in Conflict & Terrorism* 2 (2009), pp. 149–170.

in Italy too, contains several elements attractive for many far-right social movements such as a patriarchal gender arrangement, a cult of the heroic body and contempt for life. It supports the idea of overcoming coddled civilization and corrupt democracy through an elite steeled in war.

The wide variety of right-wing social movements and the different social, political and legal contexts in which they emerge and act makes a systematic study of the interactions of these movements with their respective environments impossible at this point. The same applies for the impact of such movements. Therefore, the following notes are intended to give some exemplary ideas on the complexity and width of these issues.

Interactions of right-wing social movements can take place between a particular movement and state authorities like police forces and judiciary; towards competing right-wing movements, parties or organizations; in dealing with counter-movements; regarding mainstream media; and in relation to the political system and political parties.

As social movements are not homogeneous, controversies about the appropriate strategy and tactics, the importance of violence or the issue of entering into an alliance with other political actors may lead to the split of the movement, at least as perceived by the activists themselves. As a result, they may use different framings and various tactical repertoires and they differ in the rituals used to strengthen their collective identity and so on. Counter-movements interact with right-wing movements in different ways. They may question the role of right-wing movements as legitimate claim-makers and challenge them by using frames that stress the very idea of 'sameness' instead of 'otherness' regarding the legal and social status of minority groups. Counter-movements might also confront right-wing movements by disputing their claim to the use of public spaces. In fact, since the late 1990s, a broad anti-fascist movement in Germany has been successfully suppressing many neo-Nazi marches by the blocking of roads. This has led to a change in protest tactics of the neo-Nazi movement.

Interaction with mainstream media depends on the strength of the particular right-wing movement. While fringe neo-Nazi movements do not have regular access to mainstream media and often argue that having any news is better than no news, movements like the Tea Party or the RSS are well represented in relevant parts of mass media. However, every right-wing movement seeks to have tactical media under its own control.[91]

[91] R. Sophie Statzel, 'Cybersupremacy: The New Face and Form of White Supremacist Activism', in Megan Boler (ed.), *Digital Media and Democracy* (Cambridge, MA: MIT Press, 2008), pp. 405–428.

State authorities, media and counter-movements can contribute to the stigmatization of a right-wing social movement under particular conditions. In reaction, movements themselves as well as individuals related to the movements act out stigma management that can take various forms. Individuals may conceal and disclose their political identity and movements might tone down their confrontational framing.[92] The effect of acts of repression like the arrest of leaders or the banning of parties on right-wing social movements rests on several factors: the social cohesion and ideological unity of the group, the extent and duration of the repressive measure, the possibility of evasion opting to do something similar elsewhere and so on.[93]

The impact of right-wing social movements on political decisions can range from zero to substantially altering the political agenda. Taking the Jewish settler movement as an example, Oded Haklai shows that the impact of a right-wing movement can be generated by the penetration of the state apparatus.[94] This leads to a situation in which the state loses enforcement capacity vis-à-vis the penetrating right-wing social movement. As a result, the movement can go ahead with the establishment of Jewish settlements deemed illegal in many cases even according to Israeli law. Regarding the Russian DNPI, the event that triggered the emergence of the movement—the killing of a Spartak Moscow football fan by a group of six men from the Northern Caucasus—and the subsequent racist riots were denounced at the time by the government as the result of football fanaticism. During the following months, however, the Russian government implemented a two-pronged strategy. On one hand, it condemned the riots and banned DNPI, but on the other hand it reinforced an ethno-racial understanding of Russianness constructed in marked contrast to the alleged 'wildness' and 'laziness' of Russian citizens racialized as 'Caucasians'.[95] Considering the Tea Party movement as a final example, it can be said that the Tea Party movement has been able to make relevant inroads into the Republican

---

[92] Peter Simi and Robert Futrell, 'Negotiating White Power Activist Stigma', *Social Problems* 1 (2009), pp. 89–110.

[93] Theodore McLauchlin and Wendy Pearlman, 'Out-Group Conflict, In-Group Unity? Exploring the Effect of Repression on Intramovement Cooperation', *Journal of Conflict Resolution* 1 (2012), pp. 41–66; Jennifer Earl, 'Political Repression: Iron Fists, Velvet Gloves, and Diffuse Control', *Annual Review of Sociology* 37 (2011), pp. 261–284.

[94] Oded Haklai, 'Religious-Nationalist Mobilization and State Penetration', *Comparative Political Studies* 6 (2007), pp. 713–739.

[95] Zakharov, 'The Social Movement'.

Party. During the 2010 primaries, Tea Party candidates defeated more mainstream competitors. Also, the list of proposed legislative items brought forward by the Republican leadership under the title 'Pledge to America in November 2010' was clearly influenced by the Tea Party movement.[96] However, any assessment of the impact of social movements must keep in mind that there is a dynamic system at work. The success of a social movement might lead to its weakening or even dissolution because it has reached its major aims or it causes counter-activities that might reduce its influence.

FUTURE RESEARCH

While there is a growing number of theoretical embedded research on individual right-wing social movements, there is still the question of according to which criteria scholars speak of a right-wing movement instead of a party or lobby-group, particularly in terms of the movements' emergence, political profile, framing and protest activities. Such academic work should be done more often by operationalizing and empirically testing of the underlying definition of what a social movement is made of. If combined with a diachronic comparative perspective it might lead us to new insights regarding the relative grade of social movementization of a particular political actor. In general, there is need for more systematic and comparative studies both diachronic and synchronic. This might show that we are facing quite different political entities although the name of the particular group or movement has remained the same for decades. Finally, the interactions of right-wing social movements with societal, political and state actors need further elaboration, not least because many right-wing movements struggle for 'uncivil' aims.

FURTHER READING

Regarding the fact that social movement research for a long time had a strong focus on progressive social and political movements there is very limited work on right-wing social movements that the topic introduce systematically. A systematizing approach should include presenting and discussing definitions as well as marking out what political/social protagonist should be considered under the term of right-wing social movement, e.g. in distinction to a political party. Essential reading in this sense are some book

---

[96] Edward Ashbee, 'Bewitched—The Tea Party Movement', p. 162–163.

chapters and journal contributions published more recently such as Kathleen Blee and Kimberly A. Creasap in the *Annual Review of Sociology* (2010, pp. 269–286), Neil Davidson from a Marxian perspective in the volume on *Marxism and Social Movements* edited by Colin Barker et al. (Leiden/ Bosten: Brill, 2013, pp. 277–297), and the encyclopaedic overview by Sivan Hirsch-Hoefler and Cas Mudde in the *Wiley-Blackwell Encyclopedia of Social & Political Movements* (Vol. III, 2013, pp. 1116–1124). As a monograph *Right-wing Extremism as a Social Movement* edited by Bert Klandermans and Nonna Mayer (London: Routledge, 2006) has definitely to be mentioned with its rich empirical findings.

So far, most research on right-wing social/political movements is presented in the form of case studies. For the US context this covers the Ku Klux Klan with seminal work like Rory McVeigh's *The Rise of the Ku Klux Klan. Right-wing Movements and National Politics* (Minneapolis: University of Minnesota Press, 2009) as well as the often groupuscular White supremacist, Christian Identity and neo-Nazi movements to which authors like Pete Simi and Robert Futrell with *American Swastika. Inside the White Power Movement's Hidden Spaces of Hate* (Lanham, MD: Rowman & Littlefield, 2010), Carolyn Gallaher with *On the Fault Line. Race, Class, and the American Patriot Movement* (Lanham, MD: Rowman & Littlefield, 2003) and Michael Barkun with *Religion and the Racist Right: The Origins of the Christian Identity Movement* (Chapel Hill: University of North Carolina Press, 1994) contributed to our understanding significantly. Finally, *The Terrorist Next Door: The Militia Movement and the Radical Right* by Daniel Levitas (New York: Dunne, 2002) on the phenomenon of US militias is still a path-breaking read.

Most recently, the US Tea Party movement has gained growing academic attention. While there are many studies on its ideological profile, membership structure and its impact on the Republican Party, Christine Trost and Lawrence Rosenthal (eds), *Steep: The Precipitous Rise of the Tea Party* (Berkeley: University of California Press, 2012), and Nella Van Dyke's and David S. Meyer's *Understanding the Tea Party Movement* (Burlington: Ashgate, 2014) help to follow it from a social movement theories perspective. The Tea Party movement lucidly set in a wider context has been covered in some timely work by David R. Dietrich in his *Rebellious Conservatives. Social Movements in Defense of Privilege* (Basingstoke: Palgrave-Macmillan, 2014) and by Isaac William Martin in his *Rich People's Movements. Grassroots Campaigns to Untax the One Percent* (Oxford: Oxford University Press, 2013).

The broad range of right-wing social and political movements in contemporary Europe is discussed in articles on Russia and Eastern Europe like Nikolay Zakharov's *The Social Movement Against Immigration as the Vehicle and the Agent of Racialization in Russia*, as part of the volume *Beyond NGO-ization. The Development of Social Movements in Central and Eastern Europe* edited by Kerstin Jacobsson and Steven Saxonberg (Farnham: Ashgate, 2013, pp. 169–189) and Dennis Zuev's *The Movement Against Illegal Immigration: Analysis of the Central Node in the Russian Extreme-Right Movement* published in *Nations and Nationalism* 16 (2010), pp. 261–284. It is also worth looking into Đorđe Tomić's *'On the "Right" Side? The Radical Right in the Post-Yugoslav Area and the Serbian Case* to be found in *Fascism* 2 (2013), pp. 94–114. For the Italian situation Casa Pound is the most relevant contemporary right-wing social movement. Pietro Gattinara, Caterina Froio and Matteo Albanese have discussed this movement in relation to the latest financial crisis in Europe (*Fascism* 2 2012, pp. 234–258).

For the UK, one of the most relevant recent studies on the English Defence League might be Joel Busher's *The Making of Anti-Muslim Protest* (London: Routledge, 2016), while a look at my chapter in *Digital Media Strategies of the Far Right in Europe and the United States* (edited by Helga Druxes and Patricia Simpson, Lanham, MD: Lexington 2015, pp. 177–190) will probably help to understand the Identiarian Movement active in Austria, France and Germany.

While research on right-wing social and political movements definitely has a strong focus on North American and European contexts and history there is some relevant work on Asia and Latin America. The latter is often related to right-wing paramilitary groups like in Leigh A. Payne's *Uncivil Movements. The Armed Right Wing and Democracy in Latin America* (Baltimore, MD: Johns Hopkins University Press, 2000). Regarding the Asian context, excellent research is available on Hindu nationalism, a good starting point is *The Hindu Nationalist Movement and Indian Politics, 1925 to the 1990s* by Christophe Jaffrelot (London: Hurst & Co., 1993).

In order to get some basic information on right-wing social and political movements it might also be helpful to visit some encyclopaedic work like Stephen E. Atkins's *Encyclopedia of Right-Wing Extremism in Modern American History* (Santa Barbara, CA: ABC Clio, 2011) or Cyprian Blamires's two volume *Historical Encyclopedia of World Fascism* (Santa Barbara, CA: ABC Clio, 2006).

CHAPTER 22

The Global Justice Movement: Resistance to Dominant Economic Models of Globalization

Britta Baumgarten

Resistance to dominant economic models of globalization has a long history that reaches back to various movements, protests and campaigns,
as for example the Tupac Amaru uprising (1780–1781) or the anti-slave
trade movement (which peaked between 1787 and 1807).[1] This chapter
focusses on one of the most recent incarnations, the 'global justice movement' (GJM). The recent mobilizations by the Indignados and the Occupy
movements do not form part of this movement. These current movements entered the scene in 2011 and became prominent for their large
street protests and occupations of public spaces. They are mainly directed
towards their respective national governments, claiming more democracy

[1] Zahara Heckscher, 'Long before Seattle. Historical Resistance to Economic Globalization',
in Robin Broad (ed.), *Global Backlash. Citizen Initiatives for a Just World Economy* (Lanham,
MD: Rowman & Littlefield, 2002).

B. Baumgarten (✉)
Centre for Research and Studies in Sociology, University Institute of Lisbon,
Lisbon, Portugal

© The Author(s) 2017
S. Berger, H. Nehring (eds.), *The History of Social Movements in
Global Perspective*, DOI 10.1057/978-1-137-30427-8_22

647

and protesting against austerity programmes. According to Dieter Rucht in this volume 'a social movement can be defined as a network of individuals, groups and organizations that, based on a sense of collective identity, seek to bring about social change (or resist social change) primarily by means of collective public protest'.[2] In order to speak about a movement as an entity, there has to exist a certain degree of consensus of what activists perceived as a grievance and how problems and solutions are defined. The actors within movements also need to be related to each other, at least in the sense that they consider their struggles as related. Similarities in action forms and internal practices also have to exist in a meaningful way in order for observers to be able to talk about movements. These criteria are also important when we decide whether to consider a movement as a new movement or as a continuity of an existing movement. Although some claims and practices are very similar to the GJM's, the organizational structure of the current protests differs and the international ties of the GJM are hardly used by these new movements. As the current mobilizations have a lot in common with the global justice movement and as there already exists some comparative research on these movements that reveals the continuities between the GJM and the current mobilizations,[3] this chapter will occasionally highlight connections and similarities as well as differences and discontinuities between these movements.

It is not easy to define the global justice movement: its diversity and global scope resist any straightforward classification. Researchers discuss whether the label of what I call here 'global justice movement' is appropriate. In the literature we find also the terms 'no-global movement', 'anti-globalization movement', 'alter-globalization movement' or 'alternative globalization movement' and 'movement for a globalization from below'. These terms are contested because there is disagreement about the main objectives of the movement. These have been described as 'anti-capitalist',

[2] Dieter Rucht, 'Social Movements—Some Conceptual Challenges', Chap. 2 in this volume.

[3] Ron Hayduk, 'Global Justice and OWS. Movement Connections', *Socialism and Democracy* 26 (2012), pp. 43–50; Eduardo Romanos, 'Collective Learning Processes within Social Movements. Some Insights into the Spanish 15M/Indignados Movement', in Christina Flesher Fominaya and Laurence Cox (eds), *Understanding European Movements. New Social Movements, Global Justice Struggles* (London: Routledge, 2013), pp. 203–217.

[4] Marco Giugni, Marko Bandler and Nina Eggert, 'The Global Justice Movement. How Far Does the Classic Social Movement Agenda Go in Explaining Transnational Contention?',

'anti-corporate' or 'anti-globalization'.[4] In light of the great diversity of actors and aims some authors speak about global justice movements in the plural.[5] The great variety of labels illustrates the difficulties social science research has in classifying the GJM.[6] In face of the same difficulty the labels for the actual mobilizations are labelled in broad terms, such as 'Indignados', referring to Stéphane Hessels essay 'Indignez-vous',[7] 'Occupy', referring to action forms, or 'Arab Spring', referring to regions. It is also important to bear in mind that the activists themselves label their events in an all-encompassing way. For example, 15M was chosen as a name for the occupation of Puerta del Sol in Madrid referring only to the date of the event (15 May 2011), similarly the worldwide protests 15O (15 October 2011).[8]

A major slogan of the GJM is 'unity in diversity', which indicates a common identity and the valuation of internal differences within the movement. The GJM consists of various actors around the globe, including NGOs, grassroots organizations, political parties and individuals. During its time in existence it has launched many different campaigns, from debt relief over the Tobin tax to environmental issues. The description 'movement of movements'[9] fits the GJM well, because many movements like

Civil Society and Social Movements Programme Paper 24 (2006), p. 2; Yousaf Ibrahim, 'Understanding the Alternative Globalisation Movement', *Sociology Compass* 3 (2009), pp. 394–416, here p. 397.

[5] Ulrich Brand, 'Contradictions and Crises of Neoliberal–Imperial Globalization and the Political Opportunity Structures for the Global Justice Movements', *Innovation: The European Journal of Social Science Research* 3 (2012), pp. 283–298; Dieter Rucht, 'Social Forums as Public Stage and Infrastructure of Global Justice Movements', in Jackie Smith, Scott Byrd, Ellen Reese and Elizabeth Smythe (eds), *Handbook on World Social Forum Activism* (Boulder, CO: Paradigm, 2011), pp. 11–28.

[6] Breno Bringel and Enara E. Muñoz, 'Dez anos de Seattle, o movimento antiglobalização e a ação coletiva transnacional', *Ciências Sociais Unisinos* 1 (2010), pp. 28–36, here p. 30.

[7] Stéphane Hessel and Marion Duvert, *Time for Outrage!* (New York: Twelve, 2011).

[8] Britta Baumgarten, 'Geração à Rasca and Beyond. Mobilizations in Portugal after 12 March 2011', *Current Sociology* 4 (2015), pp. 457–473; Benjamin Tejerina and Ignacia Perugorría, 'Continuities and Discontinuities in Recent Social Mobilizations. From New Social Movements to the Alter-Global Mobilizations and the 15M', in Tejerina and Perugorría (eds), *From Social to Political. New Forms of Mobilization and Democratization* (Bilbao: Bizkaia Aretoa, 2012), pp. 89–107.

[9] Giugni, Bandler and Eggert, 'Justice Movement'.

ecological, women's or indigenous movements played an important role in the GJM. Indeed, many activist groups that played a role in other social movements presented in this volume have also been part of the GJM, although the main part of their activities has not been related to it. The global justice movement developed out of a great variety of earlier movements and shares most of their claims and values. Breno Bringel has developed five characteristics for the GMJ, apart from its diversity: (1) the spectacular character of many of its action forms; (2) its use of Internet based communication technologies; (3) its horizontal structure of decision making that goes along with a decentralized network-like structure; (4) the principle of 'think global, act local'; and (5) the movement's radical claims against the prevailing socio-economic models. It unites various sectors of the political and social Left and uses the prominent slogan 'Another World is Possible' to confront Margaret Thatcher's often repeated 'There is No Alternative'.[10] What is new about the movement since the 1990s is a denser cooperation and the orientation of events towards the large international meetings of the political and economical elite. The movement became publicly visible in counter protests and the Social Forum Process: events around which the international cooperation within the movement is structured. 'Many of the most visible civil society gatherings have been explicitly, and often antagonistically, related to events of the global elite.'[11] The Social Forum Process consists of various large international meetings of activists that meet to debate alternatives to the current economic and political system, to network and to jointly protest against this system. An important question of definition that has an impact on the functioning of the Social Forum Process remains unresolved, however: Is it an event or a movement?[12]

In what follows I will describe the GJM in more detail, taking into consideration the driving forces for this kind of activism and the key conflicts. Moreover, I outline the actors, their action forms, debates and framings.

---

[10] Bringel and Muñoz, 'Movimento Antiglobalização', p. 30; Geoffrey Pleyers, *Alterglobalization. Becoming Actors in the Global Age* (Cambridge: Polity Press, 2010).

[11] Teivo Teivanen, 'The World Social Forum and Global Democratisation. Learning from Porto Allegre', *Third World Quarterly* 4 (2002), pp. 621–632, here p. 622.

[12] Andy Scerri, 'The World Social Forum. Another World Might Be Possible', *Social Movement Studies* 1 (2012), pp. 111–120.

The main movement events will be described from a chronological and geographical perspective.

THE DEVELOPMENT OF THE GJM IN DIFFERENT PHASES

There is no consensus about when the global justice movement actually began:

> Many say that it started in Seattle. Others maintain that it began five hundred years ago, when colonialists first told indigenous peoples that they were going to have to do things differently if they were to 'develop' or be eligible for 'trade'. Others argue that the movement began on 1 January 1994 when the Zapatistas launched their uprising with the words 'Ya basta!' on the nights NAFTA [North American Free Trade Association] became law in Mexico. It all depends on whom you ask.[13]

Resistance against economic globalization, however, goes back several centuries.[14] For example, Zahara Heckscher mentions the cases of the Tupac Amaru uprising (1780/1781), the anti-slave trade movement (which peaked between 1787 and 1807), the campaign against the colonization of the Congo, the First International Workingmen's Association (founded 1864) and the anti-imperialist movement.[15] These examples are connected to today's GJM, but they were not part of the movement. They were single-issue campaigns and movements. And although we can find organization and protest with a global perspective, the degree of globalization was far lower than in today's movements.

According to Elizabeth Smythe, the establishment of free trade agreements across the Americas and Asia were a starting point for the movement to become global. For example, in 1985, Canada and the United States signed a free trade agreement, followed by a tri-lateral free trade agree-

---

[13] Naomi Klein, 'Reclaiming the Commons', in Luc Reydams (ed.), *Global Activism Reader* (New York: Continuum, 2011), pp. 341–346, p. 341.

[14] Giugni, Bandler and Eggert, 'Justice Movement', p. 4; Robin Broad, 'The Historical Context', in idem (ed.), *Global Backlash. Citizen Initiatives for a Just World Economy* (Lanham, MD: Rowman & Littlefield, 2002), pp. 65–76.

[15] Heckscher, 'Historical Resistance'. See also the chapter on moral movements in this volume.

ment with Mexico in 1991.[16] The counter-summit protests started around the same time as protests 'outside the closed doors of inter-governmental decision making on global issues'.[17] In this first phase activists struggled for access to inter-governmental organizations.[18]

The activism of the 1990s was closely connected to hope that various UN conferences would help to solve the global problems that the movements sought to address. Examples include the UN conferences on environment and development in 1992, on human rights in 1993, on population in 1994, on social development in 1995 and on housing in 1997. In this period, the movements argued for the strengthening of multi-lateral agreements and of regulatory mechanisms; they aimed to increase attention on social concerns, to establish information regimes and to defend, and expand, access into global arenas.[19] In these years early anti-free trade networks became active, which are important for the later World Social Forum process. There were, for example, the European farmer's association, the Hemispheric Social Alliance (HSA) or the International Forum on Globalization (IGFG) 1993.[20] These early anti-free trade networks held international meetings long before the first World Social Forum (WSF), such as the meeting to form the International Forum on Globalization (IFG) in 1994, the 1996 Zapatistas' 'meeting for Humanity and Against Neoliberalism' and meetings following their example in Spain (1997) and Brazil (1999).[21] 'People's Global Action (PGA), a network to facilitate organizing across borders, grew out of a 1998 meeting in Geneva

[16] Elizabeth Smythe, 'Our World is not for Sale! The WSF Process and Transnational Resistance to International Trade Agreements', in Smith, Byrd, Reese and Smythe, *Handbook*, p. 168.

[17] Mario Pianta, Frederico S. Silva and Duccio Zola, 'Global Civil Society Events. Parallel Summits, Social Fora, Global Days of Action (Update)', in Helmut Anheier, Marlies Glasius and Mary Kaldor (eds), *Global Civil Society 2004/2005* (London: Sage, 2004), p. 2.

[18] Jackie Smith, *Social Movements for Global Democracy* (Baltimore, MD: Johns Hopkins University Press, 2008), p. 97.

[19] Smith, *Social Movements*, pp. 95–97.

[20] Smythe, 'Our World is not for Sale!', p. 168; Smith, *Social Movements*, pp. 100–101.

[21] Agnieszka Paczynska, 'Turtles, Puppets and Pink Ladies. The Global Justice Movement in a Post-9/11 World', *Working Papers in Global Studies* 1, (August 2008), p. 4; Rucht, 'Social Forums', p. 13.

of over 400 representatives of grassroots organizations and NGOs from 71 countries.'[22] The contemporary activist practices in the global north, as part of the alternative globalization movement, in some respects emanated from the Zapatistas in the global south, a movement that became publicly visible in January 1994 when NAFTA took effect.[23] In this period also falls the World Bank (WB)/International Monetary Fund (IMF) fiftieth anniversary party that gave rise to the campaign Fifty Years is Enough.[24]

The movement's milestones have been the G8, IMF and WTO summits. The GJM attended (and disrupted or influenced to differing degrees) the summits in Birmingham in 1998, Seattle in 1999, Prague in 2000 and Genoa in 2001. Each of these events was accompanied by a panoply of fringe events and protests.[25] Table 22.1 shows an overview of the biggest events related to the GJM (events with more than 50,000 participants are marked in italics, those with more than 100,000 are marked in bold):

The counter-summit protests are the starting point of a new phase of activism of the GJM. The massive protests against the WTO meeting in Seattle 1999 were the most outstanding event in terms of media attention and impact on further global meetings.[27] After Seattle, the world summits were organized in more remote places. In contrast to these increasingly secretive meetings that were protected from any large-scale protests, the WSF process was initiated as an alternative, participative way of joint debate about solutions. It aimed at creating alternatives to formal politics, changing values of the predominant socio-political order and providing alternative venues for global problem solving.[28] The Jubilee 2000 campaign was a major campaign run during these years in order to campaign for debt relief.[29]

---

[22] Hayduk, 'Global Justice', p. 45.

[23] Ibrahim, 'Alternative Globalisation Movement', p. 395.

[24] Smith, *Social Movements*, pp. 100–101.

[25] Duncan Green and Matthew Griffith, 'Globalization and Its Discontents', *International Affairs* 1 (2002), pp. 49–68, here p. 53.

[26] Paczynska, 'Turtles, Puppets', pp. 9–12; Smith, *Social Movements*, p. 101; Rucht, 'Social Forums', p. 14; Scerri, 'World Social Forum'.

[27] Giugni, Bandler and Eggert, 'Justice Movement', p. 3; Jackie Smith, 'Globalizing Resistance. The Battle of Seattle and the Future of Social Movements', *Mobilization: An International Journal* 1 (2001), pp. 1–19.

[28] Smith, *Social Movements*, p. 97.

[29] Smith, *Social Movements*, pp. 100–101.

Table 22.1   GJM events

Year	Event	Number of participants
1996	Intercontinental Gathering for Humanity and Against Neoliberalism, Chiapas	3,000
1998	G8, Birmingham	70,000[a]
1998	WTO, Geneva	2,000–3,000
1998	WB/IMF, Washington	200–300
1999	*WTO, Seattle*	*50,000–70,000*
1999	WB/IMF, Washington	1,000
1999	G8, Berlin	800–1,000
2000	WB/IMF, Washington	7,000–10,000
2000	*WB/IMF, Prague*	*10,000–15,000*
2000	*G8, Okinawa*	*70,000*
2001	*WSF, Porto Alegre*	*20,000–30,000*
2001	WTO, Doha	1,000
2001	**G8, Genoa**	**100,000–250,000**
2002	*WSF, Porto Alegre*	*40,000–60,000 (150,000*[b]*)*
2002	*ESF, Florence*	*40,000–60,000*
2002	**EU summit, Barcelona**	**300,000**
2002	*WB/IMF, Washington*	*40,000–50,000*
2002	G8, Calgary	2,000–3,000
2002	**Anti-war, Florence**	**1,000,000**
2003	**Anti-war protests, 800 cities**	**10–12 million**
2003	**ESF, Paris**	**100,000**
2003	*WSF, Porto Alegre*	*70,000–75,000*
2003	WTO, Cancun	2,000–3,000
2003	WB/IMF, Doha	Demonstrations banned by law
2003	*G8, Evian*	*50,000–100,000*
2004	WSF, Mumbai	80,000–90,000 (115,000[b])
2004	WB/IMF, Washington	2,000–3,000
2004	G8, Savannah	1,000–2,000
2005	**WSF, Porto Alegre**	**155,000–200,000**
2005	WTO Meeting, Hong Kong	5,000–10,000
2005	WB/IMF, Washington	200
2005	**G8, Edinburgh**	**225,000**
2006	**WSF Caracas**	**80,000**
	WSF Bamako	**11,000**
	WSF Karachi	**20,000**
2006	WB/IMF, Singapore	Demonstrations banned by law
2006	G8, St. Petersburg	150–300
2007	*WSF Nairobi*	*66,000 (57,000*[b]*)*

(continued)

Table 22.1 (continued)

Year	Event	Number of participants
2007	WB/IMF, Washington	300
2007	*G8, Heiligendamm*	*25,000–80,000*
2009	*WSF, Belem*	*100,000*[b]
2011	*WSF, first in 35 places, then centralized in Dakar*[c]	*70,000*[c]

Source: Paczynska; except: [a]Smith; [b]Rucht and [c]Scerri[26]

In 2001, the 'Social Forum Process' began in Porto Alegre. In opposition to the World Economic Forum that has met every year since 1971 in Davos, it emphasizes social issues, is hosted in countries of the global south and thought of as a meeting of people instead of elites. The first World Social Forum was organized by eight founding organizations and hosted by the Workers' Party (*Partido dos Trabalhadores*, PT) in Porto Alegre. There were around 20,000 participants from 100 countries, amongst them were 436 members of parliament. The number of participants grew rapidly to 150,000 participants at the WSF the following year, which was organized by more or less the same actors.[30] Thereafter, the WSF was organized by a broader and more international team and moved away from Porto Alegre, leaving many organizational tasks to local committees. Another important event for the GJM was 11 September 2001. 'Both activists and observers agree that a fundamental turning point in the evolution of the global justice movement were the attacks on the Twin Towers and the Pentagon on September 11, 2001. [...] Although large scale demonstrations have faded in the United States, the global justice movement rather than disintegrating and fading into oblivion has developed a variety of other tactics and strategies to push forward its agenda.'[31] Parallel to the War on terror peace becomes more important in the Social Forums after 2002.[32] There were WSFs in Mumbai (2004), Caracas (Venezuela), Bamako (Mali) and Karachi (Pakistan) (all 2006), Nairobi (Kenya) (2007), Belem (Brazil) (2008) and Dakar (Senegal) (2011).[33] After the first WSF, national forums rapidly spread, especially in the global south.[34]

[30] Rucht, 'Social Forums', pp. 13–14.
[31] Paczynska, 'Turtles, Puppets', p. 1.
[32] Pianta, Silva and Zola, 'Global Civil Society Events'.
[33] Rucht, 'Social Forums', p. 14.
[34] Pianta, Silva and Zola, 'Global Civil Society Events', p. 3.

The most recent phase of the movement so far is characterized by a focus on work at the local level and enhanced coordination via Internet, including various blogs and sites dedicated to counter information, for example, the Indymedia pages that are broadly used as a way of delivering information independent from the mainstream media. The increasing commercialization, the establishment and bureaucratization of the Social Forums led to the creation of counter-forums that ran parallel to the forums and served as a space for the more radical groups.[35]

There is disagreement among scholars about how to evaluate the current state of the global justice movement. On the one hand, scholars such as Breno Bringel argue that the GJM has died as a unitary actor but nonetheless enjoys good health; it merely no longer has the basic characteristics that it had at the beginning. Identities have become more diverse, and many activists today no longer define themselves as part of the GJM. Its ideas and practices, however, continue to be relevant, such as the global–local connection of transnational collective action and a broad repertoire of action that has been developed by the movement over the past decades.[36] The global–local connection has also gained new prominence: 'activists want to change the world starting locally with their neighborhood assemblies'.[37] Scholars such as Dieter Rucht, on the other hand, do not regard the GJM as dead. On the contrary, he mentions factors that have contributed to strengthening the movement: the growing relevance of transnational problems, the vast potential of movements in the global south, the availability of Internet as a tool for coordination and communication, and the past processes of learning from mistakes and negative experiences.[38] The GJM has lost some of its force during the last five years for several reasons. It is difficult to sustain a movement at the high intensity the GJM had between 1999 and 2006.[39] Global summits involve a substantial amount of personal and material resources and are therefore hard to sustain by actors that are usually not well endowed with such resources. Every day practices at the local level are also not without limits, however.

[35] Bringel and Muñoz, 'Movimento Antiglobalização', p. 32–34.
[36] Bringel and Muñoz, 'Movimento Antiglobalização', p. 35.
[37] Pleyers, *Alter-globalization*, p. 52.
[38] Rucht, 'Social Forums', p. 27.
[39] Bringel and Muñoz, 'Movimento Antiglobalização', p. 34.

They are less resource intensive, but 'most of the time, they have scarcely any impact on public debate'.[40] Especially in the United States the developments after 9/11 hampered activists.[41] Nevertheless, counter-summits and the Social Forum Process continue to the present day. The tenth European Social Forum took place in Florence in November 2012. The movement relates to the new wave of protest and probably regains force due to the new worldwide protests. In February 2012, it was decided to locate the WSF 2013 in Tunis, Tunisia.[42] Some authors go as far as to see Occupy as a part of the GJM.[43] Although many activists involved in Occupy Wall Street have experiences in the GJM, the new waves of protests are not a simple continuation of the GJM.[44]

THE GJM'S CRITIQUE OF GLOBALIZATION

In spite of its diversity, the GJM has common aims and opponents. According to Ulrich Brand, neo-liberal globalization is the defining context for the GJM: 'a competitive strategy to restore economic growth and strengthen the power of capital on the local, national and international levels'.[45] Lauren Langman highlights five major dysfunctions of the global economy that gave rise to the GJM: (1) the ongoing redistribution of wealth from poor to rich countries; (2) the erosion of the autonomy of state policy; (3) the universalization of a homogenized popular culture that increasingly serves economic interests; (4) the destruction of the environment; and (5) continuing human rights violations.[46] These problems, all attributed to the global economic system, are also a reason for the GJM's broad nature, encompassing various single-issue groups. The movement holds a specific way of economic globalization responsible for social, environmental, political and other problems. This way of 'economic integration goes back centuries, and so do critiques claiming the negative social, economic and environmental impacts, resistance and the development of

---

[40] Pleyers, *Alter-globalization*, p. 87.
[41] Hayduk, 'Global Justice', p. 49.
[42] Scerri, 'World Social Forum', p. 6.
[43] Brand, 'Contradictions and Crises', p. 295.
[44] Hayduk, 'Global Justice', p. 43.
[45] Brand, 'Contradictions and Crises', p. 287.
[46] Lauren Langman, 'From Virtual Public Spheres to Global Justice: A Critical Theory of Internetworked Social Movements', *Sociological Theory* 1 (2005), pp. 42–74.

alternatives'.[47] Important parts of this way of economic integration are institutions, like the World Bank, the International Monetary Fund and the World Trade Organization that all emerged from the Bretton Woods meeting in 1944.[48] But those institutions alone cannot be regarded as driving forces behind the movement. Rather the crises of the economic and social system that these institutions could not prevent, but rather intensified, are regarded as grievances[49] related to the movement. 'During the last few decades, policies and reforms have been guided by the neo-liberal agenda of efficiency, competitiveness and world market orientation, transformation of the state, and the partial privatization of public services and social welfare programs such as pension insurance. [...] Thus, the essentially state-mediated wage relation is eroded and devolved back to the firm level, resulting in a massive loss of power for wage-earners and organized labor.'[50] A growing distance between the citizens and the centres of political decision making, not only resulting from the loss of power of the nation state, but also from negative experiences with political decision makers, is one of the driving forces for the GJMs search for a more participatory democracy.[51] 'Many critiques of global capitalism point to the fact that it prevents citizens from participating in the most crucial decisions that affect their lives.'[52] Representative democratic institutions have lost legitimacy as they 'have become increasingly ineffective at representing and responding to popular interests under neoliberalism'.[53]

At the level of the economy, according to Duncan Green and his colleague, several events have fostered the development of the GJM 'the oil crisis and the suspension of dollar convertibility in 1972 marked the end of the "long boom" of post-1945 Keynesianism. They also triggered

---

[47] Broad, *Global Backlash*.

[48] Smith, *Social Movements*, p. 55.

[49] Brand, 'Contradictions and Crises'. Doug McAdam, 'Conceptual Origins, Current Problems, Future Directions', in Doug McAdam, John D. McCarthy and Mayer N. Zald (eds), *Comparative Perspectives on Social Movements. Political Opportunities, Mobilizing Structures, and Cultural Framings* (Cambridge: Cambridge University Press, 1996), pp. 23–40, p. 25.

[50] Brand, 'Contradictions and Crises', p. 287.

[51] Bringel and Muñoz, 'Movimento Antiglobalização', p. 31.

[52] Smith, *Social Movements*, p. 220.

[53] Jackie Smith and Nicole Doerr, 'Democratic Innovation in the U.S. and European Social Forums', in Smith, Byrd, Reese and Smythe, *Handbook*, p. 343.

the meteoric rise of the global capital markets which made earning and keeping "market confidence" an increasingly important determinant of government policies.' Mexico's near-default on its foreign debt in 1982 and the collapse of Soviet communism (in 1989) were two important events that marked the end of the post-war era of import-substituting industrialization. Several developing countries suffered from large foreign indebtedness. The Asian crisis of 1997 (caused in part by excessive liberalization of financial markets which was then misdiagnosed, aggravated and perpetuated by the IMF) was perhaps the most significant event to undermine neo-liberal theory. But also important were the Mexican peso crisis of 1994 and the catastrophe of free market reform in Russia. The political influence of the IMF, World Bank and the international capital markets increased and the idea of downsizing the state gained importance. There was a certain 'consensus over the model of global economic and political management promoted by global institutions and the most powerful state players—a model variously titled "neoliberalism" or the "Washington consensus"'.[54] To put these ideas into practice, there were various attempts at deregularization and promotion of free trade, like the General Agreement on Tariffs and Trade (GATT) that started in 1986 with negotiations on agriculture, trade-related aspects of intellectual property rights (TRIPS), trade related investment measures (TRIMs) and a General Agreement on Trade Services (GATS). In 1995, the Organization for Economic Cooperation and Development (OECD) launched negotiations on a multi-lateral investment agreement that were linked to GATT negotiations and the North American Free Trade Agreement (NAFTA).[55]

In terms of events, the big international summits and negotiations to create the large free trade zone NAFTA and the Multilateral Agreement on Investment were a major driving force behind the GJM. 'The movement gathered momentum as the secret negotiations between members of the Organization for Economic Cooperation and Development (OECD) on Multilateral Agreement on Investment became public in early 1997'.[56] 'Social movements and NGOs recognized the need to create and strengthen global networks to challenge international trade and investment agreements, the key drivers of global neoliberal policies.'[57] But it was not only the inter-

[54] Green and Griffith, 'Globalization', pp. 51–52.
[55] Smythe, 'Our World is Not for Sale!', p. 169.
[56] Paczynska, 'Turtles, Puppets', p. 4.
[57] Smythe, 'Our World is Not for Sale!', p. 167.

national economic summits that gave force to the GJM. Further, the failure of the UN summits and the loss of confidence in NGOs to resolve the problem of growing worldwide inequality, called for alternative approaches.[58] With regard to organizational infrastructure and international cooperation it is important to note that the NGO sector grew vastly. NGOs were 'increasingly funded by international organizations, such as private foundations, the United Nations and the World Bank'.[59] The development of infrastructure, including offices and resources for travel, supported the rise of long-term cooperation at the international level. In the mid-1990s cooperation became easier through the rise of Internet-based communication.

THE KEY SOCIAL, POLITICAL, ECONOMIC AND CULTURAL CONFLICTS ADDRESSED AND FRAMED BY THE GJM

Against this structural backdrop, GJM activists framed their campaign against developments that redefine the function of national governments in the sense of reducing distributive functions of the welfare state and their capacity to control multi-national companies, as well as marginalizing welfare- and human rights-oriented international organizations, especially those connected to the UN. It is also against a culture-ideology based on a certain type of consumerism favouring big business and delegitimizing opponents of neo-liberalism.[60] In the face of the developments described above, 'Social movements and NGOs recognized the need to create and strengthen global networks to challenge international trade and investment agreements, the key drivers of global neoliberal policies.'[61]

The fields of activity of the GJM are very broad. The different actors within the movement have different thematic foci, but the issues are not just loosely connected. There is a quite coherent framework of ideas about grievances and responsibilities. 'Development, economic issues and democracy continue to characterise the main field of activities of the organizations involved in the organization of global events [...]. Labour and trade unions, environment, human rights and peace follow.'[62] Trade liberalization has been one of the major issues in the WSF since 2001,

---

[58] Bringel and Muñoz, 'Movimento Antiglobalização', p. 31.
[59] Paczynska, 'Turtles, Puppets', pp. 3–4.
[60] Smith, *Social Movements*, p. 69.
[61] Smythe, 'Our World is Not for Sale!', p. 167.
[62] Pianta, Silva and Zola, 'Global Civil Society Events', pp. 3–4.

but perhaps the most important issue at stake is the nature of democracy and political representation. The WSF challenges the 'loss of legitimacy of representative democratic institutions, which have become increasingly ineffective at representing and responding to popular interests under neo-liberalism'.[63] On this issue it is very close to the demands of the current movement in Spain that also connects various issues under the main claim for democracy from below. Besides the Social Forums that usually embrace a broad collection of issues, there have been several thematic forums, for example, on education, health, democracy and human rights.[64]

Social movements 'frame, or assign meaning to and interpret events and conditions in ways that are intended to mobilize potential adherents and constituents, to garner bystander support, and to demobilize antagonists'.[65] In terms of diagnostic framing, neo-liberalism by the GJM is defined as the main cause of various grievances. The GJM argue that the 'dominant form of economic globalisation is not inevitable'. But Guigni and colleagues argue that neo-liberalism for many of the groups within the GJM is not enough to mobilize. They 'suggest "mid-range" or intermediate-level frames that link the struggle against neoliberalism to more specific issues and claims and which allow for the mobilisation of many different kinds of networks'.[66] Moreover, many of the protest groups are not generally against capitalism. They aim at reducing 'some of the perceived harmful effects of policies and practices by global political institutions and corporations'.[67] Economic globalization is framed as a force that leads to a 'race to the bottom' with regard to labour standards, provision of welfare or ecological issues, to name but a few concerns. Further, the global economy is accused of undermining democratic

[63] Smythe, 'Our World is Not for Sale!', p. 167; Smith and Doerr, 'Democratic Innovation', p. 343.

[64] Marlies Glasius and Jill Timms, 'The Role of Social Forums in Global Civil Society. Radical Beacon or Strategic Infrastructure', in Marlies Glasius, Mary Kaldor and Helmut Anheier (eds), *Global Civil Society 2005–2006* (London: Sage, 2006), p. 205.

[65] David A. Snow and Robert D. Benford, 'Ideology, Frame Resonance, and Participant Mobilization', in Bert Klandermans, Hans P. Kriesi and Sidney Tarrow (eds), *From Structure to Action: Comparing Social Movement Research Across Cultures. International Social Movement Research*, Vol. 1 (London: JAI Press, 1988), pp. 197–217, p. 198.

[66] Giugni, Bandler and Eggert, 'Justice Movement', p. 15.

[67] Ibrahim, 'Alternative Globalisation Movement', p. 398.

institutions.[68] The rejection of global neo-liberalism, however, does not mean a rejection of globalization. According to Mario Pianta and his colleagues most actors in the GJM favour alternative forms of 'globalisation from below' or 'humanised globalisation', placing civil society and human beings centre stage. Only 4% call themselves 'anti-globalisation'.[69]

Finding solutions to the problems caused by neo-liberalism is more complicated. A large part of the movement favours 'transformation instead of revolution'.[70] One partial solution practised is to defend established rights. This, however, is not enough. 'Parallel to the struggle against neoliberalism, the GJM calls for greater participation of citizens in decision-making processes and arenas, both at the local and global level.'[71] The movement claims 'more people-centered than market-centered forms of global governance' and deglobalization.[72] This concept of deglobalization involves: 'reducing dependence on foreign investment, redistribution of income and land, de-emphasizing growth and maximising, abandoning market governance, constant monitoring of state and market by civil society, reorient production towards away from remote goods'.[73] Most activists support the desire to 'shrink or sink global financial institutions to eliminate unfair advantage of rich countries and cooperations [...] strengthen economic governance at global level through, for example Tobin tax [...] debt relief for poor countries [...] strengthen state sovereignty [...]emphasize local economic empowerment [...] promote human rights'.[74] Local grievances and local resistance are always connected to economic neo-liberal policies and to global processes.[75]

Comparing the GJM to other movements, we see that the values and issues of the GJM do not differ fundamentally from those of the wave of contention that has preceded it, namely those of the new social movements.[76] They, for example, all aspire to equality, democracy from below or an alternative ecologically sound way of living. With regard to the claim

---

[68] Smith, *Social Movements*, p. 6.
[69] Pianta, Silva and Zola, 'Global Civil Society Events', p. 6.
[70] Pleyers, *Alter-globalization*, p. 91.
[71] Giugni, Bandler and Eggert, 'Justice Movement', p. 6.
[72] Smith, *Social Movements*, p. 4.
[73] Smith, *Social Movements*, p. 205.
[74] Smith, *Social Movements*, p. 6.
[75] Paczynska, 'Turtles, Puppets', p. 4.
[76] Giugni, Bandler and Eggert, 'Justice Movement', p. 15.

for more participatory democracy, the Indignados[77] and Occupy movements also employ new forms of participatory decision-making and techniques of deliberative democracy.[78]

FORMS OF PROTEST

GJM activists' framing of the issues at stake also has implications for the forms of protest they have adopted. The GJM is characterized by two large forms of protest events: 'mass demonstrations and protest activities addressed against major international governmental or private institutions or organizations on the one hand, and social forums on the other'.[79] Both of these most visible forms of the GJMs were mainly organized in the shape of large counter-summits, running simultaneous to global summits and often organized near the summits.[80]

Pianta's study about global civil society events included a breakdown of such events in 2003 and 2004: 30% of all events were social forums, 26% were parallel summits with regional conferences (European Union, American or Asian government meetings), 21% were meetings organized independently from official summits, 9% were parallel events to UN conferences, 7% were counter protests to IMF, World Bank or WTO meetings and 7% were counter protests to G8 summits.[81] About 50% of protest events take place around such meetings. Taking into consideration the novelty and impact of these meetings, Rucht has therefore argued that 'the World Social Forum (WSF) process is the most important manifestation of the contemporary global justice movements (GJMs)'.[82] As for the most common forms of activism, survey data shows that demonstrations and petitions are very common, 'while confrontational tactics such as blockade and occupation have been applied by roughly one-quarter of them [...] GJMOs do not fall into groups using moderate forms of action and other groups using radical means. Instead, confrontational action forms are appended to the moderate repertoire.'[83]

[77] Romanos, 'Collective Learning Processes'.
[78] Hayduk, 'Global Justice', p. 44.
[79] Giugni, Bandler and Eggert, 'Justice Movement', p. 7.
[80] Rucht, 'Social Forums', p. 12.
[81] Pianta, Silva and Zola, 'Global Civil Society Events', p. 3.
[82] Rucht, 'Social Forums', p. 11.
[83] Dieter Rucht and S. Teune, 'Forms of Action of Global Justice Movement Groups. Do Conceptions and Practices of Democracy Matter?', in Della Porta, *Democracy*, pp. 171–193, pp. 177–178.

While large and visible events contributed to the fame of the GJM, these events are just one part of the movement. Rucht describes the WSF as 'not an event but a global communication network resting only in part on a visible infrastructure'.[84] Similarly, Jackie Smith states: 'The notion of the WSF as a "process" signals the idea that the meetings themselves are not the main purpose. Instead, the goal of most organizers is to facilitate the exchange of ideas, to expand and deepen activist networks, and to provide new spaces in which people can reflect on and help realize alternatives to neoliberal globalization.'[85] The Social Forums are open to everybody who opposes global neo-liberalism, except for right-wing extremists and groups using violence. Further, political parties and elected government officials in their official capacity are in principle excluded, a practice not consistently followed. The idea of the forums is to give voice to every participant. Due to its standing, however, there have been many prominent speakers who naturally attract a greater audience. This star cult is criticized and the WSFs in 2005 and 2007 avoided promoting prominent speakers.[86] 'The basic format of the forum itself resembled in many ways the civil society conferences that paralleled UN global conferences of the 1990s. It also mirrors a model forged by feminist activists in Latin America, who gathered in what they called encuentros.'[87] The Social Forums also have a lot in common with the assemblies of the 15M in Spain. Both are open to different ideas which are regarded as enriching. The organizational structure of the movements is not hierarchical but made of open assemblies, working groups and networks of cooperation with a constant change in positions and no spokespersons. The local and the global level are connected in a framework and there is a rather pragmatic variance between different types of organizations that takes into consideration the different possibilities of each actor.[88]

---

[84] Rucht, 'Social Forums', p. 16.

[85] Jackie Smith, Scott Byrd, Ellen Reese and Elizabeth Smythe, 'Introduction', in Smith, Byrd, Reese and Smythe, *Handbook*.

[86] Rucht, 'Social Forums', pp. 18–19.

[87] Smith, *Social Movements*, p. 208.

[88] Tomás Nistal, 'Antecedents, Achievements and Challenges of the Spanish 15M Movement', in Tejerina and Perrugorría, *From Social to Political*, pp. 74–88, here p. 84.

[89] Glasius and Timms, 'Social Forums', p. 223.

There is a divide between deliberation versus struggle: some actors of the GJM put deliberation in first place.[89] They usually favour a WSF that is as open as possible to new ideas, values and debate for its own sake. For the groups that favour struggle, open debates are not enough; they are aiming to construct a counter power. The positions are two extremes in a continuum. 'The most vibrant debates have occurred over the WSFs inability or rather its unwillingness to take strategic decisions.'[90] To see the forum as a place for debate instead of a unified actor avoids building common positions and statements. Thus, while an open structure is usually praised, there was an increasing disaffection with the movement's failure to generate political decisions or actions.[91]

KEY ACTORS AND MOVEMENTS OF THE GJM

The diversity of the key actors and movements that make up the GJM reflect the movements' diversity in terms of its aims and forms of protests.

The GJM comprises a broad variety of activists and their groups and organizations. They not only meet at Social Forums and counter summits, but also launch independent political campaigns.[92] Marco Guigni and colleagues 'distinguish between two basic types of mobilizing structures: (i) formal organizations—for example, the Association for the Taxation of Financial Transactions for the Aid of Citizens (ATTAC); and (ii) informal networks— that is, the web of interpersonal contacts and exchanges among movement activists and participants'.[93] Jackie Smith further distinguishes various streams of organization: anti-free trade activism, transnational labour, transnational environmentalism, women's rights, Tobin tax and peace.[94]

There is already some substantial research on the actors who are involved in the organization of Social Forums. 'The first WSF was organized by a group of seven representatives of the groups that launched the

[90] Smith, Byrd, Reese and, Smythe, *Handbook*.
[91] Rucht, 'Social Forums', pp. 20–21.
[92] Brand, 'Contradictions and Crises', p. 290.
[93] Giugni, Bandler and Eggert, 'Justice Movement', p. 8.
[94] Smith, *Social Movements*, pp. 102–103.
[95] Rucht, 'Social Forums', p. 19.
[96] Pianta, 'Global Civil Society Events', p. 3.

events. From 2002 onwards, the WSF is organized by the International Council that meets a few times but coordinates the WSF mainly via the Internet. Local committees handle logistical and technical questions and set the programme. The International Council includes several hundred groups and networks (e.g. 100 in 2003 and 156 in 2010).'[95] 'In a few cases, typically, World Social Fora, there are more than 400 organizations are involved [in the organization of the events]. Generally, however, the number of organizations working together has more manageable size, below 24 in a quarter of cases, between 25 and 49 in 30 per cent of cases, between 50 and 199 in 23 per cent of cases.'[96]

Within the GJM are many different types of actors, for example, non-governmental organizations, anarchist groups, environmental groups, actor networks, PGA, autonomists, indigenous movements, Socialists, anti-corporate and anti-war groups.[97] These actors vary not only in terms of their political orientation, preferred action forms or access to resources and alliances; they can also be distinguished by the nature of their organizational structures, which has often grown over years. We can distinguish two main types of organizational structure, the horizontal and vertical.[98] Groups with a more vertical structure (such as trade unions) typically practise elections and have hierarchies, while the more horizontal groups are against such hierarchical organizational structures and practices. 'Old Left organizations were predominantly founded before 1968 and tend to have more than 100,000 individual members. Most New Left, anarchist, or autonomous groups were founded between 1969 and 1989 and are more likely to have between 100 and 1,000 members. Most new social movement groups were founded in the same period, but have a larger membership (1,000–10,000 members). Solidarity, peace, or human rights organizations were predominantly founded between 1990 and 1999 (a considerable number, however, also before 1968 or between 1969 and 1989) and tend to have between 1,000 and 10,000 members. Finally, new groups acting primarily on the global level were founded in the years 2000 and after, and are mostly small (with up to 100 individual mem-

---

[97] Ibrahim, 'Alternative Globalisation Movement', p. 397.

[98] Rucht, 'Social Forums', p. 22. Glasius and Timms, 'Social Forums', p. 222.

[99] Herbert Reiter, 'Participatory Traditions within the Global Justice Movement', in Della Porta, *Democracy*, pp. 50–51.

[100] Rucht, 'Social Forums', pp. 14–15.

bers).'[99] A closer look at the structure of the participants of the Social Forums shows the importance of activist groups and organizations: 'the bulk of participants are members or formal delegates of political or social groups such as Indigenous associations, farmer's movements, trade unions, and NGOs. In addition, independent activists, intellectuals, artists, and unaffiliated young people take part.'[100] Amongst the European Social Forum in Florence (2002) participants, 34.6% belonged to a political party, 36.6% were tied to unions, 52.7% to social movements and 41.5% to NGOs.[101]

Apart from the large visible forums and protest events, there are various important, albeit less visible, groups working at the local level all over the world. Geoffrey Pleyers subsumes this main organizational principle of the GJM as follows: 'Activists want to change the world starting locally with their neighborhood assemblies.'[102] Alternative solutions are practised in these small-scale groups and projects. This principle is repeated within the actual assemblies, such as when the Spanish 15M spread to the 'Barrios' after the central occupation of Puerta del Sol.[103]

Looking at the organizational structure of the movements we find a lot of continuities, for example, an 'overlap between the WSF International Council and Our World network, the network that first protested against WTO'.[104] According to Hayduk many activists involved in Occupy Wall Street come 'directly out of the Anti-Globalization movement'.[105] The 15M in Spain is connected to the Spanish anarchist movements. My own observations in Portugal, by contrast, show very little connection between the current anti-austerity movements and the GJM, especially to the Social Forum processes. Although transnational cooperation was regarded as important, almost all movements during their first year of existence did not have institutionalized transnational ties. Exchange of ideas was mainly done via personal contacts, Erasmus students and by well-known groups via the Internet. In my study

[101] Donatella Della Porta, *The Social Bases of the Global Justice Movement. Some Theoretical Reflections and Empirical Evidence from the First European Social Forum* (New York: UNRISD/UN Publications, 2005), p. 11.

[102] Pleyers, *Alter-globalization*, p. 41.

[103] Nistal, 'Antecedents, Achievements and Challenges', p. 76.

[104] Smythe, 'Our World is Not for Sale!', p. 172.

[105] Hayduk, 'Global Justice', p. 43.

[106] Baumgarten, 'Geração à Rasca and Beyond'.

[107] Romanos, 'Collective Learning Processes'; Mayo Fuster Morell 'The Free Culture and 15M Movements in Spain: Composition, Social Networks and Synergies', *Social Movement Studies* 3–4 (2012), pp. 386–392, here p. 388; Baumgarten, 'Geração à Rasca and Beyond'.

about Portugal I did not find the use of earlier ties from the GJMs.[106] The recent Spanish 15M movement also involved a large number of people without experience in civil society groups and organizations. Further, many of the groups involved in organizing are new.[107] So, although some groups and activists have been involved in earlier struggle, in terms of actors the recent movements are not simple continuities of the GJM.

KEY GEOGRAPHICAL AREAS OF THE GJM

The GJM is a globalized movement, with actors and events placed all over the world. It is based on transnational networks of transnational, national and local actors. There are, however, some especially important spaces that shaped the movement. The counter summits have always taken place near the summits of the World Bank, the WTO or the IMF. In spite of all the difficulties connected to places such as Davos or Doha, including banishment of protest, high police presence or difficulties reaching remote places, the activists protest as close as possible to the venue of the respective summit. In terms of the Social Forums, Porto Alegre in south Brazil plays an important role. The WSF process started here and was shaped especially by Brazilian and French actors. In contrast to the counter summit protests, Porto Alegre was chosen because of its favourable infrastructure.

Even though the movement is global, the networks of actors involved in the movements are embedded in national contexts. Their daily work takes place in the local arenas, often targeting local and national politics. Participants in global protest events and Social Forums come predominantly from the country the event takes place in. The geographical distribution of participants in the WSF in Porto Alegre 2005 illustrates this nicely: 80% of participants came from Brazil, 8.8% from other Latin American countries and 4.5% from Europe.[108] The counter summit protest in Seattle in 1999 was dominated by US activists, and the largest

---

[108] Peter J. Smith and Elizabeth Smythe, '(In)Fertile Ground? Social Forum Activism in its Regional and Local Dimensions', in Smith, Byrd, Reese and Smythe, *Handbook*, p. 31.
[109] Giugni, Bandler and Eggert, 'Justice Movement', p. 13.
[110] Pianta, 'Global Civil Society Events', p. 3.

contingent of participants in any WSF is always from the respective host country.[109] 'National associations and NGOs always are key actors in the organization of global civil society events, joining in most cases with international NGOs and networks. Still, local groups continue to play a key role in most events.'[110]

If local and national actors play a greater role in events, then it is worth looking at the distribution of events to map the key geographical areas of the global movement. Based on an analysis of 43 civil society events in 2003 and the first six months of 2004, Pianta and colleagues count one third of the events in Latin America, one quarter in Europe, one fifth in Asia and Oceania, 12% in North America and 7% in Africa. In a larger study focussed on Social Forum events, Smith counts 600 events between 2001 and 2006.[111] More than half of them (306) took place in Europe, 70 in South America, 38 in Africa, 28 in North America and 5 in Oceania. The distribution of organizations involved in the planning of the events in this time period are also unequally distributed: 354 come from Europe, 125 from South America, 62 from Africa, 39 from North America and 15 from Oceania. These differences are caused mainly by the local and national Social Forums in that time period being predominantly in Europe; the European Social Forum is the biggest Social Forum after the WSF.[112] Further, between 2001 and 2004 there were about 183 local Social Forums in Italy and about the same number in Greece.[113] The two countries were, therefore, the most important places for local Social Forum activism. Thus, regarding events the movement has an emphasis in Latin America and Europe.

During its time in existence, the movement became more decentralized.[114] The organizational structure of the WSF shifted especially between 2003 and 2005. It not only grew in size, but also developed a more horizontal design. With technical innovations on the Internet some of the preparatory processes were shifted to this arena.[115]

[111] J. G. Smith (2011) 'Creating Spaces for Global Democracy: The World Social Forum Process in Reydams', *Global Activism*, pp. 347–375.
[112] Glasius and Timms, 'Social Forums', p. 205.
[113] Smith, *Social Movements*, p. 212.
[114] Bringel and Muñoz, 'Movimento Antiglobalização', 34.
[115] Scott C. Byrd and Lorien Jasny, 'Transnational Movement Innovation and Collaboration. Analysis of World Social Forum Networks', in Smith, Byrd, Reese and Smythe, *Handbook*, pp. 355–372, here pp. 362–363.
[116] Pleyers, *Alter-globalization*, p. 93.
[117] Smith, *Social Movements*, p. 212.

From 2005 onwards, we can observe a process of deregionalizing away from Brazil. This process was accompanied by the emergence of a self-organizing structure and a more open consultation process with regard to the themes the protests should address. These processes have led to more cooperation and networking before the forum takes place. By decentralizing, the movement is following the idea of the Zapatistas to 'resist wherever you are'.[116] Decentralization was also initiated by the organizers of the forums, who aimed at a broader participation, especially of those people who cannot travel long distances.[117] To make participation easier for those people who are not used to international events, furthermore, the language question became important. Already at the 2005 WSF there were 16 official languages and 533 official interpreters.[118]

The tension between 'the global' and 'the local' as Tejerina puts it, is not only a tension within the GJM but also in the actual movements, although these are not so globalized yet.[119] According to Tejerina: 'the alter-global movement has opted for pursuing "glocal" actions. As a consequence, it has been in permanent oscillation between the fixed (here and now) and the mobile (there and before-after). This option has defined the alter-global movement and given it specificity when compared to previous processes of mobilization. Many 15M militants, particularly the youngest ones, have shown a global or "international vocation"; they are aware of the importance of raising support in other countries.'[120]

IMPACT AND OUTCOMES

Outcomes of social movements are difficult to measure. They not only include political impact, but also, for example, long-term cultural shifts and movement-internal developments. In general outcomes develop in complex processes and thus often cannot be attributed to a single movement or campaign. Compared to other movements of this volume, the GJM is still quite young. Its impact and outcomes are already in evidence,

---

[118] Glasius and Timms, 'Social Forums', p. 199. About the issue of language in the WSFs and ESFs see: Nicole Doerr, 'Deliberative Discussion, Language, and Efficiency in the World Social Forum Porcess', *Mobilization* 4 (2008), pp. 395–410.

[119] Baumgarten, 'Geração à Rasca and Beyond'.

[120] Tejerina and Perrugorra, 'Continuities and Discontinuities', p. 100.

[121] Smith, *Social Movements*, p. 14.

[122] Smith, *Social Movements*, p. 207.

however. The first phase of the GJM in particular contributed to the strengthening of multi-lateral institutions and to the democratization of global politics.[121] 'The extraordinary success of the WSF lies in the fact that it emerged from an extensive history of transnational activism that had built a foundation of network ties capable of spreading the word about the initiative and of providing resources and motivation for participants.'[122]

On the discursive level there is an important visible impact of various campaigns of the movement: 'growing numbers of public officials are echoing claims of social movement actors to demand efforts to strengthen democracy'. In recent years the current system is criticized even by important spokespersons 'who were once (and may still be) sympathetic to the neoliberal agenda'.[123]

The GJM was not only successful in changing discourses but also left its imprint on politics. 'The GJM are, and have been, able to politicize certain aspects of capitalist globalization, but by and large they have been unable to intervene in those power relations. The power of capital and its allies in the political system, science and the media still seems too strong for the broader societal alternatives to be born.'[124] Nevertheless, the protests had a tangible political impact: 'Politicians recognized a need to respond to public disquiet, for example in the G8's decision to put debt on the agenda at its 1998 Birmingham summit, or when Chancellor Schröder and Prime Minister Jospin ordered a study of the Tobin Tax in 2001. In 1999, the IMF committed itself to the 2015 targets for halving world poverty, drawn up by the OECD and agreed at the UN Millennium Summit in Geneva in June 2000.'[125] Debt relief as a political issue was mainly introduced to the world by the Jubilee 2000 campaign. The idea of debt relief became prominent, as well as the practices of codes of conduct, for example, promoted in the movements Clean Clothes Campaigns. Business practices are under closer observation by the public and consumers and exploitation and inequalities have become more visible—also because of the various campaigns by the

[123] Smith, *Social Movements*, pp. 11 and 58.
[124] Brand, 'Contradictions and Crises', pp. 295–296.
[125] Green and Griffith, 'Globalization', pp. 60–61.
[126] Paczynska, 'Turtles, Puppets', p. 15.
[127] Green and Griffith, 'Globalization', pp. 54–55.

GJM.[126] The campaign against the Multilateral Agreement on Investment was successful. The Agreement was rejected. Furthermore, the idea of corporate social responsibility has gained importance during recent years.[127] Those partial successes have strengthened the reformists within the movement.

At a fundamental level, the GJM also contributed to the democratization of society: not only through its demands but moreover by its own practices of organization and meetings.[128] Especially the Social Forums helped to spread the model of participatory budget assemblies which was already practised in Porto Alegre before the World Social Forum. In terms of internal outcomes the movement has developed practices of decision-making and participation. Bonds between various types of activists groups all over the world have been strengthened. The GJM has developed an infrastructure as a 'node of information, communication, and organization of different kinds of movements acting on different levels'.[129] It remains a question for further research, however, to what extent this infrastructure serves the actual movements. A lack of international contacts in the first phase of the actual movements in some countries rather suggests that these could not easily be taken up. Between the actors of the GJM, however, there are many long-term and often-institutionalized contacts that, for example, resulted in joint campaigns and international NGOs and associations.

CONCLUSION

This chapter has shown that the GJM is extremely difficult to conceptualize. Due to its great diversity, many boundaries that usually define a social movement are blurred. Its inner coherence can also not be easily discovered. The movement includes actors that are not usually part of social movements, such as party politicians and state actors at the Social Forums. Furthermore, as the movement is made of a conjuncture of earlier movements, it is a question of definition to identify the beginning of the movement. While the counter protests belong to the classical repertoire of social movements,

---

[128] Giugni, Bandler and Eggert, 'Justice Movement', p. 6.
[129] Rucht, 'Social Forums', p. 24.
[130] Smith, 'Creating Spaces', p. 348.
[131] Teivanen, 'The World Social Forum', p. 624.

Social Forums are described as 'autonomous gathering'.[130] This issue gives rise to the question of whether a Social Forum can still be meaningfully analysed under the rubric of 'social movements'. I regard the Social Forums as events organized by a social movement. There is, however, no consensus in the literature as to whether to regard the WSF as an arena or as an actor.[131] In practice, this problem is connected to the question of whether the Social Forum should communicate a position on political issues, or whether it should just be a meeting place where diverse opinions are debated.

Despite its great diversity of actors and aims, this chapter has shown how the GJM can be conceptualized as one movement. There is a feeling of belonging to this global movement amongst its actors. Joint events and campaigns are important to keep the cooperation between actors alive, but the movement has also developed an infra-structure of cooperation that includes not only informal contacts, but also long-term cooperation and global networks of the GJM actors.

Some of the GJM's main characteristics can also be found within the new Indignados and Occupy movements. They have in common the spectacular character of action forms, Internet-based communication and the radical claims against the system. The new movements, nevertheless, do not share the GJM's orientation towards counter events. They are also far less globalized in their organizational structure and their claims. The GJM has developed a global network over time, including a high frequency of contacts, meetings and joint events. The activists of the current movements do not use this network. They keep informed about what happens in other countries and plan global days of action via the Internet, but do not have this structure of regular global meetings and joint activities of the GJM. Although the new protest movements refer to each other, each movement also is much more embedded in its national context.

In terms of issues and their framing, the GJM is closely related to the Indignados and the Occupy movement. The GJM and these movements, however, are not connected by a common identity, and the key actors are for the most part not the same. These new movements profited to some extent from the experiences of the GJM. The practices of deliberation,

[132] Baumgarten, 'Geração à Rasca and Beyond'.

open meetings, the ideas of unity in diversity and to 'walk slowly because it is a long way to go' were taken from the GJM. Some groups of the GJM played an important role, especially in the US Occupy movement and in Spain. The current movements, however, did not profit so much from established transnational contacts. Cooperation at the transnational level is still in its beginning and mainly restricted to joint days of action, exchanging information via Facebook and mailing lists, personal contacts and some instances of inviting speakers from abroad.[132] The detailed analysis of the GJM's impact on these contemporary movements, their similarities and differences remains a question for future research.

FURTHER READING

There are various good publications on the global justice movement: Jackie Smith, *Social Movements for Global Democracy* (Baltimore, MD: Johns Hopkins University Press, 2008) analyses global activism taking into account its economic and political context. Robin Broad (ed.), *Global Backlash. Citizen Initiatives for a Just World Economy* (Lanham, MD: Rowman & Littlefield, 2002) provides an overview over the GJM including its historical roots. The collective volume edited by Donatella Della Porta, *The Global Justice Movement. Cross-National and Transnational Perspectives* (Boulder, CO: Paradigm, 2007), resulted from a comparative research project and provides a good introduction to the global justice movement in various European countries and in the United States. Another collective volume by Della Porta, *Democracy in Social Movements* (Basingstoke: Palgrave Macmillan, 2009), is dedicated to the question of how democracy is practiced within the GJM. Luc Reydams (ed.), *Global Activism Reader* (New York: Continuum, 2009) is an edited collection on global activism that covers various areas of the GJM: global labour, human rights, women's rights, environment, peace, social justice and democracy. In this volume we find a part dedicated to global justice struggles providing overviews of the world social forum process and the historical roots of the global justice movement.

A very good introduction to social forums is the collective volume by Jackie Smith, Scott Byrd, Ellen Reese and Elizabeth Smythe (eds), *Handbook on World Social Forum Activism* (Boulder, CO: Paradigm,

2011). It provides detailed information on the social forum process, participants, its idea of democracy and different issues of the social forums, including resistance to international trade agreements and labour solidarity. Furthermore, there is a part on the connections between the local and the global and a part on democratic innovations developed in the social forums. There is a large amount of literature on the issue of democracy and the social forums, including case studies on internal practices and surveys on the participants of the forums. A collection of case studies on practices in social forum meetings is provided by Donatella Della Porta, *Meeting Democracy: Power and Deliberation in Global Justice Movements* (Cambridge: Cambridge University Press, 2013). Nicole Doerr, 'Deliberative Discussion, Language, and Efficiency in the World Social Forum Process', *Mobilization* 13 (2008), pp. 395–410 work on the role of language in the social forum meetings is relevant. An overview of the structure of participants in the social forums can be found in Chap. 4 of the collective volume by Jackie Smith, Scott Byrd, Ellen Reese and Elizabeth Smythe (eds), *Handbook on World Social Forum Activism* (Boulder, CO: Paradigm, 2011) that I have already mentioned above.

Global Civil Society is a yearbook published by Marlies Glasius, Mary Kaldor and Helmut Anheier from 2001 to 2012. The yearbook can be consulted at the website of LSE, Department of International Development (e.g. Global Civil Society Yearbook 2001 is available at: www.lse.ac.uk/internationalDevelopment/research/CSHS/civilSociety/yearBook/contentsPages/2001.aspx). There are various contributions about struggles of resistance against the current economic model in general, the global justice movement and the social forums in these yearbooks.

Elizabeth Smythe, *Our World is Not for Sale! The WSF Process and Transnational Resistance to International Trade Agreements* (in J. Smith et al. (eds), *Handbook on World Social Forum Activism*, Boulder, CO: Paradigm, 2011) focusses on resistance against trade agreements in the world social forum process.

A wealth of publications covers the recent wave of protest against austerity. Tova Benski, Lauren Langman, Ignacia Perugorría and Benjamín Tejerina edited the special issue 'From Indignation to Occupation: A New Wave of Global Mobilization' (*Current Sociology* 4, 2013), including cases of social movements from various countries protesting against austerity and looking for alternative ways of democracy. The journal *Social Movement Studies* published a special issue 'Occupy!' (3–4, 2012) with case studies from various cities and contributions that try to connect cases of Occupy to other protests and social movements. For example, in 'The Indignados of Spain. A Precedent to Occupy Wallstreet', Ernesto Castañeda connects the Spanish case to Occupy Wall Street (*Social Movement Studies* 3–4, 2012).

Donatella Della Porta and Alice Mattoni edited the collective volume *Spreading Protest. Social Movements in Times of Crisis* (Essex: ECPR Press Studies, 2014) with a specific focus on the travel of ideas between the Arab Spring, the Indignados, Occupy and the various movements against austerity in Europe.

The collective volume *Understanding European Movements: New Social Movements, Global Justice* edited by Cristina Flesher Fominaya and Laurence Cox (London: Routledge, 2013) attempts to show the role of European movements as precursors for the global justice movement and also includes some connections to the recent anti-austerity protests. Other authors have worked on the connections between recent protests and the global justice movement, like Ron Hayduk, *Global Justice and OWS. Movement Connections* (Socialism and Democracy 2, 2013).

CHAPTER 23

The 'Arab Spring' in Global Perspective: Social Movements, Changing Contexts and Political Transitions in the Arab World (2010–2014)

Nora Lafi

INTRODUCTION

The objects of this chapter are to investigate the pertinence of the use of the concept of 'social movement' for analysing the developments that the Arab world has been the theatre of during the last few years and, through a critical reading of such developments, to re-frame the role of such movements in comparison with other determinants. The definition of a social movement adopted here relates to the existence and action of a network of individuals and groups that share a certain sense of collective destiny and collectively ask for social and political change though various forms of protest.[1] The interpretation of what happened in the Arab world since 2010 is, however, a highly delicate operation, as the processes initiated by social

[1] See Dieter Rucht's Chap. 2 in this volume.

N. Lafi (✉)
Zentrum moderner Orient, Berlin, Germany

© The Author(s) 2017
S. Berger, H. Nehring (eds.), *The History of Social Movements in Global Perspective*, DOI 10.1057/978-1-137-30427-8_23

movements often turned into civil wars, coups d'état and/or conservative political developments. Both local claims and international geo-strategy are also entangled in the determination of the various chains of events and so it is difficult to judge the precise role of social movements in sparking the events that led, or not, according to the place, to regime change.[2] The more time passes after the events the more investigators are becoming suspicious regarding the role of social movements. It seems that the season of revolutionary romanticism that accompanied and immediately followed the events is becoming the object of much more circumspect interpretations. A further difficulty is added by the fact that the perception of the existence and characteristics of a civic sphere in the cultural context of the Arab world has been the object of lasting culturalist *clichés*. The very existence and role in society of expressions coming from the civic sphere is thus to be analysed historically and anthropologically in order to assess the nature of contemporary protests. In this chapter I argue that one of the conditions necessary in order to explain the logics of mobilization of social movements is to re-evaluate the historical dimension of the civic sphere in the region.[3] Contemporary social movements, but also their evolution since 2011, cannot be understood without a look at the history of mobilization in this cultural context. I will thus study here the roots of the civic dimension in the Arab world and follow its developments and limits throughout the events which marked the region since 2010.

It all began in Tunisia, in the city of Sidi Bouzid, when on 17 December 2010, Mohamed Bouazizi, a young street-vendor set himself on fire, as a sign of protest against the harassing practices of the local police and against the situation of youth in the country in general.[4] He died a few days later in hospital. His individual protest provoked a series of demonstrations, first in Sidi Bouzid and then in the whole country, which eventually led to the departure of President Ben Ali. On 25 January

---

[2] On this dimension, see: Katerina Dalacoura, 'The 2011 Uprisings in the Middle-East: Political Change and Geopolitical Implications', *International Affairs* 1 (2012), pp. 63–79. See also: Hamid Dabashi, *The Arab Spring (2012). The End of Postcolonialism* (London: Zed Books, 2005), p. 272.

[3] On such a necessity, see also: Augustus R. Norton (ed.), *Civil Society in the Middle East* (Leiden: Brill, 2005), p. 353.

[4] For a presentation of these events: Leila Dakhli, 'Une lecture de la révolution tunisienne', *Le Mouvement Social* 3 (2011), pp. 89–103. For a reflection on the actual nature of the initial incident that sparked the unrest: Abdelhamid Largueche, 'Cette gifle qui n'a jamais eu lieu … en hommage à Fadia, fille de Sidi Bouzid', *L'autre* 12, (2011–2012), pp. 216–217.

2011, a wave of protests began in Egypt, from Cairo to Alexandria and Tanta, culminating in the occupation of Tahrir Square in Cairo which, after violent episodes of repression, eventually led to the overthrowing of President Mubarak.[5] In Yemen, on 27 January, a massive demonstration against the regime of President Saleh was organized, starting a one-year long process of unrest.[6] On 13 February, protests against the Gaddafi regime also began in Benghazi, Libya. The events soon sparked a civil war in the country which, following a massive foreign military intervention, resulted in regime change. In Syria, demonstrations against the al-Assad regime began on 25 March, sparking a process of repression and then a civil war that turned into the most tragic event in the region in decades. Many other countries of the broader region, from Bahrain to Morocco were also affected by movements of protest which did not, however, result in regime change or civil wars. This series of events was quickly labelled the 'Arab Spring', echoing what happened in Europe in 1848[7] and in Prague in 1968. However, many questions arise, both about the nature of the events, and the role of social movements in their occurrence and development. Each of the terms within the 'Arab Spring' expression also deserve to be discussed.[8] The 'Arab' identity of the movements is not evident, as Arab nationalism, or even the claim to a common Arab identity, was not necessarily among the ideologies at stake and no real transnational Arab movement was involved as such (this does not mean, as I shall illustrate, that transnational movements, such as the mass media or Islamist political activism, were not involved). The term 'Spring' is also highly controversial, beyond considerations of the calendar, as the 2010–2014 events evolved into a season which is not best labelled a flourishing spring. In some cases and from some perspectives, the period also took a dark turn as conservative and sometimes right-wing extremist movements took over and as civil wars turned out to be devastating.

---

[5] On these events: Dina Shebata, 'The Fall of the Pharaoh: How Hosni Mubarak's Reign Came to an End', *Foreign Affairs* 3 (2011), pp. 3–10.

[6] See: Vincent Durac, 'Yemen's Arab Spring: Democratic Opening or Regime Maintenance?', *Mediterranean Politics* 2 (2012), pp. 161–178.

[7] This historical parallel has been explored by: Kurt Weyland, 'The Arab Spring: Why the Surprising Similarities with the Revolutionary Wave of 1848?', *Perspectives on Politics* 4 (2012), pp. 917–934.

[8] For a such a discussion: Gilbert Achcar, *Le peuple veut. Une exploration radicale du soulèvement arabe* (Paris: Errance, 2013), p. 432.

However, beyond a critique of the terminology, what is certain is that something decisive occurred in the region during these years and that there was a communicative effect between each single country involved.[9] The object of this chapter is to analyse the logics at stake in this historical phenomenon and to discuss the role of various forms of social movements, compared to other possible factors such as international geo-strategy, or the complex logics of the power systems and of their transformation and/or preservation. Beyond a discussion of the pertinence of the term, understanding this 'Arab Spring' is indeed no easy task due to a highly complex entanglement of factors. There is no common explanation for the unrests, from Tunis to Cairo or Sanaa, and as things evolved completely differently in each place, any attempt to reduce interpretations of the events to one simple narrative would be in vain. The social movement rubric, however, might allow for an evaluation of the genuine social dimension of the events and the functioning of local societies and their civic spheres. Whatever the answer is to the question of their role and of the limits of social movements involved, examining this dimension might bring into light other factors and help gauge their influence on the course of events. Understanding the role of social movements is also crucial as it invites one to question the very nature of societies.

Between mobilization according to existing or new networks, geo-strategy and the logic of the political systems, it is not easy to determine for any of the cases which element proved decisive. Many aspects will be uncovered only by historians of the future, when, for example, the archives of the different administrations and secret services involved are revealed. Immediate history is always delicate.[10] But in all cases, even where more complicated issues were at stake, mobilizations occurred and illustrated the existence of strong social movements in the Arab world, as well as the dynamics of their present reconfiguration and impact on social and political change. These movements addressed a variety of themes, from the corruption of the regimes to the disastrous situation of young people without a job,[11] and generated a variety of forms of mobilization. What is

[9] On such developments: Stephan Rosiny, 'The Arab Spring: Triggers, Dynamics and Prospects', *GIGA Focus* 1 (2012), pp. 1–8.

[10] For a reflection on the immediate history of the Arab Spring: Mathieu Guidere, 'Histoire immédiate du "Printemps arabe"', *Le Débat* 168 (2012), pp. 129–145.

[11] On the Arab Spring as the expression of a new vision of political action: Sari Hanafi, 'The Arab Revolutions: the Emergence of a new political subjectivity', *Contemporary Arab Affairs* 2 (2012), pp. 98–113. On the role of the youth: Michael Hoffmann and Amaney Jamal,

certain is that because of what happened in the Arab world between 2010 and 2014, the whole relationship between the theory of social movements and its applications to societies of the region must be revised. Indeed, the sociology of social movements has always had difficulties when considering the Arab world.[12] Social movements in the region had mostly been analysed according to the degrees of conformity with the pre-existing theoretical proposals formulated in other cultural contexts. Of course, many among such elements are important, but they might also mask other dimensions. Research about social movements in the Arab world has long had difficulties in considering aspects beyond Arab nationalism, labour activism and later, political Islam, and with the latter dimension the eternal question of deciding whether right-wing movements of religious inspiration qualify or not for the category.[13] In the case of the Arab world, this discussion remains central, as political Islam has proved itself as one of the driving forces of protest in recent decades and has been acting according to methods pertaining to social movements, even if it was not central during the first phases of the events that led and then constituted the Arab Spring.[14] Even if single events, from bread riots in Jordan[15] or Algeria[16] in the 1980s and 1990s to the miners' protest in Tunisia in the

'The Youth and the Arab Spring: Cohort Differences and Similarities', *Middle-East Law and Governance* 1 (2012), pp. 168–188 and Emma Murphy, 'Problematizing Arab Youth: Generational Narratives of Systemic Failure', *Mediterranean Politics* 1 pp. (2012), pp. 5–22.

[12] For theoretical explorations dealing with such difficulties: Olivier Fillieule, Eric Agrikoliansky and Isabelle Sommier (eds), *Penser les mouvements sociaux. Conflits sociaux et contestations dans les sociétés contemporaines* (Paris: La Découverte, 2010), p. 327. See also: Holger Albrecht (ed.), *Contentious Politics in the Middle East: Political Opposition under Authoritarianism* (Gainesville: University Press of Florida, 2010), p. 252; Martin Beck, Cilja Harders and Annette Jünemann (eds), *Der Nahe Osten im Umbruch. Zwischen Transformation und Autoritarismus* (Wiesbaden: Verlag für Sozialwissenschaften, 2009), p. 333; Jerome Beinnin and Frederic Vairel (eds), *Social Movements, Mobilization and Contestation in the Middle East and North Africa*, (Palo Alto, CA: Stanford University Press, 2011), p. 308.

[13] For a reflection on such debates: Asef Bayat, *Making Islam Democratic: Social Movements and the Post-Islamist Turn* (Palo Alto, CA: Stanford University Press, 2007), p. 291.

[14] Researchers have illustrated how political Islam used mobilization and networking methods inspired by social movements. See, for example: Quintan Wiktorowicz (ed.), *Islamic Activism: A Social Movement Theory Approach* (Bloomington: Indiana University Press, 2004), p. 316.

[15] Lamis Andoni and Jillian Schwedler, 'Bread Riots in Jordan', *Middle East Report* 201 (1996), pp. 40–42.

[16] Claude Liauzu, *Enjeux urbains au Maghreb: crises, pouvoirs et mouvements sociaux* (Paris: L'Harmattan, 1985), p. 218.

1990s,[17] or political agitation in Egypt have benefited from some atten-tion by scholars, discussions on the nature of social movements have long been controversial.[18] A consensus began to emerge, however, during the 2000s about the qualification of social movement applied to agitations in the region, from Morocco to Iraq or Palestine.[19] Historians working in the field of labour history and history from below also helped shape this kind of analysis.[20] Even before the 2010 outbreaks, some studies underlined the role of new media in mobilization and the emergence of new forms of protest.[21] But overall, there was a shared difficulty in understanding the nature of social movements in the region. A reason, arguably the main reason, for this relates to the fact that the civic dimension in such a cul-tural context has always tended to be underestimated. Civic mobilization tended to be seen as the expression of a class of Westernized intellectuals or labour militants with minimal roots in society and with few echoes into its cultural background. As for the activism of Islamist militants, it was seen as corresponding to a secret society model whose success was explained by an investment in social issues. There was also the ambiguity deriving from the fact that most of the liberation movements of the era of the independences turned into dictatorships. What might have begun as a social movement against foreign occupation and domination often turned into an apparatus of oppression and repression, making it difficult to historically root reflections on social movements. This is why I argue

[17] Didier Le Saout and Marguerite Rollinde Marguerite (eds), *Emeutes et mouvements sociaux au Maghreb* (Paris: Karthala, 1999), p. 381.

[18] Bernard Duterme (ed.), *Etat des résistances dans le Sud—2010. Monde arabe* (Paris/Louvain-la-Neuve: Editions Syllepse/Centre Tricontinental, 2009), p. 233.

[19] Mounia Bennani-Chraibi and Olivier Fillieule, *Résistances et protestations dans les sociétés musulmanes* (Paris: Presses de Sciences Po, 2003), p. 424.

[20] Stephanie Cronin (ed.), *Subalterns and Social Protest. History from Below in the Middle East and North Africa* (London: Routledge 2008), p. 322.

[21] Franck Mermier, *Mobilisation et nouveaux medias dans l'espace arabe* (Paris: Maisoneuve et Larose, 2003), p. 438; Yves Gonzalez-Quijano and Christophe Varin, *La société de l'information au Proche-Orient. Internet au Liban et en Syrie* (Beirut: Presses de l'Université Saint-Joseph, 2006), p. 211; Jean-Philippe Bras and Larbi Chouikha (eds), *Médias et tech-nologies de communication au Maghreb et en Méditerranée* (Tunis: IRMC 2002), p. 158. Khadija Mohsen-Finan, *Les médias en Méditerranée* (Arles: Actes Sud 2009), p. 398; Romain Lecompte, 'Internet et la reconfiguration de l'espace public tunisien: le rôle de la diaspora', *TIC et Sociétés* 1:2 (2009), pp. 199–229 ; Charles Hirschind, 'New Media and Political Dissent in Egypt', *Revista de Dialectologia y Tradisiones Populares* 1 (2010), pp. 137–153; François Polet (ed.), *Globalizing Resistance: the State of Struggle* (London: Pluto, 2004), p. 321.

in this chapter that, in order to understand the logics of mobilization in the Arab world today, a new examination of the roots of civil society in the region is necessary and that this examination must go back to the rich cultural and social heritages that societies possessed even before colonial times. One of the necessary conditions for explaining the logics of mobilization in the region today, is the re-evaluation of the historical dimension of the civic sphere and the social consistency of the networks it has given birth to. The structure of the present chapter mirrors this ambition: after a presentation of the various forms of social mobilization in societies of the region on the *longue durée*, it proposes a different look at the nature of the mobilization processes that occurred between 2010 and the present time, and then focusses on the question of the various difficulties that arose during transition processes and constituted constant new challenges to social movements.

THE HISTORICAL ROOTS OF CIVIC MOBILIZATION IN THE ARAB WORLD

It is only, indeed, with a historically grounded and informed perspective on the roots of social movements and civic action in the Arab world, that contemporary movements can be explained beyond the dimension of *clichés*. The main *cliché* is that every type of social movement is an echo to an import from the West, from nationalist sentiments to trade unions and, more recently, to Facebook-related phenomena. Without underestimating the importance of all these elements, which have proven pivotal in many circumstances, I argue here that such imports only gain importance when they are articulated in the context of deeper sentiments of civic identity and action that are historically rooted in societies of the region. The civic dimension in cities of the Islamic world and its capacity to constitute networks of mobilization for social movements has various origins. The historiography has, with few exceptions,[22] long tended to underestimate their relevance, but studies now converge in reinterpreting this dimension.

---

[22] Claude Cahen, 'Mouvements populaires et autonomisme urbain dans l'Asie musulmane du moyen age', *Arabica* 5 (1958:3), pp. 225–250, 6 (1958:1), pp. 25–56 and 6 (1959:3), pp. 233–265; André Raymond, 'Urban Networks and Popular Movements in Cairo and Aleppo (End of the 18th–beginning of the 19th c.)', *Urbanism in Islam* 2 (1989), pp. 219–271.

Among the medieval Islamic roots of the civic sphere in an Islamic context, various elements need to be emphasized.

Firstly, there is group identity and its articulation within space and society. In cities of the Arab world, since medieval times, quarters and neighbourhoods, as well as streets, were the object of the construction of a civic identity, which had expressions in group solidarity and in the social value given to space. The same applies to professional organizations and confessional communities. All these groups potentially constitute vectors of mobilization in case of the rupture of the equilibrium of governance or in case of degenerating conflict. There was also a dimension of patronage, notables being able to mobilize their clientele. Protest was morally justified when certain conditions, like the respect of governance procedures, were not satisfied, or when codified procedures of mediation in cases of conflict had been bypassed, in contradiction to the duties of the rulers. Excessive violence in the repression of demonstrations has also always been amongst the manifestations of a rupture of the governance pact. Under the Ottoman Empire, combining with other heritages such as imperial Byzantine, medieval Islamic characteristics were subject to a process of re-interpretation in the framework of the building of the Ottoman imperial apparatus and ideology. The right to petition, for example, of medieval—and even ancient—origins, was recognized as a fundamental element of the pact of governance and became a central feature in Ottoman governance practices. At the level of the city, its neighbourhood and streets, the networks of civic identity were recognized and inserted into the old imperial regime's governance system. In case of conflict or failed respect of mediation procedures, mobilization occurred along the vectors of civic conscience and could lead to violent episodes of unrest or revolt.[23] In such cases, streets and guilds, but also mosques (or churches and synagogues), could function as bases for mobilization. With the Ottoman reforms of the second part of the nineteenth century, the new imperial ideology somehow lost direct contact with this expression of collective identity and civic conscience in promoting modern solutions of governance based upon new

[23] Nora Lafi, 'From a Challenge to the Empire to a Challenge to Urban Cosmopolitanism? The 1819 Aleppo Riots and the Limits of the Imperial Urban Domestication of Factional Violence', in Ulrike Freitag and Nora Lafi (eds), *Urban Governance Under the Ottomans: Between Cosmopolitanism and Conflict* (London: Routledge, 2014), pp. 58–75. See also: Nora Lafi, 'Violence factieuse, enjeux internationaux et régulation ottomane de la confictualité urbaine à Tripoli d'Occident entre XVIIIe et XIXe siècles', *Hypothèses* (2013), pp. 395–404.

principles. This tendency was accentuated in colonial times, with further ambiguities, as modernity became an instrument of foreign domination.

But the social networks of civic identity and potential mobilization remained, even if not fully integrated into the governance system as during the time of the old regime. The solidarities which they expressed remained strong. The question of modern governance and its relationship with inherited characteristics of the civic sphere cannot be resolved, of course, by mere analogy. The long season of nationalisms and ideologies during the times of the independences brought along many new features,[24] which themselves are much more complex than a mere mirroring of Western-inspired styles of mobilization. There are also new civic contexts at stake in current situations, and not everything can be reduced to the importance of the traditional background. Old civic habits, however, which were not necessarily integrated into administrative schemes or even into modern representations of what mobilization is, are still present and explain a lot about the dynamics of mobilization in the societies of the contemporary Arab world[25]: morale as a reason for discontent, the ways of propagation of protest, the forms of solidarity at work: not everything is characterized by the internet or Facebook, and what happened in 2011 in many cities of the region reflects various past events and logics.

These old logics can indeed become vectors of mobilization, the nature of which is understandable only in the light of historical and anthropo-logical explorations. In contemporary social movements, from the point of view of historical anthropology, many features reflect developments rooted in this past, from the mobilization of 'women against injustice', to the collective defence of neighbourhood space with improvised bar-ricades, to the activity of gangs of young men or to the moral justifica-tions of legitimate unrest. Present-day social movements in the Arab world are in no way merely imports of Western thinking, democracy or human rights. Although the importance of these concepts and the techniques of mobilization inspired from the 'West', is not to be negated, they are also the response of societies with a rich history of civic identity to specific traumatisms.

---

[24] John Chalcraft, *The Striking Cabbies of Cairo. Crafts and Guilds in Egypt, 1863–1914* (Albany: State University of New York Press, 2005), p. 285.

[25] Diane Singerman, *Avenues of Participation: Family, Politics, and Networks in Urban Quarters of Cairo* (Princeton, NJ: Princeton University Press, 1995), p. 335.

The 2010–2014 Events in Perspective: Social Movements and Mobilization Networks

Theoretical reflections on social movements have illustrated how protests generally relate to the conjunction between profound causes of discontent among a certain category of the population and more specific and immediate causes, giving to previously organized networks the momentum for civic mobilization or facilitating the emergence of new networks. Such logics are clearly traceable in what happened in Tunisia at the end of 2010: the country was experiencing a long-lasting protest in mining and industrial cities of the south against the concentration of the benefits of growth in the urbanized centres of the north of the country; there was also, in such urbanized centres, a growing exasperation with the corruption of the regime (and more precisely with the kleptocratic tendencies of the family of the wife of President Ben Ali), the intrusive and violent practices of the police serving the dictatorship, but also a frustration against the unequal distribution of the benefits of liberalization and consumerism. Until the moment of the 2010 unrests, no connection had been efficiently built by activists between these main causes of exasperation, which corresponded to very different social backgrounds: the miners, their families and the jobless youth in the south and the new middle-class in the north.[26] But then the Bouazizi tragedy created a momentum and allowed a kind of merger (at least at the scale of perception, not necessarily at the scale of social movements and of their sociology) between various claims for change.[27] In the past, similar causes had not resulted in the same consequences.[28] In Egypt, the causes for discontent were also diverse, but the same kind of merger happened in the winter of 2011, under the influence of the Tunis events, between the anger of educated youth and the frustration of the lower classes against both the lack of freedom and economic difficulties. This resulted in the occupation of Tahrir Square and in the birth of a hybrid social movement in which young intellectuals, gangs of violent young men and then members of the Muslim Brotherhood and Salafist

---

[26] Béatrice, Hibou, 'Tunisie: économie politique et morale d'un mouvement social', *Politique africaine* 1 (2011), pp. 5–22.

[27] Zeineb Touati, 'La révolution tunisienne: interaction entre militantisme de terrain et réseaux sociaux', *L'année du Maghreb* 8 (2012), pp. 121–141.

[28] Myriam Catusse, Blandine Destremau and Eric Verdier (eds), *L'Etat face aux 'débordements' du social au Maghreb. Formation, travail, protection* (Paris: Karthala, 2010), p. 468.

activists shared the same space.[29] In Libya, protests in Benghazi began as contestations of the unequal regional distribution of the benefits of oil extraction and as protests against the brutal repression operated by the regime against the first demonstrations. In all places where protest movements appeared, from Syria to Yemen[30] and also Bahrein, one of the causes for unrest, beyond claims for justice, democracy, freedom of speech or regime change, was indeed the protest against police or military violence and in general against the repression of nascent social movements. Causes such as corruption, authoritarianism, injustice, the effects of globalization or those of the 2009 economic crisis are also among the conditions for mobilization,[31] but the spark which made things possible came from what Barrington Moore defined as anger and moral outrage.[32] What made this moral outrage grow is the use of live ammunition against the first demonstrations from Tunis to Cairo, Benghazi, Damascus and Bahrein. The killing of young demonstrators resulted in regimes losing what was left of their moral legitimacy, and when the various regimes utilized militias or instrumentalized gangsters in order to attack protesters, this sentiment only grew, facilitating mobilization at the local level through which neighbourhoods protected themselves. The absence of political liberalization in the context of escalating demands by the population is also to be counted among the causes for mobilization.

But beyond such causes (for mobilization, not necessarily directly for regime change), what counts in a social movement is the existence of vectors of mobilization along existing or newly formed networks. In the case of the Arab Spring, these networks were very diverse and varied according to the place. In Tunisia, where it all began, networks related to the labour movement proved pivotal, from trade unions to the solidarity network which was born in support of the miners of Gafsa (composed of miners and former miners, but also of their wives and relatives as well as of

[29] Zeinab Abdul-Magd, 'Occupying Tahrir Square: the Myths and the Realities of the Egyptian Revolution', *South-Atlantic Quarterly* 3 (2012), pp. 165–172; Emad El-Din Shahin, 'The Egyptian Revolution: The Power of Mass Mobilization and the Spirit of Tahrir Square', *The Journal of the Middle-East and Africa* 1 (2012), pp. 46–69.

[30] Laurent Bonnefoy, 'Les révolutions sont-elles exportables? L'effet domino à la lumière du cas yéménite', *Mouvements* 66 (2011), pp. 100–116.

[31] See Britta Baumgarten's Chap. 22 in this volume.

[32] Barrington Moore, *Injustice: the Social Bases of Obedience and Revolt* (London: Sharpe, 1978), p. 540.

members of the Tunisian Left).[33] This network had been organizing mobilizations for almost a decade and proved very efficient when it was given momentum by the course of events. It already had its spokespersons, its slogans and was ready for generalization of its social and political claims. Spatial solidarities also proved decisive, with mobilization occurring along the lines of streets and neighbourhoods, according to ties of solidarity anchored in the older forms of local civic conscience.

In other countries, by contrast, labour-related mobilization networks do not seem to have played a decisive role. In this regard, Tunisia, with its rich history of unionism might be an exception. In other countries, the left was represented by various types of political networks. Just as— once the movement had started—Tunisian left-wing political parties and non-recognized political organizations served as powerful relays (mainly in Tunis) of the slogans and claims of the Gafsa, Kasserine and Sidi Bouzid demonstrators, so, in Egypt, structured organizations of the left played a role in the mobilization which led to the occupation of Tahrir Square. They were not the force behind the initial protests but, on various occasions, they provided structural support in spite of their narrow influence over the youth in revolt. In other countries of the region though, it cannot be said that political parties of the left proved instrumental to the mobilizations, for the simple reason that in many cases they were too marginal.

What made mobilization during the Arab Spring distinctive is to be found in other dimensions. One such dimension relates to the role of information and communication technologies. This is the question of the Facebook and Twitter revolution.[34] Such innovations, made available to the educated youth of many Arab countries by the economic liberalization of the telecommunications sector and by the belief of censorship authorities that the intrusive control they exercised would prevail against the

---

[33] Michael Bechir Ayari, *S'engager en régime autoritaire: gauchistes et islamistes dans la Tunisie indépendante,* (Institut d'études politiques d'Aix en Provence/IREMAM, PhD, 2009); Larbi Chouikha and Vincent Geisser, 'Retour sur la révolte du bassin minier: retour sur les cinq leçons politiques d'un conflit social inédit', *L'Année du Maghreb* 6 (2010), pp. 415–426; Amin Allal, 'Trajectoires révolutionnaires en Tunisie', *Revue française de science politique* 32 (2012), pp. 821–841.

[34] Francesca Comunello and Giuseppe Anzera, 'Will the Revolution be Tweeted? A Conceptual Framework for the Understanding of the Social Media and the Arab Spring', *Islam and Christian-Muslim Relations* 4 (2012), pp. 453–470; David Faris, 'La révolte en réseau: le printemps arabe et les médias sociaux', *Politique étrangère* 1 (2012), pp. 99–109; Philip Howard and Muzammil Hussein, *Democracy's Fourth Wave? Digital Media and the Arab Spring* (Oxford: Oxford University Press, 2013), p. 145.

illusion of liberty that these technologies created, proved powerful tools of mobilization. The conjunction of new means of messaging, which made the organization of demonstrations easier, and of new paths to publish images (of the harsh repression for example), which made moral outrage spread more quickly, is definitely one of the most striking characteristics of the Arab Spring.[35] However, these techniques, which turned informal mobilizations into social movements almost instantaneously, only proved successful because of the existence of a social milieu of young people, frustrated by the various dictatorships and by the limits upon their own personal and collective development that these contexts imposed. There was no Facebook or Twitter revolution as such.[36] What is also interesting is the entanglement of scales: Twitter and Facebook, as well as YouTube, were used both as local instruments of mobilization among an indistinct group of protesters (but who shared common values and modes of recognition) and as a media tool targeting national and international audiences. Blogs, such as those of Lina Ben Mhenni in Tunisia, were also used as tools to relay information and spread opinion.[37] In Tunisia, during the crucial days of the demonstrations against the regime, old media forms, like the radio, also played an important role: when demonstrators took control of a radio station they began to spread information contradicting regime propaganda. In Egypt, blogs had played an important role since the assassination of Khaled Said in 2010.[38] This gave social movements in Tunisia and then in Egypt a transnational dimension.[39] This aspect developed further through the Arabic-speaking news channels which almost immediately built an epic narrative of the events in the region.[40] The role of Al-Jazeera in this regard is to be analysed as both instrumental in the spreading of information and slogans, as well as of a sentiment of common

[35] Habibul H. Khondker, 'Role of the New Media in the Arab Spring', *Globalizations* 5 (2011), pp. 675–679.

[36] Michael B. Ayari, 'Non les Révolutions tunisienne et égyptienne ne sont pas des Révolutions 2.0', *Mouvements* 66 (2011), pp. 56–61.

[37] Marta Severo and Thimothée Giraud, 'Nouveaux regards sur le cyber-activisme: une cartographie de la blogosphère des révoltes arabes', *Proceeding of the conference: Mouvements sociaux en ligne, cyber activisme et nouvelles formes d'expression en Méditerranée* (Tunis: IRMC, 2011).

[38] Delphine Pagès El-Karoui and Leila Vignal, 'Les racines de la révolution du 25 janvier en Egypte: une réflexion géographique', *Echogéo online Journal* (2011).

[39] Romain Lecompte, 'Révolution tunisienne et internet: le rôle des médias sociaux', *L'année du Maghreb* 7 (2011), pp. 389–418.

[40] Théo Corbucci, 'Les Quatre Vies d'Al-Jazeera', *Géo-économie* 62 (2012), pp. 89–96.

destiny, and it is regarded as highly ambiguous in its treatment of the various local realities and their insertion into a rhetoric mirroring a specific political and geostrategic agenda. Al-Jazeera's role had been tagged as such for a long time,[41] but during the period of the Arab Spring, information on this channel tended to become a vector of propagation of precise ideas pertaining to a very conservative agenda.

Mosques also played a role in the structuration of protests as social movements: many demonstrations began after the Friday prayer and inside the demonstrations in Egypt, for example, groups were organized according to the geography of mosques. In Egypt, Coptic churches also played an important role in providing not only a sentiment of common belonging, but also in providing networks of mobilization.[42] Even if right-wing conservative Muslim activists were neither in the Tunisian nor the Egyptian movements during their very first stages, they quickly joined in, developing networks of mobilization around the mosques and, as it turned out, within the structures of the Muslim Brotherhood. This has been particularly true in Egypt (in Tunisia, the mobilization of the conservative Islamists mostly appeared once the regime had been ousted). The transnational dimension of the social and political networks of the Muslim Brotherhood is another important factor in the development of mobilization in the region.[43] It has also played a crucial role in the political restructuring in the aftermaths of the Arab Spring.[44] Developments, however, were very diverse according to the country and they illustrated between 2012 and 2014 how the Muslim Brotherhood remained exposed to reversals of fortune.

There is now a consensus among researchers in describing its networks as constituting a social movement, but its ephemeral access to power cannot be understood simply as the success of a social movement. It responded to much more complex stakes, strategies and compromises. The interpretation of the growing importance of Salafist movements in Tunisia and

---

[41] Olfa Lamloum, *Al-Jazira: miroir rebelle et ambigu du monde arabe* (Paris: La Découverte 2004), p. 143.

[42] Laure Guirguis, 'Les Frères, les Coptes et la Révolution', *Outre-Terre* 29 (2011), pp. 373–387; Fatiha Kahoues, 'Les Frères musulmans et les chrétiens dans la révolution égyptienne', *Confluences Méditerranée* 79 (2011), pp. 147–160.

[43] Stephan Malthaner, *Mobilizing the Faithful: Militant Islamist Groups and their Constituencies* (Frankfurt: Campus, 2011), p. 273.

[44] Carrie Wickham, 'The Muslim Brotherhood and Democratic Transition in Egypt', *Middle-East Law and Governance* 1–2 (2011), pp. 204–223.

in Egypt is also difficult: they have developed methods of mobilization inspired by those of the Muslim Brotherhood, but they also use methods of intimidation and public space violence.[45] There is also the activity of what can be described as the Jihadist international, with its archipelago of local groups and its global ideology. Its role in mobilizing the Arab Spring, as well as its importance in the following period of protest from Libya to the civil war in Syria, should not be underestimated. Jihadists have used many mobilization strategies that resemble those of other social movements, and the sociology of the members of such movements, which comprises an elite of educated ideologists and troops of poor young men is also to be taken into account. This kind of complexity indicates that the interpretation of the Arab Spring in terms of social movement theory should not be undertaken without, at the same time, evaluating the influence of other issues. The variety of actors in the Arab Spring is extreme, they range from Labour activism related networks to global Jihad. All categories took part at one level or another in what can be described as a social movement. However, this does not mean that social movements were the single cause for regime change.

FROM SOCIAL MOVEMENTS TO REGIME CHANGES: COMPLEX PROCESSES OF TRANSITION

Until 2013, any narrative of the Arab Spring which focussed predominantly on the mechanical link between the emergence of social movements, their role in the departure of dictators and political transitions could only end in the description of what appeared to be the seizure of the various movements by conservative Islamist political parties, from Tunisia to Egypt and even Syria.[46] The fact that in Tunisia the *Ennahda* movement had to negotiate with other parties as its political dominance was rejected, and that in Egypt the Muslim Brotherhood was violently ousted from power by a coup d'état, suggests a need to revise this perspective.[47] Even

---

[45] Fabio Merone and Francesco Cavatorta, 'Salafist Mouvance and Shiekhism in the Tunisian Democratic Transition', *Working Papers in International Studies*, Dublin City University (2012); Bernard Rougier, 'Elections et mobilisations dans l'Egypte post-Moubarak', *Politique étrangère* 1 (2012), pp. 85–98.

[46] John Bradley, *After the Arab Spring: How Islamists Hijacked the Middle-East Revolts* (London: Macmillan, 2012), p. 256.

[47] Paolo Gerbaudo, 'The Roots of the Coup', *Soundings: A Journal of Politics and Culture* 54 (2013), pp. 104–113.

before these events however, the idea of seizure by conservative Islamists needed to be complemented not only by a critical examination of the very nature of the social movements involved—insisting, for example, on the Muslim Brotherhood as a social movement and even on the Salafist movements as part of a network partly operating at this scale, as illustrated above—but also by a framing of the influence of social movements in more complex contexts. These contexts include dimensions such as the inner logic of transformation of political and institutional apparatuses, nego-tiations, mediations, accommodations and geo-strategy. Comparisons between the various countries involved also need to be made in relation to the specificity of each context.

All dictatorships look alike in their active limitation of individual and collective freedoms and in their methods of brutal repression, but the fact that some revolts of the Arab Spring were against right-wing regimes backed by the United States (Tunisia, Egypt) and some others against what was left of the heritage of left-wing revolutions and struggles for national independence backed by Russia (Libya, Syria) has to be under-lined. The situation in Yemen was more complex but was also a heritage of the Cold War. There is indeed a post-Cold War dimension to the Arab Spring, since many of the contested regimes had been put in place in the context of the rivalry between blocks in the Mediterranean until 1990.[48] The unfolding of the Arab Spring is to be understood in the context of a new international situation, but also in that of the persistence in the region of strong geo-strategic stakes whose shape has been changed by 30 years of Islamist activism and by the rise of new actors like Saudi Arabia and Qatar. The role of social movements in the Arab Spring cannot be anal-ysed outside this context.

The first question to arise is that of the role of social movements in causing the fall of regimes in the region. Again, the narrative of dictators leaving power when faced with contestations on the street is too limited and cannot suffice to explain the dynamic of events. It cannot be said, either, that regime changes in Tunisia and Egypt were mere coups d'état. Only when archival material has become available will historians of the future be able to evaluate the relative weight of the different factors at stake. What can be said for now is that it must have been something in between. This is quite clear for Tunisia, where available evidence tends to underline the existence of an attempt to prevent the total collapse of the

---

[48] Curtis Ryan, 'The New Arab Cold War and the Struggle for Syria', *MERIP* 262 (2013).

system of power through the ousting of President Ben Ali by a commando of special forces, which might have forced him to leave the country. It is not possible at this point to assess the exact role of President Obama in this decision, but what is certain is that the situation in Tunis was monitored closely in Washington and that the figure of President Ben Ali (who himself, having followed political training in the US, came to power in 1987 through a coup d'état), had become continuously less acceptable.[49]

This does not mean that social movements had no role in regime change, or that the process was finished at this stage: on the contrary, it only opened a new period. In Egypt, developments took more time to unfold, but the link between what happened on Tahrir Square, the palace's power games and foreign pressures is still to be analysed. In Yemen, the transition was much more complicated and all the previously described factors were mixed with tribal, generational and regional stakes, as well as with the heritage of a decade or more of radical Islamist struggle.[50] In Libya, it is clear that regime change was made possible only by a massive foreign military intervention, following the transformation of the first demonstrations in Benghazi into a civil war once the former Jihadist guerrilla forces, which had been fighting the regime for two decades,[51] had joined the movement and seized weapons in military cantonments. In the case of Libya, it is extremely difficult to follow the fate of the social movement component of the rebellion, as it was overwhelmed by both foreign bombings and Jihadist militia action. In present-day Syria, too, social movements, networks of the Muslim Brotherhood and Jihadist groups affiliated to Al-Qaeda and later ISIS all fight the Assad regime with different strategies and sponsors. In some contexts of the Arab Spring, the hypothesis according to which social movements themselves might have been manipulated in order to become instruments for the promotion of regime change by foreign secret services cannot be excluded. In spite of signs of previous similar clandestine action in Ukraine, the Balkans and the Caucasus, however, the individual elements are too fragile to allow us to build a theory. The distinction between the international promotion of democracy by means of social movement-style mobilizations and geo-strategic

---

[49] Mansouria Moqhefi, 'Washington face aux revolutions arabes', *Politique étrangère* 3 (2011), pp. 631–643.

[50] Laurent Bonnefoy, *Salafism in Yemen. Transnationalism and Religious Identity* (New York: Columbia University Press, 2011), p. 336.

[51] Luis Martinez, 'Révolution, contestation et insurrection en Libye (1969–2011)', *Tumultes* 38: 39 (2012), pp. 173–186.

manipulations remains difficult, given the absence of primary sources. The presence of *agents provocateurs* is also difficult to confirm. All these issues invite us, however, to place the role of social movements in regime changes in a broader context.

A similar logic applies to the reading of the political and institutional restructurings which have taken place in the wake of the collapse of the regimes in the region. The general narrative is now that of the confiscation of the various revolutions by conservative Islamists and then of a backlash of the old regime through a coup, as in Egypt. The question of political Islam is crucial here. However, its role cannot be reduced to a mechanical vision. We have seen here how the networks of mobilization and civic action of the Muslim Brotherhood had been active for decades. In the accession to power of members of the Brotherhood, various factors have to be taken into account, from a kind of historical deal with President Obama, who might have lifted the previous implicit US veto to such a transition in exchange for promises of moderation towards Israel, to the electoral success of a social movement deeply rooted into local societies.

Such transitions happened in Tunisia and Egypt, where conservative Islamists won the post-revolution elections.[52] In these countries, the situation of the political class is very different. In Tunisia, after various phases of transition, the Islamist party Ennahda has decided to abandon power in face of the mobilization of the opposition against its dominance and to concentrate again on activism in society. Almost no social movement representative is part of the new system, and the ephemeral ministerial career of former blogger Slim Amamou in 2011 is very telling. The Tunisian government under Ennahda was composed mostly of Ennahda militants or affiliates, many of whom have spent years in prison, and former judges, lawyers and diplomats. In Egypt, most of the ministers under President Morsi had a background identity as Muslim Brotherhood militants. Under General Sisi, the situation is more that of a return to power of representatives of the old regime. The heritage of the Tahrir social movements is divided between those who accepted the coup against Morsi as a revenge against the Muslim Brotherhood and those who try to continue expressing voices of dissent. In an even more

---

[52] David Sarquis, 'Democratization after the Arab Spring: the Case of Egypt's Political Transition', *Politics and Policy* 5 (2012), pp. 871–903.

chaotic situation like Libya, where extremist Jihadists keep challenging the more moderate political class composed of conservative Islamists trained in the US, the influence of the social movement dimension is more difficult to follow. Western powers themselves, after having made an alliance with Jihadists against the regime of Colonel Gaddafi, hesitated between several options. In Syria the situation degenerated into a long civil war in which not only Syrian militants fought against the troops of the Assad regime but also in which many foreign powers intervened more or less directly, from Saudi Arabia to Qatar, from the United States, Great Britain and France to Russia and to the Lebanese Hezbollah, and from Turkey to Israel on their respective borders. Numerous militants belonging to the sphere of international Jihad also came to the country. The renunciation of direct military intervention by the United States and France probably arose following warnings by Israel[53] of the dangers of an alliance with Jihadist militias of the Al-Qaeda archipelago as in Libya, and the difficulties that US-trained political figures experienced in rallying consensus at the various junctures of the rebellion (in spite of the fact that these men were better trained than those sent to Iraq ten years earlier). In that case, the influence of social movements in Aleppo, Homs and Damascus is difficult to assess, even if signs of a growing influence of the Islamic Brotherhood and of its networks abound. If we add the manipulations operated by the secret services of countries like Saudi Arabia, Turkey and Qatar in support of either conservative Islamist movements or even armed Jihadists, the picture could appear quite dark.[54] However, not every element of the Arab Spring can be reduced to a mere international game of geo-strategic calculations, and the complexity of the situation at this scale does not mean social movements were or are irrelevant. In many cases, they were driving forces for change and they enforced an adaptation of the systems. The Arab Spring also witnessed the emergence of various forms of civic action and mobilization which truly changed the face of the region and the attitude of the population in the face of power.

---

[53] Daniel Byman, 'Israel's Pessimistic View of the Arab Spring', *Washington Quarterly* 3 (2011), pp. 123–136; Laurent Greilsammer, 'Israel face au printemps arabe', *Politique étrangère* 1 (2012), pp. 123–134.

[54] Madawi al-Rasheed, 'Sectarianism as Counter-Revolution: Saudi Responses to the Arab Spring', *Studies in Ethnicity and Nationalism* 3 (2011), pp. 513–526, Hala Kodmani, 'L'implication du Qatar dans les révolutions arabes: stratégie d'influence ou OPA?', *Confluences Méditerranéennes* 84 (2011), pp. 77–85.

Conclusion

A general interpretation of the period will, of course, be the task of historians of the future. What can already be said, however, is that between 2010 and 2014 the face of the Arab world changed, not only geo-strategically but also in citizens' own perception of their role in politics and in the civic life of their countries, cities and neighbourhoods. Will the whole movement result in a kind of transnational counter-revolution in which conservative Islamism and neo-military dictatorships take over? Or will political diversity and democracy find its way through the troubles of the times? What is certain is that a new situation has emerged, characterized by a new appetite for freedom of speech, for debates and for a critical relationship to power.[55] In Tunisia, since the revolution, hardly a day goes by without a civic movement expressing its claim for justice. Radios and newspapers experience an inedited season of intense debate.[56] Despite the growing pressures on the streets from radical Salafists and their stance against women or those who do not share their views, and despite the ambiguous relationship between this faction and conservative Islamists, civil society has reached a new level in which many organizations are extending their networks. One can also say that in a way, in spite of harsh conflicts, the gap between the governance sphere and civil society has been reduced. The deep economic crisis the country is now confronted with is, however, a challenge to this moment of freedom and civic exaltation.[57] In Egypt however, the season of relative liberty as for freedom of speech seems to be over. In Libya the situation of civic activists and women may paradoxically be even worse now than it was before the fall of the previous regime: Jihadist militias or other militias are still controlling the streets and justice is often reduced to merely a demonstration of violence.[58] Predictions for Syria are not good either, civil war is still raging and, on the battle-

---

[55] Sari Hanafi (ed.), *Al-shabab wa-l-thawra wa-l-dimuqratiyya*, Special issue (2011) Idafat, p. 13.

[56] Kmar Bendana, *Chronique d'une transition* (Tunis: Script 2011), p. 213; Zeineb Touati, 'Presse et révolution en Tunisie: rôle, enjeux et perspectives', *ESSACHESS* 1 (2012), pp. 139–150.

[57] Béatrice Hibou, 'Macroéconomie et domination politique en Tunisie: du 'miracle économique benaliste aux enjeux socio-économiques du moment révolutionnaire', *Politique africaine* 124 (2012), pp. 127–154.

[58] International Crisis Group, *Trial by Error: Justice in Post-Qhadafi Libya*, Middle-East and North-Africa Report, 140, April 17, 2013.

field, Jihadist militias, now the object of foreign attacks and bombings, are fighting various elements.[59]

However, in order to understand the dynamics of the Arab Spring, it is also important to analyse what happened in places where social movements did not result in regime change. In Algeria, for example, social movements have been very active for decades, under a variety of forms, from labour-related to conservative Islamists. The context of the chaos created by regime change in neighbouring countries has resulted, it seems, in the emergence of a kind of consensus between the regime and activists from the civil society not to expose the country, which experienced a deadly civil war in the 1990s, to such a risk.[60] In Morocco, in spite of various forms of contestation emanating from social movements and from radical Islamists, the royalist consensus eventually resisted.[61] The same kind of phenomenon seems to have prevailed in Jordan, in Qatar and Saudi Arabia where the expression of claims coming from civil society has been totally frozen at the local level by repression.[62] In Bahrain, too, claims for justice and communal equity have been repressed by force.[63] As for Palestine, social movements (closely controlled by the Palestinian Authority and Hamas in the West Bank and in Gaza respectively) never really dared to benefit from the regional momentum in order to boost their claims for internal democracy

[59] Thomas Pierret, 'Syrie: l'Islam dans la révolution', *Politique étrangère* 4 (2011), pp. 879–891.

[60] Werner Ruf, *Die algerische Tragödie. Vom Zerbrechen des Staates einer zerrissenen Gesellschaft* (Münster: Agenda Verlag, 1997), p. 171; Salim Chéna, 'L'Algérie dans le printemps arabe entre espoirs, initiatives et blocages', *Confluences méditerranéennes* 77 (2011), pp. 105–118; Alhouari Addi, 'Le régime algérien après les révoltes arabes', *Mouvements* 66 (2011), pp. 89–97.

[61] Myriam Catusse and Frédéric Vairel, 'Question sociale et développement: les territoires de l'action publique et de la contestation au Maroc', *Politique africaine* 120 (2011), pp. 5–23; Pierre Vermeren, 'Le Maroc: une royale exception?', *Raison présente*, 181 (2012), pp. 105–113.

[62] Samuel and Tally Helfont, 'Jordan between the Arab Spring and the Gulf Cooperation Council', *Orbis* 1 (2012), pp. 82–95; Mansouria Moqhefi, 'Qatar: forces et faiblesses d'un activisme', *Politique étrangère* 4 (2012), pp. 849–861; Toby Matthiesen, 'A Saudi Spring? The Shi'a Protest Movement in the Eastern Province, 2011–2012', *The Middle-East Journal* 4 (2012), pp. 628–659; Jean-François Seznec, 'La révolte arabe et le vide politique en Arabie Saoudite', *Outre-Terre* 29 (2011), pp. 489–492.

[63] Miriam Joyce, *Bahrain, From the Twentieth Century to the Arab Spring* (New York: Palgrave, 2012), p. 184; David Mc Murray and Amanda Ufheil-Somers, *The Arab Revolts. Dispatches on Militant Democracy in the Middle-East* (Bloomington: Indiana University Press, 2013), p. 259.

and against the Israeli occupation and colonization.[64] Here, the ambiguity of the national liberation movement becoming a regime was at a very different stage than in other countries of the region. As for the Arab minority in Israel, in spite of a vague feeling of solidarity with what happened in the region and in spite of the existence of strong networks of civic action, it did not join in the rhetoric of the Arab Spring.[65]

The extreme diversity of situations explains why scholars should not consider the Arab Spring as a single moment in time and in space and as one trans-national or regional movement, but as one of the decisive moments in a complex evolution in which many factors interacted. As for social movements, they are also to be followed during the aftermaths of the revolutions, civil wars, regime changes or even apparent situations of stability: research on civil society in the Arab world must now embrace a situation in which fundamental questions about the coherence of social movements and the mobilization potential of societies in the region are beginning to be answered. At the same time, new questions and directions of research are now emerging, including the conservative Muslim activists' passage from opposition to power, the cultural marginalization of part of the activists from the Left, the impact between radical Islam, civil society and the stakes of power and the role of women in society between activism and renewed forms of oppression.[66] This is all happening in a context where the international stakes, with the risk of constant instrumentalization of local claims by foreign powers, remain high.

FURTHER READINGS

Literature about the Arab Spring and the role of social movements has been overwhelming since 2011. Many of the most important contributions have been evoked in the chapter. They concentrate on specific aspects

---

[64] Roger Heacock, 'La révolution arabe de 2011 et son printemps palestinien', *Confluences Méditerranéennes* 77 (2011), pp. 131–137.

[65] Nida Shoughry, *Israeli-Arab Political Mobilization: Between Acquiscence, Participation and Resistance* (Basingstoke: Palgrave Macmllan, 2012), p. 217.

[66] Valentine Moghadam, *From Patriarchy to Empowerment: Women's Participation, Movements, and Rights in the Middle East, North Africa, and South Asia* (New York: Syracuse University Press, 2007), p. 266; Nadje Al-Ali, 'Gendering the Arab Spring', *Middle-East Journal of Culture and Communication* 1 (2012), pp. 26–31; Eva Gondorova, *The Arab Spring in Tunisia: the Role of Women in Social Movements and Decision-Making Processes*, MA Thesis 2013 (G. Yurdakul and N. Lafi supervisors), Middle-East Technical University Ankara and Humboldt Universität zu Berlin.

of what happened in the region, pertaining to gender, social media, mobilization networks, passive and active resistance against repression and the complex relationship between social movements and rebellions, as well as on the articulation of scales between local events and geopolitics.

Part of the literature has focussed on the mechanisms of protest and of mobilization triggering. As Asef Bayat states, the Arab Spring was not only a surprise, as very few observers had predicted its possibility, it also invited researchers to come to surprising conclusions compared to what they thought earlier of both the region and the social movement theory ('The Arab Spring and its Surprises', *Development and Change* 3 (2013), pp. 587–601). A few years after the start of the events indeed, and as many countries are still struggling with their often traumatic consequences, authors reflecting on social movements in general have begun to revise their opinions of what the Arab Spring illustrated. As triggering factors, apart from the study of previous low-intensity mobilizations in countries like Tunisia and Egypt that served as basis for the movements, many authors have underlined the importance of geopolitical implications. It is what Ghia Nodia calls 'The Revenge of Geopolitics': *Journal of Democracy* 4 (2014), pp. 139–150. Scholars are now insisting also on the importance of such factors in the spreading of the rebellions from Tunisia and Egypt, where mobilization happened against dictatorships backed by the United States, to Libya and Syria, dictatorships backed by Russia. Research, however, is still limited by the lack of access to primary sources as for the study of the work of possible *agents provocateurs* and of the manipulation of armed factions by foreign powers. Jean-François Bayart ('Retour sur les Printemps Arabes', *Politique Africaine* 133 (2014), pp. 153–175) insists on the link between geopolitics and logics of repression, an interpretation that Bülent Aras and Richard Falk suggest to explore further too ('Authoritarian "Geopolitics" of Survival in the Arab Spring', *Third World Quarterly* 2 (2015), pp. 322–336). In other words, the more the years pass after the mobilizations, the more scholars lose their innocence in interpreting what happened, due to a difficulty in distinguishing between spontaneous movements and geopolitical manipulations. In order to avoid the impasse of such a dichotomy, researchers focused on the global context of the events. Analyses of the impact of globalization and liberalization, for example: Imad Salamey, 'Post-Arab Spring: Changes and Challenges', *Third World Quarterly* 1 (2015), pp. 111–129, and Amin Allal, 'Retour Vers le Futur: les Origines Économiquesde la Révolution Tunisienne', *Pouvoirs* 156 (2016), pp. 17–29, insist on the importance of the transformations local societies were submitted to in the 1990s and 2000s. Other scholars insist, to the contrary, on more constant factors in local societies, influences that historical anthropology and sociology might explain: Raymond Hinnebusch, 'Historical Sociology and the Arab Spring', *Mediterranean Politics*, 1 (2014), pp. 137–140. As for violence, in the case of Egypt, the existence of groups of young men potentially becoming violent and potentially used by political factions (and/or provocateurs of the regime or of foreign powers) has also been underlined as expressing an historical constant. In present days, this dimension is expressed by the blured boundaries between football fans, groups of hooligans, political activism and street violence: Khaled Adham, 'Urban Injustice, Urban Violence and the Revolution: Reflections on Cairo', in Ulrike Freitag, Nelida Fuccaro, Claudia Ghrawi and Nora Lafi (eds), *Urban Violence in the Middle East* (Oxford: Berghahn, 2015), pp. 265–286. The understanding of this kind of mobilization/counter-mobilization is key in understanding the nature of the social movements and of their impact in society.

The more time passes, the more scholars grow critical of early enthusiastic visions of social movement mobilization processes in a digital age. Manuel Castells is one of them: *Networks of Outrage and Hope: Social Movements in the Internet Age* (New York: John Wiley & Sons, 2012). In his conclusion to this book, Castells reflects on the role of digital media during the Arab Spring in this quite pessimistic parabola: 'the life and death of networked social movements' (p. 244). Various denunciations of a wave of 'facile analyses' of the role of new media in the mobilizations of the Arab Spring have been voiced, with critical remarks about the social *clichés* this vision embodies, see Miriyam Aouragh, 'Social Media, Mediation and the Arab Revolutions', in Christian Fuchs and Vincent Mosco (eds), *Marx in the Age of Digital Capitalism* (Leiden: Brill, 2016), pp. 482–515. This trend is part of the general critical re-examination of belief in the performing power of mobilizations through the internet: Tim Markham, 'Social Media, Protest Cultures and Political Subjectivities of the Arab Spring', *Media, Culture and Society* 1(2014), pp. 89–104; Zeynep Tufekci, 'Social Movements and Governments in the Digital Age: Evaluating a Complex Landscape', *Journal of International Affairs* 1 (2014), pp. 1–16. In order to avoid to only focus on a 'digital élite' and on factors of 'emotional mobilization' (Anita Breuer, Todd Landman and Dorothea Farquhar, 'Social Media and Protest Mobilization: Evidence from the Tunisian Revolution', Democratization 4 (2015), pp. 764–792), Peter Snowdon proposed a reappraisal of the role of 'vernacular video': 'The Revolution Will be

Uploaded: Vernacular Video and the Arab Spring', *Culture Unbound* 6 (2014), p. 401–429.

The question of repression has also been at the centre of the attention dedicated by scholars to the aftermaths of the revolts. Deciphering the 'lineages of repression': Jason Brownlee, Tarek Masoud and Andrew Reynolds, *The Arab Spring: Pathways of Repression and Reform* (Oxford: Oxford University Press, 2014) that characterized the development of the events in the region between 2010 and the present day has been one of the ways used by scholars to distantiate themselves from positivist narratives. Understanding the logics of power and repression has become a major stake. This is also what Choukri Hmed proposed as for his reading of the Tunisian revolution 'Répression d'État et situation révolutionnaire en Tunisie (2010–2011)', *Vingtième Siècle, Revue d'histoire* 128 (2015), pp. 77–90.

This kind of reading also poses the question of the existence of a counter-revolution in some countries of the region, Egypt for example. Following reflections on the trauma of the confiscation of revolutions by religious conservative movements (in Egypt and Tunisia for a short period, for example; see Cilja Harders, 'Revolution I und II. Ägypten zwischen Transformation und Restauration', in Annette Jünemann and Anja Zorob (eds), *Arabellions, Politik und Gesellschaft des Nahen Ostens* (Wiesbaden, Springer, 2013), pp. 19–42, and Tarek Chamkhi, 'Ennahda as a Neo-Islamist political Party in Power (2011–2014)', researchrepository.murdoch.edu.au), academia is concentrating on the understanding of the severe disenchantment that saw armed fanatics, foreign interventions and/or new dictatorships confiscate the struggle for democracy. Saudi Arabia as promoter of counter-revolutionary regimes and the fundamental ambiguities of Western pro-democratic discourses are among the most discussed issues, see: Hassan Oz, 'Undermining the Transatlantic Democracy Agenda? The Arab Spring and Saudi Arabia's Counteracting Democracy Strategy', *Democratization* 3 (2015), pp. 479–495.

But in this situation of fundamental doubt and need for scholars to deconstruct the ambiguities of the period, some authors still think that what happened in the Arab World since the end of 2010 illustrates new modes of mobilization that are worth being inserted into a revised typology of social movements in spite of the traumatic context. David West (*Social Movements in Global Politics*, New York: John Wiley & Sons, 2014) is among them. For him, beyond aspects of failure, confiscation and instrumentalization, the Arab Spring has been a source of vitality and has participated in the present renewal of the evaluation of the potential role of social movements in political change. For Frédéric Volpi furthermore, revolutionary movements should not be seen only as for the nature of the political proposals they carried, but also as for their capacity of eclosion of new social practices ('Framing Political Revolutions in the Aftermath of the Arab Uprisings', *Mediterranean Politics* 1 (2014), pp. 153–156). Under this perspective, the Tunisian case is surely the one that supports best visions of hope, in spite of the huge challenges and difficulties that confront the country. Social movements have not only been able to boost political change in the country where it all started in 2010 and even before: they were also able to throw their weight behind the process of constitutional reform and, in general, support the diffusion into society of a renewed culture of civic debate (Mohamed Kerrou, 'Société Civile et Compromis Historique', *IEMED Quaderns*, 2015). Souheil Kaddour is among the scholars who insist on this dimension ('La Gouvernance des Droits de l'homme en Tunisie post-révolutionnaire: état des lieux, difficultés et opportunités *La revue des droits de l'homme* 6 (2014), pp. 2–15). Others have focussed on a reading of the transformation of public spaces by mobilizations since 2010, illustrating how the logics at work had long-lasting consequences (Raffaele Cattedra, Francesca Governa, Maurizio Memoli and Matteo Puttilli, *Al Centro di Tunisi*, http://webdoc.unica.it/). And even debates on the restoration of the old regime through processes of economic reconstruction (Leyla Dakhli, 'Entre fidélité et réconciliation: quelle place pour la politique dans la Tunisie révolutionnaire?', *Pouvoirs* 156 (2016), pp. 7–16) insist on the existence of a new civic sphere that is vigilant against possible abuses. In Tunisia, a new dimension of civic life and social movements has, in spite of all ambiguities and difficulties, been achieved in the aftermath of the revolution, see Mohamed Kerrou, 'New Actors of the Revolution and the Political Transition in Tunisia', in Clement Henry and Jang Ji-Hyang (eds), *The Arab Spring* (Basingstoke: Palgrave Macmillan, 2012), pp. 79–99. Hopefully such a dimension will also emerge in other countries in spite of wars, foreign manipulations, repression mechanisms and counter-revolution.

INDEX

A

Aachen, 532
Abbas, Ferhart, 243
Abd al Malek, Anwar, 250
Aberle, David F., 622
Abyssinia, 500
Addams, Jane, 423
al-Afghani, Jamal al-Din, 234, 235
Afghanistan, 108, 251–3, 258, 510,
    571, 574
Africa, 2, 11, 12, 25–6, 93, 119, 135,
    177, 211–63, 363, 367, 368,
    377, 400, 403–5, 409, 426, 455,
    459, 460, 467, 469, 470, 474,
    475, 491, 498, 499, 504–5, 508,
    525, 533, 549, 551, 558, 560,
    571, 628, 669
Ahmad, Eqbal, 258
Alaska, 433
Al-Atrash, Sultan, 244
Albania, 433
Albee, Edward, 443
Aleppo, 695
Alexander of Yugoslavia, 557

Alexandria, 230, 238, 259, 679
Algeria, 200, 225, 226, 230, 234–6,
    242, 243, 245–7, 249, 255, 259,
    505, 526, 528, 532, 558–60,
    573, 681, 697
Alsace, 595
Altiplano, 121, 137, 138
Altman, Dennis, 342
Amamou, Slim, 694
Amaru, Tupac, 564, 647, 651
Ambedkar, Bhim Rao, 27, 268, 277,
    280, 282–4
Amin, Samir, 250
anarchism, 20, 31, 33, 123, 125, 163,
    164, 198, 199, 391, 400, 436,
    457, 467, 468, 494, 498, 533,
    544, 550–5, 557, 568, 666, 667
Andhra Pradesh, 68
Angola, 196
Ankara, 234
Anthony, Susan B., 160
Antwerp, 192, 532
Araújo, Arturo, 125
Arendt, Hannah, 267, 290

© The Author(s) 2017   703
S. Berger, H. Nehring (eds.), *The History of Social Movements in
Global Perspective*, DOI 10.1057/978-1-137-30427-8

Argentina, 116, 119, 122–4, 126,
127, 129, 131, 132, 134, 139,
142, 363, 531, 565
Arnaud, Emile, 485
Arnold, David, 70
Arrighi, Giovanni, 538
Asia, 19, 27, 29, 71, 93, 99–109, 135,
163, 219, 235, 243, 251, 315,
321, 350, 400, 409, 440, 455,
459, 467, 470, 474, 475, 498,
551, 558, 573, 628, 651, 659,
663, 669
al-Assad, Bashar, 679
Asturias, 388
Atatürk, 244, 609
Augsburg, 183
Australia, 27–8, 172, 325–51, 371,
399, 412, 428, 430, 442, 469
Austria, 183, 194, 195, 199, 362,
365, 407, 421, 494, 500, 556,
593, 595, 602, 630, 636

B
Baader, Andreas, 567
Bahaguna, Sunderlal, 288–90
Bahia, 122
Bahrain, 243, 248, 256, 258, 679, 697
Bakunin, Mikhail, 391, 544
Balkans, 235, 549, 551, 559, 693
Balring, 183
Barbe Baker, Richard, 289
Barlow, Tani, 94
Barthes, Roland, 65
Barton, Clara, 365
Basel, 186, 433
Basque country, 561, 562
Batista, Fulgencio, 130
Baudrillard, Jean, 83
Bauer, Bruno, 14
Baviskar, Amita, 289, 290
Bayart, Jean-François, 12
Bayly, Christopher, 270, 274

Bebel, August, 396, 465
Beck, Ulrich, 440
Beijing, 93, 454, 472, 476, 477
Beirut, 230, 251, 572
Belem, 655
Belgium, 186, 192, 199, 200, 390,
442, 497, 517, 531
Belgrade, 519, 520, 529
Belo Monte, 122
Ben Ali, Zine El Abidine,
678, 686, 693
Ben Barka, Mehdi, 250
Bengal, 68, 74, 81, 89, 271–5, 278, 281
Benghazi, 679, 687, 693
Ben Mhenni, Lina, 689
Benenson, Peter, 375–7
Berbier, Mitch, 632
Berkeley, 521
Berlin, 199, 357, 366, 432, 470, 505,
557, 571, 595, 597, 600, 609
Berlin, Isaiah, 167
Bernardes, Artur, 127
Berne, 499
Berque, Jacques, 245
Bess, Michael, 420, 441
Bethlen, István, 601
Beukelsz, Jan, 192
Bhadra, Gautam, 70
Bhatt, Chandi Prasad, 288
Bhojpuri, 80
Biberach, 183
Bin Laden, Osama, 252, 253
Birmingham, 34, 361, 653, 671
Bismarck, Otto von, 389, 598
Blackburn, Robin, 528
Blee, Kathleen, 620
Blickle, Peter, 182
Bligh, William, 328, 330
Bloch, Ernst, 204, 594
Blühdorn, Ingolfur, 3
Bobbio, Norberto, 620
Bodelschwingh, Friedrich von, 363
Boeke, Kees, 498

Boli, John, 7
Bolivar, Simón, 128, 139
Bolivia, 42, 121, 123, 127, 130, 131, 137, 138
Bolotnikov, Ivan, 184
Bombay, 270, 281, 285, 655
Booth, William, 357, 371
Borganäs, 181
Bose, Subhas Chandra, 609
Boston, 153, 156
Bouazizi, Mohamed, 678, 686
Bouzid, Sidi, 678, 688
Bowden, Tom, 239
Brabant, 185
Brandini, Ciuto, 188
Brand, Ulrich, 657
Brazil, 116, 119, 121–4, 127, 129, 132, 133, 135, 377, 397, 412, 420, 565, 610–14, 652, 655, 668, 670
Bremen, 363
Bright, Charles, 4
Brokdorf, 430
Brower, David, 430
Bruges, 185
Brunswick, 186
Brussels, 364, 422, 491, 520
Bryce, James, 428
Bucaram, Abdala, 137
Budapest, 202, 432
Bulavin, Kondratii, 184
Bulgaria, 199, 202, 236, 556
Bursa, 234

C
Cairo, 236, 472, 679, 680, 687
Calcutta, 270, 272, 279
Calderon, Fernando, 116
Caldicott, Helen, 342
Cale, Guillaume, 180
Calhoun, Craig, 5, 16, 46
California, 163, 165, 523

Calık Ahmed, 237
Cameroon, 12, 368
Canada, 24, 146, 147, 150–3, 172, 412, 433, 532, 651
Canterbury, 181
capitalism, 19, 24, 25, 31, 65, 71, 75, 82, 84, 94, 99, 100, 105, 109, 120, 123, 124, 133, 135–7, 139, 140, 162, 176–8, 185, 188, 190, 193–6, 226, 227, 230, 234, 245, 259, 265, 272, 283, 286, 287, 290, 292, 297, 299, 305–7, 309, 310, 317, 326, 336, 364, 385, 387–400, 402, 404, 405, 407, 408, 411–13, 438, 442, 457–60, 465, 469, 471, 473, 474, 479, 518, 528, 588, 603, 612, 631, 648, 657–9, 661, 671
Caracas, 139, 655
Caracazo, 133, 134, 139
Cardoso, Ruth, 116
Caribbean, 119, 130, 146, 400, 459, 553, 558
Carlos, John, 521
Carnegie, Andrew, 497
Cascavel, 135
Castells, Manuel, 6
Castile, 186
Castro, Fidel, 131, 505, 564
Catalonia, 182, 555
Catherine the Great, 184
Caucasus, 643, 693
Ceadel, Martin, 486, 501
Certeau, Michel de, 536
Chakrabarty, Dipesh, 70, 71, 81, 86–8, 270, 398, 414, 487
Chandra, Bipan, 270
Chandra Sen, Keshab, 275
Charles I, 186, 193
Charles, Martel, 631
Charles, the Bad of Navarre, 180
Chatterjee, Partha, 65, 70, 71, 84–6, 270

Chauri Chaura, 78, 282
Chávez Frías, Hugo, 139
Chernobyl, 433
Chiapas, 152, 537
Chicago, 161, 521, 571
Chile, 119, 123, 124, 129, 138
China, 17, 33, 65, 82, 102, 106, 107,
   159, 163, 250, 251, 307, 318,
   329–31, 366, 401, 402, 412,
   413, 454, 460, 464, 490, 495,
   551, 583, 610, 614
Chirac, Jacques, 630
Chizuko, Ueno, 107
Chow, Rey, 101
Chung-Hee, Park, 307
Clavin, Patricia, 509
Clemenceau, Georges, 555
Cochabamba, 137
Collins, Randall, 548
Cologne, 186, 363
Colombia, 131, 138
colonialism, 11, 13, 19, 21, 23, 26–8,
   32, 33, 63–77, 79–82, 84–6, 98,
   99, 130, 151, 200, 213, 215,
   218–22, 226–8, 230, 232, 234,
   239–41, 245–47, 260, 266–74,
   276–82, 284–7, 290–2, 297–320,
   326–9, 332–5, 337, 351, 363,
   368, 386, 396–8, 401, 402, 404,
   409, 410, 421, 426–8, 452, 453,
   455–6, 459, 460, 462, 465,
   467–9, 473, 498, 504, 505, 524,
   549, 651, 557–61, 563, 570,
   635, 683, 685
communism, 14, 15, 25, 28, 68, 73,
   76, 125, 128, 129, 147, 163–6,
   200, 202, 238, 243, 245, 249,
   250, 279, 300–2, 303, 304,
   308–12, 338, 339, 355, 370,
   379, 399, 401–3, 406–11, 413,
   414, 416, 432, 454, 499, 501–4,
   506, 518, 522, 526, 530, 528,
   533, 555, 556, 558, 561, 566,

   568, 569, 575, 585, 594, 600,
   604, 609, 611, 612, 659
Congo, 651
Conselheiro, Antônio, 122
Constantinople, 374
Cooper, Fred, 218–21
Cooper, Sandi E., 31, 495
Copenhagen, 425
Cordoba (Argentina), 126, 127
Corumbiara, 135
Courtrai, 185
Cousteau, Jacques-Yves, 420
Creasap, Kuimberly, 620
Cremer, W. Randal, 493
Cromwell, Oliver, 193
Cuba, 126, 130–2, 460, 522, 532,
   544, 564
Curcio, Renato, 568
Cyrenaica, 234, 242
Czechoslovakia, 200, 202, 432, 520,
   531, 558

D
Dakar, 32, 215, 524–5, 655
Damascus, 240, 241, 687, 695
D'Annunzio, Gabriele, 586, 589,
   590, 593
Darmstadt, 441
Davos, 655, 668
Debs, Eugene V., 163
democracy(ies), 1–4, 17, 18, 25, 27,
   28, 35, 45, 67, 71, 86, 87, 97,
   101, 107, 116, 118–21, 126–30,
   132–4, 136–8, 140, 141, 148,
   150–3, 161, 163, 165, 166, 185,
   193, 194, 196, 198–200, 204,
   213, 215, 217, 219, 247, 250,
   251, 255, 256, 258, 266, 268,
   277, 284, 285, 287, 291, 292,
   297, 299, 301–3, 305, 307, 309,
   310–20, 331–3, 341, 389, 392,
   394, 399, 403, 406–14, 429,

437, 440, 453, 454, 460–2, 464, 469, 473, 493, 499, 504, 517, 518, 520–2, 524, 525, 531, 533, 554, 557, 558, 571, 588, 589, 598, 603, 604, 608, 613, 619, 623, 642, 647, 658, 660–3, 671, 672, 685, 687, 693, 696, 697
Díaz, Adolfo, 125
Díaz, Porfirio, 123–5
dictatorship(s), 24, 25, 27, 119, 124, 125, 129, 131–2, 139, 178, 200, 201, 299, 302, 303, 305, 306, 309, 312, 313, 406, 409, 413, 432, 453, 471, 529, 531, 594, 599, 603, 612, 613, 682, 686, 689, 691, 692, 696
Dirlik, Arif, 104, 105
Dobry, Michel, 582, 583, 585
Dodge, David Low, 492
Don, Charles Jardine, 334
Douala, 220
Doumani, Beshara, 232
Doumergue, Gaston, 606
Drescher, Seymour, 364
Dubai, 243
Dubček, Alexander, 202
DuBois, W.E.B., 161
Duffy, Charles Gavan, 335
Dunant, Henry, 365
Durham, Eunice Ribeiro, 116
Dutschke, Rudi, 517
Du Val, Gennevieve, 374
Dyke, Nella van, 638
Dylan, Bob, 570

E
East Timor, 107
Ecuador, 134, 136, 137, 435
Eder, Klaus, 622
Egypt, 229–49, 252, 254–9, 402, 403, 410, 499, 679, 682, 686, 688–94, 696

Eisenhower, Dwight D., 247
Eldorado do Carajás, 135
Elias, Norbert, 57
El Salvador, 125, 131
Elstner, Reinhold, 623
Elyachar, Julie, 257
Engelbrektsson, Engelbrekt, 181, 182
Engels, Friedrich, 14, 29, 213, 355, 356, 370, 379, 390, 465
Engels, Jens Ivo, 442
England, 28, 63, 67, 71, 79, 153, 178, 181, 193, 197–9, 235, 240–3, 246, 247, 267, 272, 274–82, 284, 289, 290, 292, 326, 327, 329–31, 333–6, 360, 362–4, 366, 367, 369, 371, 389, 392–4, 398, 399, 407, 409, 422, 426, 428, 429, 431, 434–5, 437, 465, 474, 491, 492, 495, 499–501, 504, 507–8, 511, 560, 563, 570, 573, 591, 609, 628, 629, 695
Ensslin, Gutrud, 567
Erzberger, Matthias, 557
Eschenbach, 428
Eurocentrism, 228, 385–418, 477, 487, 498, 490
Europe, 2, 17–20, 25, 29, 30, 32, 44, 45, 65, 103, 105, 135, 153, 162, 172, 175, 176, 178, 179, 184, 185, 188, 190, 192–201, 212, 214, 216, 229, 232, 237, 241, 247, 251, 252, 328, 331, 332, 340, 342, 343, 356–60, 362, 365, 366, 370, 371, 387–9, 392–6, 406–11, 432, 440, 453, 456, 459, 460, 463, 469, 475, 485, 487, 489–94, 497, 500, 501, 503–12, 517–21, 528, 529, 531–5, 544, 550, 551, 553, 555, 556, 558, 559, 561, 565, 566, 584, 593, 595, 609–13, 619, 631, 635, 668, 669, 676, 679
Evers, Tilman, 116

F
Fahn, James David, 440
Falk, Jim, 342
Fanon, Franz, 250
Farouk, 248
fascism, 14, 15, 24, 33, 45, 57, 127,
    129, 196, 242, 387, 405, 407,
    408, 410, 470, 498, 556, 557,
    566, 568, 569, 579–617, 619–46
feminism, 11, 23, 30, 31, 56, 57,
    93–111, 117, 132, 150–2, 158,
    165, 169, 171, 213, 248, 249,
    305, 316–19, 324, 335–41, 348,
    367, 395, 396, 449–54, 457,
    459, 462, 463, 465–7, 471–6,
    478, 479, 536, 537, 589, 607,
    621, 664
Ferreira, Carla, 139
Fiume, 586, 593
Flanders, 179, 180, 185, 192
Flasbarth, Jochen, 435
Florence, 185, 189, 657, 667
Foucault, Michel, 98, 379, 581
Fourier, François Charles, 390, 396
France, 2, 3, 13, 17, 20, 33, 57, 71,
    88, 102, 180, 181, 185, 187–9,
    193, 194–6, 198–200, 219–21,
    225, 226, 230, 235, 241–7, 327,
    333, 342, 348, 362, 363, 366–8,
    374, 379, 387, 390, 392, 394,
    396, 400, 411, 417, 420, 426,
    429, 431, 439, 441, 469, 475,
    489, 492, 495, 498, 500, 506,
    517, 518, 523, 525–7, 530, 531,
    534, 539, 550, 553–6, 559, 560,
    565, 566, 569, 572, 573, 578,
    582, 583, 588, 589, 593, 599,
    603–9, 621, 627, 630, 641, 668,
    674, 695
Franco, Francisco, 195
Fried, Alfred Hermann, 494
Fuentes, Carlos, 529

Fukushima, 443
Futrell, Robert, 639

G
al-Gaddafi, Mummar, 247, 679, 695
Gallagher, David, 270
Gandhi, Indira, 286, 402, 416, 422
Gandhi, Mahatma, 27, 65, 73, 78, 79,
    258, 268, 270, 275, 277, 278,
    280–2, 284, 285, 288, 373, 385,
    389, 504, 505, 512, 513
Garcia Márquez, Gabriel, 529
Garibaldi, Guiseppe, 493
Garrison, William Lloyd, 154
Garvey, Marcus, 346
Gaza, 253, 254, 697
Gdánsk, 202
gender, 13, 21, 30–2, 93, 101, 104,
    105, 108, 151, 212, 214, 219,
    227, 228, 232, 233, 239, 244,
    260, 271, 285, 286, 291, 317,
    318, 320, 342, 347–9, 395,
    450–2, 455–83, 496, 502, 551,
    562, 566, 572, 589, 620, 624,
    640, 642
' Geneva, 366, 493, 532, 652, 671
Genoa, 388, 653
Genscher, Hans-Dietrich, 429, 435
Gentile, Emilio, 580
Gent, Jan van, 181
Gelvin, James, 240, 241
George III, 198
Germany, 13, 14, 20, 33, 39, 61,
    182–4, 186, 188, 191, 194, 195,
    198, 199, 204, 252, 362, 363,
    366–9, 371, 373–6, 381, 388–92,
    394, 398, 406, 407, 419–22,
    427–31, 434–9, 441, 442, 465,
    469, 494, 497, 500, 501, 504,
    508, 517, 531, 539, 553, 556–9,
    565, 567–71, 579, 584, 585,

593–6, 598–602, 605–13,
615, 622, 623, 625, 630, 635,
640, 642
Geyer, Michael, 4
Ghana, 218, 504, 560
Giddens, Anthony, 423
Giddings, Paula, 161
Giri, V. V., 279
globalization, 1–35, 58, 68, 72, 87,
93–105, 107–9, 132, 136, 143,
171, 202, 216, 221, 222, 226,
250, 251, 254, 267, 274, 291,
292, 301, 305, 306, 317, 319,
324, 349, 351, 355, 356, 359,
360, 366, 370–4, 376, 378,
385–483, 485–491, 502–4,
506–11, 522, 525, 537, 549,
551, 554, 563, 564, 571, 574,
631, 640, 647–702
global social movement, 1–35, 118,
132, 136, 486–8, 490, 501,
509, 511
Gloria Gohn, Maria da, 116
Glubb Pasha, 247
Goldman, Emma, 164
Gömbös, Gyula, 585, 601, 602, 609
Gomes, Juan Vicente, 139
Gompers, Samuel, 162, 163, 166, 400
Gomułka, Władysław, 202
Gorbachev, Mikhail, 203, 432
Göring, Hermann, 598
Göttingen, 422
Gottlieb, Robert, 423
Gouges, Olympe de, 462
Goyet, Bruno, 605
Gramsci, Antonio, 65, 70, 76, 86, 87,
302, 594
Great Britain. See England
Greece, 233, 236, 237, 407, 409,
559, 566, 669
Greer, Germaine, 342
Gregg, Richard, 500

Griefahn, Monika, 435
Grimke, Angelina, 154
Grimke, Sarah, 154
Grohnde, 430
Grotius, Hugo, 494
Guatemala, 131
Guerrero, 124
Guevara, Che, 250, 505, 537
Guha, Ramachandra, 285, 423
Guha, Ranajit, 63, 65, 69, 75, 270
Guigni, Marco, 661, 665
Guinea, 196
Gujarat, 78, 279
Gutierrez, Lucio, 137

H
Habermas, Jürgen, 509
Habib, Sheth Haji, 499
The Hague, 470, 495, 497, 498
Haiti, 397, 410, 411
Haklai, Oded, 643
Hales, Robert, 181
Hamburg, 190, 199, 369, 370
Hanson, Pauline, 350
Hardiman, David, 70, 75, 78, 270
Hariri, Rafiq, 253
Haya de la Torre, Victor Raul, 127
Hazare, Anne, 266
Heckscher, Zahara, 651
Hegel, Georg Friedrich, 14, 271, 360,
361, 516
Helsinki, 202
Hébert, Alexandre, 526
Heyrick, Elizabeth, 361
al-Hiba, Ahmed, 242
Hidalgo, Miguel, 121
Higgins, Henry Bourne, 337
Hill, Christopher, 64
Hiroshima, 504
Hirsch-Hoefler, Sivan, 621
history from below, 76, 84, 682

Hitler, Adolf, 596–601, 608–10, 628, 635
Hobsbawm, Eric, 64, 76, 393, 556
Homs, 695
Hong Kong, 454
Hopkins, Terence K., 538
Horthy, Miklos, 585, 601
Hugo, Victor, 493
human rights, 2, 23, 29, 35, 93, 94, 99, 100, 108, 109, 132, 136, 145, 202, 254, 372–7, 379, 403, 459, 462, 463, 476, 497, 506, 652, 657, 660–2, 666, 685
Hume, A. O., 265
Hungary, 20, 33, 195, 199, 201, 202, 407, 410, 432, 583, 585, 593, 601–3, 609, 641
Hus, Jan, 191
Hwan, Chun Doo, 309, 312
Hyun, Roh Moo, 315

I
Ibrahim Pasha, 238
Ignatieff, Michael, 372
Ik-hwan, Mun, 305
immigration, 123, 124, 152, 159, 162, 163, 170, 316, 318, 330, 350, 440, 533, 568, 573, 611, 621, 624, 625, 627–9, 631, 640
India, 23, 27, 33, 63–88, 235, 236, 250, 258, 265–92, 362, 371, 373, 380, 385, 389, 402, 410, 412, 413, 416, 422, 428, 453, 460, 469, 499–501, 504–5, 512, 513, 549, 551, 583, 609, 614, 620, 624, 629, 630
Indonesia, 106, 107, 279
industrialization, 1, 17–19, 23, 25, 29, 45, 68, 69, 75, 79, 82, 84, 87, 116, 119, 120, 123, 127, 129, 130, 133, 139, 147, 151, 154,

156, 161–3, 165, 166, 177, 178, 188, 194, 217, 219, 239, 249, 278, 279, 286, 287, 294, 301, 303, 307, 308, 326, 331, 336–8, 341, 343, 345, 346, 349, 350, 385–98, 400–5, 407, 412, 413, 426, 455, 457, 458, 469, 527, 529, 531, 558, 564, 659, 686
internationalism, 9, 10, 12, 25, 30, 31, 33–5, 93, 94, 99, 101–4, 107, 108, 119, 120, 123, 127, 128, 130, 135, 136, 138, 163, 164, 171, 197–9, 213, 215, 216, 221, 251, 254, 286, 289–91, 305, 316, 319, 342, 349, 356, 359, 363, 380, 391, 393, 406, 409, 410, 414, 419, 422, 423, 426, 428, 430–3, 450, 453–5, 457, 460–70, 474–9, 485, 486, 489, 490, 491–501, 509–11, 516, 519, 524, 530, 537, 552, 554, 559, 561, 563, 566, 567, 571, 584, 593, 594, 596, 600, 601, 605, 607, 629, 631, 641, 648, 650, 652, 655, 658–60, 663, 669, 272, 675, 678, 680, 691–3, 695
Iran, 225, 229, 230, 232, 233, 235, 237, 238, 241, 243, 245, 247–9, 251, 252, 256, 258, 259, 403
Iraq, 108, 241–6, 248, 252, 253, 258, 403, 510, 574, 682, 695
Ireland, 159, 334–7, 406, 561–3, 570
Ismail (Pasha), 231
Israel, 246, 247, 251–4, 444, 694, 695
Istanbul, 233–5, 237
Italy, 33, 123, 137, 185, 195, 234, 235, 241, 242, 259, 365, 390, 407, 493, 494, 500, 501, 516, 529, 530, 535, 555, 556, 558, 559, 562, 565, 567–9, 579,

583–5, 589–603, 605–14, 617,
    619, 625, 626, 629, 636, 638,
    642, 669
Izmir, 230

J
Jaffa, 240
Japan, 103, 106–8, 299, 306, 311,
    323, 324, 366, 385, 390, 400,
    401, 408, 426, 430, 453, 458,
    464, 469, 475, 490, 491, 495,
    501, 504–12, 567, 609, 610, 614
Jelin, Elizabeth, 116
Jenin, 253, 254
Jenkins, Craig, 43
John II, 180
Jones, Kenneth, 273
Jones, William, 495
Jordan, 243, 247, 255, 681, 697
Joshi, V. P., 279
Jospin, Lionel, 671
Jung, Kim Dae, 315

K
Kadivar, Mohsen, 259
Kai-shek, Chiang, 610
Kakabadse, Yolanda, 435
Kanzō, Uchimura, 495
Kapp, Wolfgang, 594
Karachi, 655
Karim Khan, 237
Karnik, V. B., 279
Kasserine, Gafsa, 688
Kazan, 184
Kejriwal, Arvind, 265–7, 291
Kelly, Petra, 419
Kennedy, Robert, 521
Kenya, 435, 560, 655
Keohane, Robert, 509
Kerouac, Jack, 528

Khan, Hakim Ajmal, 282
Khartoum, 238
Khomeini, Ruhollah, 248, 252
Khoury, Philip, 240
Khrushchev, Nikita, 201
Ki-hun, Kang, 314
King, Martin Luther, 146, 167,
    500, 521
Ki-sŏl, Kim, 314
Kitschelt, Herbert, 623
Klandermans, Bert, 61, 587
Korea, 106–8, 297–320, 402,
    453, 469
    North, 300, 309, 310, 312, 319
    South, 27, 107, 300, 301
Kraków, 432
Kral'ovany, 432
Krämer, Augustin Friedrich, 427
Kriesi, Hanspeter, 52
al-Krim, Abd, 242, 244
Kropotkin, Pyotr, 544
Kuwait, 243, 252
Kyŏng-dae, Kang, 314

L
labour movement(s), 1, 14, 20, 24,
    25, 28–30, 32, 45, 46, 82, 123,
    126, 128, 157, 162, 164, 166,
    172, 218–22, 240, 249, 307,
    309, 311, 315, 320, 337, 343,
    380, 385–414, 493, 531, 549,
    551, 554, 555, 687
Laclau, Ernesto, 116
Ladd, William, 492
Laglösaköping, 181
Lalor, Peter, 335
Lando, Michele di, 189
Langman, Lauren, 657
La Paz, 138
Larmer, Miles, 216
La Rocque, François de, 607, 608

Latin America, 19, 24, 29, 33, 93, 115–41, 212, 222, 400, 408, 409, 411, 412, 455, 460, 467, 469, 470, 474, 475, 498, 499, 505, 531, 533, 535, 544, 550–3, 555, 556, 561, 564–6, 664, 668, 669
Latvia, 432
Lavigerie, Charles Martial Allemand, 362
Lebanon, 231, 233, 234, 237, 239, 246–9, 251–3, 258, 403, 572, 695
Le Bon, Gustave, 590, 592, 593
Leiden, 190
Leinen, Jo, 435
Lemonnier, Charles, 493
Lenin, 65, 86, 131, 195, 201, 250, 309, 339, 406, 409, 572
Lennon, John, 528
Leubas, 183
Leuven, 517
Levi-Strauss, Claude, 65, 70
Liberia, 221
Libya, 235, 241, 242, 244, 247, 248, 252, 679, 687, 691–3, 695, 696
Liebknecht, Karl, 556
Liège, 185
Lim, Jie-Hyun, 303
Lincoln, Abraham, 157
Lindau, 183
Linden, Marcel van der, 15, 18, 25, 392
Lisbon, 196
Liu, Lydia, 103
Lloyd-George, David, 389
Locke, John, 456
Loire-Atlantique, 526, 527
London, 181, 193, 199, 253, 333, 357, 369–71, 376, 392, 433, 508, 573, 574
Loudon, John, 430

Louis XVI, 193, 194
Lovelock, James, 419
Lowell, 156
Lübeck, 186
Luhmann, Niklas, 3
Lutzenberger, José, 420, 423
Luxemburg, Rosa, 526, 556
Lyon, 189

M
Maathai, Wangari, 423, 435
Mackie, Vera, 458
Madero, Francisco, 124, 125
Madras, 270, 278, 281
Maharashtra, 68, 266, 282, 293
Mahuad, Jamil, 137
Makram, Umar, 252
Malatesta, Errico, 544
Mamdani, Mahmood, 215
Manchester, 198, 369, 388, 491
Mao Zedong, 65, 82, 86, 87, 250, 401
Mariátegui, José Carlos, 128
Marighella, Carlos, 565
Marrakech, 242
Marseille, 557
Martí, Agustín Farabundo, 125, 131
Martinez-Alier, Joan, 422
Martinez, Hernandez, 125
Marx Ferree, Myra, 451
Marxism, 45, 47, 49, 50, 65, 81, 82, 86, 117, 131, 226, 250, 258, 270, 271, 283, 291, 309–11, 356, 391, 397, 398, 400, 402, 409, 410, 437, 474, 528, 566, 572, 596
Marx, Karl, 14, 29, 86, 87, 250, 355, 356, 379, 387, 390, 391, 520
Masaniello, 187
Mashriq, 239, 241, 246
mass mobilization, 49, 64, 73, 90, 241
Matthiesen, Klaus, 435

Mazzini, Guiseppe, 499
McCarthy, John, 40, 51, 52, 302, 325
McKay, Ian, 150
McVeigh, Timothy, 549
Mecca, 273
Mehmet Ali, 231
Mehta, Uday, 267
Meinhof, Ulrike, 567
Melbourne, 332, 334
Memmi, Albert, 250
Memmingen, 183
Mendes, Chico, 420, 436
Menem, Carles, 134
Menon, Nivedita, 96
Merkl, Peter, 597, 598
Metcalf, Barbara, 272
Metcalf, Thomas, 272
Mexico, 24, 121, 123–6, 129,
    136, 147, 400, 522, 523, 539,
    540, 659
Mexico City, 32, 521–3, 525
Michels, Robert, 592
Mickiewicz, Adam, 518, 529
Mies, Maria, 56
Milan, 494, 555, 556
Mirabehn (Madeleine Slade), 288
mobilization(s), 6, 9, 13, 16, 18, 19,
    25, 34, 44, 47–9, 51, 52, 63–5,
    68, 69, 71–3, 75, 85, 93, 94, 97,
    101, 106, 108, 109, 118, 124,
    135, 139, 149–51, 175, 184, 197,
    212, 221, 226, 228, 229, 235,
    236, 239–42, 244–6, 252, 256,
    258, 259, 286, 288, 300, 303,
    304, 326, 327, 332, 335–51, 360,
    361, 365, 367, 368, 393, 412,
    413, 419, 432, 442, 450–6, 458,
    460–71, 473–9, 517, 518, 524,
    532, 536, 537, 545, 551, 560,
    562, 567, 571, 582–6, 590, 593,
    594, 596, 600, 601, 604, 605,
    607, 608, 622, 625, 640, 641,

647–9, 661, 665, 670, 678, 680,
    682–91, 693–5, 698
Mombasa, 404
Mohan Roy, Raja Ram, 27, 268,
    274–5, 291
Moldavia, 184
Montgomery, 500
Moore, Barrington, 687
moral, 28, 29, 47, 101, 106, 108,
    118, 178, 188, 215, 259, 308,
    314, 332, 341, 342, 355–83,
    391, 456, 467, 468, 491, 492,
    494, 500, 511, 573, 574, 612,
    625, 633, 684, 685, 687, 689
Morales, Evo, 42, 138
Moravia, 191
Morelo, José Maria, 121
Morelos, 124
Moretti, Mario, 568
Morocco, 225, 229–31, 234–6,
    238, 241–4, 247, 250, 255, 367,
    679, 682
Morsi, Mohamed, 694
Mosca, Gaetano, 592
Moscow, 184, 411, 643
Mosonmagyaróvár, 432
Mossadegh, Mohammed, 248
Most, Johann, 544
Mott, Lucretia, 154
Mozambique, 196
Mubarak, Husni, 254, 679
Muddehave, Cas, 621
Mumbai. See Bombay
Münster, 191
Mussolini, Benito, 556, 586, 587,
    589–93, 595, 596, 599–601,
    603, 604, 606, 608, 610, 614

N
Nablus, 236
Naess, Arne, 438

Nagaland, 285
Nagasaki, 504
Naidu, Sarojini, 282
Nairobi, 655
Nantes, 518, 526, 527
Naples, 182, 187
Napoleon, 194, 230, 456
Nash, Roderick, 424
Nasser, Gamal Abdel, 246–8, 258,
    402, 403, 410
Natarajan, L., 74
nationalism(s), 18, 20, 22–4, 26, 27,
    32, 45, 66, 67, 69, 70, 72, 73,
    78, 84, 87, 89, 103, 108, 109,
    127–30, 138, 164, 218, 239–44,
    246–8, 250, 251, 267–71,
    276–80, 290, 292, 299, 300,
    303, 305, 310, 350, 380, 402,
    403, 408, 426, 436, 454, 460,
    463, 465, 468, 469, 493,
    499–501, 505, 506, 549–54,
    556–8, 561, 562, 580, 584, 592,
    594–6, 602, 603, 609, 611, 612,
    614, 624, 625, 627–30, 634,
    635, 679, 681, 683, 685
nation state, 1, 5, 6, 20, 26, 27, 67,
    85, 94–7, 106, 109, 119, 122,
    177, 195, 277, 291, 297, 299,
    306, 316, 326, 378, 406, 414,
    421, 431, 436, 458, 461, 464,
    470, 477, 493, 495, 496, 498,
    506, 509, 574, 584, 630,
    640, 658
Nehru, Jawaharlal, 270, 275, 279
Neidhardt, Friedhelm, 44
neoliberalism, 26, 98, 99, 109, 119,
    134, 136, 137, 139–41, 152,
    214, 226, 250, 255, 260, 315,
    320, 348, 349, 351, 411, 412,
    537, 629, 652, 654, 657–62, 664
Netherlands, 107, 178, 190–4, 319,
    494, 498, 529, 570, 635

New Delhi, 265
New Left, 27, 33, 45, 147, 173,
    316–18, 320, 410, 534, 537,
    549, 563–71, 570, 571, 666
new social movements, 1, 15, 24, 27,
    29, 30, 45, 46, 58, 65, 116,
    146–52, 167, 335, 343, 410,
    437, 479, 536, 662, 666
New South Wales, 328, 332, 337, 343
New York, 373, 492
New Zealand, 341, 399, 421, 469
Nicaragua, 125, 131, 622
Nicholas II, 495
Nkrumah, Kwame, 505
Noril'sk, 201
Normandy, 179
North America, 17, 18, 24, 29, 32,
    102, 104, 135, 145–72, 213,
    332, 338, 342, 346, 388, 399,
    453, 459, 475, 491, 500, 501,
    521–3, 528, 533, 537, 651,
    659, 669
North Carolina, 639
Norway, 20, 199, 496
Novočerkassk, 201
Novotny, Antonin, 202
Nuevo León, 523
Nye, Joseph, 509

O
Oaxaca, 124, 523
Obama, Barack, 148, 627, 628,
    693, 694
Offen, Karen, 451
O'Hanlon, Rosalind, 83, 85
Oise, 180
Okinawa, 502
Okupu-Mensah, Paul, 217
Old Left, 316, 317, 666
old social movements, 24, 29, 151
Omvedt, Gail, 283

Ong, Aihwa, 100
Oran, 573
Orissa, 68
Oslo, 253
Osman II, 234
Ottoman Empire. *See* Turkey
Owen, Robert, 390, 393, 396

P

Pakistan, 251, 277, 573, 655
Palestine, 231, 232, 236, 239–42,
    244–6, 248, 253, 254, 260, 561,
    567, 571, 609, 682, 697
Pandey, Gyanendra, 66, 67, 70, 75,
    77, 79–81, 85
Pankhurst, Sylvia, 465
Pape, Robert, 572
Pareto, Vilfredo, 592
Paris, 180, 194, 199, 357, 370, 491,
    493, 494, 518, 520, 530, 606
Pas de Calais, 388
Passy, Frédéric, 493
Pateman, Carole, 456
Paul, Alice, 165
Paul, Vincent de, 368
Payne, Leigh A., 622
Paz Estenssoro, Victor, 130
peace, 2, 12, 15, 30–2, 45, 119, 164,
    266, 284, 332, 337, 339, 342,
    407, 421, 422, 427, 433, 439,
    464, 465, 468, 470, 474–6, 478,
    479, 485–513, 550, 553, 561,
    563, 593, 601, 655, 660,
    665, 666
Petkov, Petko, 556
Pérez, Carloes Andrés, 134
Perón, Juan Domingos, 129
Persia. *See* Iran
Peru, 123, 126–8, 131, 138, 142, 363
Peter III, 184
Philadelphia, 155

Philippines, 106, 107, 319
Phule, Jyotirao, 279
Pianta, Mario, 662, 669
Pierce, William L., 641
Pittsburgh, 388
Pitt, William, 492
Pleyers, Geoffrey, 667
Poitiers, 630, 631, 641
Poland, 201–3, 407, 432, 518, 519,
    529, 558, 634
Polletta, Francesca, 639
Pommerolle, Marie-Emmanuelle, 12
Porto Alegre, 133, 655, 668, 672
Portugal, 121, 196, 407, 409, 531,
    540, 558, 622, 667, 668
post-colonialism, 11, 23, 27, 28,
    67–9, 71, 82, 84, 85, 89, 90, 98,
    213, 215, 220, 226–8, 232,
    266–71, 277, 278, 282, 284–7,
    290–2, 297–324, 397, 398,
    402, 404, 409, 421, 428, 453,
    455, 456, 459, 460, 473, 504,
    505, 559
Potonié-Pierre, Edmond, 493
Poujade, Robert, 429
Pound, Ezra, 626, 629
Poznań, 201
Prague, 191, 200, 202, 519–21,
    653, 679
Prestes, Luis Carlos, 127
Primo de Rivera, Miguel, 603
Prussia, 194, 195, 365–7
Puebla, 124
Pugačev, Emelian, 184
Puke, Erik, 182
Punjab, 85

Q

al-Qadir, Abd, 233
al-Qassam, Izz al-Din, 240
Qatar, 225, 243, 692, 695

al-Qawuqji, Fawzi, 244
Quataert, Donald, 262
Quang Ngai, 377
Québec, 521, 532
Quidde, Ludwig, 500
Qutb, Sayyid, 258

R
Radkau, Joachim, 423, 424, 442
Raphael, Lutz, 15
Raschke, Joachim, 623
Rasul, Abdullah, 74
Ravensburg, 186
Ray, Suprakash, 73
Razin, Stepan, 184
Reagan, Ronald, 431
Reilly, William, 435
religion(s), 21, 23, 27, 33, 34, 40, 43,
   65, 67, 69, 70, 72, 77, 80, 81,
   84, 189, 190, 193, 226, 230,
   235, 243, 244, 258, 260, 267–9,
   271–5, 283–6, 290, 291, 301,
   401, 402, 307, 312, 359, 362–4,
   369–71, 375, 377–80, 392, 421,
   451, 463, 464, 474, 491, 492,
   498, 545, 549, 550, 558, 571,
   572, 580–2, 584, 585, 588, 590,
   591–3, 596–8, 607, 612, 621,
   623, 624, 629, 631, 632, 633,
   637, 640, 681
Renzetti, Guiseppe, 599, 600
revolution(s), 2, 3, 13, 14, 17, 18, 20,
   21, 24, 25, 45, 46, 65, 73, 76,
   82, 86, 87, 119, 124, 125, 127,
   129–32, 138, 151–4, 164, 175,
   177, 186, 189, 192–6, 200, 201,
   232, 236, 237, 242, 244, 245,
   246–9, 251, 252, 258, 283, 302,
   308–14, 316, 320, 332, 338,
   339, 370, 387, 389, 391–4, 399,
   400, 401, 405, 406, 410, 411,

460, 466, 479, 489, 491, 492,
   500, 522, 528, 531–33, 537,
   538, 549–51, 555, 561, 564–66,
   569, 575, 580, 585–8, 594, 595,
   604, 611, 614, 635, 641, 662,
   678, 688, 689, 692, 694,
   696, 698
Rhee, Syngman, 300, 302, 303, 311
Richard II, 179, 181
Richardson, Louise, 546
Riga, 432
Rio de Janeiro, 124, 565, 611
Rio de la Plata, 121
Robespierre, Maximilien de, 194
Roca, Deodoro, 127
Roccca, Alfredo, 607
Rodowick, D.N., 87, 88
Romania, 184, 199, 407, 433, 556, 641
Rome, 133, 428, 554, 561, 587, 600,
   603, 605, 629
Roosevelt, Theodore, 426
Rootes, Christopher, 437
Rostow, Walt Whitman, 306
Rousseau, Jean Jacques, 456
Ruby Ridge, 637
Rucht, Dieter, 22, 33, 39–59, 147–9,
   152, 153, 172, 386, 486, 545,
   581, 583, 587, 604, 610, 614,
   648, 656, 663, 664
Russell, Bertrand, 503
Russia, 65, 87, 178, 184, 195, 199,
   200, 241, 248, 250–2, 309, 318,
   402, 403, 406, 409–11, 413,
   432, 434, 453, 501, 503, 553,
   559, 571, 621, 631, 643, 659,
   692, 695
Rustin, Bayard, 500

S
al-Sadr, Muhammad Baqir, 258
Sadr, Musa, 248, 252, 258

Said, Edward, 258
Said, Khaled, 689
Saint-Simon, Henri de, 13, 390
Sakai, Naoki, 102, 103
Saleh, Ali Abdullah, 679
Salgado, Plínio, 612, 613
Salzburg, 362
Samaj, Brahmo, 274–5, 278
Samara, 184
Sanaa, 680
Sánchez de Lozada, Gonzalo, 138
Sandino, Augusto Ceasar, 125
Sanger, Margaret, 164
Sang-jin, Kim, 305
Santiago de Chile, 124
al-Sanusi, Ahmad, 234, 235, 242, 244
Sao Paulo, 552, 565, 611
Sarmiento, Domingo Faustino, 122
Saro-Wiwa, Ken, 436
Sartori, Andrew, 274, 275
Sartre, Jean-Paul, 569
Saudi Arabia, 243, 248, 252, 254,
    274, 692, 695, 697
Schapiro, Leonard, 580
Schleyer, Hanns-Martin, 567
Schröder, Gerhard, 671
Schumacher, F. F., 289
Schwabach, 428
Schweitzer, Albert, 503
Scott, James, 71, 178
Seal, Anil, 270
Segovias, 125
Seipel, Ignaz, 556
Seitz, Karl, 556
Selim III, 231
Sembéne, Ousmane, 529
Senegal, 524–5, 655
Senghor, Léopold Sédar, 524
Sen, Sunil, 74
Sétif, 246
Sewell, William H., 228
Shah, Ghanshyam, 64, 269, 270, 279

Sharp, Gene, 500
Shehadeh, Raja, 258
Sicily, 517, 586
Simi, Pete, 639
Simmel, Georg, 4
Singer, Peter, 342
Slovakia, 202, 432, 641
Smith, Jackie, 664, 665, 674, 675
Smith, Tommie, 521
Smythe, Elizabeth, 651
social movement
    definition, 22, 40–2, 64, 148, 153,
        172, 217, 545, 614, 644, 677
    theory, 9, 35, 212, 345, 579, 582,
        588, 624–33, 691
Somalia, 253
Somers, Peggy, 511
Somoza Debayle, Anastácio, 125
Somoza García, Anastácio, 125
Sorel, Georges, 592, 593, 604
Sorj, Bernardo, 116
Soroush, Abdulkarim, 259
South Africa, 25, 212, 217, 218, 367,
    368, 377, 400, 403, 469, 499, 560
Soviet Union. See Russia
Spain, 123, 137, 187, 192, 193, 195,
    199, 241, 242, 244, 391, 407,
    409, 467, 500, 531, 534, 555,
    556, 558, 562, 566, 594, 603,
    607, 609, 652, 661, 664, 667,
    668, 674
Spalding, Hobert, 400
Speyer, 186
Spivak, Gayatri, 83
Szàlasi, Ferenc, 602
Stalin, Joseph, 201, 306, 309, 316,
    406, 453, 529, 534, 610
Stanton Cady, Elizabeth, 154, 155,
    158, 160
Stein, Lorenz von, 14
Stockholm, 133, 181, 422, 428, 429,
    431, 433

St. Petersburg, 388
Strasbourg, 186, 532
Strasser, Otto, 597, 599
subaltern studies, 22, 23, 63–88, 225, 270, 271
Sudan, 236, 253, 403
Sudbury, Simon, 181
Südtirol, 517
Sung, Kim Il, 310
Sun, Kim Hak, 107, 319
Suttner, Bertha von, 494
Sweden, 179, 181, 182, 199, 200, 407, 408, 431, 496
Switzerland, 183, 185, 199, 433, 494
Sydney, 328–30, 342, 343, 428
Syria, 234, 239, 241, 242, 244, 246, 249, 252, 253, 374, 403, 679, 687, 691–3, 695, 696
Szczecin, 202

T
T'ae-il, Chon, 307, 320
Tagore, Debendranath, 275
Tagore, Rabindranath, 275, 278
Taiwan, 106, 107, 319, 454
Tampico, 125
Tanta, 679
Tarrow, Sidney, 11, 634
Tasmania, 344, 422
Taylor, Verta638
al-Tayyib, Ahmad, 236, 238
Tel Aviv, 561
tenBroek, Jacobus, 145–7, 167
terrorism, 32, 33, 171, 201, 252, 253, 256, 300, 301, 302, 543–75, 596, 625, 629, 655
Thailand, 319
Thaite, Bertrand, 378
Thermopylae, 631
Thiong'o, Ngũgĩ wa, 529
Thomas, George, 7

Thompson, E. P., 64, 503
Thoreau, Henry David, 499
Tilly, Charles, 5, 6, 10, 41, 42, 301, 543, 550, 634
Togo, 363
Tokyo, 107, 319
Tolstoy, Leo, 499
Toshiko, Kishida, 464
Tours, 631
transnationality, 10, 20, 24, 26, 28, 29, 31–3, 35, 58, 93–111, 118, 137, 138, 164, 229, 254, 261, 262, 275, 318, 319, 326, 355, 358, 359, 364, 368, 372, 373, 375, 399, 414, 419, 422, 426–8, 430, 432, 474, 477–9, 485, 486, 488, 491, 494–503, 505, 506, 509, 511, 535–8, 549, 550, 552, 556, 560, 563, 571, 572, 574, 579–617, 620, 633, 640, 656, 665, 667, 668, 671, 674, 679, 689, 690, 696
Tripp, Charles, 229
Trotsky, Leon, 131, 526, 537
Truth, Sojourner, 464
Tunis, 251, 657, 680, 686–8, 693
Tunisia, 242, 247, 248, 255, 657, 678, 681, 686–92, 694, 696
Turin, 555
Tyler, Wat, 181

U
Ukraine, 693
uprising(s), 65, 69–74, 76, 78, 79, 85, 118, 124, 125, 127, 137, 140, 143, 175, 179–82, 184, 186, 189, 194, 195, 200, 201, 212, 220, 226, 230, 231, 235–42, 244, 245, 248, 254, 256, 257, 300, 301, 308–10, 314, 320, 328, 332, 339, 531, 647, 651

Urabi, Ahmad, 233, 236
urbanization, 308, 686
Uruguay, 116, 119, 121, 123, 132,
    363, 564, 565
USA, 460, 463, 490, 571
Uttarakhand, 287, 288
Uttar Pradesh, 79, 80, 289

V
Vadstena, 182
Vahrenholt, Fritz, 435
Vale del Mezquital, 121
Valois, Georges, 604, 605
Valparaiso, 124
Vargas, Getúlio, 129, 611–13
Venezuela, 126, 134, 139, 655
Venice, 532
Victoria, 329, 332–4
Vidin, 236
Vienna, 363, 490, 492, 556, 636
Vietnam, 147, 200, 342, 344, 377,
    410, 411, 429, 460, 502, 505,
    528, 532, 566
violence, 28, 32, 33, 49, 68, 78, 81,
    96–9, 122–5, 134–6, 138, 141,
    157, 158, 161, 172, 173, 187,
    195, 202, 226, 245, 253, 256–8,
    282, 284, 301, 302, 307, 317,
    318, 327–30, 332–5, 339–42,
    350, 373, 374, 378, 391, 430,
    439, 465, 472–4, 478, 485, 486,
    495, 496, 500, 505, 510, 522,
    543, 545–56, 558–60, 562, 563,
    568–70, 572–5, 580, 584, 585,
    587, 589, 590, 592, 593, 597,
    599, 600, 605, 608, 612, 614,
    616, 620, 622, 624, 625, 629,
    630, 633, 634, 636–8, 641, 642,
    664, 679, 684, 686, 687, 691,
    696, 700
Vorkuta, 201

W
Wallachia, 184
Wallerstein, Immanuel, 133
Wallraff, Günter, 440
Warsaw, 518–20, 529
Wałęsa, Lech, 2, 203
war, 14, 19, 20, 27, 29, 32, 102,
    106–8, 121, 125, 129, 130,
    136–8, 147, 153, 154, 156–60,
    163, 164, 167, 168, 171, 172,
    179–84, 191, 193–5, 200, 203,
    218–21, 229, 239–42, 244–6,
    250–4, 277, 279, 300–2, 305–9,
    313, 315, 317, 319, 338, 339,
    342, 344, 359, 360, 365–7,
    374, 387, 393, 394, 399–413,
    420, 426, 430, 431, 434,
    441, 453, 454, 459, 464, 468,
    470, 488–92, 494–8, 500–8,
    510, 526, 534, 549, 554–7,
    559, 560, 563, 565, 566, 569,
    571, 575, 580, 584–6, 590,
    593–5, 599, 601, 602, 604, 605,
    608, 614, 621, 623–5, 628,
    635, 641, 642, 655, 679,
    691–3, 695–7
Washbrook, David, 270
Washington, Booker T., 161
Washington, D.C., 146, 148, 469,
    537, 626, 659, 693
Weber, Thomas, 289
Weiner, Douglas, 434
Wells-Barnett, Ida B., 161
Wenglein, Carl, 428
Wichern, Johann Hinrich, 368
Wick, Hackney, 371
Williams, Eric, 364
Wilson, Woodrow, 242, 247, 499
Wittum, Johanna, 372
Wöbse, Anna, 428
Wüstenhagen, Hans-Helmuth, 429
Wyhl, 430

X

Xerxes I, 631

Y

Yemen, 247–50, 679, 687,
692, 693
Young, Crawford, 214
Yucatán, 523
Yugoslavia, 410, 432, 510, 519, 529,
557, 585, 593

Z

Zagreb, 519, 520
Zakharov, Nikolay, 631
Zald, Mayer, 40, 51, 52
Zambia, 219, 404
Zapata Emiliano, 124
Zárate, Pablo, 121
Zastoupil, Lynn, 274, 275
Zenteno, Raul Benitez, 116
Zetkin, Clara, 465, 466
Zuev, Dennis, 631